The English Legal Process

The English Legal Process

Eighth Edition

Terence Ingman LLM, PhD

of the Newcastle Law School, University of Newcastle upon Tyne

BLACKSTONE PRESS LIMITED

This edition published in Great Britain 2000 by Blackstone Press Limited,
Aldine Place, London W12 8AA. Telephone (020) 8740 2277
www.blackstonepress.com

© Terence Ingman, 1983

First edition 1983
Second edition 1987
Reprinted 1989
Third edition 1990
Reprinted 1991
Fourth edition 1992
Reprinted 1993
Fifth edition 1994
Reprinted 1995
Sixth edition 1996
Reprinted 1997
Seventh edition 1998
Reprinted 1999
Eighth edition 2000

ISBN: 1 84174 028 4

British Library Cataloguing in Publication Data
A CIP catalogue record for this book is available from the British Library

Typeset by Style Photosetting Ltd, Mayfield, East Sussex
Printed and bound in Great Britain by Antony Rowe Limited, Chippenham and Reading

Contents

1.1 Introduction — 1.2 House of Lords — 1.3 Court of Appeal — 1.4 High
Court of Justice — 1.5 Crown Court — 1.6 County courts — 1.7 Magistrates'
courts — 1.8 Judicial misconduct and immunity from suit — 1.9 Access to
justice

2.1 Court of Justice of the European Communities — 2.2 Judicial Committee of
the Privy Council — 2.3 Employment Appeal Tribunal — 2.4 Restrictive
Practices Court — 2.5 Coroners' courts — 2.6 Public funding of proceedings

3.1 Introduction — 3.2 Administrative (or statutory) tribunals — 3.3 Employment tribunals — 3.4 Domestic tribunals — 3.5 Public funding of proceedings

4.1 Introduction — 4.2 Bail — 4.3 General right to bail — 4.4 Granting bail —
4.5 Habeas corpus — 4.6 Availability of habeas corpus — 4.7 Procedure —
4.8 Successive applications for habeas corpus — 4.9 Appeals in habeas corpus
proceedings

5.1 Introduction — 5.2 Criminal contempt of court — 5.3 Civil contempt of
court — 5.4 Punishment for contempt of court — 5.5 Appeals in cases of
contempt of court

Preface

The revised text of this new edition takes account of major developments in the legal process since publication of the seventh edition two years ago. Some changes which are at the planning stage are also considered.

For the first time a solicitor has been appointed direct from practice to be a full-time High Court judge (para 1.4.2), and a woman has become President of the Family Division of the High Court (para 1.4.5.1).

The Civil Procedure Rules came into force in April 1999. They apply in both the High Court and the county courts, and constitute a new procedural code with the 'overriding objective' of enabling the court to deal with cases justly (para 1.4.6). Small claims arbitration in the county courts is now the 'small claims track' (para 1.6.4). The Rules make a number of changes to terminology. Thus, 'writ' or 'summons' becomes 'claim form', 'plaintiff' becomes 'claimant', *Anton Piller* order is a 'search order', and a '*Mareva* injunction' is a 'freezing injunction'.

A review of the practices, procedures and rules of evidence of the criminal courts is ongoing (para 1.5.6). An attempt by the government to abolish a defendant's right to choose trial by jury for an *either-way* offence was defeated in the House of Lords, but a substantially similar Bill was subsequently introduced in the House of Commons (para 1.7.6.2.2). Committal proceedings in respect of *indictable* offences were finally abolished in 1999 (para 1.7.6.3.1). The *doli incapax* rule (the common law presumption that a child between the ages of 10 and 14 is incapable of committing a crime) has been abolished (para 9.3.2.2). A Sentencing Advisory Panel has been established, and the criminal division of the Court of Appeal is now under a statutory duty to consider whether to frame new sentencing guidelines or to review existing guidelines (para 6.2.2.2). The recent miscarriages of justice involving Patrick Nicholls, Ryan James and Danny McNamee are examined (para 6.3.4).

The Treaty on European Union and the Treaties establishing the Communities have been amended by the Treaty of Amsterdam. In consequence, a number of articles of the EC Treaty were repealed and the rest were renumbered.

The jurisdiction of the Judicial Committee of the Privy Council has been extended to cover 'devolution questions' referred to it under the Government of Wales Act 1998, the Scotland Act 1998, and the Northern Ireland Act 1998 (para 2.2.3.5.). The Restrictive Practices Court will be abolished some time in 2001 (para 2.4.6). 'Industrial tribunals' have been renamed 'employment tribunals' (para 3.3). Sir Jeffery Bowman's *Review of the Crown Office List* (published in April 2000) has recommended that the Crown Office List should be renamed the 'Administrative Court' (para 11.14).

The legal aid and advice scheme is in the process of being dismantled under the provisions of the Access to Justice Act 1999. The Legal Aid Board has been replaced by the Legal Services Commission with the responsibility of establishing and developing the Community Legal Service (launched on 1 April 2000; para 1.9.2) and the Criminal Defence Service (expected to be established in October 2000; para 1.9.8). The availability of conditional fee agreements to finance civil litigation has been extended (para 1.9.3).

The new statutes noted include the Crime and Disorder Act 1998, the Competition Act 1998, the Data Protection Act 1998, the European Communities (Amendment) Act 1998, the Human Rights Act 1998, the Access to Justice Act 1999, and the Criminal Cases Review (Insanity) Act 1999.

The Human Rights Act 1998 seeks to incorporate into English law by an indirect route the rights and freedoms guaranteed by the European Convention on Human Rights (referred to in the Act as 'the Convention rights'). The Act is due to come into force in England and Wales in October 2000, and will require, among other things, a fresh approach to be taken to the judicial interpretation of United Kingdom legislation. A massive judicial training programme has been under way for some time with the object of making judges at all levels aware of potential human rights problems. Four extra High Court judges have been appointed to assist with the backlog of judicial review cases pending the implementation of the Act (para 11.14). The Convention rights have been applicable to the Scottish Executive created by the Scotland Act 1998 since 1 July 1999, and problems have already begun to emerge (para 8.10.8).

The Access to Justice Act 1999, in addition to effecting the changes to the delivery of legal services noted above, has introduced reforms to other parts of the legal process. A requirement of permission (formerly 'leave') to appeal has been imposed in almost all cases at all levels of court, and normally only one appeal against a decision is henceforth to be permitted (para 6.1 .4). Greater flexibility in the use of the time of Court of Appeal judges is to be sought (para 1.3.3.1). The metropolitan and provincial stipendiary magistracies are to be merged into a single judicial body, and the title 'stipendiary magistrate' is to be changed to the rather inelegant 'district judge (magistrates' courts)' (para 1.7.2). Justices of the peace and justices' clerks who acted in good faith are given immunity from being ordered to pay the costs in cases about how they exercised their judicial functions (para 1.8.2).

Numerous recent Court of Appeal and High Court case-law developments are incorporated, including decisions on the correct test for determining whether an employment tribunal hearing is 'in public' (*Storer* v *British Gas plc*); whether a threat is an 'insult' for the purposes of the law of contempt (*Manchester City Council* v *McCann*); offences of strict liability (*Harrow London Borough Council* v *Shah*); the purposive approach to statutory interpretation (*Oliver Ashworth (Holdings) Ltd* v *Ballard (Kent) Ltd*); the *per incuriam* doctrine (*Royal Bank of Scotland* v *Etridge (No. 2); Wahtcite* Ltd v *Ferrishurst Ltd Hughes* v *Kingston upon Hull City Council*); the duty of counsel to keep themselves up-to-date with new case law (*Copeland* v *Smith*); damages for mental distress caused by the breach of a contract to provide pleasure, relaxation or peace of mind (*Farley* v *Skinner*); and the rule against bias (*Locabail (UK) Ltd* v *Bayfield Properties Ltd; Seer Technologies Ltd* v *Abbas*).

In addition, account is taken of important pronouncements by the House of Lords on challenges in a criminal court to the validity of delegated legislation (*Boddington* v *British Transport Police*); the recovery of money paid under a mistake of law (*Kleinwort Benson Ltd* v *Lincoln City Council*); the inherent jurisdiction of the House to order the rehearing of an appeal (*R* v *Bow Street Metropolitan Stipendiary Magistrate (ex parte Pinochet Ugarte) (No. 2)*); the meaning of the word 'road' (*Cutter* v *Eagle Star Insurance Co. Ltd*); the requirement of *mens rea* in statutory offences (*B (a minor)* v *Director of Public Prosecutions*); the purposive approach to statutory interpretation (*Re Ismail; Fitzpatrick* v *Sterling Housing Association Ltd*); prospective overruling (*Kleinwort Benson Ltd* v *Lincoln City Council*) judicial law-making (*Kleinwort Benson Ltd* v *Lincoln City Council; Fitzpatrick* v *Sterling Housing Association Ltd*); the rule against bias (*R* v *Bow Street Metropolitan Stipendiary Magistrate (ex parte Pinochet Ugarte) (No. 2)*); and the effect of delay in seeking permission to apply for judicial review (*R* v *Criminal Injuries Compensation Board (ex parte A)*).

In conclusion, it is a pleasure to acknowledge once again the help received from Heather and Alistair of Blackstone Press. In the preparation of this edition, I owe an enormous debt of gratitude to Anne Henderson, a former student of mine, for her unfailing (and often unwitting) stimulation, encouragement and support.

The law is stated as at early May 2000.

Terry Ingman
Newcastle Law School
Newcastle upon Tyne
June 2000

Preface to the First Edition

In writing *The English Legal Process* it was not my intention to provide a comprehensive survey of the English legal system. Rather, my aim was to produce a topical account of some of the more important institutions and practices which form part of our legal process.

There appeared to be a need for a textbook, as opposed to a source-book, which attempted to deal with the substantive law on those matters in an informative and unsophisticated manner, and which, at the same time, did not ignore their relationship to the 'real world' and avoided the impression that our legal process was without blemish. It is for these latter reasons that areas of current controversy or difficulty are touched upon. Court delays, bail, contempt of court, miscarriages of justice, the vetting and 'nobbling' of juries, and the continuing struggle of the ordinary citizen, occasionally frustrated by the courts, to challenge abuse of power on the part of central government and other public authorities: these are some of the areas where the legal process is malfunctioning. Although in places I have ventured to be critical, I did not perceive that as my principal function. I have tried to avoid 'knocking' for its own sake. I have knocked 'the system' only where, in my view, it is in need of it.

The English Legal Process is intended mainly for first-year students at universities, polytechnics and colleges who are studying the English legal system. It is hoped that they will find it a comprehensible treatment of the subjects with which it deals and that the material contained in it will be rendered more accessible and digestible to them by the use of frequent cross-referencing and relatively short, numbered paragraphs.

The subject of remedies is often ignored or, at best, treated only cursorily in works on the legal system. Yet it is an integral and important part of the civil legal process. The inclusion in this book of chapters on remedies is designed to familiarise students at an initial stage in their career with the major forms of redress available in both private and public law. It is believed that their inclusion is further justifiable on the ground that an early introduction to remedies may prove helpful to the study and understanding of other legal subjects, such as contract, tort, administrative law, land law and equity. Students who have advanced beyond the first year of their course may find the book useful for that reason.

The law-making process is never static. Because the book covers so many diverse topics, keeping the text up to date in the face of incessant legislative and judicial outpourings has been a particularly difficult task. Many parts of the manuscript had to be rewritten at short notice, sometimes more than once, in order to take account of the latest changes in the law effected by statute or judicial decision.

Among the new statutes to be considered were two important consolidating measures, the Magistrates' Courts Act 1980 and the Supreme Court Act 1981, and others which introduced important rules into our law, such as the Contempt of Court Act 1981, the Criminal Justice (Amendment) Act 1981, the Administration of Justice Act 1982, the Criminal Justice Act 1982 and the Forfeiture Act 1982.

As is to be expected, the courts have been even more productive than Parliament. Many important new cases, too numerous to mention here, have had to be accommodated in the text. The House of Lords has been unusually active over the past two or three years. In the first quarter of 1983 alone some 15 House of Lords' decisions affecting the text have been reported.

I acknowledge with gratitude my indebtedness to those in the Law Faculty at Newcastle upon Tyne who gave me their time during the preparation of this book. Bill Elliott, Mick Rowell, Ashley Wilton, John Clark, Ian Dawson and Joanna Gray, a former student, were all imposed upon. With characteristic generosity and good nature they supplied innumerable criticisms and suggestions which rescued me from many an error. Responsibility for those errors and other shortcomings which remain is, of course, mine alone. My thanks are also due to my secretary, Christine Markham, who worked on a disgraceful manuscript with such commendable intelligence, speed, accuracy and cheerfulness, to Alistair MacQueen and Heather Saward for their assistance at every step in the publishing process, and to Derek French, who edited the manuscript so conscientiously and skilfully and succeeded in making sense out of some of my more Delphic pronouncements.

I have endeavoured to state the law as at the end of March 1983. There have been developments since then which it was not possible to include in the text. Some of them may be mentioned here.

All the provisions of the Criminal Justice Act 1982 (so far as it affects England and Wales) come into force on various dates from January to May 1983.

Sir John Donaldson MR, in an effort to facilitate further the disposal of appeals in the Court of Appeal, civil division, has given guidance on the submission of 'skeleton arguments' by counsel (see para 1.3.5 and *The Times,* 13 April 1983).

The Lord Chancellor has taken the unusual step of dismissing two lay magistrates — apparently after a complaint from the estranged wife of one of them. The two justices, who became good friends and intended to marry, had refused to resign from the bench (see para 1.8.1).

The Coroners' Society is pressing the Home Secretary to introduce legislation to reverse the decision of the Court of Appeal in *R v West Yorkshire Coroner (ex parte Smith)* [1982] 3 All ER 1098, which requires a coroner to hold an inquest into certain deaths occurring abroad if the body is brought back to England (see para 2.5.3.2).

The wisdom of conferring on magistrates' courts the power to punish summarily a contempt committed in the face of the court came into question when a man was sent to gaol by a stipendiary magistrate, under s. 12(1) of the Contempt of Court Act 1981, for whispering in the public gallery (see para 5.4.4).

In a White Paper, the Government has rejected the suggestion that there should be an independent review body to examine alleged miscarriages of justice. It is envisaged, however, that the Home Secretary will in future be prepared more readily to exercise his power to refer cases to the Court of Appeal, criminal division, under s. 17 of the Criminal Appeal Act 1968, and that the court will be prepared to make greater use of its powers to admit fresh evidence and order a retrial (see para 6.3.6 and *Miscarriages of Justice: Government Reply to the Sixth Report from the Home Affairs Committee, Session 1981 to 1982* Cmnd 8856, 1983).

Terry Ingman
Newcastle upon Tyne
April 1983

Table of Cases

Table of Statutes

Table of Secondary Legislation

Table of Reports

1

Courts of Normal Jurisdiction

1.1 INTRODUCTION

1.1.1 Civil courts and criminal courts

Civil courts exist in order to resolve disputes between private citizens or between a citizen and the state. These disputes may involve such matters as breach of contract, liability for harm in the law of tort, rights in property, marital status, or the wrongful exercise of power by some public authority. In such cases one party is seeking to obtain from the court some private remedy against the other.

Criminal courts exist in order to hear and determine accusations against persons that they have broken the criminal law. In most cases the accusation is made by someone representing the state. On a finding of guilt, the criminal courts have power to inflict punishment, commonly in the form of a fine or imprisonment.

In England and Wales there is no rigid line of demarcation between civil and criminal courts since almost all the courts exercise both types of jurisdiction. Exceptionally, the county courts are purely *civil* courts and exercise exclusively one type of jurisdiction.

1.1.2 Superior courts and inferior courts

Some courts are *superior* courts and others are *inferior* courts. Superior courts, like the House of Lords, the Court of Appeal, the High Court and the Crown Court, have unlimited jurisdiction and deal with the more important and difficult cases. Inferior courts, such as the county courts and the magistrates' courts, have limited jurisdiction and hear the less important and less difficult cases. Inferior courts, but not superior courts, are subject to the supervisory prerogative jurisdiction of the High Court, which is discussed in Chapter 11. For the unusual position of the Crown Court, which is a superior court and yet is sometimes subject to supervision by the High Court, see para 11.8.2.3.

1.1.3 Courts of record and courts not of record

Another distinction is that between *courts of record* and *courts not of record*. A court of record is one whose proceedings are kept as a permanent record in the Public Record Office. A court of record may be a superior court or an inferior court. The House of Lords, the Court of Appeal, the High Court, the Crown Court, the Restrictive Practices Court and the Employment Appeal Tribunal are superior courts of record. The county courts and the coroners' courts are inferior courts of record. Magistrates' courts are courts not of record.

A superior court of record has power to punish all forms of contempt of court (see Chapter 5) while an inferior court of record can generally only punish contempt committed in the face of the court. The distinction between a court of record and a court not of record has little meaning now that the magistrates' courts have power themselves to punish contempt committed in the face of the court (Contempt of Court Act 1981, s. 12; see para 5.4.4).

The coroners' courts are inferior courts of record and have jurisdiction, therefore, to punish contempt committed in their face (*R* v *West Yorkshire Coroner (ex parte Smith) (No. 2)* [1985] 1 All ER 100, DC). Other contempts of the coroners' courts, such as prejudicial comment in the press, are not punishable by those courts themselves but may be punished on an application to the Queen's Bench Division of the High Court (*R* v *Davies* [1906] 1 KB 32, DC, and see para 5.4.5).

Consistory courts and courts martial are courts not of record and do not, therefore, possess any inherent power to punish for contempt of court. The Queen's Bench Divisional Court may, however, punish contempts on their behalf (see para 5.4.5).

1.1.4   Courts and tribunals

The distinction between a court and a tribunal is sometimes blurred. While every court is a tribunal, not every tribunal is a court. The nomenclature used is not a sure guide. Thus, the Employment Appeal *Tribunal* is a court (see para 2.3.1) while a local valuation *court* was a tribunal only. The distinction between a court and a tribunal assumes particular importance in relation to punishment for contempt of court. The Queen's Bench Divisional Court has jurisdiction to punish a contempt committed in connection with the proceedings of an 'inferior court' (Rules of the Supreme Court (RSC) 1965, Ord. 52), but it has no general power to punish contempt of a tribunal. It does, however, have power to punish a contempt of a tribunal of inquiry established under the Tribunals and Inquiries (Evidence) Act 1921 (para 5.4.5).

In *Attorney-General* v *British Broadcasting Corporation* [1980] 3 All ER 161, the House of Lords held that a local valuation court was not an inferior court because, although it was called a 'court', its functions were essentially administrative rather than judicial. It followed that the Divisional Court had no power to punish an alleged contempt of a local valuation court arising out of a BBC television programme about the religious sect known as the Exclusive Brethren. (Note that local valuation courts were replaced on 1 May 1989 by valuation and community charge tribunals established under the Local Government Finance Act 1988; these were renamed 'valuation tribunals' by the Local Government Finance Act 1992 as from 6 March 1992.) In *General Medical Council* v *British Broadcasting Corporation* [1998] 3 All ER 426, CA, it was held that the Professional Conduct Committee of the General Medical Council is not a court. Although the Committee's function is a judicial one, it does not exercise the judicial power of the state. Its role is to exercise the self-regulatory power of the medical profession to maintain standards of professional conduct.

On the other hand, it has been held by the House of Lords that a mental health review tribunal *is* a court for the purposes of the law of contempt. Its functions are essentially judicial rather than administrative, and, in discharging them, it is exercising the judicial power of the state (*Pickering* v *Liverpool Daily Post and Echo Newspapers plc* [1991] 1 All ER 622, HL). Similarly, in *Peach Grey & Co.* v *Sommers* [1995] 2 All ER 513, DC, it was held that an employment tribunal is a court since it has many of the characteristics of a court of law and discharges judicial, as opposed to administrative, functions.

The opinion of their Lordships in *Attorney-General* v *British Broadcasting Corporation* was that a court of law is a court established to exercise the judicial power of the state. This definition has since been adopted by Parliament in s. 19 of the Contempt of Court Act 1981. It is explained in the following words of Lord Scarman in *Attorney-General* v *British Broadcasting Corporation* at pp. 181–2:

> I would identify a court in (or 'of') law, i.e., a court of judicature, as a body established by law to exercise, either generally or subject to defined limits, the judicial power of the state. In this context judicial power is to be contrasted with legislative and executive (i.e. administrative) power. If the body under review is established for a purely legislative or administrative purpose, it is part of the legislative or administrative system of the state, even though it has to perform duties which are judicial in character. . . . [T]he judicial power of the state exercised through judges appointed by the state remains an independent, and recognisably separate, function of government. Unless a body exercising judicial functions can be demonstrated to be part of this judicial system, it is not, in my judgment, a court in law.

Attorney-General v *British Broadcasting Corporation* was applied by the Judicial Committee of the Privy Council in *Badry* v *Director of Public Prosecutions of Mauritius* [1982] 3 All ER 973, in which it was said that *Attorney-General* v *British Broadcasting Corporation* had plainly established that, in the absence of any statutory provision to the contrary, the common law relating to contempt of court applied by definition only to courts of justice properly so called and to the judges of such courts of justice. It followed in the *Badry* case that the appellant's comments against a judge of the Supreme Court of Mauritius, including the statement that 'We must tear off his trousers in this country', did not constitute a contempt of court. The comments were 'vulgar, scurrilous, abusive and lacking in respect' (*per* Lord Hailsham of St Marylebone LC at p. 980) but they were directed against the judge as a commissioner or tribunal holding an inquiry into allegations of fraud and corruption and not in his capacity as a judge of the Supreme Court.

1.1.5 Courts and Legal Services Act 1990

The Courts and Legal Services Act 1990 achieved the most radical reforms in court jurisdiction and procedure since the nineteenth century, and, in relation to the legal profession, the most fundamental changes ever made. The Act represented, among other things, the government's attempt to implement the final report of the civil justice review body of June 1988 (*Report of the Review Body on Civil Justice,* Cm 394, 1988) together with the philosophy underlying its own White Paper of July 1989, *Legal Services: A Framework for the Future* (Cm 740, 1989), which, in turn, was based upon three Green Papers of January 1989 (*The Work and Organisation of the Legal Profession,* Cm 570, 1989; *Conveyancing by Authorised Practitioners,* Cm 571, 1989; *Contingency Fees,* Cm 572, 1989).

Of particular importance here are the changes made by the Act to the qualifications required for appointment as a judge. One effect of these changes is that *solicitors* are qualified for many more judicial posts than hitherto; another is that some *laymen* may become qualified. Eligibility no longer depends solely upon whether candidates happen to be barristers (or solicitors). Instead, candidates are eligible if they possess qualifications which are based upon rights of audience in the courts granted by authorised bodies. This move also reflected the government's policy of stimulating competition by an extension of rights of audience and a widening of the choice of persons qualified to provide advocacy services. This saw the beginning of the profession of 'paralegal advocate' (i.e., a person engaging in paid advocacy who is neither a barrister nor a solicitor) since the intention of the Act is to facilitate not only the removal of the Bar's monopoly on advocacy in the higher courts but also the destruction of the joint monopoly on advocacy enjoyed by barristers and solicitors alike in the lower courts.

A list of the new qualifications for judicial appointment based upon rights of audience is set out in s. 71(3) of the Act:

(a)   A 'Supreme Court qualification': i.e., a right of audience in relation to all proceedings in the Supreme Court.

(b)   A 'High Court qualification': i.e., a right of audience in relation to all proceedings in the High Court.

(c)   A 'general qualification': i.e., a right of audience in relation to any class of proceedings in any part of the Supreme Court, or all proceedings in county courts or magistrates' courts.

(d)   A 'Crown Court qualification': i.e., a right of audience in relation to all proceedings in the Crown Court.

(e)   A 'county court qualification': i.e., a right of audience in relation to all proceedings in county courts.

(f)   A 'magistrates' court qualification': i.e., a right of audience in relation to all proceedings in magistrates' courts.

1.1.6   Access to Justice Act 1999

The Access to Justice Act 1999 implements proposals contained in the White Paper of December 1998, *Modernising Justice*, Cm 4155, 1998, which was based upon several consultation papers, including *Access to Justice with Conditional Fees* (March 1998; see para 1.9.9 below), and upon Sir Jeffery Bowman's *Report to the Lord Chancellor by the Review of the Court of Appeal, Civil Division* (September 1997; see para 1.3.5 below). The Act is intended to achieve the government's declared 'twin aims' of, first, effecting a significant increase in access to justice, and, secondly, obtaining the best value for taxpayers from money spent on legal services and the courts.

The Access to Justice Act 1999 makes further sweeping changes to the way in which legal services are provided. It establishes the Legal Services Commission (replacing the Legal Aid Board), the Community Legal Service and the Criminal Defence Service. It extends the availability of conditional fee agreements and makes new provision for rights of audience before the courts.

The Act also introduces reforms to the appeal system, the deployment of judges, and court proceedings. It imposes a requirement of permission (formerly 'leave') to appeal in almost all cases at all levels of court, and provides that there should normally only be one appeal in any case. It allows greater flexibility in the use of the time of Court of Appeal judges. It merges the metropolitan and provincial stipendiary magistracy into a single judicial body, and changes the title 'stipendiary magistrate' to 'district judge (magistrates' courts)'. The requirement for lay magistrates to sit in cases committed to the Crown Court for sentence is abolished, and justices of the peace and justices' clerks are given immunity (provided they acted in good faith) from being ordered to pay the costs in cases about how they exercised their judicial functions.

1.2 HOUSE OF LORDS

1.2.1 Introduction

In cases not involving European Community legislation, the House of Lords is the highest court in the United Kingdom. (For the relationship between the House of Lords, European Community legislation and the Court of Justice of the European Communities, see para 2.1.1). Judicial decisions of the House of Lords can be overruled only by statute or by a refusal of the House to follow them in later cases. (For judicial precedent in the House of Lords, see para 9.3.2.2).

1.2.2 Composition

The president of the House of Lords as a court is the Lord Chancellor, assisted by between 7 and 12 Lords of Appeal in Ordinary (Appellate Jurisdiction Act 1947; Administration of Justice Act 1968, s. 1(1) (a)) and any peer who holds or has held high judicial office, such as a former Lord Chancellor or retired Court of Appeal judge. The Lords of Appeal in Ordinary are made life peers (Appellate Jurisdiction Act 1876, s. 6) and are often called Law Lords for short. The maximum permitted number of 12 may be increased by Order in Council (Administration of Justice Act 1968, s. 1(2)). The original number was two (Appellate Jurisdiction Act 1876, s. 6), and they were Lord Blackburn and Lord Gordon of Drumearn. At the end of 1999 there were 12 Law Lords.

Qualifications for appointment as a Lord of Appeal in Ordinary are:

(a)   The holding of high judicial office for two years (Appellate Jurisdiction Act 1876, s. 6). 'High judicial office' means 'The office of Lord Chancellor . . . or of Judge of one of Her Majesty's superior courts of Great Britain and Ireland'. (Appellate Jurisdiction Act 1876, s. 25; the reference to 'superior courts of Ireland' is now a reference to the High Court in Northern Ireland and the Court of Appeal in Northern Ireland — ibid., as amended by the Judicature (Northern Ireland) Act 1978.)

(b)   Possession of a 15-year Supreme Court qualification within the meaning of s. 71 of the Courts and Legal Services Act 1990 (para 1.1.5 above) (Appellate Jurisdiction Act 1876, s. 6, as amended by the Courts and Legal Services Act 1990).

(c)   Practice for 15 years as an advocate in Scotland, or as a solicitor entitled to appear in the Court of Session and the High Court of Justiciary (ibid.).

(d)   Practice for 15 years as a member of the Bar of Northern Ireland (ibid.).

It is not unknown, though not common, for a Law Lord to be appointed direct from the Bar without previous judicial experience. Examples are Lord Macnaghten (a Law Lord from 1887 to 1913), Lord Robson (1910–1912), Lord Macmillan (1930–1939 and 1941–1947), Lord Reid (1948–1974), and Lord Radcliffe (1949–1964). It is customary for one or two of the Law Lords to be Scottish lawyers.

1.2.3 Jurisdiction

The House of Lords has little *original* jurisdiction left. What remains includes the trial of disputed peerage claims and breaches of Parliamentary privilege in relation to itself. The jurisdiction to try fellow peers accused of crime was abolished by the Criminal Justice Act

1948. The jurisdiction of the House of Lords is now almost exclusively *appellate*. It is the final appeal court for England and Wales and Northern Ireland in both civil and criminal cases, and for Scotland in civil cases only. Final Scottish criminal appeals are heard in Edinburgh in the High Court of Justiciary.

Most appeals heard by the House of Lords come from the Court of Appeal in England. An appeal can be taken from the Court of Appeal to the House of Lords only by leave of either court (Administration of Justice (Appeals) Act 1934, s. 1(1)). In criminal cases there is the additional requirement that the appeal must involve a point of law of general public importance (Criminal Appeal Act 1968, s. 33(2)).

Every appeal to the House of Lords must be heard by at least three of the judges mentioned in para 1.2.2 (Appellate Jurisdiction Act 1876, s. 5). In practice, five of them usually sit together to form a court. Sometimes more than five may sit to hear an appeal which involves particularly difficult or important points. Thus, seven sat in the important civil case of *Cassell & Co. Ltd* v *Broome* [1972] AC 1027 and in the important criminal case of *DPP* v *Majewski* [1977] AC 443. More recently, a court of seven was assembled to hear the appeal in *Pepper (Inspector of Taxes)* v *Hart* [1993] 1 All ER 42 (para 8.10.5), and to rehear Senator Pinochet's attempt to avoid extradition to Spain on charges of crimes against humanity in *R* v *Bow Street Metropolitan Stipendiary Magistrate (ex parte Pinochet Ugarte) (Amnesty International intervening) (No. 3)* [1999] 2 All ER 97 (para 11.8.3.2.1).

Each judge may deliver his own separate judgment, called a 'speech' or 'opinion' in the House of Lords. The hearing of the appeal is not a retrial. No oral evidence is given; the judges read all the documents in the case and listen to counsel's arguments. The majority decision prevails. If for any reason the number of judges sitting is even, and the House is equally divided, the appeal is dismissed.

Although the House of Lords has an inherent jurisdiction to rehear an appeal, it is reluctant to do so except where a party has been the victim of an unfair procedure through no fault of his own. An appeal will not be reopened simply because the earlier decision is subsequently thought to be wrong. (See, e.g., *R* v *Bow Street Metropolitan Stipendiary Magistrate (ex parte Pinochet Ugarte) (No. 2)* [1999] 1 All ER 577; and see further, para 6.1.5.)

1.2.4   The House of Lords under attack

The House of Lords has existed as part of the High Court of Parliament for many centuries. (See Holdsworth, *History of English Law,* vol. 1, 7th ed., 1956, pp. 351–94.) Parliament is the oldest common-law court. Since the fifteenth century at the latest, its judicial functions have been exercised by the House of Lords alone. Until the middle of the nineteenth century any peer, whether legally qualified or not, was entitled to take part and vote in the hearing of appeals before the House with the result that it was possible for the judicial members of the House to be outvoted by the lay members. Indeed, in 1834 the House decided a case without any legally qualified judge present (Holdsworth, op. cit., pp. 376–7). The practice of allowing lay peers to take part in the judicial proceedings of the House was discontinued in 1844 on it appearing that the authority of the House of Lords as a court was being impaired (*O'Connell* v *The Queen* (1844) 11 Cl & F 155, HL; and see Radcliffe and Cross, *The English Legal System,* 6th ed., 1977, pp. 220–1). As late as 1883 a lay peer attempted to vote on an appeal, but his vote was ignored (*Bradlaugh* v *Clarke* (1883) 8 App Cas 354, HL). It is now a constitutional convention, though not law, that lay peers do not take part in the hearing of appeals.

After 1844 the judicial House of Lords was usually composed of the Lord Chancellor, and any former Lord Chancellors, or other peers who had held high judicial office, who wished to participate. Such persons tended not to be the leading judicial minds of the day. It was fortunate, therefore, that the Lord Chancellor had power to summon the judges from the Queen's Bench to advise their Lordships on the law. It is still theoretically possible to summon the judges, although it does not appear to have been done in an English appeal since *Allen* v *Flood* [1898] AC 1, HL, or in a Scottish appeal since *Free Church of Scotland* v *Lord Overtoun* [1904] AC 515.

An effort by the government to strengthen the quality of the House of Lords' bench by creating life peerages was frustrated when the House decided that the royal prerogative did not authorise the creation of a non-hereditary peerage with a right to sit in the House of Lords (*Wensleydale Peerage Case* (1856) 5 HL Cas 958, HL). The government had granted a life peerage (with the title of Lord Wensleydale) to one of the best judges of the time, Mr Baron Parke, with the object of enlisting his assistance with the dispatch of judicial business in the House of Lords. (He was described as 'Mr Baron' because he was a judge of the old Court of Exchequer, whose judges were called barons of Exchequer.) Consequent upon the decision in the *Wensleydale Peerage Case,* Parke's grant was altered so as to confer on him an *hereditary* peerage under the title of Lord Wensleydale and he sat as a judge in the House of Lords until his death in 1868.

Criticism of the composition and quality of the House of Lords as a court continued. The Judicature Act 1873 contained a section which would have abolished its appellate jurisdiction altogether. The Act was not to come into operation until 1875. In the meantime there was, in 1874, a change of government from Liberal to Conservative and it was decided not to bring into operation the section affecting the jurisdiction of the House of Lords. Instead, the House was reconstituted and revitalised, in the manner described earlier, by the Appellate Jurisdiction Act 1876, which provided for the appointment of paid professional judges with life peerages. (For the legal and political background to the Appellate Jurisdiction Act 1876, see Stevens, 'The final appeal: reform of the House of Lords and Privy Council', (1969) 80 LQR 343. See also Manchester, *A Modern Legal History of England and Wales, 1750–1950,* 1980, pp. 175–9.)

In the twentieth century, criticism has not abated; indeed, it appears to have gathered momentum. The House of Lords has been accused of being too conservative a body with a tendency towards safe, pro-Establishment decisions, such as *Liversidge* v *Anderson* [1942] AC 206, *Duncan* v *Cammell, Laird & Co. Ltd* [1942] AC 624 (para 9.3.2.2), *Secretary of State for Defence* v *Guardian Newspapers Ltd* [1984] 3 All ER 601 (para 5.2.1.4), and *Attorney-General* v *Guardian Newspapers Ltd* [1987] 3 All ER 316. *Liversidge* v *Anderson* concerned the construction of a wartime defence regulation authorising detention if the Home Secretary had reasonable cause to believe that the detainee was of hostile origin or associations. It was held that the grounds for the Home Secretary's belief could not be questioned and his statement that he had reasonable cause was final.

Attorney-General v *Guardian Newspapers Ltd,* which arose during the interlocutory stages of the *Spycatcher* litigation of 1986–1988, effectively muzzled the press for a time. The Attorney-General, acting on behalf of the government, was granted (by a majority decision of three to two) interim injunctions against some British newspapers prohibiting the publication of extracts from a book called *Spycatcher,* the memoirs of a former member of the British security service, Peter Wright. Furthermore, the injunctions were expressed in terms which prevented even the publication of material disclosed in similar court proceedings then in progress in Australia. The injunctions were granted on security grounds and in spite of the fact that the book was openly on sale in the United States and that individual copies were obtainable in the United Kingdom. Their Lordships' decision caused a furore. In letters to newspapers those responsible for it were accused, *inter alia,* of bringing the law into contempt and of 'dangerous judicial arrogance'. Lord Scarman (himself a former Lord of Appeal in Ordinary) wrote of his disappointment that the House of Lords had placed emphasis on *private* rights and obligations at the expense of 'the more fundamental law providing the right of the public to access to information already in the public domain and the public right of free speech, of which the freedom of the press is an important constituent'. (See *The Times,* 3 August 1987; for further chapters in the *Spycatcher* saga, see *Attorney-General* v *Guardian Newspapers Ltd (No. 2)* [1988] 3 All ER 545, HL, below, and *Attorney-General* v *Times Newspapers Ltd* [1991] 2 All ER 398, HL, para 5.2.2.4.8).

In 1991, the European Court of Human Rights decided that, although the granting of the original *Spycatcher* interlocutory injunctions against *The Guardian, The Observer* and the *Sunday Times* before the date of publication of the book in the United States in July 1987 was justified, the continuation of those injunctions by the House of Lords beyond that date (at which time the confidentiality of the material they sought to protect was destroyed) was not 'necessary in a democratic society' and, accordingly, constituted a violation of article 10 of the European Convention on Human Rights (*Sunday Times* v *United Kingdom (No. 2)* (1992) 14 EHRR 229, ECHR). This outcome confirmed Lord Bridge's prediction that there would be 'inevitable condemnation and humiliation' by the European Court of Human Rights if the government sought to maintain the ban on *Spycatcher (Attorney-General* v *Guardian Newspapers Ltd* [1987] 3 All ER 316, 347, quoted more fully below). At the same time, it confounded the confidently expressed opinion of Lords Templeman and Ackner that the continuation of the ban was 'necessary in a democratic society' within the meaning of art. 10 (ibid., at pp. 356 and 364 respectively.)

The House of Lords has been accused of anti-trade-union prejudice in such cases as *Taff Vale Railway Co.* v *Amalgamated Society of Railway Servants* [1901] AC 426, *Rookes* v *Barnard* [1964] AC 1129, *J. T. Stratford & Son Ltd* v *Lindley* [1965] AC 307, and *Hunt* v *Broome* [1974] AC 587. In the *Taff Vale* case, a trade union was held liable in damages for the tort of its officials in inducing strike-breakers to refuse, in breach of contract, to replace striking workmen. This decision was subsequently overruled by the Trade Disputes Act 1906. In *Rookes* v *Barnard* a union official was held liable for the obscure tort of intimidation, a decision which was promptly overruled by the Trade Disputes Act 1965. In *Stratford* v *Lindley* it was held that a boycott imposed by one union, in support of a claim to the same recognition accorded to another union, was not a trade dispute. In *Hunt* v *Broome* it was decided that a picket has no right to obstruct the highway while attempting to persuade a lorry driver to turn back.

The House of Lords has been accused of political complicity (see Griffith, *The Politics of the Judiciary,* 5th ed., 1997; Stevens, *Law and Politics: The House of Lords as a Judicial Body, 1800–1976,* 1978; Shetreet, *Judges on Trial,* 1976). The decisions attacked on this ground are those like *Roberts* v *Hopwood* [1925] AC 578, in which the Poplar Borough Council were held not entitled to pay wages to their employees well above the prevailing rate despite their statutory duty 'to pay such wages as they may think fit', *Bromley London Borough Council* v *Greater London Council* [1982] 1 All ER 129, in which it was held that the Labour-controlled GLC had acted *ultra vires* in issuing a supplementary rate precept to London boroughs in order to finance a 25 per cent cut in London Transport fares, *Council of Civil Service Unions* v *Minister for the Civil Service* [1984] 3 All ER 935 (the 'GCHQ case'), in which the House upheld the exercise of ministerial power to withdraw, on grounds of national security and without consultation, the right of a particular group of civil servants to trade union membership, and *Westminster City Council* v *Greater London Council* [1986] 2 All ER 278, where decisions of the GLC (to be implemented following its demise on 1 April 1986) to provide grants for ILEA, an arts centre and several hundred voluntary organisations were found to be *ultra vires* and void.

The continued existence of the House of Lords as a court has been called into question. The social and political backgrounds of its judges have been subjected to close scrutiny (Blom-Cooper and Drewry, *Final Appeal,* 1972; Stevens, op. cit.; Paterson, *The Law Lords,* 1982; 'Judging the Law Lords by their Records', *The Independent,* 18 February 1988). The quality and helpfulness of its judicial pronouncements have been the targets of adverse comment (Murphy and Rawlings, (1981) 44 MLR 617).

Another specific criticism of the House of Lords relates to its failure to make any adequate contribution to the development of the criminal law. Appeals to the House of Lords in criminal cases are few in number because of the strict conditions for taking such an appeal there. The appellant must obtain the leave of the court below or of the House of Lords to bring an appeal *and* a certificate from the court below that the case involves a point of law of general public importance. The paucity of criminal appeals reaching the House means that the Law Lords have little opportunity to exercise their talents in the field of criminal law. It does not, of course, explain fully why they have made such a mess of some of the criminal cases which did come before them. Two of our most distinguished commentators on the criminal law have publicly questioned whether we can afford to keep the House of Lords as an appellate criminal court (J.C. Smith, [1981] Crim LR 393; G.L. Williams, op. cit., p. 580, and (1985) 135 New LJ 24).

There are signs that some of the criticisms, although perhaps ill-founded, may have been taken to heart and that the House of Lords is becoming defensive. In a trade dispute case in 1980 Lord Scarman made a plea for comprehensively drafted trade-union legislation so as to keep the judges out of the industrial arena where they are often called upon to exercise 'a discretion which may well be misunderstood by many and which can damage confidence in the administration of justice' (*Duport Steels Ltd* v *Sirs* [1980] 1 All ER 529, HL, at p. 554). That the House of Lords is not a political court was underlined by Lord Diplock in *Bromley London Borough Council* v *Greater London Council* [1982] 1 All ER 129, at p. 159:

> It cannot be too emphatically stated that your Lordships in this appeal are not concerned with the wisdom or, indeed, the fairness of the GLC's decision to reduce by 25 per cent the fares charged in Greater London by the London Transport Executive. . . . All that your Lordships are concerned with is the legality of that decision: was it within the limited powers that Parliament has conferred by statute on the GLC?

More recently, in *R* v *Shivpuri* [1986] 2 All ER 334, a criminal case in which the House with great rapidity overruled its own previous decision in *Anderton* v *Ryan* [1985] AC 560, Lord Bridge acknowledged the force of the stinging criticism made of the latter case by Professor Glanville Williams in the *Cambridge Law Journal* ([1986] 2 All ER 334, 345, and see Williams, [1986] CLJ 33).

It cannot be said that the House of Lords has been consistently anti-trade-union in its decisions. For example, in *Allen* v *Flood* [1898] AC 1 a union representative was held not to be liable in damages for forcing an employer to dismiss some workmen. The representative's act was not *per se* unlawful and his bad motive did not make it so. In *Crofter Hand*

Woven Harris Tweed Co. v *Veitch* [1942] AC 435, union officials were held not to be liable for conspiracy to injure where their acts were calculated to further the interests of their union members. Again, in some more recent trade-dispute decisions the House of Lords has shown itself to be more enlightened than the Court of Appeal. In *Express Newspapers Ltd* v *MacShane* [1980] 1 All ER 65, it was held that the test of whether an act was done 'in furtherance of a trade dispute' was subjective. This decision was followed in *Duport Steels Ltd* v *Sirs* [1980] 1 All ER 529, and in *Hadmor Productions Ltd* v *Hamilton* [1982] 1 All ER 1042, union officials were held to be acting 'in contemplation or furtherance of a trade dispute', and therefore immune from a civil action, when threatening to induce union members employed by Thames Television to 'black' television programmes made by a third party. In *Associated British Ports* v *Transport and General Workers Union* [1989] 3 All ER 822, it was held (reversing the decision of the Court of Appeal) that the National Dock Labour Scheme 1967 (abolished by the Dock Work Act 1989 but still in force when this case was decided) did not make it unlawful for registered dock workers to go on strike. Consequently, there was no serious issue to be tried in the case and the port employers therefore failed in their attempt to obtain an interim injunction restraining the union from calling a strike. In each of these four cases the earlier decision of the Court of Appeal was reversed.

Nor can it be said that the House has always toed the Establishment line. Its decision in *Burmah Oil Co. Ltd* v *Lord Advocate* [1965] AC 75 (para 8.10.3.6) was so inconvenient to the government of the day that it was quickly overruled by statute. (See also *Conway* v *Rimmer* [1968] AC 910, in which the House overruled its decision in *Duncan* v *Cammell, Laird & Co. Ltd* [1942] AC 624, para 9.3.2.2; *R* v *Secretary of State for the Home Department (ex parte Khawaja)* [1983] 2 WLR 321, overruling in part its decision in *R* v *Secretary of State for the Home Department (ex parte Zamir)* [1980] AC 930, para 4.5; *M* v *Home Office* [1993] 3 All ER 537, holding that the courts can grant injunctions against government ministers, who may be liable for contempt of court if they disobey them, paras 5.3 and 11.11.6.) At the interlocutory stage of the *Spycatcher* litigation the House was not unanimous in its decision to impose wide-ranging interim injunctions (*see Attorney-General* v *Guardian Newspapers Ltd* [1987] 3 All ER 316, above). Lord Bridge wrote a blistering dissenting opinion in which he confessed that the decision of the majority had seriously undermined his confidence in the capacity of the common law to protect the fundamental freedoms essential to a free society. He continued (at pp. 346–7);

. . . I can see nothing whatever, either in law or on the merits, to be said for the maintenance of a total ban on discussion in the press of this country of matters of undoubted public interest and concern which the rest of the world now knows all about and can discuss freely. Still less can I approve your Lordships' decision to throw in for good measure a restriction on reporting court proceedings in Australia which the Attorney-General had never even asked for.

Freedom of speech is always the first casualty under a totalitarian regime . . . The present attempt to insulate the public in this country from information which is freely available elsewhere is a significant step down that very dangerous road . . . If the government are determined to fight to maintain the ban to the end, they will face inevitable condemnation and humiliation by the European Court of Human Rights in Strasbourg. Long before that they will have been condemned at the bar of public opinion in the free world.

Lord Oliver, the other dissentient, said (at p. 376):

> Ideas, however unpopular or unpalatable, once released and however released into the air of free discussion and circulation, cannot for ever be effectively proscribed as if they were a virulent disease . . . [T]o attempt, even temporarily, to create a sort of judicial *cordon sanitaire* against the infection from abroad of public comment and discussion is not only, as I believe, certain to be ineffective but involves taking the first steps on a very perilous path.

When the Attorney-General sought to have the *Spycatcher* injunctions made permanent at the full trial of the action between the parties, the House of Lords, to its credit, discharged the injunctions on the ground that they were not needed since all possible damage had already been done by publication of the confidential information abroad (*Attorney-General v Guardian Newspapers Ltd (No. 2)* [1988] 3 All ER 545). It was further held, contrary to the Attorney-General's claim, that it would not be appropriate to issue a general injunction restraining future publication of information about the security service. It is perhaps an unfortunate feature of this case that the opinions of some of their Lordships are punctuated by unnecessary personal attacks on Mr Wright (see *per* Lord Keith at p. 646, Lord Brightman at p. 647 and Lord Griffiths at p. 654).

The House of Lords has performed a valuable function in correcting the mistakes of the Court of Appeal. Blom-Cooper and Drewry reported in 1972 that in the period 1952 to 1968 the Court of Appeal was reversed by the House of Lords in 39.2 per cent of civil appeals and in 25 per cent of criminal appeals (*Final Appeal*, pp. 241–50). During 1998, in 26 out of 35 civil appeals (74 per cent) the decision of the Court of Appeal was reversed or varied. In the same year, the decision of the Court of Appeal was reversed in two out of the three criminal appeals to reach the House of Lords (*Judicial Statistics 1998*, Cm 4371, 1999, p. 10).

The House of Lords has moreover made some notable contributions to our jurisprudence in such well known cases as *Rylands* v *Fletcher* (1868) LR 3 HL 330 (para 9.5); *Donoghue* v *Stevenson* [1932] AC 562 (para 9.5); *Hedley Byrne & Co. Ltd* v *Heller & Partners Ltd* [1964] AC 465 (para 9.4.2); *British Railways Board* v *Herrington* [1972] AC 877 (para 9.3.2.2); *Christie* v *Leachinsky* [1947] AC 573, in which it was held that a person effecting an arrest must communicate to the detainee the reason for the arrest or else be liable for the tort of false imprisonment; *McLoughlin* v *O'Brian* [1982] 2 All ER 298, in which it was held, extending once again the boundaries of negligence, that the claimant was entitled to damages for nervous shock sustained on hearing about, and seeing the results of, an accident to her family caused by the defendants' negligence even though she was not at or near the scene of the accident at the time or shortly afterwards; *Gillick* v *West Norfolk and Wisbech Area Health Authority* [1985] 3 All ER 402, where the restricted scope of so-called 'parental rights' in a modern society was confirmed; *R* v *R (rape: marital exemption)* [1991] 4 All ER 481 (para 9.3.2.7), in which the House abolished a husband's immunity from criminal liability for the rape of his wife; *Derbyshire County Council* v *Times Newspapers Ltd* [1993] 1 All ER 1011, where it was held that local and central government bodies cannot sue for libel since it is of the highest public importance that they should be open to unfettered public criticism; *Boddington* v *British Transport Police* [1998] 2 All ER 203 (para 11.5.2.3), in which the House decided that a defendant's challenge in criminal proceedings to the validity of the delegated legislation under which he is charged can be made on *procedural* as well as *substantive* grounds; and *Kleinwort Benson Ltd* v *Lincoln City Council* [1998] 4 All ER

513 (para 9.3.2.2), where the 200 year-old common law rule that money paid under a mistake of law is not recoverable was abolished.

1.3   COURT OF APPEAL

1.3.1   Introduction

The Court of Appeal was created by the Judicature Act 1873. Under the Act as originally drafted the Court of Appeal was to have been the ultimate appeal court since the jurisdiction of the House of Lords was to be abolished. In the end, the House of Lords was reprieved and the Court of Appeal was set up to hear civil appeals only. It now also hears criminal appeals after the Criminal Appeal Act 1966 created its criminal division to replace the Court of Criminal Appeal (see now the Supreme Court Act 1981, s. 3(1)). The Court of Appeal, together with the High Court and the Crown Court, is part of the Supreme Court of Judicature (Supreme Court Act 1981, s. 1(1)). The president of the Supreme Court is the Lord Chancellor (Supreme Court Act 1981, s. 1(2)), a belated statutory recognition of his traditional *de facto* headship of the judiciary. The House of Lords, although for most purposes the 'supreme' court in the United Kingdom, is not part of the Supreme Court of Judicature. This was probably a pure oversight caused originally by the uncertainty surrounding the future of the House of Lords between 1873 and 1876. The Employment Appeal Tribunal is also not part of the Supreme Court despite the fact that High Court judges sit in it and that appeals from its decisions lie to the Court of Appeal.

1.3.2   Composition

The Court of Appeal is composed of the Lord Chancellor, any former Lord Chancellor willing to sit, any Lord of Appeal in Ordinary willing to sit, the Lord Chief Justice, the Master of the Rolls, the President of the Family Division of the High Court, the Vice-Chancellor of the Chancery Division and up to 35 Lords Justices of Appeal (Supreme Court Act 1981, s. 2, as amended). The number of Lords Justices may be increased by Order in Council. In addition, any former Court of Appeal or High Court judge, and any present High Court judge, may be requested to sit in the Court of Appeal (ibid., s. 9). A former judge can refuse the request; a judge still in office cannot do so (ibid., s. 9(3)).

The Lord Chancellor, although an *ex officio* member, never sits in the Court of Appeal and it is rare to find former Lord Chancellors, Law Lords, the President or the Vice-Chancellor sitting there. In practice, the work is done by the Lord Chief Justice, the Master of the Rolls, the Lords Justices and those High Court judges who are requested to sit on an *ad hoc* basis. To be qualified for appointment as a Lord Justice of Appeal a person must either have a ten-year High Court qualification within the meaning of s. 71 of the Courts and Legal Services Act 1990 (para 1.1.5 above) or be a High Court judge (Supreme Court Act 1981, s. 10(3)(b), as amended by the Courts and Legal Services Act 1990). Thus it is possible for a person to be appointed as a Lord Justice direct from practice without any previous judicial experience. A good example is Sir Wilfred Greene, who was appointed a Lord Justice of Appeal in 1935 after a highly successful career of 27 years at the Bar. He later became Master of the Rolls (1937–49) and a Lord of Appeal in Ordinary (1949–50).

The president of the *civil* division of the Court of Appeal is the Master of the Rolls. The president of the *criminal* division is the Lord Chief Justice (Supreme Court Act 1981, s. 3(2)). The criminal division also has a vice-president. Any number of courts of either division may sit at the same time, subject, of course, to the availability of judicial manpower (ibid., s. 3(5)).

Since January 1995, it has been possible for circuit judges, approved for the purpose by the Lord Chancellor, to sit on some appeals in the criminal division of the Court of Appeal at the invitation of the Lord Chief Justice. Circuit judges are, however, forbidden to take part in appeals against a conviction before, or a sentence passed by, a High Court judge and not more than one of them is allowed to hear any particular appeal (Supreme Court Act 1981, s. 9, as amended by, and s. 56A, as inserted by, the Criminal Justice and Public Order Act 1994, following a recommendation of the *Royal Commission on Criminal Justice* (Cm 2263, 1993)).

1.3.3   Jurisdiction

1.3.3.1   Civil division
The jurisdiction of the Court of Appeal, civil division, is mainly to hear appeals in civil cases from all three divisions of the High Court and from the county courts. Before 1935 an appeal in most cases from the county courts went first to the Divisional Court of the King's Bench Division of the High Court before going on to the Court of Appeal. This first appeal was ended by the Administration of Justice (Appeals) Act 1934. (For restrictions on the right to appeal, and for appeals to the Court of Appeal from other courts and tribunals, see para 6.1.) Since 1970 it has been possible, in certain circumstances, to 'leapfrog' the Court of Appeal and to take a civil appeal direct from the High Court to the House of Lords (para 6.1.4.1).

An appeal before the Court of Appeal, civil division, is normally heard by three judges sitting together, although any uneven number of judges not less than three (e.g., five or seven) will suffice (Supreme Court Act 1981, s. 54(2)). However, in the interests of the economic and efficient use of judicial time, the following *may* be heard by only *two* judges (ibid., s. 54(4), as amended by the Courts and Legal Services Act 1990):

(a)   Any appeal against an interlocutory order or judgment (i.e., an order or judgment which is not final).

(b)   Any application for leave to appeal.

(c)   Any appeal where, before the hearing, all the parties have filed a consent to the appeal being heard by two judges.

(d)   Any appeal of which part has been heard by three or more judges of whom one or more are unable to continue if all the parties have consented to the remainder of the appeal being heard by two remaining judges.

(e)   Any other appeal prescribed by order by the Lord Chancellor with the concurrence of the Master of the Rolls. In this category come all appeals from the county courts and appeals from the High Court in proceedings which could have been brought in a county court (Court of Appeal (Civil Division) Order 1982, SI 1982, No. 543).

The arrangements for the composition of the Court of Appeal, civil division, will be changed when the Access to Justice Act 1999 substitutes the present s. 54 of the Supreme Court Act 1981. Under the new s. 54, the court will be properly constituted if it consists of *one or more* judges. Beyond that, the Master of the Rolls will be empowered to:

(a)   give directions (with the concurrence of the Lord Chancellor) about the minimum number of judges required to sit in any *description of proceedings*;

(b)   decide how many judges should sit in any *particular proceedings*, or designate any Lord Justice of Appeal to do this for him;

(c)   give directions about what is to happen where proceedings in a case are partly heard and a judge is unable to continue.

If an appeal has been heard by two judges and they are equally divided, the case must be re-argued before an uneven number of judges not less than three before any appeal can be taken to the House of Lords (Supreme Court Act 1981, s. 54(5)). This provision also applies to appeals heard in the criminal division.

Although it seems self-evident in the interests of justice and the preservation of public confidence in the bench, it is expressly provided that a judge is not allowed to hear an appeal from one of his own decisions (ibid., s. 56). This provision, too, applies equally to appeals in the criminal division. It ousts the common law assumption that there is no inherent objection in allowing a superior court judge to hear an appeal from one of his own decisions.

1.3.3.2   Criminal division

The jurisdiction of the Court of Appeal, criminal division, is to hear appeals in criminal cases from persons convicted at the Crown Court. An appeal lies against conviction and/or sentence, but only with leave of the Court of Appeal or if the trial judge certifies that the case is fit for appeal (see further, para 6.2.2). Although they should not, strictly, be called 'appeals', the criminal division also hears cases referred to it by the Attorney-General and the Criminal Cases Review Commission (paras 6.2.2.5, 6.2.2.6 and 6.3.3). The Court of Appeal has no jurisdiction to hear appeals in criminal cases from the High Court, including a divisional court thereof (Supreme Court Act 1981, s. 18(1)(a); see further, para 6.1.4). Such appeals will normally lie direct to the House of Lords (para 6.2.1.3). An exception is that an appeal lies to the Court of Appeal from the decision of a single judge of the High Court in a case of criminal contempt of court (other than a decision on appeal to him) (para 5.5).

An appeal in the criminal division will normally be heard by three judges. In particular, the court must consist of an uneven number of judges not less than three to hear the following matters (Supreme Court Act 1981, s. 55(4), as amended):

(a)   An appeal against conviction.
(b)   An appeal against a verdict of not guilty by reason of insanity.
(c)   An appeal against a jury's finding of unfitness to plead by reason of a disability.
(d)   An application for leave to appeal to the House of Lords.
(e)   A reference by the Attorney-General of an unduly lenient sentence (see para 6.2.2.6).

An appeal by the defendant against *sentence only* may be heard by *two* judges. Where the two judges fail to agree, the case will be re-argued before an uneven number of judges, normally three (ibid., s. 55(5)).

1.3.4   Procedure

The Court of Appeal can sit anywhere in England and Wales (Supreme Court Act 1981, s. 57(1)), although it usually sits in London. The criminal division sat for the first time outside London when, in November 1979, it sat for a week in Cardiff to hear appeals from the Crown Court in Wales. It has also sat in Manchester, Liverpool, Birmingham and Bristol.

The hearing of an appeal by the Court of Appeal is not a retrial. The appeal is determined after reading the documents in the case and hearing counsel's arguments. In the civil division where the court consists of an uneven number of judges, the majority decision prevails. Each judge is entitled to deliver his own separate judgment. In the criminal division, normally only one judgment is delivered, either by the presiding judge or by another member of the court on his direction. Separate judgments can be delivered in the criminal division only where the presiding judge states that in his opinion the case involves a question of law on which it is convenient that separate judgments should be pronounced (ibid., s. 59). This rule is designed to prevent the regular recording of dissenting judgments on the criminal law where certainty is of especial importance.

1.3.5 Delay in the Court of Appeal, civil division

Changes in the procedure of the Court of Appeal, civil division, were announced by Sir John Donaldson MR in 1982 (see *Practice Note* [1982] 3 All ER 376). The changes were designed mainly to achieve a reduction in delay before the court and a saving of costs.

Procedural changes were introduced in an effort to reduce the length of oral hearings before the court. Although proposals to change to a system of written briefs and to impose time-limits on counsel's argument have been rejected, the judges are now expected to familiarise themselves before the hearing with the general background to the dispute, the judgment of the court below and the grounds of appeal. The Master of the Rolls has given guidance on the preparation of 'skeleton arguments', which counsel are expected to submit to the court at least 14 days in advance of the hearing of all appeals other than those of exceptional urgency (*Practice Direction (Court of Appeal: procedure)* [1999] 2 All ER 490). Since the purpose of a skeleton argument is to identify, but not to argue, the points involved, it should be as succinct as possible. It should state points of law and cite the principal authorities in support, including references to the relevant page numbers. Since 1985, counsel for the appellant has also been expected to submit a written chronology of events relating to the appeal (see now, ibid., at p. 500). It was hoped that the judicial intimacy with the issues involved in an appeal, resulting from a perusal of these various documents, would discourage lengthy opening addresses by counsel and shorten the hearing generally. Furthermore, where the court has prepared *written* judgments, the judges of the Court of Appeal are now encouraged to give copies to counsel, the law reporters and the press instead of wasting valuable time reading them aloud in court.

It was also hoped to achieve some reduction in delay by the use of two-man courts as sanctioned by the Supreme Court Act 1981 (para 1.3.3.1 above), although at the same time it is recognised that it is desirable to have a three-man court where the appeal raises issues of complexity or general importance (*Practice Note* [1982] 3 All ER 376, 383–4; *Wandsworth London Borough Council* v *Winder* [1984] 3 All ER 83, at p. 106, CA). In addition, changes in the Rules of the Supreme Court in 1982 made it possible for the Court of Appeal to sit in vacation in August and September to hear non-urgent appeals and applications as well as those of an emergency nature (see now *Practice Direction (Court of Appeal: procedure)* [1999] 2 All ER 490).

Each year the Master of Rolls issues a review of the work of the civil division of the Court of Appeal for the previous legal year. The review highlights such problems as the backlog of cases, dealing with hopeless appeals and the shortage of judicial manpower.

Although the Court of Appeal can itself order the hearing of appeals to be expedited, it is extremely reluctant to do so because of the knock-on effect upon other appeals. Examples of appeals in which expedited hearings will be sympathetically considered include cases in which children are likely to suffer extraordinary prejudice, or publication of allegedly unlawful material is imminent, or a party may lose his livelihood, business or home (ibid.; *Unilever plc* v *Chefaro Proprietaries Ltd* [1995] 1 All ER 587, CA).

The Court of Appeal, civil division, is an extremely busy court. Furthermore, in the vast majority of cases it is the ultimate appellate court since only a very small proportion of appeals are taken further to the House of Lords. In circumstances of real urgency, too, it is effectively the final appellate court and a party is entitled to act on its decisions in such circumstances without waiting to see whether the other party intends to appeal to the House of Lords (*C* v *S* [1987] 1 All ER 1230, CA, *per* Sir John Donaldson MR at p. 1243 — termination of pregnancy urgently required).

In November 1996, against a background of delays in the hearing of appeals caused by an ever increasing caseload, Sir Jeffery Bowman, former senior partner of Price Waterhouse Europe, was asked to chair a review of the civil division of the Court of Appeal. The terms of reference called for an examination of the rules, procedures and working methods of the Court of Appeal, the scope of its jurisdiction, the appropriate constitution of the court for different categories of case, and its legal and administrative support. The review was expected to put forward costed recommendations for improving the operating efficiency of the Court of Appeal, and it was warned that its recommendations must make best use of all available resources and must not compromise the fairness of proceedings, the quality of decisions or the independence of the judiciary.

The findings of the review were published in *Report to the Lord Chancellor by the Review of the Court of Appeal, Civil Division* (Lord Chancellor's Department, September 1997). The review concluded that the appeal process should ensure that, so far as is practical, uncertainty and delay are kept to a minimum, and it identified a private and a public purpose of appeals in civil cases. The private purpose is to correct error, unfairness or wrong exercise of discretion which has led to an unjust result. The public purpose is to ensure public confidence in the administration of justice and, in appropriate cases, to clarify and develop the law, practice and procedure and help maintain the standards of first instance courts and tribunals.

Among the major recommendations of the review were the following:

(a)   Certain appeals which presently go to the Court of Appeal should be heard at a lower level by a court or judge with a superior jurisdiction to the court or judge who made the first instance decision. For example, it is proposed that appeals in fast-track cases should be heard quickly and locally by a circuit judge from decisions of a district judge and by a High Court judge from decisions of a circuit judge.

(b)   The Court of Appeal should retain appellate jurisdiction in three situations: when an individual appeal raises an important point of principle or practice, or is one which for some other special reason ought to be considered by it; when the Master of the Rolls directs that, in certain cases or groups of cases giving rise to the same or similar issues, appeal should lie direct to it; and when Parliament lays down that a particular class of appeals should be heard by it.

(c)   The requirement for permission to appeal should be extended to all cases except those involving the liberty of the subject (appeals against committal orders and refusals to grant habeas corpus), adoption cases, and child abduction cases. The Court of Appeal should issue guidance to the lower courts on when it is expected that permission should be granted or refused and the lower courts should be required to give brief reasons for granting or refusing permission to appeal. If the proposed extension of the requirement for permission does not result in a corresponding increase in success rates on appeal, consideration should be given to requiring that applications for permission to appeal must all be made to the Court of Appeal itself.

(d)   There should be a discretion to list cases before a single member of the Court of Appeal.

(e)   Consideration should be given to the greater use of two-judge courts in appropriate cases where no fundamental point of principle or practice is involved.

(f)   There should be a power to appoint outstandingly distinguished academic or practising lawyers to sit as members of the Court of Appeal on an *ad hoc* basis.

(g)   Judicial case management should be strengthened.

(h)   Appeals should be better prepared by lawyers at a much earlier stage and realistic timetables should be set and strictly observed.

(i)   Appropriate time limits should be imposed on counsel's oral argument.

(j)   With the agreement of the parties, it should be possible for an appeal to be decided on the papers alone without hearing any oral argument at all.

(k)   Applications for permission to appeal which are manifestly ill-founded, unreasonable or vexatious should be dismissable on the papers by a single Lord Justice.

(l)   More judicial time should be spent on reading and less on sitting in court.

(m)   Information for litigants in person about the appeal process and what it can deliver should be available at an early stage.

(n)   Consideration should be given to the feasibility of a survey of the reasons why some litigants appeal and why others accept the decisions of courts of first instance.

(o)   The use of information technology should be further developed to support the court's work.

(p)   A number of internal reforms were recommended (including the eventual abolition of the post of Registrar of Civil Appeals) with a view to improving the administrative efficiency of the court.

Many of these recommendations are being implemented by the Access to Justice Act 1999, and regulations made thereunder, and by practice directions, such as *Practice Direction (Court of Appeal: procedure)* [1999] 2 All ER 490.

1.4   HIGH COURT OF JUSTICE

1.4.1   Introduction

The High Court of Justice, a superior court of record, was created as part of the Supreme Court of Judicature by the Judicature Act 1873. For administrative convenience, it comprises three divisions: the Chancery Division, the Queen's Bench Division and the Family Division. The three divisions are not, however, separate courts (see the Supreme Court Act 1981, s. 5(5)). Originally five divisions were created, corresponding to some old courts which were at the same time abolished. The original five were the Chancery Division, the Queen's Bench Division, the Common Pleas Division, the Exchequer Division and the Probate, Divorce and Admiralty (PDA) Division. In 1880, the Common Pleas and Exchequer Divisions were abolished and their jurisdiction taken over by the Queen's Bench Division. In 1971, under the provisions of the Administration of Justice Act 1970, the PDA Division was renamed the Family Division and its jurisdiction redistributed among the three divisions. The number of divisions may be increased or reduced by Order in Council on a joint recommendation of the Lord Chancellor, the Lord Chief Justice, the Master of the Rolls, the President of the Family Division and the Vice-Chancellor of the Chancery Division (Supreme Court Act 1981, s. 7(1)).

Judges of the High Court sit mainly in London but it is possible for sittings of the High Court to be held at any place in England and Wales (ibid., s. 71(1)). It is the Lord Chancellor who directs where sittings outside London shall take place (ibid., s. 71(2)). Standing directions authorise High Court civil cases to be tried at the following places: Birmingham, Bristol, Caernarvon, Cardiff, Carlisle, Chelmsford, Chester, Exeter, Leeds, Lewes, Lincoln, Liverpool, Manchester, Middlesbrough, Mold, Newcastle upon Tyne, Norwich, Nottingham, Oxford, Preston, Sheffield, Stafford, Swansea, Truro, Warwick and Winchester. The Lord Chancellor can authorise sittings at places other than these on an *ad hoc* basis. For example, in *St Edmundsbury & Ipswich Diocesan Board of Finance* v *Clark* [1973] Ch 323 Megarry J was given permission to sit in the Chancery Division at Iken in Suffolk so as to take the evidence of an 84-year-old witness who was in poor health (see also *Tito* v *Waddell (No. 2)* [1977] 3 All ER 129, para 1.4.4.4 below).

The High Court is principally a civil court. It does, however, exercise some important criminal jurisdiction. Its civil jurisdiction is virtually unlimited.

1.4.2 Composition

The High Court consists of the Lord Chancellor, who is president of the Chancery Division but never sits; the Lord Chief Justice, who presides over the Queen's Bench Division; the vice-president of the Queen's Bench Division; the President, who presides over the Family Division; the Vice-Chancellor, who is vice-president of the Chancery Division; the Senior Presiding Judge (see para 1.5.3 below); and a number of ordinary High Court judges (Supreme Court Act 1981, s. 4(1), as amended). The ordinary High Court judges are sometimes referred to as 'puisne' (i.e., lesser or assistant) judges. Their maximum number is 106. This number may be increased by Order in Council (ibid., s. 4(4)).

To be qualified for appointment as a puisne judge of the High Court a person must either have a ten-year High Court qualification within the meaning of s. 71 of the Courts and Legal Services Act 1990 (para 1.1.5 above) or have been a circuit judge for at least two years (ibid., s. 10(3)(c), as amended by the Courts and Legal Services Act 1990).

A puisne judge is appointed by the Queen on the advice of the Lord Chancellor, who assigns him or her to a particular division dependent upon the volume of business before the court. Although assigned initially to a particular division, a puisne judge can sit in any division as and when required at the request of the Lord Chief Justice made with the concurrence of the President of the Family Division or the Vice-Chancellor (Supreme Court Act 1981, s. 5(3), as amended). He can be transferred by the Lord Chancellor to another division, but only with his consent and that of the president of his present division (ibid., s. 5(2)).

In addition, judges and former judges of the Court of Appeal, former puisne judges of the High Court, circuit judges and recorders may be requested by the Lord Chancellor to sit as additional judges of the High Court (ibid., s. 9(1), (2) and (3), as amended by the Administration of Justice Act 1982, s. 58). Such requests are rare, although it is not unusual for a circuit judge to be asked to take High Court work in the provinces or for a recorder to deal with urgent High Court applications in matrimonial and wardship cases.

The Lord Chancellor may also appoint deputy judges of the High Court on a temporary basis in order to facilitate the disposal of business. The persons appointed must be qualified for appointment as puisne judges. A deputy judge has all the powers of a puisne judge of the High Court (Supreme Court Act 1981, s. 9(4) and (5), and see para 1.5.4 below). In September 1997, the Lord Chancellor for the first time appointed solicitors to sit as deputy High Court judges. The two appointees were Dr L.A. Collins QC and Mr A.L. Marriott QC. Earlier in the same year Dr Collins and Mr Marriott had become the first solicitors to be appointed Queen's Counsel. The first solicitor to be appointed as a full-time High Court judge was Sachs J, who was promoted from circuit judge in 1993. In 2000, Dr Collins became the first solicitor to be appointed as a full-time High Court judge *direct from practice*. He was assigned to the Chancery Division.

1.4.3 Queen's Bench Division

The Chancery Division is the senior division of the High Court but here it is proposed to deal first with the Queen's Bench Division because of the volume, diversity and importance of its work.

1.4.3.1 Composition
The president of the Queen's Bench Division is the Lord Chief Justice and he is assisted by a vice-president and a number of puisne judges. Over half of the total number of puisne judges of the High Court are attached to the Queen's Bench Division. This judicial strength reflects both the volume of business in the division and the fact that Queen's Bench judges spend a certain amount of time away from London on circuit in the provinces trying High Court civil actions and, as judges of the Crown Court, criminal cases.

1.4.3.2 Jurisdiction
The Queen's Bench Division acts mainly as a civil court where a single judge tries, at first instance, such cases as breach of contract and actions in tort. These cases are invariably tried by the judge sitting alone since juries are very rare in civil cases (para 7.6). Most actions are either settled or abandoned and only 1 per cent result in a trial.

1.4.3.3 The Commercial Court and the Admiralty Court
Within the Queen's Bench Division there exist the Commercial Court and the Admiralty Court (Supreme Court Act 1981, s. 6(1)).

The Commercial Court, which was officially made part of the Queen's Bench Division in 1971, hears cases which have been entered on a special commercial list kept in London, Liverpool and Manchester (ibid., s. 62(3)). The commercial list has existed since 1895, although it is only since 1971 that the cases on the list have been dealt with in a separate Commercial Court officially recognised by statute. These cases include banking and insurance disputes and the construction of mercantile documents such as negotiable instruments and charterparties. The judges of the Commercial Court are those puisne judges of the High Court nominated by the Lord Chancellor (ibid., s. 6(2)). They are usually puisne judges of the Queen's Bench Division with special knowledge and experience of commercial affairs. Ten such judges are nominated and normally five of them sit in the Commercial Court at any one time.

The advantages of the Commercial Court to the business community lie in the guidance provided by a substantial body of case law and in the court's simplified, speedier procedure. Thus, by consent of the parties, the strict rules of evidence may be relaxed so as to admit testimony which would normally be inadmissible. Moreover, the case may be decided on the documentary evidence alone, thereby saving the time and money involved in calling witnesses to give oral evidence.

In appropriate cases (for example, where the costs of litigation are likely to be out of all proportion to the amount at stake), parties are encouraged to consider the use of alternative dispute resolution, such as mediation, conciliation and arbitration, as an additional means of settling disputes (see *Practice Note (Commercial Court: alternative dispute resolution)* [1994] 1 All ER 34).

Although the Commercial Court is frequently used by foreign litigants for the resolution of international commercial disputes, the Court is a national or domestic court of England and Wales and is *not* an 'international' court (*Amin Rasheed Shipping Corpn.* v *Kuwait Insurance Co.* [1983] 2 All ER 884, HL). The very popularity of the Commercial Court has made it the victim of its own success (*Barclay's Bank plc* v *Bemister* [1989] 1 All ER 10, CA, *per* Sir John Donaldson MR at p. 12; on the problem of *delay,* see para 1.4.6 below).

The Admiralty Court became part of the Queen's Bench Division on the demise of the Probate, Divorce and Admiralty Division in 1971. Admiralty jurisdiction includes the trial of claims for damages, loss of life or personal injury arising out of a collision between ships, or as a result of any defect in a ship, claims to the possession or ownership of a ship, claims for loss of or damage to goods carried in a ship, claims for salvage and towage in respect of a ship or aircraft, and claims for wages by a master or member of the crew of a ship (Supreme Court Act 1981, s. 20, as amended). The jurisdiction over claims for salvage in respect of ships is exercisable only where the ship in question was in *tidal* waters. It does not extend to ships in peril in *non-tidal waters (The Goring* [1988] 1 All ER 641, HL, disallowing a claim for remuneration for salvage services rendered to a small passenger vessel adrift in the River Thames).

The Admiralty Court, sitting as a prize court, also exercises the prize jurisdiction of the High Court (ibid., ss. 20(1)(d), 27 and 62(2)). Prize relates to ships and aircraft, and the goods carried therein, seized by the armed forces of a belligerent. It should be noted that an appeal from the High Court in a prize case lies to the Judicial Committee of the Privy Council and not to the Court of Appeal (ibid., s. 16(2)).

The judges of the Admiralty Court are those puisne judges of the High Court nominated by the Lord Chancellor (ibid., s. 6(2)). A judge of the Admiralty Court often sits with lay nautical assessors, who are chosen from acting Masters of Trinity House and who keep the judge advised on questions of seamanship and navigation (ibid., s. 70).

In 1993, with a view to improving Admiralty Court practice and harmonising it with that of the Commercial Court, the appropriate parts of the *Guide to Commercial Court Practice* were extended to the Admiralty Court (see *Practice Note (Admiralty Court Practice)* [1993] 2 All ER 671). The two courts remain, however, separate and distinct.

1.4.3.4   The election court

Two judges of the Queen's Bench Division, sitting as an election court, have jurisdiction to pronounce upon the validity of disputed Parliamentary elections. The matter is tried in open court without a jury. The judgment of the election court takes the form of a report to the Speaker which the House of Commons is bound to act upon (Representation of the People Act 1983, ss. 120–126, 144). With leave of the election court, an appeal lies on a question of law to the Court of Appeal, whose decision is 'final and conclusive' (ibid, s. 157).

1.4.3.5   Divisional Court of the Queen's Bench Division

Two or more judges sitting together may constitute a Divisional Court of the Queen's Bench Division (Supreme Court Act 1981, s. 66(1) and (3)). The judges will usually be from the

Queen's Bench Division, although it is provided that judges from the other two divisions are qualified to sit (ibid., s. 66(4)). The Divisional Court is presided over by the senior judge present (ibid., ss. 66(5) and 13). The functions of the Queen's Bench Divisional Court are:

(a)   To supervise public authorities, inferior courts and tribunals by entertaining applications for judicial review (Chapter 11). Permission to apply for judicial review is granted (or refused) by a single judge. If permission is granted, the substantive application for judicial review is heard by the Divisional Court if it concerns a *criminal* cause or matter. If, however, it concerns a *civil* cause or matter it will normally be heard by a single judge unless the court orders it to go before the Divisional Court.

(b)   To hear applications for the writ of habeas corpus from persons who allege that they are being unlawfully detained (Chapter 4). Note, however, that an application for a writ of habeas corpus made by a parent or guardian in relation to the custody of a minor is heard in the Family Division and not in the Queen's Bench Division (Supreme Court Act 1981, sch. 1).

(c)   To hear criminal appeals on points of law by way of case stated direct from the magistrates' courts or via the Crown Court (Chapter 6).

(d)   To hear applications to punish contempts committed in inferior courts (Chapter 5).

In an effort to achieve a more economical use of judicial manpower, cases in categories (b), (c) and (d) will be heard by a single judge rather than by the Divisional Court when the relevant sections of the Access to Justice Act 1999 come into force.

1.4.4   Chancery Division

1.4.4.1   Composition
The president of the Chancery Division is the Lord Chancellor and the vice-president is the Vice-Chancellor. In practice, the Lord Chancellor never sits and the work is done by the Vice-Chancellor assisted by a number of puisne judges.

A Vice-Chancellor was first appointed in 1813 in order to assist the Lord Chancellor and the Master of the Rolls with the dispatch of judicial business in the old Court of Chancery where the backlog of undecided cases had become something of a scandal (see Holdsworth, *History of English Law,* vol. 1, 7th ed., 1956, pp. 437–45). Two additional Vice-Chancellors were appointed in 1842. The office of Vice-Chancellor disappeared in 1875 on the reorganisation of the courts and it was not revived until 1970, when the incumbent was merely nominated by the Lord Chancellor from among the puisne judges of the Chancery Division (Administration of Justice Act 1970, s. 5, repealed by the Supreme Court Act 1981, sch. 7). From 1982, however, the Vice-Chancellorship, like other judgeships of the Supreme Court, is a formal royal appointment (Supreme Court Act 1981, s. 10(1)). Sir Robert Megarry V-C, who was Vice-Chancellor when the 1981 Act came into force, had been nominated under the old procedure. However, by para 1 of sch. 6 to the 1981 Act he was deemed to have been appointed under s. 10(1) as from 1 January 1982.

1.4.4.2   Jurisdiction: original
The Chancery Division is purely a civil court, being the successor to the old Court of Chancery which was chiefly concerned with the administration of equity. Its jurisdiction covers those matters formerly dealt with by the Court of Chancery together with other matters assigned to it by various statutes. By s. 61(1) of and sch. 1 to the Supreme Court Act 1981, the jurisdiction covers all causes and matters relating to:

(a)   The sale, exchange or partition of land, or the raising of charges on land.
(b)   The redemption or foreclosure of mortgages.
(c)   The execution of trusts.
(d)   The administration of the estates of deceased persons.
(e)   Bankruptcy.
(f)   The dissolution of partnerships or the taking of partnership or other accounts.
(g)   The rectification, setting aside or cancellation of deeds or other written instruments.
(h)   Contentious probate business, including both the validity and the interpretation of wills.
(i)   Patents, trade marks, registered designs, copyright or design right.
(j)   The appointment of a guardian of a minor's estate.
(k)   Company law.

1.4.4.3   Jurisdiction: appellate

In addition to the *first instance* or original jurisdiction just set out, the Chancery Division has some *appellate* jurisdiction as follows.

(a)   A single judge may hear appeals from decisions of General or Special Commissioners on matters of taxation (Taxes Management Act 1970, ss. 56 and 56A), and appeals in insolvency cases from the county courts (Insolvency Act 1986, s. 375 and sch. 1 to the Supreme Court Act 1981).

(b)   A Divisional Court of the Chancery Division, consisting of at least two judges, may hear land registration appeals from the county courts (Land Registration Act 1925, ss. 138(1) and 143(1); RSC, Ord. 93, r. 10).

(c)   When sitting as the Patents Court, one or more judges may hear appeals from certain decisions of the Comptroller-General of Patents, Designs and Trade Marks (Patents Act 1977, s. 97(1) and (2)). The Patents Court was first established as part of the Chancery Division in 1978, under the Patents Act 1977, to take over the functions of the Patents Appeal Tribunal. The Patents Court is part of the Chancery Division now by virtue of s. 6(1) of the Supreme Court Act 1981. The judges of the Patents Court are those puisne judges of the High Court nominated by the Lord Chancellor (Supreme Court Act 1981, s. 6(2)). The Patents Court may be assisted by scientific advisers (ibid., s. 70(3)).

1.4.4.4   The hearing of High Court Chancery proceedings

Although the High Court may sit at any place in England and Wales, the highly specialised work of the Chancery Division is concentrated mainly in London. It is chiefly the Queen's Bench judges, and sometimes the Family Division judges, who undertake High Court work on circuit in the provinces, although on one celebrated occasion Megarry J took the Chancery Division beyond even the provinces. In *Tito* v *Waddell* [1975] 3 All ER 997, he held that he had power to conduct a 'view' outside the jurisdiction of the court altogether (i.e., outside England and Wales). Having visited Ocean Island and Rabi in the western Pacific, he produced, in *Tito* v *Waddell (No. 2)* [1977] 3 All ER 129, a judgment of some 180 pages (complete with table of contents) which took him more than four days to read out in court and which brought an end to litigation which had already occupied the court for 206 days. The report of *Tito* v *Waddell (No. 2),* which involved the citation of over 200 cases, occupies 195 pages in the *All England Law Reports*.

There is provision for High Court Chancery proceedings to be dealt with by the Vice-Chancellor of the County Palatine of Lancaster sitting as a High Court judge at

Birmingham, Bristol, Cardiff, Liverpool, Manchester, Preston, Leeds and Newcastle upon Tyne. The Vice-Chancellor of the County Palatine of Lancaster is able to take High Court work because he is a circuit judge (Courts Act 1971, s. 16 and sch. 2) and, as such, may be requested by the Lord Chancellor to act as a judge of the High Court under s. 9 of the Supreme Court Act 1981 (para 1.4.2 above).

1.4.5   Family Division

1.4.5.1   Composition
The Probate, Divorce and Admiralty Division was renamed 'Family Division' in 1971 (para 1.4.1 above). It is presided over by the President of the Family Division and she is assisted by a number of puisne judges. The first female President, Dame Elizabeth Butler-Sloss P, was appointed in October 1999.

1.4.5.2   Jurisdiction
The jurisdiction of the Family Division is as follows (Supreme Court Act 1981, s. 61(1) and sch. 1, as amended):

(a)   All matrimonial causes and matters (whether at first instance or on appeal).
(b)   All causes and matters (whether at first instance or on appeal) relating to:

(i)   legitimacy;
(ii)   the exercise of the inherent jurisdiction of the High Court with respect to minors, the maintenance of minors and any proceedings under the Children Act 1989, except proceedings solely for the appointment of a guardian of a minor's estate (which are dealt with in the Chancery Division);
(iii)   adoption;
(iv)   non-contentious or common-form probate business (contentious or solemn-form probate business is taken in the Chancery Division).

(c)   Applications for consent to the marriage of a minor (such applications may alternatively be made to a county court or a magistrates' court (Marriage Act 1949, s. 3(5)).
(d)   Proceedings on appeal by persons who have been punished for disobeying an order, other than for the payment of money, made by a magistrates' court in matrimonial proceedings, or proceedings under part IV of the Family Law Act 1996 (family homes and domestic violence), or with respect to the guardianship of a minor (see the Magistrates' Courts Act 1980, s. 63(3)).
(e)   Proceedings under the Children Act 1989.
(f)   Proceedings under:

(i)   part IV of the Family Law Act 1996;
(ii)   the Child Abduction and Custody Act 1985;
(iii)   the Family Law Act 1986 (including declarations of status);
(iv)   s. 30 of the Human Fertilisation and Embryology Act 1990.

(g)   Proceedings for the purpose of enforcing an order made in any of the above proceedings.
(h)   Proceedings under the Child Support Act 1991.

1.4.5.3   Divisional Court of the Family Division

An appeal lies to the High Court on family matters, such as financial provision orders, from decisions of the magistrates' courts made under the Domestic Proceedings and Magistrates' Courts Act 1978 (ibid., s. 29), from their decisions to make or refuse to make any order under the Children Act 1989 (Children Act 1989, s. 94), and from their decisions to make or refuse to make any order under part IV of the Family Law Act 1996, except for a decision to decline jurisdiction in any proceedings under part IV (Family Law Act 1996, s. 61).

An appeal under the 1978 Act will usually be heard by a Divisional Court consisting of two or more judges; if the appeal is concerned only with the amount of any periodical or lump sum payment ordered to be made it will be heard by a single judge unless the President directs otherwise (Family Proceedings Rules 1991, SI 1991, No. 1247, r. 8.2).

An appeal under the Children Act 1989 will usually be heard by a single judge unless the President directs otherwise (ibid., r. 4.22); the hearing will normally be held in open court at the nearest convenient High Court centre (see *Practice Direction* [1992] 1 All ER 864).

1.4.6   Delay in the High Court

The Report of the Royal Commission on Legal Services was generally critical of the complexities of civil procedure. Although procedural matters were outside its terms of reference, the Royal Commission noted that 'there is a close relationship between the rules of procedure and the duration and cost of litigation' and recommended a full appraisal of the practical operation of our system of civil justice (Cmnd 7648, 1979, p. 723).

In its belated response to that Report, the government announced its intention to conduct a review of civil procedure (Cmnd 9077, 1983). Work on the civil justice review, as it became known, began in 1985 with the object of finding ways to reduce the delay, cost and complexity associated with civil proceedings (notably in the Queen's Bench Division). The review, which was under the control of the Lord Chancellor's Department, was supplemented by factual surveys commissioned from independent institutions and management consultants. A number of consultation papers were issued and the final report was published in June 1988 (*Report of the Review Body on Civil Justice,* Cm 394, 1988).

Even before the outcome of the civil justice review was known, changes were introduced in the Commercial Court (para 1.4.3.3 above). The substantial increase in demand for the services of this court experienced during the 1980s was caused mainly by foreign litigants voluntarily choosing to use an English court in preference to one situated abroad. Pressure on judicial time has led to a substantial backlog of cases. In 1986, changes were made to the Rules of the Supreme Court and to practices within the Commercial Court with the object of promoting greater expedition, economy and efficiency in the conduct of commercial business. In particular, it was hoped to reduce hearing times by asking the judges to read more of the documentation in advance of the hearing and by encouraging counsel to avoid the prolonged reading aloud in court of documents and extracts from cases. The changes were summarised in a 'Guide to Commercial Court Practice' issued by the Lord Chief Justice as a *Practice Note* (1986) 136 New LJ 868.

In its final report in 1988, the civil justice review body itself recommended further changes with the object of restricting access to the Commercial Court and reducing delay. Increased fees at a level which reflected the cost of handling cases (including hearings), the introduction of a monetary limit of at least £50,000 on claims, and the strengthening of full-time judicial manpower were proposed. It was further recommended that the waiting period for a hearing should, within three years, be reduced to 12 months from the time when a trial date is given (*Report of the Review Body on Civil Justice,* Cm 394, 1988).

Proceedings in the Chancery Division of the High Court were excluded from the civil justice review because the workings of that court had already been separately investigated. In 1979, the Royal Commission on Legal Services had recommended that 'the administrative methods of the Chancery Division should be subjected to an organisation and methods examination' (Cmnd 7648, 1979, p. 727). In the same year, the Lord Chancellor appointed a two-person review body under Oliver J (a judge of the Chancery Division and later of the House of Lords) to examine the procedure and organisation of the division. The review body reported in 1981 and made nearly 100 recommendations for achieving the more expeditious and economical disposal of business (*Report of the Review Body on the Chancery Division of the High Court,* Cmnd 8205, 1981). Many of the review body's recommendations were implemented in 1982 and the exercise of Chancery jurisdiction was extended to Birmingham, Bristol and Cardiff.

Although by reason of changes made to the Rules of the Supreme Court in 1982 it is possible for High Court judges to sit in vacation to hear non-urgent cases as well as the usual emergency applications, it remains the position that the problems caused by delays in the High Court are exacerbated by the long vacation during August and September. While the Crown Court and the county courts operate fairly normally during this period, High Court judges do not sit regularly in court. Of course, it is not true to say that High Court judges do no work at all during the long vacation. In *Libyan Arab Foreign Bank* v *Bankers Trust Co.* [1989] 3 All ER 252, Staughton J, delivering in the Commercial Court on 2 September 1987 a reserved judgment which occupies 34 pages in the *All England Law Reports,* concluded with the following postscript (at p. 288):

In August of this year there were 20 working days. Fourteen of them were entirely consumed in the preparation of this judgment. In those circumstances it is a shade disappointing to read in the press and elsewhere that High Court judges do no work at all in August or September and have excessively long holidays.

It seems undeniable, however, that the long vacation does lead to under-utilisation of valuable judicial time when there is a need for increased judicial productivity in the High Court. The civil justice review body recommended that the long vacation in the High Court should be limited to August but without any overall reduction in annual judicial leave (*Report of the Review Body on Civil Justice,* Cm 394, 1988).

Further measures aimed at reducing the costs and delay associated with civil litigation in the High Court were announced in January 1995. (See *Practice Note* [1995] 1 All ER 385 (Queen's Bench and Chancery Divisions); *Practice Note* [1995] 1 All ER 586 (Family Division).) In March 1994, the Lord Chancellor appointed Lord Woolf (then a Lord of Appeal, now the Master of the Rolls) to inquire into the problems of cost, delay and complexity associated with the civil justice system. In an interim report published in June 1995, Lord Woolf proposed a three-track system comprising small claims arbitration in the county court for claims up to £3,000, a fast track for claims up to £10,000, and a multi-track for claims over £10,000 (the latter track characterised by interventionist management by teams of judges). He also advocated a greater use of technology in the courts with laptop computers for judges, video conferencing facilities and computerised filing systems (*Access to Justice: interim report to the Lord Chancellor on the civil justice system in England and Wales,* HMSO, June 1995).

Lord Woolf's final report, published in July 1996, contained some 300 recommendations, including those from the interim report. The report (*Access to Justice: final report to the*

Lord Chancellor on the civil justice system in England and Wales, HMSO, July 1996) proposes a 'new landscape' for civil litigation with the following features:

(a)   Litigation to be avoided wherever possible; people will be encouraged to use alternative methods of dispute resolution if appropriate, and to start court action as a last resort.

(b)   Litigation to be less adversarial and more cooperative.

(c)   Parties to litigation to be expected to be more open and cooperative.

(d)   The duty of expert witnesses to the court to be emphasised. Single experts, instructed by both parties, to be used whenever practicable.

(e)   Litigation to be less complex. There will be a single set of rules for the High Court and county courts. A draft of these rules was published in a separate volume at the same time as the final report.

(f)   All proceedings to be commenced by a 'claim' (instead of by writ or summons) in the same way in any court. The claim and defence will not be technical documents but will make clear the real issues between the parties.

(g)   The timescale of litigation to be shorter and more certain. All cases will progress to trial on a timetable set and monitored by the court. On the fast track there will be fixed timetables, normally of no more than 30 weeks. The court will apply strict sanctions to parties who do not comply with the procedures or timetables.

(h)   The cost of litigation to be more affordable, more predictable, and more proportionate to the value and complexity of individual cases.

The Civil Procedure Act 1997 facilitated the reform of the civil justice system by introducing new arrangements for making rules of court. The Supreme Court Rule Committee and the County Court Rule Committee were replaced by a single committee, the Civil Procedure Rule Committee, which has power to make Civil Procedure Rules 'with a view to securing that the civil justice system is accessible, fair and efficient' (s. 1(3)), and which must try to produce rules which are 'both simple and simply expressed' (s. 2(7)). The Civil Procedure Rules regulate practice and procedure in the civil division of the Court of Appeal, in the High Court and in the county courts.

The Civil Procedure Act 1997 also created an advisory body, the Civil Justice Council, for the purposes of considering how to make the civil justice system more accessible, fair and efficient, advising the Lord Chancellor and the judiciary on the development of the system, referring proposals for change in the system to the Lord Chancellor and the Civil Procedure Rule Committee, and making proposals for research (s. 6).

The Civil Procedure Rules 1998 (SI 1998, No. 3132 (CPR)), as amended, came into force on 26 April 1999. They comprise 52 Parts, together with associated practice directions, and pre-action protocols covering clinical negligence and personal injury cases. Part 1 emphasises that the Rules are a new procedural code with the overriding objective of enabling the court to deal with cases justly. In furtherance of the overriding objective, courts are required actively to manage cases. Cases are allocated under CPR, Part 26, by procedural judges to one of three tracks — the small-claims track, the fast-track, or the multi-track — taking into account a number of factors, including the financial value and the complexity of the claim.

The *small-claims track* is the normal track for:

(a)   any claim for personal injuries which has a financial value of not more than £5,000 where the claim for damages for personal injuries is not more than £1,000;

(b) any claim which includes a claim by a tenant of residential premises against a landlord for repairs or other work to the premises where the estimated cost of the repairs or other work is not more than £1,000 and the financial value of any other claim for damages is not more than £1,000; and

(c) any other claim which has a financial value of not more than £5,000.

A claim for a remedy for harassment or unlawful eviction relating to residential premises will not be allocated to the small-claims track whatever the financial value of the claim. A case involving a disputed allegation of dishonesty will not usually be regarded as suitable for the small-claims track (*Practice Direction* to CPR, Part 26). Cases generally suitable for the small-claims track include consumer disputes, accident claims, disputes about the ownership of goods, and most disputes between a landlord and tenant other than those for possession (ibid.).

The *fast-track* is the normal track for any claim for which the small-claims track is not the normal track and which has a financial value of not more than £15,000. The *multi-track* is the normal track for any claim for which the small-claims track or the fast-track is not the normal track.

Proceedings are started when the court issues a claim form (formerly a 'writ' or 'summons') at the request of the claimant (formerly the 'plaintiff'). Proceedings (whether for damages or for a specified sum) cannot be started in the High Court unless the value of the claim is more than £15,000, or, where the proceedings include a claim for damages for personal injuries, £50,000 or more (*Practice Direction* to CPR, Part 7A).

1.4.7 Judicial salaries

From April 2000 the Lord Chancellor receives a salary of £167,760 p.a. and the Lord Chief Justice £165,260 p.a. The Master of the Rolls is paid £157,390 p.a. The Law Lords, the President of the Family Division and the Vice-Chancellor earn £152,072 p.a. The Lords Justices of Appeal are paid £144,549 p.a. Puisne judges of the High Court receive salaries of £127,872 p.a. Senior circuit judges receive salaries of £103,516 p.a., and other circuit judges £95,873 p.a.

The explanation traditionally given (and equally traditionally greeted with some public scepticism) for the high level of judicial salaries is that senior barristers need adequate compensation for loss of earnings at the Bar in order to attract them to the Bench.

1.5 CROWN COURT

1.5.1 Introduction

Before the Courts Act 1971 the major criminal courts were the Assizes (which also heard civil cases) and the Quarter Sessions. One of the main criticisms of these courts was that they did not sit continuously. The Commissioners of Assize went on circuit to the counties only two or three times a year while the Quarter Sessions sat four times a year. The Assize circuits were outdated and were not based on the large centres of population thrown up by the industrial revolution. As much as one-quarter of valuable judicial time was spent simply on travelling from one Assize town on the circuit to the next. The system of criminal justice was severely strained by the increasing crime rate of the twentieth century. Accused persons spent long periods in jail awaiting trial. At the Assizes, civil cases tended to be neglected in order to get through as much of the criminal list as possible. A major defect of the Quarter Sessions was that the existence of a large number of part-time judges made it difficult to achieve any consistency in sentencing.

1.5.2   Courts Act 1971

In 1967 a Royal Commission on Assizes and Quarter Sessions was appointed under the chairmanship of Lord Beeching. It reported in 1969 and made many recommendations for the improvement of the court system in England and Wales (*Report of the Royal Commission on Assizes and Quarter Sessions,* Cmnd 4153, 1969). Most of these recommendations were implemented with unusual speed by the Courts Act 1971.

The principal changes brought about by the Courts Act 1971 may be summarised as follows:

(a)   The Assizes and Quarter Sessions were abolished (Courts Act 1971, ss. 1(2) and 3). In their place was established a single Crown Court as part of the Supreme Court of Judicature (ibid., ss. 4(1) and 1(1); see now s. 1(1) of the Supreme Court Act 1981).

(b)   The judges of the Crown Court are High Court judges, circuit judges, recorders and justices of the peace (Courts Act 1971, s. 4(2); see now s. 8(1) of the Supreme Court Act 1981 and para 1.5.4).

(c)   The High Court can sit at any place in England and Wales designated by the Lord Chancellor to take civil work (Courts Act 1971, s. 2; see now s. 71 of the Supreme Court Act 1981). The list of civil cases is no longer linked to the criminal list, although the High Court, when on circuit, often sits in the old Assize court buildings.

(d)   The Court of Chancery of the County Palatine of Lancaster and the Court of Chancery of the County Palatine of Durham and Sadberge were merged with the High Court (Courts Act 1971, s. 41). However, the office of Vice-Chancellor of the County Palatine of Lancaster was expressly preserved by s. 44(1) (para 1.4.4.4 above).

(e)   Certain ancient local courts of record which still heard some civil cases were abolished (ibid., s. 43). They were the Tolzey and Pie Poudre Courts of the City and County of Bristol, the Liverpool Court of Passage, the Norwich Guildhall Court, and the Court of Record for the Hundred of Salford.

(f)   In the place of individual local authorities, the Lord Chancellor was given overall responsibility for the court system, including the provision of administrative staff (ibid., s. 27).

(g)   The Lord Chancellor was made responsible for the summoning and empannelling of jurors in both civil and criminal cases in the High Court, Crown Court and county courts (ibid., ss. 31 and 32; provisions now contained in the Juries Act 1974, ss. 2 and 5; para 7.4).

1.5.3   Circuits, court centres and the classification of offences

The Courts Act 1971, and the administrative arrangements made thereunder by the Lord Chancellor, have produced a smoother and more unified court system in the provinces. England and Wales are divided into six circuits each with a circuit administrator, headquarters and staff. In addition, each circuit has at least two Presiding Judges from the High Court to assist with administration. A Senior Presiding Judge for England and Wales is appointed from among the Lords Justices of Appeal. Appointments to the post of Presiding Judge and Senior Presiding Judge are made by the Lord Chief Justice with the agreement of the Lord Chancellor. (These arrangements, which have existed on an informal basis since 1970, were put on a statutory footing by s. 72 of the Courts and Legal Services Act 1990.)

The Crown Court is not a local court. It is a single court which can sit anywhere in England and Wales (Supreme Court Act 1981, s. 78(1)), although sittings are usually confined within each circuit to the towns designated as court centres. When the Crown Court sits in the City of London it is known as the Central Criminal Court (often referred to as the Old Bailey), thus preserving the name of a court first established in 1834 (see Supreme Court Act 1981, s. 8(3), re-enacting the Courts Act 1971, s. 4(7)).

The six circuits with (in parentheses) some of their first-tier centres are: (i) Midland and Oxford (Birmingham, Nottingham); (ii) North-Eastern (Leeds, Newcastle upon Tyne, Sheffield); (iii) Northern (Liverpool, Manchester); (iv) South-Eastern (London, Norwich); (v) Wales and Chester (Cardiff, Chester, Swansea); (vi) Western (Bristol, Exeter, Winchester). The full list of first-tier centres appears in para 1.4.1 above.

The court centres, of which there are presently some 90, are designated as such by the Lord Chancellor (Supreme Court Act 1981, s. 78(3), formerly s. 4(6) of the Courts Act 1971). They are either first-tier, second-tier or third-tier centres. At first-tier centres, High Court judges try both civil and criminal cases while circuit judges and recorders try criminal cases only. Second-tier centres deal with criminal cases only but are served by High Court judges, circuit judges and recorders. At third-tier centres, circuit judges and recorders try criminal cases only.

For the purposes of trial in the Crown Court, criminal offences are classified according to gravity and complexity into four classes (*Practice Note* [1987] 3 All ER 1064, as amended by *Practice Note* [1995] 2 All ER 900 and *Practice Direction* [2000] 1 All ER 380; these directions were given by the Lord Chief Justice, with the concurrence of the Lord Chancellor, under s. 75(1) of the Supreme Court Act 1981, formerly s. 4(5) of the Courts Act 1971, and replaced directions first given in 1971). Class 1 offences, including murder and offences under the Official Secrets Acts, are triable only by a High Court judge except that a case of murder (or of incitement, attempt or conspiracy to commit murder) can be released from his list by a Presiding Judge for trial by a circuit judge approved for the purpose by the Lord Chief Justice. Class 2 offences, including manslaughter, unlawful abortion and rape, are tried by a High Court judge unless a particular case is released from his list by a Presiding Judge for trial by a circuit judge. A case of rape, or of a serious sexual offence of any class, can only be so released for trial by a circuit judge or recorder approved for the purpose by the Senior Presiding Judge with the concurrence of the Lord Chief Justice. Class 3 offences, covering all offences triable only on indictment and not falling into any other class, are normally tried by a High Court judge but may be tried by a circuit judge or by a recorder in accordance with general or particular directions given by a Presiding Judge. Class 4 offences, including wounding or causing grievous bodily harm with intent, robbery or assault with intent to rob, and all offences triable either way, may be tried by a High Court judge, a circuit judge or a recorder but will not normally be tried by a High Court judge. (For offences triable either way, and the procedure for determining their mode of trial, see para 1.7.6 below.)

It may be noted here that cases of serious or complex fraud which are transferred from the magistrates' courts to the Crown Court under ss. 4 and 5 of the Criminal Justice Act 1987 (see para 1.7.6.3.5 below) are triable only at the crown court centres designated for that purpose for each circuit by the Lord Chief Justice (see *Practice Note* [1998] 4 All ER 1023).

1.5.4   Composition of the Crown Court

The judges of the Crown Court are High Court judges, circuit judges, recorders and justices of the peace (Supreme Court Act 1981, s. 8(1)). The High Court judges are drawn mainly from the Queen's Bench Division.

Circuit judges, who are appointed by the Queen on the advice of the Lord Chancellor (Courts Act 1971, s. 16(1)), are full-time permanent judges. To be qualified for appointment as a circuit judge a person must:

(a)   have a ten-year Crown Court or ten-year county court qualification within the meaning of s. 71 of the Courts and Legal Services Act 1990 (para 1.1.5 above);

(b)   be a recorder; or

(c)   have held a full-time appointment for at least three years in one of the offices listed in Part 1A of sch. 2 to the Courts Act 1971 (Courts Act 1971, s. 16(3), as amended by the Courts and Legal Services Act 1990). Part 1A of sch. 2 to the Courts Act 1971 was inserted by the 1990 Act, and the appointments mentioned include Social Security Commissioner, chairman of an industrial tribunal, district judge, and stipendiary magistrate.

The many new posts of circuit judge created when the Crown Court was originally set up were, in the main, filled automatically from the ranks of existing county court judges (see Courts Act 1971, s. 16(5) and sch. 2). Before recommending any person for appointment as a circuit judge, the Lord Chancellor must take steps to satisfy himself that that person's health is satisfactory (Courts Act 1971, s. 16(4)).

A circuit judge also sits as a county court judge to hear civil cases (County Courts Act 1984, s. 5(1)). He may also be requested by the Lord Chancellor to sit as an *additional* judge of the High Court under the provisions of the Supreme Court Act 1981, s. 9(1) and (2).

A circuit judge retires at the age of 70 (Courts Act 1971, s. 17(1), as amended by the Judicial Pensions and Retirement Act 1993). A circuit judge may be removed from office by the Lord Chancellor on the ground of incapacity or misbehaviour (ibid., s. 17(4)).

Recorders are also appointed by the Queen on the advice of the Lord Chancellor. But, unlike circuit judges, recorders are part-time judges appointed for a specified period (not less than five years). The period may be extended from time to time by the Lord Chancellor, although not beyond the age of 75. The appointment of a recorder must state how often and for how long during the specified period he will be required to sit as a judge. Failure to make himself available as agreed may lead to the termination of his appointment. He may, in addition, be dismissed by the Lord Chancellor for incapacity or misbehaviour (ibid., s. 21(6)). A recorder may also sit as a judge of the county court to hear civil cases (County Courts Act 1984, s. 5(3)).

To be qualified for appointment as a recorder a person must have a ten-year Crown Court or a ten-year county court qualification within the meaning of s. 71 of the Courts and Legal Services Act 1990 (para 1.1.5 above) (Courts Act 1971, s. 21(2), as amended by the Courts and Legal Services Act 1990).

Justices of the Peace may only sit as judges of the Crown Court with a High Court judge, circuit judge or recorder. The number of justices of the peace hearing any particular case must not exceed four (Supreme Court Act 1981, s. 8(1)(c)). When the Crown Court is hearing appeals, the presence of between two and four justices along with a High Court judge, circuit judge or recorder is mandatory (ibid., s. 74(1)). In addition, justices *may* sit with a circuit judge or recorder when trying cases on indictment, except for cases listed for plea of not guilty (ibid., ss. 8(1) and 75(2); *Practice Direction* [2000] 1 All ER 380 at p. 383. When sitting with justices the judge must consult them on the question of sentence (*R* v *Newby* (1984) 6 Cr App R(S) 148, CA), and on any defence submission that there is no case to answer (*R* v *Southwark Crown Court (ex parte Mitchell)* [1994] COD 15, DC).

To add to the usual judges of the Crown Court already mentioned, judges and former judges of the Court of Appeal and former puisne judges of the High Court may be requested by the Lord Chancellor to sit in the Crown Court on an *ad hoc* basis (Supreme Court Act 1981, s. 9(1) and (2); *R* v *Lord Chancellor (ex parte Maxwell)* [1996] 4 All ER 751, DC). Such requests are rare. The request can be refused in the case of each category of additional judge mentioned (ibid., s. 9(3)).

The Lord Chancellor may also appoint deputy circuit judges, for periods of at least five years, in order to facilitate the disposal of business in the Crown Court or a county court. The persons appointed as deputy circuit judges must previously have held office as judges of the Court of Appeal or High Court or as circuit judges (Courts Act 1971, s. 24(1)(a)). A deputy circuit judge has all the powers of a circuit judge (Courts Act 1971, s. 24(2), as substituted by the Supreme Court Act 1981).

1.5.5 Jurisdiction of the Crown Court

The jurisdiction of the Crown Court is as follows:

(a)   It has exclusive jurisdiction in relation to trial on indictment for offences wherever committed (Supreme Court Act 1981, s. 46), although, as noted in para 1.5.3 above, offences are divided into four classes for the purposes of the distribution of work among the judges. Where the accused pleads not guilty, trial on indictment in the Crown Court takes place before judge and jury. In the Crown Court in 1998, 39 per cent of defendants pleaded not guilty to all charges. Of these defendants, 64 per cent were totally acquitted and 36 per cent convicted. The proportion of defendants acquitted out of all those sent for trial was 18 per cent (*Judicial Statistics 1998*, Cm 4371, 1999, pp. 64–65; for a statistical breakdown of the responsibility for acquittals as between judge and jury, see para 7.9.1.)

(b)   It hears appeals by persons convicted summarily in the magistrates' courts. This, as well as heads (c) and (d) below, was part of the jurisdiction of the old Quarter Sessions which was given to the Crown Court by the Courts Act 1971 and is preserved by the Supreme Court Act 1981, s. 45(2).

In the course of hearing an appeal, the Crown Court may correct any error in the order or judgment incorporating the decision which is being appealed against (Supreme Court Act 1981, s. 48(1)). At the conclusion of the hearing the Crown Court has power to confirm, reverse or vary any part of the decision under appeal or to remit the case with its opinion thereon to the magistrates' court which made the decision (ibid., s. 48(2), as amended). If the appeal is decided against the accused, the Crown Court has power to impose any sentence which the magistrates' court could have imposed. This power is wide enough to allow the imposition of a punishment which is *more severe,* as well as one which is less severe, than that actually inflicted by the magistrates' court (ibid., s. 48(4)). The Crown Court cannot increase the sentence in a case which has been referred to it under s. 11 of the Criminal Appeal Act 1995 by the Criminal Cases Review Commission (Criminal Appeal Act 1995, s. 11(6)).

(c)   To sentence persons committed for sentence following conviction in the magistrates' courts (para 1.7.6.2.3 below).

(d)   It has a limited civil jurisdiction which allows it to hear, in particular, licensing appeals from the magistrates' courts.

1.5.6   Delay in the Crown Court

The benefits to the legal process achieved by the reorganisation of the courts in the early 1970s are undoubted. But the problem of delay, which plagues criminal justice in England and Wales, remains unresolved. A person committed to the Crown Court to be tried must wait (sometimes in custody) an average of 13.2 weeks for the trial to begin. The worst figures are for the Northern circuit where the average waiting time is 15.1 weeks. The shortest waiting time of 10.1 weeks is on the Wales and Chester circuit (*Judicial Statistics 1998,* Cm 4371, 1999, p. 68).

In 1961, an official committee looking into the business of the criminal courts recommended that the waiting time should not exceed eight weeks on average (*Report of the Interdepartmental Committee on the Business of the Criminal Courts,* Cmnd 1289, 1961, paras 31–3, 139 and 185). In 1969, the Royal Commission on Assizes and Quarter Sessions noted that this target had not been achieved and that the problem was particularly acute in London (Cmnd 4153, 1969, para 65). The Courts Act 1971 came into force on 1 January 1972 and for that year and the following three years there was a progressive reduction in the waiting time. In 1976 there was an upturn. Since 1979, however, there has been another gradual reduction — from 17.6 weeks in 1979 to 13.2 weeks in 1998.

The *actual* waiting times compare unfavourably with the *theoretical* maximum period of eight weeks prescribed under s. 77 of the Supreme Court Act 1981 by r. 24 of the Crown Court Rules 1982 (SI 1982, No. 1109). The reason for the discrepancy between the actual and the theoretical periods is that a judge of the Crown Court has power to order that a trial need not begin within the eight-week period. Moreover, s. 77 is directory and not mandatory so that failure to comply with it (a) does not nullify the trial (*R v Urbanowski* [1976] 1 All ER 679, CA; *R v Spring Hill Prison Governor (ex parte Sohi)* [1988] 1 All ER 424, DC), and (b) does not constitute a material irregularity in the trial such as to give rise to a right of appeal (*R v Edwards* (1975) 62 Cr App R 166, CA).

The principal causes of delay in the Crown Court are the large number of defendants being committed for trial, the small number of judges available to try them, and the slowness of trial by jury, which, in turn, is due in no small measure to the increasing prolixity of counsel and judges (*R v Lawrence* [1981] 1 All ER 974, HL, *per* Lord Hailsham of St Marylebone LC at p. 975). In 1998, the Crown Court dealt with 83,210 defendants, of whom 30,000 required trial before a jury following a plea of not guilty to some or all charges (*Judicial Statistics 1998,* Cm 4371, 1999, p. 65). To cope with the bulk of this work there are only 553 full-time circuit judges and 849 part-time recorders. The average hearing time for a trial on a not-guilty plea is 9.4 hours. This represents between 1.5 and 2 court days. In London the average hearing time is 12.2 hours compared with 6.4 and 7.6 hours on the Northern and Midland and Oxford circuits respectively (ibid., p. 70).

The long delay between committal and trial has been condemned judicially as 'nothing short of a disgrace to our legal system' (*R v Lawrence* [1981] 1 All ER 974, *per* Lord Diplock at p. 979). As well as introducing anxiety and uncertainty into the life of the defendant, such delay may amount to a denial of justice since the recollection of witnesses on both sides dims as the months pass (ibid., *per* Lord Hailsham of St Marylebone LC at p. 975).

In an attempt to ensure that cases are as well prepared for trial as possible, and that sufficient information is available for a trial date to be fixed, preliminary hearings known as 'plea and directions hearings' were introduced in almost all crown court cases in July 1995 (*Practice Direction (Crown Court: Plea and Directions Hearings)* [1995] 4 All ER 379). At a plea and directions hearing, the defendant's plea is taken. If the plea is one of guilty, the judge is expected to sentence the defendant at this stage wherever possible. If the defendant pleads not guilty, the prosecution and defence are expected to assist the judge to identify the key issues of law and fact in the case in readiness for the ensuing trial before a jury.

In 1999, the government published a consultation paper, *Transforming the Crown Court* (Lord Chancellor's Department, September 1999). The paper promised the most radical changes to the Crown Court in almost 30 years with the aims of cutting delays and cancellations, improving performance, and delivering enhanced levels of service to victims of crime, witnesses and jurors. A key feature of any reform would be a system of judicial case management in which judges will be expected to monitor individual cases on a daily basis, deciding what action is needed to maintain standards and imposing sanctions, such as on-the-spot fines for poor performance by lawyers and criminal justice agencies.

Additionally, in anticipation of the commencement of the Human Rights Act 1998 during the year 2000, the Lord Chancellor established a review of the criminal courts in December 1999. The review, under the chairmanship of a Court of Appeal judge, Auld LJ, will examine the practices, procedures and rules of evidence of the criminal courts at every level, with a view to ensuring that justice is delivered fairly. Regard will be had to streamlining processes, increasing efficiency, the interests of all parties (including victims and witnesses) and the promotion of public confidence in the rule of law. It is hoped that Auld LJ will present a report by the end of December 2000. His review is complementary to the changes already signalled in *Transforming the Crown Court* (above) and to the work done by Lord Woolf on the *civil* justice system between 1994 and 1996 (para 1.4.6 above).

1.6 COUNTY COURTS

1.6.1 Introduction

The common-law courts at Westminster were unable to provide cheap justice in small cases. Between 1822 and 1827 an average of 90,000 causes were entered each year in the common-law courts, of which 30,000 were for claims of £20 or less. The cost of recovering £20 in a defended action far exceeded the amount of the claim (see Radcliffe and Cross, *The English Legal System,* 6th ed., 1977, pp. 282–4). The modern county courts were established by the County Courts Act 1846 in order to hear small civil cases at first instance. Their jurisdiction originally was over most personal actions (especially in contract and tort) involving not more than £20. That financial limit was raised progressively from £20 to £50 (1850), £100 (1903), £200 (1937), £400 (1955), £500 (1966), £750 (1969), £1,000 (1974), £2,000 (1977), and £5,000 (1981) until it was finally abolished in the wake of reforms introduced by the Courts and Legal Services Act 1990.

In its final report in 1988, the civil justice review body made a number of recommendations for change in the county courts (*Report of the Review Body on Civil Justice,* Cm 394, 1988). Among the most important were the following:

(a)   There should be no upper financial limit on the jurisdiction of the county courts.

(b)   There should be an upper tier of circuit judges (with correspondingly higher salaries) to take responsibility for heavier civil work.

(c)   Barristers as well as solicitors should be eligible for appointment as registrars.

(d)   Registrars should be given the title of judge.

(e)   While liquidated (fixed) claims not exceeding £5,000, and housing possession cases, should continue to be dealt with in the county court for the district in which the defendant lives or carries on business, or for the district in which the land is situated, in all other cases a claimant should be free to commence proceedings in any county court the claimant chooses.

(f)   Forms should be produced centrally and standardised to prevent local variations. They should be written in plain English.

(g)   Court staff should be trained to give direct help to the public in the handling of their cases.

(h)   Parties in small claims cases, and in debt and housing cases, should have a *statutory right* to be assisted or represented by a lay representative of their choice, subject to the discretion of the court.

(i)   The small claims limit should be raised from £500 to £1,000. There should be carefully monitored experiments in early evening hearings and paper adjudications in some small claims cases. Cases should normally be dealt with at a single hearing the date of which should be fixed by the court on receipt of a defence. At the hearing, the registrar should:

(i)   conduct the proceedings according to the circumstances of each case and adopt an interventionist role, dispensing with formal rules of evidence and procedure, and assuming control of questioning of the parties and their witnesses. He should be empowered to require that questions be asked through him;

(ii)   explain the legal terms he finds it necessary to use;

(iii)   give short reasons for his decision.

Many of these recommendations were subsequently implemented.

1.6.2   Composition

In England and Wales there are about 230 county courts sitting locally. The regular judges are 553 circuit judges and 362 district judges (formerly known as 'registrars'). The post of county court judge disappeared when, under the provisions of the Courts Act 1971, all existing county court judges became circuit judges (Courts Act 1971, ss. 16 and 20 and sch. 2).

All circuit judges are competent to sit in any county court, although the Lord Chancellor must specifically assign one or more circuit judges to each county court district (County Courts Act 1984, s. 5(1)).

A district judge is appointed by the Lord Chancellor from persons who have a seven-year general qualification within the meaning of s. 71 of the Courts and Legal Services Act 1990 (para 1.1.5 above) (ibid., s. 9, as amended by the Courts and Legal Services Act 1990). An appeal can be taken from the district judge's decision to the circuit judge. Apart from this right of appeal, the county courts have no appellate jurisdiction; they are civil courts of first instance.

In addition to the regular judges, every judge of the Court of Appeal and of the High Court and every recorder is, *ex officio*, competent to sit in any county court. If he consents to do so, he may sit at such times and on such occasions as the Lord Chancellor considers desirable (County Courts Act 1984, s. 5(3)). It would, however, be extremely rare to find a Court of Appeal or High Court judge sitting in a county court.

1.6.3   Jurisdiction

1.6.3.1   Introduction

The jurisdiction of the county courts is limited in three ways. First, as noted in para 1.6.3.2 below, there is sometimes a *financial* limit beyond which the county courts have no jurisdiction to hear cases. Such cases would have to be taken to the High Court, which has unlimited jurisdiction. There is, however, an exception which allows the parties to agree to give jurisdiction to the county court where the case should normally have gone to the Queen's Bench Division of the High Court (County Courts Act 1984, s. 18).

Secondly, there is a *geographical* limitation. The claimant is not allowed to pick and choose his forum. The court can deal with a case at any place that it considers appropriate (CPR, r. 2.7). Where the defendant is an individual, and the claim is for a specified amount of money and was commenced otherwise than in the defendant's home court, the proceedings will automatically be transferred by the court to the defendant's home court when a defence is filed (CPR, r. 26.2). The 'defendant's home court' means the county court for the district in which the defendant's address for service, as shown on the defence, is situated (CPR, r. 2.3). Proceedings for the recovery of land must be brought in the county court for the district in which the land is situated. (CCR 1981, Ord. 4, r. 3).

Thirdly, there are limitations on the powers of the county courts to grant remedies. They cannot grant the prerogative remedies of mandamus, certiorari and prohibition (County Courts Act 1984, s. 38(3), as substituted by the Courts and Legal Services Act 1990, reinforcing s. 1(10) of the 1990 Act which provides that the county courts are not to be given jurisdiction to hear applications for judicial review; see Chapter 11). They cannot grant search orders (*Anton Piller* orders) at all (para 10.4.2.5). Subject to certain exceptions (notably when dealing with family proceedings or when seeking to preserve the subject matter of the dispute), they cannot grant freezing injunctions (*Mareva* injunctions) (para 10.4.2.6). They cannot revoke or vary a search order made by a High Court judge. They cannot *revoke* a freezing injunction granted by a High Court judge; they can *vary* it but only if all the parties agree upon the terms of the variation. (These limitations on the granting of search and freezing relief, which do not apply to a Court of Appeal or High Court judge sitting in a county court, or to the judge of the Edmonton patents county court (para 1.6.3.3 below), are contained in the County Court Remedies Regulations 1991, SI 1991, No. 1222, made under the County Courts Act 1984, s. 38, as substituted by the Courts and Legal Services Act 1990.) Where a county court is unable to grant the appropriate remedy, application will have to be made instead to the High Court.

The county courts are entirely creatures of statute. It follows that their jurisdiction is entirely statutory, conferred either by the consolidating County Courts Act 1984 or by particular statutes of which there are many. They are extremely busy courts. In 1998, 2.2 million proceedings were commenced in the county courts as opposed to a combined total of 152,000 in the Queen's Bench Division and the Chancery Division of the High Court, although only a small fraction of proceedings ever come to trial (*Judicial Statistics 1998*, Cm 4371, 1999, pp. 19, 27, 37). When compared with the High Court, the county courts provide a speedy and inexpensive forum for the trial of civil cases.

1.6.3.2   General jurisdiction under the County Courts Act 1984

(a)   Claims founded on contract or tort, or for money due under a statute (County Courts Act 1984, ss. 15 and 16; High Court and County Courts Jurisdiction Order 1991, SI 1991, No. 724, as amended).

By s. 1 of the Courts and Legal Services Act 1990, the Lord Chancellor was empowered to confer jurisdiction on the county courts in relation to proceedings in which the High Court has jurisdiction, and *vice versa*. He was further empowered by s. 1 to allocate business between the High Court and the county courts according to criteria which include the following:

(i)   the value of a claim;
(ii)   the nature of the proceedings;
(iii)   the parties to the proceedings;
(iv)   the degree of complexity likely to be involved in any aspect of the proceedings; and
(v)   the importance of any question likely to be raised by, or in the course of, the proceedings.

These provisions gave effect to proposals made by the civil justice review body for the more rational distribution of civil cases between the High Court and the county courts and for the easier transfer of cases up and down the system. It was anticipated that the allocation of civil business to the Queen's Bench Division of the High Court would in future reflect not so much the amount at stake (although this would still be a relevant factor) but the likely complexity and importance of particular proceedings.

The Lord Chancellor exercised his powers in the High Court and County Courts Jurisdiction Order 1991 (SI 1991, No. 724, as amended.) This provides that claims which include a claim for damages for personal injuries (such as might arise in contract and tort) are to be commenced in a county court unless the value of the claim is £50,000 or more. Claims of which the value is £50,000 or more are to be tried in the High Court unless, in accordance with the criteria laid down for the transfer of claims (see below), they are more suitable for trial in a county court.

The county courts have no original jurisdiction to entertain claims for the tort of defamation (libel and slander) (County Courts Act 1984, s. 15(2)(c)). A county court may be given such jurisdiction, however, if the parties agree to it under s. 18 (para 1.6.3.1 above) or the High Court transfers the case under s. 40 (as substituted by the Courts and Legal Services Act 1990).

In addition to claims for defamation, many other proceedings commenced in the High Court are transferable to a county court under s. 40 of the County Courts Act 1984. The section gives the High Court power to order a transfer either of its own motion or on the application of a party to the proceedings. The effect of a transfer is to free High Court judges for other, more important, work and to expedite hearings.

Any transfer will be to a county court considered appropriate by the High Court having regard to the convenience of the parties and the state of business in the courts concerned (s. 40(4)). Section 40 does not apply to family proceedings (s. 40(9)). These proceedings may, however, be transferred under the Matrimonial and Family Proceedings Act 1984 (para 1.6.3.3 below).

Guidance has been given on the appropriateness of transfers under s. 40. When considering whether to transfer proceedings to a county court the High Court must have regard to the following criteria under CPR, r. 30.3:

(i)   the financial value of the claim and the amount in dispute, if different;
(ii)   whether it would be more convenient or fair for hearings (including the trial) to be held in some other court;

(iii)   the availability of a judge specialising in the type of claim in question;

(iv)   the complexity of the facts, legal issues, remedies or procedures involved;

(v)   the importance of the outcome of the claim to the public in general; and

(vi)   the facilities available at the court where the claim is being dealt with and whether they may be inadequate because of any disabilities of a party or potential witness.

In addition, it is provided by the *Practice Direction* to CPR Part 29 that certain types of proceedings are particularly suitable for trial in the High Court and, therefore, should not normally be transferred to a county court. These are cases involving:

(i)   professional negligence;

(ii)   fatal accidents;

(iii)   allegations of fraud or undue influence;

(iv)   defamation;

(v)   malicious prosecution or false imprisonment;

(vi)   claims against the police;

(vii) contentious probate claims.

(b)   Claims for the recovery of land, or in which the title to land comes into question, whatever the value of the land (s. 21).

(c)   Equity matters, such as trusts, mortgages and dissolution of partnerships, where the amount of the fund or the value of the property involved does not exceed £30,000 (s. 23).

(d)   Applications for financial-provision orders under s. 2 of the Inheritance (Provision for Family and Dependants) Act 1975, whatever the value of the deceased's estate (s. 25).

(e)   Contentious probate proceedings concerning an application for a grant or revocation of probate or letters of administration where the net value of the estate at the time of death was less than £30,000 (s. 32, as substituted by the Administration of Justice Act 1985).

(f)   Certain county courts designated by the Lord Chancellor have jurisdiction in specified admiralty proceedings. The financial limit in each case is £5,000, except in a claim for salvage where the value of the property saved must not exceed £15,000. These limits may be increased in individual cases by agreement of the parties (ss. 26 and 27).

1.6.3.3 Special jurisdiction under other statutes

(a)   Certain county courts designated by the Lord Chancellor may hear insolvency cases and may deal with all matters relating to companies with paid-up capital not exceeding £120,000 (Insolvency Act 1986, ss. 117 and 373).

(b)   The Edmonton county court has been designated by the Lord Chancellor as a patents county court with the same jurisdiction as the High Court to deal with patent and design matters, with the exception that it cannot hear appeals from the Comptroller-General of Patents, Designs and Trade Marks (Patents County Court (Designation and Jurisdiction) Order 1990, SI 1990, No. 1496, made under the authority of s. 287(1) of the Copyright, Designs and Patents Act 1988).

(c)   Certain county courts designated by the Lord Chancellor as divorce county courts have jurisdiction to hear petitions for divorce, nullity of marriage or judicial separation (Matrimonial and Family Proceedings Act 1984, s. 33). Under the special procedure applicable in the divorce county courts, the district judge examines the documentary evidence in undefended divorce cases and (if satisfied) issues a certificate which enables him or the circuit judge later to pronounce the decree nisi of divorce in open court.

(d)   County courts have jurisdiction to hear such family proceedings as are transferred to them under s. 38 of the Matrimonial and Family Proceedings Act 1984, as amended by the Matrimonial Proceedings (Transfers) Act 1988 (and see *Practice Direction* [1992] 3 All ER 151) and by the Children Act 1989. These proceedings may include wardship proceedings *except* applications for an order that a minor be made, or cease to be, a ward of court. County courts are thus able to deal with ancillary issues arising in wardship cases, such as residence, contact and education, but the High Court alone retains jurisdiction to decide whether a minor should be a ward of court or not.

(e)   All county courts have jurisdiction to hear proceedings under the Children Act 1989. The allocation of these proceedings, and other family proceedings, as between judges in county courts is governed by a *Practice Direction* [1991] 4 All ER 764.

(f)   All county courts have jurisdiction to grant orders against molestation and to exclude a spouse or a cohabitee from the home whether any other proceedings are pending or not (Family Law Act 1996, part IV; the High Court and the magistrates' courts also have jurisdiction under this statute).

(g)   Certain county courts designated by the Lord Chancellor may hear civil actions brought by individuals in respect of alleged acts of unlawful racial discrimination otherwise than in the field of employment (Race Relations Act 1976, ss. 57 and 67). The judge has power to award damages, grant injunctions and make declarations in such cases (ibid., s. 57(2)). Any damages awarded may include compensation for injury to feelings whether or not they include compensation under any other head (ibid., s. 57(4)). Damages for injury to feelings should normally not be of an exaggerated amount but should be more than a merely nominal sum (*Alexander* v *Home Office* [1988] 2 All ER 118, CA, where, on appeal, damages of £50 were increased to £500).

In addition, the Commission for Racial Equality may apply to a designated county court for an injunction to restrain *persistent* racial discrimination (ibid., s. 62). In either case the circuit judge will normally sit with two assessors, appointed by the Home Secretary for their special knowledge and experience of problems connected with race relations. If the parties consent, the judge may sit without assessors (ibid., s. 67(4)).

Complaints about unlawful racial discrimination in *employment* are dealt with by the employment tribunals and not by the county courts (Race Relations Act 1976, s. 54; para 3.3.4).

(h)   All county courts have jurisdiction to hear claims from individuals alleging unlawful sexual discrimination in the fields of education and the provision of goods, facilities, services and premises (Sex Discrimination Act 1975, s. 66(1) and (2)). Damages, injunctions and declarations are the available remedies (Sex Discrimination Act 1975, s. 66(2)). Complaints of unlawful sexual discrimination in *employment* are heard by the employment tribunals and not by the county courts (ibid., s. 63(1); para 3.3.4).

(i)   All county courts have jurisdiction to hear claims from individuals that they have been the victims of unlawful disability discrimination in the provision of goods, facilities and services (Disability Discrimination Act 1995, s. 25). Any damages awarded may include compensation for injury to feelings whether or not they include compensation under any other head (ibid., s. 25(2)). Complaints of unlawful disability discrimination in *employment* are heard by the employment tribunals and not by the county courts (ibid., s. 8; and see para 3.3.4).

1.6.4   Small claims hearings in the county courts

A scheme for the hearing of small claims using the existing county courts was introduced in 1973 by the Administration of Justice Act of that year (see now County Courts Act 1984,

s. 64, as amended by the Courts and Legal Services Act 1990). The original 1973 financial limit of £75 has been raised progressively to £100 (1974), £200 (1977), £500 (1981), £1,000 (1991), £3,000 (1996), and £5,000 (1999).

A claim which has a financial value of £5,000 or less is dealt with on the small-claims track (CPR, r. 26.6). This track is 'intended to provide a proportionate procedure by which most straightforward claims with a financial value of not more than £5,000 can be decided, without the need for substantial pre-hearing preparation and the formalities of a traditional trial, and without incurring large legal costs' (*Practice Direction* to CPR, Part 26).

The small-claims track is also the appropriate one for:

(a)   a claim for personal injuries having a financial value of not more than £5,000 where the claim for damages for personal injuries is not more than £1,000; and

(b)   a claim which includes a claim by a tenant of residential premises against his landlord for repairs (or other work) to the premises where the estimated cost of the repairs (or other work) is not more than £1,000 and the financial value of any other claim for damages is not more than £1,000 (CPR, r. 26.6).

The court can later reallocate a claim to a different track (ibid., r. 26.10).

In addition, a claim with a value above these financial limits can be allocated by the court to the small-claims track if the parties consent (ibid.), in which event the claim is treated, for the purposes of costs, as if it were proceeding on the fast-track (CPR, r. 27.14). However, such a claim will not be allocated to the small claims track, even where the parties are agreeable, unless the court is satisfied that it is suitable for that track (*Practice Direction* to CPR, Part 26).

Most hearings of small claims are conducted by the district judge, although the circuit also has jurisdiction to conduct them. There were 98,692 small claims hearings in the county courts in 1998, the vast majority of them conducted by the district judge (*Judicial Statistics 1998,* Cm 4371, 1999, p. 40). In what follows, the judge is assumed to be the district judge.

There will normally be a hearing, although this is not necessary if the parties consent to the claim being dealt with by the judge on the basis of the statements and documents filed with the court (CPR, r. 27.10).

The hearing can be held at the court (usually in the judge's room, but it may be in a courtroom), or at any other place convenient to the parties. If the hearing takes place elsewhere than at the court, for example, at the home or business premises of a party, it will not be in public (*Practice Direction* to CPR, Part 27). The general rule is that the hearing is to be in public (CPR, r. 27.2, applying r. 39.2; *Practice Direction* to CPR, Part 27). It may be in private if the parties agree (*Practice Direction* to CPR, Part 27), or if publicity would defeat the object of the hearing, or if it involves matters relating to national security, or if it involves confidential information (including information relating to personal financial matters) and publicity would damage that confidentiality, or if a private hearing is necessary to protect the interests of any child or patient, or if the judge considers it to be necessary in the interests of justice (CPR, r. 39.2).

The hearing is an informal one at which the strict rules of evidence do not apply, evidence need not be taken on oath, and the judge can limit cross-examination (CPR, r. 27.8). The judge can adopt any method of proceeding which he considers to be fair (ibid.). In particular, he can question any witness himself before allowing any other person to do so; refuse to allow cross-examination of any witness until all the witnesses have given evidence in chief; and limit cross-examination of a witness to a fixed time, or to a particular subject or issue, or both (*Practice Direction* to CPR, Part 27).

An expert cannot give evidence (whether written or oral) at a hearing without the permission of the judge (CPR, r. 27.5). In any event, expert evidence is restricted to what is reasonably required to resolve the proceedings. The expert's duty is to help the court on the matters within his expertise, and this duty overrides any obligation to the person from whom he has received instructions or by whom he is paid (CPR, r. 27.2, applying rr. 35.1 and 35.3).

The judge must give reasons for his decision (CPR, r. 27.8). They can be given as briefly and simply as the nature of the case allows. They will normally be given orally at the hearing, or, failing that, they can be given later either in writing or at a hearing fixed for that purpose (*Practice Direction* to CPR, Part 27). Where the judge decides the case without a hearing (see above), or a party has given written notice that he will not attend the hearing and does not attend it (see below), the judge will prepare a note of his reasons and the court will send a copy to each party (ibid.).

The judge has power to grant interim injunctions (CPR, r. 27.2, applying r. 25.1), but not search orders (*Anton Piller* orders) and freezing injunctions (*Mareva* injunctions) (*Practice Direction* to CPR, Part 25A), and any final remedy which could be granted if the proceedings were on the fast track or the multi-track, such as injunctions, damages and specific performance (CPR, r. 27.3).

If a party does not attend a final hearing, the judge can decide the case in his absence after taking into account that party's statement of case and any other documents he has filed, provided that that party has given the court at least seven days' written notice that he will not be attending and has, in his notice, requested the court to decide the claim in his absence. If neither party attends or gives the requisite notice, the court can strike out the claim and any defence and counterclaim. If the claimant does not attend, and does not give notice, the court can strike out the claim. If the defendant does not attend, or does not give notice, and the claimant either does attend or gives notice, the court can decide the claim on the basis of the evidence of the claimant alone (CPR, r. 27.9).

A party who did not attend, and was not represented at, the hearing of the claim, and who did not give the requisite notice to the court, can apply to have the decision set aside and the claim re-heard. This is not, technically, an appeal. The judge can only set aside the decision if the applicant had a good reason for not attending or being represented at the hearing or giving notice to the court, and has a reasonable prospect of success at the hearing (CPR, r. 27.11).

The only other grounds on which the judge's decision may possibly be set aside are that there was a serious irregularity affecting the proceedings or that the judge made a mistake of law. These grounds involve appealing against the decision (CPR, r. 27.12). An appeal from a decision of a district judge is dealt with by a circuit judge (*Practice Direction* to CPR, Part 27), who can make any order he or she considers appropriate, and can dismiss an appeal without a hearing (CPR, r. 27.12). A 'serious irregularity' consisting of misconduct on the part of the judge is very difficult to establish (*Starmer* v *Bradbury* (1994) *The Times*, 11 April, CA, where the claimant's allegations that the district judge appeared partial and lost control of the proceedings were dismissed).

At the hearing, representation of a party by a lawyer (which, for this purpose, means a barrister, a solicitor or a legal executive employed by a solicitor) or by a lay representative (see further below) is permitted (*Practice Direction* to CPR, Part 27), but must be paid for by the party personally even if he wins the case. This is because of the general rule in small claims cases that a party is not to be ordered to pay the other party's costs except in the limited circumstances permitted by the Civil Procedure Rules. Thus, pursuant to CPR,

r. 27.14 and *Practice Direction* to CPR, Part 27, some small costs can be awarded by the judge, representing, for example:

(a)   the fixed costs attributable to issuing the claim;
(b)   any court fees paid by another party;
(c)   the reasonable travel and subsistence expenses of a party or witness;
(d)   a sum not exceeding a prescribed amount for loss of earnings of a party or witness;
(e)   a sum not exceeding a prescribed amount in respect of an expert's fees.

In addition, further costs can be awarded against a party who has behaved unreasonably (CPR, r. 27.14).

A corporate party can be represented by any of its officers or employees (*Practice Direction* to CPR, Part 27).

The general rule that a party will not be ordered to pay the other party's costs is designed to discourage the employment of lawyers at small claims hearings (*Hobbs* v *Marlowe* [1978] AC 16, HL, *per* Lord Elwyn-Jones LC at p. 32). The rule has been successful in that the vast majority of parties are not represented by lawyers.

By virtue of s. 11 of the Courts and Legal Services Act 1990, the Lord Chancellor was empowered by order to provide that there shall be no restriction on the persons who may exercise rights of audience in relation to certain proceedings (including small claims hearings) in a county court. This provision implemented the civil justice review body's recommendation that in small claims cases a party should have a statutory right to be represented by a lay representative of his choice. The power was first exercised in the Lay Representatives (Rights of Audience) Order 1992 (SI 1992, No. 1966), which was revoked and replaced by the Lay Representatives (Rights of Audience) Order 1999 (SI 1999, No. 1225). This provides that any person can exercise rights of audience as a lay representative at small claims hearings, except where his client does not attend the hearing, at any stage after judgment, or on any appeal brought against the district judge's decision. Nevertheless, the court, exercising its general discretion to hear anybody, can hear a lay representative even in circumstances excluded by the 1999 Order (*Practice Direction* to CPR, Part 27).

The conduct of lay representatives is governed by other provisions of s. 11 of the Courts and Legal Services Act 1990. The county court may refuse to hear a person who otherwise has a right of audience under the section if he is behaving in an unruly manner in any proceedings (s. 11(4)). A person exercising a right of audience under s. 11 may be disqualified by order of the judge from exercising that right in any county court if the judge has reason to believe that that person has intentionally misled the court, or otherwise demonstrated his unsuitability to exercise that right, whether in the current or any other proceedings (s. 11(6)). The judge must give his reasons for making the order, which can be appealed against to the Court of Appeal (s. 11(7), (8)). An order may be revoked at any time by any judge of a county court (s. 11(9)).

Small claims were the subject of a consultation paper published in 1986 as part of the civil justice review (*Civil Justice Review, Consultation Paper No. 2: Small Claims in the County Court,* Lord Chancellor's Department, September 1986; for recommendations contained in the review body's final report, see para 1.6.1 above). The consultation paper was based on the findings of a factual survey conducted by a firm of management consultants.

The consultation paper reached a number of important conclusions. There appeared to be a high level of satisfaction among litigants, including those who lost their cases. Neither costs nor the procedure involved seemed to be a deterrent to would-be suitors. Although (not surprisingly) small claims were processed more quickly than ordinary litigation, some county courts were taking an unacceptably long time to decide cases. In view of this the consultation paper suggested that, as far as possible, the preliminary hearing should be dispensed with and the case decided at a single hearing.

Preliminary hearings were routinely used by some district judges as an opportunity to give directions for the preparation and conduct of the case and to assist with the isolation of the issues between the parties. The change advocated by the civil justice review body was achieved in 1992 by amendment to the County Court Rules. The relevant county court rule has since been revoked and replaced by arrangements contained in the Civil Procedure Rules 1998. A preliminary hearing can only be held where:

(a)   the judge considers that special directions are needed to ensure a fair hearing, and it appears necessary for a party to attend at court to ensure that he understands what he must do to comply with the special directions, or

(b)   to enable the judge to dispose of the claim on the basis that one or other of the parties has no real prospect of success at a final hearing, or

(c)   to enable the judge to strike out a statement of case or part of a statement of case on the basis that the statement, or the part to be struck out, discloses no reasonable grounds for bringing or defending the claim (CPR, r. 27.6).

Furthermore, the judge, when considering whether to hold a preliminary hearing, must have regard to the desirability of limiting the expense to the parties of attending court (ibid.).

At or after the preliminary hearing, any appropriate directions are given, the date of the final hearing is fixed (if it has not been fixed already), the parties are given at least 21 days' notice of that date unless they agree to accept less notice, and they are informed of the amount of time allowed for the final hearing. If all the parties agree, the preliminary hearing can be treated as the final hearing of the claim (ibid.).

The factual survey found that most claims were about goods and services, and it appeared that the small claims scheme was used as much by local traders and professional firms as by ordinary consumers.

The major defect in dealing with small claims has been the lack of effective enforcement procedures against recalcitrant defendants. It was, therefore, pleasantly surprising to find that, in the survey sample, 65 per cent of successful claimants said that they were paid all or a substantial part of the money awarded to them. Nevertheless, there remained the fact that about 25 per cent of successful claimants had been paid nothing at all by the date of the survey. The claimant who has obtained judgment is provided with remedies by the law but is given little assistance in enforcing those remedies.

Similar conclusions were reached in another survey published some ten years later. This study — based upon a sample of 3,000 small claims cases — revealed a high level of satisfaction with the way cases were handled in the county courts, that 70 per cent of claimants were businesses seeking payment of unpaid bills, and that 60 per cent of defendants were individuals. Unfortunately, enforcement remained a problem. According to the survey, the proportion of successful claimants who actually received all or part of their claim had fallen to 54 per cent, while the proportion who received nothing at all had risen to 36 per cent (*Handling Small Claims in the County Courts*, National Audit Office, March 1996, HMSO).

A research study conducted by Professor John Baldwin and published in 1996 found that, while over 80 per cent of litigants were satisfied with the way in which small claims hearings were conducted, many successful claimants would not use the small claims procedure again because of their dissatisfaction with the enforcement system. Most district judges thought that the presence of lawyers in small claims hearings was more detrimental than helpful, and concern was expressed at the failure of litigants in person to understand the concept of having to prove their case. They often arrived at the court without supporting documentation or witnesses, and were clearly in need of some prior instruction on procedure and on the validity of their claim or defence (*Small Claims Procedures in County Courts in England and Wales*, October 1996).

In a consultation paper published in November 1997, the Lord Chancellor expressed his belief that the success and popularity of the small claims procedure justified its extension to more cases. Concern was voiced at the increasing presence of lawyers at small claims hearings. It was felt that if legal representation were to become common, the small claims procedure might cease to have the advantages usually identified by litigants and might become increasingly formal, complex and expensive. The consultation paper invited views on whether there should be a study to examine the feasibility of prohibiting legal representation in small claims cases (*Access to Justice – the Small Claims Procedure: A Consultation Paper*, Lord Chancellor's Department, November 1997).

In an accompanying press release, the Lord Chancellor acknowledged that there were problems with enforcement. He stated that work was in hand to improve the efficiency and effectiveness of county court bailiffs and that a wider review of the current methods of enforcement, including their scope and success rates, would commence in 1998. The first phase of the review, involving an examination of the efficiency, effectiveness and accessibility of the enforcement methods available in the civil courts, began in April 1998 and is expected to be completed by June 2000. A number of related consultation papers have been published by the Lord Chancellor's Department.

1.7 MAGISTRATES' COURTS

1.7.1 Introduction

The office of magistrate or justice of the peace dates back to 1195 when Richard I appointed 'keepers of the peace' to pursue, arrest and punish those who offended against the King's peace. In 1363 a statute provided that the justices should meet at least four times a year in each county. These meetings, which existed in addition to the petty sessions of local magistrates, became known as the Quarter Sessions and lasted until finally abolished by the Courts Act 1971. Originally the magistrates had many administrative as well as judicial duties. They were responsible for such local government activities as the poor law, highways and bridges, and weights and measures. Responsibility for the administration of local government was transferred from the justices to elected local authorities in the nineteenth century.

1.7.2 District judges (magistrates' courts)

Most of what follows in para 1.7 is concerned with magistrates' courts composed of lay justices. However, it should be mentioned here that in addition to lay justices there are, in London and some of the larger provincial towns, some 93 district judges (magistrates' courts) who sit alone and exercise the same jurisdiction as a bench of lay magistrates (Justices of the Peace Act 1997, s. 10D, as inserted by the Access to Justice Act 1999). They are full-time, paid appointments made by the Queen on the recommendation of the Lord Chancellor from persons who have a seven-year general qualification within the meaning of s. 71 of the Courts and Legal Services Act 1990 (para 1.1.5 above) (Justices of the Peace Act 1997, s. 10A, as inserted by the Access to Justice Act 1999).

District judges (magistrates' courts) can be removed from office by the Lord Chancellor, but only on the ground of incapacity or misbehaviour (ibid.). By virtue of the Judicial Pensions and Retirement Act 1993, they normally retire at the age of 70, but, if it is desirable in the public interest, they may be authorised on an individual basis by the Lord Chancellor to continue in office for a year at a time up to the age of 75.

The Lord Chancellor may also appoint deputy district judges (magistrates' courts) on a temporary basis in order to facilitate the disposal of business. The persons appointed as deputies must be qualified for appointment as district judges (magistrates' courts). Deputy district judges (magistrates' courts) have all the judicial powers of district judges (magistrates' courts). They may be removed from office by the Lord Chancellor for incapacity or misbehaviour (Justices of the Peace Act 1997, s. 10B, as inserted by the Access to Justice Act 1999).

District judges (magistrates' courts) were formerly called 'stipendiary magistrates'. They were renamed by the Access to Justice Act 1999. The Act also abolished the office of 'metropolitan stipendiary magistrate' formerly held by stipendiary magistrates appointed to sit in the Inner London area. The resultant merger of the provincial and metropolitan professional magistracy into a unified judicial body was intended to increase speed and efficiency in the magistrates' courts.

1.7.3   Appointment and training of lay magistrates

Lay magistrates are appointed and removed on behalf of the Queen by the Lord Chancellor in consultation with local advisory committees (Justices of the Peace Act 1997, s. 5(1)). Each county has a local advisory committee, usually under the chairmanship of the Lord-Lieutenant of the county with the rest of its membership remaining secret to discourage lobbying. Names are put forward to the local advisory committee by interested bodies, such as political parties, trade unions and chambers of commerce. In addition, the committee may, if it wishes, advertise for candidates to put themselves forward. Candidates may be interviewed. The details of those found to be acceptable by the committee are sent to the Lord Chancellor, who makes the final decision on appointments.

There is no formal limit on the number of lay magistrates that can be appointed. At present there are some 30,000 magistrates (51 per cent men and 49 per cent women) in England and Wales dispensing justice in approximately 700 magistrates' courts. Lay magistrates are unqualified and unpaid, although they are expected to attend courses of instruction (Justices of the Peace Act 1997, s. 64) and they are paid allowances for travel, subsistence and loss of earnings (ibid., s. 10).

A magistrate must be resident within 15 miles of the area for which he is commissioned and his jurisdiction only extends within his particular commission area (ibid., s. 6(1)) though he may sit in the *Crown Court* at a place outside his commission area (Supreme Court Act 1981, s. 8(2)).

With effect from September 1998 there has been a new style of training which places greater emphasis on learning through the experience of actually sitting in court. The object is to allow magistrates to demonstrate that they have acquired the knowledge and skills necessary for their work. Attendance at courses still plays a part in the training process, but emphasis is placed upon learning by sitting as a magistrate supported and assisted by specially selected colleagues trained to act as monitors. The new training scheme is also designed to emphasise equality of treatment for all who appear in the magistrates' courts regardless of race, creed, colour, ethnic origin, gender, religion, disability or sexual orientation.

1.7.4   The supplemental list and retirement

Lay magistrates do not officially 'retire'. At the age of 70 their names are entered in 'the supplemental list'. Also placed in the supplemental list are the names of justices who have become unfitted to sit on the bench, whether by reason of age or infirmity or for declining or neglecting to perform their functions (Justices of the Peace Act 1997, s. 7). A justice may also ask to be placed in the list (ibid.). Justices whose names are on the supplemental list cannot sit in a magistrates' court or sign any information or warrant. They may, however, sit in the Crown Court if under the age of 72 and authorised to do so by the Lord Chancellor, and they may also perform minor administrative duties, such as authenticating signatures or written declarations not made on oath (ibid., s. 9).

1.7.5   Justices' clerks

1.7.5.1   Appointment
Every bench of lay magistrates is assisted by a justices' clerk appointed by the local magistrates' courts committee usually from persons who have a five-year magistrates' court qualification within the meaning of s. 71 of the Courts and Legal Services Act 1990 (Justices of the Peace Act 1997, s. 43). The justices' clerk is assisted by deputies and court clerks.

1.7.5.2   Function of the clerk to the justices
The main duty of a justices' clerk is to advise the lay magistrates on matters of law (including procedure and practice), and he may tender such advice even when not specifically requested if he thinks he should do so (see Justices of the Peace Act 1997, s. 45, as amended by the Access to Justice Act 1999, and *Practice Directions* [1981] 2 All ER 831; [1954] 1 All ER 230). The magistrates are not bound by law to accept their clerk's advice as they are independent and are responsible for making their own decisions and fixing their own sentences.

It has been said to be of 'fundamental importance that justice should not only be done but manifestly and undoubtedly be seen to be done' (*R* v *Sussex Justices (ex parte McCarthy)* [1924] 1 KB 256, DC *per* Lord Hewart CJ at 259; and see para 11.8.3.2.1). In accordance with this principle, the justices' clerk should not *instruct* the magistrates what their actual decisions should be or what sentence to impose, and, further, should not even *appear* to be taking part in decisions. To this end, the justices' clerk should not normally retire with the magistrates when they consider their verdict. But he may legitimately be called in by them to give advice on matters of law (including procedure and practice). He should not, however, be a party to findings of fact. Any request to the clerk to accompany them while they retire should be made by the justices clearly and in open court (*R* v *Eccles Justices (ex parte Fitzpatrick)* (1989) 89 Cr App R 324, DC). It is recognised as good practice that the clerk should return to the court before the justices rather than stay with them throughout the whole of their retirement, although so to stay is not regarded as improper in itself.

1.7.6   Functions of magistrates' courts

1.7.6.1   Introduction
The functions of magistrates' courts include the following:

(a)   To exercise summary criminal jurisdiction.
(b)   To act as examining justices during committal proceedings in the preliminary examination of persons accused of offences triable either way after it has been decided that the offence should be tried at the Crown Court.
(c)   To exercise some civil jurisdiction.

1.7.6.2   Summary criminal jurisdiction

1.7.6.2.1   Classification of offences.   Magistrates try mainly *summary* offences; i.e., offences which are triable without a jury, such as most motoring offences. The case must be heard by at least two, and not more than three, justices (or a district judge (magistrates' court)) (Magistrates' Courts Act 1980, s. 121(1); Justices of the Peace Act 1997, s. 15(1)). Magistrates may try a case in the absence of the accused but they cannot sentence him to imprisonment or detention in his absence (Magistrates' Courts Act 1980, s. 11(1) and (3)).

About 90 per cent of defendants accused of summary offences plead guilty (*Report of the Committee on the Distribution of Criminal Business between the Crown Court and Magistrates' Courts* (James Committee), Cmnd 6323, 1975, para 221). This contrasts with the proportion of accused persons pleading guilty to all charges in the Crown Court, which stands at the lower figure of 61 per cent (*Judicial Statistics 1998*, Cm 4371, 1999, p. 64).

Following conviction for a summary offence, the magistrates may, in general, impose a prison sentence not longer than the period specified in the statute creating the offence, or six months, whichever is the shorter (Magistrates' Courts Act 1980, s. 31(1) and (2)). If the defendant has been convicted of two or more summary offences the magistrates may impose consecutive prison sentences, but these must not exceed six months in the aggregate (ibid., s. 133(1)). Many summary offences are not punishable by imprisonment at all.

The maximum fine for a summary offence is such sum as may be specified in the statute creating the offence, or £1,000, whichever is the higher (ibid., s. 34(3), as amended). Before deciding upon the amount of a fine to be imposed on an offender who is an individual, the magistrates must inquire into the defendant's financial circumstances and, when fixing the amount, must take these into account (so far as they are known, or appear, to the court) together with the other circumstances of the case. The amount of any fine imposed must be such as in the opinion of the court reflects the seriousness of the offence (Criminal Justice Act 1991, s. 18, as amended).

Other sentences available to the court for dealing with adult offenders include absolute discharge, conditional discharge, probation, community service order and compensation order. The latter sentence has assumed increasing importance in recent years and is designed, *inter alia,* to relieve the victim of a crime from the burden of having to sue the offender for damages in a civil court. In that respect a compensation order differs from a fine. The compensation is payable to the victim whereas a fine is payable to the State. Compensation orders were introduced by s. 35 of the Powers of Criminal Courts Act 1973, although before that Act was amended in 1982 they were not regarded as separate sentences in their own right but could only be imposed in addition to some other sentence. They may now be made instead of, as well as in addition to, dealing with the defendant in any other way (Powers of Criminal Courts Act 1973, s. 35(1), as substituted by the Criminal Justice Act 1982). In order to encourage greater use of them, it is provided that a court which does not make a compensation order must give reasons for not doing so (ibid., s. 35(1), as amended by the Criminal Justice Act 1988). The maximum amount of compensation a magistrates' court can order is £5,000 (Magistrates' Courts Act 1980, s. 40(1), as amended). This figure may be raised (or lowered) by the Home Secretary by statutory instrument (ibid., s. 143, as amended). In fixing the amount of any compensation payable, the magistrates must take into account the defendant's means (Powers of Criminal Courts Act 1973, s. 35(4)).

The magistrates' courts also have jurisdiction to try offences *triable either way*; i.e. offences which are triable *either* summarily by magistrates or on indictment in the Crown Court. Following summary conviction of the defendant for an offence triable either way, the magistrates' powers of punishment are limited to a maximum of six months' imprisonment for any one offence and a maximum fine of £5,000 (Magistrates' Courts Act 1980, ss. 31(1), 32(1) and 32(9), as amended; see further para 1.7.6.2.3 below). If the magistrates convict the defendant summarily of two or more offences triable either way, they may impose consecutive prison sentences of up to 12 months in the aggregate (ibid., s. 133(2)).

The Criminal Law Act 1977, giving effect to the main recommendations of the James Committee, provided for three classes of offence as regards modes of trial:

(a) *Offences triable only summarily.* There are hundreds of these. All summary offences are created by statute and most of them are of a relatively minor nature.

(b) *Offences triable only on indictment.* These are the most serious crimes and include treason, murder, manslaughter and rape. These offences remain triable only in the Crown Court.

(c) *Offences triable either way.* These are the offences listed in sch. 1 to the Magistrates' Courts Act 1980 or which are made triable either way by individual statutes.

1.7.6.2.2 Procedure for determining the mode of trial in the case of offences triable either way. The Criminal Law Act 1977 laid down a procedure for determining the mode of trial of offences triable either way. The procedure is now set out in the Magistrates' Courts Act 1980, ss. 17A–26. This particular jurisdiction may be exercised by a single justice (Magistrates' Courts Act 1980, s. 18(5)).

In the case of an accused person aged 18 or over, the magistrates' court must decide whether the offence is more suitable for summary trial or trial on indictment. The first step is to ascertain whether (if the offence were to proceed to trial) the accused would plead guilty or not guilty (Magistrates' Courts Act 1980, ss. 17A–17C, as inserted by the Criminal Procedure and Investigations Act 1996). The charge is read to the accused and the court explains to him in ordinary language that (a) he may indicate his plea; (b) if he indicates that he would plead guilty the court will try him summarily; and (c) he may be committed for sentence to the Crown Court under s. 38 of the Magistrates' Courts Act 1980 (para 1.7.6.2.3 below). The court then asks the accused about his plea, and, if he indicates that he would plead guilty, proceeds to try him summarily.

If the accused indicates that he would plead not guilty, or fails to indicate any plea at all, the court does not at that point proceed to try him summarily but will instead reach a decision whether the offence is more suitable for summary trial or trial on indictment after taking into account the following matters: the nature of the case; whether the circumstances make the offence one of a serious character; whether the punishment which a magistrates' court could inflict would be adequate; any representations about mode of trial made by the prosecution and the accused; any other circumstances which appear to make either mode of trial more suitable (ibid., s. 19(1) to (3)). (Guidelines to help magistrates decide whether or not to commit 'either way' offences for trial in the Crown Court are set out in a *Practice Note* [1990] 3 All ER 979. This states that, in general, 'either way' offences should be tried summarily unless a case has one or more specified aggravating features *and* the magistrates' court considers that its sentencing powers are inadequate.) However, if the prosecution is being conducted by the Attorney-General, the Solicitor-General or the Director of Public Prosecutions and he applies for the offence to be tried on indictment, the magistrates' court must accept this and proceed as examining justices only (ibid., s. 19(4)). In any event, the accused may be deprived of trial by jury if the prosecution decides to charge a lesser offence on the same facts (*R* v *Canterbury etc. Justices (ex parte Klisiak)* [1981] 2 All ER 129, DC; *R* v *Liverpool Stipendiary Magistrate (ex parte Ellison)* [1990] RTR 220, DC).

If, after considering the relevant matters, the court decides that *summary* trial is more suitable the court must explain its decision to the accused in ordinary language and then ask him whether he consents to summary trial or wishes to be tried by a jury (Magistrates' Courts Act 1980, s. 20(1) to (3)). It must also be explained to the accused that if he is tried summarily and is convicted, he may be committed for sentence to the Crown Court if the magistrates, having had information about his character and antecedents, are of opinion that greater punishment should be inflicted than they have power to inflict for the offence (ibid., s. 20(2)(b)).

If the accused consents to be tried summarily, the magistrates proceed with a summary trial. If he does not consent to be tried summarily, the magistrates proceed as examining justices only (ibid., s. 20(3)(a) and (b)).

An accused person who intends to plead guilty and who consents to summary trial may be allowed to *re-elect* for jury trial in the Crown Court if he had not properly understood the nature and significance of his earlier choice (*R* v *Birmingham Justices (ex parte Hodgson)* [1985] 2 All ER 193, DC).

Where two or more accused are jointly charged, the right of election as to mode of trial provided by s. 20(3) of the Magistrates' Courts Act 1980 is given to each accused individually and not to all the accused collectively. The election of one accused is not affected, therefore, by a different election by a co-accused person. Accordingly, where one accused elects summary trial but a co-accused elects trial by jury the magistrates should proceed to try the former summarily but, in relation to the latter, should act as examining justices only (*Nicholls* v *Brentwood Justices* [1991] 3 All ER 359, HL).

If, after considering the relevant matters, the court decides that trial *on indictment* is more suitable, the court must tell the accused that its decision is that it is more suitable for him to be tried by a jury (ibid., s. 21). This decision is final and the magistrates then proceed to act as examining justices only.

Normally the accused must be present in court during the proceedings for determining the mode of trial of an offence triable either way (ibid., s. 18(2)). But if the accused is represented by counsel or a solicitor, his presence is not required if he consents to the proceedings being conducted in his absence and the court is satisfied that there is a good reason for so proceeding (ibid., s. 23). This would cover, for example, the illness of the accused. Proceedings cannot continue in the accused's absence, and would need to be adjourned, if he is *not* represented. In addition, the court may proceed in the absence of the accused, and without his consent, where it is not practicable to proceed in his presence because of his disorderly conduct before the court (ibid., s. 18(3)). Where the accused is not present, the procedure outlined above is followed with appropriate modifications. In particular, the accused's consent to summary trial may be signified by the barrister or solicitor (if any) representing him (ibid., ss. 18(3) and 23(2) to (5); and see *R* v *Horseferry Road Magistrates' Court (ex parte K)* [1996] 3 All ER 719, DC).

Where an offence is triable either way and the magistrates' court has started to try it summarily, the court may, at any time before the conclusion of the prosecution evidence, change from summary trial to committal proceedings (ibid., s. 25(2), as amended). The consent of the accused is not required. However, the magistrates cannot change from summary trial to committal proceedings where the accused has pleaded guilty because, on a guilty plea, no 'evidence for the prosecution' within the meaning of s. 25(2) is given so that there is no evidence 'before the conclusion of' which the magistrates could make the switch (*Chief Constable of West Midlands Police* v *Gillard* [1985] 3 All ER 634, HL). If the court has started to inquire into the offence as examining justices it can change, at any time during the inquiry, to summary trial if that appears after all to be more suitable (ibid., s. 25(3)). But the accused must consent to the change after it has been explained to him in ordinary language that summary trial now appears to be more suitable and that if he is convicted before the magistrates he could be committed to the Crown Court for sentence (ibid., s. 25(4)). If the magistrates find that the evidence does not support the either-way offence with which the accused is charged but that it does support some other offence *triable summarily,* they may proceed, under s. 25(3), to try the lesser offence summarily (*R* v *Cambridge Justices (ex parte Fraser)* [1985] 1 All ER 668, DC).

The procedure outlined above for determining the mode of trial of an offence triable either way only applies where the accused is aged 18 or over. In the case of *children* (aged 10 or more but under 14) and *young persons* (aged 14 or more but under 18) different considerations apply. Such a person appearing before a magistrates' court charged with an indictable offence must normally be tried summarily (ibid., s. 24(1)). This does not mean that he is necessarily deprived of the right to choose trial by jury. If he becomes 18 at any time before he appears or is brought before the court on the occasion when it decides on the mode of trial he is entitled to elect trial by jury (*Re Daley* [1982] 2 All ER 974, HL, reversing the decision of the Divisional Court *sub nom. R* v *Tottenham Juvenile Court (ex parte ARC)* [1982] 2 All ER 321, disapproving *R* v *Amersham Juvenile Court (ex parte Wilson)* [1981] 2 All ER 315, DC, and applying *R* v *St Alban's Juvenile Court (ex parte Godman)* [1981] 2 All ER 311, DC). If, however, he becomes 18 *after* the mode of trial is decided (but before the actual trial) the decision about mode of trial is not affected. Thus, if summary trial was ordered he must be tried summarily and not committed to the Crown Court for trial by jury (*R* v *Nottingham Justices (ex parte Taylor)* [1991] 4 All ER 860, DC, explaining *Re Daley,* above, and disapproving in part *R* v *St Alban's Juvenile Court (ex parte Godman),* above).

There are in any event three exceptional cases where a child or young person will not be tried summarily but will be committed for trial to the Crown Court. First, where the offence charged is *homicide*. Secondly, where a *child or young person* is charged with an offence for which the penalty in the case of an adult is 14 years' imprisonment or more, and the magistrates' court considers that if he is found guilty of the offence it ought to be possible to sentence him to a long period of detention (Magistrates' Courts Act 1980, s. 24(1)(a), as amended). Thirdly, where a *child or young person* is charged jointly with an adult (aged 18 or over) and the magistrates' court considers it necessary in the interests of justice to commit them both for trial to the Crown Court (ibid., s. 24(1)(b)). In the case of the first two exceptions, the child or young person may also be committed for trial for any other indictable offence with which he is charged at the same time if the charges for both offences could be joined in the same indictment (ibid., s. 24(1A), as inserted by the Crime and Disorder Act 1998). In the case of the third exception, the court may also commit the child or young person for trial for any other indictable offence with which he is charged at the same time (whether jointly with an adult or not) if the charges for both offences could be joined in the same indictment (ibid., s. 24(2), as amended by the Crime and Disorder Act 1998).

In 1993, the *Report of the Royal Commission on Criminal Justice* (Cm 2263, 1993) controversially recommended the abolition of the defendant's right to choose trial by jury for an either-way offence. It was proposed that where the Crown Prosecution Service and the defence are unable to agree on mode of trial a magistrates' court should determine it, and that legislation should specify the various factors (including the defendant's potential loss of reputation) to be taken into account by the magistrates in deciding the matter. The Criminal Justice (Mode of Trial) Bill of 1999 would have given effect to these recommendations, but it was defeated in the House of Lords in early 2000. The government decided not to proceed with it and to introduce another Bill in the same parliamentary session. The Criminal Justice (Mode of Trial) (No. 2) Bill was introduced in the House of Commons in February 2000.

1.7.6.2.3   Committal to the Crown Court for sentence.   There are statutory limits on the punishments that may be imposed by a magistrates' court. There is a maximum sentence of imprisonment of six months for offences triable either way (Magistrates' Courts Act 1980, s. 32(1)), though the court may impose consecutive sentences of up to 12 months in the aggregate in the case of two or more offences triable either way (ibid., s. 133(2)). The maximum fine that can be inflicted is £5,000 (ibid., s. 32(9), as amended). For many offences the prescribed punishment is less than these maxima. For example, many offences are not punishable by imprisonment at all and others are punishable by a maximum fine substantially less than £5,000. The maximum fine of £5,000 may be raised (or lowered) by the Home Secretary by statutory instrument (ibid., s. 143, as amended).

In certain cases the magistrates' powers of punishment will be inadequate. It is accordingly provided that if a person aged 18 or over has been convicted summarily of an offence triable either way he may sometimes be committed instead to the Crown Court for sentence. There are two such cases. The first is where the magistrates are of opinion that the offence, or the combination of the offence and one or more offences associated with it, is so serious that greater punishment should be inflicted than they have power to impose. The second is where a violent or sexual offence has been committed and the magistrates are of the opinion that a custodial sentence longer than they have power to impose is necessary to protect the public from serious harm from the defendant (ibid., s. 38, as substituted by the Criminal Justice Act 1991 and subsequently amended).

On a committal for sentence the Crown Court will inquire into the circumstances of the case in the same way as if the defendant had been convicted there. Prosecuting counsel will give details of the facts and the defence counsel or solicitor will present a plea in mitigation of sentence. The Crown Court may impose any sentence up to the maximum prescribed for that particular offence if it were tried on indictment (Powers of Criminal Courts Act 1973, s. 42, as amended).

1.7.6.2.4   Youth courts   A child (aged ten or over but under 14) or young person (aged 14 or over but under 18) will normally be tried in a youth court. This is a magistrates' court sitting for that purpose and composed of justices from a special panel. There must be three justices on the bench to hear a case and at least one of them must be a woman and at least one must be a man.

The procedure in a youth court is aimed at avoiding both the criminal environment of the magistrates' court and excessive publicity. A youth court must not sit in a room which has been or will be used, within one hour, for sittings of a court other than a youth court (Children and Young Persons Act 1963, s. 17(2)). Among the persons allowed to be present are the justices, court officers, the parties and their legal representatives, witnesses, newspaper reporters, and other persons authorised by the court to be present (Children and Young Persons Act 1933, s. 47(2), as amended). The attendance at court of a parent or guardian may be required in any case, and is mandatory in the case of a child or young person under the age of 16, unless it would be unreasonable to require such attendance in the circumstances (ibid., s. 34A, as inserted by the Criminal Justice Act 1991). The name or photograph of any person under the age of 18 appearing in the case must not be published in any newspaper or broadcast without the authority of the court (Children and Young Persons Act 1933, s. 49, as substituted by the Criminal Justice and Public Order Act 1994, and amended by the Crime and Disorder Act 1998). The words 'conviction' and 'sentence' must not be used in connection with children and young persons (ibid., s. 59).

The punishments available to a youth court are different from those that may be imposed by the magistrates' court. In the case of a *child,* there is a maximum permitted fine of £250 (Magistrates' Courts Act 1980, ss. 24(4) and 36(2), as amended). A child may be made the subject of a supervision order, compensation order, attendance centre order or secure training order (if aged not less than 12). In the case of a *young person,* the maximum permitted fine is £1,000 (ibid., ss. 24(3) and 36(1), as amended). He may be made the subject of a supervision order, compensation order, community service order (if aged 16), attendance centre order, a sentence of detention in a young offender institution (if aged 15) or secure training order (if aged 14).

The maximum permitted fines may be raised (or lowered) by the Home Secretary by statutory instrument (Magistrates' Courts Act 1980, s. 143, as amended by the Criminal Justice Act 1982). In some circumstances the court is under a duty to order that any fine imposed on, or compensation awarded against, a child or young person shall be paid instead by the parent or guardian of the child or young person (Children and Young Persons Act 1933, s. 55, as substituted by the Criminal Justice Act 1982 and subsequently amended). In the case of a young person of at least 16, the court has a power but not a duty to make such an order (ibid.). The court has power to bind over the parents and guardians of children and young persons who are under the age of 16 (Criminal Justice Act 1991, s. 58, as amended).

The minimum age for a sentence of *imprisonment,* as opposed to detention in a young offender institution, is 21 (Criminal Justice Act 1982, s. 1(1); the prohibition against prison sentences for those under 21 applies equally to cases of contempt of court: *R v Selby Justices (ex parte Frame)* [1991] 2 All ER 344, DC, para 5.4.4). Sentences of *Borstal training* were abolished by the Criminal Justice Act 1982 and replaced by *detention centre* orders and sentences of *youth custody.* They, in turn, were abolished and replaced in 1988 by *detention in a young offender institution.*

No *criminal* proceedings at all can be brought against a child under the age of ten because of the irrebuttable presumption that he is incapable of committing a crime (Children and Young Persons Act 1933, s. 50, as amended by the Children and Young Persons Act 1963). Ten is the so-called age of criminal responsibility in English law. A child under that age who gets into trouble and who is, for example, beyond parental control may be brought before a family proceedings court (see para 1.7.6.4.2 below) in *care* proceedings, which are *civil*, and in which he may be made the subject of, *inter alia*, a care order or a supervision order involving the local authority. Alternatively, the child may be made the subject of a child safety order under the Crime and Disorder Act 1998.

In criminal proceedings against a child aged between ten and 14, it was formerly the case that the prosecution had to prove beyond reasonable doubt not only that he committed the offence but also that he knew that what he was doing was seriously wrong as opposed to merely naughty or mischievous. This rebuttable common law presumption had attracted much criticism in recent years and in 1994 an attempt was made to get rid of it by judicial decision in *C* v *Director of Public Prosecutions* [1994] 3 All ER 190, DC. Here the Queen's Bench Divisional Court, departing from some of its own earlier decisions, held that the presumption was no longer part of English law. However, the Divisional Court was reversed on appeal to the House of Lords ([1995] 2 All ER 43), although their Lordships also expressed dissatisfaction with the presumption and called upon Parliament to review it. It was finally abolished by the Crime and Disorder Act 1998.

The presumption that a boy under the age of 14 is incapable of sexual intercourse was abolished by the Sexual Offences Act 1993.

The Children and Young Persons Act 1969 made provision for a completely new way of treating children and young persons. But after more than 20 years the relevant provisions (ss. 4 and 5) were repealed by the Criminal Justice Act 1991 without ever having been brought into force. The proposed procedure was aimed broadly at the replacement of criminal proceedings by care proceedings.

1.7.6.3 Committal proceedings before examining justices

1.7.6.3.1 Introduction. The object of committal proceedings is to decide whether there is a prima facie case against the accused; i.e., whether there is sufficient evidence to put him on trial. Committal proceedings are held in the magistrates' court in respect of an offence triable either way where it has been decided that the offence should, in fact, be tried at the Crown Court (para 1.7.6.2.2 above). Committal proceedings for *indictable* offences were abolished by the Crime and Disorder Act 1998 with effect from January 1999. When conducting committal proceedings the magistrates are known as 'examining justices'. They must normally sit in open court unless the 'ends of justice', or a particular statutory provision, require privacy (Magistrates' Courts Act 1980, s. 4(2)). The jurisdiction may be exercised by a single justice (ibid., s. 4(1)).

In the exercise of its supervisory jurisdiction over inferior courts the Queen's Bench Division of the High Court has power to interfere with (and, if necessary, quash) committal proceedings if the magistrates have wrongly declined to exercise, or have acted outside, their jurisdiction (*R* v *Wells Street Metropolitan Stipendiary Magistrate (ex parte Westminster City Council)* [1986] 3 All ER 4, DC), or if the committal proceedings are an abuse of the process of the court owing to, for example, the staleness of the offence (*R* v *Telford Justices (ex parte Badhan)* [1991] 2 All ER 854, DC, para 11.9.3.2), or if there has been an error of law, as where the magistrates admit into the proceedings evidence which is legally inadmissible (*Williams* v *Bedwellty Justices* [1996] 3 All ER 737, HL).

Before the changes effected by the Criminal Procedure and Investigations Act 1996 there were two types of committal proceedings — *old-style* proceedings (commonly referred to as *full committals*) and *new-style* proceedings (commonly referred to as *paper committals*).

In old-style committal proceedings, the prosecutor was able to make an opening speech outlining the facts to the justices. Prosecution evidence, both written and oral, was then called and witnesses appearing in person gave their evidence on oath and could be examined, cross-examined and re-examined. The evidence was taken down by the justices' clerk or his assistant and read over to the witness. At the close of the prosecution evidence the defence could submit that there was no case to answer. If no such submission was made, or was made but was rejected, the accused could give evidence and call witnesses.

Old-style committal proceedings were lengthy and in the overwhelming proportion of cases the accused was committed for trial anyway. An alternative procedure, new-style committal proceedings, which was not so wasteful of the time of everyone involved, was introduced in 1967. In new-style committal proceedings the justices were able to commit the accused for trial without considering the evidence if all of it consisted of written statements exchanged beforehand and it was not objected to by either the prosecution or the defence.

The cost of committal proceedings was rising because of the larger number of proceedings taking place and because old-style ('full') committal proceedings, which were the more expensive, had increased as a proportion of all committal proceedings. This proportion rose from 8 per cent in 1981 to 13 per cent in 1986 (*Committal Proceedings: A Consultation Paper*, Home Office and Lord Chancellor's Department, 1989). A limited study conducted on behalf of the government in 1987 found that the average hearing time was 1 hour and 15 minutes for full committals and 6.7 minutes for paper committals. The cost to the magistrates' courts service alone was about £4 million a year (£2.7 million for full committals and £1.3 million for paper committals). This sum did not include the extra costs of the Crown Prosecution Service or of legal aid (op. cit.).

Old-style committal proceedings had clearly been unsatisfactory for some time before the Criminal Procedure and Investigations Act 1996. When cases collapse at the Crown Court the cost is high in terms of time and money. The high acquittal rate on the direction of the judge in the Crown Court (para 7.9.1) suggested that many cases were being committed for trial on weak prosecution evidence. The reluctance of examining justices (sometimes sitting alone) to take the responsibility of refusing to commit defendants for trial in full committals undoubtedly contributed to the increasing unmanageability of Crown Court lists.

In 1981, the *Report of the Royal Commission on Criminal Procedure* (Cm 8092, 1981) proposed the abolition of committal proceedings, and in 1986 the *Report of the Committee on Fraud Trials* (HMSO, 1989) recommended that consideration be given to extending to other offences the suggested new procedure (since implemented in relation to cases of serious or complex fraud) whereby committal proceedings are by-passed but the accused has the right to make an application to the Crown Court to have the charge dismissed on the ground of the insufficiency of the evidence against him (see para 1.7.6.3.5 below). However, a government consultation paper published in 1989 expressed no enthusiasm for such an extension (*Committal Proceedings: A Consultation Paper*, Home Office and Lord Chancellor's Department, 1989).

In 1993, the abolition of committal proceedings was recommended in the *Report of the Royal Commission on Criminal Justice* (Cm 2263, 1993). In their place, it was envisaged that defendants would, within specified time limits, make submissions of no case to answer to the Crown Court (in respect of offences triable only on indictment) or to the magistrates' court (either-way offences). Acting on the recommendations of the Royal Commission, the government decided to abolish committal proceedings and to replace them with a 'transfer for trial' procedure. This was to be achieved by the substitution of new sections in the Magistrates' Courts Act 1980 by the Criminal Justice and Public Order Act 1994. By 1996, however, the Government had concluded that the proposed 'transfer for trial' procedure was too complex and would not produce the desired efficiency gains. Accordingly, the relevant provisions of the Criminal Justice and Public Order Act 1994 were repealed by the Criminal Procedure and Investigations Act 1996 without ever having been brought into force. Thus, the replacement of committal proceedings by the 'transfer for trial' procedure never became law.

However, committal proceedings in respect of *indictable* offences were subsequently abolished in 1999 by the Crime and Disorder Act 1998, which provides that when an adult appears before a magistrates' court charged with an indictable offence the court 'shall send him forthwith to the Crown Court for trial' (ibid., s. 51(1)). He may be sent for trial either in custody or on bail (ibid., s. 52(1)). He can apply to the judge for the charge to be dismissed, and the judge must dismiss the charge if it appears to him that the evidence is insufficient for a jury to convict (ibid., sch. 3). If the charge is dismissed, no further proceedings can be brought in respect of it except by use of the voluntary bill of indictment procedure (ibid., and see para 1.7.6.3.4 below). On an application to have a charge dismissed, reporting restrictions operate which are similar to those applicable to reports of committal proceedings (ibid., and see para 1.7.6.3.3 below).

The transfer procedure in relation to war crimes established by the War Crimes Act 1991 was abolished for England and Wales by the Criminal Procedure and Investigations Act 1996. Thus, the decision whether to send persons accused of war crimes for trial to the Crown Court is now taken in committal proceedings. The transfer procedure applicable in cases of serious or complex fraud (para 1.7.6.3.5 below), and in certain cases involving children (para 1.7.6.3.6 below), is unaffected.

1.7.6.3.2 Procedure. Instead of 'transfer for trial', a modified form of committal proceedings was introduced by the Criminal Procedure and Investigations Act 1996. Old-style committals were abolished. At committal, the accused is not asked to plead to the charge since this is a preliminary hearing and not his trial. He can be represented by a legal representative (Magistrates' Courts Act 1980, s. 122(1), as amended). Only *documentary evidence tendered by the prosecution* in the form of written statements and depositions, together with any exhibits, is admissible at committal (Magistrates' Courts Act 1980, s. 5A. as inserted by the Criminal Procedure and Investigations Act 1996). Thus, witnesses can no longer be called to give *oral* evidence and be cross-examined. However, the defendant's right to ask the justices to consider an oral submission that there is insufficient evidence to put him on trial by jury is preserved (Magistrates' Courts Act 1980, s. 6(2), as substituted by the Criminal Procedure and Investigations Act 1996).

The accused must normally be present when the evidence is tendered unless he is ill (and is legally represented) or his disorderly conduct makes his presence impracticable (ibid., s. 4(3) and (4), as amended by the Criminal Procedure and Investigations Act 1996). If the accused is *not represented*, the proceedings cannot continue in his absence and must be adjourned.

If the justices decide, after considering the prosecution evidence, that there is a prima facie case to answer they must commit the accused to the Crown Court for trial (ibid., s. 6(1), as substituted by the Criminal Procedure and Investigations Act 1996; for the rules about which location of the Crown Court the accused should be sent to for trial, see para 1.5.3 above). If the examining justices are not satisfied that there is a prima facie case, they must discharge the accused unless he is in custody for some other cause (ibid.). It should be noted that such a discharge is not an 'acquittal'; it follows that the accused may be proceeded against on a later occasion on exactly the same charge by use of the voluntary bill of indictment procedure (para 1.7.6.3.4 below).

The justices can commit the accused for trial without considering either the contents of the documentary evidence or any exhibits unless (a) the accused has no legal representative acting for him, or (b) the accused's legal representative has asked the justices to consider a submission that there is insufficient evidence to put the accused on trial by jury (ibid.).

1.7.6.3.3   Restrictions on reports of committal proceedings.   In old-style committal proceedings evidence was normally given only by the prosecution, the accused reserving his defence. Before 1967 this evidence was widely reported in sensational cases, thus making it difficult to find an unbiased jury for the actual trial later. Considerable adverse publicity was given to the committal proceedings involving Dr John Bodkin Adams in 1957. In particular, mention was made before the justices of the deaths of other patients of Dr Adams in addition to the one patient for whose murder he later stood trial. No further mention of these deaths was made at the trial and no evidence about them was given. The Adams case led to the setting up of the Tucker Committee on Proceedings Before Examining Magistrates, which reported in 1958 and recommended restrictions on reports of committal proceedings. But no change in the law was made until the passing of the Criminal Justice Act in 1967. The law is now contained in the Magistrates' Courts Act 1980.

Printed and broadcast reports of committal proceedings are required to be limited to the following matters (Magistrates' Courts Act 1980, s. 8(4)):

(a)   The identity of the court and the names of the examining justices.

(b)   The names, ages, addresses and occupations of the accused and witnesses.

(c)   The offence with which the accused is charged.

(d)   The names of the legal representatives engaged in the case.

(e)   Any decision of the court to commit or not commit for trial.

(f)   Where the court commits the accused for trial, the charge on which he is committed and the court to which he is committed.

(g)   Where the proceedings are adjourned, the date and place to which they are adjourned.

(h)   Any arrangements for bail on committal or adjournment.

(i)   Whether legal aid was granted to the accused.

It is a summary offence to report or broadcast any information not listed above. The proprietors, editors and publishers of newspapers or periodicals, and the BBC, independent television companies, and their senior programme executives, are liable to a fine (ibid., s. 8(5)). Proceedings for this offence cannot be instituted without the consent of the Attorney-General (ibid., s. 8(6)).

The reporting restrictions must be lifted by the justices if the accused makes an application to that effect (ibid., s. 8(2)). Where there are two or more accused and one of them objects to the lifting of reporting restrictions, the justices must not lift the restrictions unless it is in the interests of justice to do so. The court must hear representations on the matter from the accused before making its decision (ibid., s. 8(2A) added by the Criminal Justice (Amendment) Act 1981). This provision is designed to stop the kind of prejudice suffered by Jeremy Thorpe in *R* v *Holmes and others* (22 June 1979, unreported; para 7.7), in which the committal proceedings were widely reported after reporting restrictions had been lifted in respect of *all* the accused on the application of only *one* of them.

If there is disagreement among co-accused as to whether committal proceedings should be reported, the burden of satisfying the magistrates that it is 'in the interests of justice' that they should make an order lifting reporting restrictions is placed, by the Magistrates' Courts Act 1980, s. 8(2A), on those accused who wish to have the proceedings reported. They will have to make out a powerful case. The phrase 'the interests of justice' mentioned in s. 8(2A) refers to the interests of justice as affecting the accused before the court since only they are entitled to make representations on the matter. The 'interests of justice' so-defined require, as a paramount consideration, that *all* the accused should have a fair trial. In deciding whether to lift reporting restrictions the magistrates must balance the conflicting views of the co-accused and take into account the rule contained in s. 8(1) that, prima facie, committal proceedings should not be reported (*R* v *Leeds Justices (ex parte Sykes)* [1983] 1 All ER 460, DC). The magistrates have no power to lift restrictions in relation to some only of the co-accused. The restrictions must be lifted in respect of the committal proceedings as a whole, or not at all.

If the restrictions are lifted, reporting in the media ceases to be confined to the matters specified above. Full reporting is possible, including details of the evidence, subject to the understanding that official secrets must not be divulged and subject to what is said below about the Contempt of Court Act 1981. Even if the reporting restrictions are not lifted, the evidence given at committal proceedings may be published at the end of those proceedings if the accused is not committed or at the end of the *trial* if he *is* committed (Magistrates' Courts Act 1980, s. 8(3)). By this time, however, the evidence will have lost much of its news value.

The reporting restrictions outlined above operate *in addition to* any other statutory limitations on reports of court proceedings (ibid., s. 8(7)). By s. 4(2) of the Contempt of Court Act 1981, a court has a discretion to order that the publication of any report of legal proceedings held in public be postponed for such period as the court thinks necessary. But a court, including a magistrates' court, can only make such an order 'where it appears necessary for avoiding a substantial risk of prejudice to the administration of justice' in the proceedings before it or in any other proceedings which are pending or imminent (see further, *R* v *Horsham Justices (ex parte Farquharson)* [1982] 2 All ER 269, CA, and para 5.2.2.4.5).

1.7.6.3.4   The voluntary bill of indictment.   Voluntary bill of indictment is a procedure which may be used by the prosecution to avoid committal proceedings altogether, or to cut them short if they have already commenced, or to circumvent the justices' refusal to commit for trial. The application can be made only to, and leave to prefer a bill granted only by, a High Court judge (Administration of Justice (Miscellaneous Provisions) Act 1933, s. 2(2)(b); Indictments (Procedure) Rules 1971 (SI 1971, No. 1253), and note that his decision to grant or refuse leave to prefer a bill is not challengeable by judicial review in the High Court: *R* v *Manchester Crown Court (ex parte Williams and Simpson)* [1990] Crim LR 654, DC). The proceedings are held in chambers although judgment on the application may be given in open court.

The proceedings are essentially *ex parte* and, therefore, the defendant has no right to be heard or to make representations. It has been said that there is nothing inherently unjust in denying the defendant any right to be heard in these exceptional proceedings since he will have the right to be heard at his trial (*R* v *Raymond* [1981] 2 All ER 246, CA). However, the High Court judge has a discretion to receive written representations from the defendant, although the discretion is exercised only in exceptional circumstances (see *Practice Note* [1991] 1 All ER 288). There is probably no discretion to hear *oral* representations by or on behalf of the defendant. The application to prefer a bill of indictment is usually dealt with solely on the basis of the documents which accompany the application (*R* v *Raymond,* at p. 255).

If the defendant wishes to challenge the granting of leave to prefer a bill of indictment, it seems that the correct procedure is for him to appeal to the Court of Appeal. It would appear that neither a circuit judge nor even another High Court judge has jurisdiction, at the actual trial on the indictment, to review the original decision to grant leave to prefer a bill (*R* v *Rothfield* (1937) 26 Cr App R 103, CCA; *R* v *Raymond* at p. 255).

The voluntary bill procedure is an exceptional and potentially oppressive one. For these reasons it is provided that the application must state why it is desired to prefer a bill of indictment instead of or in addition to committal proceedings. In addition, there must accompany the application the proposed bill of indictment and the proofs of the evidence of the witnesses whom it is proposed to call in support of the charges at the trial. The application must contain a statement that that evidence will be available at the trial and that the case disclosed by the proofs is, to the best of the knowledge, information and belief of the applicant, substantially a true case (Indictments (Procedure) Rules 1971, rr. 8 and 9).

The commonest circumstances giving rise to the use of the voluntary bill procedure are as follows:

(a)   Where there are a number of co-defendants and some of them have already been committed for trial. Delay and hardship to them can be avoided by bringing the rest to trial by means of the voluntary bill procedure.

(b)   Where committal proceedings before the justices are taking an unreasonable length of time or are being seriously disrupted. Thus, in an unreported case in October 1981 a High Court judge granted leave to prefer a bill of indictment to send fifteen black youths for trial on charges of murder and riot. The reason was that committal proceedings at Croydon magistrates' court would not be completed within a reasonable time. In twelve working days, only nine prosecution witnesses had been heard. The accused were represented by eleven barristers and two solicitors. The Director of Public Prosecutions intervened and applied for a bill of indictment in order to save time. (See *The Guardian,* 22 October 1981.) In *R* v *Raymond* [1981] 2 All ER 246, CA, a bill of indictment was sought because the committal proceedings were being seriously disrupted. Mr Raymond was described by the Court of Appeal as 'a practised disturber of court proceedings', having also interrupted other committal proceedings in 1979 (see [1981] 2 All ER 246 at p. 256).

(c)   Where the justices have refused to commit the defendant for trial. Committal proceedings are not a trial and, therefore, since there is no acquittal, the prosecution can bring fresh committal proceedings against the same person on exactly the same charge. In these circumstances, however, it would be quicker to use the voluntary bill procedure.

The use of the voluntary bill procedure may be illustrated by reference to the strange sequence of events following the death of Barry Prosser (see *The Guardian,* 23 and 24 October 1981). Mr Prosser died in August 1980 in a prison cell at Winson Green, Birmingham. His death was due to shock caused by severe injuries, including a ruptured stomach and oesophagus and bruising all over the body. In February 1981, the Birmingham stipendiary magistrate refused to commit for trial a prison officer, Melvyn Jackson, on a charge of murdering Mr Prosser. In April 1981, a coroner's jury, after hearing evidence for eight days, returned a verdict of unlawful killing in relation to the death of Mr Prosser. In September 1981, fresh committal proceedings were brought against Melvyn Jackson and two other prison officers, Eric Smith and Howard Price. This time a different stipendiary magistrate in Birmingham decided that there was no case to answer. In October 1981, after a public outcry, the Director of Public Prosecutions applied for leave to prefer a bill of indictment so that the whole affair could be investigated at a public trial. Leave was granted. The three officers were duly tried for murder at the Crown Court at Leicester in March 1982 and all three were acquitted.

Another controversial use of the voluntary bill procedure occurred in May 1986 and was seen by some as an example of the executive overriding the decision of an 'unco-operative' magistrate in the interests of good relations between the United Kingdom and Indian governments. Four Sikhs appeared in committal proceedings before a stipendiary magistrate in Leicester charged with conspiracy to murder the Indian Prime Minister during his visit to this country in October 1985. There was disagreement between the prosecution and the bench over the extent to which one of the prosecution witnesses, an undercover policeman, should disclose his name and force. The prosecution called no further evidence and the accused were discharged. However, three of them were immediately re-arrested and the Director of Public Prosecutions (apparently at the instigation of the Attorney-General) applied to a High Court judge for leave to prefer a bill of indictment. Leave was granted and the three accused were committed for trial to the Crown Court (see *The Guardian*, 24 May 1986). At their trial in December 1986, two were convicted and the other was acquitted. On another occasion, the magistrates found there was no prima facie case to answer and refused to commit for trial a policeman charged with raping a female colleague. The Crown Prosecution Service obtained leave to prefer a voluntary bill of indictment and the policeman stood trial at the Crown Court at Northampton. He was acquitted (see *The Independent*, 9 November 1989).

1.7.6.3.5   Transfer to the Crown Court of cases of serious or complex fraud.   The *Report of the Committee on Fraud Trials* (HMSO, 1986) recommended a new procedure designed to avoid complicated and lengthy committal hearings in cases of serious and complex fraud. This recommendation was implemented by ss. 4–6 of the Criminal Justice Act 1987, the effect of which is to by-pass committal proceedings and allow such cases to be transferred direct to the Crown Court.

If a person has been charged with an indictable offence and, in the opinion of a designated authority (or of one of its officers acting on its behalf), the evidence (a) would be sufficient for the person charged to be committed for trial, and (b) reveals a case of fraud of such seriousness or complexity that it is appropriate that the management of the case should be taken over without delay by the Crown Court, the designated authority (or one of its officers) may give the magistrates' court a notice of transfer certifying that opinion (Criminal Justice Act 1987, s. 4(1)). Upon the giving of a notice of transfer, the functions of the magistrates' court in relation to the case cease. The notice of transfer must be given before committal proceedings have commenced (ibid.). The 'designated authorities' are the Director of Public Prosecutions, the Director of the Serious Fraud Office, the Commissioners of Inland Revenue, the Commissioners of Customs and Excise, and the Secretary of State (ibid., s. 4(2)).

Although the defendant is deprived of the filter of magistrates' committal proceedings, he has instead the right to apply to the Crown Court before trial for the transferred charge to be dismissed on the ground that the evidence disclosed would not be sufficient for a jury properly to convict him of it (i.e., that there is no prima facie case against him; ibid., s. 6(1)). If the charge is dismissed at this stage no further proceedings can be brought in respect of it except by use of the voluntary bill of indictment procedure (ibid., s. 6(7) and see para 1.7.6.3.4 above). There are restrictions on media reports of applications to have charges dismissed (ibid., s. 11). The restrictions are similar to those which operate in relation to reports of committal proceedings in the magistrates' courts (para 1.7.6.3.3 above).

1.7.6.3.6 Transfer to the Crown Court of cases of sexual offences, and offences of violence or cruelty, involving children.   The Criminal Justice Act 1991, s. 53, as amended, and sch. 6, enables the Director of Public Prosecutions to serve a notice of transfer in such cases if he is of the opinion: (a) that the evidence of the offence would be sufficient for the person charged to be committed for trial; (b) that a child who is alleged to be the victim of, or a witness to, the offence will be called as a witness at the trial; and (c) that, for the purpose of avoiding any prejudice to the child's welfare, the case should be taken over and proceeded with without delay by the Crown Court. The notice of transfer, which must be given before committal proceedings have commenced, causes the functions of the magistrates' court to cease in relation to the transferred case. The Act contains similar provisions about applications for dismissal and media reporting restrictions as apply in cases of serious or complex fraud (para 1.7.6.3.5 above).

1.7.6.4 Civil jurisdiction

1.7.6.4.1 Introduction.   The magistrates' courts have jurisdiction to hear family proceedings, particularly under the Domestic Proceedings and Magistrates' Courts Act 1978, the Children Act 1989, and part IV of the Family Law Act 1996 (family homes and domestic violence). They have powers over the recovery of the council tax and charges for water, gas and electricity. As licensing justices, magistrates are responsible for granting, revoking and renewing licences for the sale of liquor.

1.7.6.4.2 Family proceedings courts.   In the magistrates' court, perhaps the most important and time-consuming aspect on the civil side is the jurisdiction, first conferred by s. 4 of the Matrimonial Causes Act 1878, over family proceedings. When a magistrates' court is dealing with family proceedings it is called a 'family proceedings court' (Magistrates' Courts Act 1980, s. 67(1), as amended). The term 'family proceedings' includes adoption proceedings (ibid., s. 65(1)), which, before 1979, were dealt with, somewhat anomalously, in the juvenile court (now called the youth court). 'Family proceedings' also include applications for residence and contact orders under the Children Act 1989, proceedings under part 1 of the Domestic Proceedings and Magistrates' Courts Act 1978 (Magistrates' Courts Act 1980, s. 65(1), as amended), and proceedings under part IV of the Family Law Act 1996. Proceedings under part I of the 1978 Act enable the magistrates to order financial provision, which may take the form of periodical payments and/or a lump sum (not exceeding £1,000), to be made by a spouse in cases of failure to provide reasonable maintenance for the other spouse or any child of the family. Part IV of the Family Law Act 1996 confers jurisdiction on the magistrates to make occupation orders and non-molestation orders in cases of domestic violence.

1.7.6.4.2.1 Family panels.   A lay justice cannot sit in a family proceedings court unless he is a member of a family panel, which comprises only lay justices specially appointed to deal with family proceedings (Magistrates' Courts Act 1980, s. 67(2), as amended by the Access to Justice Act 1999). Under s. 66(1) of the Magistrates' Courts Act 1980, as substituted by the Access to Justice Act 1999, a family proceedings court must be composed of:

(a)   two or three lay justices; or

(b)   a district judge (magistrates' courts) as chairman sitting with one or two lay justices; or

(c)   a district judge (magistrates' courts) sitting alone if it is not practicable for him to sit with one or two lay justices.

Except where the court is composed of a district judge (magistrates' courts) sitting alone, it must, so far as practicable, include both a man and a woman (ibid., s. 66(2), as substituted by the Access to Justice Act 1999).

A district judge (magistrates' courts) is qualified to hear family proceedings if he has been nominated by the Lord Chancellor to do so; he does not have to be a member of a family panel (ibid., s. 67(2), as amended by the Access to Justice Act 1999).

1.7.6.4.2.2   Restrictions on attendance at family proceedings.   The hearing and determination of family proceedings must be kept separate from other business dealt with by the magistrates' court so far as this is consistent with efficiency (Magistrates' Courts Act 1980, s. 69(1)). When family proceedings (other than *adoption* proceedings) are being heard the only persons entitled to be present are:

(a)   Officers of the court.

(b)   The parties, their legal representatives, witnesses and other persons directly concerned in the case. This would include social workers and probation officers.

(c)   Representatives of newspapers or news agencies.

(d)   Any other person who the court may in its discretion permit to be present. But permission must not be refused to 'a person who appears to the court to have adequate grounds for attendance' (ibid., s. 69(2)). This would probably include a trainee solicitor and a law student and, possibly, a close relative of one of the parties.

In the case of *adoption* proceedings, only persons in categories (a) and (b) above are entitled to be present; those in categories (c) and (d) are excluded (ibid., s. 69(3)).

Although in *any* family proceedings witnesses are generally entitled to be present, the court still retains its discretion to exclude them until they are called for examination (ibid., s. 69(6)). When hearing *any* family proceedings which involve indecent evidence the court may exclude everyone during the taking of the evidence except officers of the court, the parties and their legal representatives, and other persons directly concerned in the case. But the magistrates can only do this if they think it is necessary in the interests of the administration of justice or of public decency (ibid., s. 69(4)).

1.7.6.4.2.3   Restrictions on newspaper and broadcast reports of family proceedings.   The only information that may be published is as follows (Magistrates' Courts Act 1980, s. 71(1A)):

(a)   The names, addresses, and occupations of the parties and witnesses.

(b)   The grounds of the application, and a concise statement of the charges, defences, and counter-charges in support of which evidence has been given.

(c)   Submissions on any points of law arising in the proceedings and the decision of the court on the submissions.

(d)   The decision of the court and any observations made by the court in giving it.

In the case of *adoption* proceedings the information that may lawfully be published is limited to categories (c) and (d) above; information in categories (a) and (b) must not be published (ibid., s. 71(2)).

Breach of these reporting restrictions is a summary offence punishable by a fine. A prosecution may be started only with the consent of the Attorney-General. The restrictions do not forbid the publication of otherwise prohibited particulars in a newspaper or periodical of a technical nature which is bona fide intended for circulation among members of the legal or medical professions (ibid., s. 71(3)–(5)).

1.7.7   Future of magistrates' courts

It has traditionally been a criticism of appointments to the lay magistracy that they are political in character and made by the Lord Chancellor from a limited social class. This problem occupied a Royal Commission in 1910 and again in 1948 (*Report of the Royal Commission on Justices of the Peace,* Cd 5250, 1910; *Report of the Royal Commission on Justices of the Peace,* Cmd 7463, 1948). The position has undoubtedly improved since the efforts of the Labour government which took office in 1964. Some of the mystique surrounding magisterial appointments has disappeared and newspaper advertisements inviting people to put themselves forward for consideration can sometimes be seen.

Moreover, since the Employment Protection Act 1975, it has been theoretically less difficult for working people to secure time off work in order to perform their duties as magistrates. An employer is bound by statute (currently the Employment Rights Act 1996) to permit an employee who is a lay magistrate to take time off during working hours to enable him to perform his duties (Employment Rights Act 1996, s. 50(1)). How much time off the employee is entitled to will depend on what is reasonable in the circumstances bearing in mind particularly how much time off the employee has already been allowed and the effect of the employee's absence on the employer's business (ibid., s. 50). There is no express statutory duty on the employer to pay the employee during the time he takes off to act as a magistrate. An employee who is not allowed time off (or sufficient time off) can complain to an industrial tribunal, which can award him such compensation as is just and equitable in the circumstances (ibid., s. 51(1), (3) and (4)).

It is a common criticism of lay justices that they do not know the law. But this is to misunderstand their role in the judicial process. The duty to act judicially and impartially with an appreciation of the basics of procedure and evidence is, in their case, far more important than the acquisition of a detailed knowledge of substantive law (see *Report of the Royal Commission on Justices of the Peace,* Cmd 7463, 1948, para 89). For this they are entitled to ask for the advice of their professional clerk. It is obviously preferable for the magistrates to get their decisions right in the first place, but when, inevitably, mistakes are made they can be rectified by an appeal to a higher court. There is an appeal to the Crown Court on points of law and fact, and a further appeal from there to the Queen's Bench Division of the High Court on a point of law only. Alternatively, on a point of law, an appeal can be taken direct from the magistrates' court to the High Court by way of 'case stated' (para 6.2.1). Any excess of jurisdiction, or violation of the principles of natural justice, on the part of the magistrates can be cured by an application for judicial review made to the Divisional Court of the Queen's Bench Division, which may quash the offending decision by an order of certiorari (Chapter 11).

Lack of uniformity in sentencing is a constant source of concern. Precise uniformity is impossible to achieve unless Parliament were to lay down fixed penalties for each offence.

This would be most undesirable as it would exclude that flexibility which the court needs in order to arrive at the most appropriate penalty in the light of any mitigating circumstances. Variations in sentences for the same offence are inevitable as long as there is a system in which Parliament lays down a *maximum* but *no minimum* penalty. There are many thousands of lay magistrates exercising the same jurisdiction throughout England and Wales, and local and individual attitudes towards particular offences are bound to be reflected in the sentences imposed for them.

Magistrates are not kept in ignorance of the sentences they can impose (cf. *Report of the Royal Commission on Justices of the Peace,* Cmd 7463, 1948, para 90). They may seek the opinion of their clerk. Moreover, the Home Office handbook, *The Sentence of the Court* (first published by HMSO in 1964), advises magistrates (and other judges) of their powers in dealing with offenders and gives guidance on how to exercise those powers. The Magistrates' Association, established in 1921, also provides information and organises conferences at which problems can be aired. The Queen's Bench Division of the High Court, in its decisions on appeal from the magistrates' courts, gives guidance on sentencing.

It is sometimes said that magistrates are too old. It is probably true that most would not put themselves forward for appointment until the passing of those years which involve the heaviest family commitments. Some, no doubt, wait until retirement approaches. Magistrates are removed to the supplemental list at the age of 70 and are then usually unable to perform any judicial functions (Justices of the Peace Act 1997, ss. 7(2) and 9(1)). There is, as it were, a presumption of senility. Yet there is nothing wrong with old age *per se.* Problems arise when it is associated with mental infirmity, or lack of touch with the outside world, or political or social bias. But these failings, which may disturb both judgment and behaviour, are found in persons of all ages. A lay magistrate of any age may be removed to the supplemental list if it is expedient, because of infirmity 'or other like cause', that he should not exercise judicial functions, or if he declines or neglects to take a proper part in the exercise of his judicial functions (ibid., s. 7(4)). The ultimate sanction is removal from office by the Lord Chancellor, although this is a course resorted to only rarely.

Perhaps a greater problem is the extent to which a magistrates'court may be dominated by its clerk and/or the police. The justices' clerk is there to advise and assist, not to dictate or even to be seen taking an over-active part in the decision-making process (para 1.7.5.2 above). The expression 'police court' is an unfortunate misnomer, a relic of the days when the magistrates' court was often situated in the same building as, or next door to, the local police station. But the suspicion remains in some quarters that, on a conflict of evidence, the magistrates are too ready to accept the 'official', police version. Police officers are frequent witnesses and may come to be on reasonably familiar terms with the bench.

Some magistrates' courts exposed themselves to a certain amount of criticism during the miners' strike of 1984–85. The criticisms were made mainly in relation to the imposition of wide bail conditions and the appearance of 'conveyor-belt justice'. The dispensing of 'group justice' (i.e., putting into the dock together defendants who have been arrested on different occasions or at different places) was condemned by the Lord Chief Justice (*R v Mansfield Justices (ex parte Sharkey)* [1985] 1 All ER 193, DC, *per* Lord Lane CJ at p. 203).

In another context, the growing practice among some magistrates of claiming anonymity has been declared unlawful (*R v Felixstowe Justices (ex parte Leigh)* [1987] 1 All ER 551, DC). Open justice, it was said, demands that the names of those who sit in judgment should be known. It is an 'occupational hazard', which magistrates and other judges should accept, that they will occasionally be subjected to criticism, and even vilification, and that they will be pestered by persons who bear some grievance (ibid., *per* Watkins LJ at pp. 560–61).

Other problems have arisen over the extent to which a magistrates' court may sit in private or protect the identity of a defendant or witness. Section 121(4) of the Magistrates' Courts Act 1980 provides that a magistrates' court 'shall sit in open court'. That provision notwithstanding, it seems that the court has *inherent* jurisdiction to exclude the public and the press, and to sit in private, if the administration of justice so requires. Such a course should, however, be regarded as exceptional and there must be a compelling reason for deciding to sit in private (*R* v *Governor of Lewes Prison (ex parte Doyle)* [1917] 2 KB 254, C; *R* v *Malvern Justices (ex parte Evans)* [1988] 1 All ER 371, DC, *per* Watkins LJ at p. 378). Similarly, a magistrates' court has inherent jurisdiction to take steps to protect the identity of a defendant or witness, but only in those rare cases where disclosure of that identity would interfere with the administration of justice (*Attorney-General* v *Leveller Magazine Ltd* [1979] AC 440, HL; *R* v *Evesham Justices (ex parte McDonagh)* [1988] 1 All ER 371, DC, in which the magistrates' decision to prohibit publication of the defendant's home address was declared unlawful on the ground that, being concerned with a desire to spare the defendant from harassment from his former wife, it had nothing to do with the administration of justice).

In view of the fact that some 97 per cent of criminal cases begin and end in the magistrates' courts, it would be manifestly impracticable to abolish them without providing for their replacement by whatever system was considered to be more desirable. The appointment of large numbers of district judges (magistrates' courts) would bring the advantage of full-time professionalism and mitigate further the problem of lack of uniformity in sentencing. But, assuming that a sufficient supply of persons was available with the requisite knowledge of the law and with other judicial attributes, the financial cost would be enormous. Such a move would also seriously undermine the involvement of the layman in the administration of justice. The *Report of the Royal Commission on Justices of the Peace,* published in 1948, recommended that 'both on principle and on grounds of practical convenience' lay magistrates should be retained (Cmnd 7463, paras 213–24). At the same time, however, the Royal Commission encouraged the appointment of more professional magistrates as and when desirable. Addressing the Council of the Magistrates' Association in July 1997, the Lord Chancellor, Lord Irvine of Lairg, reassured lay magistrates that their efforts were appreciated by the government, that they were not an endangered species, and that there was no truth in recent reports that they were under threat of replacement by professional magistrates. He referred to lay magistrates as 'the backbone of the criminal justice system', and praised them for their voluntary work across the whole of the country and for offering excellent value for money.

On the civil side, magistrates' courts continue to play an important role in family proceedings. In their training there is now a greater emphasis on family law. Their jurisdiction over family proceedings, which for so long lagged behind the modern social policy underlying the reformed divorce law, has been substantially recast in recent years.

A report published by the Home Office in 1989 highlighted the inefficiency and lengthy delays in processing criminal cases through the magistrates' courts (*Scrutiny Report on Magistrates' Courts,* Home Office, 1989). As a result, the Magistrates' Courts Service Inspectorate was established as an independent national agency charged with the task of inspecting, and reporting upon, the organisation and administration of magistrates' courts. Executive responsibility for magistrates' courts was transferred from the Home Office to the Lord Chancellor's Department on 1 April 1992. The Police and Magistrates' Courts Act 1994 gave effect to proposals for the administration of magistrates' courts set out in the White Paper, *A New Framework for Local Justice* (Cm 1829, 1992).

The relevant provisions are now contained in the Justices of the Peace Act 1997 (as amended by the Access to Justice Act 1999), under which the Lord Chancellor is empowered to combine magistrates' courts committee areas, to amend the constitution of magistrates' courts committees, and to intervene if a magistrates' court committee fails to perform its statutory duties. Each magistrates' courts committee area is required to appoint a justices' chief executive to be responsible for the day to day administration of the area, subject to the direction of the committee. Regulations require each magistrates' courts committee to keep accounts and provide for those accounts to be audited. At the request of a magistrates' court committee, the Audit Commission may undertake 'value for money' studies of the performance of the committee's functions. The Magistrates' Courts Service Inspectorate is placed on a statutory footing.

In order to safeguard the independence of justices' clerks and staff in relation to their legal functions, it is provided that advice given to magistrates in individual cases shall be free from management direction (Justices of the Peace Act 1997, s. 48, as amended by the Access to Justice Act 1999).

It may be proper to conclude that, in spite of the criticisms made of them and the upheaval to which they have been subjected in recent years, magistrates' courts seem assured of an active part in the judicial process for a long time ahead if men and women of the right quality and motivation can be recruited to the bench.

1.8   JUDICIAL MISCONDUCT AND IMMUNITY FROM SUIT

1.8.1   Judicial misconduct

Before the Revolutionary Settlement of 1701 the judges were dismissible at the King's pleasure. Now, as a direct result of the Act of Settlement (1701), judges of the House of Lords, Court of Appeal and High Court hold office during good behaviour, subject to a power of removal by Her Majesty on an address presented to her by both Houses of Parliament (Appellate Jurisdiction Act 1876, s. 6 (House of Lords); Supreme Court Act 1981, s. 11(3) (Court of Appeal and High Court)). The Lord Chancellor is an exception. Since he is a government minister he can be dismissed at any time by the Queen on the advice of the Prime Minister. He is expressly excluded from the security of tenure normally associated with superior court judges (Supreme Court Act 1981, s. 11(1)).

Save for the rare dismissal of a Lord Chancellor occasioned by political or other exigency, no judge of a superior court in England has been removed from office since the Act of Settlement of 1701. The Conservative Lord Chancellor, Viscount Kilmuir, resigned in 1962 at the instance of the Prime Minister, Mr Macmillan, during the major Cabinet reshuffle known as the 'night of the long knives'. Lord Macclesfield LC was dismissed for corruption in 1725, a fate which had befallen Francis Bacon (Lord St Albans) a century earlier. In 1865, Lord Westbury LC, while not actually dismissed, resigned after allegations of nepotism and abuse of patronage had been made against him. (For the cases of Bacon, Macclesfield and Westbury, see Gibb, *Judicial Corruption in the United Kingdom,* 1957, pp. 1–51.) During the course of 1987 there were no fewer than three Conservative Lord Chancellors. Lord Hailsham of St. Marylebone LC (the incumbent between 1970 and 1974, and again from 1979) was prevailed upon to resign by the Prime Minister, Mrs Thatcher, in June 1987. He was replaced by Lord Havers LC, the former Attorney-General, who resigned on health grounds after only four months in office. His successor, appointed in October 1987, was one of the Scottish Law Lords, Lord Mackay of Clashfern LC.

An *Irish* judge was removed from office in 1830. He was Sir Jonah Barrington. He was found to have misappropriated £700 paid into the Admiralty Court of Ireland. Having fled to France, an address was presented by Parliament to the Crown and he was dismissed from office (see Gibb, op. cit., pp. 64–72).

English judges have generally shown themselves to be above corruption and, on the whole, impeccably behaved. Judicial misbehaviour is much more of a problem in the USA (see, e.g., Morrick, 'Judicial misconduct in the USA', (1978) 128 New LJ 400). It must be noted, however, that even if it were possible to define with any precision 'good' or 'bad' behaviour, it is still difficult to get rid of an English judge of the High Court and above. The Lord Chancellor has no legal power to dismiss, although, as effective head of the judiciary, he may privately suggest resignation in the guise of voluntary early retirement. Thus, Hallett J was persuaded to resign by Viscount Kilmuir LC following serious criticism by the Court of Appeal in *Jones* v *National Coal Board* [1957] 2 QB 55 that he interrupted counsel too much and asked too many questions. Harman J resigned in April 1998 following criticism by the Court of Appeal of his conduct of a case in which he had delayed giving judgment for 20 months after the conclusion of the hearing (see *The Times*, 14 February 1998 and *Goose* v *Wilson Sandford & Co.* (1998) *The Times*, 19 February, CA). What is needed for *compulsory* removal is nothing short of a joint address presented to the Queen by both Houses of Parliament.

The retiring age for a judge of the Court of Appeal or High Court is 70 (Supreme Court Act 1981, s. 11(2), as amended by the Judicial Pensions and Retirement Act 1993). A judge may, by giving written notice to the Lord Chancellor, resign his office at any time before reaching retirement age (Supreme Court Act 1981, s. 11(7)), although resignation other than for reasons of health or old-age is rare. Lord Devlin caused controversy when he resigned as a Lord of Appeal in Ordinary in 1964 at the early age of 58. He explained many years later that he had found life as a Law Lord 'utterly boring' (see *The Times*, 11 June 1985; he died in 1992 at the age of 85). There was more controversy in 1970 when Fisher J resigned from the High Court bench in order to go into the City at a greatly enhanced salary. Lord Denning had already decided to retire as Master of the Rolls in 1982 at the age of 83 before it became clear that he could not carry on much longer following the discovery of a possible libel in his book *What Next in the Law*. He tells his own story of his retirement in *The Closing Chapter* (1983, Section One). He had previously maintained that he would die in office, being quoted more than once as saying that he had 'all the Christian virtues except resignation'. He was able to sit on the bench to such an advanced age because he was appointed before a statutory retirement age was introduced for judges in 1959. He died in March 1999 at the age of 100.

There is provision for vacating the office of a Court of Appeal or High Court judge who is so ill as to be incapable of both the performance of his duties and resignation. The procedure requires the Lord Chancellor, acting on a medical certificate and with the concurrence of senior judges, to make a written declaration that the office has been vacated. The judge in question is then deemed to have resigned (Supreme Court Act 1981, s. 11(8) and (9)).

Circuit judges and recorders do not enjoy the same security of tenure as their senior judicial colleagues. Although the Crown Court is part of the Supreme Court of Judicature, circuit judges are not judges of the Supreme Court for the purposes of appointment, tenure of office and precedence (Supreme Court Act 1981, s. 151(4)). Their position remains governed by the Courts Act 1971. Circuit judges and recorders can be removed by the Lord Chancellor, without the intervention of Parliament, for incapacity or misbehaviour.

A circuit judge was removed in 1983 after pleading guilty to, and being fined on, charges of evading customs duty on cigarettes and whisky. In 1985, another was allegedly threatened with dismissal unless he abided by the so-called 'Kilmuir rules' which seek to provide guidance to judges about participation in journalism and appearances on radio and television. (These 'rules' were abolished by a later Lord Chancellor, Lord Mackay of Clashfern LC in 1987.) The same judge was 'seriously rebuked' by the Lord Chancellor in 1990 after describing the Lord Chief Justice as an 'ancient dinosaur living in the wrong age'. In 1992, a circuit judge was rebuked for kissing a court usher in his chambers. The same judge was rebuked in 1997 for using a racially offensive expression during the course of a trial. In 1999, a circuit judge was severely reprimanded, but not dismissed, following conviction for a drink-driving offence. Another circuit judge resigned in the same year. This judge, who had been suspended on full pay since November 1995, was tried in March 1998 for conspiracy to commit offences under the Theft Act 1978 while in practice as a solicitor. The jury failed to reach a verdict, and in October 1998 the Attorney General imposed a permanent stay on any further prosecution by entering a *nolle prosequi* ('unwilling to prosecute'). The judge's resignation pre-empted any decision by the Lord Chancellor to remove him from office. It was known that the Lord Chancellor was considering whether the evidence disclosed in the judge's trial would justify removing him for misbehaviour.

Recorders, who are part-time judges, may also be removed by the Lord Chancellor for failing to sit as often as agreed. Another sanction available against recorders is not to extend their appointment on the expiry of the specified period (para 1.5.4 above).

District judges can be removed from office by the Lord Chancellor, without the intervention of Parliament, for incapacity or misbehaviour (County Courts Act 1984, s. 11). A district judge of the Principal Registry of the Family Division who had been convicted of a drink-driving offence was 'severely reprimanded' (but not dismissed) by the Lord Chancellor in 1989. Another district judge was reprimanded for the same reason in 1993. The same district judge was charged with a similar offence in 1997. However, before the case was heard it became apparent that he was no longer able to perform his judicial duties on account of alcohol dependence and depression, and he was allowed to retire from the bench on grounds of ill-health. At his subsequent trial, he was convicted and sent to prison for 28 days.

A district judge (magistrates' courts) is dismissible by the Lord Chancellor, but only on the ground of incapacity or misbehaviour (Justices of the Peace Act 1997, s. 10A(3), as substituted by the Access to Legal Services Act 1999; and see para 1.7.2 above). Lay magistrates are removable completely from office by the Lord Chancellor without showing cause. One was removed in 1997 after the Lord Chancellor got to hear of a 'mooning' incident in which she was photographed exposing her bottom during an argument (see *The Times*, 18 September 1997, under the headline 'JP who exposed bottom loses her seat'). There is no official retiring age for lay magistrates but they are put on the 'supplemental list' at the age of 70 and thereupon cease to exercise judicial functions. Lay magistrates may request to be put on the supplemental list before they reach the age of 70. Alternatively, their names may be placed there if the Lord Chancellor is of opinion that they are unfit to sit on the bench by reason of age or infirmity or a refusal or neglect to perform their functions (paras 1.7.3 and 1.7.4 above).

1.8.2   Immunity from suit

Judicial immunity from suit means that a judge of a *superior* court (such as the High Court) cannot be sued for damages for acts done in his judicial capacity in good faith, even though he has acted mistakenly or in ignorance of his powers. Immunity from suit enables a judge to perform his duties with complete independence and freedom from fear of repercussions. Although he cannot succeed in a civil action for damages, the hapless litigant who is damaged in some way at the hands of the judiciary is not totally without a remedy. He may, for example, appeal against the judge's decision to a higher court (Chapter 6) or seek to have it set aside by *certiorari* (Chapter 11). If he has been imprisoned he may try to secure his release by taking habeas corpus proceedings (Chapter 4). Such a judge is only liable in a civil action for damages if he was not acting judicially, knowing that he had no jurisdiction to do what he did.

An example of judicial immunity is provided by the case of *Sirros* v *Moore* [1975] QB 118, CA, in which a civil action was brought against a circuit judge. The claimant, a Turkish citizen, had overstayed his sojourn in England and a magistrates' court recommended his deportation. However, the stipendiary magistrate specifically ordered that he was not to be detained pending the Home Secretary's decision on the deportation recommendation. The claimant had then appealed to the Crown Court against the magistrate's recommendation. His appeal was dismissed and he left the court. The circuit judge, obviously under the impression that the claimant was in custody, ordered the police to stop him. He was arrested outside the court, refused bail, and sent to prison to await the Home Secretary's decision. He was released after taking habeas corpus proceedings and now brought a civil action for the torts of assault and false imprisonment against the police and the circuit judge. The Court of Appeal held that the claimant's detention was unlawful but that no action lay against the circuit judge, notwithstanding his mistaken belief that he had power to detain the claimant, because he had acted judicially and in good faith. Nor were the police liable since what they did was done on the judge's instructions and, for that reason, they were entitled to immunity from suit.

Prior to 1991, magistrates, as judges of *inferior* courts, had a more limited form of immunity from suit under the Justices of the Peace Act 1979. They could, for example, be civilly liable for acts done without, or in excess of, jurisdiction even though sitting judicially at the time. The opportunity was taken in the Courts and Legal Services Act 1990 to amend the 1979 Act so as to give magistrates the same immunity from suit as that enjoyed by judges of superior courts. A justice of the peace is now immune from civil action for anything done or omitted to be done while executing his duty as a magistrate *and* acting within his jurisdiction, even though he has acted mistakenly or in ignorance of his powers (Justices of the Peace Act 1997, s. 51). If he goes outside his jurisdiction while purporting to execute his duty as a magistrate he will be liable to be sued, but only if it is proved that he acted *in bad faith,* such as where he knew he had no jurisdiction to do what he did (Justices of the Peace Act 1997, s. 52). Furthermore, a justice of the peace is immune from paying *costs* in any proceedings in respect of any act or omission in the execution (or purported execution) of his duty as a justice (Justices of the Peace Act 1997, s. 53A, as inserted by the Access to Justice Act 1999). The immunity does not extend to any proceedings in which the justice is himself being tried for an offence or in which it is proved that he acted in bad faith (ibid.).

It should be noted that other participants in the legal process may have immunity from suit in respect of things said or done by them as participants. This immunity extends to the parties to a case, witnesses, advocates and jurors. Thus, a witness or advocate cannot be sued in slander for anything in his remarks that may be defamatory. In *Munster* v *Lamb* (1883) 11 QBD 588, CA, for example, a solicitor was held not liable in slander for things said in court about a third party while representing a person on a criminal charge.

Immunity from suit does not, however, give the participants complete freedom to say and do as they please. A witness who tells lies may fall foul of the crime of perjury and an advocate whose conduct falls below professionally accepted standards may be disciplined by his professional body. Moreover, every participant in court proceedings, with the exception of the judge, is subject to the law of contempt of court. Acting under the apparent protection of immunity from suit, Ronald Smith, while appearing before a magistrates' court in August 1981 for non-payment of rates, suddenly announced the name of the alleged murderer of his daughter, Helen Smith, who died in Saudi Arabia in 1979 after or during an illegal drinking party. This outburst was not punished. It could be argued that such a statement, being irrelevant to the proceedings in hand, may not have attracted immunity from suit and, in any case, was probably a contempt of the magistrates' court under s. 12(1)(b) of the Contempt of Court Act 1981 (para 5.4.5). When, in November 1982, Mr Smith interrupted the inquest into the death of his daughter to repeat the allegation, he was fined £50 for contempt of court by the coroner in the exercise of his inherent jurisdiction to punish contempts committed in the face of a coroner's court (*R* v *West Yorkshire Coroner (ex parte Smith) (No. 2)* [1985] 1 All ER 100, DC).

1.9   ACCESS TO JUSTICE

1.9.1   Introduction: Access to Justice Act 1999

It is axiomatic that making available the elaborate structure of courts outlined in the preceding paragraphs is useless in itself unless those courts are accessible, regardless of financial status, to those with meritorious cases. Litigation is expensive. Its cost can be prohibitive even to a commercial company or to a rich individual.

To many people, litigation, or even the obtaining of legal advice, is impossible unless the cost is subsidised in some way. The state has for some considerable time accepted responsibility in this area, although the financial limits imposed on eligibility for assistance have never been over-generous.

There is always a danger that justice may be denied to those who fall outside the financial eligibility limits and who, contrary to the presumption, cannot afford to proceed out of their own pockets. There is also the problem of tribunals, before the vast majority of which state financial assistance is simply not available at all. Many view this omission as an ironic denial of justice given that Parliament created many of these tribunals for the protection and assistance of ordinary citizens who have then been denied the public funding with which to assert their rights adequately (see further, Chapter 3).

A scheme for the provision of legal aid and advice to those who could not otherwise afford to employ a lawyer to assist with advice, or in the bringing or defending of proceedings, was introduced by the Legal Aid and Advice Act 1949. The Act of 1949 was repealed and replaced by the Legal Aid Act 1974, which, as subsequently amended, governed the scheme until 1 April 1989 when it, in turn, was repealed and replaced by the Legal Aid Act 1988. The avowed purpose of the 1988 Act, as set out in s. 1, was

to establish a framework for the provision . . . of advice, assistance and representation which is publicly funded with a view to helping persons who might otherwise be unable to obtain advice, assistance or representation on account of their means.

It was a feature of the new arrangements that the scheme was regulated to a much greater extent by means of delegated, rather than primary, legislation. The 'framework' supplied by the Act was supplemented by detailed regulations made under the authority of the Act by the Lord Chancellor, who had the very wide power to make such regulations as appeared to him necessary or desirable for giving effect to the Act or for preventing abuses of it.

Among the major changes to the scheme effected by the Legal Aid Act 1988 and regulations made thereunder were:

(a) the transfer of responsibility for the administration of legal aid from the Law Society (where it had rested since 1949) to the Legal Aid Board established by the Act; and

(b) the power given to the Legal Aid Board, acting under the direction of the Lord Chancellor, to provide advice, assistance and representation by means of contracts with, or grants or loans to, other persons or bodies, such as Citizens' Advice Bureaux, law centres and designated firms of solicitors.

The range of legal services available under the scheme expanded considerably since 1949.

At the same time, public expenditure on legal aid and advice spiralled out of control in recent years. The overall net cost rose from £650m (1990) to £1,285m (1994), £1,475m (1996), and £1,604m (1998). Much of the blame for this was placed upon lawyers, whose fees accounted for some 90 per cent of the legal aid bill. It also became evident that more money was being paid out each year to help fewer people.

From 1992, successive governments indicated a determination to bring expenditure within reasonable limits. The Conservative Lord Chancellor, Lord Mackay of Clashfern, attacked the problem of escalating costs in 1993 by making new, more stringent, regulations on financial eligibility, and by imposing standard fees for the remuneration of solicitors performing criminal legal aid work in the magistrates' courts. Further progress was made by his introduction of conditional fee agreements in 1995.

The funding of civil litigation on a contingency basis was suggested in the Green Paper, *Contingency Fees*, (Cm 572, 1989) published in 1989. The US contingency fee model, under which the lawyer claims a percentage of a client's damages if he wins a case but receives no fee if he loses, was rejected in favour of a system which does not give the lawyer a stake in the client's damages but instead allows him, if the case is won, to receive his usual fee together with a success fee.

Following the Green Paper, conditional fee agreements were authorised by s. 58 of the Courts and Legal Services Act 1990, which came into force in July 1993 and provided for such agreements to be allowed in proceedings specified by the Lord Chancellor, who was also given power to prescribe the maximum permitted percentage success fee. Section 58 prohibited the use of conditional fee agreements in criminal proceedings and in most family proceedings.

In 1995, after a lengthy period of consultation with senior judges, the legal profession, consumer bodies and other interested organisations, the maximum percentage success fee was fixed at 100 per cent and three types of proceedings were prescribed in which conditional fee agreements were to be available, namely, personal injury cases, insolvency proceedings, and cases before the European Court of Human Rights.

The Conservative Government's further proposals to deal with the funding crisis in legal aid provision, contained in its White Paper of 1996, *Striking the Balance: the Future of Legal Aid in England and Wales* (Cm 3305, 1996), were quickly overtaken when the Labour Government elected in May 1997 decided to pursue its own, more radical agenda under the guidance of Lord Irvine of Lairg LC. This involved removing most civil cases from the scope of legal aid and the substitution of public funding by private funding in the form of conditional fee agreements.

In the light of research commissioned by the Lord Chancellor's Advisory Committee on Legal Education and Conduct, the results of which were presented in *The Price of Success: Lawyers, Clients and Conditional Fees* (Policy Studies Institute, 1997), the new government published a Consultation Paper in March 1998, *Access to Justice with Conditional Fees*, in which it signified its intention to widen the availability of conditional fee agreements and to limit severely the provision of legal aid, which was to be focused where it was most needed and would do most good. Thus, legal aid in some form would remain available (to those who qualified for it on financial grounds) for social welfare matters, such as employment, housing, debt, and state benefits, and for judicial review and other proceedings against officialdom and bureaucracy.

With legal aid costs increasing year by year ahead of inflation, the government's aim was to modernise the funding of civil litigation so that the civil justice system was accessible not just to the rich or the very poor, but to everyone who needed it. Criminal cases would continue to be excluded from the conditional fee scheme, as would family cases, but it was proposed to allow conditional fee agreements to be used in most other civil cases. The successful claimant's success fee and insurance premium under an extended conditional fee system would be recoverable as disbursements from the loser so that the winner's damages were left intact. The scope of conditional fee agreements was extended to all civil cases, except family cases, in July 1998.

A limited fund was envisaged from which to provide financial support in cases involving very high costs that occurred during the transitional period in which funding shifted from legal aid to conditional fee agreements. The investigative costs of establishing the merits of a claim in some cases are enormous; on present financial structures, few lawyers' firms would be able to carry the risk of losing such cases. The transitional fund would also be used to assist with cases excluded from legal aid but which have a significant, wider public interest. Cases involving novel points of law, the resolution of which is likely to have a practical impact as opposed to satisfying academic curiosity, would be included.

Legal aid would be removed from cases which are weak and unlikely to succeed. This would be achieved by making the merits test more stringent so that only cases with a strong prospect of success will be supported with taxpayers' money. Further, it was intended that by some undetermined future date all legal aid work, both civil and criminal, would be done only by providers of legal services who have a contract with the Legal Aid Board (or its successor), which would be able to agree the price to be paid for the majority of cases.

The government also indicated its intention to create a Community Legal Service, varying from area to area according to local needs, to provide a coherent scheme based upon existing information and advice sources. The aim of the Community Legal Service would be to create effective procedures for the enforcement of those legal rights, such as housing, welfare, consumer and employment rights, that substantially impinge upon the lives of the socially excluded and economically disadvantaged.

The government expressed its keenness to investigate other alternative funding mechanisms for paying lawyers' bills. It wished to encourage the extended use of legal-expenses insurance and of membership litigation schemes operated by legal-expenses insurers, trade unions and motoring organisations.

The culmination of all this activity was the Access to Justice Act 1999, which, when fully implemented, will result in the most significant changes in the funding of court proceedings since the legal aid and advice scheme was introduced in 1949. That scheme, outlined in earlier editions of this book, is being replaced by a Community Legal Service and a Criminal Defence Service authorised by the 1999 Act.

On 1 April 2000, the Legal Services Commission (created by the Access to Justice Act 1999, s. 1), the Community Legal Service (ibid., s. 4), and the Funding Code (ibid., s. 5) were established, and the scope of conditional fee agreements (ibid., s. 27) was extended.

The Legal Services Commission replaces the Legal Aid Board and will develop and maintain the Community Legal Service and the Criminal Defence Service (ibid., s. 12: expected to be established in October 2000). The Commission will allocate funds to priority areas through contracts, and will work in partnership with funders of legal services, including local authorities.

The Commission has set priorities at both national and local levels to ensure that resources are spent on the areas of greatest need (ibid., s. 6). The Commission has also introduced contracting for legal services (ibid.). Contracts are placed with 'quality-assured' providers only. These include firms of solicitors, law centres, advice bureaux, and other non-profit-making agencies. Community Legal Service Partnerships have been formed between local authorities, charities, and advice providers.

The previous civil and family legal aid budget was replaced by the Community Legal Service Fund, the size of which is fixed by the Lord Chancellor. The Fund is to be administered by the Commission in a way which obtains the best possible value-for-money for taxpayers. All applications for funding must meet the tests set out in the Funding Code (approved by Parliament), which replaces the former civil/legal aid merits test.

The Code sets less stringent tests for higher priority cases and more stringent tests for lower priority cases, such as money claims. It will thus be harder to get funding for lower priority cases (and impossible if the case is unmeritorious) than under the previous legal aid scheme. Strict cost-benefit tests must be satisfied to ensure that funding is justified, and the Code also allows the Commission to refuse funding where there are alternative ways of resolving a dispute or funding litigation.

The Commission is not allowed to fund certain services as part of the Community Legal Service (Access to Justice Act 1999, s. 6(6) and sch. 2). Those excluded services are, *inter alia*:

(A)   services consisting of the provision of help (beyond the provision of general information about the law and the legal system and the availability of legal services) in relation to—

    (i)   allegations of negligently caused injury, death or damage to property, apart from allegations relating to clinical negligence;

    (ii)   conveyancing;

    (iii)   boundary disputes;

    (iv)   the making of wills;

    (v)   trust law;

    (vi)   defamation or malicious falsehood;

    (vii)   company or partnership law; or

    (viii) other matters arising out of the carrying on of a business.

(B)   Advocacy in any proceedings *except*—

    (i)   proceedings in—

      (a)   the House of Lords in its judicial capacity;

(b) the Judicial Committee of the Privy Council in the exercise of its jurisdiction under the Government of Wales Act 1998, the Scotland Act 1998, or the Northern Ireland Act 1998;

(c) the Court of Appeal;

(d) the High Court;

(e) any county court;

(f) the Employment Appeal Tribunal; or

(g) any mental health review tribunal;

(ii) proceedings in the Crown Court—

(a) for the variation or discharge of an order under s. 5 of the Protection from Harassment Act 1997;

(b) which relate to an order under ss. 4 or 10 of the Crime and Disorder Act 1998; or

(c) under s. 8 of the Crime and Disorder Act 1998 where the order is made by virtue of s. 8(1)(c);

(iii) proceedings in a magistrates' court—

(a) for or in relation to an order under Part I of the Domestic Proceedings and Magistrates' Courts Act 1978 (financial provision);

(b) under the Children Act 1989;

(c) under s. 30 of the Human Fertilisation and Embryology Act 1990;

(d) under ss. 20 or 27 of the Child Support Act 1991;

(e) under Part IV of the Family Law Act 1996 (family homes and domestic violence);

(f) for the variation or discharge of an order under s. 5 of the Protection from Harassment Act 1997; or

(g) under ss. 1, 2, 8 or 11 of the Crime and Disorder Act 1998.

The Lord Chancellor is empowered to amend the list of excluded services by adding new services to it, or by omitting or varying any services (Access to Justice Act 1999, s. 6(7)). He also has power to direct the Commission to fund any excluded service or, if requested by the Commission, to authorise its funding in an individual case (ibid., s. 6(8)). This power would, for example, enable the Lord Chancellor to direct that non-clinical personal injury cases (which are excluded services) should be funded because there are high investigative or overall costs, or because they involve wider issues of public interest.

Criminal proceedings in the magistrates' courts and Crown Court (which are excluded services) will be funded under the Criminal Defence Service (para 1.9.8, below).

It will be seen that most personal injury cases are outside the scope of the Community Legal Service; they will be funded instead by conditional fee agreements (para 1.9.3, below). Cases of clinical negligence, and other personal injury not caused by negligence (e.g., claims against the police for assault and battery), are within the scope of the Service.

Public funding under the former legal aid scheme was not available for proceedings in defamation (i.e., libel and slander). However, in *Joyce v Sengupta* [1993] 1 All ER 897, CA, it was held that legal aid could be granted in a claim for the analogous, but separate, tort of malicious falsehood even though this involved the circumvention of the rule that legal aid was not available for defamation proceedings. Malicious falsehood is based upon the malicious making of a false statement about the claimant; if the statement constitutes both malicious falsehood and defamation, the claimant can choose which cause of action to pursue. The list of excluded services in sch. 2 to the Access to Justice Act 1999 continues the prohibition on the public funding of defamation proceedings, and, at the same time, extends it to malicious falsehood. The public funding aspect of the decision in *Joyce* v *Sengupta* is thus overruled.

1.9.2 The Community Legal Service

1.9.2.1 Levels of service
The Funding Code (Part 1 — Criteria) provides that the Commission will fund the following levels of service as part of the Community Legal Service:

(a) Legal Help;
(b) Help at Court;
(c) Approved Family Help (either General Family Help or Help with Mediation);
(d) Legal Representation (either Investigative Help or Full Representation);
(e) Support Funding (either Investigative Support or Litigation Support);
(f) Family Mediation;
(g) Other services authorised by the Lord Chancellor from time to time.

'Legal Help' includes advice on how the law applies in particular circumstances.

'Help at Court' covers help and advocacy for a client in relation to a particular hearing without formally acting as a legal representative.

'Approved Family Help' is help in relation to a family dispute, including assistance in resolving the dispute by negotiation or otherwise.

'Legal Representation' covers legal representation for a party to proceedings (including litigation and advocacy services) or for a person who is contemplating taking proceedings.

'Support Funding' authorises the same services as Legal Representation but is limited to partial funding of proceedings which are otherwise being pursued privately under, or with a view to, a conditional fee agreement. 'Investigative Support' is support funding limited to investigation of the strength of a proposed claim with a view to a conditional fee agreement. 'Litigation Support' covers partial funding of high-cost litigation which is proceeding under a conditional fee agreement.

'Family Mediation' covers mediation of a family dispute, including an assessment of whether mediation appears suitable to the dispute.

1.9.2.2 Standard criteria: financial eligibility
An application for funding for any level of service *will* be refused, *inter alia*, if:

(a) it relates to law other than the law of England and Wales, except where this is permitted by or under s. 19 of the Access to Justice Act 1999; or
(b) the client is not financially eligible.

In addition, an application *may* be refused if it appears unreasonable to grant funding in the light of the client's conduct in connection with this or any other application or in connection with any proceedings.

The financial eligibility conditions are contained in the Community Legal Service (Financial) Regulations 2000 (SI 2000, No. 516) made under s. 7 of the Access to Justice Act 1999.

The following services, *inter alia*, are available without reference to the client's financial resources and without payment of any contribution:

(a)   services consisting exclusively of the provision of general information about the law and legal system and the availability of legal services;

(b)   initial legal advice consisting of such amount of Legal Help as is authorised under a contract to be provided without reference to the client's financial resources;

(c)   Legal Representation in certain proceedings under the Children Act 1989;

(d)   Legal Representation in proceedings before a mental health review tribunal under the Mental Health Act 1983, where the client's case or application to the tribunal is, or is to be, the subject of the proceedings.

A client is eligible for:

(a)   Legal Help, Help at Court, and Legal Representation before the Immigration Appeal Tribunal and an adjudicator if his weekly disposable income does not exceed £84, and his disposable capital does not exceed £1,000;

(b)   Family Mediation if his weekly disposable income does not exceed £180 and his disposable capital does not exceed £3,000; a client who is eligible for Family Mediation is also eligible for Help with Mediation in relation to family mediation;

(c)   Legal Representation in respect of family proceedings before a magistrates' court, other than proceedings under the Children Act 1989 or Part IV of the Family Law Act 1996, if his weekly disposable income does not exceed £180, and his disposable capital does not exceed £3,000;

(d)   Legal Representation (other than as provided for in (a) and (c) above), General Family Help, and Support Funding if his disposable income does not exceed £8,067 p.a., but he may be refused such services where:

(i)   his disposable capital exceeds £6,750; and

(ii)   it appears to the assessing authority that the probable cost of the funded services would not exceed the contribution payable by him.

Those in receipt of certain state benefits, like income support and income-based jobseeker's allowance, are automatically eligible since they are deemed to have disposable incomes and disposable capital which do not exceed the limits specified.

No contribution is payable in respect of services provided under (a) and (b), above. In the case of (c), above, a weekly contribution is payable of one-third of the amount by which the client's weekly disposable income exceeds £76. In the case of (d), above, a contribution is payable where his disposable income exceeds £2,723 p.a., or his disposable capital exceeds £3,000. Contributions are payable to the assessing authority, which also has the responsibility for calculating them.

A service supplier must not provide any funded service to the client prior to the assessment of resources unless in accordance with Funding Code procedures, or they are authorised to do so by the Legal Services Commission in a contract. When making an application, the client must provide the assessing authority with the information necessary to enable it to determine whether he satisfies the financial eligibility conditions and to calculate his disposable income and disposable capital.

Disposable income is what is left of the client's weekly income after deducting income tax, national insurance contributions, prescribed allowances in respect of his spouse or partner, children and other dependants, and a reasonable amount in respect of regular maintenance payments for a former partner, a child, or a relative who is not a member of his household.

The client's *disposable capital* ignores the amount or value of the subject matter of the dispute to which the application relates, the first £100,000 of the value of his interest in his house, and (unless the circumstances are exceptional having regard in particular to the quantity or value of the items concerned), his furniture, clothing and tools of his trade. His disposable capital is what is left of his cash, savings, investments, and other valuable items after deducting prescribed allowances in respect of his spouse or partner, children and other dependants.

In calculating the disposable income and disposable capital of the client, the resources of his partner are treated as his resources unless he has a contrary interest in the dispute in respect of which the application is made.

Except where eligibility is being assessed under (d), above, where the client is a child the resources of a parent, guardian or any other person who is responsible for maintaining him, or who usually contributes substantially to his maintenance, are treated as his resources, unless, having regard to all the circumstances, including the age and resources of the child and any conflict of interest, it appears inequitable to do so.

If it appears to the assessing authority that the person concerned, with intent to reduce the amount of his disposable income or disposable capital, has:

(a) directly or indirectly deprived himself of any resources; or

(b) transferred any resources to another person; or

(c) converted any part of his resources into resources which under the Regulations are to be wholly or partly disregarded,

the resources in question are still treated as part of his resources.

The client must inform the assessing authority immediately of any change in his financial circumstances which has occurred since assessment of his resources, and which might affect the terms on which he was assessed as eligible to receive funded services.

1.9.2.3 Specific criteria
Applications for particular levels of service must satisfy both the standard criteria which apply to all levels of service (para 1.9.2.2, above) and certain specific criteria.

1.9.2.3.1 Legal Help.
Help may only be provided if:

(a) there is sufficient benefit to the client to justify work or further work being done, and

(b) it is reasonable for funding to come from the Community Legal Service Fund having regard to any other potential sources of funding.

1.9.2.3.2 Help at Court.
The two specific criteria for Legal Help (above) apply. In addition, Help at Court may only be provided if:

(a)   advocacy is appropriate and will be of real benefit to the client; and

(b)   Legal Representation is not more appropriate to the proceedings given their contested nature or the nature of the hearing.

1.9.2.3.3   Legal Representation and Support Funding.   An application *will* be refused if the case has been, or is likely to be, allocated to the small-claims track (see para 1.6.4, above).

An application *may* be refused if:

(a)   alternative funding is available (e.g., through insurance, but not by means of a conditional fee agreement); or

(b)   there are alternatives to litigation which should be tried first; or

(c)   other levels of service appear more appropriate; or

(d)   it appears unreasonable to fund representation.

In addition, *Full Representation* will be refused if the case is suitable for a conditional fee agreement and the client is likely to be able to avail himself of one. It will also be refused if prospects of success are 'unclear' (not fitting into any other category because further investigation is needed), 'borderline' (not better than 50 per cent) and the case has no significant wider public interest, or 'poor' (clearly less than 50 per cent so that the claim is likely to fail).

If the claim is primarily for damages and has no significant wider public interest, Full Representation will be refused unless:

(a)   prospects of success are 'very good' (80 per cent or more) and likely damages exceed likely costs;

(b)   prospects of success are 'good' (60–80 per cent) and likely damages exceed likely costs by a ratio of 2:1; or

(c)   prospects of success are 'moderate' (50–60 per cent) and likely damages exceed likely costs by a ratio of 4:1.

If the claim is not primarily for damages and has no significant wider public interest, Full Representation will be refused unless the likely benefits from the proceedings justify the likely costs, so that a reasonable private-paying client would be prepared to litigate.

1.9.2.3.4   Approved Family Help, Family Mediation, and Legal Representation in family proceedings.   General Family Help may only be provided where there is sufficient benefit to the client to justify work or further work being done. It may be refused if either mediation or legal help is more appropriate.

Help with Mediation may only be provided if:

(a)   the client is participating, or has reached an agreement or settlement, in family mediation and is in need of the services provided by Help with Mediation; and

(b)   there is sufficient benefit to the client to justify work or further work being done.

It may be refused if Legal Help is more appropriate.

Legal Representation in family proceedings is available only as Full Representation; Investigative Help is not available. Moreover, the specific criterion relating to the small-claims track, and the specific criteria for Full Representation (para 1.9.2.3.3, above) concerning conditional fee agreements and prospects of success, do not apply to applications for Legal Representation in family proceedings.

In private law domestic violence cases in which an injunction, committal order, or other order protecting a person from harm, is sought, Legal Representation will be refused if:

(a) the prospects of obtaining the order are 'poor' (clearly less than 50 per cent so that the application is likely to fail); or

(b) the likely benefits for the client do not justify the likely costs.

In family proceedings concerning financial provision, Legal Representation *will* be refused if:

(a) in accordance with the Funding Code (Part 2 — Procedures), the case must first be referred to a mediator in order to decide whether mediation is suitable; or

(b) if prospects of success are—

(i) 'borderline' (not better than 50 per cent) or 'unclear' (not fitting into any other category because further investigation is needed), unless the case has overwhelming importance for the client or a significant wider public interest; or

(ii) 'poor' (clearly less than 50 per cent so that the application is likely to fail); or

(c) the likely benefits for the client do not justify the likely costs.

It *may* be refused if:

(a) mediation is more appropriate; or

(b) reasonable attempts have not been made to resolve the dispute (by negotiation or otherwise) without recourse to legal proceedings.

1.9.2.3.5 Special cases. The Funding Code (Part 1 — Criteria) lays down additional criteria applicable in cases of emergency and in special cases, such as very expensive cases, judicial review and other claims against public authorities, clinical negligence, housing, mental health, and immigration.

1.9.2.4   The statutory charge

It may happen that the amount of costs (if any) recovered for a successfully funded client, together with his own contribution (if any), is not sufficient to reimburse the Community Legal Service Fund in respect of the sums actually expended by the Legal Services Commission in funding the services for the client. In this event, the Commission has a first charge (known as 'the statutory charge') on any property recovered or preserved by him in any proceedings or in any compromise or settlement of any dispute (Access to Justice Act 1999, s. 10(7)). This means, for example, that any damages awarded in proceedings may be swallowed up by the Community Legal Service Fund before they are ever received by the funded claimant.

The Community Legal Service (Financial) Regulations 2000 (SI 2000, No. 516) lay down detailed rules about the statutory charge. Maintenance payments and (unless the circumstances are exceptional having regard in particular to the quantity or value of the items concerned), the client's furniture, clothing and tools of his trade are exempt from the charge. In certain family proceedings, the first £2,500 of any lump sum, or of the value of any property (e.g., the matrimonial home), recovered by the client is exempt. There are provisions for postponement of the charge, the payment of interest and for substitution of the charged property.

In the case of Legal Help or Help at Court, the statutory charge may sometimes be in favour of the supplier of the service. The supplier, with the authority of the Commission, can waive either all or part of the amount of the statutory charge where its enforcement would cause grave hardship or distress to the client or would be unreasonably difficult because of the nature of the property. The Commission itself can, if it considers it equitable to do so, waive some or all of the amount of the statutory charge in cases of 'wider public interest', which means the potential of proceedings to produce real benefits for individuals other than the client (apart from any general benefits which normally flow from proceedings of the type in question).

1.9.2.5   Costs against a funded client

By virtue of s. 11(1) of the Access to Justice Act 1999, except in prescribed circumstances, costs ordered against a client in relation to proceedings funded for him must not exceed an amount which is reasonable for him to pay having regard to all the circumstances, including:

(a)   the financial resources of all the parties, and
(b)   their conduct in connection with the dispute.

Detailed rules for assessing financial resources are contained in the Community Legal Service (Costs) Regulations 2000 (SI 2000, No. 441).

The limit, imposed by s. 11(1), on costs awardable against a funded client is referred to as 'cost protection' in the Community Legal Service (Cost Protection) Regulations 2000 (SI 2000, No. 824), which prescribe the circumstances in which cost protection does not apply.

1.9.2.6   Costs of a successful non-funded party

Section 11(4) of the Access to Justice Act 1999, and regulations made thereunder in the Community Legal Service (Cost Protection) Regulations 2000, provide for the recovery of costs against the Legal Services Commission in certain circumstances.

A non-funded party appearing in proceedings against a funded party may, at the discretion of the court which finally determines the proceedings, be awarded all or part of his costs from the Community Legal Service Fund (other than any costs that the client is required to pay under a s. 11(1) costs order), provided that:

(a)   the non-funded party wins the case; and
(b)   cost protection applies; and
(c)   as regards costs incurred in a court of first instance, the proceedings were begun by the funded party and the court is satisfied that the non-funded party will suffer severe financial hardship unless the costs order is made (on the meaning of 'severe financial hardship', see *Adams* v *Riley* [1988] 1 All ER 89; *R* v *Greenwich London Borough Council (ex parte Lovelace) (No. 2)* [1992] 1 All ER 679, CA); and
(d)   in any case, the court is satisfied that it is just and equitable in the circumstances that the costs should be paid out of public funds (for what is 'just and equitable' in this context, see *Hanning* v *Maitland (No. 2)* [1970] 1 QB 580, CA).

In determining whether conditions (c) and (d) are satisfied, the court is to have regard to the resources of the non-funded party and of his partner. However, the partner's resources are not taken into account where the partner has a contrary interest in the funded proceedings.

1.9.3 Conditional fee agreements

Section 58(2) of the Courts and Legal Services Act 1990 (as substituted by the Access to Justice Act 1999) defines a conditional fee agreement as:

> an agreement with a person providing advocacy or litigation services which provides for his fees and expenses, or any part of them, to be payable only in specified circumstances.

If such an agreement satisfies all the statutory conditions, it is not unenforceable by reason only of its being a conditional fee agreement (ibid., s. 58(1)).

In essence, a conditional fee agreement is one by which a legal representative supplying advocacy or litigation services agrees with his client that fees and expenses are to be payable on a 'no win, no fee' basis. The legal representative usually agrees that he will be paid nothing if the case is lost, but that he will take a 'success fee' (or percentage 'uplift' on his normal fee) if the case is won. This arrangement has the advantage for the client that he does not have to worry about paying his own legal representative if he loses the case. He may, however, still be liable to pay his successful opponent's costs, although this possibility can be insured against.

Criminal proceedings and family proceedings are excluded from the scope of enforceable conditional fee agreements (ibid., s. 58A, as inserted by the Access to Justice Act 1999). Proceedings under s. 82 of the Environmental Protection Act 1990 for an order that a statutory nuisance be put right are included; however, the agreement in such a case cannot provide for a success fee (ibid., and Conditional Fee Agreements Order 2000 (SI 2000, No. 823)).

All civil proceedings, except family proceedings, are thus within the scope of enforceable conditional fee agreements which may provide for a success fee. The maximum percentage success fee is fixed at 100 per cent of the normal fee (Conditional Fee Agreements Order 2000). In addition, regulations have been made governing conditional fee arrangements generally (Conditional Fee Agreements Regulations 2000 (SI 2000, No. 692)). These specify the minimum information to be contained in agreements, including the details of any success fee, and provide that agreements must be signed by the client and the legal representative, except where the agreement is between a legal representative and an additional legal representative.

Subject to rules of court, the successful party's success fee is recoverable from the losing party (Courts and Legal Services Act 1990, s. 58A, as inserted by the Access to Justice Act 1999), as is the premium paid for litigation costs and/or liability insurance (Access to Justice Act 1999, s. 29).

The aim of the conditional fee legislation is to widen access to justice, particularly for those who fall outside the financial eligibility limits for public funding and who are deterred from going to court by the costs of litigation. Under a conditional fee agreement, the costs risk is transferred from the client (or the taxpayer) to the legal representative, who is given an incentive to take on cases by means of the success fee which is intended to be proportionate to the risk of failure. In practice, it seems that the average percentage success fee charged by legal representatives is 43 per cent. In addition, it appears that they voluntarily limit the success fee to no more than 25 per cent of any damages recovered by the client.

1.9.4   Duty solicitor schemes in criminal cases before the magistrates' courts

1.9.4.1   Extent
These schemes, which hitherto had existed solely on a voluntary basis, were put on a statutory footing in 1982, following a recommendation of the *Royal Commission on Legal Services* (Cmnd 7648, 1979). They became fully operational during 1984 and 1985 in various parts of England and Wales. The schemes are now operated under the control of the Legal Services Commission. The object of the schemes is to make assistance by way of representation (ABWOR) and advice and assistance available in connection with certain criminal proceedings before magistrates' courts (including youth courts). The services are provided by solicitors designated by the Legal Services Commission to attend at those courts. It is not compulsory for defendants to use the schemes. They may instead instruct their own solicitors privately.

ABWOR may be given under the schemes to a client who has not previously received, and is not receiving, representation under full criminal legal aid or under ABWOR in connection with the same proceedings, for the purpose of:

(a)   making an application for bail;

(b)   an appearance in court where the client is in custody and wishes the case to be concluded at that appearance, unless the solicitor advising him considers that the case should be adjourned in the interests of justice or of the client;

(c)   an appearance in court as a result of a failure to obey an order of the court, where such failure may lead to the client being at risk of imprisonment;

(d)   safeguarding the interests of a client who is not in custody but who in the opinion of the solicitor requires ABWOR;

(e)   an appearance in court as a result of a failure to pay a fine or other sum which he was ordered on conviction to pay, and such failure may lead to the client being at risk of imprisonment.

In situations (a) to (d) above, ABWOR is excluded from the duty solicitor schemes in the case of committal proceedings, proceedings in which the client pleads not guilty, and, unless the solicitor considers the circumstances to be exceptional, proceedings in connection with a non-imprisonable offence. However, advice and assistance, and full criminal legal aid, remain available for these proceedings.

Solicitors who are authorised to give ABWOR under the schemes may also be authorised to give *advice and assistance* in the form of:

(a)   advice to a defendant who is in custody;

(b)   advice to a defendant who is before the court as a result of a failure to pay a fine or other sum which he was ordered on conviction to pay, or to obey an order of the court, where such failure may lead to his being at risk of imprisonment;

(c)   advice, where in the opinion of the solicitor the defendant requires it, to a defendant who is not in custody;

(d)   assistance to a defendant to make an application for representation in respect of any subsequent appearance before the court.

Neither ABWOR nor advice and assistance can be provided under the duty solicitor schemes if a legal aid order is in force, or if advice and assistance is otherwise being given, in respect of the proceedings (Legal Aid Act 1988, s. 8(5)).

1.9.4.2 Eligibility
ABWOR and advice and assistance under the statutory schemes are provided to the defendant free of charge. There is no merits test, no means test, and no contributions are payable. Duty solicitors are remunerated out of the legal aid fund.

1.9.5 Advice and assistance for persons in police stations

1.9.5.1 Extent
From 1 January 1986, duty solicitor schemes were extended to cover persons who had been arrested and held in custody in police stations *and* persons who were voluntarily at police stations helping the police with their enquiries. These schemes, which are provided on a 24-hour a day basis and operate in some 94 per cent of police stations in England and Wales, are limited to the giving of *advice and assistance*. There is a prospective cost limit of £90. The schemes are coordinated by the use of a centrally-manned telephone answering system operational throughout England and Wales. This is intended to enable duty solicitors to be contacted promptly at any time of the day or night.

The schemes currently authorise the giving of advice and assistance to any person who:

(a) is arrested and held in custody at a police station or other premises; or

(b) is being interviewed in connection with a serious service offence under the Army Act 1955, the Air Force Act 1955 or the Naval Discipline Act 1957; or

(c) is a volunteer; i.e., someone who, for the purpose of assisting with an investigation, attends voluntarily at a police station or at any other place where a constable is present, or accompanies a constable to a police station or any such other place without having been arrested.

Suspects who require advice and assistance are not compelled to use the statutory schemes. They may instead consult their own solicitors privately, although there are some important limitations on the exercise of this right (see Police and Criminal Evidence Act 1984, s. 58).

In 1989, the published results of research carried out in 10 police stations revealed serious defects in the working of the schemes which, in some places, were on the verge of collapse (A. Sanders et al, *Advice and Assistance at Police Stations and the 24 Hour Duty Solicitor Scheme*, Lord Chancellor's Department, 1989). There was found to be a low take-up rate with less than 20 per cent of suspects receiving advice and assistance. Response rates were slow; some solicitors were reluctant to respond at all, especially at night. Some who did attend at the police station left after giving advice but before interrogation of the suspect began. A solicitor was present in only 14 per cent of all interrogations. An inescapable conclusion from this research appeared to be that some duty solicitors were taking payments under false pretences (see A. Sanders and L. Bridges, (1990) 140 New LJ 85, 86). As for the police, it was found that they were less than enthusiastic about informing suspects fully of their rights.

Research conducted later for the Royal Commission on Criminal Justice discovered other deficiencies (J. Baldwin, *The Conduct of Police Investigations*, HMSO 1992, pp. 25–52; see also J. Baldwin, (1992) 142 New LJ 1762). For the purposes of this research 400 videotaped and 200 audiotaped police station interviews were examined. In 30.3 per cent of the interviews legal representatives were present; these were more often articled clerks or other unqualified persons than solicitors. For the most part they played no active role in the proceedings, being either completely silent or confining themselves to passive note-taking. A number of instances were identified where representatives failed to protect suspects from unfair police practices. On some occasions when there *was* an intervention on behalf of the suspect the police reacted to it in a hostile fashion.

In the *Report of the Royal Commission on Criminal Justice* (Cm 2263, 1993) it was recommended that police training should include instruction in the role which solicitors are expected to play in the criminal justice system. The Law Society was urged to ensure that solicitors are more aware of their responsibilities when advising clients at police stations, and it was proposed that the Legal Aid Board (since replaced by the Legal Services Commission) should fund occasional empirical research as a means of checking on the quality of performance of legal representatives at police stations.

1.9.5.2   Eligibility
Advice and assistance is provided to the suspect free of charge. There is no merits test, no means test, and no contributions are payable. Duty solicitors are remunerated out of the legal aid fund. They are entitled to payment for stand-by duty not resulting in advice or assistance, and there are enhanced rates of payment for work done outside normal office hours.

1.9.6   Legal aid in criminal cases

1.9.6.1   Method of application
Because it is desirable that decisions about legal aid should be made more speedily in *criminal,* as opposed to *civil,* proceedings, applications are normally made to the court itself rather than to the Legal Services Commission. This paragraph concentrates on the provision of criminal legal aid in the *trial* courts, namely, the magistrates' courts and the Crown Court.

It should be noted that legal aid for proceedings in the Crown Court may be granted either by the Crown Court itself or by the magistrates' court which committed the defendant for trial or sentence (Legal Aid Act 1988, s. 20(2) and (4)). Moreover, magistrates inquiring into an offence as examining justices can make a single legal aid order which covers both the committal proceedings *and* any subsequent trial at the Crown Court (Legal Aid Act 1988, s. 20(5) and regulations).

An application for a legal aid order is made either to the justices' clerk (or chief clerk in the case of the Crown Court) on a prescribed form, or orally to the court, which may, if it wishes, refer it to the clerk for determination. It is usual for the clerk of the court to be entrusted with making decisions about legal aid. The clerk or the court may grant or refuse the first application. Where the application is refused, the applicant must be notified on a prescribed form that refusal is on one or both of the following grounds:

(a)   that it does not appear to the court or the clerk desirable to make an order in the interests of justice (see para 1.9.7.3.1 below); or
(b)   that it appears to the court or the clerk that the applicant's disposable income and disposable capital make him ineligible for legal aid (see para 1.9.7.3.2 below).

If legal aid is refused, whether by the clerk or by the court itself, the applicant has a right to *renew* his application either orally to the court or to the clerk. If the application is renewed to the clerk, the clerk cannot refuse it; he must either grant it or refer it to the court (or to a single justice of the peace in the case of a magistrates' court). If the application is renewed to the court, the court can grant or refuse it or refer it to the clerk.

A person charged with an indictable offence who is refused legal aid by the magistrates' court may *renew* his application to the *Crown Court,* where the refusal rate is very small. Ninety eight per cent of all applications to the Crown Court for legal aid are successful, and 97 per cent of defendants tried there are legally aided.

1.9.6.2 Extent

Criminal legal aid normally extends to preparation of the case *and* representation by a solicitor and counsel. However, it does not cover representation by counsel in bail proceedings in a magistrates' court or in other proceedings before a magistrates' court unless the offence charged is an indictable one *and* the unusual gravity or difficulty of the case makes representation by both solicitor and counsel desirable (Legal Aid Act 1988, s. 2(7) and regulations). An application for representation by counsel in these latter circumstances is made to the justices' clerk, who may grant or refuse it. If it is refused, the applicant may *renew* his application to the court.

A legal aid order can provide for the services of *two* counsel at a trial in the Crown Court:

(a)   on a charge of murder; or
(b)   where the case is one of exceptional difficulty, gravity or complexity and the interests of justice require that the defendant should have the services of two counsel.

1.9.6.3   Eligibility

1.9.6.3.1   Merits test.   The criminal trial courts do not have an unfettered discretion to grant legal aid. Two points are of particular importance here. First, s. 21 of the Legal Aid Act 1988 says that legal aid *must* be granted in the following cases if the defendant is financially eligible for it:

(a)   where a person is committed for trial on a charge of murder;
(b)   where the prosecution appeals, or applies for leave to appeal, to the House of Lords;
(c)   on an application for bail by a person charged with an offence before a magistrates' court who has, without legal representation, been remanded in custody and who appears at a remand hearing at which he may be again remanded or committed in custody, and is not, but wishes to be, legally represented;
(d)   for sentencing proceedings where a person is to be sentenced or otherwise dealt with for an offence by a magistrates' court or the Crown Court and is to be kept in custody to enable enquiries or a report to be made to assist the court.

Secondly, s. 21 of the Act also stipulates that legal aid *may* be granted, provided that the defendant is financially eligible for it, if it is 'desirable to do so in the interests of justice'. Where there is any doubt whether legal aid should be granted the doubt *shall* be resolved in the accused's favour (Legal Aid Act 1988, s. 21(7)). It was accepted by successive Lord Chancellors that the question whether or not it was 'desirable in the interests of justice' to grant legal aid was to be determined in accordance with some non-statutory criteria suggested in the *Report of the Departmental Committee on Legal Aid in Criminal Proceedings* (Cmnd 2934, 1966). These so-called 'Widgery criteria' (named after the chairman of the Committee) have now been put down in statutory form in s. 22 of the Legal Aid Act 1988. They apply to trials in the magistrates' courts *and* the Crown Court *and* to appeals to the Crown Court against conviction. They are as follows:

(a) That the offence charged is a grave one in the sense that, if it is proved, the accused is likely to lose his liberty or livelihood or suffer serious damage to his reputation.

(b) That the determination of the case may involve consideration of a substantial question of law.

(c) That the accused may be unable to understand the proceedings or to state his own case because of his inadequate knowledge of English, mental illness or other mental or physical disability.

(d) That the nature of the defence involves the tracing and interviewing of witnesses or expert cross-examination of a witness for the prosecution.

(e) That legal representation of the accused is in the interests of someone other than the accused (as, for example, in the case of sexual offences against young children when it is undesirable that the accused should cross-examine the witness in person).

This list of criteria is not exhaustive since the Act says that the factors to be taken into account merely 'include' those mentioned (s. 22(2)) and the Lord Chancellor is empowered to vary the factors listed by amending factors in the list or by adding new ones to it (s. 22(3)).

1.9.6.3.2   Means test and contributions.   A court must not make a legal aid order unless it appears that the applicant's disposable income and disposable capital are such that he is eligible for legal aid (Legal Aid Act 1988, s. 21(5)). To that end, the applicant is normally required to supply a written statement of his means before legal aid can be granted (ibid., s. 21(6)).

If the accused person to whom legal aid has been granted appears able to afford to pay part of the costs himself the court will make a legal aid contribution order against him (ibid., s. 23(1)). The contribution may be payable in one sum out of savings or by instalments out of income (ibid., s. 23(5) and regulations). No contribution will be ordered where the accused's *disposable income* is £50 p.w. or less *and* his *capital* is £3,000 or less. If his disposable income and/or his capital are beyond these free limits, he will be ordered to pay a contribution from income and/or capital calculated according to a formula laid down by regulations made under the authority of the legislation. A legal aid contribution order can be varied (upwards or downwards) if the accused's means change (ibid., s. 24(5) and regulations).

If it turns out that the contribution paid exceeds the costs actually incurred, the balance will be refunded to the contributor (ibid., s. 23(7)). If the accused is acquitted, or is successful on appeal, or if the proceedings against him are withdrawn or discontinued, the court has power (but is not obliged) to remit or order the repayment of any contribution due from or paid by him (ibid., s. 24(5) and regulations).

These contribution rules laid down by legislation in 1982 first came into effect in 1984. The courts had limited powers before 1984 to order contributions but did so comparatively seldom. The new rules, under which significantly more contribution orders are made, caused controversy because they were blatantly designed to save public funds at the expense of those accused of crime and overruled the view of the Royal Commission on Legal Services, which in 1979 had recommended the total abolition of contributions for magistrates' courts proceedings.

1.9.7 Legal aid in contempt proceedings

By s. 29 of the Legal Aid Act 1988, legal aid in the form of representation may be made available to a person in proceedings against him for contempt committed in the face of the court or in the immediate vicinity of the court (see further, para 5.4.6). This provision applies to the magistrates' courts, the county courts and to the superior courts as defined (s. 29(1) and (3)). Representation is ordered by the appropriate court itself and not by the Legal Services Commission (s. 29(2)).

No *means* test is specified, but there is a *merits* test. The court may grant legal aid only 'if it appears to the court to be desirable to do so in the interests of justice' (ibid.).

The Act does not confer any *right* to legal aid; the court has a *discretion* to grant it or not. Nevertheless, s. 29 is a potentially useful measure for helping to prevent the injustice that might otherwise occur in the case of an unrepresented defendant in what are usually very hasty proceedings.

1.9.8 The Criminal Defence Service

Section 12 of the Access to Justice Act 1999 requires the Legal Services Commission to 'establish, maintain and develop' a Criminal Defence Service 'for the purpose of securing that individuals involved in criminal investigations or criminal proceedings have access to such advice, assistance and representation as the interests of justice require'. When established (expected to be in October 2000), the matters dealt with in paras 1.9.4–1.9.7 (duty solicitor schemes and public funding of criminal and contempt proceedings) will be included within the scope of the Criminal Defence Service.

'Criminal proceedings' include criminal trials, appeals and sentencing hearings, extradition hearings, binding over proceedings, appeals on behalf of a convicted person who has died, proceedings for contempt committed in the face of any court, and such other proceedings before any court or other body as may be prescribed by the Lord Chancellor (Access to Justice Act 1999, s. 12). It is understood that this power will be used to prescribe Parole Board reviews of discretionary life sentences.

The Legal Services Commission is empowered to secure advice, assistance and representation services through contracts with legal representatives in private practice. Alternatively, these services will be available through salaried defenders employed directly by the Commission or by non-profit-making organisations. All contractors will have to meet quality-assurance standards.

Salaried defenders employed by the Commission, or by any bodies established by the Commission, will be subject to a code of conduct prepared by the Commission. The code will include duties: to avoid discrimination, to protect the interests of the individuals for whom services are provided, to the court, to avoid conflicts of interest, of confidentiality, and to act in accordance with professional rules.

The Commission is required to provide such *advice and assistance* as it considers appropriate for individuals who are arrested and held in custody at a police station or other premises, and for individuals involved in criminal investigations in other circumstances to be prescribed by the Lord Chancellor in regulations (ibid., s. 13). The new arrangements are expected to cover advice and assistance provided by duty solicitors at a magistrates' court, at a solicitor's office, to a 'volunteer' at a police station, or to someone being interviewed about a 'serious service offence'.

The courts will continue to be responsible for granting *representation* to defendants according to the interests of justice (ibid., s. 14 and sch. 3). The criteria for determining the 'interests of justice' of an individual are set out in sch. 3 and are very similar to the current criteria. They are:

(a)   whether the individual would be likely to lose his liberty or livelihood or suffer serious damage to his reputation;

(b)   whether the proceedings may involve consideration of a substantial question of law;

(c)   whether the individual may be unable to understand the proceedings or to state his own case;

(d)   whether the proceedings may involve the tracing, interviewing or expert cross-examination of witnesses on behalf of the individual; and

(e)   whether it is in the interests of another person that the individual be represented.

The Lord Chancellor is empowered to amend this list by adding new factors or by varying any factor.

- In most cases, as at present, representation will be granted by a magistrates' court and will also cover proceedings in the Crown Court if the case ends up there (ibid., sch. 3).

The courts will no longer have to conduct a means test before deciding whether to grant representation. The system of means-testing every defendant will be abolished, although in the more expensive cases defendants will continue to pay towards the cost of their defence when they can afford to do so. A Crown Court judge (but not a magistrates' court) will have power to order a defendant to pay some or all of the cost of his defence, which can include the cost of any earlier representation in a magistrates' court (ibid., s. 17). The Commission will be able to investigate the defendant's means in order to assist the judge. Regulations may provide for the defendant's assets to be frozen during the investigation (ibid.).

A person granted representation will usually be able to select any representative who is willing to act for him (ibid., s. 15). Regulations may provide for this freedom of choice to be limited in cases of prescribed descriptions (ibid.) so that the defendant will instead have a representative assigned to him. It is envisaged that this will cover the case of an otherwise unrepresented defendant charged with a serious sexual offence against a child given that such a defendant is forbidden to cross-examine child witnesses directly.

The funding of the Criminal Defence Service is the responsibility of the Lord Chancellor, who is required to pay to the Legal Services Commission the cost of advice, assistance and representation funded by the Commission (ibid., s. 18). Thus, the Criminal Defence Service (like the criminal legal aid scheme before it, but unlike the Community Legal Service Fund) will be demand-led.

2

Courts of Special Jurisdiction

2.1 COURT OF JUSTICE OF THE EUROPEAN COMMUNITIES (THE EUROPEAN COURT)

2.1.1 Introduction

By the European Communities Act 1972, the United Kingdom became a member of the European Communities on 1 January 1973. The Communities are:

(a) The European Coal and Steel Community established in 1951 by the Treaty of Paris (the ECSC Treaty).

(b) The European Economic Community established in 1957 by the Treaty of Rome (the EEC Treaty).

(c) The European Atomic Energy Community established in 1957 by the second Treaty of Rome (the Euratom Treaty).

As from November 1993, the European Economic Community and the EEC Treaty were renamed, respectively, the 'European Community' and the 'EC Treaty' by the Treaty on European Union (TEU, signed at Maastricht in 1992). At the same time the TEU created the 'European Union', a completely new body based upon the European Communities. The TEU was approved by the United Kingdom Parliament in the European Communities (Amendment) Act 1993. With effect from May 1999, the TEU and the Treaties establishing the Communities were amended by the Treaty of Amsterdam (signed at Amsterdam in 1997). A number of articles of the EC Treaty were repealed, and the rest were renumbered. The Treaty of Amsterdam was approved by the United Kingdom Parliament in the European Communities (Amendment) Act 1998.

The other member states of the European Union are (in 2000) France, the Federal Republic of Germany, Italy, Belgium, Holland, Luxembourg, Denmark, the Republic of Ireland, Greece, Spain, Portugal, Austria, Finland and Sweden.

Since the accession of the United Kingdom, the Court of Justice of the European Communities has stood above the House of Lords as the ultimate court. However, this is so only in disputes with a European flavour. (For the content of European Community law, see para 8.9.) In internal, domestic cases the House of Lords remains the final appeal court in the United Kingdom. The Court of Justice of the European Communities was first established in 1954 as the Court of Justice of the European Coal and Steel Community. It was renamed in 1958. The court, which sits in Luxembourg, is often referred to simply as 'the European Court', but it is not to be confused with the European Court of Human Rights, which sits in Strasbourg, nor with the International Court of Justice, which sits at The Hague.

2.1.2   Composition

The European Court consists of 15 judges chosen from among persons who are eligible for appointment to the highest judicial posts in their own countries or who are jurists of recognised competence (EC Treaty, art. 165 (now art. 221), as amended). They are appointed by the governments of the member states. Their appointment is for six years initially, although reappointment is permissible. The court has a president, who is appointed from among themselves by the judges. The presidency is held for three years (ibid., art. 167 (now art. 223)).

The court is assisted in its work by nine advocates-general, who must have the same qualifications for appointment as the judges. The advocate-general assigned to a particular case delivers an opinion in which he indicates the issues raised and the reasoned conclusions he has reached. The opinion is not binding on the court, although it will, of course, be taken into account when the court is considering its decision.

It is the practice of the European Court to deliver only one judgment so that it is never known whether there were any dissentients among the judges. The judgment often consists of a series of terse propositions from which it is difficult to extract any *ratio decidendi*. (For the meaning of *ratio decidendi* and the role of judicial precedent in the European Court, see paras 9.2 and 9.3.2.1.) For this reason, the usually fuller opinion of the advocate-general can be of considerable assistance in understanding what the court has decided.

For the hearing of most cases, the court sits in plenary session, i.e., the case is heard by all 15 judges sitting together.

2.1.3   Jurisdiction

2.1.3.1   Introduction

The vast majority of cases heard by the European Court are brought by member states or by the institutions of the European Union or are referred to it by national courts. It has only limited power to deal with cases brought by individual citizens.

In February 1986, the Single European Act was signed and made important amendments to the Treaties. That Act was ratified by the United Kingdom Parliament in the European Communities (Amendment) Act 1986. The Single European Act added a new art. 168A (now art. 225) to the EC Treaty. Article 168A (art. 225) provided for a new *Court of First Instance of the European Communities* to be attached to the European Court with jurisdiction to decide at first instance certain classes of case brought by natural or legal persons. There is a right of appeal to the European Court from a decision of the Court of First Instance, but only on points of law. If an appeal is successful, the European Court must quash the decision and either give final judgment itself or refer the case back to the Court of First Instance for final judgment.

The members of the Court of First Instance are appointed by the governments of the member states from persons whose independence is beyond doubt and who possess the ability required for appointment to judicial office. By paragraph 1 of art. 168A (art. 225) (as amended by TEU), references for a preliminary ruling under art. 177 (now art. 234) (para 2.1.3.3 below) are expressly excluded from the jurisdiction of the Court of First Instance. These matters continue to be dealt with by the European Court itself, while the Court of First Instance relieves pressure on the European Court by dealing with, *inter alia,* claims by the employees of Community institutions ('staff cases'), claims by companies fined under Community monopolies and competition law, coal and steel cases arising under the ECSC

Treaty, and other direct actions concerning legal entities and persons. It is quite possible that, in the future, further areas of jurisdiction will be transferred by the Council from the European Court to the Court of First Instance.

2.1.3.2   Breach of obligation under the treaties

The European Court has jurisdiction to hear complaints that a member state has not fulfilled its obligations under the treaties, to decide whether the Council of Ministers and the Commission of the European Communities have acted legally, and to decide disputes between member states about the subject-matter of the treaties (EC Treaty, arts. 169–76 (now arts. 226–233), 182 (now art. 239)). In *Re Tachographs: EC Commission v UK* [1979] 2 CMLR 45, CJEC, a complaint against the United Kingdom was upheld for failing to implement a regulation which provided for the compulsory installation of tachographs in lorries used to carry dangerous goods. In *EC Commission v UK, Case No. 124/81* [1983] 2 CMLR 1, CJEC, the United Kingdom was found to have failed to fulfil its obligations under art. 30 (now art. 28) of the EC Treaty. Article 30 (art. 28) prohibits, as between member states, 'quantitative restrictions on imports and all measures having equivalent effect'. The United Kingdom was held to be in violation of this prohibition by making imports of UHT (ultra-heat treated) milk and cream subject to a system of prior individual import licences and a second heat treatment and repacking. These measures were held to be equivalent in effect to quantitative restrictions on imports. In *United Kingdom v Council of the European Union* [1996] 1 All ER (EC) 877, CJEC, the United Kingdom complained that the Council had acted unlawfully in adopting Council Directive 93/104 on the 48-hour working week. The complaint was unsuccessful and the United Kingdom failed in its attempt to have the Directive annulled by the European Court.

The European Court can impose a financial penalty on a member state which has not complied with the judgment of the Court following a finding that the member state is in breach of its Treaty obligations (EC Treaty, art. 171 (now art. 228), as amended by TEU).

2.1.3.3   References under article 177 (now art. 234) of the EC Treaty

The European Court has jurisdiction to give preliminary rulings on references made to it by United Kingdom courts under art. 177 (234) of the EC Treaty. It has similar jurisdiction under art. 41 of the ECSC Treaty and art. 150 of the Euratom Treaty. Article 177 (234) of the EC Treaty (as amended by TEU) is here set out in full:

The Court of Justice shall have jurisdiction to give preliminary rulings concerning:

(a)   the interpretation of this treaty;

(b)   the validity and interpretation of acts of the institutions of the Community and of the European Central Bank;

(c)   the interpretation of the statutes of bodies established by an act of the Council, where those statutes so provide.

Where such a question is raised before any court or tribunal of a member state, that court or tribunal may, if it considers that a decision on the question is necessary to enable it to give judgment, request the Court of Justice to give a ruling thereon.

Where any such question is raised in a case pending before a court or tribunal of a member state, against whose decisions there is no judicial remedy under national law, that court or tribunal shall bring the matter before the Court of Justice.

2.1.3.3.1   The meaning of article 177 (now art. 234).   Article 177 (234) is designed to
secure the uniform judicial interpretation of European Community law (*Sociale Verzekerin-
gsbank* v *H.J. Van der Vecht* [1968] CMLR 151, 161, CJEC; *H. P. Bulmer Ltd* v *J. Bollinger
SA* [1974] Ch 401, CA, *per* Lord Denning MR at p. 425). A reference for a preliminary
ruling may be made by a national court without any application from the parties and,
although a party may seek to persuade the court to make a reference, the decision belongs
to the national court. If a national court makes a reference under art. 177 (234), the national
proceedings will be stayed pending receipt of the preliminary ruling from the European
Court. In the meantime, it is the responsibility of the national court to protect the parties'
Community law rights by granting interim relief if that is required in the circumstances
(*Amministrazione delle Finanze dello Stato* v *Simmenthal SpA* [1978] 3 CMLR 263, CJEC).
The effectiveness of the reference system established by art. 177 (234) would be undermined
if the national court were not able to award interim relief until after receipt of the European
Court's preliminary ruling (*Factortame Ltd* v *Secretary of State for Transport (No. 2)* [1991]
1 All ER 70, CJEC).

Where a rule of national law is the sole impediment to the granting of interim relief in
such cases, Community law insists that it is the obligation of the national court to set aside
that rule of national law (ibid.). In the case of an English court this may involve defying
the hitherto accepted common law by subjecting the Crown to an interlocutory injunction
and/or by disapplying a statute of the United Kingdom Parliament (*Factortame Ltd* v
Secretary of State for Transport (No. 2), above, where the House of Lords, in response to a
preliminary ruling from the European Court, granted an interlocutory injunction against the
Secretary of State for Transport which, in effect, disapplied certain statutory regulations,
made under the Merchant Shipping Act 1988, pending final judgment by the European Court
on the merits of the case; see further, para 8.7).

It will be observed that under the second paragraph of art. 177 (234) there is a discretion
whether or not to refer the question to the European Court (the 'court or tribunal *may . . .*').
Under the third paragraph, however, there is a positive duty to refer the question (the 'court
or tribunal *shall . . .*'). In relation to the English legal system, the third paragraph of art.
177 (234) certainly applies to the House of Lords since, under English law (the 'national
law'), there is no appeal ('judicial remedy') from decisions of the House. It is still an open
question whether the Court of Appeal, like the House of Lords, is *bound* to refer a question
in those cases where it is effectively the final appellate court. It must be remembered that
no appeal at all is possible from the Court of Appeal to the House of Lords in probate
proceedings which emanated from a county court or in insolvency proceedings which
emanated from the Chancery Division (para 6.1.5). Moreover, in all other cases, an appeal
from the Court of Appeal to the House of Lords lies only with leave of either court.

The third paragraph of art. 177 (234) is open to two interpretations. First, it only makes
a reference compulsory in the case of the highest judicial body of a member state. This is
the construction favoured by Lord Denning MR (*H.P. Bulmer Ltd* v *J. Bollinger SA* [1974]
Ch 401, CA, at pp. 420–1; the other members of the court, Stamp and Stephenson LJJ, did
not commit themselves on the question). Secondly, it imposes an obligation to refer on any
national court, not necessarily the highest in the land, whose decision is (or may be) final
in a particular case. This wider interpretation is the one favoured by the European Court
itself and seems to have received the greater support of the two (*Costa* v *ENEL* [1964]
CMLR 425, CJEC; Bridge, (1975–6) 1 EL Rev 13, at pp. 18–19).

The wider interpretation was preferred in *SA Magnavision NV* v *General Optical Council
(No. 2)* [1987] 2 CMLR 262, DC, where the Queen's Bench Divisional Court was prepared

to assume that it was a final court in a criminal case for the purposes of the third paragraph of art. 177 (234), having prevented a further appeal to the House of Lords by refusing to certify under s. 1 of the Administration of Justice Act 1960 (para 6.2.1.3) that the case before it involved a point of law of general public importance. (See further on this case, para 2.1.3.3.3.)

The *Magnavision* approach was approved in *Chiron Corp* v *Murex Diagnostics Ltd* [1995] All ER (EC) 88, CA, in which it was said that the Court of Appeal is a court of last resort for the purposes of the third paragraph of art. 177 (234) in those cases where there is no right of appeal against its decision to the House of Lords. Lord Denning's statement in *H.P. Bulmer Ltd* v *J. Bollinger SA* ([1974] Ch 401 at p. 420) that 'short of the House of Lords, no other English court is bound to refer a question to the European Court at Luxembourg' was said to be mistaken ([1995] All ER (EC) 88 *per* Balcombe LJ at p. 93). Where, however, there is a right of appeal to the House of Lords but the Court of Appeal refuses leave to appeal, the court of last resort is the House of Lords and not the Court of Appeal (*Chiron Corp* v *Murex Diagnostics Ltd*, above; see further on this case, para 2.1.3.3.3).

2.1.3.3.2   Exercise of the discretion under the second paragraph of article 177 (now art. 234).   The second paragraph of art. 177 (234) applies to any United Kingdom court or tribunal below the House of Lords where the decision in a particular case is not final. Thus, in the exercise of the discretion, references to the European Court have been made by the Court of Appeal (*Macarthys Ltd* v *Smith* [1979] 3 All ER 325, CA, and [1981] 1 All ER 111, CJEC and CA; para 2.1.3.3.3); the High Court (*Van Duyn* v *Home Office* [1975] Ch 358; para 2.1.3.3.3); the Employment Appeal Tribunal (*Burton* v *British Railways Board* [1982] 3 All ER 537, CJEC); and even by a magistrates' court (*R* v *Marlborough Street Stipendiary Magistrate (ex parte Bouchereau)* [1977] 3 All ER 365, DC; *R* v *Plymouth Justices (ex parte Rogers)* [1982] 2 All ER 175, DC).

Guidelines for the exercise of the discretion under art. 177 (234) were suggested by Lord Denning MR in *H.P. Bulmer Ltd* v *J. Bollinger SA* [1974] Ch 401, CA, at pp. 420–5. It is important to appreciate, however, that these guidelines have been criticised on the ground that some of them are unduly restrictive and, if followed, will reduce the number of opportunities for asking the European Court to resolve doubts about important principles of Community law (Bridge (1975–6) 1 EL Rev, p. 20). The guidelines appear to have been accepted by Stephenson LJ in the *Bulmer* case (at p. 430), but not with any great enthusiasm. In addition, it may be argued that the Court of Appeal has no power to lay down any guidelines at all since the discretion under art. 177 (234) is vested directly in national courts and should not be limited by a national appellate court (see *Bethell* v *Sabena* [1983] 3 CMLR 1, *per* Parker J at p. 4). Lord Denning's guidelines are:

(a)   A reference to the European Court should only be made if a ruling of that court is necessary to enable the English court to give judgment in the case. 'Necessary' means that the ruling would be conclusive of the case. If other matters remained to be decided, then the ruling would not be 'necessary' within the meaning of art. 177 (234). In a criminal trial on indictment, for example, this means that it would rarely be proper for the Crown Court judge to seek a preliminary ruling before the facts of the alleged offence have been established. It is generally preferable for the trial judge himself to decide the question of Community law that has arisen and to have his decision reviewed on appeal through the hierarchy of our national courts (*R* v *Henn* [1980] 2 All ER 166, HL).

(b)   There is no need to refer a question which has already been decided by the European Court in a previous case. This guideline is open to objection. Since the European Court is not bound by its own previous decisions, it may be advisable for an English court to submit the same question where it considers that the previous decision of the European Court may have been wrong or where there are new factors which ought to be put before the Court.

(c)   There is no need to refer a point which is reasonably clear and free from doubt. This is the so-called *acte clair* doctrine. Where it arises there is no need to interpret the law but only to apply it. It has been said that magistrates' courts in particular should exercise considerable caution before referring a question to Europe and should generally decide any question of European Community law themselves. If their decision is wrong it can be appealed against to a higher English court, which is a more suitable forum to assess the appropriateness of a reference and to formulate the question to be referred (*R* v *Plymouth Justices (ex parte Rogers)* [1982] 2 All ER 175, DC, *per* Lord Lane CJ at p. 182).

(d)   In deciding whether to make a reference, the English court must consider all the circumstances. Of particular consequence are factors such as not overloading the European Court with references, the length of time which may elapse before a ruling can be obtained, the difficulty and importance of the point to be referred, the expense involved in obtaining a ruling, and the wishes of the parties.

None of these matters is expressly mentioned in art. 177 (234). Nevertheless in the *Bulmer* case itself time and expense were important factors in the decision to refuse to refer the question to Europe. The view of the Court of Appeal was that the point was important but not difficult and should be decided by the English courts. In *Maxim's Ltd* v *Dye* [1978] 2 All ER 55, Graham J found it unnecessary to refer a point to Europe. He mentioned the expense involved in obtaining a European ruling and said that he could decide the point himself. By contrast, the Court of Appeal in *Macarthys Ltd* v *Smith* [1979] 3 All ER 325 concluded that it would be less expensive and more convenient to send the case to the European Court than to the House of Lords (see especially *per* Lawton LJ, at p. 334).

It should be noted that the costs of a reference to the European Court are included as part of the proceedings before the English court, so that, for example, a legal aid order in criminal proceedings covers an application for a ruling to the European Court (*R* v *Marlborough Street Stipendiary Magistrate (ex parte Bouchereau)* [1977] 3 All ER 365, DC).

(e)   The discretion to refer the case or not belongs to the English court and not to the European Court. This means that the European Court cannot be asked to give guidance on how the discretion should be exercised and that a party cannot complain to the European Court about the exercise of the discretion one way or the other by the English court. The appropriate remedy for a party who wishes to challenge the decision to refer or not to refer is to appeal to a higher English court.

On its own initiative and without the agreement of the parties, the Court of Appeal has power to withdraw a reference it has already made under art. 177 (234). However, it is reluctant to do so unless it is clear that the reference will serve no useful purpose (*Royscot Leasing Ltd* v *Commissioners of Customs and Excise* [1999] 1 CMLR 903; (1998) *The Times*, 23 November, CA).

2.1.3.3.3   References under the third paragraph of article 177 (now art. 234).   In *CILFIT* v *Ministro della Sanita* [1983] 1 CMLR 472, CJEC, the European Court provided guidance for national courts failing within the third paragraph of art. 177 (234). The national court is not bound to refer a question to the European Court if the question is not relevant, i.e., if the answer to the question could have no influence on the outcome of the case. This guideline is similar to Lord Denning's guideline at (a) in para 2.1.3.3.2 above.

The national court can rely on previous rulings of the European Court and need not refer the same questions again. However, the national court is always entitled to make a fresh reference on the same point if it sees fit (cf Lord Denning's guideline at (b) in para 2.1.3.3.2 above).

The national court need not make a reference where the correct application of European Community law is so obvious as to leave no room for reasonable doubt. The European Court has thus approved the *acte clair* doctrine, although not in such wide terms as Lord Denning had expressed it in the *Bulmer* case (see para 2.1.3.3.2 above, at (c)). According to the European Court, the question whether or not there is reasonable doubt must be assessed by the national court having regard to the special characteristics of Community law, the peculiar problems presented by its interpretation, and the risk of causing conflicts of legal rulings within the European Union (*CILFIT* v *Ministro della Sanita,* above). Lord Denning's view of the *acte clair* doctrine must now be taken to have been modified in the light of this opinion from the European Court.

It is too late to make a reference to the European Court once judgment has been given by the national court because such a case can no longer be said to be 'pending' before the national court within the meaning of the third paragraph of art. 177 (234), and any decision by the European Court on such a reference could not be described as a 'preliminary ruling' (*SA Magnavision NV* v *General Optical Council (No. 2)* [1987] 2 CMLR 262, DC); *Chiron Corp* v *Murex Diagnostics Ltd* [1995] All ER (EC) 88, CA). In the *Magnavision* case the Queen's Bench Divisional Court would not have made a reference even if it had not been too late to do so, since, applying the *acte clair* doctrine, the judges found the relevant point of European Community law to be quite clear. In the *Chiron* case, it was pointed out in approving the *Magnavision* decision that a preliminary ruling by the European Court under art. 177 (234) should logically precede the judgment of the national referring court. Once, therefore, the Court of Appeal has given final judgment in a case it has no power to make a reference under art. 177 (234).

2.1.3.3.4 Some references to Europe by the English courts. The first reference to Europe by an English court was made by a High Court judge in *Van Duyn* v *Home Office* [1974] 3 All ER 178, Pennycuick V-C, and [1975] Ch 358, CJEC, a case which arose out of the United Kingdom government's dislike of Scientology. The Church of Scientology was established in the USA as a pseudo-philosophical cult. Opposition to it was based on its alienation of members of families, its indoctrination of children and its harm to the individual personality. Whilst not actually unlawful in the United Kingdom, the Home Office was anxious to prevent it spreading and in 1968 began refusing admission to the United Kingdom to foreign 'students' of Scientology and declining to extend the short-term entry permits of some of those already here. In *Schmidt* v *Home Secretary* [1969] 2 Ch 149, CA, this practice was upheld, although more recently the Home Office has abandoned it.

Miss Van Duyn was a Dutch national and a practising Scientologist. She was offered work as a secretary by the Church of Scientology in England but the Home Office refused her leave to enter the United Kingdom on the ground of her undesirability. She brought an action for a declaration that the attitude of the Home Office was in breach of the provisions of the EC Treaty (art. 48 (now art. 39)) and regulations relating to freedom of movement for workers of member states. Pennycuick V-C stayed the proceedings and referred the following question to the European Court for a ruling: whether a member state could refuse leave to enter its territory on the ground of association with an organisation whose activities were deemed to be contrary to the public good. The European Court answered the question in the affirmative and said it was immaterial that the organisation is not actually unlawful and that nationals of the member state are permitted to work for it.

The first case to be referred to the European Court by the Court of Appeal was *Macarthys Ltd* v *Smith* [1979] 3 All ER 325, CA. Macarthys Ltd employed a man to manage a stockroom at £60 per week. He left their employment and four and a half months later they appointed a woman, Mrs Smith, to manage the stockroom in his place at only £50 per week. Mrs Smith claimed to be entitled to equal pay under s. 1(2)(a)(i) of the Equal Pay Act 1970. The Employment Appeal Tribunal found in her favour and the employers appealed to the Court of Appeal. It was held that there should be a reference to the European Court for a ruling, under art. 177 (234) of the EC Treaty, asking whether the British Equal Pay Act was out of step with art. 119 (now art. 141) of the EC Treaty, which must take priority in the event of a conflict. By the Equal Pay Act 1970, s. 1(2):

> An equality clause is a provision which relates to terms (whether concerned with pay or not) of a contract under which a woman is employed (the 'woman's contract'), and has the effect that:
>
> (a)   where the woman is employed on like work with a man in the same employment:
>
> (i)   if (apart from the equality clause) any term of the woman's contract is or becomes less favourable to the woman. . . . that term of the woman's contract shall be treated as so modified as not to be less favourable.

By the EC Treaty, art. 119 (141):

> Each member state shall . . . ensure and subsequently maintain the application of the principle that men and women should receive equal pay for equal work.

The contrast in legislative and literary styles between the two provisions is striking (see *per* Lord Denning MR, [1979] 3 All ER 325, 329). What exercised the minds of the judges in the Court of Appeal was whether they applied only when the man and the woman were doing like or broadly similar work side by side at the same time, or whether they extended to cases where the woman was employed on like work *in succession to* the man. It was held by Lawton and Cumming-Bruce LJJ that the British legislation was limited to the former situation. Lord Denning MR dissented, being of the opinion that both the Equal Pay Act and art. 119 (141) were wide enough to cover the latter situation as well. However, all three judges agreed that there was sufficient doubt over the meaning of art. 119 (141) to justify a reference to the European Court, although Lord Denning did not suffer the same degree of dubiety as his two colleagues. While he thought that art. 119 (141) was 'reasonably clear' (p. 330) and said that he had 'no doubt' about its true interpretation (p. 331), Lawton LJ commented with some acerbity that his own doubts placed him under a judicial duty not to guess what art. 119 (141) meant but to find out from the European Court (p. 334). That court held that there must be equal pay for equal work whether the man and the woman were working side by side or successively, thus vindicating the judgment of Lord Denning. In the light of this ruling from Europe, the Court of Appeal later dismissed the appeal of Mrs Smith's employers ([1981] 1 All ER 111, CJEC and CA).

The first case to be referred to the European Court by the House of Lords was a criminal case, *R* v *Henn* [1980] 2 All ER 166, CJEC and HL. One of the main points at issue in the case was whether a total prohibition on the import into the United Kingdom of pornographic articles constituted a 'quantitative restriction on imports' within art. 30 (now art. 28) of the EC Treaty and, if so, whether it was justified on 'grounds of public morality' within art. 36 (now art. 30). (See also *Conegate Ltd* v *Customs and Excise Commissioners* [1986] 2 All ER 688, CJEC and DC — the inflatable dolls case — in which *R* v *Henn* was considered.)

Another case referred to the European Court for a preliminary ruling by the House of Lords was *Garland* v *British Rail Engineering Ltd* [1982] 2 All ER 402, CJEC and HL, a seemingly simple dispute which eventually occupied the time of five different tribunals and produced considerable judicial disagreement. The case began in an industrial tribunal in February 1977 and went successively to the Employment Appeal Tribunal, the Court of Appeal, the House of Lords and the European Court. The question at issue was whether the employers had discriminated against a female employee in the matter of free travel facilities on retirement. The case was not finally disposed of until April 1982, when the House of Lords, in the light of the European Court's opinion on Community law, decided it in favour of the female employee. The House of Lords was responsible for making the final decision in the case because the European Court itself can neither rule on the consistency of national law with Community law nor interpret national law. Its function under art. 177 (234) is limited to giving rulings on the interpretation of the Treaty and on the interpretation and validity of secondary Community legislation (see *Costa* v *ENEL* [1964] CMLR 425, CJEC).

In *Stoke-on-Trent City Council* v *B & Q plc* [1993] 1 All ER 481, CJEC, the House of Lords had used art. 177 (234) to refer to the European Court some questions on the interpretation of art. 30 (28) and its applicability to s. 47 of the Shops Act 1950, which, with some exceptions, forbade Sunday trading. The European Court laid down that the prohibition against quantitative restrictions on imports, and measures equivalent thereto, contained in art. 30 (28) did not apply to national legislation prohibiting Sunday trading since the legislation did not discriminate between the sale of imported and domestic goods and its restrictive effect was not disproportionate to its aim. In the light of this ruling, the House of Lords three months later in *Stoke-on-Trent City Council* v *B & Q plc* [1993] 2 All ER 297 dismissed the appeal of B & Q (brought under the 'leapfrog' procedure: see para 6.1.4.1) against the decision of Hoffmann J at first instance in *Stoke-on-Trent City Council* v *B & Q plc* [1991] 4 All ER 221. (See further on this case, para. 8.7, and note that s. 47 of the Shops Act was repealed by the Sunday Trading Act 1994.)

2.2 JUDICIAL COMMITTEE OF THE PRIVY COUNCIL

2.2.1 Composition

Before 1833 the Crown prerogative to hear appeals from courts in all the dominions was exercised through a lay committee of the whole Privy Council. Since the Judicial Committee Act of 1833, all such appeals have been heard by a special committee created by that Act and called the Judicial Committee of the Privy Council. The Judicial Committee is composed of the Lord President of the Council, the Lord Chancellor, ex-Lord Presidents, the Lords of Appeal in Ordinary, other members of the Privy Council who hold or have held high judicial office (para 1.2.2) in the United Kingdom, and privy counsellors who hold or have held the office of chief justice or judge in a superior court in Australia, Canada or in any other superior court in the Commonwealth named by Order in Council. In addition, the Queen may appoint two other privy counsellors as members of the Judicial Committee (Judicial Committee Act 1833, s. 1; Appellate Jurisdiction Act 1876, s. 6; Judicial

Committee Act 1881; Appellate Jurisdiction Act 1887, s. 3; Judicial Committee Amendment Act 1895, s. 1; Appellate Jurisdiction Act 1908, s. 3(1)).

Among the superior courts 'named' are those in Barbados, Sri Lanka, Ghana, Trinidad and Tobago, the Bahamas, Jamaica and the Eastern Caribbean. South Africa was removed from the list in 1962.

Any member of the Judicial Committee may resign by written notice to the Lord President of the Council (Appellate Jurisdiction Act 1908, s. 4).

When exercising its jurisdiction, under the Government of Wales Act 1998, the Scotland Act 1998, and the Northern Ireland Act 1998, to determine 'devolution questions' (para 2.2.3.5, below), membership of the Judicial Committee is limited to the Lord Chancellor, the Lords of Appeal in Ordinary, and judges of the Court of Appeal, the Court of Appeal in Northern Ireland, the Scottish Court of Session, the High Court, and the High Court in Northern Ireland. All such members mentioned are eligible whether serving or retired.

2.2.2   Procedure

As a matter of convenience, the Judicial Committee sits in London. Appeals are heard at the bar of the Privy Council; the judges do not wear robes. Each appeal must be heard by at least three members of the Committee (Court of Chancery Act 1851, s. 16: 'An Act to improve the Administration of Justice in the Court of Chancery and in the Judicial Committee of the Privy Council'). In practice, five usually sit. The court is most commonly made up of Lords of Appeal in Ordinary. For this reason, decisions of the Judicial Committee carry strong persuasive authority but they are not absolutely binding on English courts. (For judicial precedent in relation to the Judicial Committee, see para 9.3.2.9.)

Technically, the Committee's decision in a case is not a judgment but *advice* to Her Majesty (Judicial Committee Act 1833, s. 3). This is why the judgment usually ends with some such formula as, 'The Committee will humbly advise Her Majesty that this appeal be dismissed [or allowed]'. In practice, the advice is always followed and is implemented by an Order in Council. On the day fixed for delivery of judgment, it is the practice of the Committee to announce the result of the appeal in open court. The reasons for the decision are not read in full; instead the parties and the press are supplied with printed copies. In theory, the advice to Her Majesty should be unanimous. For this reason, the practice was for only one judgment to be prepared so that it was never known publicly whether there had been any dissension among the judges. This is still the normal practice, although, since 1966, it has been possible for a member of the Committee to publish a dissenting judgment (Judicial Committee (Dissenting Opinions) Order dated 4 March 1966).

2.2.3   Jurisdiction

The jurisdiction of the Judicial Committee of the Privy Council extends to Commonwealth appeals, appeals from professional bodies in disciplinary cases, prize appeals, ecclesiastical appeals and certain other matters.

2.2.3.1   *Commonwealth jurisdiction*
The Judicial Committee hears appeals from courts in Her Majesty's dominions outside the United Kingdom and from the independent members and associate members of the Commonwealth, except for independent Commonwealth countries that have stopped sending their final appeals to London either because special legislation has been passed or because

Her Majesty has ceased to be head of state there. Among the territories whose final appeals are still heard by the Committee are the Bahamas, Barbados, Bermuda, British Antarctic Territory, the Channel Islands, the Falkland Islands, Fiji, Gibraltar, Jamaica, the Isle of Man, New Zealand and the Seychelles. The jurisdiction of the Committee has been specially extended to the republics of the Gambia, Trinidad and Tobago, and Mauritius, where the Queen is not Head of State though she is recognised as Head of the Commonwealth. The appeal from a republic either lies to the head of state (who refers it to the Judicial Committee) or it is expressed as lying to the Committee itself and not to the Queen in Council.

The jurisdiction has been ended in Aden, Australia, Botswana, Burma, Canada, Cyprus, Ghana, Guyana, Hong Kong, India, Kenya, Malaysia, Malta, Nigeria, Pakistan, Sierra Leone, Singapore, Sri Lanka, Tanzania and Uganda, among others. Aden and Burma did not become members of the Commonwealth on independence. Pakistan left the Commonwealth in 1972; although she was readmitted as a member in 1989, the jurisdiction of the Committee was not revived. The same is true of South Africa, which was not a member of the Commonwealth between 1962 and 1994. The jurisdiction of the Committee in relation to Malaysia, an independent monarchy not owing allegiance to the Queen, was terminated at the end of 1984. Appeals from Australia on *state* law ceased to lie to the Judicial Committee in 1986 (Australia Act 1986, s. 11), thus completing the process of withdrawal begun in 1968 when the Australian Parliament abolished appeals to the Committee on *federal* law. The final appeal court from all Australian courts, both state and federal, is now the High Court of Australia. The right of appeal to the Committee from the republic of Singapore was abolished in 1994. The Committee was replaced as the final appellate court for Hong Kong by the Hong Kong Court of Final Appeal when that territory became a Special Administrative Region of China on 1 July 1997. Arrangements for two serving United Kingdom Law Lords to sit occasionally in the Hong Kong Court of Final Appeal as non-permanent judges were completed in January 1998 when Hong Kong's Provisional Legislative Council endorsed the appointment of the first two nominees, Lord Nicholls of Birkenhead and Lord Hoffmann.

Most of the appeals heard by the Judicial Committee are in *civil* cases. The Committee in particular does not sit as a court of appeal against *criminal sentence* and will not grant special leave to appeal in criminal cases unless there has been a substantial injustice, such as where the appellant has been denied a fair trial because of a violation of the principles of natural justice (*Ibrahim* v *R* [1914] AC 599, PC; *Practice Note* (1932) 48 TLR 300; *Badry* v *Director of Public Prosecutions of Mauritius* [1982] 3 All ER 973, PC).

The Judicial Committee has recently re-emphasised that unless some other matter is specifically referred to it under s. 4 of the Judicial Committee Act 1833 (para 2.2.3.5 below) its Commonwealth jurisdiction is as an appellate court only. Accordingly, it cannot, for example, act as a court of first instance to adjudicate upon a question of the constitutionality of a mandatory sentence of death where that question has not yet been determined by the appellate courts of the country concerned (*Walker* v *R* [1993] 4 All ER 789, PC, *per* Lord Griffiths at p. 791).

The continuing influence of the Judicial Committee within the Commonwealth is illustrated by the case of *Pratt* v *Attorney-General for Jamaica* [1993] 4 All ER 769, PC, in which it was held that the state's failure to carry out a death sentence as swiftly as practicable after sentence amounted to 'inhuman or degrading punishment or other treatment' contrary to the Jamaican constitution. The Judicial Committee commuted from death to life imprisonment the sentences of two men, thus rescuing them from 'death row' where they had been for almost 15 years. The fate of 105 other prisoners who had been awaiting execution for more than five years (23 of them for longer than 10 years) also depended upon the outcome of the appeal. *Pratt* was applied in *Guerra* v *Baptiste* [1995] 4 All ER 583, PC, an appeal from Trinidad and Tobago, and considered in *Henfield* v *Attorney-General of the Commonwealth of the Bahamas* [1996] 3 WLR 1079, PC, in both of which the death sentence was commuted.

Pratt, Guerra and *Henfield* were considered in another appeal from the Bahamas, *Fisher* v *Minister of Public Safety and Immigration* (1997) *The Times*, 26 December, PC, where, by a majority, it was held that when considering whether execution has become 'inhuman' within the *Pratt* principle (i.e., by reason of delay in carrying out the death sentence), it is not, as a general rule, appropriate to take into account *pre-trial* delay as opposed to delay occurring after imposition of the sentence of death. Pre-trial delay is only to be considered in exceptional circumstances where it is sufficiently serious. In a powerful dissenting opinion, Lord Steyn argued that the view of the majority was contrary to the language, purpose and spirit of the relevant article of the constitution of the Bahamas. He said that humanity and decency should allow the court to take into account in all cases the fact, if proved, that for several years before sentence a defendant may have been held 'in appalling conditions with a noose constantly dangling before his mind's eye', or that the state may have taken a deliberate decision to delay his trial for several years, or that there may have been an inexcusable failure to bring him to trial for many years.

2.2.3.2   Disciplinary jurisdiction

The Judicial Committee of the Privy Council hears appeals from persons in the United Kingdom whose names have been ordered by the appropriate disciplinary committee to be erased from certain professional registers. This jurisdiction extends to medical practitioners, dentists, opticians, veterinary surgeons, chiropodists, occupational therapists, physiotherapists, osteopaths, chiropractors and others. The appeal lies as of right without leave.

2.2.3.3   Prize jurisdiction

The Judicial Committee hears appeals in prize cases from decisions of the High Court sitting as a prize court (Supreme Court Act 1981, s. 16(2)). (For the meaning of 'prize', see para 1.4.3.3.)

2.2.3.4   Ecclesiastical jurisdiction

The wide jurisdiction to hear appeals from ecclesiastical courts ended in 1963. However, the Judicial Committee still hears appeals from decisions of the Arches Court of Canterbury and the Chancery Court of York given in causes of faculty not involving a matter of doctrine, ritual or ceremonial (Ecclesiastical Jurisdiction Measure 1963, ss. 7 and 8). (A 'faculty' is a power granted by the consistory court of a diocese authorising an alteration to consecrated land or buildings, including the fabric, furnishings, decorations and ornaments.)

2.2.3.5   Other jurisdiction

The Judicial Committee has power to entertain an application for a declaration that a person purporting to be a member of the House of Commons is disqualified or has been disqualified at any time since his election (House of Commons Disqualification Act 1975, s. 7(1) and (2)). For the purpose of determining any preliminary issue of fact, the Committee may order the issue to be tried in the High Court, the Court of Session, or in the High Court in Northern Ireland, depending on the location of the constituency involved (ibid., s. 7(4)).

Her Majesty may make a special reference to the Judicial Committee asking it to hear or consider any matter whatsoever (Judicial Committee Act 1833, s. 4). The special reference need not necessarily be concerned with a judicial decision and, in the past, this procedure has been used in such diverse matters as the conduct and powers of colonial judges, the privileges of the Jersey Bar, boundary disputes between dominions and the eligibility of a person to sit and vote in the House of Commons. The Committee advises the Queen on the outcome of the reference in the same way as on an appeal.

Under the Government of Wales Act 1998, the Scotland Act 1998, and the Northern Ireland Act 1998, 'devolution questions' may be referred to the Judicial Committee for determination. In relation to Scotland and Northern Ireland, for example, these include the question of whether any provision in a Bill would be within the legislative competence of the Scottish Parliament or the Northern Ireland Assembly, respectively. The Acts provide that the decision of the Judicial Committee on a devolution question is binding in all legal proceedings, except proceedings before the Judicial Committee itself.

2.3 EMPLOYMENT APPEAL TRIBUNAL

2.3.1 Introduction

The Employment Appeal Tribunal was established in 1976 as the successor to the ill-fated National Industrial Relations Court (NIRC) which was created under a Conservative government by the Industrial Relations Act 1971. The NIRC became unpopular with certain trade unions chiefly because of the exercise of its jurisdiction over 'unfair industrial practices'. This unpopularity led to a refusal of recognition and to open defiance of its orders on the part of some unions, resulting in the imprisonment of some members for contempt of court. The President of the Court, Sir John Donaldson, at that time a judge of the High Court, was accused of political prejudice. (For the political background, see Denning, *The Closing Chapter,* 1983, pp. 164–78. Sir John Donaldson's involvement in the controversy surrounding the NIRC, and the claims of other more likely candidates, made him a surprising choice as Master of the Rolls in 1982 as successor to Lord Denning, although, paradoxically, some saw the appointment as a reward for Sir John's services to the NIRC.) The Labour Party committed itself to the repeal of the Industrial Relations Act 1971 and the abolition of the NIRC. These objectives were achieved, on the return of a Labour government, by s. 1(1) and (3) of the Trade Union and Labour Relations Act 1974 (since repealed).

The NIRC was abolished on 31 July 1974 and, for a time, appeals in employment cases were heard by the Divisional Court of the Queen's Bench Division. On 30 March 1976, the Employment Appeal Tribunal came into existence. It was created as from that date by s. 87 of the Employment Protection Act 1975 (see now s. 20(1) of the Employment Tribunals Act 1996). Although called a 'tribunal' for psychological reasons in view of the trade union movement's distaste for courts, it is, in fact, a superior court of record (Employment Tribunals Act 1996, s. 20(3)). Thus, it has power to punish for contempt of court and is not subject to the supervisory jurisdiction of the Queen's Bench Division.

2.3.2 Composition

The Employment Appeal Tribunal consists of those High Court and Court of Appeal judges nominated by the Lord Chancellor, at least one judge of the Scottish Court of Session nominated by the Lord President of that Court, and lay members appointed by Her Majesty on the joint recommendation of the Lord Chancellor and the Secretary of State for Employment (Employment Tribunals Act 1996, s. 22(1)). The judicial members cannot be nominated unless they consent (ibid., s. 22(4)). One of the judicial members is appointed president by the Lord Chancellor (ibid., s. 22(3)). The lay members are persons with special knowledge or experience of industrial relations and are representatives of employers and of workers (ibid., s. 22(2)). There are no independent lay members. A lay member can be removed by the Lord Chancellor, after consultation with the Secretary of State, on the grounds of incapacity, misbehaviour, bankruptcy or absence from sittings of the tribunal for longer than six months without the permission of the president (ibid., s. 25(4)). A lay member can resign at any time by written notice to the Lord Chancellor and the Secretary of State (ibid., s. 25(2)).

The Employment Appeal Tribunal has a central office in London but is authorised to sit at any place in Great Britain in any number of divisions concurrently (ibid., ss. 20(2) and 28(1)). An appeal must normally be heard by a judge with either two or four lay members who represent employers and workers in equal numbers. However, with the consent of the parties, an appeal may be heard by a judge sitting with one lay member or by a judge sitting with three lay members (ibid., s. 28(2), (3)). In all cases the judgment of the tribunal is prepared and read by the judge.

2.3.3   Jurisdiction

The jurisdiction of the Employment Appeal Tribunal is largely limited to the hearing of appeals. Unlike the NIRC, it has no original jurisdiction over such matters as 'unfair industrial practices'. The appeals come mainly from employment tribunals on questions of law arising in cases decided under various statutes. The matters covered include redundancy, equal pay, written particulars of contracts of employment, sex discrimination (in the field of employment only), racial discrimination (in the field of employment only), disability discrimination (in the field of employment only), unfair dismissal, unlawful deductions from wages, and unlawful refusal of employment, or of the services of an employment agency, on grounds related to trade union membership. Cases involving sexual, racial or disability discrimination in fields other than employment are heard at first instance by the county courts, with an appeal lying to the Court of Appeal (para 1.6.3.3). In addition, the tribunal hears appeals on questions of law or fact from certain decisions of the Certification Officer, an official responsible for certifying various matters in relation to trade unions (Trade Union and Labour Relations (Consolidation) Act 1992, ss. 9 and 95).

The Employment Appeal Tribunal has *original* jurisdiction over two matters. First, it has the power to hear an application for compensation from a person who has been unreasonably excluded or expelled from membership of a trade union and who has not been admitted or readmitted at the time of the application. This right to claim compensation only arises where there is a union membership agreement in existence (ibid., ss. 174 and 176 as substituted by the Trade Union Reform and Employment Rights Act 1993; para 3.4.2).

Secondly, it has the power to hear an application for compensation from a person who has been unjustifiably disciplined by a trade union if, at the time of the application, the decision to discipline him has not been withdrawn or the trade union has failed to take all necessary steps for ensuring the revocation of any disciplinary measure already imposed (ibid., s. 67; para 3.4.2).

2.3.4 Procedure

The procedure before the Employment Appeal Tribunal is relatively quick, informal, simple and cheap. Any party may appear in person or be represented by counsel or by a solicitor or by a representative of a trade union or an employers' association or by any other person he chooses (Employment Tribunals Act 1996, s. 29(1)). There are no strict rules of evidence. The judge is not robed and may be addressed simply as 'sir'. There is no bench or witness-box. The parties and their representatives sit at tables and may address the tribunal sitting down.

The tribunal can order the attendance and examination of witnesses and the discovery of documents. It has power to enforce its own orders, although contempt of court can only be punished by, or with the consent of, the judge (ibid., s. 36(4)). Unlike proceedings in the ordinary courts, each party is normally responsible for paying his own costs even if he is successful in the appeal. The tribunal can order a party to pay the costs of another party only where the proceedings were unnecessary, improper or vexatious or where there has been unreasonable delay or other unreasonable conduct in bringing or conducting the proceedings (ibid., s. 34).

2.3.5 Appeals

The decision of the Employment Appeal Tribunal is final on any question of *fact,* except in the case of committal for contempt of court. On a question of *law,* an appeal lies to the Court of Appeal or, in the case of Scottish proceedings, to the Court of Session. Leave to appeal must first be obtained from the tribunal or from the Court of Appeal (or Court of Session in the case of Scottish proceedings) (Employment Tribunals Act 1996, s. 37). A further appeal lies, with leave, to the House of Lords.

2.4 RESTRICTIVE PRACTICES COURT

2.4.1 Introduction

The Restrictive Practices Court was established by the Restrictive Trade Practices Act 1956. Its composition and procedure are now regulated by the Restrictive Practices Court Act 1976. The court is a superior court of record (Restrictive Practices Court Act 1976, s. 1(1)).

2.4.2 Composition

The Restrictive Practices Court consists of five judges and not more than ten lay members (Restrictive Practices Court Act 1976, s. 1(2); these numbers may be increased by the Lord Chancellor under ibid., s. 4). The judges are three puisne High Court judges nominated by the Lord Chancellor, one judge of the Court of Session nominated by the Lord President, and one judge of the Supreme Court of Northern Ireland nominated by the Lord Chief Justice of Northern Ireland (ibid., s. 2(1)). A judge cannot be nominated unless he consents. One of the judicial members is appointed president of the court by the Lord Chancellor.

The lay members are appointed by the Queen, on the recommendation of the Lord Chancellor, from among persons with knowledge or experience of industry, commerce or public affairs. The period of office of a lay member is determined at the time of his appointment and must not be for less than three years. He is eligible for reappointment. A lay member can be removed by the Lord Chancellor for inability or misbehaviour, or on the ground of any employment or interest which appears to the Lord Chancellor to be incompatible with the functions of a member of the court. A lay member may resign at any time by written notice to the Lord Chancellor (ibid., s. 3(1) and (2)).

The central office of the Restrictive Practices Court is in London, although the court has authority to sit at any place in the United Kingdom. It may sit in any number of divisions concurrently and either in public or in private (ibid., s. 6(3), (4) and (6)). Each case must normally be heard by a presiding judge sitting with at least two other members. However, if a case involves only issues of law it may be heard by a judge alone (ibid., s. 7(1)). The opinion of the judge or judges sitting as members of the court must prevail on any question of law. That apart, the decision of the court is taken by all members sitting. If there is a difference of opinion, the majority decision prevails. If the voting is equal, the presiding judge has a second or casting vote. The judgment of the court must always be delivered by the presiding judge (ibid., s. 7(2) and (3)).

2.4.3 Jurisdiction

The jurisdiction of the Restrictive Practices Court is to determine whether restrictive agreements and information agreements relating to the supply of goods or services are valid or whether they are contrary to the public interest and void (Restrictive Trade Practices Act 1976, s. 1). The operation of a declaration made by the court may be suspended pending the submission of revised agreements to the court for approval (Competition Act 1980, ss. 25 and 26). Proceedings are normally taken before the court by the Director General of Fair Trading.

2.4.4 Procedure

The Restrictive Practices Court can order the attendance and examination of witnesses and the discovery of documents. It has power to enforce its own orders, although contempt of the court can only be punished by, or with the consent of, a judge who is a member of the court (Restrictive Practices Court Act 1976, s. 9(3) and (4)).

2.4.5 Appeals

An appeal may be taken from a decision of the Restrictive Practices Court on a question of law only, unless the proceedings were brought under part III of the Fair Trading Act 1973 (consumer protection) when an appeal lies on a question of fact as well as law. Depending on the location of the proceedings, the appeal lies, without leave, to the Court of Appeal, the Court of Session or the Court of Appeal in Northern Ireland (Restrictive Practices Court Act 1976, s. 10). A further appeal lies, with leave, to the House of Lords.

2.4.6 Abolition of the Restrictive Practices Court

The Competition Act 1998 introduces new investigation and enforcement procedures into competition law. From 1 March 2000, it increased the powers of the Director General of Fair Trading and established the Competition Commission. Appeals from decisions of the Director General lie to an appeal tribunal of the Commission (Competition Act 1998, ss. 46–48). An appeal lies from a decision of the appeal tribunal either on a point of law or on the amount of any penalty imposed. Depending on the location of the proceedings, the appeal lies to the Court of Appeal, the Court of Session in Scotland, or the Court of Appeal in Northern Ireland. Permission to appeal is required either from the appeal tribunal or from the appropriate appellate court (ibid., s. 49).

When fully in force, the Competition Act 1998 will repeal the Restrictive Practices Court Act 1976 and the Restrictive Trade Practices Act 1976, thus signalling the abolition of the Restrictive Practices Court. This is expected to happen some time after 1 March 2001. In the meantime, the Restrictive Practices Court will continue, under transitional provisions, to deal with references already made to it.

2.5 CORONERS' COURTS

2.5.1 Introduction

Coroners were first appointed in the twelfth century in order to assist the sheriffs in their criminal jurisdiction. Coroners also kept watch on the sheriffs, whose honesty was suspected by the King in connection with royal revenues, such as fines and forfeitures, which were due from persons convicted of serious crimes ('Pleas of the Crown').

The coroners also kept a roll of local crimes to present to the royal judge on his next visit to the area and held inquiries or 'inquests' into cases of unexplained death and 'deodand'. A deodand (literally, 'to be given to God', *deo dandum)* was an animate or inanimate object which had caused the death of a human being. It was forfeited to the King, or to the lord of the manor, to be put to pious uses in order to appease the wrath of God. The commonest deodands were said to be horses, oxen, carts, boats, millwheels and cauldrons (Pollock and Maitland, *History of English Law,* 2nd ed., 1898, vol. 2, pp. 473–4). Deodand was abolished in 1846 after the claiming of a railway engine had demonstrated that its continued existence could prove an expensive barrier to progress. The investigation of unexplained deaths remains the chief function of the coroner's court, although the purpose is no longer to add to the royal revenues through fines but to satisfy the public conscience (see *R v West Yorkshire Coroner (ex parte Smith)* [1982] 3 All ER 1098, CA, *per* Donaldson LJ at p. 1108).

Most of the law relating to coroners' courts is contained in the Coroners Act 1988, which consolidated (with some amendments) legislation passed between 1844 and 1983.

2.5.2 The coroner

By law, coroners must be appointed by the appropriate local authority for each coroner's district in a metropolitan county or Greater London, for each non-metropolitan county and for the City of London (Coroners Act 1988, s. 1(1)). For appointment as a coroner, a person must either have a five year general qualification within the meaning of s. 71 of the Courts and Legal Services Act 1990 or be a registered medical practitioner of at least five years' standing (ibid., s. 2(1), as amended by the Courts and Legal Services Act 1990).

A coroner may be removed from office by the Lord Chancellor for inability or misbehaviour in the discharge of his duty (Coroners Act 1988, s. 3(4)). Alternatively, a coroner who has been convicted of the criminal offence of corruption or of wilful neglect of his duty or of misbehaviour in the discharge of his duty may be ordered by the court of conviction to be removed from office and to be disqualified from acting as coroner (ibid., s. 3(6)).

The Lord Chief Justice and all the puisne judges of the High Court are *ex officio* coroners, although they are never called upon to act in that capacity.

2.5.3 Jurisdiction

2.5.3.1 Treasure

At common law, treasure trove was coin, plate or bullion, made of gold or silver, which had been hidden and of which the true owner was unknown. Any money or coin or other object not containing a substantial amount of gold or silver was not treasure trove. (This is Coke's definition (3 Co Inst 132), preferred to all others by the Court of Appeal in *Attorney-General of the Duchy of Lancaster* v *G.E. Overton (Farms) Ltd* [1982] 1 All ER 524; para 9.4.4.)

The Treasure Act 1996, which was fully in force by 24 September 1997, replaced the common law rules on treasure trove with a statutory code. 'Treasure trove' was abolished and replaced with 'treasure', which is defined in s. 1 as including, *inter alia*, any found object (except a single coin) containing at least 10 per cent precious metal (i.e., gold or silver) and at least 300 years old. Coins are only treasure in two circumstances: (a) if there are at least two of them in the same find and they are at least 300 years old and contain 10 per cent precious metal, or (b) there are at least ten of them and they are at least 300 years old.

In addition, the Secretary of State has power to alter the meaning of 'treasure' so as to (a) exclude from the definition any class of object which would otherwise be treasure, and (b) include within the definition any designated class of object which he considers to be of outstanding historical, archaeological or cultural importance (s. 2).

Treasure belongs, subject to any prior interests and rights, to any franchisee of the Crown (e.g., the Duchy of Cornwall, the Duchy of Lancaster and the City of London) or to the Crown itself (s. 4).

The coroner must be notified of any find if the finder believes, or has reasonable grounds for believing, that the found object is treasure (s. 8(1)). Failure to notify is a criminal offence (s. 8(3)). Any doubt about whether an object is treasure will be resolved by a coroner's inquest, which will be held without a jury unless the coroner orders otherwise (s. 7). Before an inquest the coroner must notify the British Museum or the National Museum of Wales (s. 9).

In the case of treasure which vests in the Crown and is to be transferred to a museum, the Secretary of State must decide whether a reward is to be paid by the museum and, if so, how much. The reward must not exceed the treasure's market value as determined by the Secretary of State. Payment of the reward is not enforceable against a museum or the Secretary of State (s. 10).

The Secretary of State is responsible for devising a code of practice, dealing with such matters as rewards and to whom treasure should be offered. The code may also include guidance for people who search for, or find, treasure (s. 11).

2.5.3.2 Deaths

The coroner has jurisdiction to inquire into violent or unnatural deaths, sudden deaths where the cause is unknown, and deaths in prison (Coroners Act 1988, s. 8(1)).

As long as the body is now lying within his district, the coroner has jurisdiction to hold an inquest into such a death which occurred outside England and Wales (*R* v *West Yorkshire Coroner (ex parte Smith)* [1982] 3 All ER 1098, CA, in which *certiorari* was granted to quash the coroner's decision not to hold an inquest into the death of Helen Smith made on the ground that the death had occurred abroad). It is not obligatory for a coroner holding an inquest to view the body (ibid., s. 11(1)). The coroner has power to order the exhumation of the body of a person buried within his district (ibid., s. 23(1)). In the case of a sudden death from an unknown cause, the coroner may order a post-mortem examination of the body (ibid., s. 19(1)). If this shows that the death was from natural causes the coroner is not compelled to hold an inquest (ibid., s. 19(3)) unless the deceased died in prison (ibid., s. 19(4), and see *R* v *Greater Manchester North District Coroner (ex parte Worch)* [1987] 3 All ER 661, CA).

A death is natural or unnatural depending upon its cause, which is essentially a practical question of fact. An otherwise natural death is not converted into an unnatural death (requiring the holding of an inquest under s. 8(1) of the Coroners Act 1988) solely by the presence of other facts (such as unavoidable delay in treating the deceased's medical condition) which might have contributed to the death if, taking all the evidence together, the death is due to a natural cause. Where, therefore, the deceased died from a severe asthmatic attack before the delayed arrival of an ambulance it was held that death was due to natural causes rather than the late arrival of the ambulance and that the coroner had correctly decided that an inquest was unnecessary (*R* v *Poplar Coroner (ex parte Thomas)* [1993] 2 All ER 381, CA). Asthma is not a rare condition so that a death resulting from it cannot be regarded as 'unnatural'; it may be otherwise with rare diseases like typhoid and Legionnaires' disease (*R* v *Poplar Coroner (ex parte Thomas)*, above, *per* Dillon LJ at p. 385).

2.5.4 Procedure

An inquest must be held in public except where the coroner considers that privacy is desirable in the interest of national security (Coroners Rules 1984 (SI 1984, No. 552), r. 17). This rule has two purposes. First, to allow interested parties and members of the public to hear the evidence of the circumstances of a death; secondly, to prevent the public from hearing evidence which affects national security. The coroner at an inquest which does not involve national security is not prevented by the rule from allowing a witness to give evidence out of public sight from behind a screen. Such an inquest is still 'held in public' (*R* v *Newcastle upon Tyne Coroner (ex parte A)* (1998) *The Times*, 19 January, where a member of the Northumbria Police armed response team obtained an order of certiorari quashing the coroner's decision not to allow him to give evidence while screened from public sight).

The proceedings and evidence are to be directed solely towards ascertaining who the deceased was; how, when and where he came by his death; and the particulars required to be registered concerning the death. Neither the coroner nor the jury (if there is one) must express any opinion on any other matters (ibid., r. 36).

In particular, no verdict should be framed in such a way as to appear to determine any question of criminal liability on the part of a named person or any question of civil liability (ibid., r. 42). There appears to be a conflict between this prohibition and a verdict which states that the cause of death was aggravated, or contributed to, by 'lack of care'. This formula is increasingly used following the death in hospital or in prison of a person who, unable to look after himself, was being cared for by others and the death was due to starvation or exposure, or similar causes, brought about by the failure of his carers to look after him properly. The apparent conflict is, however, avoided if the verdict simply records that 'death was aggravated, or contributed to, by lack of care' and omits all reference to any particular hospital, prison or person. Such a verdict is acceptable because it contains no suggestion that a legal duty of care has been broken giving rise to potential criminal liability for manslaughter or civil liability for negligence (*R* v *East Berkshire Coroner (ex parte Buckley)* (1992) *The Times*, 1 December, DC; *R* v *North Humberside and Scunthorpe Coroner (ex parte Jamieson)* [1994] 3 All ER 972, CA; *R* v *Surrey Coroner (ex parte Wright)* [1997] 1 All ER 823). 'Lack of care' signifies neglect, and neglect is only appropriate as part of a verdict where there is a direct causal link between the neglect and the death. Thus, while it is not neglect merely to present a prison inmate with opportunities to kill himself, it might be otherwise if a prison officer failed to intervene in a prisoner's obvious ongoing attempt at suicide (*R* v *North Humberside and Scunthorpe Coroner (ex parte Jamieson)*, above).

In most cases the coroner has a *discretion* to summon a jury to the inquest (Coroners Act 1988, s. 8(4)). In a few cases, to be considered in para 2.5.6 below, the coroner *must* summon a jury. A coroner's jury consists of between seven and eleven persons (ibid., s. 8(2)). In order to sit on a coroner's jury a person must be qualified under the Juries Act 1974 (Coroners Act 1988, s. 9(1) and see paras 7.2 and 7.3 for the Juries Act 1974).

Prospective jurors must in general be summoned formally in writing (Coroners Act 1988, s. 8(2)(a); Coroners Rules 1984, r. 45). There is an exception where a jury would be otherwise *incomplete*. Here, the coroner can require any person(s) in the vicinity of the place of the inquest to be summoned without written notice (for example, by informal oral communication with them) in order to make up the correct number of jurors required (Coroners Rules 1984, r. 48; this provision is analogous to s. 6 of the Juries Act 1974 (see para 7.4), which applies to the informal summoning of jurors to the Crown Court, High Court and county courts). There is, however, no power to summon an *entire* jury by means of an informal oral communication (*R* v *Merseyside Coroner (ex parte Carr)* [1993] 4 All ER 65, DC, in which inquest proceedings were declared to be a nullity where the entire jury of nine had been obtained informally from a pool of jurors waiting at the nearby Crown Court).

A coroner has no *statutory* power to discharge a juror. It is not certain whether he has a *common law* power to do so without having to start the inquest all over again with a fresh jury. It has been suggested, *obiter*, that a coroner has a common law power to discharge a juror and to continue the inquest provided that the number of jurors does not fall below the minimum number of seven (*R* v *Merseyside Coroner (ex parte Carr)*, above, *per* Neill LJ at p. 73).

At the inquest witnesses attend and give evidence on oath. If necessary, their attendance can be compelled. The procedure is inquisitorial, unlike the procedure in the ordinary courts of law. There is no right to legal representation, although it may be allowed at the coroner's discretion. Thus, while legal representation was permitted to the Anti-Nazi League by the Hammersmith coroner at the Blair Peach inquest in 1979 (para 2.5.6 below), it was denied to the Foreign Office by the West Yorkshire coroner at the inquest in 1982 into the death in Saudi Arabia of the British nurse, Helen Smith. Interested parties or their representatives are permitted to question witnesses. 'Representatives' include authorised advocates (as defined in s. 119(1) of the Courts and Legal Services Act 1990) and not just barristers and solicitors (Coroners Rules 1984, r. 20(1), as amended by the Coroners (Amendment) Rules 1999 (SI 1999, No. 3325)). Within his limited role in the legal process, it is somewhat anomalous that a coroner has wider powers than those of a High Court judge. Unlike the latter, the coroner decides which witnesses to call and then takes an active part in their examination. If the evidence given at the inquest is likely to be of a technical nature, the coroner is entitled to invite an assessor to sit with him if he considers it necessary to do so. Under the control of the coroner, the assessor can examine witnesses who give technical evidence. However, he must not be allowed to give expert evidence himself since that could create the impression that the assessor's evidence was accorded by the coroner greater weight than it deserved (*R* v *Surrey Coroner (ex parte Wright)* [1997] 1 All ER 823).

With the exception of the coroner's summing-up to the jury, no person is allowed to address the jury (or the coroner) on the *facts* (Coroners Rules 1984, r. 40). The coroner must, however, allow submissions on the *law* to be made to him, such as a submission (made in the absence of the jury) about what verdict ought or ought not to be left to the jury. A coroner's failure to do so may amount to a violation of natural justice leading to the quashing of the inquest by the High Court (*R* v *Southwark Coroner (ex parte Hicks)* [1987] 2 All ER 140, DC; *R* v *East Berkshire Coroner (ex parte Buckley)* (1992) *The Times*, 1 December, DC).

Where a jury has been used at the inquest, its verdict need not be unanimous as long as there are not more than two dissentients (Coroners Act 1988, s. 12(2)). The jury cannot return a verdict of murder, manslaughter or infanticide against a named person (ibid., s. 11(6)). The appropriate verdict in such circumstances is that the deceased was killed unlawfully. The standard of proof required for a verdict of unlawful killing is the standard applicable in criminal cases, namely, satisfaction beyond reasonable doubt (*R* v *West London Coroner (ex parte Gray)* [1987] 2 All ER 129, DC; *R* v *Wolverhampton Coroner (ex parte McCurbin)* [1990] 2 All ER 759, CA). If criminal proceedings are already pending in respect of the death, the inquest is adjourned until the outcome of those proceedings is known (ibid., s. 16(1)). The coroner may then resume the adjourned inquest if he thinks there is sufficient cause to do so (ibid., s. 16(3)). However, the finding of the inquest must not be inconsistent with the outcome of the criminal proceedings (ibid., s. 16(7)). The decision whether to resume an adjourned inquest under s. 16(3) is clearly of a highly discretionary nature. The coroner, however, need only be satisfied that there is 'sufficient cause' for a resumption; it is not necessary that there should be exceptional circumstances (*R* v *Inner West London Coroner (ex parte Dallaglio)* [1994] 4 All ER 139, CA; see further on this case, para 2.5.5 below).

If, before the conclusion of an inquest, the coroner is informed by the Lord Chancellor that (a) a public inquiry conducted or chaired by a judge is being, or is to be, held into the circumstances of the death, and (b) the Lord Chancellor considers that the cause of death is likely to be adequately investigated by the inquiry, the coroner must adjourn the inquest unless there is an 'exceptional reason' not to do so (Coroners Act 1988, s. 17A(1), as inserted by the Access to Justice Act 1999). If the inquest is adjourned, the Lord Chancellor must send the coroner the findings of the public inquiry as soon as reasonably practicable after their publication (ibid., s. 17A(3)). The inquest must not be resumed by the coroner unless in his opinion there is an exceptional reason for doing so (ibid., s. 17A(4)). If the inquest is not resumed, the coroner must send to the registrar of deaths a signed certificate stating the findings of the public inquiry (ibid., s. 17A(6)). These provisions significantly reduce the possibility that concurrent inquests and public inquiries into the same deaths will produce inconsistent findings of fact.

Other verdicts suggested by the Coroners Rules 1984 include death from natural causes, death from dependence on drugs or non-dependent abuse of drugs, death by accident or misadventure (in effect, there is no distinction between these two words; in modern parlance, 'accident' is to be preferred: *R* v *Portsmouth Coroner (ex parte Anderson)* [1988] 2 All ER

604, DC), that the deceased killed himself, and an open verdict for use where the evidence does not fully disclose the cause of death. It should be noted that *suicide* is never to be presumed. It must be proved by evidence and, if it is not, the appropriate verdict is an open one (*R* v *Cardiff Coroner (ex parte Thomas)* [1970] 3 All ER 469, DC; *R* v *HM Coroner for the City of London (ex parte Barber)* [1975] 3 All ER 538, DC). Suicide is not an appropriate verdict unless the death has ensued within a year and a day of a self-inflicted injury (*R* v *Inner West London Coroner (ex parte De Luca)* [1988] 3 All ER 414, DC). In the case of a death caused by casual glue-sniffing, the appropriate verdict is death by solvent abuse, or a similar verdict, rather than the more offensive and uninformative one of death by drug abuse (*R* v *Inner South London Coroner (ex parte Kendall)* [1989] 1 All ER 72, DC).

2.5.5   Judicial review of coroner's proceedings

It is not possible to appeal against the finding of a coroner's inquest. The proceedings are, however, subject to judicial review in the High Court, which has an inherent common law power of supervision over inquests, and, on an application by an interested private citizen, may be quashed by certiorari for fraud, excess or refusal of jurisdiction, violation of the principles of natural justice, or for an error of law made within the coroner's jurisdiction. (For the distinction between an appeal and judicial review, see para 11.12.) In *R* v *Inner West London Coroner (ex parte Dallaglio)* [1994] 4 All ER 139, CA, a coroner's decisions were quashed by certiorari on the ground of his apparent bias. The case arose following the deaths in August 1989 of 51 people in a collision on the River Thames between the dredger *Bowbelle* and the passenger launch *Marchioness.* Inquests were opened but adjourned pending the outcome of criminal proceedings against the master of the dredger. In an official letter, the coroner described some relatives and survivors as 'mentally unwell', and, at a meeting with journalists, he referred to one bereaved mother as 'unhinged'. He later decided, first, not to accede to a request from some of the bereaved families to remove himself from the proceedings on the ground of apparent bias, and, secondly, not to resume the inquests. It was held that the coroner's unfortunate choice of words had given rise to a real possibility that he had unconsciously allowed himself to become biased against the relatives. His decisions were quashed and the matter was remitted to a different coroner for a fresh decision on whether there should be a resumption of the inquests. (A different coroner ordered the inquests to be resumed and, in April 1995, a coroner's jury brought in a verdict of unlawful killing. See *The Times,* 8 April 1995, and see further on this case, para 11.8.3.2.1.)

Instead of judicial review, the matter may be taken to the High Court, in the form of a statutory application to quash the inquest, by or with the authority of the Attorney-General under s. 13 of the Coroners Act 1988. Under this statutory procedure the grounds for interference are probably wider than those available to the court at common law, extending as they do to 'fraud, rejection of evidence, irregularity of proceedings, insufficiency of inquiry, the discovery of new facts or evidence or otherwise' (ibid., s. 13(1)). The High Court has power to quash an inquest and order a fresh one on these grounds where it is necessary or desirable in the interests of justice to do so. It is not necessary to show a *probability* that a fresh inquest would produce a different verdict; a *possibility* of a different verdict is sufficient (*Re Rapier (deceased)* [1986] 3 All ER 726, DC, in which it was the coroner himself who made, through the Attorney-General, the successful statutory application to quash; but note *R* v *Inner London North District Coroner (ex parte Linnane) (No.*

2) [1991] COD 12, DC, and *R* v *West Berkshire Coroner (ex parte Thomas)* (1991) *The Times,* 25 April, DC, in both of which a fresh inquest was refused despite irregularities in the course of the original inquest). If the High Court decides to interfere, its powers are limited to quashing the proceedings and ordering a fresh inquest. It has no power to substitute a verdict for one wrongly returned at the inquest, although such a power has been said to be desirable (*R* v *Birmingham and Solihull Coroner (ex parte Secretary of State for the Home Department)* (1990) *The Independent,* 2 August, DC, *per* Watkins LJ).

Although it is possible to seek to have an inquest quashed by combining an application under s. 13 of the Coroners Act 1988 with an application for judicial review, it has been held to be preferable to proceed under s. 13 in cases where the Attorney-General has given his authority under that section (*R* v *West Berkshire Coroner (ex parte Thomas),* above).

Section 13 may also be used to compel the holding of an inquest in cases where the coroner refuses or neglects to hold one which ought to be held.

2.5.6 Circumstances in which a coroner's jury is compulsory

There are some circumstances in which the summoning of a jury is compulsory. By s. 8(3) of the Coroners Act 1988, the coroner *must* have a jury in cases of:

(a)   Deaths in prison.

(b)   Deaths occurring in police custody or resulting from an injury caused by a police officer in the purported execution of his duty.

(c)   Deaths caused by an accident, poisoning or disease, notice of which is required to be given to a government department under any statute or to a health and safety at work inspector.

(d)   Deaths occurring 'in circumstances the continuance or possible recurrence of which is prejudicial to the health or safety of the public'.

Category (b) was introduced in 1982 following public disquiet over, *inter alia,* the number of deaths occurring in police custody. 'Police custody' for this purpose does not necessarily involve direct physical control of a person. Thus, a man was held to have died 'in police custody', within the meaning of s. 8(3)(b) of the Coroners Act 1988, where he died in a hospital without a police guard. The man had become ill and had been moved to the hospital from the police station at which he had begun to serve a term of imprisonment because of overcrowding in the prisons. The court granted an order of mandamus directing the coroner to summon a jury (*R* v *Inner London North District Coroner (ex parte Linnane)* [1989] 2 All ER 254, DC). The man's son was concerned that any neglect in his father's care should be publicly exposed. When at the subsequent inquest the jury returned a verdict of death from natural causes, the coroner having refused to call as a witness a doctor consulted by the son and having withdrawn the issue of lack of care from the jury, the son applied under s. 13 of the Coroners Act 1988 (see para 2.5.5 above) to have the inquest quashed. It was held that, although there had been 'rejection of evidence' and 'insufficiency of inquiry' on the part of the coroner within the meaning of s. 13, the application would be dismissed since it would be wrong to order a fresh inquest 21 months after the death and there was little evidence to show lack of care by the police (*R* v *Inner London North District Coroner (ex parte Linnane) (No. 2)* [1991] COD 12, DC).

The words in category (d) fell to be construed by the Court of Appeal in *R* v *Hammersmith Coroner (ex parte Peach)* [1980] 2 All ER 7, CA, a case which was decided before the addition of category (b) to the list. A teacher from New Zealand, Blair Peach, was killed in Southall while watching a demonstration which turned into a riot. It was alleged that the violent blow to the head which killed the deceased was struck by a police officer. It was further alleged that the weapon used was much heavier than a police truncheon. Police inquiries unearthed a number of unauthorised weapons in the lockers of policemen who had been present at the demonstration. The coroner refused to summon a jury to the inquest and the deceased's family applied to the Divisional Court of the Queen's Bench Division for orders of certiorari and mandamus. The Divisional Court refused the orders but, on appeal, the Court of Appeal granted certiorari to quash the coroner's decision to sit without a jury and granted mandamus to compel him to have a jury when the inquest resumed.

The Court of Appeal held that the true construction of the words in category (d), above, was that the coroner must sit with a jury if the circumstances of the death were such that similar fatalities might recur and it was reasonable to expect that proper action ought to be taken by some responsible public body to prevent that happening. In the present case, there was reason to suspect that the death had resulted from the unauthorised use of a potentially lethal weapon by a police officer. In that situation the presence of a jury was required because, if that suspicion was confirmed, it would be reasonable to expect the police authority to take action to prevent it happening again. The possible recurrence of those circumstances would be 'prejudicial to the health or safety of the public' (see the other examples given by Lord Denning MR, [1980] 2 All ER 7 at p. 10).

There need be no causative link between the deceased's death and the circumstances in which it occurred. Accordingly, a coroner must summon a jury if the deceased has died in circumstances the continuance or possible recurrence of which would be prejudicial to public health or safety even though they may not have caused the deceased's death (*R v Inner London North District Coroner (ex parte Linnane)* [1989] 2 All ER 254, DC).

If the circumstances of the case come within s. 8(3)(d), the coroner must summon a jury even though the death took place abroad. In the case of *In re Neal (coroner: jury)* (1995) *The Times*, 9 December, DC, the death occurred in a holiday apartment in Spain and was caused by carbon monoxide gas emanating from a water heater. The Surrey coroner sat without a jury and returned an open verdict. The deceased's father applied under s. 13 of the Coroners Act 1988 to have the inquest quashed and a fresh one ordered. In deciding that the coroner should have sat with a jury, the court said it was just as important that travellers to Spain should be protected from the dangers of gas heaters as those who stayed at home. However, the court, in the exercise of its discretion, declined to quash the inquest: the case was an old one, the death having occurred two years earlier, and in the circumstances an open verdict could not be impugned as irrational.

2.6 PUBLIC FUNDING OF PROCEEDINGS

Public funding is available for proceedings in most of the courts discussed in this chapter.

The Court of Justice of the European Communities can itself grant public funding. However, in the case of an application for a preliminary ruling under art. 177 (now art. 234) (para 2.1.3.3 above) it will only do so if public funding is not available under the domestic law of the country from which the reference emanated. This is because the reference is regarded as a step in the national proceedings and the Court of Justice will normally leave questions of costs and funding to be determined by the national court. Public funding under our domestic Community Legal Service is available in such proceedings originating in courts in England and Wales.

Public funding is available for proceedings in the Employment Appeal Tribunal (Access to Justice Act 1999, sch. 2).

Public funding is *not* available for proceedings in the Judicial Committee of the Privy Council (except in relation to its jurisdiction under the Government of Wales Act 1998, the Scotland Act 1998, or the Northern Ireland Act 1998: ibid.), or in coroners' courts. For access to justice and public funding, see para 1.9.

3

Tribunals

3.1 INTRODUCTION

Alongside the ordinary civil courts already described in Chapters 1 and 2 there exist many hundreds of tribunals dealing with a wide variety of disputes arising between the individual citizen and the state or between citizen and citizen. The proliferation of tribunals has been a special feature of the development of judicial administration in England and Wales over recent decades. The number of tribunals and their importance have increased so significantly that it is no longer justifiable to regard tribunals merely as an appendage to the ordinary courts of law. They are an integral part of the ordinary legal process, a position which has been reached largely due to the implementation of the *Report of the Committee on Administrative Tribunals and Enquiries* (the Franks Committee), Cmnd 218, 1957. Most of the committee's recommendations were implemented by the Tribunals and Inquiries Act 1958, since repealed and replaced by the Tribunals and Inquiries Act 1971, which, in turn, was repealed and replaced by the Tribunals and Inquiries Act 1992.

The distinction between a court and a tribunal was noted in para 1.1.4. Tribunals are regarded as inferior to the ordinary courts of law, even though for the most part they are independent in the exercise of their various jurisdictions. Because of this inferiority, and by reason of the fact that even tribunals described as 'administrative' are exercising *judicial* functions, they are subject to the supervisory prerogative jurisdiction of the High Court so that complaints of unlawful conduct on the part of tribunals may lead to the granting of remedies against them by the Queen's Bench Division (Chapter 11).

The workload of tribunals greatly exceeds that of the county courts. As with the county courts, most of the cases heard by tribunals are small cases. Even in a small case, however, the outcome is of great importance to the parties directly involved. Some matters heard by tribunals involve substantial sums of money, as in the case of industrial injuries claims determined by social security appeal tribunals, or claims for redundancy payments or compensation for unfair dismissal determined by employment tribunals. Others may involve the deprivation of a person's freedom, as in the decision of a mental health review tribunal that a patient should not be discharged from compulsory detention.

In this chapter it is proposed to examine (i) administrative tribunals, which have been established by statute to resolve a myriad of specific disputes; (ii) employment tribunals, an important species of administrative tribunal, which hear certain defined disputes arising out of the employment relationship; and (iii) domestic tribunals, which are usually established privately in order to enforce discipline within a profession or trade union.

3.2 ADMINISTRATIVE (OR STATUTORY) TRIBUNALS

3.2.1 Reasons for existence

Administrative tribunals are established, in the main, to resolve disputes between a private citizen and a central government department, such as claims to social security benefits, disputes which require the application of specialised knowledge or experience, such as the assessment of compensation following the compulsory purchase of land, and other disputes which by their nature or quantity are considered unsuitable for the ordinary courts, such as fixing a fair rent for premises or immigration appeals.

The main reasons for the creation of administrative tribunals may be identified as the relief of congestion in the ordinary courts of law, the provision of a speedier and cheaper procedure than that afforded by the ordinary courts, and the desire to have specific issues dealt with by persons with an intimate knowledge and experience of the problems involved. Thus, tax experts sit as Special Commissioners of income tax, surveyors sit on the Lands Tribunal, and medical practitioners sit on medical boards and medical appeal tribunals to determine medical questions under the industrial injuries scheme.

3.2.2 Defects in the tribunal system

Several criticisms of administrative tribunals are common.

(a) In the case of a few tribunals, *legal representation* is not permitted. However, before the vast majority of tribunals representation *is* allowed, whether by a lawyer, trade union official, social worker or other person.

(b) A more fundamental criticism is that, with a few exceptions *public funding* is not available for representation in tribunal proceedings. (See further, para 3.5 below.)

(c) Some tribunals decide disputes to which the government minister who appointed the members of the tribunal is a party. This makes it difficult for a tribunal to achieve the *appearance* of impartiality, although there is no evidence of bias *in fact* towards a minister's case. The Franks Committee recommended that all chairmen of tribunals should be appointed by the Lord Chancellor and that other members should be appointed by the Council on Tribunals. (The Council was established by the Tribunals and Inquiries Act 1958. It consists of up to 15 members and exists to supervise the working of specified tribunals. It must be consulted before new procedural rules are made.) These proposals were not acceptable to the government of the day, although in many cases a compromise formula has been reached under which the Lord Chancellor appoints a panel of chairmen from which the appropriate minister makes his selection. Ordinary members are usually appointed by the appropriate minister, but quite often they are not dismissible without the consent of the Lord Chancellor.

(d) There remain a few instances where tribunals are not obliged to give *reasons for their decisions.* However, in the case of the vast majority of tribunals reasons for decisions must now be given if requested (Tribunals and Inquiries Act 1992, s. 10). The reasons may be furnished either in writing or orally and are taken to form part of the decision of the tribunal and, as such, to be incorporated in the record (ibid., s. 10(6)), even if given orally. This provision enables the High Court, on an application for judicial review, to quash a tribunal's decision for error of law on the face of the record if any reason given is bad in law (para 11.8.3.3).

(e) Sometimes there is *no right of appeal* against a tribunal's decision, although an application for judicial review is not an 'appeal' and may therefore be made to the High Court, on the grounds of error of law on the face of the record, violation of the principles of natural justice, or excess of jurisdiction, notwithstanding the fact that an 'appeal' is precluded. (For the distinction between an appeal and judicial review, see para 11.12.) Since administrative tribunals are statutory bodies, a right of appeal can only be conferred by statute. In fact, a right of appeal does exist from the decisions of most tribunals, although Parliament has not prescribed a uniform appellate procedure. In some instances, an appeal lies from one tribunal to another; in others, it lies from a tribunal to a minister. Or, again, an appeal may lie from a tribunal to a court of law.

3.2.3   Control of administrative tribunals

To a large extent the criticisms of administrative tribunals mentioned in para 3.2.2 are countered by other rules of law. Thus, tribunals are obliged to observe the principles of natural justice, namely, that no man may be a judge in his own cause (the rule against bias) and that both sides to the dispute must be heard and, moreover, given a hearing which is fair (see further, para 11.8.3.2). Administrative tribunals are public statutory bodies inferior to the ordinary courts of law and, as such, they are subject to the supervision of the Queen's Bench Division of the High Court, which, on an application for judicial review of a tribunal's decision, may issue the prerogative remedies of certiorari, mandamus and prohibition. It may do so for a variety of reasons, such as where there has been a violation of the principles of natural justice, or where the tribunal has refused to exercise its jurisdiction in a particular case or has exceeded or threatened to exceed its jurisdiction, or where the tribunal has made an error of law. (For judicial review and the prerogative remedies, see Chapter 11.)

3.2.4   Examples of administrative tribunals

There are over 2,000 tribunals falling under the supervision of the Council on Tribunals. The enormous variation from one tribunal to another in terms of composition, jurisdiction, procedure and appeal machinery makes it difficult to describe and compare tribunals. One common factor is that they were all created by Act of Parliament. Some examples of the more important administrative tribunals are the Immigration Appeal Tribunal, employment tribunals, the Lands Tribunal, medical appeal tribunals, mental health review tribunals, valuation tribunals, rent tribunals, rent assessment committees, General Commissioners of income tax, Special Commissioners of income tax, Social Security Commissioners, social security appeal tribunals and the traffic commissioners.

3.3   EMPLOYMENT TRIBUNALS

3.3.1   Introduction

The employment tribunals, which sit locally, were originally established as 'industrial tribunals' with a somewhat limited role by the Industrial Training Act 1964, since when their jurisdiction has been expanded considerably — notably under the employment legislation of the 1960s and 1970s. Their composition, jurisdiction and procedure are now regulated by the Employment Tribunals Act 1996 and regulations made thereunder by the Secretary of State for Employment.

'Industrial tribunals' were renamed 'employment tribunals' by the Employment Rights (Dispute Resolution) Act 1998 with effect from 1 August 1998.

3.3.2 Composition

When hearing a case, each employment tribunal is normally composed of a legally qualified chairman sitting with two lay members. However, with the consent of the parties a case can be heard by the chairman and one lay member. Some proceedings may be heard by the chairman sitting alone (Employment Tribunals Act 1996, s. 4).

The chairman, who is appointed by the Lord Chancellor, must have a seven-year general qualification within the meaning of s. 71 of the Courts and Legal Services Act 1990 (Employment Tribunals (Constitution and Rules of Procedure) Regulations 1993 (SI 1993, No. 2687), reg. 5(1)). The lay members are taken from panels appointed by the Secretary of State after consultation with appropriate organisations representing employers and employees respectively (ibid.).

3.3.3 Procedure and appeals

An employment tribunal normally sits in public, except where it is in the interests of national security or of confidentiality to sit in private (Employment Tribunals Act 1996, s. 10(2)). It has been held that the correct test for deciding whether a hearing is in public is not whether any member of the public is prevented from attending it, but whether he is able to attend if he wishes to do so. Thus, a hearing conducted in an office within a secure area and behind a locked door with a push-button coded lock is not a public hearing because the coded door lock is a physical barrier preventing all access to the public and eliminating any chance of a member of the public 'dropping in' to see how the tribunal proceedings are conducted. The fact that no one actually attempts to gain access is irrelevant — the tribunal is sitting in private when it has no jurisdiction to do so (*Storer* v *British Gas plc* [2000] 2 All ER 440, CA).

The proceedings are comparatively informal as the strict rules of evidence do not apply. Any party may appear before an employment tribunal in person or be represented by counsel or by a solicitor or by a representative of a trade union or an employers' association or by any other person whom he desires to represent him (ibid., s. 6). This right to representation is an unqualified right, and the tribunal has no power to stop a party's chosen representative from acting or to order that party to represent himself (*Bache* v *Essex County Council* (2000) *The Times*, 2 February, CA).

The tribunal will normally only award costs against a party if he has acted frivolously or vexatiously in relation to the proceedings. The decision of the tribunal may be unanimous or by majority. An appeal lies to the Employment Appeal Tribunal from most decisions of an employment tribunal, but the appeal can be taken only on questions of *law* as opposed to *fact*.

3.3.4 Jurisdiction

The jurisdiction of the employment tribunals includes the following matters:

(a)   Questions relating to written particulars of employment (Employment Rights Act 1996, ss. 1 and 11; and see *Mears* v *Safecar Security Ltd* [1982] 2 All ER 865, CA).

(b)   Questions relating to redundancy payments (ibid., s. 163).

(c)   Disputes relating to equality clauses under the equal pay legislation (Equal Pay Act 1970, s. 2 as substituted by the Sex Discrimination Act 1975, sch. 3).

(d)   Complaints of unfair dismissal (Employment Rights Act 1996, s. 111).

(e)   Appeals against improvement and prohibition notices under the health and safety legislation (Health and Safety at Work etc. Act 1974, s. 24).

(f)   Complaints of unlawful sexual discrimination in employment (Sex Discrimination Act 1975, s. 63). As a result of the Sex Discrimination and Equal Pay (Remedies) Regulations 1993 (SI 1993, No. 2798) there is now no limit on the amount of compensation an employment tribunal can award for unlawful acts of sexual discrimination. These regulations were made in consequence of *Marshall* v *Southampton and South West Hampshire Area Health Authority (No. 2)* [1993] 4 All ER 586, CJEC, in which the European Court held that it was contrary to Community law to have an upper limit to the compensation payable for discriminatory dismissal. The abolition of the upper limit led to such high awards being made against the Ministry of Defence for unlawfully dismissing servicewomen on the ground of pregnancy that the Employment Appeal Tribunal found it necessary to lay down guidelines for employment tribunals when assessing compensation in such cases (*Ministry of Defence* v *Cannock* [1995] 2 All ER 449, EAT).

(g)   Complaints of unlawful racial discrimination in employment (Race Relations Act 1976, s. 54). By virtue of the Race Relations (Remedies) Act 1994 there is now no limit on the amount of compensation an employment tribunal can award for unlawful acts of racial discrimination. The same rule thus applies to both sexual and racial discrimination. As mentioned above, the upper limit on compensation for sexual discrimination was removed in 1993 in response to the decision of the European Court in *Marshall* v *Southampton and South West Hampshire Area Health Authority (No. 2)*.

(h)   Complaints relating to maternity pay; time off work for trade union activities, for public duties or to look for work or training; refusal to provide a written statement of reasons for dismissal; and failure to provide an itemised pay statement (Employment Rights Act 1996, ss. 70 (maternity pay), 51 (public duties), 54 (seeking work or training), 93 (written reasons for dismissal), and 11 (itemised pay statement); Trade Union and Labour Relations (Consolidation) Act 1992, ss. 146, 168 and 170 (trade union activities)).

(i)   Complaints of unlawful deductions from wages (Wages Act 1986, s. 5).

(j)   Complaints of unreasonable exclusion or expulsion from a trade union where there exists a union membership agreement (Trade Union and Labour Relations (Consolidation) Act 1992, s. 174; see para 3.4.2 below).

(k)   Complaints from individuals of having been unjustifiably disciplined by a trade union (ibid., s. 66; see para 3.4.2 below).

(l)   Complaints of unlawful refusal of employment, or of the services of an employment agency, on grounds related to trade union membership (ibid., ss. 137 and 138).

(m)   Complaints of unlawful disability discrimination in employment (Disability Discrimination Act 1995, s. 8). Consistent with the treatment of awards for unlawful sexual and racial discrimination, there is no upper limit on the amount of compensation awardable for unlawful disability discrimination.

(n)   In addition, the Lord Chancellor has power to confer jurisdiction on the employment tribunals to hear claims for damages for breach of the contract of employment or of any other contract connected with employment, excluding claims for damages for personal injuries (Employment Tribunals Act 1996, s. 3). The Lord Chancellor did not exercise this power until 1994, although it had existed since 1971 (Industrial Relations Act 1971, s. 113, replaced by s. 109 of the Employment Protection Act 1975, which, in turn, was replaced by s. 131 of the Employment Protection (Consolidation) Act 1978; the provision is now contained in s. 3 of the Employment Tribunals Act 1996). The failure of the Lord Chancellor before 1994 to implement s. 131 of the Employment Protection (Consolidation) Act 1978, or either of its predecessors, had attracted considerable judicial criticism (see, e.g., *Treganowan* v *Robert Knee & Co. Ltd* [1975] ICR 405 *per* Phillips J at p. 411; *Secretary of State for Employment* v *Globe Elastic Thread Co.* [1980] AC 506, HL, *per* Lord Wilberforce at p. 519; *O'Laoire* v *Jackel International Ltd* [1990] ICR 197, CA, *per* Lord Donaldson MR at p. 207; *Barlow* v *Whittle* [1990] ICR 270, EAT, *per* Wood J at p. 275; *Delaney* v *Staples* [1992] 1 All ER 944, HL, *per* Lord Browne-Wilkinson at p. 952).

The employment tribunals have been given jurisdiction to adjudicate upon contract claims made by both employees and employers which arise, or are outstanding, on the termination of the employee's employment. Excluded are claims for breach of a contractual term relating to intellectual property, restraint of trade, the provision of living accommodation, or the imposition of an obligation of confidence. There is a limit of £25,000 on the amount of compensation that can be ordered to be paid in these proceedings (Employment Tribunals Extension of Jurisdiction (England and Wales) Order 1994 (SI 1994, No. 1623)).

3.4 DOMESTIC TRIBUNALS

3.4.1 Introduction

Most domestic tribunals are set up by private bodies for their own internal purposes. Examples are the disciplinary committees of a trade union, professional association, university or college. These domestic tribunals differ from administrative tribunals in that the latter are set up by *statute* to decide matters of a more *public* nature. Some domestic tribunals, however, are created by statute, such as the bodies mentioned earlier which have been established to regulate conduct in particular professions (para 2.2.3.2).

3.4.2 Control by the ordinary courts of law

All domestic tribunals, however created, are subject to the control of the ordinary courts of law in two ways. First, a domestic tribunal must observe the principles of natural justice. If it fails to do so, its proceedings may be challenged in the courts. For example, in *R* v *Aston University Senate (ex parte Roffey)* [1969] 2 QB 538, DC, it was made clear that a student ought not to be expelled from his university (not even for failing his examinations twice) without first being given an opportunity of making representations in his own defence. On the facts of this particular case, however, relief was refused because of the applicants' delay in seeking it.

Secondly, a domestic tribunal, however created, must not exceed its jurisdiction as laid down in its rules or its statute of creation. For example, a trade union which acted *ultra vires* (beyond its powers) by expelling a member for some conduct not covered by its rules could be sued for a declaration (*Kelly* v *NATSOPA* (1915) 84 LJKB 2236, CA) that the expulsion was wrongful and for an injunction (*Lee* v *Showmen's Guild* [1952] 2 QB 329, CA) to prevent the union from acting on the wrongful expulsion. The expelled person may, in addition, be awarded damages for breach of the contract that exists between a member and his trade union, the basis of which is the union rules. If the wrongful expulsion has caused financial loss, as where the claimant was unable to find another job because of the operation of a closed shop, which happened in *Bonsor* v *Musicians' Union* [1956] AC 104, HL, the damages may be quite substantial.

In relation to trade union membership, there are special statutory procedures which exist *in addition to* the common law position just discussed. First, a person has the right not to be excluded or expelled from a trade union except in accordance with statute (Trade Union and Labour Relations (Consolidation) Act 1992, s. 174(1), as substituted by the Trade Union Reform and Employment Rights Act 1993). If this right is infringed, a complaint may be made to an employment tribunal, which, if it finds that the complaint is well founded, must make a declaration to that effect (Trade Union and Labour Relations (Consolidation) Act 1992, s. 174(5) and s. 176(1), as substituted by the Employment Rights Act 1996). An appeal lies to the Employment Appeal Tribunal, on any question of *law,* from the decision of the employment tribunal (Employment Tribunals Act 1996, s. 21(1)). Having first obtained a declaration, the complainant may then apply for an award of monetary compensation. If at the time of such application the complainant has been admitted or readmitted to membership of the union, the application for compensation is made to an employment tribunal. If he has not been so admitted or readmitted, the application is made to the Employment Appeal Tribunal (Trade Union and Labour Relations (Consolidation) Act 1992, s. 176(2)). Where an employment tribunal has jurisdiction, an appeal lies from the tribunal's decision to the Employment Appeal Tribunal, on a question of *law* (Employment Tribunals Act 1996, s. 21(1)).

Secondly, a person who is or has at any time been a member of a trade union has the right not to be unjustifiably disciplined by that union (Trade Union and Labour Relations (Consolidation) Act 1992, s. 64). If this right is violated, a complaint may be made to an employment tribunal, which, if it finds that the complaint is well founded, must make a declaration to that effect (ibid., s. 66(1) and (3)). An appeal lies, on a question of *law* only, from the decision of the employment tribunal to the Employment Appeal Tribunal (Employment Tribunals Act 1996, s. 21(1)). The successful complainant may then make an application for compensation from the trade union and/or the return of any fine imposed on him by the union. If at the time of the application the decision to discipline him has been withdrawn, or the union has taken all necessary steps for ensuring the revocation of any disciplinary measure already imposed, the application for compensation is made to an employment tribunal. If these conditions are not satisfied, the application is made to the Employment Appeal Tribunal (Trade Union and Labour Relations (Consolidation) Act 1992, s. 67(1) and (2)). Where an employment tribunal has jurisdiction, an appeal lies, on a question of *law* only, from the tribunal's decision to the Employment Appeal Tribunal (Employment Tribunals Act 1996, s. 21(1)).

3.4.3 Remedies against domestic tribunals

It has been seen that all domestic tribunals are under an obligation to observe the principles of natural justice and to act within their powers. A breach of either obligation may lead to the intervention of the ordinary courts of law at the suit of an interested party. There is, however, a difference in the remedies available according to the type of tribunal involved. For unlawful conduct on the part of domestic tribunals exercising functions which are purely *private,* the appropriate remedies are the private law remedies of declarations, injunctions and damages. The powers of such voluntary tribunals exist within the field of private contract law and the prerogative remedies of certiorari, mandamus and prohibition, which operate in the field of public law, are not available against them. They are not public bodies performing public duties (*R* v *Criminal Injuries Compensation Board (ex parte Lain)* [1967] 2 QB 864, DC, *per* Lord Parker CJ at p. 882).

The legal position remains the same after the introduction in 1978 of a new procedure for claiming public-law remedies, called an 'application for judicial review'. Thus, in *R* v *British Broadcasting Corporation (ex parte Lavelle)* [1983] 1 All ER 241 it was held that an application for judicial review was not available as a procedure for challenging the decision of a disciplinary tribunal set up by the BBC. The appropriate remedy against a tribunal of this character is to seek damages, or an injunction or declaration, in ordinary private-law proceedings for breach of contract, although, if such a remedy has already been inappropriately claimed in an application for judicial review, the court has a discretion to allow the proceedings to continue as if they had been begun as an ordinary action by writ (RSC, Ord. 53, r. 9(5); para 11.11.6). This is a sensible provision which obviates the necessity to refuse the application and compel the claimant to start the action all over again, with a consequent throwing away of legal costs, before a different court.

On the other hand, the prerogative remedies *are* available against domestic tribunals exercising functions of a *public* nature (see *R* v *Panel on Takeovers and Mergers (ex parte Datafin plc)* [1987] 1 All ER 564, CA; para 11.11.2).

3.5 PUBLIC FUNDING OF PROCEEDINGS

Public funding for representation is available in proceedings before the Lands Tribunal, the Commons Commissioners, immigration adjudicators, the Immigration Appeal Tribunal, and mental health review tribunals. It is also available in the Employment Appeal Tribunal, but this is a court rather than a tribunal (see paras 1.1.4 and 2.3.1).

Research has shown that representation before tribunals significantly improves a claimant's chances of success. However, public funding is not available for most administrative tribunal proceedings. Thus, for example, although there is an unrestricted right to representation in such important tribunals as employment tribunals, social security appeal tribunals, Social Security Commissioners and medical appeal tribunals, no public funds are available to assist with the cost of representation. Persons involved in proceedings before such tribunals may, however, qualify for other forms of help under the Community Legal Service.

For access to justice and public funding, see para 1.9.

4

Bail and Habeas Corpus

4.1 INTRODUCTION

Bail and the writ of habeas corpus provide two separate methods of securing freedom from custody. Bail is the appropriate method where a person has been charged with a criminal offence and is in lawful custody awaiting trial, while habeas corpus proceedings lie where a person has been detained *unlawfully* and whether that detention has arisen out of a criminal case, such as a wrongful arrest by a police officer, or a civil case, such as a false imprisonment by a private citizen.

4.2 BAIL

Bail is the release from custody, pending a criminal trial, of a defendant on the promise that money will be paid if he absconds. Decisions on bail involve the balancing of competing interests. A person is presumed innocent of a criminal charge until he is proved guilty of it. This well-known principle suggests that no one should ever be kept in detention awaiting trial. Yet it is impossible to release all defendants on bail because of the danger that they might abscond, interfere with witnesses or commit further offences. At the same time, there is a reasonably held fear that some defendants, who could quite safely be bailed, are locked away, thereby adding to the problem of the already overcrowded prison population.

In an effort to mitigate some of these difficulties, new provisions relating to bail were introduced by the Bail Act 1976. This Act (s. 3(2)) abolished personal recognizances (sums payable by the defendant himself if he failed to appear for trial), although recognizances still remain for sureties (persons who 'stand bail' for the defendant). Recognizances from the defendant were replaced by a duty imposed upon him to surrender to custody (Bail Act 1976, s. 3(1)). This duty is enforceable in criminal proceedings for the offence of absconding while on bail (ibid., s. 6(1)). This offence is committed by a person who, having been released on bail in criminal proceedings, fails without reasonable cause to surrender to custody (ibid.). The offence is punishable either on summary conviction or as if it were a criminal contempt of court (ibid., s. 6(5)). It is not triable on indictment (*Schiavo* v *Anderton* [1987] QB 20, DC; *Practice Note* [1987] 1 All ER 128; *Murphy* v *DPP* [1990] 2 All ER 390, DC).

Absconding while on bail is not, and never has been, a contempt of court. It follows that it is punishable only under the Bail Act 1976 and not under the Contempt of Court Act 1981 (*R* v *Reader* (1987) 84 Cr App R 294, CA; *R* v *Lubega* (1999) *The Times*, 10 February, CA. For punishment under the Contempt of Court Act 1981, see para 5.4). The phrase in s. 6(5) of the Bail Act 1976, 'punishable . . . as if it were a criminal contempt of court', is merely a device to allow the Crown Court, on committal for sentence under s. 6(6), to deal with both the absconding offence and the original offence at the same time so as to avoid two sets of proceedings.

When a person on bail has surrendered to the custody of the court by reporting at the appropriate time to the appropriate official, he is not guilty of the offence of absconding under s. 6(1) if, before his case is called, he leaves the court building without permission given by or on behalf of the court. Such conduct would, however, render him liable to arrest under s. 7(2) (*DPP* v *Richards* [1988] 3 All ER 406, DC). A solicitor's mistake about the date on which his client is due to attend court may, depending upon all the circumstances, amount to a 'reasonable cause' within the meaning of s. 6(1) for the client's failure to surrender to custody (*R* v *Liverpool Stipendiary Magistrate (ex parte Santos)* (1997) *The Times*, 23 January, DC, *per* Staughton LJ).

The Bail Act 1976 also creates a general, though qualified, *right* to bail (s. 4), requires magistrates' courts and the Crown Court to give reasons for *refusing* bail (s. 5(3)), and requires those courts to give reasons for *granting* bail to persons charged with certain serious offences (sch. 1, pt. I, as amended by the Criminal Justice Act 1988).

4.3 GENERAL RIGHT TO BAIL

Subject to s. 25 of the Criminal Justice and Public Order Act 1994, and subject to sch. 1 of the Bail Act 1976, s. 4 of the 1976 Act provides that bail *shall* be granted to:

(a) A person accused of an offence who appears before a magistrates' court or the Crown Court in connection with proceedings for the offence.

(b) A person accused of an offence who applies to a court for bail in connection with the proceedings.

(c) A person who, having been convicted of an offence, appears before a magistrates' court to be dealt with for breach of a probation or community service order.

(d) A person who has been convicted of an offence and whose case has been adjourned for reports to be obtained before sentence.

Save in cases (c) and (d) above, there is no right to bail as regards proceedings on or after a person's conviction for an offence.

4.3.1 Qualifications

Schedule 1 to the Bail Act 1976, as amended, contains provisions which qualify the general right to bail. Where the offence of which the defendant is accused is punishable with imprisonment, he need not be granted bail in the following circumstances:

(a) If the court is satisfied that there are substantial grounds for believing that the defendant, if released on bail, would:

(i)   fail to surrender to custody, or
(ii)   commit an offence while on bail, or
(iii) interfere with witnesses or otherwise obstruct the course of justice.

(b) If the court is satisfied that the defendant should be kept in custody for his own protection or, if he is a child or a young person, for his own welfare.

(c) If the defendant is already in custody in pursuance of a court sentence.

(d) If it has not been practicable for want of time to obtain sufficient information to enable the court to make its decision on bail.

(e)   If the defendant, having been released on bail, has been arrested for absconding or breaking the conditions of his bail.

(f)   If the offence is one triable on indictment or either way and the defendant was on bail in criminal proceedings on the date of the offence.

Whenever the court is considering the grounds mentioned in (a)(i), (ii), (iii) and (f) above, all relevant factors must be taken into account, including the nature and seriousness of the offence, the character, antecedents, associations and community ties of the defendant, and his record in satisfying his obligations under previous grants of bail (Bail Act 1976, sch. 1, pt I, para 9). In *R* v *Vernege* [1982] 1 All ER 403, CA, it was said to be a 'relevant factor' that it is in the interests of a defendant charged with murder that he should be examined by a doctor with a view to establishing the state of his mind at the time of the offence. The committing magistrates should, therefore, consider remanding in custody a defendant charged with murder so that the necessary reports can be prepared.

Where the offence of which the defendant is accused is *not* punishable with imprisonment, sch. 1 provides that bail may be withheld only in the circumstances mentioned in (b), (c) and (e) above, or where the court believes, in view of a previous failure to surrender to custody, that the defendant would abscond if released on bail (ibid., sch. 1, pt II).

Further qualifications apply in the case of murder, manslaughter, rape, attempted murder and attempted rape. If the defendant is charged with one of these serious offences, and is granted bail after representations have been made about any of the grounds specified in (a)(i)–(iii) above, the court must give the reasons for its decision to grant bail (sch. 1, pt I, para 9A, as inserted by the Criminal Justice Act 1988). This provision does not forbid the granting of bail to defendants charged with the serious offences mentioned, but the obligation to give reasons may make the court more hesitant about granting it. Furthermore, a defendant charged with, or convicted of, one of these offences who has a previous conviction for any of them and, in the case of manslaughter, was sentenced to imprisonment or long-term detention, can only be granted bail if the court is satisfied that there are exceptional circumstances which justify it (Criminal Justice and Public Order Act 1994, s. 25, as amended by the Crime and Disorder Act 1998).

4.4   GRANTING BAIL

Bail may be granted by the police or by a court, usually a magistrates' court or the Crown Court. However, a person charged with *treason* can only be granted bail by a High Court judge or the Home Secretary (Magistrates' Courts Act 1980, s. 41).

4.4.1   Police bail

The police have power to grant bail to arrested persons without the necessity for any court appearance. When a magistrate issues a warrant for arrest he may endorse it for bail, i.e., he may endorse the warrant with a direction that the person to be arrested is to be released on bail subject to a duty to appear before a magistrates' court on the date specified and with the amount in which any surety is to be bound (Magistrates' Courts Act 1980, s. 117(1) and (2)). Such a warrant is described as 'backed for bail' and, if the defendant is taken to a police station following his arrest, it is the duty of the custody officer to release the defendant on bail as directed in the endorsement. The duty to let the defendant go is, however, subject to the officer's approving any surety offered in compliance with the endorsement (ibid., s. 117(3)), as substituted by the Police and Criminal Evidence Act 1984).

In considering the suitability of a proposed surety, regard *may* be had, *inter alia,* to that person's financial resources, his character and any previous convictions, and his proximity (whether in point of kinship, place of residence or otherwise) to the defendant (Bail Act 1976, s. 8(2)). The same criteria apply when bail has been granted by a court. Note that this list of factors to be taken into account is neither mandatory nor exhaustive. A proposed surety who is rejected by the police may apply to a court to determine his suitability (ibid., s. 8(5)). It is a criminal offence for the defendant to agree with a surety to indemnify the surety against loss of his recognizance. Both parties may be liable. Proceedings for this offence need the consent of the Director of Public Prosecutions (ibid., s. 9).

The police also have powers, under ss. 37 and 38 of the Police and Criminal Evidence Act 1984, to grant bail to persons arrested either without a warrant or under a warrant not endorsed for bail. These powers are subject to s. 25 of the Criminal Justice and Public Order Act 1994, para 4.3.1 above. Where the defendant has been bailed under the Police and Criminal Evidence Act 1984 to appear before a magistrates' court, the court has power to fix a later date for his appearance and to enlarge the recognizances of any sureties for him (Magistrates' Courts Act 1980, s. 43(1), as substituted by the Police and Criminal Evidence Act 1984).

Until 1995 the police had no power to impose conditions when granting bail. The Royal Commission on Criminal Justice recommended that the police should be given this power (*Report*, Cm 2263, 1993), and it was conferred by the Criminal Justice and Public Order Act 1994. The police can attach conditions if this appears to be necessary for ensuring that the defendant surrenders to custody, does not commit an offence while on bail, or does not interfere with witnesses or otherwise obstruct the course of justice (Bail Act 1976, s. 3, as extended by s. 3A (inserted by the Criminal Justice and Public Order Act 1994)). The police have no power to impose a condition that the defendant live in a bail hostel (Bail Act 1976, s. 3A).

The police must give reasons for imposing or varying bail conditions (Bail Act 1976, s. 5A, as inserted by the Criminal Justice and Public Order Act 1994). This requirement is designed to help the defendant to decide whether to request a variation, or a further variation, of bail conditions. Any conditions imposed by the police may, on the application of the defendant, later be varied by the police (Bail Act 1976, s. 3A) or by a magistrates' court (Magistrates' Courts Act 1980, s. 43B, as inserted by the Criminal Justice and Public Order Act 1994). In each case, the varied conditions may be more onerous than those originally imposed.

A defendant released on bail by the police subject to a condition that he attend at a police station may be arrested without warrant if he fails to attend (Police and Criminal Evidence Act 1984, s. 46A, as inserted by the Criminal Justice and Public Order Act 1994).

4.4.2 Bail in the magistrates' courts

Bail is available at many stages of proceedings before magistrates:

(a) Where a defendant is first brought before a magistrates' court and the hearing is adjourned because, for example, the prosecution is not ready to proceed with its case, the court will remand the defendant either in custody or on bail (Magistrates' Courts Act 1980, s. 128(1)).

(b)   Where a defendant is committed for trial to the Crown Court the magistrates may commit either in custody or on bail (ibid., s. 6(3); for committal proceedings, see para 1.7.6.3).

(c)   Where a defendant has been convicted summarily and the magistrates decide to commit him to the Crown Court for sentence, they may commit either in custody or on bail (ibid., s. 38; for committal to the Crown Court for sentence, see para 1.7.6.2.3).

(d)   Where a defendant has been convicted summarily and the magistrates adjourn the proceedings in order to consider sentence, they will remand the defendant either in custody or on bail (ibid., s. 128(1)).

In common with other courts, the magistrates' courts *may* impose conditions when granting bail, although the power to do so is qualified. If conditions are imposed they must only be such as appear to the court to be necessary to ensure that the defendant surrenders to custody, does not commit an offence while on bail, does not interfere with witnesses or otherwise obstruct the course of justice, makes himself available for the purpose of enabling inquiries or a report to be made to assist the court in dealing with him for the offence with which he is charged (Bail Act 1976, s. 3(6)), or, where the condition is that the defendant live in a bail hostel or probation hostel, that it is necessary to impose that condition in order to assess his suitability for a period of residence in a probation hostel should he be convicted of the offence (ibid., sch. 1, pt 1, para 8, as amended by the Criminal Justice Act 1988). If this latter condition is imposed on the defendant, the further condition that he must comply with the rules of the hostel may be added (ibid., s. 3(6ZA), as inserted by the Criminal Justice Act 1988).

A court has no power to impose conditions to achieve any purposes other than those just mentioned (ibid., sch. 1, pt I, para 8, as amended by the Criminal Justice Act 1988). Appropriate conditions would include the surrender of the defendant's passport, keeping away from specified places and persons, and reporting to a police station at specified times. In imposing conditions, magistrates are entitled to use their knowledge of local events and conditions (*R* v *Mansfield Justices (ex parte Sharkey)* [1985] QB 613, DC, in which a bail condition was upheld that the defendants should not picket or demonstrate during the miners' strike of 1984–85 otherwise than peacefully at their own place of work).

Any conditions imposed by a court may later be varied by that court on the application of the defendant, the prosecutor or a constable (Bail Act 1976, s. 3(8)). If bail was originally granted unconditionally, conditions may later be imposed by the court on the application of any of the same persons (ibid.). Breach of a bail condition renders the defendant liable to arrest without warrant by a constable (ibid., s. 7(3)). A defendant so arrested must be brought before a justice of the peace within 24 hours of his arrest (ibid., s. 7(4)). If this provision is not strictly observed, the defendant is automatically entitled to be released since there is no power to detain him further under s. 7(5), which is dependent upon proper compliance with s. 7(4) (*R* v *Governor of Glen Parva Young Offender Institution (ex parte G)* [1998] 2 All ER 295, DC, where the defendant had been brought into the *precincts* of a magistrates' court within the 24-hour period but had not been 'brought before a justice of the peace' until two hours after the expiry of that period, and, on an application for a writ of habeas corpus, his continued detention was declared unlawful).

In one circumstance the court must impose conditions if it grants bail. A court granting bail to a person accused of murder must impose conditions requiring the accused to attend an institution or place and there to submit to an examination by two medical practitioners for the purpose of enabling medical reports to be prepared on his mental condition (Bail Act

1976, s. 3(6A), added by the Mental Health (Amendment) Act 1982). These conditions must be imposed by the court which grants bail and not later by the same or a different court (*R v Central Criminal Court (ex parte Porter)* [1992] Crim LR 121, DC). They need not be imposed, however, where satisfactory reports on the accused's mental condition have already been obtained. Medical reports on the accused's mental state at the time of the offence are essential in order that any plea of diminished responsibility may be properly investigated. Since it is now mandatory for a person released on bail on a murder charge to undergo a medical examination it will not be necessary to remand the accused in custody merely in order to achieve the same purpose (see *R v Vernege* [1982] 1 All ER 403, CA, para 4.3.1 above).

There is a prima facie right to bail whenever the defendant appears before a magistrates' court (e.g., on remand), or the Crown Court, in connection with proceedings for the offence with which he is charged, or whenever he applies for bail (Bail Act 1976, s. 4). If, for example, a magistrates' court refuses bail to the defendant, it is bound to consider granting bail on every subsequent occasion on which he appears before the court, whether or not an application for bail has been made. At the *first* hearing following the one at which bail was refused, the defendant can support an application for bail with any argument of fact or law that he wishes, including any argument already used previously.

At hearings *subsequent* to this one, the court is not obliged to hear arguments which it has heard previously, although it may do so if it wishes (ibid., sch. 1, pt IIA, as inserted by the Criminal Justice Act 1988). At this stage, the court may fulfil its duty to consider the grant of bail merely by continuing its refusal of bail without going into the merits of the defendant's unchanged application. For his part, a defendant who wishes to have an application for bail considered in full would need to show that there are new circumstances which were not before the court on previous occasions. These new provisions represent an attempt to put down in statutory form the decision of the Divisional Court in *R v Nottingham Justices (ex parte Davies)* [1980] 2 All ER 775.

It is not clear, either from the statute or the case law, what new circumstances will suffice to entitle the defendant to have his right to bail fully considered. In *R v Crown Court at Reading (ex parte Malik)* [1981] 1 All ER 249, DC, at p. 251, Donaldson LJ said, *obiter,* that committal for trial would usually represent a sufficient change of circumstances for this purpose. In *R v Slough Justices (ex parte Duncan and Embling)* (1982) *The Times,* 24 July, a differently constituted Divisional Court, not following this dictum, held that committal did not necessarily amount to such a change of circumstances.

The requirement to show a change of circumstances would, without more, deprive many defendants of any effective means of securing bail. A defendant who is denied bail can, as explained below, apply to a High Court judge in chambers but legal aid will not normally be granted for such an application (Legal Aid Act 1988, s. 19(4)). There is, however, a limited right to make a legally aided application to the *Crown Court* against a magistrates' court's refusal of bail. A person remanded in *custody* by magistrates prior to summary trial or committal proceedings, or after summary conviction and before sentence, can apply to the Crown Court for bail (Supreme Court Act 1981, s. 81(1)(g), as added (with effect in 1983) by the Criminal Justice Act 1982 in response to criticism of the *Nottingham Justices* decision). This application may be legally aided since it is provided that representation for the purpose of criminal proceedings in a court extends to any preliminary or incidental proceedings, including bail proceedings, whether in that or another court (Legal Aid Act 1988, s. 19(2), replacing earlier provisions). The Crown Court can only grant bail on such an application if the magistrates' court has certified that it heard full argument on the defendant's bail application before rejecting it (Supreme Court Act 1981, s. 81(1J), and see *Practice Direction* [1983] 2 All ER 261).

In certain circumstances, the prosecution can apply to a magistrates' court for reconsideration of a decision to grant bail made by the court or by the police (Bail Act 1976, s. 5B, as inserted by the Criminal Justice and Public Order Act 1994). An application for a reconsideration can only be made where:

(a)   the defendant is charged with an indictable offence or an either-way offence and not with a summary offence only; and

(b)   the application is based on new information which was not available to the court or the police at the time when the original decision to grant bail was made.

On an application for reconsideration of a bail decision, the court may impose or vary bail conditions or withhold bail altogether. However, the defendant's general right to bail is preserved since it is provided that the court cannot refuse bail except in accordance with s. 4(1) and sch. 1 of the Bail Act 1976 (see paras 4.3 and 4.3.1 above).

Where a magistrates' court refuses bail or grants it subject to conditions, the defendant may apply to the High Court and a judge in chambers may, subject to s. 25 of the Criminal Justice and Public Order Act 1994, grant bail or vary the conditions (Criminal Justice Act 1967, s. 22(1), as amended). The application should be made to a judge of the Queen's Bench Division, either in London or at the place where sittings of the High Court are held which is nearest to the court where the defendant was refused bail (*Practice Note* [1976] 1 All ER 736).

There is no appeal against the High Court judge's refusal to grant bail. Nor can the defendant make a renewed application 'to any other judge or to a Divisional Court' (RSC, Ord. 79 r. 9(12)). The Lord Chancellor has no jurisdiction, either original or appellate, to hear an application for bail (*Re Kray* [1965] Ch 736 (Lord Gardiner LC)). In *R v Crown Court at Reading (ex parte Malik)* [1981] 1 All ER 249, DC, it was held that the words 'any other judge' mean any other judge in the *High Court* and do not, therefore, preclude a subsequent application to a judge of the *Crown Court* in a proper case. The fact that legal aid will not normally be granted for a High Court application makes an approach to the Crown Court (under the provisions mentioned above) a much more attractive alternative.

In response to the growing problem of 'bail bandits' Parliament passed the Bail (Amendment) Act 1993. A 'bail bandit' is a person who commits further offences (especially burglary and crimes involving vehicles) while on bail. The Act is a useful, though somewhat limited, measure which gives to the *prosecution* on certain strict conditions a right of appeal to the Crown Court against the decision of a magistrates' court to grant bail.

The right of appeal arises only where the prosecution is conducted by or on behalf of the Director of Public Prosecutions, or by a person prescribed for the purposes of the 1993 Act by the Secretary of State, and:

(a)   representations were made against the granting of bail; and

(b)   after those representations were made a magistrates' court granted bail to a person charged with, or convicted of—

(i)   an offence punishable by a prison sentence of five years or more, or

(ii)   an offence under s. 12 of the Theft Act 1968 (taking a conveyance without authority — 'joyriding') or s. 12A of the same Act (aggravated vehicle-taking).

The prescribed prosecuting authorities include the Director of the Serious Fraud Office, the Secretary of State for Trade and Industry, the Secretary of State for Social Security, the Commissioners of Customs and Excise, and the Commissioners of Inland Revenue.

The right of appeal can only be exercised if the prosecution gives both oral and written notice of appeal. *Oral notice* must be given to the magistrates' court at the conclusion of the proceedings in which bail was granted and before the defendant has been released from custody. *Written notice* must be served on the magistrates' court *and the defendant* within two hours of the conclusion of the proceedings. If oral notice of appeal is successfully given, the magistrates' court must remand the defendant in custody until the appeal is determined or otherwise disposed of. If the prosecution fails within the two-hour period to serve one or both of the written notices the appeal is deemed to have been disposed of.

The actual hearing of the appeal at the Crown Court must begin (though not necessarily be completed) within 48 hours from the date on which oral notice of appeal was given, excluding weekends and public holidays. The proceedings on appeal are by way of rehearing at which the defendant can either be remanded in custody or granted bail subject to such conditions (if any) as the judge thinks fit. Probably due to an oversight, the Bail (Amendment) Act 1993 is silent about the length of time for which the judge can order the defendant to be remanded in custody following a successful appeal by the prosecution. The courts, however, have filled the lacuna by deciding that this period should not exceed eight days (*R* v *Governor of Pentonville Prison (ex parte Bone)* (1994) *The Times*, 15 November, DC).

4.4.3 Bail in the Crown Court

Subject to s. 25 of the Criminal Justice and Public Order Act 1994 (para 4.3.1 above), the Crown Court has power to grant bail, under the Supreme Court Act 1981, s. 81(1) (as amended), in the following circumstances:

(a) Where a defendant has been committed in custody for trial or sentence to the Crown Court, or has been sent in custody to the Crown Court for trial under s. 51 of the Crime and Disorder Act 1998.

(b) Where a defendant is in custody following a sentence imposed by a magistrates' court and he is in the process of appealing to the Crown Court against his sentence or conviction.

(c) Where a defendant is in the custody of the Crown Court pending the disposal of his case by that court.

(d) Where a defendant's case has been determined by the Crown Court and he has applied to that Court to state a case for the opinion of the High Court.

(e) Where a defendant has applied to the High Court for an order of certiorari to remove proceedings in the Crown Court in his case into the High Court, or has applied to the High Court for leave to make such an application. The granting of bail in this situation is limited to proceedings in the Crown Court on appeal from the magistrates' court since the High Court has no jurisdiction to make an order of certiorari where the Crown Court is acting as a court of trial on indictment (Supreme Court Act 1981, s. 29(3), and see para 11.8.2).

(f) Where a defendant has been remanded in custody by a magistrates' court after summary conviction but before sentence or where a case is adjourned prior to or during committal proceedings or summary trial.

(g) Where a defendant is appealing against conviction or sentence from the Crown Court to the Court of Appeal he may be granted bail by the Crown Court, but only if a

Crown Court judge has certified that the case is fit for appeal. Alternatively, the defendant may apply for bail to the Court of Appeal (para 4.4.5 below).

When the Crown Court grants bail in any of these circumstances, the time during which the defendant is free on bail does not count as part of any term of imprisonment or detention under his sentence (Supreme Court Act 1981, s. 81(1)).

An application to the Crown Court for bail will normally be heard at the location of the Crown Court where the proceedings out of which the application arises took place or are pending (*Practice Direction* [1981] 3 All ER 443). The application may be heard in chambers (Crown Court Rules 1982, r. 27). An application to the Crown Court for bail by a person charged with a class 1 offence will be heard by a High Court judge sitting in the Crown Court or by a circuit judge nominated for that purpose by a presiding judge. An application by a person charged with a class 2 offence may be heard by a High Court judge or by a circuit judge or, if a presiding judge so authorises, by a recorder. An application by a person charged with an offence in class 3 or class 4 may be heard by any judge of the Crown Court. A presiding judge has an overall discretion to direct that any particular application for bail shall be heard by a High Court judge (*Practice Direction* [1981] 3 All ER 443; for the classification of offences for Crown Court purposes, see para 1.5.3).

As long as it is within his power as outlined above, a judge of the Crown Court may grant bail even though a previous application before a High Court judge in chambers has failed (*R v Crown Court at Reading (ex parte Malik)* [1981] 1 All ER 249, DC). The applicant must inform the Crown Court of any earlier bail application made to the High Court or the Crown Court in the course of the same proceedings (Crown Court Rules 1982, r. 20(1)). It has been stated, *obiter,* that renewed applications cannot be made to other Crown Court judges unless there has been a change of circumstances. This is because the jurisdiction to grant bail belongs to the Crown Court itself and not to the individual judges who exercise that jurisdiction in practice (*R v Crown Court at Reading per* Donaldson LJ at p. 253). If bail is refused by the Crown Court, the defendant may apply to the High Court under the jurisdiction discussed earlier (ibid.).

4.4.4   Bail in the High Court

The High Court has power to grant bail, or to vary the conditions attached to bail, where bail has been refused, or granted subject to conditions, by a magistrates' court or the Crown Court.

In addition, the High Court may, subject to s. 25 of the Criminal Justice and Public Order Act 1994 (para 4.3.1 above), grant bail where an application has been made for an order of certiorari or for a case to be stated by the Crown Court (Criminal Justice Act 1948, s. 37 as amended).

4.4.5   Bail in the Court of Appeal, criminal division

The Court of Appeal may, subject to s. 25 of the Criminal Justice and Public Order Act 1994 (para 4.3.1 above), grant bail where:

(a)   an appeal is pending to the Court of Appeal (Criminal Appeal Act 1968, s. 19, as amended);

(b)   a retrial has been ordered by the Court of Appeal following an appeal (ibid., s. 8(2), as amended); or

(c)   an appeal is pending to the House of Lords from the Court of Appeal (ibid., s. 36, as amended).

The power of the Court of Appeal to grant bail under (a) above is not affected by the limited power of the Crown Court to grant bail pending an appeal to the Court of Appeal (para 4.4.3 above).

4.5 HABEAS CORPUS

The writ of habeas corpus is designed to protect the personal freedom of those who have been illegally detained in prison, hospital or private custody. In former times the writ began with the Latin words *habeas corpus,* meaning 'You must have the body'. The writ is addressed to the detainer and commands him to 'have the body' of the detainee before the court on the specified day and time. It is an ancient prerogative writ emanating, originally, from the King himself. The power to issue it is now exercised by the courts.

It can be used to secure a release from unlawful detention in both criminal and civil cases. A 'criminal case' in this context means a detention (for example, in police custody) that may be followed by the trial of the detainee for an alleged offence. A civil case is one which will not result in the trial of the detainee on a criminal charge; examples are the detention of children by persons not entitled to their custody and the wrongful detention of persons as mental patients in hospitals.

Unlike the prerogative orders of certiorari, prohibition and mandamus, habeas corpus is not a discretionary remedy. It is available as of right, though good cause must be shown. If the evidence discloses a prima facie case that the detention is unlawful, the court is under a duty to issue the writ. Since every detention is prima facie unlawful the burden of proof is on the detainer to justify it.

This is now the position in *immigration* cases, too, despite an earlier decision of the House of Lords to the contrary. In *R* v *Secretary of State for the Home Department (ex parte Zamir)* [1980] AC 930, the House of Lords had held that the decision of the Home Office to detain an immigrant could only be interfered with if the *detainee* showed that there was no evidence on which the decision could have been reached or that it was one which no reasonable person would have reached. The House was quickly called upon to reconsider the *Zamir* case, and in *R* v *Secretary of State for the Home Department (ex parte Khawaja)* [1983] 2 WLR 321, HL, it was decided not to follow it (see para 9.3.2.2). Instead, the House of Lords laid down that the burden is on the *Home Office* to prove to the satisfaction of the court on the balance of probabilities (the burden of proof applicable in civil cases) that the applicant is an illegal immigrant and that his detention is therefore justified. This is so whether the decision of the Home Office is challenged in proceedings for habeas corpus, as in the *Zamir* case, or in proceedings for judicial review, as in the *Khawaja* case. Because the liberty of the subject is involved, the Home Office will need to show probability of a high degree.

The person responsible for the illegal detention is not punished by the writ of habeas corpus, but its issue frees the detainee and thus allows him to pursue his ordinary remedies against the wrongdoer. These would include an action for damages for the torts of assault, battery and false imprisonment.

4.6 AVAILABILITY OF HABEAS CORPUS

Habeas corpus proceedings may be brought not only against a public authority but also against any private person suspected of detaining another unlawfully. Their scope is not limited to the police and prison governors. Thus, habeas corpus has been granted where a husband would not allow his wife out of the house (*R v Jackson* [1891] 1 QB 671, CA), where children have been unlawfully detained (*Barnardo v Ford* [1892] AC 326, HL), and where the Vice-Chancellor of Cambridge University imprisoned a woman for 'walking with a member of the University' (*ex parte Daisy Hopkins* (1891) 61 LJQB 240, DC). Proceedings also lie against the Crown and its servants (*Home Secretary v O'Brien* [1923] AC 603, HL).

Habeas corpus proceedings are available to all persons within the Queen's protection, including foreigners (*R v Governor of Brixton Prison (ex parte Kolczynski)* [1955] 1 QB 540, DC; *Re Castioni* [1891] 1 QB 149, DC; *R v Secretary of State for the Home Department (ex parte Khawaja)* [1983] 2 WLR 321, HL, *per* Lord Scarman at p. 344).

Since habeas corpus is available only where the court or person had no lawful authority to detain, a person detained as the result of a decision that was lawfully made but erroneous cannot secure his release by habeas corpus. The appropriate remedy in this situation would be for him either to *appeal* against the decision to a higher court or to challenge it in *judicial review* proceedings (*R v Secretary of State for the Home Department (ex parte Cheblak)* [1991] 2 All ER 319, CA (a case which arose out of the Gulf War of 1991); *R v Secretary of State for the Home Department (ex parte Muboyayi)* [1991] 4 All ER 72, CA; for judicial review proceedings, see para 11.11). A decision to detain is erroneous (as opposed to unlawful) where the person taking it, although it is within his power to do, has made a procedural error, has misunderstood the relevant law, has failed to take account of relevant matters, has taken into account irrelevant matters, or has acted perversely (*R v Secretary of State for the Home Department (ex parte Cheblak)*, above, *per* Lord Donaldson MR at p. 323; *R v Secretary of State for the Home Department (ex parte Muboyayi)*, above, *per* Lord Donaldson MR at p. 80). If detention is allowed to continue after such a decision is set aside in successful appellate or judicial review proceedings, the detention is unlawful and habeas corpus proceedings can be used to secure release from it (*R v Secretary of State for the Home Department (ex parte Cheblak) per* Lord Donaldson MR at p. 323).

4.7 PROCEDURE

Any person, whether the detainee himself or some other person on his behalf, may make an application, supported by an affidavit, to a judge in court or, if the judge so directs, to the Divisional Court of the Queen's Bench Division. (Cases involving the custody of children are dealt with by the Family Division (RSC, Ord. 54, r. 11).) In vacation, the application may be made to a single judge in chambers. In an emergency at night or at weekends, the application may be made anywhere, such as the judge's home (as in *R v Governor of Brixton Prison (ex parte Soblen)* [1963] 2 QB 243, CA).

Initially, the application is made *ex parte*. But if a prima facie case for the release of the detainee is made out, the court will usually adjourn the application until a named day so that notice to the respondent can be given. Argument on the merits of the application then takes place, *inter partes,* on the day named. If the court decides that the detention is unlawful it may order the release of the detainee without issuing the actual writ of habeas corpus (RSC, Ord. 54, r. 4(1); *Barnardo v Ford* [1892] AC 326, HL). There is, therefore, usually no need to produce the prisoner in court.

In exceptional cases the court has power to issue the writ immediately on the ex parte application. A notice accompanying the writ warns the respondent that disobedience to the writ will result in proceedings for contempt of court. The respondent must make a return to the writ setting out the reasons for the detention. On the appointed day, argument on the return to the writ takes place and the detainee is either released or continued in detention.

4.8 SUCCESSIVE APPLICATIONS FOR HABEAS CORPUS

Where a criminal or civil application for the writ of habeas corpus has been made, no further application can be made on the same grounds, whether to the same or another court or judge, unless fresh evidence is adduced, and no such application can in any case be made to the Lord Chancellor (Administration of Justice Act 1960, s. 14). This statutory rule was enacted to prevent a detainee going from judge to judge until he found one sympathetic to his case. The statutory rule was anticipated in a series of cases immediately before 1960 in which it was held that successive applications on the same grounds were not possible (*Re Hastings (No. 1)* [1958] 1 WLR 372, DC; *Re Hastings (No. 2)* [1959] 1 QB 358, DC; *Re Hastings (No. 3)* [1959] Ch 368, CA).

Even if the application for the writ of habeas corpus is made on a new ground, or on an old ground supported by fresh evidence so as to satisfy s. 14 of the Administration of Justice Act 1960, the court still retains its inherent jurisdiction to dismiss the application on the ground that it is an abuse of the process of the court (*R* v *Governor of Brixton Prison (ex parte Osman) (No. 4)* [1992] 1 All ER 579, DC. The applicant in this case had made five previous unsuccessful applications to the Divisional Court: see *R* v *Governor of Pentonville Prison (ex parte Osman)* [1989] 3 All ER 701, *R* v *Governor of Pentonville Prison (ex parte Osman) (No. 2)* (1988) 133 SJ 121, *R* v *Governor of Pentonville Prison (ex parte Osman) (No. 3)* [1990] 1 All ER 999, *R* v *Governor of Brixton Prison (ex parte Osman) (No. 2)* (1990) *The Times,* 17 December. The present (sixth) application was dismissed as an attempt to use the machinery of the court for an improper purpose, namely to prevent or delay the applicant's extradition to Hong Kong to face serious criminal charges of dishonesty. Mr Osman was finally deported in December 1992 after a further unsuccessful application in *R* v *Governor of Brixton Prison (ex parte Osman) (No. 5)* (1992) *The Times,* 26 November).

4.9 APPEALS IN HABEAS CORPUS PROCEEDINGS

A right of appeal in habeas corpus proceedings, both criminal and civil, was granted in 1960 against an order for release as well as against the refusal of an order. Thus, either the applicant or the respondent may appeal. In civil cases the appeal is made from the Queen's Bench Division of the High Court to the Court of Appeal and thence to the House of Lords. In criminal cases the appeal is made direct from the High Court to the House of Lords, and, although permission to appeal is required, a certificate that a point of law of general public importance is involved is not (Administration of Justice Act 1960, s. 15, as amended by the Access to Justice Act 1999).

Pending the outcome of a prosecution appeal from the High Court to the House of Lords in criminal habeas corpus proceedings, the High Court has power to order that the applicant be detained or not be released except on bail. If no such order is made and the applicant is released unconditionally he cannot be detained again if the appeal goes against him in the House of Lords (ibid., ss. 5 and 15; *United States Government* v *McCaffery* [1984] 2 All ER 570, HL, where the Divisional Court was severely criticised for making an unqualified order for the release of a fugitive offender whose extradition was being sought by the government of the USA).

5

Contempt of Court

5.1 INTRODUCTION

Contempt of court has traditionally been classified as either criminal or civil, although in recent years this classification has been criticised as 'unhelpful and almost meaningless' (*Jennison* v *Baker* [1972] 2 QB 52, CA, *per* Salmon LJ at p. 61; see also *Home Office* v *Harman* [1982] 1 All ER 532, HL, *per* Lord Scarman at p. 542; *Attorney-General* v *Newspaper Publishing plc* [1987] 3 All ER 276, CA, *per* Sir John Donaldson MR at p. 294 and Lloyd J at p. 306). The abolition of the distinction between criminal and civil contempt was recommended in 1974 by the *Phillimore Committee on Contempt of Court* (Cmnd 5794, 1974, paras 170–6), but so far there has been no legislative move to abandon it.

Criminal contempt is a non-arrestable common-law offence punishable by imprisonment and/or a fine or an order to give security for good behaviour. Alternatively, the court may grant an injunction to restrain a repetition of the contempt, as in *Attorney-General* v *Times Newspapers Ltd* [1974] AC 273, HL (the 'thalidomide case', see para 5.2.2.3). Criminal contempt extends to such matters as insulting behaviour in the face of the court or conduct which interferes with the proper administration of justice, both criminal and civil. The offence of criminal contempt is triable summarily without a jury. Trial of the offence on indictment is obsolete.

In *Attorney-General* v *Times Newspapers Ltd* [1991] 2 All ER 398, the term 'contempt of court' was criticised by the House of Lords as 'inaccurate and misleading' and as 'a less than happy description' of a concept designed to promote the effective administration of justice rather than (as is commonly supposed) the dignity of judges (see especially [1991] 2 All ER 398 *per* Lord Ackner at pp. 406–7, Lord Oliver at p. 413 and Lord Jauncey at p. 423). This criticism is consistent with earlier *dicta*, and their Lordships re-emphasised Lord Diplock's statement in *Attorney-General* v *Leveller Magazine Ltd* [1979] AC 440, HL, at p. 449 that

> . . . although criminal contempt of court may take a variety of forms they all share a common characteristic: they involve an interference with the due administration of justice, either in a particular case or more generally as a continuing process. *It is justice itself that is flouted by contempt of court . . .*

(Italics supplied. See to the same effect *Re Johnson* (1888) 20 QBD 68, CA, *per* Bowen LJ at p. 74; *Jennison* v *Baker* [1972] 2 QB 52, CA, *per* Salmon LJ at p. 61; *Attorney-General* v *Times Newspapers Ltd* [1974] AC 273, HL, *per* Lord Cross at p. 322.)

Civil contempt, sometimes called contempt in procedure, consists of disobedience to the judgments or orders of the court or a breach of an undertaking given to the court. In essence, civil contempt is a *private wrong* to the person entitled to the benefit of the order or undertaking, although contempt proceedings are not an action in tort even where the contempt has incidentally been committed during an action in tort (*Express and Star* v *National Graphical Association (1982)* [1986] ICR 589, CA). Civil contempt is also a *criminal offence* punishable by imprisonment and/or a fine under the inherent jurisdiction of the court. Alternatively, an injunction may be granted against the contemnor. Because proceedings for civil contempt are criminal in nature the standard of proof required to establish the contempt is the criminal standard, i.e., proof beyond reasonable doubt (*Dean* v *Dean* [1987] 1 FLR 517, CA).

The High Court has power to impose a fine of an unlimited amount. The power has been used to inflict swingeing fines on trade unions which have defied court orders made during industrial disputes. Thus, in 1983 the NGA was fined a total of £675,000 for contempt, and, in 1984, the NUM and the TGWU were each fined £200,000.

A further remedy, not available in cases of criminal contempt, is a writ of sequestration under which the contemnor's property is placed temporarily in the hands of sequestrators, who manage the property and receive the rents and profits from it until the contempt is purged. Property cannot be sold by sequestrators without a court order. Since sequestration is available only against a person or body in contempt, the court has no jurisdiction to sequestrate assets for an *apprehended* contempt or for a contempt which has already been purged (*Inland Revenue Comrs* v *Hoogstraten* [1984] 3 All ER 25, CA).

Sequestration is regarded as a drastic remedy and one to be resorted to sparingly. It is a particularly appropriate method of enforcing court orders against a company or its directors, or against a trade union, especially where the contempt consists of a refusal to pay a sum of money. The assets of the NUM were sequestrated during the miners' strike of 1984–85, and, in 1986, SOGAT '82 was fined £25,000 and had its assets sequestrated for contempt of orders made in legal proceedings arising out of the disputed move of Times Newspapers from Fleet Street to Wapping.

The court declined to make sequestration orders in *Director of Public Prosecutions* v *Channel Four Television Co. Ltd* [1993] 2 All ER 517, DC, in which the defendants were held to be in contempt of an order of a circuit judge, made under the Prevention of Terrorism (Temporary Provisions) Act 1989, requiring them to produce to a constable specified documents (from which the identity of their source of information could be obtained) relating to a broadcast television programme which had made allegations of collusion between members of the Royal Ulster Constabulary and loyalist terrorists. Sequestration was considered inappropriate in the circumstances; it could have had the effect of putting the defendants out of business (and their employees out of work) without achieving its purpose since the defendants were adamant that they would not reveal their source of information (see [1993] 2 All ER 517 *per* Woolf LJ at pp. 531–2). The defendants were instead fined £75,000. The case of the NUM was distinguished because there it was possible, by the appointment of a sequestrator, to prevent the union from continuing to defy orders of the court.

Normally, proceedings for civil contempt will be commenced either by the litigant in whose favour the court order was made or by the Attorney-General. It seems, however, that where neither the litigant nor the Attorney-General commences proceedings the court itself may act in exceptional cases of clear contempt where it is urgent and imperative for the contempt to be punished immediately (*Clarke* v *Chadburn* [1985] 1 All ER 211, *per* Sir Robert Megarry V-C at p. 215; *Re M and others (minors) (breach of contact order: committal)* [1999] 2 All ER 56, CA).

5.2 CRIMINAL CONTEMPT OF COURT

5.2.1 Interference with the proper administration of justice in the courts

5.2.1.1 Interrupting court proceedings
Any words or acts which obstruct or interfere with the proper administration of justice in the courts, and are calculated to do so, are punishable as criminal contempts. Thus, in a much-publicised case in May 1993 a young man was sentenced to 14 days' imprisonment for interrupting the proceedings during a trial in the Crown Court at Cardiff. His contempt consisted of wolf-whistling at a female juror from the public gallery (*R* v *Powell* (1993) *The Times*, 3 June, CA; he was released on bail after 24 hours on application to the High Court and, within six days, the Court of Appeal, while confirming that he was guilty of contempt, quashed the sentence of imprisonment on the ground that it was an inappropriate punishment in the circumstances).

It is usual, though not essential, for the words or acts to be spoken or done in the courtroom itself (*Balogh* v *Crown Court at St Alban's* [1974] 3 All ER 283, CA, *per* Lord Denning MR at p. 287, Stephenson LJ at p. 292 and Lawton LJ at p. 294). Assaulting, insulting or abusing the judge, whether in court or outside, is a contempt, as is interference with jurors, witnesses or the parties to, or the lawyers appearing in, a case. (See further on interference with jurors, para 5.2.1.5 below.) The prohibition on interfering with witnesses extends to interference with proper and reasonable attempts by a party's lawyers to identify and interview potential witnesses (*Connolly* v *Dale* [1996] 1 All ER 224, DC, where a detective superintendent of police was held guilty of contempt).

In *Morris* v *Crown Office* [1970] 2 QB 114, CA, some students supporting the Welsh Language Society staged a demonstration in the High Court in London and interrupted the proceedings there. They were found to be in contempt of court and some of them were sent to prison for three months while others were fined. On appeal, the Court of Appeal affirmed that their conduct amounted to contempt and that the judge had power to deal with them summarily as he did. However, those imprisoned were released and were instead bound over to be of good behaviour and to keep the peace.

In *Balogh* v *Crown Court at St Alban's,* Balogh, a bored solicitor's clerk, made preparations to introduce laughing gas through a ventilation duct into the courtroom. For this purpose he stole a cylinder of nitrous oxide from a hospital. He was apprehended before he could carry out his plan and was charged with the theft of the cylinder. He was taken before the senior judge in the court building, Melford Stevenson J, who was the judge presiding in the courtroom next to the courtroom in which Balogh was engaged. The judge regarded Balogh's conduct as serious and sentenced him to six months' imprisonment for contempt of court. Balogh appealed, contending, *inter alia,* that he was not in contempt of the judge's court because it was the proceedings in the court next door that he had intended to subvert.

The Court of Appeal reaffirmed the inherent jurisdiction of superior court judges to punish summarily, of their own motion, for contempt of court whenever there had been a gross interference with the course of justice in a case which was being tried or was about to be tried. This power existed whether the judge had seen the contempt with his own eyes or it had merely been reported to him; it was not limited to cases of contempt committed in the face of the court. It was emphasised, however, that the power should only be used where the contempt had been proved beyond reasonable doubt and where it was urgent and imperative for the judge to act immediately to prevent justice being obstructed or undermined. On the facts, Balogh was not guilty of contempt of court because he had not gone far enough to commit it. His acts were preparatory acts falling short of contempt. In addition, the Court of Appeal made it clear that, even if Balogh had been in contempt, the judge should not have exercised his summary jurisdiction to punish it. There was no sufficient urgency and it was not imperative to act immediately as Balogh was already in custody on a charge of theft.

5.2.1.2   Scandalising the court

Conduct which scandalises the court or otherwise lowers its authority is a contempt. Thus, scurrilous abuse of a judge, attacks on his personal character or imputations of partiality are all punishable. In 1900, the writer of an article in a local newspaper, the *Birmingham Daily Argus,* was proceeded against for publishing comments which attacked the personal qualities of Darling J as a judge. The article was held to be a scurrilous personal abuse of the judge and a contempt of court. The writer was fined £100 and ordered to pay costs of £25 (*R v Gray* [1900] 2 QB 36, DC). In 1928, the editor of the *New Statesman* was proceeded against after making allegations of bias against Avory J. The editor was found to be in contempt, although he was not imprisoned or fined but merely ordered to pay the costs of the proceedings (*R v New Statesman (Editor)* (1928) 44 TLR 301, DC. See also *R v Wilkinson* (1930) *The Times,* 16 July, in which the *Daily Worker* was punished for contempt, having described Swift J as a 'bewigged puppet exhibiting a strong class bias').

It is not contempt to criticise judges for their judicial conduct as long as the comments are fair and made in good faith. In *R v Commissioner of Police of the Metropolis (ex parte Blackburn) (No. 2)* [1968] 2 QB 150, CA, Quintin Hogg, before he became Lord Chancellor and restored to the peerage as Lord Hailsham of St Marylebone, published an article in *Punch* which was highly critical of a certain decision on the gaming laws, said mistakenly to be a decision of the Court of Appeal. It was, in fact, a decision of the Queen's Bench Divisional Court. The decision was under appeal to the Court of Appeal and Raymond Blackburn, who was involved in the case, asked that Court for an order declaring that Quintin Hogg was in contempt. It was held, however, that the article, although it was inaccurate and perhaps in bad taste, did not amount to a contempt of court. (For the Court of Appeal's decision on the enforcement of the gaming legislation, see *R v Commissioner of Police of the Metropolis (ex parte Blackburn)* [1968] 2 QB 118, CA; and see para 11.10.3.)

The law of contempt of court applies only to courts of justice properly so called and to judges of such courts of justice. It follows that scandalous comments made about a judge otherwise than in his capacity as a member of such a court cannot amount to contempt (*Attorney-General v British Broadcasting Corporation* [1980] 3 All ER 161, HL; *Badry v Director of Public Prosecutions of Mauritius* [1982] 3 All ER 973, PC; para 1.1.4).

5.2.1.3   Impeding access to the courts

It is a contempt to impede a person's right of access to the courts. In *Raymond v Honey* [1982] 1 All ER 756, HL, the governor of Albany Prison stopped a letter written by an inmate to his solicitor because the letter contained an allegation that an assistant governor had committed theft. The inmate thereupon prepared an application to the High Court for leave to commit the governor to prison for contempt arising out of the stopping of his letter. The governor also stopped the application.

The House of Lords held that the governor was in contempt of court in stopping the application since his conduct amounted to a denial of the inmate's right of access to the courts. The governor was not, however, subjected to any punishment for his contempt. It was further held that the stopping of the inmate's letter to his solicitor was *not* a contempt since there was not enough evidence to show that it had effectively obstructed the proper administration of justice. (Note, however, that in *R* v *Secretary of State for the Home Department (ex parte Leech) (No. 2)* [1993] 4 All ER 539, CA, it was held that rule 33(3) of the Prison Rules 1964 (SI 1964, No. 388), which allows a governor to read and stop any letter, was *ultra vires* s. 47(1) of the Prison Act 1952 insofar as it purported to apply to correspondence between prisoners and their legal advisers. As from 1 April 1999, the Prison Rules 1964 were replaced by the Prison Rules 1999 (SI 1999, No. 728).)

5.2.1.4   Refusing to answer questions in court
It is a contempt committed in the face of the court for a witness in legal proceedings to refuse to be sworn or to refuse to answer a question without lawful excuse. In *R* v *Samuda* (1989) 11 Cr App R(S) 471, CA, the defendant was found guilty of contempt for refusing to give evidence against a person whom he alleged had attempted to murder him. The Court of Appeal regarded the contempt as serious in the circumstances and decided that the appropriate sentence was one of six months' imprisonment). A victim of violence and a witness to the attack who both refused to give evidence at the attacker's trial (which consequently collapsed) were found to be in contempt in *R* v *Holt* (1996) *The Times*, 31 October, CA, although their custodial sentences were reduced on appeal. It was pointed out in this case that difficulties might be avoided if more use was made of s. 23 of the Criminal Justice Act 1988, which provides that a written statement made by a witness may be admissible as evidence where the witness is too afraid to give oral evidence. (See also the guidance given by the Court of Appeal in *R* v *Montgomery* [1995] 2 All ER 28, CA, para 5.4.1 below.) A lawful excuse for failing to give evidence may be based on the fear of self-incrimination, on privilege, on the irrelevance of the question, or on a genuine fear of reprisal if the fear is so real and compelling that the witness could not reasonably be expected to ignore it (*R* v *K* (1983) 78 Cr App Rep 82, CA; *R* v *Lewis* (1992) *The Times*, 19 November, CA, where the judge's finding of contempt was set aside and the sentence of nine months' imprisonment imposed on the defendant for the 'contempt' was quashed).

Journalists have no special privilege entitling them not to reveal in court the source of their information. In 1963, three journalists refused to divulge to a tribunal of inquiry the source of their information relating to William Vassall, the Admiralty spy. An application was made to the High Court for an order that the journalists were in contempt of the tribunal. It was held that they were. One of them received a six months' suspended prison sentence (*Attorney-General* v *Clough* [1963] 1 QB 773). The sentence was suspended in the hope that he would change his mind and identify his informant. He did not. However, the informant identified himself and the journalist did not serve his sentence. The other two journalists were sent to prison for terms of six months and three months respectively (*Attorney-General* v *Mulholland; Attorney-General* v *Foster* [1963] 2 QB 477, CA).

By s. 10 of the Contempt of Court Act 1981, it is now provided that no court has power to order a person to disclose, nor is any person guilty of contempt for refusing to disclose, the source of any information contained in a publication for which he is responsible, unless the court is satisfied that disclosure is necessary in the interests of justice or national security or for the prevention of disorder or crime. The section expressly recognises the public interest in allowing newspapers to protect their sources, subject only to the demand for disclosure made by the four overriding public interests mentioned in the section (*Re an inquiry under the Company Securities (Insider Dealing) Act 1985* [1988] 1 All ER 203, HL, *per* Lord Griffiths at p. 207; *X Ltd* v *Morgan-Grampian (Publishers) Ltd* [1990] 2 All ER 1, HL, *per* Lord Bridge at p. 7, Lord Oliver at p. 16 and Lord Lowry at p. 18). However, s. 10 will make no difference to a case like that above involving the three journalists since it was 'in the interests of . . . national security' that they should reveal their sources. The public interest in the ability of the press to protect its sources may, on occasion, have to give way to the wish of a betrayed employer to identify a disloyal employee who has disclosed confidential information to, and whose identity is being shielded by, the press (*Camelot Group plc* v *Centaur Communications Ltd* [1998] 1 All ER 251, CA, below).

The scope of s. 10 was considered by the House of Lords in *Secretary of State for Defence* v *Guardian Newspapers Ltd* [1984] 3 All ER 601, a case in which the request of the government for the return of a copy of a 'leaked' secret memorandum was resisted by *The Guardian* on the ground that the markings on the document would be likely to identify the 'leaker'. The House of Lords, by a majority of three to two, decided that disclosure of the source of information was necessary in the interests of national security. The risk to national security lay in the possibility that, unless identified, the 'leaker' might in future leak other classified documents with more serious consequences. Their Lordships were unanimous in the view that the burden of proving that one or more of the four exceptions applied (the interests of justice, the interests of national security, the prevention of disorder, the prevention of crime) is on the party seeking the disclosure order. The standard of proof required is that applicable in civil proceedings generally, namely, the balance of probabilities.

The House of Lords has since held that the phrase 'prevention of . . . crime' in s. 10 is to be construed in a wide rather than a narrow fashion. It is a reference to the prevention of a particular identifiable future crime (*Re an inquiry under the Company Securities (Insider Dealing) Act 1985* [1988] 1 All ER 203, HL).

In *X Ltd* v *Morgan-Grampian (Publishers) Ltd* [1990] 2 All ER 1, the House of Lords was called upon to consider directly for the first time the phrase 'in the interests of justice' in s. 10. William Goodwin, a trainee journalist employed by the publishers of a weekly journal, *The Engineer,* intended to write an article based on confidential information about a company's financial affairs which had come into his possession. He refused to hand over to the company the notes from which the source of his information could be identified.

The House of Lords held unanimously that disclosure was necessary in the interests of justice even though the information was not 'contained in a publication' as required literally by s. 10. Their Lordships were of the opinion that s. 10 applies equally to a source of information contained in an *intended* publication since the underlying purpose of the statutory protection of sources is as valid before publication as after it (see especially [1990] 2 All ER 1 *per* Lord Bridge at p. 7 and Lord Lowry at p. 17). Their Lordships were further of the opinion that the phrase 'in the interests of justice' was not to be confined as referring only to the administration of justice in the course of legal proceedings in a court of law. Lord Diplock's *dictum* to the contrary in *Secretary of State for Defence* v *Guardian Newspapers Ltd* [1984] 3 All ER 601, HL, at p. 607, was expressly disapproved. The House in *X Ltd* v *Morgan-Grampian (Publishers) Ltd* said it was in the interests of justice that persons should be able to exercise their legal rights, and to protect themselves against legal wrongs, with or without commencing proceedings (see especially [1990] 2 All ER 1 *per* Lord Bridge at p. 9 and Lord Oliver at p. 17).

When Mr Goodwin continued to refuse to disclose his source, he was fined £5,000 for contempt by Hoffmann J in the High Court: see *The Times,* 11 April 1990. The order requiring him to reveal his source, and the fine imposed upon him for declining to do so, were later held by a majority of the European Court of Human Rights to be violations of his right to freedom of expression under art. 10 of the European Convention on Human Rights: see *Goodwin* v *United Kingdom* (1996) *The Times*, 28 March, ECHR.

Even if the case falls within one of the four exceptional categories mentioned in s. 10, disclosure of a source of information will not be ordered by the court unless it is 'necessary' to do so. 'Necessary' means something more than merely 'useful' or 'expedient' and something less than 'indispensable'. It has been suggested that the nearest paraphrase is 'really needed' (*Re an inquiry under the Company Securities (Insider Dealing) Act 1985* [1988] 1 All ER 203, HL, *per* Lord Griffiths at p. 209; *X Ltd* v *Morgan-Grampian (Publishers) Ltd* [1990] 2 All ER 1, HL, *per* Lord Oliver at p. 16). Thus, in *Maxwell* v *Pressdram Ltd* [1987] 1 All ER 656 the Court of Appeal upheld the trial judge's decision not to order disclosure because, although it may have been 'relevant', 'important' or 'desirable', disclosure was not 'necessary' in the interests of justice in the context of the claimant's libel action. In *X* v *Y* [1988] 2 All ER 648, a health authority was refused an order against a journalist and his newspaper to compel disclosure of the identities of health authority employees who had supplied information from hospital records about two doctors who were continuing in general practice despite having contracted AIDS. Disclosure was held not to be necessary for the prevention of crime since it was not the health authority's function to prevent crime and a criminal investigation was unlikely to ensue even if the source of the information were disclosed.

In *Saunders* v *Punch Ltd* [1998] 1 All ER 234, it was held not to be necessary in the interests of justice to order disclosure of a source of information protected by legal professional privilege. An anonymous article in the defendants' magazine led the claimant, the former chairman and chief executive of Guinness plc, to believe that the defendants were in possession of unpublished records of meetings between him and his solicitors. At these meetings, a Department of Trade and Industry inquiry into alleged fraudulent activities at Guinness plc was discussed. The claimant obtained an injunction to prevent further publication, and applied for an order compelling the defendants to divulge the source of their information. It was decided that the public interest in receiving the information was not outweighed by the interests of justice, and that the claimant was already sufficiently protected by the injunction already obtained.

On the facts of *Camelot Group plc* v *Centaur Communications Ltd* [1998] 1 All ER 251, CA, the opposite conclusion was reached. It was held that the public interest in enabling the claimants (organisers of the National Lottery) to identify a disloyal employee who had 'leaked' a copy of the claimants' draft accounts to the defendants (who revealed them in their publication *Marketing Week*) outweighed the public interest in enabling the defendants to protect their sources of information, and that a disclosure order was necessary in the interests of justice. Applying *X Ltd* v *Morgan-Grampian (Publishers) Ltd* [1990] 2 All ER 1, HL, and the *Camelot* case, above, it was held in *Michael O'Mara Books Ltd* v *Express Newspapers plc* (1998) *The Times*, 6 March, that it was in the interests of justice that the deputy editor of *The Express* newspaper should disclose the name of the person who had supplied him with a photocopied typescript of a book entitled, *Fergie — Her Secret Life*.

In determining whether it is 'necessary' to compel the revelation of a source of information, the court may also consider whether the applicant for the order has himself taken steps to discover the source of the leak — apart from applying to the court — and whether the leaked information was of great importance (*Broadmoor Hospital* v *Hyde* (1994) *The Times*, 18 March).

5.2.1.5   Contempt in relation to juries

A person may be punished for contempt committed in the face of the court if he fails to attend the court in answer to a jury summons or if, having answered the summons, he is not available to serve as a juror or is unfit for service by reason of drink or drugs. Alternatively, he may be prosecuted summarily for an offence under the Juries Act 1974 (Juries Act 1974, s. 20(1) and (2)). He is not liable to be punished if he can show some reasonable cause for his failure to attend or for not being available when called on to serve as a juror (ibid., s. 20(4)). A juror may also be punished for contempt if he refuses to be sworn or if he misbehaves in court. It is a contempt for a juror to refuse to give a verdict with the intention of interfering with the administration of justice. In *R* v *Schot* (1997) *The Times*, 14 May, CA, two jurors who had been given prison sentences by the trial judge for refusing, on conscientious grounds, to return a verdict were held on appeal not to have been guilty of contempt. Although they had probably committed the *actus reus* of contempt, there was no evidence that they had done so with the requisite *mens rea* (i.e., with the intention of interfering with the administration of justice).

Another rule, contained in s. 8(1) of the Contempt of Court Act 1981, affects both jurors and outsiders and is designed to preserve the secrets of the jury-room in the interests of the proper administration of justice. By this subsection, it is a contempt to obtain, disclose or solicit any particulars of statements made, opinions expressed, arguments advanced or votes cast by members of a jury in the course of their deliberations in any legal proceedings, whether criminal, civil or in a coroner's court. Proceedings for contempt under s. 8 can only be instituted by or with the consent of the Attorney-General or on the motion of a court having jurisdiction to deal with the contempt (Contempt of Court Act 1981, s. 8(3)).

There are two exceptional cases where it is not a contempt to disclose particulars (or to publish them once disclosed). First, where the particulars are disclosed in the legal proceedings in question for the purpose of enabling the jury to arrive at their verdict or in connection with the delivery of that verdict (ibid., s. 8(2)(a)). Secondly, where the particulars are disclosed in evidence in any subsequent legal proceedings for an offence alleged to have been committed in relation to the jury in the earlier proceedings (ibid., s. 8(2)(b)). There is, however, no exception allowing disclosure of jury-room deliberations for the purpose of an appeal against conviction or for the purpose of research into the practical workings of the jury system. The *Report of the Royal Commission on Criminal Justice* (Cm 2263, 1993) recommended that s. 8 should be amended so as to permit research into how juries arrive at their verdicts.

Since there is no exception to jury secrecy in relation to appeals, lawyers and others must take care not to fall foul of s. 8 by interviewing or taking statements from jurors after the trial (*R* v *McCluskey (Kevin)* (1994) 98 Cr App Rep 216, CA; *R* v *Mickleburgh* (1994) *The Times*, 26 July, CA; *R* v *Young* [1995] QB 324, CA; *R* v *Khan* (1995) *The Times*, 14 April, CA; *R* v *Schot* (1997) *The Times*, 14 May, CA, above). Furthermore, the trial judge should not be approached with enquiries relating to the jury because, after verdict and sentence, he is regarded as *functus officio* ('having performed his function' and, therefore, no longer having jurisdiction). In such cases, the guidance of the Court of Appeal should be sought instead (*McCluskey, Mickleburgh, Young* and *Khan*, above). The Court of Appeal is, however, bound by s. 8 like everyone else and cannot, therefore, inquire into what went on in the jury room. In *R* v *Young* (the 'ouija board case', above), the Court of Appeal held that it was entitled to inquire only into what happened during the jury's retirement at an hotel and not into what happened thereafter in the jury room. It authorised an inquiry under the direction of the Treasury Solicitor and a senior police officer, and ordered affidavits (limited to what, if anything, happened at the hotel) to be taken from each of the 12 jurors and from the two bailiffs looking after them at the hotel. (See further on this case, para 7.7.)

The scope of s. 8(1) was considered in *Attorney-General* v *Associated Newspapers Ltd* [1994] 1 All ER 556, HL. Here the *Mail on Sunday* had published an article referring to statements, opinions and arguments made during their deliberations by some members of the jury in the much-publicised 'Blue Arrow' fraud trial of 1991–92, including the thoughts of some jurors on the evidence, the opinion of one member of the jury that another juror did not understand what the trial was about and had only agreed with the verdict because he wanted to get home, remarks made by another juror about the defendants, and comments on how other jurors had been persuaded to change their minds in the jury room. The newspaper had not obtained its information directly from the jurors but from transcripts of interviews with them conducted by persons who had advertised in another newspaper offering a reward to jurors who contacted a box number.

The Attorney-General brought proceedings for contempt under s. 8(1) of the Contempt of Court Act 1981 against the publishers of the *Mail on Sunday*, its editor and one of its journalists. Their somewhat feeble defence was that the prohibition against disclosure of jury deliberations was limited to disclosure by members of the jury and did not apply where the information had been obtained indirectly from another source. The defendants were found to be in contempt and were fined £30,000, £20,000 and £10,000, respectively. On appeal to the House of Lords, it was held that the meaning of s. 8(1) is plain and unambiguous and that the word 'disclose' in the subsection applies not only to disclosure of jury deliberations by a member of the jury to a friend or neighbour but also to disclosure to the public at large by a non-juror who has acquired the information directly or indirectly. This interpretation is confirmed by reference to the mischief which the subsection was intended to remedy. That mischief comprised not only disclosure by individual jurors but also publication of the forbidden particulars to the general public (ibid., *per* Lord Lowry at p. 564; see further on s. 8, para 7.7).

Quite apart from the statutory contempt created by s. 8, any interference, or attempted interference, with a juror for what he has done in the discharge of his duty is an interference with the proper administration of justice and, therefore, a contempt at common law (*R* v *Martin* (1848) 5 Cox CC 356). Thus, in *R* v *Palache* (1993) 14 Cr App R(S) 294, CA, the defendant was guilty of common law contempt by threatening the jury after it returned a guilty verdict against her mother. The defendant's conduct (making remarks in the presence of the jury about the effect of their verdict, banging a water carafe against a glass screen, and moving towards the jury with the carafe in her hand before being stopped by the clerk of the court) was described as a 'grave contempt'. In *Attorney-General* v *Judd* (1994) *The Times*, 15 August, DC, the defendant's deliberate harassment at a car-boot sale of a member of the jury which had tried him was held to be a common law contempt. He was also found to have violated s. 8 of the Contempt of Court Act 1981 by asking the juror how many jurors had found him guilty.

5.2.1.6 Tape recorders in court

By s. 9 of the Contempt of Court Act 1981, it is a contempt to use in court, or bring into court for use, a tape recorder or other instrument for recording sound, except with the leave of the court, which may be granted subject to conditions. This contempt under s. 9 is probably one of strict liability and not dependent upon proof of *mens rea* (*Re Hooker* [1993] COD 190, DC; see further on this case, para 5.4.4 below). It is also a contempt under s. 9 to publish a recording of legal proceedings by playing it in the hearing of the public or any section of the public or to dispose of the recording with a view to such publication. For these contempts the court may, in addition to punishing the contemnor in the normal way, order the tape recorder or any recording made with it, or both, to be forfeited. They may then be sold or otherwise disposed of in such manner as the court directs (ibid., s. 9(3)). It should be noted that s. 9 does not apply to the making or use of sound recordings as official transcripts of legal proceedings (ibid., s. 9(4)).

The taking of photographs and the making of portraits or sketches in court are criminal offences under s. 41 of the Criminal Justice Act 1925. The restrictions on recording, photographic and drawing activities are based essentially on the desire to uphold the dignity of the judicial process.

In the light of s. 9 of the Contempt of Court Act 1981, a Supreme Court *Practice Direction* [1981] 3 All ER 848 on the use of tape recorders was issued jointly by the Lord Chief Justice, the Master of the Rolls, the President of the Family Division and the Vice-Chancellor of the Chancery Division. It lists the following factors as relevant to the exercise of the court's discretion to grant, withhold or withdraw leave to use tape recorders or to impose conditions:

(a)   Whether there is any reasonable need on the part of the applicant for leave, be he a litigant or a press or broadcasting representative, for the recording to be made.

(b)   Whether there is a risk that the recording could be used to brief witnesses waiting out of court.

(c)   Whether the use of the tape recorder would disturb the proceedings or distract or worry any witnesses or other participants.

The *Practice Direction* further provides that consideration should always be given to the imposition of conditions on the use of a recording made with leave of the court. It also emphasises that the transcript of a permitted recording is intended for the use of the person given leave to make it and is not meant to be used as, or to compete with, the official transcript of the proceedings.

5.2.2   Prejudicing a fair trial in particular proceedings: the *sub judice* or strict liability rule

5.2.2.1   Introduction
It is of the first importance that legal proceedings should be tried fairly in our courts and that they should not be 'tried' in advance on television or in the press. There is an ever-present danger that unrestrained public discussion of the issues arising in a case may prejudice a subsequent fair trial by reason of the effect that discussion might have on the minds of prospective jurors and witnesses.

The *sub judice* rule is designed to deter prejudicial comment so as to secure a fair trial in both criminal and civil proceedings. At common law it was a contempt, *irrespective of intention,* to interfere with the outcome of particular legal proceedings by publishing prejudicial comments. The rule was made the subject of important changes by the Contempt of Court Act 1981, which refers to it as the 'strict liability rule', so-called because breach of it does not depend upon proof of any intention to interfere with the trial. It is sometimes referred to as 'statutory contempt' (see, e.g., *Re Lonrho plc* [1989] 2 All ER 1100, HL, *per* Lord Bridge at p. 1113) in order to distinguish it from common law contempt, which continues to exist in this area but for which a person cannot be liable unless there was an *intention* to interfere with the trial. (See further on the post-1981 common law, para 5.2.2.4.8 below.)

5.2.2.2 The position at common law

The common law position is well illustrated by some of the cases involving the press, which, along with the broadcasting media, are particularly affected by this aspect of contempt of court.

In 1949, the *Daily Mirror* was fined £10,000 and its editor sent to prison for three months. Their contempt was in suggesting the names of persons who may have been murdered by John George Haigh, the so-called 'acid bath murderer', who at the time had been charged with only one murder (*R* v *Bolam (ex parte Haigh)* (1949) 93 SJ 220, DC). In 1957, W.H. Smith & Son Ltd were fined £50 for contempt in distributing the American magazine *Newsweek,* containing highly prejudicial material which had not been given in evidence, during the trial of Dr John Bodkin Adams for murder (*R* v *Griffiths (ex parte Attorney-General)* [1957] 2 QB 192, DC; this case was decided before the defence of innocent publication or distribution was first introduced in 1960; para 5.2.2.4.4 below. For examples of how *criminal* contempt at common law can arise in the context of *civil* litigation, see para 5.2.2.4.8 below).

In 1974, the *Socialist Worker* and its editor, Paul Foot, were each fined £250 for publishing the names of two blackmail victims after the trial judge had directed that they should be referred to only as Mr Y and Mr Z (*R* v *Socialist Worker (ex parte Attorney-General)* [1975] QB 637, DC). However, in *Attorney-General* v *Leveller Magazine Ltd* [1979] AC 440, the House of Lords found that the defendants were not in contempt for disclosing the name of a witness whom the magistrates' court had allowed to be referred to only as Colonel B. The magistrates had given no positive direction to the press not to publish his name and Colonel B himself had given evidence from which his identity could be discovered.

This type of disclosure is now dealt with by s. 11 of the Contempt of Court Act 1981, which bears a close resemblance to some of the speeches in *Attorney-General* v *Leveller Magazine Ltd.* Section 11 appears to confirm rather than confer a power to withhold matters from publication. It provides that where a court allows a name or other matter to be withheld from the public in proceedings before the court, the court may give such directions prohibiting the publication of that name or matter in connection with the proceedings as appear to be necessary for the purpose for which it was withheld.

In the *Leveller* case the majority of the House of Lords was of the opinion that for the purposes of liability at common law there had to be a clear direction or order restricting publication since it was not contempt to ignore a mere request not to publish. In view of this it seems reasonable to suppose that the court, when exercising its discretion under s. 11, must be seen clearly to be giving directions and not merely making a request. Section 11 does not impose strict liability and so a person cannot be guilty under it unless he knew of the court's order prohibiting publication. At the same time, as long as the court has allowed a name to be withheld and has given directions under s. 11 it would now seem to be immaterial that the defendant, as in the *Leveller* case, has discovered the name by deduction from the evidence given in the proceedings. However, if the court has not first allowed the name to be withheld from the public in the particular proceedings it has no jurisdiction to give a direction under s. 11 prohibiting publication of the name. Any such direction purported to be made can be ignored by the press and others (*R* v *Arundel Justices (ex parte Westminster Press Ltd)* [1985] 2 All ER 390, DC).

The power contained in s. 11 to authorise the witholding of information from the public is an exception to the principle of open justice. Accordingly, the court must exercise the power very sparingly and only in exceptional circumstances where it can be shown to be necessary. It is, for example, inappropriate for a magistrates' court to make an order under s. 11, prohibiting publication of the defendant's name and business addresses and the allegations made against him, in order to protect the defendant's business from damage and possible closure (*R* v *Dover Justices (ex parte Dover District Council)* (1991) 156 JP 433, DC). In *R* v *Legal Aid Board (ex parte Kaim Todner)* [1998] 3 All ER 541, CA, a firm of solicitors sought permission to apply for judicial review of the Legal Aid Board's decision to terminate its franchise. At the same time, the firm applied for an order under s. 11 forbidding disclosure of its identity on the ground that its interests would be seriously damaged if the Board's reasons for terminating the franchise were made public. The judge's decision to refuse to make a s. 11 order was affirmed by the Court of Appeal, which held that, in the absence of special circumstances, there is no justification for according special treatment to the legal profession with regard to anonymity.

In *Birmingham Post and Mail Ltd* v *Birmingham City Council* (1993) *The Times*, 25 November, DC, it was held that it is in the interests of the public and of the fair administration of justice for a court to make an order under s. 11 prohibiting publication of the name and address of a person with a notifiable disease (in this case tuberculosis) against whom an *ex parte* order has been made under public health legislation requiring his removal to hospital. It was further held, however, allowing the newspaper's appeal, that the prohibition order should be limited in time because once the opportunity to challenge the hospital order has gone the interests of justice are no longer involved and a desire to protect the privacy of, or prevent embarrassment to, the patient does not in itself justify the continuance of the prohibition order.

Although the *sub judice* rule is capable of applying to *all* legal proceedings, whether criminal or civil, original or appellate, it was considered most unlikely that the courts would treat as contempt, either at common law or under the statutory strict liability rule, a public discussion of the merits of a pending civil action which was to be tried by a judge sitting without a jury or a public discussion of a civil or criminal case which was pending before the Court of Appeal or House of Lords (*R* v *Duffy (ex parte Nash)* [1960] 2 QB 188, DC; *Vine Products Ltd* v *Green* [1966] Ch 484; *Attorney-General* v *British Broadcasting Corporation* [1979] 3 All ER 45, CA, reversed on other grounds at [1980] 3 All ER 161, HL). A professional judge, it was said, can be relied upon to be completely uninfluenced by anything he reads in the newspapers or sees on television (*Attorney-General* v *British Broadcasting Corporation*, CA, above, *per* Lord Denning MR at p. 52; in the House of Lords, Lord Salmon agreed with this statement (p. 169) but Viscount Dilhorne did not (p. 163)). As Lord Bridge pointed out in the *Lonrho* contempt case ([1989] 2 All ER 1100 at p. 1117 and see below), it is common to find in legal journals discussion and criticism of decisions at first instance or of the Court of Appeal which are subject to pending appeals, and, in the newspapers, criticism of criminal convictions, sentences and awards of damages in libel cases.

The view shared by Lord Denning and Lord Salmon was vindicated by the subsequent decision of the House of Lords in the unusual case of *Re Lonrho plc* [1989] 2 All ER 1100, which arose out of an alleged attempt to influence the judges of the highest appellate court. Lonrho plc had been unsuccessful in its bid to acquire House of Fraser plc (and with it the Harrods department store), which was instead taken over by the Al Fayed brothers. As a result of pressure from Lonrho, the Secretary of State for Trade and Industry appointed inspectors to inquire into the Al Fayed take-over. He referred the inspectors' report to the Director of the Serious Fraud Office and the Director of Public Prosecutions and decided not to publish it before the Serious Fraud Office had completed its investigations and any resulting prosecutions had been completed. The Secretary of State later decided, without giving any reasons, that it would not be appropriate to refer the Al Fayed take-over bid for House of Fraser to the Monopolies and Mergers Commission.

At this stage, Lonrho applied to the Queen's Bench Divisional Court for judicial review of the Secretary of State's decisions. The application was granted by the Divisional Court, but that decision was reversed by the Court of Appeal on an appeal by the Secretary of State. Lonrho appealed to the House of Lords. Before the appeal was heard a copy of the inspectors' report came into the possession of Lonrho's chief executive who passed it on to the editor of *The Observer* newspaper, which was owned by Lonrho and which supported Lonrho's campaign against the Al Fayed take-over. A special mid-week edition of *The Observer* was published containing extracts from the inspectors' report. The Secretary of State obtained an injunction to prevent further distribution of the special edition but he was too late to stop the sale of 200,000 copies. Lonrho itself sent some copies by post to persons on a mailing list. Four of the five Law Lords who were listed to hear Lonrho's appeal in the judicial review proceedings received a copy.

The House of Lords took a serious view of the matter and, of its own motion as a superior court within the meaning of s. 19 of the Contempt of Court Act 1981 (see para 5.4.2 below), instituted contempt proceedings. It was alleged that Lonrho and its advisers were in contempt in that they had (a) attempted to influence the decision of the Law Lords in the pending proceedings, and (b) pre-empted that decision by resorting to self-help to obtain the very remedy they were seeking from the courts (disclosure of the inspectors' report). It was held that Lonrho and its advisers had not committed contempt of court because (a) the possibility that the Law Lords would be influenced by *The Observer* special edition was too remote, and (b) pre-empting the decision of the court could not amount to impeding or prejudicing the course of justice. Lord Bridge said (at pp. 1116–7):

> Before proceedings have come to trial and before the facts have been found, it is easy to see how critical public discussion of the issues and criticism of the conduct of the parties, particularly if a party is held up to public obloquy, may impede or prejudice the course of the proceedings by influencing the conduct of witnesses or parties in relation to the proceedings. If the trial is to be by jury, the possibility of prejudice by advance publicity directed to an issue which the jury will have to decide is obvious. The possibility that a professional judge will be influenced by anything he has read about the issues in a case which he has to try is very much more remote . . . So far as the appellate tribunal is concerned, it is difficult to visualise circumstances in which any court in the United Kingdom exercising appellate jurisdiction would be in the least likely to be influenced by public discussion of the merits of a decision appealed against or of the parties' conduct in the proceedings.

5.2.2.3   The 'thalidomide case'

The cases on the *sub judice* rule described at the beginning of para 5.2.2.2 are eclipsed by the litigation in the 1970s in the 'thalidomide case', *Attorney-General* v *Times Newspapers Ltd* [1972] 3 All ER 1136, DC; [1973] 1 QB 710, CA; [1974] AC 273, HL; [1979] 2 EHRR 245, European Court of Human Rights. Between 1958 and 1961 the Distillers Co. Ltd manufactured and marketed a sedative which contained the drug thalidomide. The sedative was said to be safe for pregnant women but, in fact, many of those who used it gave birth to babies with serious deformities. Some 460 such children were born. Writs were issued against Distillers claiming damages for negligence. Some 70 actions were settled out of court, but by the middle of 1972 there were 389 claims outstanding.

In September 1972, the *Sunday Times* published the first of what was intended to be a series of articles to draw attention to the plight of the children. The article urged Distillers to make a larger out-of-court settlement than they had offered hitherto. Distillers complained to the Attorney-General that the article was a contempt of court because some claims were still pending, but the Attorney decided to take no action. However, the editor of the *Sunday Times* made preparations to publish a second article intended to show that Distillers had not exercised due care to ensure that thalidomide was safe for pregnant women before they put it on the market. The editor sent a copy of the second article to the Attorney-General, who commenced contempt proceedings for an injunction to restrain the proprietors of the newspaper from publishing the second article. The Queen's Bench Divisional Court granted the injunction but the Court of Appeal refused it. The House of Lords allowed the Attorney-General's appeal and sent the case back to the Divisional Court with a direction to grant the injunction.

The reasons given by the Law Lords for their decision were, first, that it was a contempt to publish comments on a specific issue which was before the court for determination where those comments gave rise to a real risk that the fair trial of the action would be prejudiced. Secondly, it was a contempt to use improper pressure to induce a litigant to settle a case on terms which were not agreeable to him.

The matter did not rest there, however, for Times Newspapers Ltd took the issue before the European Court of Human Rights, alleging that the House of Lords' decision violated art. 10 of the European Convention on Human Rights which protects the right to freedom of expression. The case was before the European Court of Human Rights for over four years pending judgment in April 1979. Meanwhile, in 1976, the Attorney-General had applied successfully to the Divisional Court to have the injunction discharged on the ground that by then most of the children's actions against Distillers had been settled. This was a tactical blunder because the Human Rights Court at Strasbourg was able to question whether the injunction had been necessary in the first place.

The European Court of Human Rights eventually decided, by 11 votes to nine, that the House of Lords' decision in the thalidomide case was a violation of the right of freedom of expression. The injunction had not been necessary in a democratic society for maintaining the authority of the courts since there was no social need which outweighed the public interest in freedom of expression.

5.2.2.4 Contempt of Court Act 1981

5.2.2.4.1 Introduction. The Contempt of Court Act 1981 was enacted to reform the law, partly to take account of the decision of the Human Rights Court in the thalidomide case in 1979 and partly to implement some of the recommendations of the *Phillimore Committee on Contempt of Court* which sat between 1971 and 1974 (Cmnd 5794, 1974). The changes effected by the Act relate particularly, although not exclusively, to the *sub judice* or strict liability rule. It should be noted that, by s. 7 of the 1981 Act, proceedings for contempt under the strict liability rule can only be commenced by or with the consent of the Attorney-General or on the motion of a court having jurisdiction to deal with the contempt. This includes the House of Lords, which, in *Re Lonrho plc* [1989] 2 All ER 1100, of its own motion commenced contempt proceedings against a multinational corporation (see para 5.2.2.2 above).

Although it is a matter of great importance to newspaper publishers and the like, no guidelines are laid down for the exercise of the Attorney-General's discretion to prosecute under the strict liability rule. Thus, although no proceedings were taken at common law (the 1981 Act was not then in force) in respect of almost universally irresponsible press speculation following the arrest in January 1981 of Peter Sutcliffe, the so-called 'Yorkshire ripper', the publishers and editor of the *Daily Mail* were proceeded against (unsuccessfully) for publishing an article at the time of the trial of Dr Arthur (*Attorney-General* v *English* [1982] 2 All ER 903, HL, para 5.2.2.4.6 below), as were the publishers of five newspapers for reports concerning Michael Fagan, the so-called 'Buckingham Palace intruder' (*Attorney-General* v *Times Newspapers Ltd and others* (1983) *The Times,* 12 February, DC).

5.2.2.4.2   Definition of 'strict liability rule' and 'publication'.   Section 1 of the Contempt of Court Act 1981 defines the strict liability rule as 'the rule of law whereby conduct may be treated as a contempt of court as tending to interfere with the course of justice in particular legal proceedings regardless of intent to do so'. It is provided that the strict liability rule applies only to 'publications' and, moreover, only to publications which create a *substantial* risk that the course of justice in the proceedings in question will be *seriously* impeded or prejudiced (Contempt of Court Act 1981, s. 2(2)). Whether this is so is essentially a question of fact. This provision has, it seems, relaxed the law since, according to the House of Lords in *Attorney-General* v *Times Newspapers Ltd* [1974] AC 273, the common-law position was that the risk need only have been *real* (not *substantial*) that the proceedings would be impeded or prejudiced (not necessarily *seriously* so). 'Publication' includes any speech, writing, broadcast or other communication in whatever form, which is addressed to the public at large or any section of the public (Contempt of Court Act 1981, s. 2(1)). The 'risk' referred to in s. 2(2) must be a practical and not a theoretical risk (*Attorney-General* v *Guardian Newspapers Ltd* [1992] 3 All ER 38, DC).

Section 2 was considered by the Court of Appeal in *Attorney-General* v *News Group Newspapers Ltd* [1986] 2 All ER 833. In 1984, Ian Botham, a well-known cricketer, began libel proceedings against the editor and owners of the *Mail on Sunday*. The case was set down for trial no earlier than March 1987. In April 1986, the *News of the World* proposed to publish the same allegations against Ian Botham as had been made the subject of the libel suit against the *Mail on Sunday*. The Attorney-General brought proceedings under the strict liability rule to stop publication in the *News of the World*. It was held that his action was premature and the injunction granted at first instance in the High Court to restrain publication was discharged. The Court of Appeal said that 'substantial risk' and 'serious prejudice' mentioned in s. 2 provide stringent tests for the making of a restraining order. Such factors as the place of trial, the nature of the proposed publication, and the proximity of publication to the date of trial are important in deciding whether, under ss. 1 and 2, the strict liability rule applies. The Court of Appeal decided that, although the libel proceedings in question were 'active' (because the case had been set down for hearing: see para 5.2.2.4.3), the date fixed for trial was so far ahead of the proposed publication that it did not create a substantial risk of serious prejudice to the trial of the libel action. Similarly, in *Attorney-General* v *Independent Television News Ltd and others* [1995] 2 All ER 370, DC, an attempt to have the defendants, ITN and the publishers of the *Daily Mail, Today*, the *Daily Express* and the *Northern Echo*, fined for contempt failed because, *inter alia*, there had been a gap of some nine months between the offending news item and the subsequent trial.

Attorney-General v *Birmingham Post and Mail Ltd* [1998] 4 All ER 49, DC, was concerned with the publication of a newspaper article *during* the trial in Birmingham of a number of defendants charged with various serious offences, including murder. The article in the *Birmingham Post* did not name any of the defendants but suggested that the murder had been committed by members of a notorious criminal gang who were connected with drug dealing. At the trial, the defendants had denied belonging to any gang and the prosecution had never alleged that the offences charged were connected with drug dealing. The trial judge stopped the trial and discharged the jury. The Attorney-General later applied to have the newspaper proprietors fined for contempt under the strict liability rule. It was held that the article had created a substantial risk that the trial was seriously prejudiced and the proprietors were fined £20,000. Of particular relevance was the possibility that those members of the jury who had read the article might have been influenced by it to view the evidence given in court in a different, unjustified light.

5.2.2.4.3 'Active' proceedings. The strict liability rule will not apply to a publication unless the proceedings in question are 'active' at the time of the publication (Contempt of Court Act 1981, s. 2(3) and sch. 1).

Briefly, *criminal* proceedings are active, as appropriate, from the time of (a) arrest without warrant; or (b) the issue of a warrant for arrest; or (c) the issue of a summons to appear; or (d) the service of an indictment or other document specifying the charge; or (e) oral charge. They are concluded by acquittal, sentence, discontinuance or by operation of law.

Civil proceedings are active from the time the case is set down for hearing or when a date for the trial or hearing is fixed.

Appellate proceedings are active only from the time when they are commenced (ibid., sch. 1). There is thus freedom to comment on a case between the conclusion of the proceedings at first instance and the initiation of an appeal. Depending on their type, appellate proceedings are usually commenced (a) by application for leave to appeal or to apply for judicial review, or by notice of such an application, or (b) by notice of appeal. Appellate proceedings cease to be active when they are disposed of, abandoned, discontinued or withdrawn. However, where the court in appellate *criminal* proceedings remits the case to the court below, or orders a new trial or a *venire de novo* (para 6.3.2.3), any further or new proceedings which result are treated as active from the conclusion of the appellate proceedings (ibid., sch. 1, para 16). Since the strict liability rule applies to such a case in the interval between the conclusion of the appellate proceedings and the start of the fresh proceedings, there is no unfettered freedom of comment.

5.2.2.4.4 Innocent publication or distribution. By s. 3 of the Contempt of Court Act 1981, innocent publication or distribution is a defence to a charge of criminal contempt under the strict liability rule. This statutory defence was first introduced by s. 11 of the Administration of Justice Act 1960, which is now repealed and replaced by s. 3 of the 1981 Act. A publisher is not in contempt if at the time of publication, and having taken all reasonable care, he does not know and has no reason to suspect that relevant proceedings are active (Contempt of Court Act 1981, s. 3(1)). A distributor is not in contempt if at the time of distribution, and having taken all reasonable care, he does not know that the publication contains prejudicial material and has no reason to suspect that it is likely to do so (ibid., s. 3(2)). The burden of proving this defence is on the publisher or distributor (ibid., s. 3(3)).

Section 3(1) was initially relied upon in *Solicitor-General* v *Henry and News Group Newspapers Ltd* [1990] COD 307, DC, in which contempt proceedings were instituted against the publishers and editor of a Sunday newspaper in respect of a prominently-featured article about the disappearance in Bristol of Shirley Banks. The *News of the World* revealed that a named man, who had been arrested for, *inter alia,* the abduction of Mrs Banks (and in respect of whom criminal proceedings were, therefore, 'active' (see para 5.2.2.4.3 above)), had previous convictions for rape and robbery. He was described in the article as a 'sex beast'. It was not disputed that the article created a substantial risk that the course of justice in the proceedings would be seriously prejudiced within the meaning of s. 2 of the Contempt of Court Act 1981. Accordingly, its publication would constitute a contempt under the strict liability rule unless the defendants could rely successfully on the defence provided by s. 3(1).

It was accepted that neither the editor nor anyone else at the *News of the World* knew about the arrest on the abduction charge. Since the man had already been arrested on a robbery charge, and was in custody, his arrest for abduction did not involve taking him into custody and nobody besides those immediately concerned would be likely to know that the second arrest had happened. The question was, therefore, whether the defendants had 'taken all reasonable care' and had 'no reason to suspect' that relevant proceedings were active. When it became clear during the course of the hearing that, on the facts, the defendants could not realistically expect the protection of s. 3(1) they abandoned their defence. The Divisional Court decided that, in the particular circumstances of the case, no penalty would be imposed on the editor but that the publishers of the *News of the World* would be fined a comparatively modest £15,000.

5.2.2.4.5   *Postponement of publication of reports.*   By s. 4(1) of the Contempt of Court Act 1981, it is not a contempt under the strict liability rule to publish contemporaneously and in good faith a fair and accurate report of legal proceedings held in public. However, under s. 4(2), a court has a discretion to order that publication of reports of a case before it be postponed.

Some judges had claimed the power to order postponement at common law. Thus, publication of reports was postponed in *R v Clement* (1821) 4 B & Ald 218, at the time of the Cato Street conspiracy trials, and at the time of the Poulson trials in the 1970s. Section 4(2) of the Contempt of Court Act 1981 now puts the discretion on a statutory footing. Under the Act, a court may order postponement of publication only 'where it appears to be necessary for avoiding a substantial risk of prejudice' in the proceedings or in any other proceedings which are pending or imminent.

Section 4(2) thus lays down two requirements for the making of a postponement order. The court must consider, first, whether publication would create 'a substantial risk of prejudice' and, secondly, whether the order 'appears to be necessary' for the avoidance of that risk. If there is no substantial risk of prejudice then no order should be made. If there *is* a substantial risk an order should still not be made unless it is necessary to do so. If it is necessary to make an order its terms should be no wider than is consistent with avoiding the risk of prejudice (*Ex parte Telegraph plc* [1993] 2 All ER 971, CA, where it was held that the trial judge had failed to consider whether his order under s. 4(2) containing all manner of restrictions, and made after he had ordered separate trials for groups of defendants charged with serious drug offences, was necessary; it was varied on appeal by restricting the postponement of publication only to the names of, and any material which might identify, the defendants in the later trials).

The postponement of publication under a s. 4(2) order may be for such period as the court thinks necessary for the purpose of avoiding the risk of prejudice.

Section 4(2) applies only to a 'report of legal proceedings held in public'. A film of a person being arrested for drug offences, taken by a television camera crew for a programme about drug trafficking, is not a report of 'legal proceedings held in public'. Accordingly, magistrates have no jurisdiction to order that publication of the film be postponed. If in such a case a breach of the strict liability rule is feared, the appropriate remedy is an application to the High Court for an injunction to prevent publication (*R v Rhuddlan Justices (ex parte HTV Ltd)* [1986] Crim LR 329, DC).

A judge's decision under s. 4(2) ordering or refusing to order postponement of publication will rarely involve a question of law, and the Court of Appeal has held that his decision is not likely to be interfered with on appeal unless he has exercised his discretion on a fundamentally flawed basis (*Re Saunders* (1990) *The Times,* 8 February).

To publish a report of proceedings in defiance of a postponement order made by a court under s. 4(2) may itself constitute a contempt. There was disagreement on this question in the Court of Appeal in *R v Horsham Justices (ex parte Farquharson)* [1982] 2 All ER 269, although the opinions there expressed were all *obiter.* Lord Denning MR thought that the defiance of a postponement order would not be a contempt under the statute unless it would also be a contempt at common law (at p. 284). Shaw and Ackner LJJ thought that s. 4 of the Contempt of Court Act 1981 had created a new head of contempt and that publication in defiance of a postponement order would be a contempt regardless of the position at common law (at pp. 290 and 295 respectively). It is clear that a publisher who defies a postponement order made under s. 4(2) is deprived of the statutory defence under s. 4(1) since the report would not be published 'in good faith'. As for other sanctions, the better view appears to be that of Lord Denning. The publisher, it seems, would not be in contempt unless the report caused, within the meaning of the common law, a real risk of prejudice to particular legal proceedings. This was certainly the view of the House of Lords, expressed before the Act was passed, in *Attorney-General v Leveller Magazine Ltd* [1979] AC 440, in which it was said that a breach of the order not to reveal Colonel B's name would not be a contempt unless the breach interfered with the administration of justice (at pp. 453, 465 and 472 *per* Lord Diplock, Lord Edmund-Davies and Lord Scarman respectively).

R v Horsham Justices was the first case in which the courts had to consider the effects of a postponement order under s. 4. On 23 June 1981 a magistrates' court hearing committal proceedings granted an application under s. 3(2) of the Criminal Justice Act 1967 to have reporting restrictions removed. (Note that s. 3(2) of the 1967 Act was replaced as from 6 July 1981 by s. 8(2) of the Magistrates' Courts Act 1980. For restrictions on the reporting of committal proceedings, see para 1.7.6.3.3.) At a later stage in the committal proceedings, the same court made an order under the Contempt of Court Act 1981 prohibiting publication of any report of the proceedings until the commencement of any subsequent trial. This order was challenged in proceedings for judicial review by a journalist, his newspaper (the *West Sussex County Times)* and his union.

The Court of Appeal held that the general restrictions on reporting contained in the Contempt of Court Act 1981 are capable of applying to committal proceedings at the same time as the specific restrictions on the reporting of committal proceedings contained in s. 3(2) of the Criminal Justice Act 1967. There is no conflict between the two statutory provisions since they impose restrictions in different situations and for different purposes. Thus, s. 3 of the 1967 Act is concerned with the prevention of prejudice to the interests of the accused in committal proceedings. On the other hand, the 1981 Act is concerned with the situation in which publication of proceedings, whether or not prejudicial to the accused, might be a contempt of court because, for example, it might prejudice other persons and other trials or because it might disclose the real name of a witness when the judge had ordered the use of a pseudonym or it might report what took place *in camera*. It was accordingly held in the *Horsham Justices* case that the magistrates did have jurisdiction under the 1981 Act to make a postponement order. However, on the facts, their order was quashed as being too wide. The case was sent back to the magistrates for them to reconsider whether it was necessary to postpone publication of all the committal proceedings or whether a postponement of publication of part of the proceedings would suffice.

It is clear from the *Horsham Justices* case that postponement orders made under s. 4(2) of the Contempt of Court Act 1981 will need to be formulated in precise terms. To that end, a *Practice Note* [1983] 1 All ER 64 provides that such an order must be in writing and must state (a) its precise scope; (b) the time at which it shall cease to have effect, if appropriate; and (c) the specific purpose of making the order. (For a case where the *Practice Note* was not properly observed, see *Re Central Independent Television plc and others* [1991] 1 All ER 347, CA, below.) The same requirements are extended by the *Practice Note* to orders made under s. 11 of the 1981 Act prohibiting the publication of any name or other matter in connection with proceedings before the court (para 5.2.2.2 above). It is envisaged that a court will give notice to the press that an order has been made under s. 4(2) or under s. 11 and that the court staff will be prepared to answer enquiries about specific cases. But it is emphasised that reporters of cases and their editors remain responsible for ensuring that there is no breach of any order and that *they* should take the initiative in making enquiries if there is doubt in any particular case.

In addition to observing the requirements of the *Practice Note*, it has been suggested that a judge making an order under s. 4(2) should in some situations make it clear at the time whether the very fact that he has made the order can be published — with or without details of its terms. This suggestion was made in the context of the view, expressed *obiter*, that publishing the terms of an order made under s. 4(2) may itself possibly amount to a contempt unless the report of the order can be construed as 'a report of legal proceedings held in public' within the meaning of s. 4(1) (*Attorney-General* v *Guardian Newspapers Ltd* [1992] 3 All ER 38, DC, *per* Mann LJ at p. 46).

The court has an inherent discretion to hear representations from the news media both before and after making an order under s. 4(2) postponing reports of proceedings (*R* v *Beck (ex parte Daily Telegraph plc)* (1991) [1993] 2 All ER 177, CA; *Attorney-General* v *Guardian Newspapers Ltd* [1992] 3 All ER 38, DC; *R* v *Clerkenwell Magistrates' Court (ex parte Telegraph plc)* [1993] 2 All ER 183, DC, where a stipendiary magistrate's decision, made on the ground that he had no jurisdiction to hear representations, refusing to hear from five national newspapers their representations on why an order he had made under s. 4(2) should be discharged, was quashed and the matter remitted to him for reconsideration).

The principle of open justice requires that legal proceedings are held in open court to which the press and public are admitted, that evidence given in the proceedings is communicated publicly, and that dissemination of fair and accurate reports of the proceedings to the public at large is not discouraged (*Attorney-General* v *Leveller Magazine Ltd* [1979] AC 440, HL, *per* Lord Diplock at p. 450). While recognising that there are exceptions (both by statute and at common law) to the basic principle, the courts have stressed that any departure from it in an individual case rests on necessity and not on what the judge in his discretion regards as expedient or convenient (*Scott* v *Scott* [1913] AC 417, HL, *per* Viscount Haldane LC at p. 437).

Maintenance of the principle of open justice makes it essential to take seriously the disquiet expressed in the media over recent years about the number of postponement orders being made under ss. 4 and 11 and about the increasing number of occasions on which members of the public are excluded from criminal trials. Such orders made by *magistrates' courts* can be challenged in an application to the High Court for judicial review. However, this procedure is not available where the order is made by the *Crown Court* in relation to a trial on indictment (Supreme Court Act 1981, s. 29(3); see para 11.8.2). Instead, a right of appeal has been provided which enables 'a person aggrieved' to appeal against orders made by the Crown Court postponing reports of a trial on indictment, or postponing publication of details emerging in it, or excluding the public from the trial (Criminal Justice Act 1988, s. 159).

The appeal lies to, and only with the leave of, the Court of Appeal, criminal division (ibid., s. 159(1)). The decision of the Court of Appeal (which may confirm, reverse or vary the order appealed against: ibid., s. 159(5)) is final, there being no further appeal to the House of Lords (ibid., s. 159(1)). When hearing an appeal under s. 159, the function of the Court of Appeal is to form its own view of what is the best order to make based on the material placed before it; its function is not limited simply to reviewing the judge's order made at first instance (*R v Beck (ex parte Daily Telegraph plc)* (1991) [1993] 2 All ER 177, CA, *per* Farquharson LJ at p. 180; *Ex Parte Telegraph plc* [1993] 2 All ER 971, CA, *per* Lord Taylor CJ at p. 977).

The first appeals under the new procedure provided by s. 159 of the Criminal Justice Act 1988 were brought by Mr Tim Crook, a freelance journalist whose job involved supplying national news organisations with reports of legal proceedings. The appeals in *Re Crook* [1992] 2 All ER 687, CA, arose out of the exclusion of the public for short periods from two unrelated trials on indictment at the Central Criminal Court. The appeals were unsuccessful. The Court of Appeal held that, in the circumstances, neither judge could be faulted for acting as he did since the exclusions were ordered for the purpose of hearing applications during which information could be imparted which, if made public, might prejudice the administration of justice. As the judge could not know until he had been given further information whether the administration of justice would be prejudiced if that information was disseminated, it was appropriate that it should be given in the absence of the public. An alternative argument of the appellant was that, even if it was right to exclude the public, the Press should not have been excluded. That argument also failed. The Court of Appeal was of the view that if exclusion of the public was necessary it would not usually be right to make an exception in favour of the Press because to do so would genuinely aggrieve other members of the public with as much interest in the proceedings, such as the victim's family or the defendant's family.

In *Re Crook,* the Court of Appeal took the opportunity to offer guidance to judges on the exclusion of the public from proceedings. Each application for exclusion must be considered on its individual merits and the public must only be excluded when it is strictly necessary. A judge should not adjourn into chambers as a matter of course, but only if he believes that something might be said which would be more appropriately heard in private than in public. If he does decide to sit in chambers he should return to open court if, and as soon as, it becomes apparent that it was not necessary, after all, to exclude the public.

In *Re Central Independent Television plc and others* [1991] 1 All ER 347, the Court of Appeal held that s. 159 of the Criminal Justice Act 1988 can be used to appeal against an order which is spent and where, therefore, the challenge to it is largely academic. To hold that an order wrongly made cannot be reversed on appeal simply because it has ceased to operate would undesirably lessen the effectiveness of s. 159 (ibid., *per* Lord Lane CJ at p. 351). In this case, the trial judge in the Crown Court had made an order under s. 4(2) of the Contempt of Court Act 1981 which prohibited the reporting of a trial by radio and television on one particular evening. The members of the jury had retired to consider their verdict and were spending the night at an hotel. The judge took the view that the jury should be able to listen to the radio, or watch television, without the possibility of being prejudiced by media reports of the trial. Three broadcasting companies appealed against the order, as 'persons aggrieved' by it, under s. 159 of the Criminal Justice Act 1988.

Allowing the appeal, the Court of Appeal held that the judge's order was not necessary because, in the circumstances, reports of the proceedings on radio and television would not have created a substantial risk of prejudice to the administration of justice. The court said, *obiter,* that even if there is a substantial risk of prejudice to the administration of justice, s. 4(2) should not be used to ban reporting of criminal trials on radio and television merely for the convenience of a jury which has to spend the night at an hotel since it is more appropriate to order the jury to be denied access to radio and television ([1991] 1 All ER 347 *per* Lord Lane CJ at p. 350).

One further point arising from *Re Central Independent Television plc and others* relates to the question of costs. On the hearing of an appeal under s. 159, the court has power 'to make such order as to costs as it thinks fit' (s. 159(5)(c)). The Court of Appeal decided that, by necessary implication, this provision must include payment out of 'central funds' (meaning 'money provided by Parliament': see the Interpretation Act 1978, s. 5 and sch. 1) and, accordingly, it was ordered that the costs of the successful appellants be paid out of central funds. The decision of the Court of Appeal on this point was later overruled in *Steele Ford & Newton* v *Crown Prosecution Service* [1993] 2 All ER 769, HL. Here the House of Lords held that, in the absence of express clear terms, a statute cannot be interpreted as conferring on the court by implication a power to order costs to be paid out of central funds since such an interpretation would amount to judicial legislation and a trespass upon Parliament's exclusive control over the raising and expenditure of public revenue. The rest of *Re Central Independent Television plc and others* is unaffected by their Lordships' decision in *Steele Ford & Newton* v *Crown Prosecution Service*.

There is no right of appeal under s. 159 against a judge's decision *not* to exclude the public from the proceedings. This is because s. 159(1)(b) refers only to 'any order restricting the access of the public to the whole or any part of a trial on indictment or to any proceedings ancillary to such a trial' and not to an order refusing to restrict such access (*R* v *Salih* (1994) *The Times*, 31 December, CA).

5.2.2.4.6 Bona fide discussion. Section 5 of the Contempt of Court Act 1981 is a particularly liberalising measure. It provides that a publication made as part of 'a discussion in good faith of public affairs or other matters of general public interest is not to be treated as a contempt of court under the strict liability rule if the risk of impediment or prejudice to particular legal proceedings is merely incidental to the discussion'. This section clearly recognises that it is in the public interest that there should be no suspension of public debate of public issues merely because there is an incidental risk of prejudice to particular legal proceedings. If the terms of s. 5 are satisfied, the strict liability rule has no application so that the publication in question will be a contempt only if an *intention* to impede or prejudice particular legal proceedings can be proved.

Section 5 of the 1981 Act was considered by the House of Lords in *Attorney-General* v *English* [1982] 2 All ER 903. The *Daily Mail* published an article by Malcolm Muggeridge written in support of someone who was seeking election to Parliament as a pro-life candidate. The article was concerned with the preservation of the sanctity of human life. It alleged that handicapped babies had been and were likely to be allowed to die of starvation and by other means. The article was published in the same week that Dr Leonard Arthur, a well-known consultant paediatrician, went on trial for the murder of a Down's syndrome baby by starvation, although the article made no mention of Dr Arthur's trial.

The Attorney-General applied to the Divisional Court of the Queen's Bench Division for an order for committal against the proprietors of the *Daily Mail* and its editor, Mr David English, for contempt under the 1981 Act. It was not suggested that the article was intended to influence Dr Arthur's trial; instead, the Attorney-General relied on the strict liability rule contained in s. 1 of the Act. The editor and publishers relied on s. 5 of the Act. The Divisional Court held that publication of the article was a contempt of court. The editor was not punished but the owners of the *Daily Mail* were fined £500. On appeal, the House of Lords held that the editor and publishers were not in contempt and their appeal was allowed. Although publication of the article created the risk of serious prejudice to Dr Arthur's trial within the meaning of s. 2(2) of the Act, the trial had not been mentioned in the article. The risk of the jury reading the article and allowing it to prejudice their minds against Dr Arthur on evidence which did not justify a finding of guilty was 'merely incidental' to the discussion contained in the article.

As for Dr Arthur himself, the judge at his trial directed a verdict of not guilty on the murder charge but left to the jury a charge of attempted murder. Dr Arthur was acquitted of that charge in November 1981. He died at the age of 57 on Christmas Day 1983 after a long illness.

The following points on s. 5 and on some other provisions of the Contempt of Court Act 1981 emerge from the judgment of Lord Diplock in *Attorney-General* v *English* [1982] 2 All ER 903, at pp. 918–20, a judgment with which the other Law Lords expressly agreed.

(a)   Section 5 of the Act must be read together with s. 2(2) (para 5.2.2.4.2 above). They both state criteria by which a publication is to be held not to constitute a contempt despite its tendency to impede or prejudice particular legal proceedings. Section 5 is not a defence to the strict liability rule. The burden of proof, therefore, is not on the defendant to exonerate himself. Instead, the burden lies on the prosecution to prove that the publication caused a substantial risk of impediment or prejudice to the proceedings within the meaning of s. 2(2), and then, if the publication was part of a wider discussion on a matter of general public interest, that the risk of impediment or prejudice was not merely incidental to the discussion.

(b)   The purpose of s. 5 is to prevent the gagging of bona fide public discussion in the media of controversial matters of general public interest merely because there exist contemporaneous legal proceedings in which some particular instance of those controversial matters may be in issue.

(c)   The word 'discussion' in s. 5 is not limited to the airing of views and the debating of principles and arguments. It includes the making of accusations.

(d)   The correct test under s. 5 is whether the risk created by the words actually chosen by the author was 'merely incidental to the discussion', i.e., no more than an incidental consequence of expounding the main theme of the discussion.

(e)   The principal beneficiaries of any mitigation of the strict liability rule brought about by the Act are the press and the broadcasting media since it is usually their publications which are 'addressed to the public at large or any section of the public'. Public speeches also fall within the definition of 'publication' in s. 2(1) (para 5.2.2.4.2 above). However, unless such speeches are reported by the media, they are likely to be exonerated by s. 2(2) on the ground that their limited reception does not create a substantial risk of serious interference with particular legal proceedings.

(f)   The risk referred to in s. 2(2) has to be assessed at the time of publication and not in the light of subsequent events. Thus, a newspaper article which, at the date of publication, violates the strict liability rule does not cease to be a contempt merely because it can be shown that, as events turned out, it did not affect the outcome of the proceedings in question. To hold otherwise would encourage trial by the media.

(g)   The expression 'substantial risk' in s. 2(2) is intended to exclude a risk which is remote. A slight or trivial risk of serious prejudice is not enough, nor is a substantial risk of slight prejudice.

(h)   The course of justice in *criminal* proceedings is seriously impeded or prejudiced within the meaning of s. 2(2) whenever the outcome of the trial, or the need to discharge the jury before verdict, is put at risk.

(i)   There is a suggestion that s. 5 of the 1981 Act may not provide protection in circumstances like those in the thalidomide case, *Attorney-General* v *Times Newspapers Ltd* [1974] AC 273, HL (para 5.2.2.3 above). In *Attorney-General* v *English* [1982] 2 All ER 903, Lord Diplock said that the offending article was in nearly all respects the antithesis of the offending article in the thalidomide case. In *Attorney-General* v *Times Newspapers Ltd* the whole subject of the article was the pending civil actions against Distillers and the whole purpose of it was to put pressure on Distillers in the lawful conduct of their defence in those actions. It would therefore be difficult to argue that the risk of prejudice to the proceedings was 'merely incidental' to the discussion in the article. (See also *Attorney-General* v *TVS Television Ltd* (1989) *The Independent,* 7 July, DC, where the subject matter of the discussion was so closely related to the particular proceedings that the admitted risk of prejudice was more than merely incidental to the discussion. A television company and the publishers of a free newspaper were fined £25,000 and £5,000 respectively for contempt under the strict liability rule.) In *Attorney-General* v *English*, on the other hand, the article did not mention Dr Arthur's trial and the risk of prejudice to it could properly be described as merely incidental to the discussion of the wider issues contained in the article (see [1982] 2 All ER 903, 920). If Lord Diplock's interpretation of s. 5 is correct, it would seem that the 1981 Act has failed to take account of the majority judgment of the European Court of Human Rights in the thalidomide case.

5.2.2.4.7   Some miscellaneous provisions.   Finally on the reform of the strict liability rule, it is provided by s. 6 of the Contempt of Court Act 1981 that:

(a)   The Act does not prejudice any defence available at common law to a charge of contempt under the strict liability rule.

(b)   The Act does not extend the strict liability rule beyond the limits previously set by the common law.

(c)   The Act does not restrict liability for contempt in respect of conduct which is *intended* to impede or prejudice the administration of justice.

5.2.2.4.8   Preservation of the common law.   Section 6(c) of the Contempt of Court Act 1981 is important because it preserves the common law of contempt in those cases where the strict liability rule cannot apply; as, for example, where the proceedings alleged to have been prejudiced were not active at the time of publication (for 'active' proceedings see para 5.2.2.4.3 above). In *Attorney-General* v *Times Newspapers Ltd* [1991] 2 All ER 398, HL, it was argued before the House of Lords on behalf of the defendants that the effect of s. 6(c) was to prevent the further development of the law of contempt otherwise than under the strict liability rule. Their Lordships' opinion was that s. 6(c) had no such effect, being merely a savings clause in respect of the existing common law (ibid., *per* Lord Brandon at p. 402, Lord Ackner at p. 413 and Lord Oliver at p. 414; this case is dealt with more fully below).

Common law contempt is of potentially wider application than the strict liability rule. While under s. 1 of the Contempt of Court Act 1981 the strict liability rule is limited to interference with 'particular legal proceedings', it has been held that common law contempt may be committed where there are no proceedings at all pending or imminent at the time of publication. It was so decided by a two-man Divisional Court in *Attorney-General v News Group Newspapers Ltd* [1988] 2 All ER 906, DC. This was a case in which the proprietors of the *Sun* newspaper were fined £75,000 for common law contempt in publishing allegations that a named doctor had raped an eight-year old girl, even though at the time of publication no proceedings against the doctor were pending or imminent (and, therefore, the strict liability rule did not apply). It was said that, although the need for a free press is axiomatic, 'the press cannot be allowed to charge about like a wild unbridled horse' (ibid., *per* Watkins LJ at p. 921).

What was thought to have been decided in *Attorney-General v News Group Newspapers Ltd* was thrown into doubt when in the later case of *Attorney-General v Sport Newspapers Ltd* [1992] 1 All ER 503, a differently constituted two-man Divisional Court was unable to agree on the point. Bingham LJ (at pp. 515–6) thought that the *News Group* decision, though admittedly extending the boundaries of common law contempt as previously understood, should be followed. Hodgson J (at p. 536) was of the opinion that the common law of contempt began to apply only from the time when relevant proceedings were pending and that, accordingly, the *News Group* case was wrongly decided. In his view, conduct committed before proceedings came into existence which was deliberately prejudicial to the administration of justice was more appropriately punished by the ordinary criminal law relating to perversion of the course of justice than by extending the scope of common law contempt.

Liability for common law contempt remains dependent upon proof of *intention* to interfere with the administration of justice. Without such an intention there will be no liability. In *Attorney-General v Sport Newspapers Ltd* [1992] 1 All ER 503, DC, proceedings were brought against the publishers and editor of *The Sport* newspaper following appearance of a front-page story in which a man wanted by the police for questioning about the disappearance of a 15-year old girl was described as a 'vicious rapist' and 'sex monster'. Bingham LJ and Hodgson J were unanimous in holding that, on the facts, the defendants were not guilty since they lacked the necessary *mens rea*. Proceedings for contempt under the strict liability rule were not possible in this case because, unlike the superficially similar case of *Solicitor-General v Henry and News Group Newspapers Ltd* [1990] COD 307, DC (para 5.2.2.4.4 above), criminal proceedings against the wanted man were not 'active' at the time of publication.

According to the Court of Appeal in *Attorney-General v Newspaper Publishing plc* [1987] 3 All ER 276, the requisite intention in common law contempt is a *specific* intention and not mere recklessness (ibid., *per* Sir John Donaldson MR at p. 304 and Lloyd LJ at p. 310). In the absence of an admission or other overt proof, the necessary intention can be implied from the contemnor's conduct and all the circumstances. It need not be the sole intention of the contemnor and may exist even though there is no wish to interfere with the administration of justice (ibid.).

A case which illustrates clearly the relationship between common law contempt and the strict liability rule is *Attorney-General v Hislop* [1991] 1 All ER 911, CA. Here, contempt proceedings were brought against the publishers and editor of the satirical magazine, *Private Eye*. Shortly before the trial of Sonia Sutcliffe's libel action against *Private Eye* (see *Sutcliffe v Pressdram Ltd* [1990] 1 All ER 269, CA, para 7.9.2.), two articles appeared in the magazine suggesting that Mrs Sutcliffe, wife of the 'Yorkshire Ripper', had known what her husband was doing at the time of the murders and either did nothing about it or gave him an alibi by lying to the police and that she was defrauding the Department of Social Security. The Attorney-General alleged that publication of the articles had created a real and substantial risk of serious prejudice to the fair trial of the libel action in that the articles had been published with the intention of persuading Mrs Sutcliffe to drop her libel action or of prejudicing potential jurors in the action. The Court of Appeal held that, in relation to the improper pressure put on Mrs Sutcliffe, the defendants were in contempt both at common law (since *intention* to deter Mrs Sutcliffe had been established) and under the strict liability rule. With regard to the prejudicing of potential jurors, however, there was contempt only under the strict liability rule since there had been no intention to influence prospective jurors. Each defendant was fined £10,000.

It is quite common for questions of *criminal* contempt to arise out of allegations of interference with the administration of *civil* justice (see, for example, *Attorney-General v Hislop*, above). The issue in *Attorney-General v Times Newspapers Ltd* [1991] 2 All ER 398, HL — another chapter in the *Spycatcher* saga (see para 1.2.4) — was whether a person who knowingly interfered with the administration of justice in civil proceedings between two other persons was guilty of criminal contempt even though he was not named in any court order and had not assisted in the breach of any court order by a party against whom it was made.

During the currency of interlocutory injuctions, granted by the High Court to the Attorney-General against *The Guardian* and *The Observer* to restrain the publication by those newspapers of confidential *Spycatcher* information pending the trial of actions for breach of confidence, certain other newspapers, including *The Independent*, published extracts from Peter Wright's *Spycatcher* memoirs. The Attorney-General instituted contempt proceedings and, at the trial of a preliminary issue, Sir Nicolas Browne-Wilkinson V-C held that the publishers and editor of *The Independent* were not guilty of criminal contempt since they were not parties to the confidentiality proceedings involving *The Guardian* and *The Observer* and were not named in the injunctions granted in those proceedings. (See *Attorney-General v Newspaper Publishing plc* [1988] Ch 333.) On appeal, the Court of Appeal reversed the Vice-Chancellor's decision (ibid.). In the meantime, the first instalment of a proposed serialisation of *Spycatcher* appeared in the *Sunday Times*. The Attorney-General immediately commenced proceedings against the publishers and editor of that newspaper. The proceedings were for criminal contempt at common law, which requires proof of an *actus reus* together with *mens rea*. The strict liability rule contained in the Contempt of Court Act 1981 did not apply because the breach of confidence actions against *The Guardian* and *The Observer* were not 'active proceedings' within the meaning of the 1981 Act at the date of the *Sunday Times'* relevant publication. The *Sunday Times* proceedings were heard together with the continuing proceedings against the publishers and editor of *The Independent*. Morritt J held that all the defendants were in contempt of court and he imposed fines of £50,000 on the publishers of *The Independent* and the *Sunday Times*. The Court of Appeal affirmed the finding of contempt but discharged the fines on the ground that, as a matter of justice, it would not be proper in the exceptional circumstances of the case to impose any penalty for the contempt. (See *Attorney-General v Newspaper Publishing plc and others* (1990) *The Times,* 28 February.)

The publishers and editor of *The Independent* appealed no further; the case of *Attorney-General* v *Times Newspapers Ltd* [1991] 2 All ER 398, HL, is concerned with the appeal of the publishers and editor of the *Sunday Times*. The House of Lords unanimously dismissed the appeal, holding that the defendants' conduct amounted to contempt since they had (*knowingly*, on their own admission) interfered with the administration of justice in the breach of confidence actions brought by the Attorney-General against *The Guardian* and *The Observer*. The trial of those actions was rendered largely academic when the *Sunday Times* placed in the public domain part of the very material which the Attorney-General claimed should remain confidential. The House of Lords had no difficulty in rejecting the defence that, as the defendants had acted of their own volition and had not aided and abetted the other newspapers to disobey the injunctions granted against them, there could be no contempt. It was made quite clear that the defendants were not in contempt for disobeying orders which were not binding on them (*civil* contempt) but for interfering with the proper administration of justice (*criminal* contempt). ([1991] 2 All ER 398, HL, *per* Lord Ackner at p. 409, Lord Oliver at p. 415 and Lord Jauncey at p. 426.) To have held the defendants liable for civil contempt in the circumstances of this case would have been to alter the status of an injunction from an order operating *in personam* to one operating *in rem* or *contra mundum* (ibid., *per* Lord Oliver at pp. 420–1 and Lord Jauncey at pp. 426–7).

Four subsidiary arguments advanced on behalf of the defendants were also rejected. First, it was contended that to hold the defendants liable would be to widen the law of criminal contempt. Their Lordships denied that their decision would have this effect; they replied that they were not widening the law but merely applying established principles to novel circumstances (*per* Lord Ackner at p. 412, Lord Oliver at p. 421 and Lord Jauncey at pp. 426–7).

Secondly, it was argued that s. 6(c) of the Contempt of Court Act 1981, under which nothing in the earlier provisions of the Act 'restricts liability for contempt of court in respect of conduct intended to impede or prejudice the administration of justice', prevented the further development of the law of contempt otherwise than under the strict liability rule. This argument has already been dealt with above.

Thirdly, it was suggested that there was no contempt because whatever confidentiality remained was destroyed when the *Spycatcher* book was shortly afterwards published in the United States. The House retorted that the *actus reus* of contempt has to be judged at the date when it was committed and that a defendant cannot seek to excuse himself by saying that someone else was also about to nullify the court's order (*per* Lord Ackner at p. 413 and Lord Oliver at p. 421).

Fourthly, it was said that a finding of contempt would conflict with the European Convention on Human Rights, art. 10 of which states that everyone has the right to freedom of expression, including the freedom to receive and impart information without interference by public authority. However, as Lord Oliver pointed out (at p. 421) it is proper to subject that freedom, in accordance with the rest of art. 10, to such restrictions or penalties as may be prescribed by law and are necessary in a democratic society for the purposes of, *inter alia*, protecting the rights of others, preventing the disclosure of information received in confidence or maintaining the authority of the judiciary. His Lordship thought that the contempt proceedings were 'clearly necessary for maintaining the authority of the judiciary, if for nothing else' (ibid.).

In *Attorney-General* v *Newspaper Publishing plc* [1997] 3 All ER 159, CA, the Court of Appeal declined to extend *Attorney-General* v *Times Newspapers Ltd* [1991] 2 All ER 398, HL, any further than was necessary and found the publishers and editor of *The Independent*, together with one of its journalists, not guilty of contempt arising from breaches of a court order since neither the *actus reus* nor the *mens rea* of contempt had been established against them. Although the order in question had not been made against the world at large or against the media, the defendants were indirectly bound by it as third parties. However, the breaches committed by the defendants were minor and did not amount to a *significant* interference with the administration of justice (the *actus reus*). There was insufficient evidence that the breaches were specifically intended so to interfere (the *mens rea*).

It has been held to be a criminal contempt for a person who is not a party to the proceedings, first, to inspect without leave of the court the documents on the court file if it is known that leave is required, or, secondly, to gain access to the court file by deceiving court officials or by subterfuge (*Dobson* v *Hastings* [1992] 2 All ER 94, where, on the facts, a *Daily Telegraph* journalist and her editor were found by Sir Donald Nicholls V-C not to be in contempt since the extracts from the court file had not been obtained by trickery or dishonesty on the part of the journalist and their publication by the newspaper was not done with an intention to interfere with the administration of justice).

5.3   CIVIL CONTEMPT OF COURT

It is a civil contempt, sometimes called a contempt in procedure, to disobey a judgment or order of the court or to act in breach of an undertaking given, either expressly or by implication, to the court. Thus, it is a civil contempt to disobey a decree of specific performance, to act contrary to the terms of an injunction, to defy a prerogative order of mandamus, prohibition, certiorari or habeas corpus, or to fail to honour an implied undertaking given to the court not to make improper use of documents disclosed on discovery (as in *Home Office* v *Harman* [1982] 1 All ER 532, HL).

In the important case of *M* v *Home Office* [1993] 3 All ER 537, HL, the House of Lords held that government departments and ministers acting in their official capacity are subject to the law of civil contempt and that, although the sanctions of imprisonment, fines and sequestration of assets are not appropriate, an order for costs could be made against them to emphasise the seriousness of the contempt.

In *M* v *Home Office*, the Home Secretary (Mr Kenneth Baker) had disobeyed an order of a High Court judge requiring him to procure the return to this country of a citizen of Zaire whose claim for political asylum he had rejected and who had been removed from the United Kingdom despite having made an application for leave to apply for judicial review of the Home Secretary's decision. At first instance, the judge, relying upon *Factortame Ltd* v *Secretary of State for Transport (No. 1)* [1989] 2 All ER 692, HL (see para 11.11.6), had taken the view that neither the Crown nor its officers were subject to the coercive jurisdiction of the court. A majority of the Court of Appeal, in finding Mr Baker personally to be in contempt (see [1992] 4 All ER 97), pointed out that *Factortame (No. 1)* was only concerned with the granting of injunctions and did not lay down that ministers were immune from contempt proceedings. No penalty was imposed for the contempt. However, as a mark of the court's displeasure Mr Baker was ordered to pay the costs of the proceedings personally, although he was indemnified in this respect out of public funds. This was the first time that a minister of the Crown had been found to be in contempt of court.

The order made by the Court of Appeal was affirmed by a unanimous House of Lords, subject to a variation whereby 'Secretary of State for Home Affairs' was substituted for 'Kenneth William Baker' as the person against whom the finding of contempt had been made. The earlier finding against Mr Baker personally had been made because the Court of

Appeal was of the opinion that, while individual ministers of the Crown and civil servants, being natural persons with legal personality, could be liable for civil contempt of court in respect of their personal acts or omissions, the Crown and government departments could not be so liable since they lacked sufficient legal personality.

The House of Lords disagreed with this opinion, holding that the Crown and government departments *are* invested with adequate legal personality for the purposes of the law of contempt (see [1993] 3 All ER 537 *per* Lord Woolf at pp. 566–7). Their Lordships further held that ministers acting in their official capacity, and government departments, are subject to other coercive aspects of the court's jurisdiction and may, therefore, have interim injunctions granted against them. (This feature of *M* v *Home Office* is dealt with more fully in para 11.11.6.)

The danger inherent in exempting ministers of the Crown from the coercive jurisdiction of the court was emphasised in the speech of Lord Templeman when he said (at p. 541) that

> . . . the argument that there is no power to enforce the law by injunction or contempt proceedings against a minister in his official capacity would, if upheld, establish the proposition that the executive obey the law as a matter of grace and not as a matter of necessity, a proposition which would reverse the result of the Civil War.

Although a civil contempt is punishable by committal to prison, it has been held that imprisonment should not be ordered if it is possible to ensure obedience to the order of the court in some other way. In *Danchevsky* v *Danchevsky* [1975] Fam 17, CA, the parties were divorced and the court made an order that the matrimonial home be sold. Mr Danchevsky refused to recognise the divorce and the court order for sale. By a further court order he was required to give up possession of the house and to cooperate in the sale. He did not comply with this order and was committed to prison for contempt of court. He appealed against the committal order and the Court of Appeal held that it should not have been made because there was available a reasonable alternative method of securing obedience to the order of the court which did not involve committing Mr Danchevsky to prison. An order for possession could have been enforced by a warrant for possession and the court could have ordered, under what is now s. 39 of the Supreme Court Act 1981, that the conveyance of the house to the purchaser be executed by some third person in place of Mr Danchevsky. All three judges in the Court of Appeal were agreed that, in the circumstances of the case, it would be pointless to send him to prison.

5.4 PUNISHMENT FOR CONTEMPT OF COURT

5.4.1 Introduction

At common law the superior courts had the power to commit a contemnor to prison for an unlimited time or to impose a fine unlimited in amount. It was not uncommon, for example, for a person who had disobeyed a court order or committed a contempt in the face of the court to be kept in prison until he had 'purged his contempt' by apology and an undertaking to obey the order of the court. Section 14 of the Contempt of Court Act 1981, which applies to both civil and criminal contempts (*Linnett* v *Coles* [1986] 3 All ER 652, CA), abolished the unlimited prison sentence as a penalty for contempt. Moreover, a person who has already been committed to prison once for failing to comply with a court order (civil contempt) cannot be sent to prison again for a continuing breach of the same order (*Kumari* v *Jalal* [1996] 4 All ER 65, CA).

A court, whether sitting at first instance or on appeal, has no power to make a probation order in a contempt case, although the Court of Appeal has said that as a punishment for criminal contempt such a power would be beneficial (albeit in a small number of cases) and has expressed the hope that Parliament will consider conferring it by statute (*R* v *Palmer* [1992] 3 All ER 289, CA).

Sentencing guidelines for some criminal contempts were laid down by the Court of Appeal in *R* v *Montgomery* [1995] 2 All ER 28, CA. First, interfering with the proper administration of justice should attract an immediate custodial sentence unless the circumstances are quite exceptional. In most cases, however, a moderate prison term will suffice. Secondly, there is no rule of law or practice that interfering with jurors should automatically be visited with a higher sentence than refusing to give evidence as a witness. The outcome of each case depends upon its particular circumstances. Thirdly, it is desirable to allow a witness who has refused to give evidence the opportunity to reconsider his position in the light of legal advice. Therefore, unless there are good reasons for dealing with the contempt quickly, the sentencing for such a contempt should be left until the end of the main trial or, at least, the end of the prosecution's case. Fourthly, it is essential to a fair sentence that the defendant be afforded the opportunity to give evidence of his reasons for refusing to testify and/or the opportunity to apologise to the court. (*R* v *Montgomery*, above, *per* Potter J; this was a case in which a sentence of 12 months' imprisonment for refusing, through fear, to give evidence against ten persons on charges of conspiracy to damage property was reduced on appeal to one of three months' imprisonment.)

5.4.2 Superior courts

A superior court can now only commit a person to prison for contempt for a fixed term of up to two years on any one occasion (Contempt of Court Act 1981, s. 14(1)). However, it retains its power to impose an unlimited fine. For the purpose of the Act, 'superior court' means the Court of Appeal, the High Court, the Crown Court, the Courts-Martial Appeal Court, the Employment Appeal Tribunal and any other court exercising in relation to its proceedings powers equivalent to those of the High Court. It also includes the House of Lords when sitting as a court (Contempt of Court Act 1981, s. 19; see *Re Lonrho plc* [1989] 2 All ER 1100, HL). In addition, for the purposes of s. 14 of the Contempt of Court Act 1981, a county court is to be treated as a superior court and not as an inferior court (ibid., s. 14(4A), added by the County Courts (Penalties for Contempt) Act 1983 and reversing the decision of the House of Lords in *Peart* v *Stewart* [1983] AC 109).

In the case of young offenders the court's powers of punishment are subject to ss. 1 and 9 of the Criminal Justice Act 1982. By s. 1(1) of that Act, all courts are forbidden to commit to prison for any reason, or to pass a sentence of imprisonment upon, a person under the age of 21. By s. 9(1), a person under 21 but not less than 18 years of age may, if the court is of the opinion that no other method of dealing with him is appropriate, be committed to be detained for contempt of court for a term not exceeding the term of imprisonment to which he would be subject but for his age. In forming its opinion that no other method of dealing with the young offender is appropriate, the court *must* take into account all the information available to it about the circumstances of the contempt (including any aggravating or mitigating factors) and *may* take into account any information available to it about the young offender (Criminal Justice Act 1982, s. 1(5), as substituted by the Criminal Justice Act 1991). Where a *magistrates' court* (but no other court) commits a young offender to be detained under s. 9(1), the reason for its opinion that no other method of dealing with him is appropriate must be stated in open court and specified in the warrant of commitment (Criminal Justice Act 1982, s. 1(5A), as inserted by the Criminal Justice Act 1991).

In a case concerning civil contempt, *Mason* v *Lawton* [1991] 2 All ER 784, CA, it appears that the relevant provisions of the Criminal Justice Act 1982 were overlooked at first instance. The defendant had been sentenced to two years' imprisonment by a county court, acting under s. 14(1) of the Contempt of Court Act 1981, for breaches of non-molestation orders. At the time of his committal the defendant was aged 20. The Court of Appeal held (independently of *R* v *Selby Justices (ex parte Frame)* [1991] 2 All ER 344, DC, which was not cited (see para 5.4.4 below)) that the committal order was unlawful by reason of s. 1(1) of the Criminal Justice Act 1982 since the defendant was under the age of 21. He should have been ordered to be detained in a young offender institution under s. 9(1) of the 1982 Act. Applying its own decision in *Linnett* v *Coles* [1986] 3 All ER 652 (para 5.5 below), the court exercised its jurisdiction under s. 13(3) of the Administration of Justice Act 1960 to substitute the correct order.

5.4.3   Inferior courts

Where an inferior court has power to commit for contempt, the committal must be for a fixed term not exceeding one month on any one occasion. Where an inferior court has power to impose a fine for contempt, the fine must not exceed £2,500 on any one occasion (Contempt of Court Act 1981, s. 14(1) and (2), as amended by the Criminal Justice Act 1991). This sum may be altered by the Home Secretary by statutory instrument (Magistrates' Courts Act 1980, s. 143, as amended).

The powers of a county court to deal with *criminal* contempts, such as contempts committed in the face of the court or in the immediate vicinity, are less severe than those for civil contempts.

By s. 118(1) of the County Courts Act 1984, a circuit judge, district judge, assistant district judge or deputy district judge has power to deal with any person who:

(a)   wilfully insults the judge of a county court, or any juror or witness, or any officer of the court during his sitting or attendance in court, or in going to or returning from the court; or
(b)   wilfully interrupts the proceedings of a county court or otherwise misbehaves in court.

The judge can order any officer of the court, with or without the assistance of any other person, to take the offender into custody and detain him until the rising of the court. In addition, the judge may, if he thinks fit, send the contemnor to prison for a specified period not exceeding one month or impose a fine not exceeding £2,500, or he may do both (County Courts Act 1984, s. 118(1), as amended by the Criminal Justice Act 1991). This sum may be altered by the Home Secretary by statutory instrument (Magistrates' Courts Act 1980, s. 143, as amended by the County Courts Act 1984).

A threat is an 'insult' within the meaning of s. 118(1)(a). In *Manchester City Council* v *McCann* [1999] 2 WLR 590, CA, a defendant in a county court case said to a neighbour returning home from court having just given evidence against the defendant, 'I'll fucking have you, you bastard', or words to that effect. The circuit judge held that, as the alleged contempt had not been committed in the face of the court, he had no jurisdiction to make an order under section 118. Not surprisingly, the Court of Appeal held that the judge was wrong since s. 118(1)(a) was not limited to contempts committed in the face of the court but clearly conferred the power to commit a person for contempt for wilfully insulting a witness returning from court. The Court of Appeal adopted a purposive approach to the statutory provision — so that insulting a witness included making threats — in view of the need to deal summarily and immediately with threats to the proper conduct of county court proceedings. Since the defendant's behaviour represented a direct and unacceptable challenge to the process of the court, the application to commit for contempt was sent back to the judge for reconsideration.

5.4.4 Magistrates' courts

The Contempt of Court Act 1981 gave the magistrates' courts power to punish a contempt committed in the face of the court or in the immediate vicinity. By s. 12(1):

A magistrates' court has jurisdiction . . . to deal with any person who:

(a)   wilfully insults the justice or justices, any witness before or officer of the court or any solicitor or counsel having business in the court, during his or their sitting or attendance in court or in going to or returning from the court; or

(b)   wilfully interrupts the proceedings of the court or otherwise misbehaves in court.

In the event of such a contempt the court may order any officer of the court, or any constable, to take the offender into custody and detain him until the court rises. In addition, the court may, if it thinks fit, commit the offender to custody for a specified period not exceeding one month or impose a fine not exceeding £2,500, or both (Contempt of Court Act 1981, s. 12(2), as amended by the Criminal Justice Act 1991). This sum may be altered by the Home Secretary by statutory instrument (Magistrates' Courts Act 1980, s. 143, as amended).

The justices' clerk is an 'officer of the court' for the purposes of s. 12(1)(a) and describing the clerk's case-listing system as 'ridiculous' may possibly amount to wilfully insulting him (*R v Tamworth Magistrates' Court (ex parte Walsh)* [1994] COD 277, DC; the court, however, did not have to decide the point since the magistrates' finding of contempt was quashed on other grounds — see para 5.4.7 below).

It has been held that the word 'wilfully' in s. 12(1)(b) qualifies the phrase 'otherwise misbehaves in court' as well as the phrase 'interrupts the proceedings of the court'. It follows that where it is alleged that the defendant's use of a tape recorder amounts to 'otherwise misbehaving in court' there is no power to punish for contempt under s. 12(2) unless it can be established that the 'misbehaviour' is 'wilful' in the sense that it involves an element of defiance or is such that a court should not reasonably be expected to tolerate it (*Re Hooker* [1993] COD 190, DC).

A committal to custody by magistrates under s. 12 is not a 'summary conviction' for the purposes of s. 21(1) of the Powers of Criminal Courts Act 1973 (see para 1.7.6.2.1) so that it is possible for the offender to be sentenced to imprisonment even though he is not legally represented in court (*R v Newbury Justices (ex parte Du Pont)* (1983) *The Times,* 15 November, DC).

In *R v Havant Magistrates' Court and Portsmouth Crown Court (ex parte Palmer)* [1985] Crim LR 658, DC, it was decided that a threat is not an 'insult' within the meaning of

s. 12(1)(a) of the Contempt of Court Act 1981. Accordingly, it was held that a witness in a magistrates' court case who, after giving evidence, threatened to 'get' the accused and his solicitor while they were awaiting the verdict could not be dealt with by the magistrates for contempt. This decision was disapproved by the Court of Appeal in *Manchester City Council* v *McCann* [1999] 2 WLR 590, CA (para 5.4.3 above), and may be regarded as no longer good law. Section 12(1)(a) of the Contempt of Court Act 1981 is in similar terms to s. 118(1)(a) of the County Courts Act 1984, except that the category of protected persons also covers solicitors and counsel, and in *Manchester City Council* v *McCann* it was held that a threat *is* an 'insult' within the meaning of s. 118(1)(a) of the 1984 Act.

The wording of s. 12(1)(b) seems to suggest that 'wilfully interrupting the proceedings of' a magistrates' court is only a contempt if the act causing the interruption takes place *inside* the court. It has been held, however, that this is not the case and that it may be contempt whether the act causing the interruption takes place *inside* or *outside* the court. Accordingly, the use of a loudhailer in the street outside the court building may constitute a contempt under s. 12(1)(b) if it prevents witnesses in court from being heard (*Bodden* v *Commissioner of Police of the Metropolis* [1989] 3 All ER 833, CA). The use of the word 'wilfully' makes it clear that the defendant cannot be punished without proof of *mens rea*. 'Wilfully' means that the defendant must either *intend* his act to be an interruption or *recklessly risk* that result (ibid., *per* Beldam LJ at p. 837).

The wisdom of conferring on magistrates' courts the power to punish summarily contempt committed in the face of the court is open to question in view of some of the trivial incidents reported in the newspapers. In 1983, a man was sent to gaol for a week (but was released after four days) by a stipendiary magistrate for whispering in the public gallery. In the same year a man was committed for seven days by lay justices for chuckling at the back of the court. In 1984, a teenager was fined £50 for contempt because he giggled in the public gallery when a prison officer fell off his chair.

5.4.5 Contempts punishable by the Divisional Court of the Queen's Bench Division

The magistrates' courts have no power to punish a contempt not falling within s. 12(1) of the Contempt of Court Act 1981. However, other contempts of magistrates' courts, such as a breach of the strict liability rule, can be punished by the Divisional Court of the Queen's Bench Division. The coroners' courts, as inferior courts of record, have power to punish contempt committed in the face of the court, but other contempts of coroners' courts can only be punished by the Queen's Bench Divisional Court. By virtue of RSC, Ord. 52, r. 1(2), the Divisional Court can also punish contempts of other inferior courts which have no inherent power to do so themselves, such as consistory courts, courts martial and tribunals of inquiry set up on an *ad hoc* basis under the Tribunals and Inquiry (Evidence) Act 1921.

A local valuation court was held not to be an 'inferior court' because its functions were essentially administrative and it was not a court of law established to exercise the judicial power of the State. It followed that the law relating to contempt of court had no application to a local valuation court (*Attorney-General* v *British Broadcasting Corporation* [1980] 3 All ER 161, HL, para 1.1.4; note that as from 1 May 1989, local valuation courts were replaced by valuation and community charge tribunals established under the Local Government Finance Act 1988, and that as from 6 March 1992 these tribunals were renamed 'valuation tribunals' by the Local Government Finance Act 1992). The Professional Conduct Committee of the General Medical Council has been held not to be a court since, although its function is a judicial one, it does not exercise the judicial power of the state (*General Medical Council* v *British Broadcasting Corporation* [1998] 3 All ER 426, CA). In contrast, a mental health review tribunal has been held to be a court for the purposes of the law of contempt. Its functions are essentially judicial and, in discharging them, it is exercising the judicial power of the State within the meaning of s. 19 of the Contempt of Court Act 1981 (*Pickering* v *Liverpool Daily Post and Echo Newspapers plc* [1991] 1 All ER 622, HL, overruling on this point *Attorney-General* v *Associated Newspapers Group plc* [1989] 1 All ER 604, DC; see further, para 1.1.4).

Furthermore, it has been held that an employment tribunal is an 'inferior court' for the purposes of the law of contempt since it has many of the characteristics of a court of law and discharges judicial, as opposed to administrative, functions. It follows that the Divisional Court has jurisdiction to punish contempt of an employment tribunal (*Peach Grey & Co.* v *Sommers* [1995] 2 All ER 513, DC).

5.4.6   Emergency legal aid

Section 29 of the Legal Aid Act 1988 provides that a person charged with a contempt committed in the face of the court or in the immediate vicinity may be granted emergency legal aid by the court. This provision applies to the magistrates' courts, the county courts and all superior courts (Legal Aid Act 1988, s. 29 (1) and (3)). It follows the recommendation of the *Phillimore Committee* (Cmnd 5794, 1974, para 32) and goes some way towards meeting the criticisms of 'instant justice' expressed by the Court of Appeal in *Balogh* v *Crown Court at St Alban's* [1974] 3 All ER 283 (see further, para 5.4.7 below). However, there is no *right* to legal aid. The court has a *discretion* to grant it 'if it appears to the court to be desirable to do so in the interests of justice'.

When the Criminal Defence Service created by the Access to Justice Act 1999 is established (expected to be in October 2000), s. 29 of the Legal Aid Act 1988 will be repealed. Public funding for proceedings arising out of contempt committed in the face of the court will thereafter be included within the scope of that Service (see further on the Criminal Defence Service, para 1.9.8).

5.4.7   Summary punishment of contempts committed in the face of the court

A major criticism of the power to deal summarily with contempts committed in the face of the court has not been met by the Contempt of Court Act 1981. Indeed, the power has been *extended* to magistrates' courts by s. 12 of the Act (para 5.4.4 above). Where the same person is both victim and judge in his own cause the court is not impartial and it is virtually impossible to be certain that justice is being done. (See *Director of Public Prosecutions* v *Channel Four Television Co. Ltd* [1993] 2 All ER 517, DC, *per* Woolf LJ at pp. 520–21, commenting on the danger of a judge acting as a prosecutor in his own cause when dealing with an alleged contempt of failing to produce information in defiance of an order made by him under the Prevention of Terrorism (Temporary Provisions) Act 1989. See also *Re M and others (minors) (breach of contact order: committal)* [1999] 2 All ER 56, CA.)

It must be remembered that there is no jury present to determine independently the question of guilt or innocence. In *Balogh* v *Crown Court at St Alban's* [1974] 3 All ER 283, the Court of Appeal was of the opinion that the summary jurisdiction should be exercised sparingly and only in the clearest and gravest cases. Other cases should, in the main, be referred to the Attorney-General for him to decide whether to apply, under RSC, Ord. 52, to the Divisional Court of the Queen's Bench Division for an order committing the defendant to prison. (See also *R* v *Schot* (1997) *The Times*, 14 May, CA, para 5.2.1.5 above.)

It is of the utmost importance that wherever possible a defendant should be allowed legal representation before a finding of contempt is made against him (*Balogh* v *Crown Court at St Alban's*, CA, above; *R* v *Powell* (1993) *The Times*, 3 June, CA, the 'wolf-whistle case', para 5.2.1.1 above; *R* v *Bromell* (1995) *The Times*, 9 February, CA, in which a finding of contempt was quashed as being unsafe when the judge had refused to hear the defendant's counsel except on the question of sentence; *R* v *Tamworth Magistrates' Court (ex parte Walsh)* [1994] COD 277, DC, where a finding was quashed because magistrates had acted unreasonably in summarily committing a solicitor for criticising the court listing system without giving him the opportunity to seek legal representation).

5.5 APPEALS IN CASES OF CONTEMPT OF COURT

Before 1960 there was no right of appeal to a higher court in a case of criminal contempt, although there was such a right in a case of civil contempt. Section 13 of the Administration of Justice Act 1960 introduced a right of appeal in cases of criminal contempt and provided a uniform procedure for appeal in cases of both criminal and civil contempt.

The defendant has the right of appeal in all cases of contempt; in the case of criminal contempt, the appeal lies against both conviction and sentence. The person who originally applied to have the defendant punished can appeal if the application was to have the defendant committed to prison (Administration of Justice Act 1960, s. 13(2)). The court hearing the appeal has power to reverse or vary the decision of the court below and to make such order as may be just (ibid., s. 13(3)). This includes the power to order a rehearing of the case before a different judge (*Duo* v *Duo* [1992] 3 All ER 121, CA, where a rehearing was ordered because justice had not been seen to be done at the first hearing in that the defendant had been denied the opportunity of properly presenting his case against an application to commit him to prison for contempt) and the power to substitute such other fine or sentence of imprisonment as the court considers just (*Linnett* v *Coles* [1986] 3 All ER 652, CA; *Mason* v *Lawton* [1991] 2 All ER 784, CA; *Delaney* v *Delaney* [1996] 1 All ER 367, CA). In exceptional circumstances a 'just' prison sentence could be a longer one than that imposed at first instance (*Linnett* v *Coles,* above; *Wilson* v *Webster* (1998) *The Times*, 5 March, CA, in which the defendant's prison term was increased from 14 days to three months on an appeal by the *applicant*). The appellate court has power to release the defendant on bail pending the outcome of his appeal (ibid., s. 13(3)). This is an important power since there are no special provisions for expediting the hearing of appeals in contempt cases, although the Court of Appeal has said that it tries to hear such appeals within a day or two (*Balogh* v *Crown Court at St Alban's* [1974] 3 All ER 283 *per* Lord Denning MR at p. 290).

The arrangements for the hearing of contempt appeals are as follows:

(a) In cases of contempt of a magistrates' court under s. 12 of the Contempt of Court Act 1981, appeal lies to the Crown Court (Contempt of Court Act 1981, s. 12(5), applying s. 108 of the Magistrates' Courts Act 1980).

(b) In cases of contempt of a county court or any other inferior court from which appeals generally lie to the Court of Appeal, appeal lies to the Court of Appeal (Administration of Justice Act 1960, s. 13(2) as amended).

(c)   In cases of contempt of an inferior court not falling under (a) or (b) above (e.g., a coroner's court), appeal lies to the High Court (ibid., s. 13(2), as amended by the Access to Justice Act 1999).

(d)   For contempt of the Crown Court, appeal lies to the Court of Appeal (ibid.).

(e)   From the decision of a single judge of the High Court in a contempt case (other than a decision on appeal), appeal lies to the Court of Appeal (ibid.).

(f)   From the decision of a single judge of the High Court on an appeal, or of the Court of Appeal, appeal lies to the House of Lords (ibid.). Permission to appeal must first be obtained either from the High Court or the Court of Appeal, as appropriate, or from the House of Lords itself. If the appeal is against a decision given on appeal from a lower court, the High Court or Court of Appeal must, in addition, certify that the case involves a point of law of general public importance. If the appeal to the House of Lords is against a decision at first instance of the High Court or Court of Appeal in a contempt case, permission to appeal may be granted without such a certificate (ibid., s. 13(4)).

6

Appeals and the Correction of Miscarriages of Justice

6.1 APPEALS IN CIVIL CASES

6.1.1 From the magistrates' courts

Appeals from the magistrates' courts in licensing matters go to the Crown Court (Courts Act 1971, s. 8 and sch. 1; Supreme Court Act 1981, s. 45). Appeals from the magistrates' courts in family proceedings lie to the Family Division of the High Court (Supreme Court Act 1981, s. 61 and sch. 1).

6.1.2 From the county courts

Appeals from the county courts in insolvency proceedings go to a single judge of the Chancery Division of the High Court (Insolvency Act 1986, s. 375 and sch. 1 to the Supreme Court Act 1981).

Appeals from the county courts in all other proceedings go to the Court of Appeal, civil division (County Courts Act 1984, s. 77(1)). An appeal lies on a question of law or fact, and, on a question of law, can be based on a point which was not raised in the county court (*Pittalis* v *Grant* [1989] 2 All ER 622, CA).

An appeal rarely lies as of right as the Lord Chancellor has power to prescribe classes of proceedings in which there is to be no right of appeal without the permission either of the county court judge or of the Court of Appeal (Access to Justice Act 1999, s. 54(1)).

The circumstances in which permission to appeal is or is not required are the same as for appeals taken from the High Court to the Court of Appeal, civil division (see para 6.1.4, below).

6.1.3 From the Employment Appeal Tribunal

Appeals from the Employment Appeal Tribunal lie to the Court of Appeal, civil division, on points of *law*. Permission to appeal, granted either by the Employment Appeal Tribunal or by the Court of Appeal, is required. On questions of *fact*, the decision of the Tribunal is final (except in a case of committal for contempt of court) and is not subject to appeal to the Court of Appeal (Employment Tribunals Act 1996, s. 37). Nor, since the Employment Appeal Tribunal is a superior court of record, is its decision on a question of fact subject to judicial review in the High Court (for the distinction between an appeal and judicial review, see para 11.12).

6.1.4 From the High Court

Unless the leapfrog procedure (described in para 6.1.4.1 below) is used, appeals from all three divisions of the High Court in civil cases lie to the Court of Appeal, civil division (Supreme Court Act 1981, s. 16(1)).

With a view to reducing the number of hopeless appeals, s. 54(1) of the Access to Justice Act 1999 enables rules of court to be made stipulating that any right of appeal to the Court of Appeal may be exercised only with permission. By the Civil Procedure Rules 1998, Part 52 (which came into force on 2 May 2000), every appeal requires permission, except an appeal against:

(a) the making of a committal order;
(b) a refusal to grant habeas corpus; or
(c) an order made under s. 25 of the Children Act 1989 (secure accommodation orders).

Permission to appeal can be given either by the court below or by the Court of Appeal itself (CPR, Part 52). No *appeal* lies against a decision to give or refuse permission, but this does not affect any right under rules of court to make a *further application* for permission to the same or another court (Access to Justice Act 1999, s. 54(4)). Accordingly, where the court below refuses an application for permission to appeal, a further application for permission can be made to the Court of Appeal, and where the Court of Appeal, without a hearing, refuses permission to appeal, the person seeking permission can request the decision to be reconsidered at a hearing (CPR, Part 52).

Permission to appeal will only be given where:

(a) the court considers that the appeal would have a real prospect of success; or
(b) there is some other compelling reason why the appeal should be heard (ibid.).

An order giving permission can limit the issues to be heard and can be made subject to conditions (ibid.).

An appeal is not usually a rehearing of the case, but is limited to a review of the decision of the lower court unless:

(a) a practice direction makes different provision for a particular category of appeal; or
(b) the court considers that in the circumstances of an individual appeal it would be in the interests of justice to hold a rehearing (ibid.).

The court will not usually allow oral evidence, or evidence which was not before the lower court, to be presented. It does, however, have power to order otherwise (ibid.)

The court will allow an appeal where the decision of the lower court was:

(a) wrong; or
(b) unjust because of a serious procedural or other irregularity in the proceedings (ibid.).

Guidance for dealing with applications for permission to appeal is given in *Practice Direction (Court of Appeal: procedure)* [1999] 2 All ER 490. The guidance stresses that permission to appeal should normally be given or refused by the court below. Where the appeal is concerned with a point of law, permission should not be given unless there is a real prospect of the Court of Appeal reaching a different conclusion on the point which will materially affect the outcome of the appeal.

Where permission to appeal is sought from the Court of Appeal, all legally represented applicants must (and litigants in person are strongly encouraged to) provide a skeleton argument (ibid.). This is a document which helps the court to deal efficiently with applications for permission to appeal by identifying and summarising the points to be relied upon without arguing them fully (see further, para 1.3.5).

Section 55(1) of the Access to Justice Act 1999, and Part 52 of the Civil Procedure Rules, impose limitations on second appeals. Where there has already been one appeal against the decision in question, for example, from a district judge to a circuit judge in the county court, or from a master to a judge in the High Court, no appeal can be taken to the Court of Appeal without the permission of the Court of Appeal itself. Such permission cannot be given unless:

(a)   the appeal would raise an important point of principle or practice, or

(b)   there is some other compelling reason for the Court of Appeal to hear the appeal.

In a *criminal* cause or matter, not even the criminal division of the Court of Appeal has jurisdiction to hear an appeal from a judgment of the High Court, with the exception of an appeal from a single judge of the High Court in proceedings for criminal contempt of court (Supreme Court Act 1981, s. 18(1)(a); and see para 5.5). Criminal appeals from the High Court will normally lie direct to the House of Lords (para 6.2.1.3 below).

A judgment of the High Court is regarded as being given in a criminal cause or matter if that judgment could lead to a criminal trial or punishment. In *R* v *Stipendiary Magistrate at Lambeth (ex parte McComb)* [1983] 1 All ER 321, CA, the civil division of the Court of Appeal held that it had jurisdiction to hear an appeal from a decision of the Divisional Court of the Queen's Bench Division in judicial review proceedings relating to exhibits to be used in a criminal prosecution. The decision of the Divisional Court was not itself one which could lead to a trial or punishment and so was not a judgment of the High Court in 'a criminal cause or matter'. It followed that the Court of Appeal was not precluded from hearing an appeal against it. In *Re O* [1991] 1 All ER 330, CA, it was held that restraint and charging orders made by the High Court under Part VI of the Criminal Justice Act 1988, with the object of preserving assets for later availability as the potential targets of any confiscation order made in criminal proceedings, are merely collateral to those criminal proceedings and are civil in character. They are not made 'in a criminal cause or matter' and, accordingly, the Court of Appeal has jurisdiction to hear an appeal against them.

On the other hand, an order of a High Court judge in criminal proceedings allowing inspection of bank accounts is made in 'a criminal cause or matter' and, therefore, no appeal lies to the Court of Appeal against the making of the order (*Bonalumi* v *Secretary of State for the Home Department* [1985] 1 All ER 797, CA; see also *R* v *Secretary of State for the Home Department (ex parte Dannenberg)* [1984] 2 All ER 481, CA; *Day* v *Grant* [1987] QB 972, CA; *Carr* v *Atkins* [1987] QB 963, CA; *R* v *Secretary of State for the Home Department (ex parte Garner)* [1990] COD 457, CA; *Cuoghi* v *Governor of Brixton Prison* (1997) *The Times*, 24 July, CA; *R* v *Blandford Magistrates' Court (ex parte Pamment)* [1991] 1 All ER 218, CA, in all of which it was held that no appeal lay).

6.1.4.1   The leapfrog procedure

There has existed since 1969 a procedure for missing out, or 'leapfrogging', the Court of Appeal so as to enable an appeal to be taken from the High Court direct to the House of

Lords (Administration of Justice Act 1969, ss. 12–15). The procedure is little used; for example, in 1998 there were only four leapfrog appeals (*Judicial Statistics 1998,* Cm 4371, 1999, p. 10). The conditions which must be satisfied before such a direct appeal can be taken are that:

(a) the trial judge has granted a certificate of satisfaction (Administration of Justice Act 1969, s. 12), and
(b) the House of Lords has given leave to appeal (ibid., s. 13).

As to (a), a trial judge can only grant a certificate if all the parties consent *and* the case involves a point of law of general public importance which is *either* concerned wholly or mainly with the construction of a statute or of a statutory instrument, *or* is one where the trial judge is bound by a previous decision of the Court of Appeal or the House of Lords (ibid., s. 12(1) and (3)). The granting of a certificate by the trial judge is discretionary. No appeal is possible against the granting or refusal of a certificate (ibid., s. 12(5)).

As to condition (b), the application for leave to appeal is determined by the House of Lords without a hearing (ibid., s. 13(3)). If leave is granted, any appeal to the Court of Appeal from the decision of the trial judge is precluded (ibid., s. 13(2)(a)).

6.1.5   From the Court of Appeal

An appeal may be taken from the Court of Appeal to the House of Lords. Leave of either court is required (Administration of Justice (Appeals) Act 1934, s. 1(1)). If the Court of Appeal refuses leave to appeal, a party may nevertheless apply to the Appeal Committee of the House of Lords for leave to appeal. The Appeal Committee has existed since 1934 in order to consider, in private, petitions to the House for leave to appeal. Each petition must be heard by at least three judges (Administration of Justice (Appeals) Act 1934, s. 1(2)). The fact that the Appeal Committee grants or refuses leave to appeal in any particular case does not indicate either disapproval or approval of the decision of the court below (*Wilson v Colchester Justices* [1985] 2 All ER 97, HL). This is so in the case of *criminal* as well as *civil* appeals.

The House of Lords is able to deal only with a limited number of cases each year and it is important for the proper development of the law that those cases should be chosen carefully (ibid., *per* Lord Roskill at p. 100). The Appeal Committee must not be confused with the Appellate Committee, which has existed since 1948 and which hears the actual appeal sitting in a committee room rather than in the chamber of the House.

As the ultimate appellate court, the House of Lords has an inherent jurisdiction (albeit rarely exercised) to rehear an appeal, and to rescind or vary an order made earlier in the proceedings, with a view to correcting any injustice that may have occurred. Thus, in *Cassell & Co. Ltd v Broome (No. 2)* [1972] AC 1136, HL, the House later varied a costs order made in the main proceedings because the parties had not had a fair opportunity to present argument on the question of costs. (See further on this litigation, para 10.2.2.) In *R v Bow Street Metropolitan Stipendiary Magistrate (ex parte Pinochet Ugarte) (No. 2)* [1999] 1 All ER 577, HL, Senator Pinochet was successful in his petition to have an earlier decision of the House set aside on the ground of bias on the part of one of the Law Lords involved in the case. A rehearing before a differently constituted Appellate Committee of the House was ordered. (See further on the *Pinochet* litigation, para 11.8.3.2.1.) The House is reluctant to reopen an appeal, and will certainly not do so merely on the ground that the earlier decision is now thought to be wrong. It seems that an appeal will only be reopened where a party has been the victim of an unfair procedure through no fault of his own (*Pinochet (No. 2)* [1999] 1 All ER 577, *per* Lord Browne-Wilkinson at pp. 585–86, the other Law Lords agreeing with him).

A civil appeal is usually taken to the House of Lords on a question of law, although the appeal can be on a question of fact, such as the quantum of damages. In a civil appeal to the House of Lords which involves a question of law, there is no statutory requirement that the question must necessarily be one of general public importance (cf. criminal appeals, para 6.2.2.4 below), although as a matter of *practice,* leave to appeal is liable to be refused by the Appeal Committee if the petition does not raise an 'arguable point of law of general public importance' (*Procedure Direction* [1988] 2 All ER 831).

In some instances the decision of the Court of Appeal is declared by statute to be final. It follows that no further appeal is possible in these instances to the House of Lords. The decision of the Court of Appeal is final, for example, in any appeal from a county court in probate proceedings (County Courts Act 1984, s. 82) and in any appeal from the Chancery Division of the High Court in insolvency proceedings (Insolvency Act 1986, s. 375(2)).

6.2 APPEALS IN CRIMINAL CASES

6.2.1 Appeal following summary trial

An appeal may lie from the magistrates' court to the Crown Court or, by way of case stated, to the Queen's Bench Division of the High Court.

6 2.1.1 Appeal to the Crown Court

If the defendant pleaded guilty, an appeal lies from the magistrates' court to the Crown Court *against sentence only.* There is no appeal to the Crown Court against *conviction* if the defendant pleaded guilty before the justices. If, on the other hand, the defendant pleaded not guilty, he can appeal to the Crown Court against either conviction or sentence or both (Magistrates' Courts Act 1980, s. 108(1)).

An appeal to the Crown Court takes the form of a complete rehearing of the case with witnesses but without a jury. The Crown Court has power to confirm, reverse or vary the decision under appeal, and may impose any sentence which the magistrates' court could have imposed, whether more or less severe than that actually inflicted (Supreme Court Act 1981, s. 48(2) and (4)). It is anomalous that the Crown Court can increase sentence whereas the Court of Appeal, which is superior to the Crown Court, cannot do so on an appeal by the defendant (see paras 6.2.2.2 and 6.2.2.6 below). Where the case has been referred to the Crown Court by the Criminal Cases Review Commission under s. 11 of the Criminal Appeal Act 1995, the Crown Court cannot increase the sentence (Criminal Appeal Act 1995, s. 11(6)).

A further appeal lies, at the instance of either the defence or the prosecution, from the decision of the Crown Court by way of case stated to the High Court, but only on the grounds that the decision is wrong in law or was given in excess of jurisdiction (Supreme Court Act 1981, s. 28(1)). In a few licensing and gaming matters the decision of the Crown Court is final and cannot be appealed against (ibid., s. 28(2)).

6.2.1.2 Appeal to the Queen's Bench Division of the High Court

As an alternative to appealing to the Crown Court, an appeal may sometimes be taken direct to the High Court by way of case stated from the magistrates' court. Either the defence or the prosecution may take advantage of this procedure. But it is available only where it is alleged that the justices' decision is wrong in law or was given in excess of jurisdiction (Magistrates' Courts Act 1980, s. 111(1); note that the decision may be wrong in *law* because of a perverse finding on the *facts*). The party so appealing will lose his right to appeal to the Crown Court (ibid., s. 111(4)). It has been held that a challenge to the *sentence* imposed by a magistrates' court should be made by way of appeal to the Crown Court and not by way of case stated to the High Court unless the exceptional hardship of the sentence amounts to an excess of jurisdiction (*Tucker* v *Director of Public Prosecutions* [1992] 4 All ER 901, DC; *R* v *Ealing Justices (ex parte Scrafield)* (1993) *The Times*, 29 March, DC).

The High Court may affirm, reverse or vary the decision under appeal, or remit the case to the magistrates' court with its opinion, or 'make such other order . . . as it thinks fit' (Supreme Court Act 1981, s. 28A, as substituted by the Access to Justice Act 1999; this provision was formerly contained in s. 6 of the Summary Jurisdiction Act 1857). It has been held that the words 'make such other order . . . as it thinks fit' empower the High Court to order a rehearing before the same or a different bench of justices provided that a fair trial is still possible (*Griffith* v *Jenkins* [1992] 1 All ER 65, HL).

An appeal to the High Court is not a rehearing. The case is decided on the documents and after considering arguments on points of law put forward by counsel for the parties.

The procedure by way of case stated is set in motion when either the defendant or the prosecutor makes written application to the magistrates' court to 'state a case' for the opinion of the High Court. The application must include a statement of the point of law on which the opinion of the High Court is required (Magistrates' Courts Rules 1981 (SI 1981, No. 552), r. 76(1), and see *R* v *Croydon Justices (ex parte Lefore Holdings Ltd)* [1981] 1 All ER 520, CA). The case stated by the magistrates will usually include a statement of the original information laid against the defendant, the facts as found by the justices, the submissions of the parties, the cases cited (if any), the decision of the justices and the question for decision by the High Court.

The magistrates can refuse to state a case only if, in their opinion, the application is frivolous (Magistrates' Courts Act 1980, s. 111(5)). Refusal to state a case may enable the applicant to seek, by way of judicial review, an order of mandamus to compel the magistrates to state a case (ibid., s. 111(6)). Thus, in *R* v *West Midlands Magistrates (ex parte PMS International Group plc* [1993] COD 455, DC, mandamus was issued in circumstances where there was no basis upon which the magistrates could reasonably have concluded that the application to state a case was frivolous. They had given no reasons for their decision and the case involved a substantial legal point about the admissibility of evidence which clearly affected the defence's conduct of its case.

6.2.1.3   Appeal to the House of Lords from the Queen's Bench Division of the High Court

A further appeal may be taken by either party from the High Court to the House of Lords. This is so whether the case reached the High Court via the Crown Court or direct from the magistrates' court. But the appeal to the House of Lords will only lie if:

(a)   the High Court has certified that the case involves a point of law of general public importance; *and*

(b)   the High Court or the House of Lords has given leave to appeal on it appearing that the point is one which ought to be considered by the House of Lords (Administration of Justice Act 1960, s. 1, as amended by the Access to Justice Act 1999).

6.2.2 Appeal following trial on indictment

6.2.2.1 Appeal against conviction

Against *conviction* in the Crown Court, the defendant may appeal to the Court of Appeal, criminal division, but only with leave of the Court of Appeal or if the trial judge grants a certificate that the case is fit for appeal (Criminal Appeal Act 1968, s. 1(2), as substituted by the Criminal Appeal Act 1995). This new provision, which applies whether the appeal is on a question of law, or of fact, or on a question of mixed law and fact, makes it more difficult to appeal against a Crown Court conviction. Before 1996, an appeal against conviction from the Crown Court to the Court of Appeal lay as of right (i.e., without leave) on a question of law.

Although the trial judge has power to facilitate an appeal by certifying that the case is fit for appeal, it has been held that he should not exercise the power unless the case has 'exceptional features' (*R* v *Bansal* (1998) *The Times*, 29 December, CA). It follows that most applications for leave will be made to the Court of Appeal itself, where it may be granted by a single judge. If the single judge refuses leave, the appellant can have his application considered by the full court (ibid., s. 31). If the single judge grants leave on some grounds but refuses it on other grounds, the leave of the full court is required in order to pursue those grounds on which the single judge refused leave (*R* v *Jackson* [1999] 1 All ER 572, CA; *R* v *Cox* [1999] 2 Cr App Rep 6, CA).

The actual appeal against conviction must be heard by at least three judges in the Court of Appeal (Supreme Court Act 1981, s. 55(4)).

It should be noted that, unlike the case of summary trial, a defendant may appeal against conviction even if he pleaded guilty at his trial on indictment in the Crown Court. On an appeal against conviction only, the Court of Appeal has no power to interfere with the sentence imposed on the defendant by the Crown Court.

The defendant is allowed only one appeal. If that is unsuccessful he cannot bring a second appeal even if he wishes under s. 23 of the Criminal Appeal Act 1968 to call fresh evidence (*R* v *Pinfold* [1988] 2 All ER 217, CA). Nor can he go back to the Court of Appeal where the House of Lords has decided his appeal and either dismissed it or directed that his conviction be restored, albeit that he now wishes to pursue grounds of appeal which were not considered by the House of Lords (*R* v *Berry (No. 2)* [1991] 2 All ER 789, CA, approved by the House of Lords in *R* v *Mandair* [1994] 2 All ER 715, HL).

6.2.2.2 Appeal against sentence

Against the *sentence* of the Crown Court, the defendant may appeal to the Court of Appeal with leave of the Court of Appeal (Criminal Appeal Act 1968, ss. 9(1) and 11(1) as amended by the Criminal Justice Act 1982). Leave may be granted by a single judge of that court or, if he refuses it, by the full court. Leave of the Court of Appeal to appeal against sentence is not required if the Crown Court judge who passed the sentence grants a certificate that the case is fit for appeal against sentence (ibid.). The actual appeal against sentence may be heard by two judges.

No appeal is possible against a sentence which is fixed by law (Criminal Appeal Act 1968, s. 9(1)), such as life imprisonment for murder.

On an appeal by the defendant against sentence, the Court of Appeal cannot *increase* the sentence but is limited to confirming it, or reducing it, or varying it from one form of detention to another (Criminal Appeal Act 1968, s. 11(3); cf. the wider power of the Crown Court under s. 48(4) of the Supreme Court Act 1981; para 6.2.1.1 above).

While not being able to increase a sentence in an individual case on appeal by the defendant, the Court of Appeal has an *inherent* power, exercisable while hearing appeals, to provide sentencing guidelines for Crown Court judges. Twice in the 1980s, for example, the Court of Appeal gave guidance on sentencing for the offences of rape and attempted rape (see *R* v *Roberts* [1982] 1 All ER 609 and *R* v *Billam* [1986] 1 All ER 985). In *R* v *Stewart* [1987] 2 All ER 383, CA, guidance was given on appropriate sentences for offences involving fraud on the public purse. More recently, new sentencing guidelines have been provided for offences of domestic burglary (*R* v *Brewster* (1997) *The Times*, 4 July, CA), for the possession of lysergic acid diethylamide (LSD) (*R* v *Hurley* (1997) *The Times*, 5 August, CA), and for firearms offences (*R* v *Avis* (1997) *The Times*, 19 December, CA).

With effect from July 1999, the Court of Appeal's *inherent* power was effectively replaced by a *statutory duty*, imposed by s. 80 of the Crime and Disorder Act 1998, to consider whether to frame new sentencing guidelines or to review existing guidelines. The duty arises when the defendant is given leave to appeal against sentence, or when leave is given to the Attorney-General to refer an unduly lenient sentence under s. 36 of the Criminal Justice Act 1988 (see para 6.2.2.6 below), or when the court receives a proposal from the Sentencing Advisory Panel that guidelines should be framed or revised (Crime and Disorder Act 1998, s. 80(1)). If the Court of Appeal decides to frame or revise guidelines, it must notify the Sentencing Advisory Panel (ibid., s. 81(2)) and it must have regard to:

(a)   the need to promote consistency in sentencing;
(b)   the sentences imposed by courts in England and Wales for offences of the relevant category;
(c)   the cost of different sentences and their relative effectiveness in preventing reoffending;
(d)   the need to promote public confidence in the criminal justice system; and
(e)   the views of the Sentencing Advisory Panel (ibid., s. 80(3)).

The Sentencing Advisory Panel was established under the authority of s. 81 of the the Crime and Disorder Act 1998 with a view to assisting the Court of Appeal by providing advice and information, particularly on the matters specified in (b) and (c) above.

In the light of perceived public misunderstanding of custodial sentences, the Lord Chief Justice handed down a *Practice Note* in January 1998 exhorting the courts to explain, at the time of sentencing, the practical effect of their sentences in terms of the actual period to be served and conditions applicable on release (*Practice Note (custodial sentences: explanation)* [1998] 1 All ER 733). The object is to ensure that, in future, custodial sentences are understood by defendants, victims and members of the public. No form of words is prescribed, although the *Practice Note* does contain suggested statements which, suitably adapted, can be used as model explanations by sentencers. Four separate statements are provided for use according to whether the defendant is a short-term prisoner subject, or not subject, to licence, a long-term prisoner, or a prisoner subject to a discretionary life sentence.

6.2.2.3   *Section 29(1) of the Criminal Appeal Act 1968*
A deterrent against appealing to the Court of Appeal is contained in s. 29(1) of the Criminal Appeal Act 1968, which says that

> The time during which an appellant is in custody pending the determination of his appeal shall, subject to any direction which the Court of Appeal may give to the contrary, be reckoned as part of the term of any sentence to which he is for the time being subject.

Two former Lord Chief Justices have said that appellants with no merit in their appeals cannot expect to be given any credit under this provision (*Practice Note* [1970] 1 All ER 1119, Lord Parker CJ; *Practice Note* [1980] 1 All ER 555, Lord Widgery CJ). Thus, a convicted defendant may find that, on the direction of the Court of Appeal, the three months or so that he spent in prison awaiting the inevitable outcome of his unmeritorious appeal will have to be served all over again.

6.2.2.4 Appeal to the House of Lords from the Court of Appeal

A further appeal may be taken by either the defendant or the prosecutor from the Court of Appeal, criminal division, to the House of Lords. But this appeal will only lie if:

(a) the Court of Appeal has certified that the case involves a point of law of general public importance; *and*

(b) the Court of Appeal or the House of Lords has given leave to appeal on it appearing that the point is one which ought to be considered by the House of Lords (Criminal Appeal Act 1968, s. 33(2)).

Pending the outcome of the appeal in the House of Lords, the Court of Appeal has power to order that the defendant be detained or not be released except on bail. If no order for detention is made and the defendant is allowed to go free he cannot be detained again if the appeal goes against him in the House of Lords (ibid., s. 37; *R* v *Hollinshead* [1985] 2 All ER 769, HL, where the Court of Appeal was criticised for refusing to make an order under s. 37 which meant that the defendants went completely unpunished for conspiracy to defraud electricity boards when their convictions were restored by the House of Lords).

For the purpose of disposing of an appeal, the House of Lords can exercise any powers of the Court of Appeal or remit the case to that Court (ibid., s. 35(3)). For example, if the Court of Appeal does not deal with a ground of appeal which is relevant to whether a conviction should be allowed to stand, the House can either deal with that ground itself or send the matter back to the Court of Appeal to be dealt with (*R* v *Mandair* [1994] 2 All ER 715, HL). If a ground of appeal has been left undetermined by the Court of Appeal, attention should be drawn to that fact in the appeal documents (ibid., at p. 723 *per* Lord Mackay of Clashfern LC).

Before 1996, if the defendant died before an appeal could be started, or before a remitted appeal could be determined, the right of appeal died with him and the Court of Appeal had no jurisdiction to hear, or to continue to hear, the appeal (*R* v *Kearley (No. 2)* [1994] 3 All ER 246, HL). This could cause hardship to the family of a deceased defendant upon whom a financial penalty had been imposed because there was no procedure for challenging the penalty and recovering any money paid under it. Parliament was called upon to consider remedying this unjust situation (ibid., at pp. 253–254 *per* Lord Jauncey, the other Law Lords agreeing with him) and a response was provided in the Criminal Appeal Act 1995, which inserted a new s. 44A into the Criminal Appeal Act 1968 allowing a person approved by the Court of Appeal to begin or continue an appeal. The first case under s. 44A was *R* v *W (crime: pursuing deceased's appeal)* (1997) *The Times*, 8 January, CA. Here, a widow was allowed to pursue her deceased husband's appeal against conviction for indecently assaulting his daughter. However, the appeal was dismissed on the merits.

The Royal Commission on Criminal Justice (*Report*, Cm 2263, 1993) recommended the repeal of the requirement in (a) above that before a criminal appeal can be taken to the House of Lords the Court of Appeal must certify that the case involves a point of law of general public importance. This requirement does not apply to civil appeals and if the Royal Commission's recommendation is implemented it would in theory make it easier to appeal to the House of Lords in a criminal case, although leave to appeal ((b) above) would still be needed.

6.2.2.5   *Section 36 of the Criminal Justice Act 1972: the Attorney-General's reference of points of law*

It will be appreciated that the prosecution has no right of appeal to the Court of Appeal following an *acquittal* on indictment, not even on a point of law. There is, however, provision for a 'reference' to be made by the Attorney-General in such a case. By s. 36(1) of the Criminal Justice Act 1972:

> The Attorney-General may, if he desires the opinion of the Court of Appeal on a point of law which has arisen in the case, refer that point to the court, and the court shall, in accordance with this section, consider the point and give their opinion on it.

This provision merely confers on the Attorney-General a *discretion;* he cannot be compelled to make a reference. The acquittal of the defendant is not affected by the opinion of the Court of Appeal. His identity must not be revealed in the Court of Appeal without his consent. He may appear before the court to present argument or be represented by counsel with his costs paid out of central funds (Criminal Justice Act 1972, s. 36(2), (5) and (7)). The Court of Appeal may refer the point of law to the House of Lords if of the opinion that it ought to be considered there (ibid., s. 36(3)).

The Attorney-General's reference to the Court of Appeal is a useful procedure for clearing up doubtful points in the criminal law, a branch of English law where certainty is particularly important. The procedure is an exception to the practice of the English courts not to give advisory opinions on academic points of law. The procedure, however, is little used — perhaps because it is thought only to be appropriate for determining exceptionally difficult points of law. The Criminal Justice Act 1972 contains no such limitation and, as Lord Widgery CJ has said,

> It would be a mistake to think, and we hope people will not think, that references by the Attorney-General are confined to cases where very heavy questions of law arise and that they should not be used in other cases. On the contrary, we hope to see this procedure used extensively for short but important points which require a quick ruling of this court before a potentially false decision of law has too wide a circulation in the courts. (*Attorney-General's Reference (No. 1 of 1975)* [1975] QB 773, CA, at p. 778).

The importance of preserving the anonymity and acquittal of the defendant is illustrated by a reference determined in 1981, *Attorney-General's Reference (No. 4 of 1980)* [1981] 2 All ER 617, CA, which concerned the serious crime of manslaughter. The case also illustrates how the procedure by way of reference can be used to determine simple but important points of law so as to provide future guidance for the Crown Court. (See also *Attorney-General's Reference (No. 1 of 1991)* [1992] 3 All ER 897, CA, where the procedure was used to establish that s. 1(1) of the Computer Misuse Act 1990, which creates the offence of securing unauthorised access to a computer, does not on its plain and natural meaning require the use of two computers; *Attorney-General's Reference (No. 3 of 1994)* [1997] 3 All ER 936, HL, in which it was held that a person can be charged with the manslaughter of a child who, though born alive, subsequently dies where that person has deliberately and unlawfully injured either the child while a foetus *in utero* or the mother carrying the child.)

6.2.2.6 Section 36 of the Criminal Justice Act 1988: the Attorney-General's reference of unduly lenient sentences

The prosecution cannot appeal to the Court of Appeal against the *sentence* imposed on the defendant. However, by s. 36(1) of the Criminal Justice Act 1988:

> If it appears to the Attorney-General . . . that the sentencing of a person in a proceeding in the Crown Court has been unduly lenient . . . he may, with the leave of the Court of Appeal, refer the case to them for them to review the sentencing of that person; and on such a reference the Court of Appeal may —
>
> (i)   quash any sentence passed on him in the proceeding; and
> (ii)   in place of it pass such sentence as they think appropriate for the case and as the court below had power to pass when dealing with him.

The Attorney-General thus has a *discretion* to refer unduly lenient sentences; he cannot be compelled to make a reference. He does, however, require leave of the Court of Appeal to refer the case. Leave must be applied for within 28 days from the day when the original sentence was passed (Criminal Justice Act 1988, sch. 3). 'Sentence' has the same meaning as in the Criminal Appeal Act 1968, namely 'any order made by a court when dealing with an offender', except that it does not include an interim hospital order under the Mental Health Act 1983 (Criminal Justice Act 1988, s. 35(6)). Accordingly, absolute and conditional discharges and even an order deferring sentence (*Attorney-General's Reference (No. 22 of 1992)* [1994] 1 All ER 105, CA) can be referred under s. 36 as well as sentences by way of imprisonment and fines.

An unduly lenient sentence may be referred whether the defendant pleaded not guilty or guilty. When dealing with the Attorney-General's reference of a sentence imposed after a plea of guilty, the Court of Appeal is not bound by any indication of sentence given by the trial judge before the defendant decided to plead guilty (*Attorney-General's Reference (No. 40 of 1996)* [1997] 1 Cr App R(S) 357, CA; *Attorney-General's Reference (No. 17 of 1998)* [1999] 1 Cr App R(S) 407, CA, in which a two-year suspended prison sentence was set aside and a two-year immediate prison sentence substituted).

The hearing at which the sentence is reviewed under s. 36 must be conducted before three judges of the Court of Appeal (Supreme Court Act 1981, s. 55(4)(aa), as inserted by the Criminal Justice Act 1988). The defendant is entitled to be present at the hearing. If he is represented by counsel he is entitled to payment of his costs out of central funds (Criminal Justice Act 1988, sch. 3). In conducting its review, the question which the Court of Appeal must ask itself is whether the sentence imposed by the trial judge is 'outside the range of sentences which the judge, applying his mind to all the relevant factors, could reasonably consider appropriate' *(Attorney-General's Reference (No. 4 of 1989)* [1990] 1 WLR 41, CA).

The Court of Appeal has power to increase or decrease the sentence (ibid., s. 36(1)(ii)). The time spent by the defendant in custody pending the outcome of the review is taken into account (ibid., sch. 3). The term of any sentence of imprisonment imposed by the Court of Appeal as a result of the review begins to run, unless otherwise directed, from the time when it would have begun to run if passed originally by the Crown Court (ibid).

When the Court of Appeal has concluded its review, a point of law involved in the sentence may be referred, by either the Attorney-General or the defendant, to the House of Lords for its opinion (Criminal Justice Act 1988, s. 36(5)). A reference to the House of Lords requires the leave of the Court of Appeal or the House itself, and leave must not be granted unless the Court of Appeal has certified that the point of law involved is one of general public importance *and* it appears to the Court of Appeal or the House of Lords that the point is one which ought to be considered by the House (ibid., s. 36(6)).

Section 36 of the Criminal Justice Act 1988 was enacted as a result of the view taken by the government that public confidence in the criminal justice system was being undermined by what it regarded as the unduly lenient sentences imposed for some serious offences. It should be noted, however, that the power of the Court of Appeal under s. 36 is not limited to *increasing* a referred sentence; it may, instead, *confirm* or even *reduce* a sentence if it is not satisfied that it is unduly lenient (*Attorney-General's Reference (No. 4 of 1989)* [1990] 1 WLR 41, CA, where probation was substituted for two concurrent 18-month suspended prison sentences imposed for incest and indecent assault). When the new procedure under s. 36 first came into force it was limited to sentences imposed for indictable offences. It has since been extended to cover sentences imposed by the Crown Court for the *either-way* offences of indecent assault, threats to kill, cruelty to persons under the age of 16, and attempts or incitements to commit any of these crimes.

The new procedure was first used in *Attorney-General's Reference (No. 1 of 1989)* [1989] 3 All ER 571, CA, in which the Court of Appeal quashed a sentence of three years' imprisonment imposed on the defendant after his conviction for incest and substituted a sentence of six years' imprisonment. The Court also provided (under its inherent jurisdiction) general sentencing guidelines for the offence of incest.

In *Attorney-General's Reference (No. 3 of 1989)* and *Attorney-General's Reference (No. 5 of 1989)* (1989) 11 Cr App R(S) 486, CA, the Court of Appeal made legal history when, for the first time, it substituted custodial sentences for the non-custodial penalties imposed by the Crown Court. These two unrelated cases concerned defendants who had been convicted of causing death by reckless driving, an offence under the Road Traffic Act 1988, s. 1, which carried a maximum sentence of five years' imprisonment (Road Traffic Offenders Act 1988, sch. 2, pt 1; note that s. 1 of the Road Traffic Act 1988 was substituted by the Road Traffic Act 1991 with the effect that the offence of causing death by *reckless* driving was abolished and replaced by the offence of causing death by *dangerous* driving, and that the maximum sentence for the offence was raised to 10 years' imprisonment by the Criminal Justice Act 1993). One defendant had been put on probation for two years by the Crown Court while the other had been fined £2,500. In the case of the first defendant, the Court of Appeal substituted a sentence of 15 months' imprisonment. The second defendant, who was aged 19 and could not, therefore, be sent to prison (see para 1.7.6.2.4), was sentenced to 21 months' detention in a young offender institution.

In a much-publicised case in 1993, a 15 year-old youth on his conviction for rape was made the subject of a three year supervision order with a condition that he attend a special activity programme, and his parents were ordered to pay £500 compensation to the victim so that she could have a holiday. The Court of Appeal held that the sentence was too lenient; it was set aside and replaced by a sentence that the youth serve two years' detention in a young offender institution (*Attorney-General's Reference (No. 3 of 1993)* [1993] Crim LR 472, CA).

In *Attorney-General's Reference (No. 17 of 1990)* (1991) 92 Cr App R 288, CA, sentences totalling four years were increased to seven years and guidelines were provided on the sentencing appropriate for sexual attacks on young children.

On granting leave to the Attorney-General to refer an unduly lenient sentence, the Court of Appeal comes under a statutory duty to consider whether to lay down new sentencing guidelines or to review existing guidelines for the relevant category of offence (Crime and Disorder Act 1998, s. 80; see para 6.2.2.2 above).

6.2.2.7 Section 54 of the Criminal Procedure and Investigations Act 1996: quashing of tainted acquittals

The Royal Commission on Criminal Justice (*Report*, Cm 2263, 1993) recommended that where a person is convicted of conspiracy to pervert the course of justice by interfering with the jury in a trial which resulted in the defendant's acquittal it should be possible for the defendant to be tried again for the same offence. Section 54 of the Criminal Procedure and Investigations Act 1996 implements this proposal in an extended form. It deals with the mischief of 'tainted' acquittals obtained by interfering with, or intimidating, a juror or witness, and is targeted mainly at criminals who use money, threats or violence to evade conviction. The section applies to acquittals in respect of offences alleged to be committed on or after 15 April 1997.

Where a person has been acquitted of an offence and the same or another person has been convicted of an administration of justice offence involving interference with, or intimidation of, a juror or witness (or potential witness) in any proceedings which led to the acquittal, and it appears to the convicting court that there is a real possibility that, but for the interference or intimidation, the acquitted person would not have been acquitted, the court must certify that it so appears (s. 54(1), (2)). The court must not so certify if, because of lapse of time or for any other reason, it would be contrary to the interests of justice to take proceedings against the acquitted person for the offence of which he was acquitted (s. 54(5)). If a court does so certify, an application can be made to the High Court for an order quashing the acquittal and, if the High Court makes such an order, proceedings can then be taken against the acquitted person for the offence of which he was acquitted (s. 54(3), (4)).

For the purposes of s. 54, 'administration of justice offences' are the offence of perverting the course of justice, the offence under s. 51 of the Criminal Justice and Public Order Act 1994 of intimidating or harming, or threatening to harm, jurors, witnesses or persons assisting in the investigation of offences, and an offence of aiding, abetting, counselling, procuring, suborning or inciting another person to commit perjury under s. 1 of the Perjury Act 1911 (Criminal Procedure and Investigations Act 1996, s. 54(6)).

The High Court cannot quash an acquittal under s. 54 of the Criminal Procedure and Investigations Act 1996 unless four conditions are satisfied (ibid., s. 54(3)). These conditions are set out in s. 55 and are as follows:

(a)   it is likely that, but for the interference or intimidation, the acquitted person would not have been acquitted;

(b)   it would not be contrary to the interests of justice, because of lapse of time or for any other reason, to take proceedings against the acquitted person for the offence of which he was acquitted;

(c)   the acquitted person has been given a reasonable opportunity to make written representations to the court; and

(d)   it appears that the conviction for the administration of justice offence will stand.

6.3   CORRECTION OF MISCARRIAGES OF JUSTICE

6.3.1   Section 36 of the Criminal Justice Act 1972: the Attorney-General's reference of points of law

Section 36 of the Criminal Justice Act 1988: the Attorney-General's reference of unduly lenient sentences

Section 54 of the Criminal Procedure and Investigations Act 1996: quashing of tainted acquittals

For the prosecution, there is the Attorney-General's reference to the Court of Appeal under s. 36 of the Criminal Justice Act 1972. However, as noted in para 6.2.2.5 above, an opinion of the court which is favourable to the prosecution does not affect the acquittal of the defendant.

In addition, the Court of Appeal has power, under s. 36 of the Criminal Justice Act 1988, to correct a miscarriage of justice occurring in the sentencing process by increasing an unduly lenient sentence brought to its attention by the Attorney-General (para 6.2.2.6 above), and, in appropriate cases, the High Court can quash tainted acquittals under s. 54 of the Criminal Procedure and Investigations Act 1996 (para 6.2.2.7 above).

6.3.2   Section 2(1) of the Criminal Appeal Act 1968
Section 142 of the Magistrates' Courts Act 1980

Mechanisms for correcting miscarriages of justice suffered by defendants convicted at the Crown Court, and by defendants convicted and sentenced by a magistrates' court, are provided by s. 2(1) of the Criminal Appeal Act 1968 and s. 142 of the Magistrates' Courts Act 1980, respectively. The latter provision is dealt with in para 6.3.2.4 below.

Section 2(1) of the Criminal Appeal Act 1968 (as amended by the Criminal Appeal Act 1995) provides as follows:

Subject to the provisions of this Act, the Court of Appeal—

(a)   shall allow an appeal against conviction if they think that the conviction is unsafe; and

(b)   shall dismiss such an appeal in any other case.

Under this new provision there is now only one ground for allowing an appeal — the unsafeness of the conviction. Two other grounds (available before 1996) of a wrong decision of any question of law and a material irregularity in the trial have been abolished as separate grounds. They are relevant now only as 'thought processes' in considering the safety of a conviction. It follows that the Court of Appeal has no power to allow an appeal where it is dissatisfied in some way with what happened at the trial but does not also think that the conviction is unsafe (*R* v *Chalkley* [1998] 2 All ER 155, CA). On the other hand, if a wrong decision of a question of law, or a material irregularity in the trial, leads the Court of Appeal to the conclusion that the conviction is unsafe, the appeal must be allowed. It has also been held that the concept of 'lurking doubt' should no longer be employed in the Court of Appeal as it is undesirable to place a gloss on the 'unsafe' test formulated by Parliament in the amended s. 2(1), which has the advantages of brevity and simplicity (*R* v *Farrow* (1998) *The Times*, 20 October, CA).

The proviso to s. 2(1), under which the Court of Appeal could dismiss an appeal if no miscarriage of justice had actually occurred notwithstanding the fact that the point raised in the appeal might be decided in favour of the defendant, has also been abolished, although it emerged in *R* v *Foley* (1997) *The Times*, 17 March, CA, that some senior barristers were unaware of its abolition more than a year after the event. Despite the abolition of the proviso, it is still possible for an appeal to be dismissed where, for example, justice was not seen to be done at the trial but the Court of Appeal is satisfied that justice was, in fact, done and that the defendant's conviction is safe (*R* v *Chalkley*, above).

It was under s. 2(1) of the Criminal Appeal Act 1968 that the convictions of the 'Winchester Three' were quashed as unsafe in *R* v *McCann and others* (1990) 92 Cr App

R 239, CA, following prejudicial comments in the media by, *inter alia,* the then Secretary of State for Northern Ireland (Mr Tom King) and a retired senior judge (Lord Denning). In 1987, the three defendants (John McCann, Finbar Cullen and Martina Shanahan) had been discovered close to the home of the Secretary of State for Northern Ireland and were arrested under the Prevention of Terrorism (Temporary Provisions) Act 1984 (since repealed and replaced by the Prevention of Terrorism (Temporary Provisions) Act 1989). They were tried in 1988 for conspiracy to murder the Secretary of State and conspiracy to murder persons unknown. Each defendant chose not to give evidence. While counsel were making their closing speeches to the jury, the Home Secretary announced the Government's intention to change the law on an accused's right to silence. This announcement received wide publicity in the press and on radio and television. Tom King and Lord Denning in separate television interviews used words which conveyed the impression that in terrorist cases a failure to answer questions or to give evidence was tantamount to an admission of guilt.

An application to discharge the jury, and for a retrial, was dismissed by the trial judge, Swinton Thomas J, who instead merely warned the jury, in his summing-up, to disregard any broadcasts on the right to silence. After deliberating for 15 hours, the jury returned a verdict of guilty on each count by a majority of ten to two. On appeal against conviction, the Court of Appeal held that the impact of the media coverage on the fairness of the trial could not be overcome by any direction to the jury and that the judge ought to have discharged the jury and ordered a retrial. The defendants' appeals were allowed and their convictions set aside on the ground that they were unsafe. (Note that the Court of Appeal itself was unable to order a retrial because this was not a fresh evidence case and the relevant part of the Criminal Justice Act 1988 which conferred a more general power to order a retrial (para 6.3.2.2 below) was not in force at the relevant time.)

If the Court of Appeal allows an appeal under s. 2(1), and does not order a retrial, it must quash the defendant's conviction. The quashing of the conviction operates as a direction to the trial court to enter an acquittal (Criminal Appeal Act 1968, s. 2(3)). Section 2(1) does not empower the Court of Appeal to declare the innocence of the defendant. That is a function exerciseable only by a jury; the Court of Appeal is solely concerned with whether a conviction can be allowed to stand (*R v McIlkenny and others* [1992] 2 All ER 417, CA; this is the case of the 'Birmingham Six' — for the full story, see para 6.3.4 below).

6.3.2.1 Receiving fresh evidence

At the hearing of an appeal, the Court of Appeal has power to admit fresh evidence (even though it was available but not called at the trial) if to do so is necessary or expedient in the interests of justice (Criminal Appeal Act 1968, s. 23(1)). The discretion to admit fresh evidence may be exercised (but only in very exceptional cases) where the reason that the evidence was not given at the trial was the defendant's unequivocal plea of guilty (*R v Lee* [1984] 1 All ER 1080, CA).

The Court of Appeal, in deciding whether to admit any evidence, must consider in particular whether that evidence appears to be capable of belief, whether it might render the defendant's conviction unsafe, whether it would have been admissible at the trial, and whether there is a reasonable explanation for the failure to adduce it at the trial (Criminal Appeal Act 1968, s. 23(2), as substituted by the Criminal Appeal Act 1995).

The Court of Appeal, having received and considered the fresh evidence, may allow the appeal against conviction and, if the interests of justice so require, may order a retrial. Alternatively, it may simply allow the appeal and quash the conviction without ordering a retrial (see para 6.3.2.2 below).

By s. 23A of the Criminal Appeal Act 1968 (as inserted by the Criminal Appeal Act 1995), on an appeal against conviction the Court of Appeal can direct the Criminal Cases Review Commission to investigate and report on any matter if:

(a)   the matter is relevant and ought to be resolved before the case is decided;

(b)   the matter is likely to be resolved by the court as a result of the investigation; and

(c)   the matter cannot be resolved without an investigation.

Copies of such a direction must be made available to the appellant and the respondent, and after the Commission has reported to the Court of Appeal on the matter the Court of Appeal must notify the appellant and the respondent of that fact and may make available to them the Commission's report and any statements and opinions which accompanied it.

6.3.2.2   Ordering a retrial under section 7 of the Criminal Appeal Act 1968

Before the summer of 1989 the Court of Appeal, on allowing an appeal, had statutory power to order a retrial instead of quashing the defendant's conviction in only one specific instance, namely where the appeal was allowed by reason of fresh evidence received by the Court on appeal (see para 6.3.2.1 above). In other cases the defendant who successfully demonstrated that his conviction was unsafe was permitted to go free even though there may have been overwhelming evidence of his guilt.

The law was changed by the Criminal Justice Act 1988 so as to provide the Court of Appeal with a *general* power to order a retrial. This new discretion is not limited to fresh evidence cases but is exerciseable whenever the Court of Appeal allows an appeal against conviction under s. 2(1) of the Criminal Appeal Act 1968 and the interests of justice require the defendant to be retried (Criminal Appeal Act 1968, s. 7(1), as amended by the Criminal Justice Act 1988).

The new trial must not be for a completely different offence, but only for (a) the offence of which the defendant was convicted at the original trial, *or* (b) an offence of which he could have been convicted at the original trial (for example, manslaughter instead of murder), *or* (c) an offence charged in an alternative count of the indictment in respect of which the jury was discharged from giving a verdict in consequence of convicting the defendant of another offence (Criminal Appeal Act 1968, s. 7(2)).

Where a retrial has been ordered and the new trial has not begun within two months, leave of the Court of Appeal is required for it to take place (ibid., s. 8(1), as amended by the Criminal Justice Act 1988). After two months the defendant can apply to the Court of Appeal to set aside the retrial order and to direct the trial court to enter a verdict of acquittal (ibid., s. 8(1A), inserted by the Criminal Justice Act 1988). On an application by the prosecution under s. 8(1), or by the defendant under s. 8(1A), the Court of Appeal can only grant leave for the retrial to take place if satisfied that there has been no undue delay (ibid., s. 8(1B), inserted by the Criminal Justice Act 1988).

The Court of Appeal is not under a duty to order a retrial on allowing an appeal against conviction. Instead, it may simply quash the conviction without ordering a retrial (ibid., s. 2(1) and (2)). This course might be adopted where the alleged crime was committed many years earlier and the passage of time would make it difficult to arrive at the truth in a new trial, or where sensational press coverage of a trial has created a real risk of prejudice against the defendant. It was for this latter reason that the Taylor sisters were not ordered to be retried (para 6.3.4 below). On the other hand, a retrial was ordered by the Court of Appeal in the case of Susan Whybrow and Dennis Saunders whose convictions were quashed on the ground that the trial judge's frequent interventions (sometimes sarcastic and scornful) during their evidence had gone so far beyond the bounds of legitimate judicial conduct as to deprive the defendants of a fair trial (*R* v *Whybrow*; *R* v *Saunders* (1994) *The Times*, 14 February, CA). They had been convicted at the Crown Court at Norwich of conspiracy to murder Mrs Whybrow's husband by making it look as though his sit-on lawnmower had accidentally toppled over and either crushed him or caused him to fall into a pond and drown. At the second trial, held at the Old Bailey, they were acquitted by the jury (see *The Times*, 22 March 1994). They had already served prison sentences for conspiracy to cause grievous bodily harm to Mr Whybrow, a charge to which they had pleaded guilty at the original trial.

6.3.2.3 Venire de novo

Most appeals against conviction come before the Court of Appeal under s. 2(1) of the Criminal Appeal Act 1968 (see para 6.3.2 above). However, the ground for allowing an appeal mentioned in s. 2(1) presupposes that the trial itself was perfectly valid. This ground is not appropriate where the basis of the defendant's appeal is that his trial was a *nullity*. Where the trial was a nullity the Court of Appeal has an inherent common law power to order a *venire de novo* (in effect, a new trial or, perhaps more accurately, a *proper* trial). However, the court is not bound to order another trial. Where the Court of Appeal decides that the trial was a nullity it does not 'quash' the 'conviction' since, technically, there is no 'conviction' to 'quash'. Instead, it orders the purported conviction to be 'set aside and annulled' (*R* v *Booth* (1998) *The Times*, 26 November, CA).

The Court of Appeal has no jurisdiction to order a *venire de novo* where a material irregularity occurred during a trial which was validly commenced and which was validly concluded by a conviction following an unequivocal verdict of guilty from the jury. In *R* v *Rose and others* [1982] 2 All ER 731, HL, Newton Rose was charged with murder and three other men were charged with attempting to pervert the course of justice. After the jury had retired, the judge privately sent messages to the jury through the clerk of the court imposing a time-limit within which he required them to reach a majority verdict failing which he threatened to discharge them. The jury convicted the defendants by a majority of ten to two. The defendants appealed against their convictions, alleging that the judge had applied improper pressure on the jury to reach a verdict. The Court of Appeal allowed their appeals on the ground that there had been a material irregularity in the proceedings which required that the convictions should be quashed. The court, however, refused to order a *venire de novo* (see [1982] 2 All ER 536). The Crown appealed, contending that a new trial should have been ordered. The House of Lords affirmed the decision of the Court of Appeal, holding that there was no power to order a retrial since the first trial had been validly commenced and had been validly concluded by a properly constituted jury returning an unequivocal verdict of guilty followed by a sentence imposed by the trial court.

In *R* v *Rose and others* the House of Lords at the same time confirmed that there are some circumstances in which the Court of Appeal does have inherent jurisdiction to order a *venire de novo* consequent upon the discovery of a material irregularity in the course of the trial. First, a new trial may be ordered where a procedural irregularity has meant that the first 'trial' was never validly commenced and was, therefore, void *ab initio*. Examples are where the 'trial' takes place before a court which has no jurisdiction to try the offence with which the defendant is charged, or where two defendants charged on separate indictments are tried together at the same hearing by the same jury. Secondly, there is power to order a new trial where the first trial, although validly commenced, has concluded without a properly constituted jury returning a valid verdict. Examples are where the defendant changes his plea of not guilty to one of guilty during the course of the hearing and the judge discharges the jury without obtaining a verdict of guilty from them, or where the jury's verdict is ambiguous.

It seems that the irregularity must be one of procedure. A new trial will not be ordered where, for instance, the judge's direction to the jury contains a mistake or the judge has left some issue to the jury which should not have been left. It is also clear that the procedural irregularity must be *fundamental*. It must be so serious that the hearing may properly be described as a mistrial or nullity (*R* v *Rose and others* [1982] 2 All ER 536, CA, *per* Lord Lane CJ, delivering the judgment of the court, at p. 542). Writing in the *Law Quarterly Review* ((1955) 71 LQR 100), Sir Robin Cooke identified seven categories of cases in which retrials had been ordered. His list was approved by the House of Lords in *R* v *Rose and others,* and is as follows:

(a)   Where a trial has been conducted on the basis that the defendant has pleaded guilty when he actually pleaded not guilty (*R* v *Scothern* [1961] Crim LR 326, CCA).

(b)   Misjoinder of defendants (*Crane* v *DPP* [1921] 2 AC 299, HL).

(c)   Failure to take the verdict of the jury when there is a change of plea from not guilty to guilty (*R* v *Hancock* (1931) 100 LJ KB 419, CCA).

(d)   Irregularity in the committal proceedings (*R* v *Gee* [1936] 2 KB 442, CCA).

(e)   Personation of juror (*R* v *Wakefield* [1918] 1 KB 216, CCA).

(f)   Denial of right of challenge of juror (*R* v *Williams* (1925) 19 Cr App R 67, CCA).

(g)   Judge unqualified to act as such (*R* v *Cronin* [1940] 2 All ER 242, CCA).

To this list, the Court of Appeal has added an eighth category, namely where the jury's verdict is so ambiguous or ill-expressed that the court could not give judgment on it (*R* v *Rose and others* [1982] 2 All ER 536 *per* Lord Lane CJ at p. 542). This, too, was approved by the House of Lords in *R* v *Rose and others.* The Court of Appeal has since ordered a *venire de novo* in a case where the defendant's trial was a nullity by reason of the fact that the bill of indictment was not signed by 'the proper officer of the court' (as required by s. 2(1) of the Administration of Justice (Miscellaneous Provisions) Act 1933) but merely initialled by a judge (*R* v *Morais* [1988] 3 All ER 161, CA; but see *R* v *Laming* (1990) 90 Cr App R 450, CA, where the trial was held not to be a nullity by reason only of the fact that a two-page indictment had not been signed by the court clerk immediately after the last count but only on the first page).

In *R* v *Comerford* [1998] 1 All ER 823, CA, the Court of Appeal refused to order a *venire de novo* in a case where the defendant had been convicted by an anonymous jury, the members of which had been given police protection by the trial judge and allowed to be called and sworn by numbers rather than by names. It was held that if it is reasonably thought to be desirable to withhold jurors' names in order to thwart suspected jury-nobbling, the trial is valid provided that the defendant's right to challenge jurors is preserved (see *R* v *Williams,* above). On the facts, it was held that the defendant had not been deprived of his right of challenge; accordingly, his trial was a valid one. (See further on *R* v *Comerford,* para 7.5.1.)

6.3.2.4   Section 142 of the Magistrates' Courts Act 1980

The magistrates' courts have power to reopen cases in order to rectify mistakes. That power was extended when s. 142 of the Magistrates' Courts Act 1980 was amended by the

Criminal Appeal Act 1995 with effect from 1 January 1996. It is still, however, of somewhat limited scope.

A magistrates' court can at any time vary or rescind a sentence or other order imposed or made by it if it appears to be in the interests of justice to do so, unless the Crown Court (by way of an appeal) or the High Court (by way of case stated) has already dealt with the matter (Magistrates' Courts Act 1980, s. 142(1), (1A)).

After convicting a person, a magistrates' court can at any time direct that the case should be heard again by different justices (whether the person pleaded guilty or not guilty) if it is in the interests of justice to do so, unless the Crown Court (by way of an appeal) or the High Court (by way of case stated) has already dealt with the matter (ibid., s. 142(2), (2A)). Where a magistrates' court gives a direction that the case should be heard again by different justices, the conviction (and any consequent sentence or other order) is treated as a nullity and has no effect (ibid., s. 142(3)).

The decision of a magistrates' court under s. 142 can be challenged in the High Court in judicial review proceedings.

The ambit of s. 142 has been limited by judicial decision. The purpose of the section is to enable a magistrates' court to rectify mistakes. It does not extend to allowing a defendant to obtain a rehearing in circumstances where he pleaded guilty before the magistrates and is, therefore, unable to appeal to the Crown Court. It has been held that it is not 'in the interests of justice' to allow s. 142 to be so used since the interests of justice include the interests of the courts and the public that there should be certainty and an end to litigation (*R v Croydon Youth Court (ex parte Director of Public Prosecutions)* [1997] 2 Cr App Rep 411, DC).

6.3.3 The Criminal Appeal Act 1995: the Criminal Cases Review Commission's reference

Before April 1997, a person convicted on indictment could have his case referred by the Home Secretary to the Court of Appeal for review under s. 17 of the Criminal Appeal Act 1968. This provision was repealed with effect from 31 March 1997 by the Criminal Appeal Act 1995, thereby abolishing the Home Secretary's power to refer cases back to the Court of Appeal. The responsibility for referring possible miscarriages of justice back to the court was taken over by a new body created by the 1995 Act, the Criminal Cases Review Commission. The Commission came into existence on 1 January 1997 and took on its casework responsibilities at the end of March 1997, when it inherited some 250 cases from the Home Office.

The Criminal Cases Review Commission can at any time refer to the Court of Appeal the conviction and/or sentence (except a sentence fixed by law) of any person tried in the Crown Court (Criminal Appeal Act 1995, s. 9). Moreover, it can at any time refer to the Crown Court the conviction and/or sentence of any person tried by a magistrates' court (ibid., s. 11). The reference of a case back to the Court of Appeal or to the Crown Court can be made on the Commission's own initiative or after an application made by, or on behalf of, the convicted person (ibid., s. 14). The reference is treated for all purposes as an appeal by the person against the conviction and/or sentence (ibid., ss. 9(2), (3) and 11(2), (3)). When a case is referred back to the *Crown Court*, the sentence actually imposed by the magistrates' court cannot be increased (ibid., s. 11(6)).

The Commission must not make a reference unless:

(a)   an appeal against conviction or sentence has been decided or leave to appeal against it has been refused; and

(b)   in the case of a *conviction*, it considers there is a real possibility that the conviction would not be upheld because of an argument, or evidence, not raised at the trial or on appeal; or

(c)   in the case of a *sentence*, it considers there is a real possibility that the sentence would not be upheld because of an argument on a point of law, or information, not raised at the trial or on appeal (ibid., s. 13).

In considering whether to refer a case to the Court of Appeal or to the Crown Court, the Commission must take into account any application or representations made to the Commission by or on behalf of the defendant, any other representations made to the Commission in relation to the application, and any other matters which appear to the Commission to be relevant (ibid., s. 14(2)). In considering whether to refer a case to the *Court of Appeal*, the Commission can at any time refer any point arising in the case to the Court of Appeal for its opinion; the Court of Appeal is obliged to consider the point referred and to provide the Commission with its opinion thereon (ibid., s. 14(3)).

When the Commission makes a reference it must give to the Court of Appeal or to the Crown Court a statement of its reasons for making the reference, and must send a copy of that statement to every person who is likely to be a party to any proceedings on the appeal arising from the reference (ibid., s. 14(4)). When the Commission decides not to make a reference following an application made by, or on behalf of, the defendant, it must give a statement of the reasons for its decision to the person who made the application (ibid., (s. 14(6)).

The Criminal Cases Review (Insanity) Act 1999 makes it clear that the Commission has the power to refer to the Court of Appeal a case in which the verdict returned was the now obsolete 'guilty but insane'.

A decision by the Commission not to refer a case to the Court of Appeal is susceptible to challenge in an application for judicial review (*R* v *Criminal Cases Review Commission (ex parte Pearson)* [1999] 3 All ER 498, DC, where, however, the challenge failed).

6.3.4   Pardon and compensation

Miscarriages of justice do still occur in spite of the above provisions which are designed to prevent or remedy them. The commonest causes of miscarriages of justice are said to be wrongful identification of the defendant, false confessions, perjury by a co-defendant or witness, police misconduct and bad trial tactics on the part of defence lawyers.

It is worth noting here that the Court of Appeal will not treat incompetent advocacy as rendering a conviction 'unsafe', within the meaning of s. 2(1) of the Criminal Appeal Act 1968 (see para 6.3.2 above) unless the advocacy is 'flagrantly incompetent' (*R* v *Gautam* (1987) *The Times,* 4 March, CA, applied in *R* v *Ensor* [1989] 2 All ER 586, CA).

When a wrongful conviction comes to light, the Home Secretary, acting under the royal prerogative, may pardon the defendant. A free pardon relieves the defendant from all penalties and punishments resulting from the conviction. But the conviction itself still stands and cannot be quashed by the Crown. It can only be quashed by the Court of Appeal under the Criminal Appeal Act 1968 (*R* v *Foster* [1984] 2 All ER 679, CA; but note that the quashing of a conviction does not operate as a declaration of the defendant's innocence — *R* v *McIlkenny and others* [1992] 2 All ER 417, CA, para 6.3.2 above).

As a result of changes made by the Criminal Appeal Act 1995, the Home Secretary is now able to seek the assistance of the Criminal Cases Review Commission in connection with the prerogative of mercy. He can refer to the Commission any matter arising in his consideration of whether to recommend the exercise of the prerogative of mercy in relation to a conviction and on which he desires its assistance. The Commission is then obliged to consider the referred matter and to give a statement of its conclusions on it to the Home Secretary, who, in considering whether to recommend mercy, must treat the Commission's statement as conclusive of the matter referred (Criminal Appeal Act 1995, s. 16(1)). In addition, the Commission can in any case express its opinion to the Home Secretary that he should consider whether to recommend the exercise of the prerogative of mercy in relation to that case. If it does so, the Commission must supply the Home Secretary with the reasons for its opinion (ibid., s. 16(2)).

The royal prerogative of mercy is a flexible power capable of being exercised in many different circumstances. Accordingly, it is within the Home Secretary's powers to grant a *partial* or *conditional* pardon, or a *posthumous* pardon, in recognition of the fact that a mistake has been made in the administration of the criminal justice system. This is illustrated by *R v Secretary of State for the Home Department (ex parte Bentley)* [1993] 4 All ER 442, DC, the case in which the sister of Derek Bentley challenged the decision taken in 1992 by the then Home Secretary, Kenneth Clarke, not to grant a posthumous pardon to her brother. (The public law aspects of this case are discussed more fully in para 11.5.2.1.)

Derek Bentley was convicted with Christopher Craig in 1952 of the murder by shooting of PC Sidney George Miles. Bentley and Craig were together on the roof of a warehouse in Croydon when they were disturbed by police officers, and Craig, who was carrying a gun, fired the fatal shot. Bentley, aged 19 with a mental age of 11, was sentenced to death (the mandatory sentence for murder at that time), but Craig, then aged 16, was too young for the death penalty and was sentenced to be detained during Her Majesty's pleasure. (He was released from custody in 1963 and maintains that Bentley never uttered the famous ambiguous words 'Let him have it, Chris'.)

The jury had recommended mercy for Bentley, and two senior civil servants at the Home Office advised the Home Secretary of the day, Sir David Maxwell Fyfe (who later became Viscount Kilmuir LC), to act on this recommendation and to reprieve Bentley and commute the death sentence to one of life imprisonment. However, the Home Secretary decided to ignore the recommendation and advice; Bentley was hanged at Wandsworth prison on 28 January 1953, his appeal against conviction having been dismissed earlier.

Kenneth Clarke's refusal to pardon Bentley was based upon what emerged as a long established policy of successive Home Secretaries that a free pardon should be granted only if the moral as well as the technical innocence of the convicted person can be established. Mr Clarke did not believe that Derek Bentley was either morally or technically innocent, although he made it clear that had he been Home Secretary in 1953 he would have reprieved Bentley.

On an application for judicial review of Mr. Clarke's decision, it was held in effect that in considering the case as one for a *free* (i.e., 'unconditional' or 'full') pardon he had directed his mind to the wrong question. He had not given any, or sufficient, consideration to the possibility of granting some other form of pardon which would be suitable to the circumstances of the particular case, such as a *conditional* pardon whereby the penalty is removed on condition that a lesser sentence is served. If Bentley had been reprieved in 1953, the substitution of a sentence of life imprisonment would have constituted a conditional pardon and the court in 1993 could see no objection in principle to the grant of a posthumous conditional pardon where a death sentence had already been carried out. It was said that the grant of such a pardon would be a recognition by the State that a mistake had been made and that a reprieve should have been granted, and that it was wrong to regard the prerogative of mercy as a power only to be exercised in cases falling into specific categories, or as no more than an 'arbitrary monarchical right of grace and favour', when, in truth, it is now a constitutional safeguard against mistakes in the criminal justice system (see *R* v *Secretary of State for the Home Department (ex parte Bentley)* [1993] 4 All ER 442 *per* Watkins LJ at pp. 454–5).

The court was further of the opinion that there was a compelling argument that even by the standards of 1953 the then Home Secretary's decision was clearly wrong (ibid., *per* Watkins LJ at p. 455). Although it was not considered appropriate to make any formal order, the unusual step was taken of inviting the Home Secretary to look at the matter again and to examine whether it would be just to exercise the royal prerogative of mercy in a way which would give recognition to the generally accepted view that Bentley should have been reprieved 40 years earlier.

Less than four weeks after this decision a new Home Secretary (Michael Howard) granted to Derek Bentley a partial posthumous pardon which recognised that he should not have been executed. Bentley's conviction was, of course, left intact (see *R* v *Foster* [1984] 2 All ER 679, CA, above). In November 1997, it was announced that the question of Bentley's conviction was to be referred back to the Court of Appeal by the Criminal Cases Review Commission in the light of new medical evidence and submissions about irregularities at the trial (see *The Times*, 7 November 1997). The conviction was quashed by the Court of Appeal in July 1998 (*R* v *Bentley* (1998) *The Times*, 31 July, CA). At first, Bentley's family was refused compensation (see *The Times*, 13 April 1999), but the Home Secretary changed his mind after four weeks (see *The Times*, 13 May 1999) in the light of fresh legal advice on the impact of *R* v *Secretary of State for the Home Department (ex parte Garner)* (1999) *The Times*, 4 May, DC (see below).

Prior to 1988, a person who was pardoned, or whose conviction was quashed, had no *right* to compensation even though he may have spent many years in prison before the miscarriage of justice came to light. He might, however, have been granted an *ex gratia* payment in recognition of hardship suffered, although such payments were extremely rare.

With effect from October 1988, the Criminal Justice Act 1988 introduced a statutory scheme of compensation for the victims of miscarriages of justice. The statutory scheme confers a *right* to compensation but only in the limited circumstances laid down in the Act. Cases falling outside the scope of the statutory scheme will continue to be dealt with under the *ex gratia* scheme, which, by its very nature, involves no right to compensation.

As amended by the Criminal Appeal Act 1995, s. 133 of the Criminal Justice Act 1988, which was passed in order to give effect to art. 14.6 of the International Covenant on Civil and Political Rights 1966, provides as follows:

(1)   Subject to subsection (2) below, when a person has been convicted of a criminal offence and when subsequently his conviction has been reversed or he has been pardoned on the ground that a new or newly discovered fact shows beyond reasonable doubt that there has been a miscarriage of justice, the Secretary of State shall pay compensation for the miscarriage of justice to the person who has suffered punishment as a result of such conviction or, if he is dead, to his personal representatives, unless the non-disclosure of the unknown fact was wholly or partly attributable to the person convicted.

(2)   No payment of compensation under this section shall be made unless an application for such compensation has been made to the Secretary of State.

(3)   The question whether there is a right to compensation under this section shall be determined by the Secretary of State.

(4)   If the Secretary of State determines that there is a right to such compensation, the amount of the compensation shall be assessed by an assessor appointed by the Secretary of State.

(5)   In this section 'reversed' shall be construed as referring to a conviction having been quashed —

(a)   on an appeal out of time; or

(b)   on a reference . . . under the Criminal Appeal Act 1995 . . .

(6)   For the purposes of this section a person suffers punishment as a result of a conviction when sentence is passed on him for the offence of which he was convicted . . .

Thus, under the statutory scheme the Home Secretary has a *duty* (and not merely a *discretion*) to pay compensation. That duty only arises, however, in the limited circumstances outlined in s. 133. In particular,

(a)   there must have been a conviction; and

(b)   the conviction must have been reversed outside the normal appeal process, or the convicted person pardoned, on the basis of a new or newly discovered fact; and

(c)   that fact must show beyond reasonable doubt that there has been a miscarriage of justice; and

(d)   a positive application for compensation under s. 133 must be made to the Home Secretary.

Since the phrase 'new or newly discovered fact' qualifies the words 'his conviction has been reversed' in subsection (1) as well as the word 'pardoned', it follows that there is no right to compensation under s. 133 where a conviction has been quashed on the ground of

(a)   wrongful admission of evidence at the trial (*R* v *Secretary of State for the Home Department (ex parte Bateman)* [1993] COD 493, DC); or

(b)   invalidity of a by-law (*R* v *Secretary of State for the Home Department (ex parte Howse)* [1993] COD 494, DC).

Section 133 is intended to apply to natural persons only and not to corporate bodies. Accordingly, a company, not being a 'person' within the meaning of s. 133(1), has no right to compensation under the statutory scheme (*R* v *Secretary of State for the Home Department (ex parte Atlantic Commercial (UK) Ltd)* (1997) *The Times*, 10 March).

The Home Secretary is solely responsible for deciding whether there is a right to compensation in individual cases (Criminal Justice Act 1988, s. 133(3)). If his decision is in the affirmative, the actual compensation payable is not assessed by the Home Secretary but by an assessor appointed by him (ibid., s. 133(4)). Those eligible for appointment are lawyers practising in the United Kingdom, persons who hold or have held judicial office in the United Kingdom, and members of the Criminal Injuries Compensation Board (ibid., sch. 12). The amount of the award is calculated using the principles applied in the assessment of damages in the law of tort. The relevant factors include loss of earnings during any period of imprisonment, loss of future earning capacity, damage to reputation, hardship (including mental suffering, injury to feelings and inconvenience), costs incurred in the original proceedings and in establishing innocence, and expenses incurred as a result of imprisonment (including family expenses). In assessing compensation attributable to suffering, damage to reputation or similar damage, the assessor must have regard in particular to the seriousness of the offence of which the applicant was convicted and the severity of the sentence imposed upon him, the way in which the offence was investigated and prosecuted, and any other convictions of, and sentences imposed upon, the applicant (ibid., s. 133(4A), as inserted by the Criminal Appeal Act 1995).

The *ex gratia* scheme of payments, which is part of the royal prerogative, continues to operate for those miscarriages of justice not covered by the new statutory scheme. The Home Secretary has a complete discretion in the matter of *ex gratia* payments and, as long as he has followed his own stated policy and has acted fairly, his refusal to make an award is not subject to judicial review (*R* v *Secretary of State for the Home Office (ex parte Chubb)* [1986] Crim LR 809, DC; *R* v *Home Secretary (ex parte Weeks)* (1988) *The Guardian,* 23 February, DC; *R* v *Secretary of State for the Home Department (ex parte Harrison)* [1988] 3 All ER 86, DC).

The Home Secretary's policy (as outlined in *R* v *Secretary of State for the Home Department (ex parte Bateman)* [1993] COD 494, DC, above) is to make an *ex gratia* payment provided that:

(a)   the claimant has spent time in custody following a wrongful conviction or charge which resulted from serious default on the part of the police or some other public authority; or

(b)   there are exceptional circumstances such as the emergence of facts which completely exonerate the claimant.

The trial judge is not a public authority for the purposes of (a) above (*R* v *Secretary of State for the Home Department (ex parte Harrison),* above). However, his errors or misconduct may constitute 'exceptional circumstances' for the purposes of (b), and the Home Secretary should at least consider in every case where judicial misconduct is alleged whether it was so gross as to give rise to exceptional circumstances. Failure to do this amounts to an improper fetter on the exercise of his discretion (*R* v *Secretary of State for the Home Department (ex parte Garner)* (1999) *The Times,* 4 May, DC). Since it is impossible for a company to have 'spent time in custody' it follows that such a corporate body is not covered by the *ex gratia* scheme (*R* v *Secretary of State for the Home Department (ex parte Atlantic Commercial (UK) Ltd)* (1997) *The Times,* 10 March).

It seems that an *ex gratia* payment will not be made unless, *inter alia,* on a balance of probabilities the claimant was more likely than not to have been innocent of the crime for which he was convicted (see *R* v *Secretary of State for the Home Department (ex parte Harrison),* above, at p. 88). This aspect of the *ex gratia* scheme has been criticised on the ground that it enables the Home Secretary to make a decision on the guilt or innocence of the claimant. The amount of an *ex gratia* award is assessed by a leading barrister on the same principles as those mentioned above in relation to the statutory scheme. The level of compensation offered in these cases is not over-generous. The value of liberty is often put at a lower figure than the value of a person's reputation.

Perhaps the most serious (and the most widely-publicised) miscarriage of justice was that involving the so-called 'Guildford Four'. In October 1989, on a reference by the Home Secretary under s. 17 of the Criminal Appeal Act 1968 (since repealed by the Criminal

Appeal Act 1995: see para 6.3.3 above) the Court of Appeal quashed the convictions of four people who had been deprived of their liberty for over 14 years. Patrick Armstrong, Gerard Conlon, Paul Hill and Carole Richardson were tried before Donaldson J and a jury in October 1975. They were convicted of conspiracy to cause explosions and of five murders arising from the bombing of a public house in Guildford a year earlier, and also of causing an explosion likely to endanger life at another public house in Guildford on the same day. In addition, Patrick Armstrong and Paul Hill were convicted of two murders arising from the bombing of a public house in Woolwich. The 'Guildford Four' were convicted solely on the basis of confessions, which they retracted at the trial; there was no corroborating scientific or identification evidence.

Messrs Armstrong, Conlon and Hill were sentenced to life imprisonment. Carole Richardson, who was under 18 at the time of the alleged offences, was ordered to be detained during Her Majesty's pleasure. Their applications for leave to appeal against conviction were refused in October 1977 by the Court of Appeal, and in January 1987 the Home Secretary refused to refer the case back to that court under s. 17 of the Criminal Appeal Act 1968. He did, however, order an inquiry to be carried out by the Avon and Somerset police into the way in which the case had been investigated in 1974–5. A reference back to the Court of Appeal was finally made in January 1989 in the face of mounting pressure from the media, senior churchmen, politicians and two retired Law Lords. The grounds on which the reference was made related particularly to new alibi and medical evidence in the case of Carole Richardson.

Before the reference came on for hearing, the Director of Public Prosecutions announced publicly that, in the light of further new evidence discovered by the Avon and Somerset police, it 'would be wrong for the Crown to seek to sustain the convictions' (see *The Times,* 18 October 1989). An expedited hearing of the reference was arranged and it emerged that some of the original investigating police officers had perjured themselves and presented fabricated evidence at the trial. This revelation rendered the convictions unsafe and they were quashed (see *R* v *Richardson and others (1989) The Times,* 20 October, CA). Three of the 'Guildford Four' were released immediately. Paul Hill, who had earlier been convicted in Belfast (and sentenced to life imprisonment) on a separate murder charge, was later released on bail pending the outcome of an investigation into the safeness of that conviction. (Three police officers were subsequently prosecuted for conspiring to pervert the course of justice; they were acquitted by a jury: see *The Times,* 20 May 1993.)

Since the case of the 'Guildford Four', other disturbing examples of actual or potential miscarriages of justice have come to light. In April 1990, the convictions of the 'Winchester Three' were quashed as unsafe after they had failed to obtain a fair trial on terrorist charges (*R* v *McCann and others* (1990) 92 Cr App R 239, CA, para 6.3.2 above). Despite spending many months in prison awaiting trial and the outcome of their appeal, the 'Winchester Three' did not qualify for compensation under s. 133 of the Criminal Justice Act 1988. Their convictions were neither reversed on the ground of a 'new or newly discovered fact' nor on an appeal out of time or on a reference by the Home Secretary under what was then s. 17 of the Criminal Appeal Act 1968. (See *R* v *Secretary of State for the Home Department (ex parte Bateman)* [1993] COD 494, DC, above.)

The story of the 'Maguire Seven' began at the time of the arrest of two of the 'Guildford Four', which had led the police to visit the Maguire home in December 1974 where seven people were apprehended. They were charged with unlawful possession of an explosive substance. No explosives were found on the premises but there were traces of nitroglycerine on the hands of the male defendants and on plastic gloves used by Mrs Maguire. The

'Maguire Seven' — Anne Maguire and her husband Patrick Maguire, two of their children (Patrick aged 13 and Vincent aged 16), Sean Smyth (Mrs Maguire's brother), Giuseppe Conlon (Mrs Maguire's brother-in-law and the father of Gerard Conlon, one of the 'Guildford Four'), and Patrick O'Neill (a family friend) — were convicted in 1975 after a trial before Donaldson J and a jury. They were given custodial sentences of between four and 14 years. Their appeals against conviction were dismissed by the Court of Appeal in 1977. One of them, Giuseppe Conlon, died in prison in 1980.

In June 1990, several years after the last of them had been released from prison, the Director of Public Prosecutions and the Home Secretary announced that the convictions of the 'Maguire Seven' could not be allowed to stand (see *The Independent,* 15 June 1990). Their case was referred to the Court of Appeal under s. 17 of the Criminal Appeal Act 1968 and eventually their convictions were quashed as unsafe on the ground that their hands could have been innocently contaminated by nitroglycerine (*R* v *Maguire and others* [1992] 2 All ER 433, CA).

The 'Birmingham Six' — Richard McIlkenny, Hugh Callaghan, Gerard Hunter, Patrick Hill, Billy Power and John Walker — were tried by Bridge J (later Lord Bridge, a Lord of Appeal in Ordinary) and a jury in 1975. They were convicted of murder and sentenced to imprisonment for life; the trial judge said that they had been convicted on the 'clearest and most overwhelming evidence' he had ever heard. They were allegedly the Birmingham pub bombers of 1974 responsible for the deaths of 21 people. They were refused leave to appeal against their convictions in 1976; Lord Widgery (then the Lord Chief Justice) said there was no evidence that they had been knocked about in custody 'beyond the ordinary'. In 1987, the Home Secretary referred the case to the Court of Appeal under s. 17 of the Criminal Appeal Act 1968, but the appeal was dismissed at the end of the hearing in the following year; Lord Lane CJ described as 'wholly incredible' the defendants' contention that the police had conspired to present a false case against them (see *The Independent,* 29 January 1988).

The Home Secretary announced in August 1990 that their case was to be referred to the Court of Appeal for a second time under s. 17 of the 1968 Act (see *The Independent,* 30 August 1990). After spending more than 16 years in prison their convictions were quashed in 1991 as unsafe in the light of fresh scientific evidence (including electrostatic document analysis (ESDA) of police interview notes) and fresh evidence of police ill-treatment of them. (The defendants were released from prison on 14 March 1991; the Court of Appeal's reasons for quashing their convictions are reported in *R* v *McIlkenny and others* [1992] 2 All ER 417, CA.) The release of the 'Birmingham Six' led to demands that Lord Lane CJ should resign in view of his part in the perpetuation of the miscarriage of justice; a national newspaper editorial declared that it 'is time he threw in his wig' (*The Independent,* 15 March 1991). One hundred Members of Parliament signed an all-party Commons motion seeking to implement a procedure which would lead to his dismissal by the Queen. The dismissal of a senior judge is notoriously difficult to achieve (see para 1.8.1); the motion was not supported by the Government or the House of Lords and was not proceeded with. (Lord Lane CJ took early retirement a year later in April 1992 at the age of 73, and was replaced by Lord Taylor CJ.)

Three former police officers involved in the 'Birmingham Six' investigation were later prosecuted for perjury and conspiracy to pervert the course of justice. However, after legal argument the judge withdrew the case from the jury on the ground that the defendants would not receive a fair trial due to prejudicial publicity and that to proceed with the trial would amount to an abuse of process (see *The Times,* 16 October 1993).

In September 1991, the Home Secretary referred the cases of Judith Ward, Winston Silcott and Mark Braithwaite to the Court of Appeal under s. 17 of the Criminal Appeal Act 1968 (see *The Independent,* 18 and 27 September 1991). Miss Ward was sentenced to imprisonment for life in 1974 following the deaths of 12 people caused by the bombing of a coach on the M62 in Yorkshire. The reference was made because the cases of the 'Maguire Seven' and the 'Birmingham Six' had cast doubt on the scientific evidence relied upon by the prosecution at Miss Ward's trial. Messrs Silcott and Braithwaite received life sentences as a result of their convictions for the murder of PC Keith Blakelock during the riot at Broadwater Farm, Tottenham, in 1985. The case of the third man convicted for the Broadwater Farm murder, Engin Raghip, had already been referred to the Court of Appeal.

The 'Tottenham Three' referrals were made because of doubts over the genuineness of their confessions to the police. Their convictions were quashed on the grounds that police notes of an interview with Silcott had been tampered with (demonstrated by electrostatic document analysis (ESDA)), the police officer in charge of the case had lied under oath at their trial in 1987, fresh psychological evidence about Raghip's level of intelligence had been wrongly excluded at an earlier Court of Appeal hearing presided over by Lord Lane CJ in 1988 at which leave to appeal against conviction was refused, and that Braithwaite had been wrongly denied access to legal advice during police interviews. For what is believed to be the first time ever, the Court of Appeal apologised for the fact that the defendants had suffered as a result of the shortcomings of the criminal justice system (*R v Silcott and others* (1991) *The Independent,* 6 December). Messrs Raghip and Braithwaite went free. Winston Silcott, who was alleged to have murdered PC Blakelock while on bail awaiting trial for another offence, remained in prison to continue a sentence imposed upon him following conviction for an earlier murder. In November 1998, the Criminal Cases Review Commission refused to refer his conviction for the earlier murder to the Court of Appeal (see *The Times,* 19 November 1998).

Judith Ward was released on bail in May 1992 and her convictions were quashed the following month on the grounds that they were unsafe and unsatisfactory and that there had been a material irregularity in the course of the trial. The material irregularity consisted of the prosecution's failure to disclose evidence to the defence which cast doubt on the prosecution case. The convictions were unsafe and unsatisfactory for two reasons. First, the fresh forensic evidence available before the Court of Appeal rendered the scientific case against Miss Ward insupportable. Secondly, in view of her mental state at the time of the trial no reliance should have been placed on the confessions she had made to the police. (See *R v Ward* [1993] 2 All ER 577, CA.)

In October 1991, the Home Secretary ordered a fresh police inquiry into the circumstances leading to the conviction in 1978 of four men for the killing of Carl Bridgewater, a 13 year-old newspaper delivery boy who was shot dead when he disturbed intruders at a farmhouse in Staffordshire. Michael Hickey, Vincent Hickey and James Robinson were convicted of murder; Patrick Molloy was convicted of manslaughter and died in prison. Mr Molloy's confession had implicated the other three defendants; the inquiry was ordered, *inter alia,* in the light of new evidence provided by language experts which raised questions about the reliability of that confession (see *The Independent,* 1 November 1991). After studying the inquiry report, the Home Secretary declined to refer the case back to the Court of Appeal (see *The Independent,* 4 February 1993). However, the case was referred back three-and-a-half years later by a different Home Secretary after it had emerged that evidence of fingerprints found on the boy's bicycle, and not belonging to the defendants, had been withheld at the trial (see *The Times,* 27 July 1996). In February 1997, the 'Bridgewater

Three' were released on bail pending the outcome of the appeal (see *The Times*, 21 February 1997).

In February 1992, Stefan Kiszko's conviction for murder 16 years earlier was quashed on the basis of scientific evidence (available at the time of the trial but, for some inexplicable reason, not produced) which showed that he could not have been the killer. Traces of sperm had been found on the clothing of the victim, an 11-year-old girl. Mr Kiszko was infertile and incapable of secreting sperm (see *The Independent,* 19 February 1992). Mr Kiszko died in December 1993 at the age of 41. In 1994, a retired police detective superintendent and a retired Home Office forensic scientist were charged with perverting the course of justice in Mr Kiszko's case (see *The Times*, 12 May 1994).

The Darvell brothers, Wayne and Paul, from Swansea were convicted in 1986 of murdering the manageress of a sex-shop. Their convictions were quashed in July 1992 after the Home Secretary had referred their case to the Court of Appeal and it was found, *inter alia*, that police records of interviews with Wayne Darvell had been altered so as to produce false admissions that his brother had committed the murder. Lord Taylor CJ, on behalf of the Court of Appeal, apologised to the brothers for the ordeal they had been put through (see *The Independent*, 1 August 1992).

In December 1992, the convictions of the 'Cardiff Three' (Stephen Miller, Yusef Abdullahi and Tony Paris) were quashed. They had stood trial in 1990 for the murder of a prostitute in Cardiff and were found guilty. Two other men, John Actie and his cousin, Ronnie Actie, who stood trial with them were acquitted.

Police interviews of Stephen Miller were central to the prosecution's case against all three convicted men. These interviews had been conducted in a bullying fashion. Miller, who was on the borderline of mental handicap, denied any participation in the murder more than 300 times but eventually 'confessed' after 13 hours of questioning spread over five days. The interviews were recorded on 19 tapes.

The Court of Appeal held that the trial judge had been wrong to allow evidence of the interviews to be introduced in evidence since the interviews were oppressive and the confession obtained was unreliable. The convictions of all three men were regarded as unsafe. In delivering the judgment of the Court of Appeal, Lord Taylor CJ was severely critical both of the interviewing police officers and of Miller's former solicitor, who was present throughout much of the interviewing but did not intervene to prevent the police asking questions, or making comments, which were improper (i.e., oppressive, threatening or insulting), or to advise his client to remain silent (*R* v *Miller and others* (1992) *The Independent*, 17 December, CA).

Michelle and Lisa, the Taylor sisters, were found guilty in July 1992 of murdering the wife of a man with whom Michelle had allegedly had an affair. Their convictions were quashed on appeal in June 1993 for two reasons. First, there had been a failure by the police detective sergeant in charge of the case to disclose (even to the prosecution) the existence of a statement by a witness that the second woman he saw leaving the victim's home around the time of the murder might have been black. The Taylor sisters are white and the witness's later statement made for the purposes of the trial described the two women he had seen as 'blonde'. The police also failed to disclose that this witness had written to Barclays Bank (the victim's employers) before the trial claiming the £25,000 reward offered for information about the murder.

Secondly, the press coverage of the trial (described as 'unremitting, extensive, sensational, inaccurate and misleading') had created a real risk of prejudice against the defendants. It was for this reason that the Court of Appeal did not think it appropriate to order a retrial. The papers in the case were ordered to be sent to the Attorney-General for him to consider whether to institute proceedings for contempt of court against any newspaper (*R* v *Taylor* (1993) *The Times*, 15 June, CA). When after a lengthy delay the Attorney-General decided that it was not appropriate to start proceedings, the Taylor sisters were granted leave to apply for judicial review of his decision (see *The Times*, 7 December 1994). It was ultimately held, however, that it was not reviewable because of the well-established principle (exemplified in *Gouriet* v *Union of Post Office Workers* [1978] AC 435, HL, para 11.6) that the courts will not review the exercise of the Attorney-General's discretion in relation to decisions taken in the execution of his public office (*R* v *Attorney-General (ex parte Taylor)* (1995) *The Times*, 14 August, DC). In October 1995, a trial on a charge of wounding with intent was stopped by the judge two weeks before it was due to begin because of what he described as the 'unfair, outrageous and oppressive' press coverage of the case. The defendant was the boyfriend of an actress appearing in the television series, *Eastenders*. Once again, the case papers were ordered to be sent to the Attorney-General so that contempt proceedings could be considered (see *The Times*, 5 October 1995). In the event, proceedings under the 'strict liability' contempt rule (see para 5.2.2.4.2) were taken against the publishers of the *Daily Mirror*, the *Daily Star*, the *Sun*, *Today*, and the *Daily Mail*. The proceedings were unsuccessful, however, it being held that the press coverage of the case had not created any greater risk of prejudice than that which had already been generated over previous years by the saturation publicity given to the couple's relationship (*Attorney-General* v *MGN Ltd and others* [1997] 1 All ER 456, DC).

In June 1993, the Court of Appeal when quashing the conviction of Ivan Fergus, by then aged 16, took the unusual step of declaring not only that the conviction was unsafe and unsatisfactory but also that Mr Fergus was 'wholly innocent'. He had been convicted in November 1991 of assault with intent to rob — largely on the basis of wrongful identification evidence provided by a short-sighted bank clerk. He was sentenced to 15 months' youth custody but was released pending his appeal after serving six months of the sentence.

The conviction was quashed for a number of reasons. The main ground was the failure of the police to disclose, first, a photograph of the defendant taken at the time of his arrest at the age of 13, and, secondly, a crime report containing the first details given to the police by the victim. These documents, which were disclosable under a common law duty of disclosure, would have revealed that Mr Fergus was not the perpetrator of the crime. Other grounds were that the trial judge should have withdrawn the case from the jury; that the judge's summing up amounted to a material irregularity in its failure to put adequately to the jury specific weaknesses in the identification evidence; that the defendant's former counsel and solicitor had failed to prepare and conduct his defence properly; that the defendant had not had a fair trial due to the failure of the police to take statements from alibi witnesses. (See *R* v *Fergus* (1993) *The Times*, 30 June, CA.)

John Berry was convicted in 1983 of making explosive substances otherwise than for a lawful object, contrary to the Explosive Substances Act 1883, and was sentenced to eight years' imprisonment (later reduced to six years on appeal). The explosive substances in question were electronic timers and there was unchallenged scientific evidence from the prosecution that these devices could be used only for military or terrorist activities. Mr Berry's defence, which does not seem to have been put with any great vigour at the trial, apparently was that the timers were made not for the benefit of terrorists but for a lawful object, namely for sale to the Syrian government under a legitimate contract. In 1984, the Court of Appeal allowed his appeal against conviction but, on a further appeal by the Crown, the House of Lords restored it (see *R* v *Berry* [1984] 3 All ER 1008, HL).

While his case was before the House of Lords, and sensing that the Crown's appeal was likely to succeed, Mr Berry fled to Spain during an adjournment. He was expelled from Spain in 1989 and was arrested on his return to the United Kingdom. In 1990, he made an unsuccessful application to have his appeal reheard by the Court of Appeal on the basis that there were grounds which had not been considered by the House of Lords in 1984 (see *R v Berry (No. 2)* [1991] 2 All ER 789, CA, para 6.2.2.1 above).

Subsequently, the case was referred back to the Court of Appeal by the Home Secretary and Mr Berry's conviction was quashed in September 1993 (see *R v Berry (No. 3)* [1994] 2 All ER 913, CA). Fresh evidence had cast sufficient doubt on the original scientific evidence about the uses of electronic timers as to render the conviction unsafe and unsatisfactory. Furthermore, the trial judge's summing up was criticised by Lord Taylor CJ as 'muddled' in that it gave no clear indication that if the timers were being supplied to the Syrian government that was a good defence and the jury should not concern itself with how the timers were to be used by that government. It is somewhat ironic that the same summing up was described as being 'distinguished by its clarity and care' when the case was before the House of Lords in 1984 (*R v Berry* [1984] 3 All ER 1008, HL, *per* Lord Roskill at p. 1009; see also Bernard Levin, 'Long Sentences for Judges', *The Times*, 15 October 1993). John Berry had spent three and a half years in prison.

In 1995 the convictions of four men — Colin Phillips, Stuart Blackledge, Bryan Mason and Paul Grecian — were set aside in controversial circumstances. They had been convicted in 1992 of breaking an arms embargo by selling 300,000 artillery fuses to Iraq under an export licence which listed Jordan as the end-user. Three were given suspended one-year prison sentences, and the fourth was fined. The Court of Appeal subsequently decided that the withholding of government documents had prevented the men from mounting a proper defence at their trial. Indeed, it was the non-availability of these documents which had pressurised the men into pleading guilty. The documents, for which government ministers had successfully invoked public interest immunity from disclosure, would have shown that within government circles there was widespread knowledge of, and complicity in, an arms trade with Iraq (see *The Times*, 8 November 1995). The political pressure generated by this case prompted the government to establish an inquiry under Sir Richard Scott, Vice-Chancellor of the Chancery Division of the High Court, into the so-called 'arms to Iraq affair'. The *Scott Report* was published in February 1996 and was highly critical of the behaviour of some ministers and civil servants (*Report of the Inquiry into the Export of Defence Equipment and Dual-Use Goods to Iraq and Related Prosecutions*, 15 February 1996). There were, however, no resignations in its immediate aftermath.

The case of Mahmood Hussein Mattan was the first to be referred to the Court of Appeal by the Criminal Cases Review Commission under s. 9 of the Criminal Appeal Act 1995. Mr Mattan was hanged at Cardiff prison in 1952 following his conviction for murder. In 1998, his conviction was quashed as unsafe after the evidence of the main prosecution witness was found to be unreliable. The Court of Appeal welcomed the creation of the Criminal Cases Review Commission and expressed profound regret that it had taken 46 years for Mr Mattan's conviction to be shown to be unsafe. It further suggested that capital punishment is not an appropriate ultimate sanction in a criminal justice system which is human and, therefore, fallible, and that no one associated with the system can afford to be complacent (see *The Times*, 25 February 1998 and *R v Mattan* (1998) *The Times*, 5 March, CA).

The murder conviction of John Roberts was quashed in 1998 after he had spent 15 years in jail. The only evidence against Mr Roberts was his confession, which he retracted at his trial in 1983. He appealed unsuccessfully against his conviction in 1984. However, it emerged ten years later that he had been denied proper access to a solicitor during his interviews with the police, and new psychological tests showed that he was vulnerable to making false confessions. Had such tests been available at the time of the trial, the trial judge would have been bound to exclude the confession evidence and there would have been no case to leave to the jury (see *The Times*, 20 March 1998).

Patrick Nicholls and Ryan James had their murder convictions quashed in 1998 when it transpired that the victim in each case had not been murdered at all. Mr Nicholls had spent 23 years in jail following conviction for the murder of an elderly widowed friend who, according to the evidence of two pathologists, had been suffocated and beaten about the face. She had actually died from a heart attack. The Court of Appeal expressed its 'great regret' that Mr Nicholls had been wrongly convicted on flawed evidence and had spent such a long time in jail (see *The Times*, 13 June 1998). Mr James was convicted in 1995 of poisoning his wife with a horse sedative, but the later discovery of a suicide note rendered his conviction unsafe. It appeared that his wife killed herself but made her death look like murder in order to gain revenge on Mr James for having an affair with another woman (see *The Times*, 29 July 1998).

Danny McNamee was convicted in 1987 of conspiracy to cause explosions in London. His conviction was quashed in 1998 because of the emergence of fresh evidence and because, at the time of the trial, the prosecution had failed to disclose relevant material to the defence. The Court of Appeal, however, reminded Mr McNamee that having his conviction quashed did not mean that he was innocent (see *The Times*, 18 December 1998).

6.3.5 Shortcomings of the existing facilities for correcting miscarriages of justice

Dissatisfaction with the facilities provided by English law for the correction of miscarriages of justice has been growing in recent years. The failure to detect and correct miscarriages of criminal justice is attributable in large measure to deficiencies in the system for appealing against conviction following trial on indictment. An appeal lies to the Court of Appeal only if that court grants leave to appeal or if the trial judge has certified that the case is fit for appeal (Criminal Appeal Act 1968, s. 1, para 6.2.2.1 above). The appeal is decided by the Court of Appeal on the documents and on counsel's legal argument; the hearing of the appeal is not a retrial. It is a hearing at which the burden of proof is shifted from the prosecution to the appellant (who, in effect, is presumed to be guilty) since it is the appellant who has to satisfy the Court of Appeal under s. 2(1) of the Criminal Appeal Act 1968 that his conviction cannot be allowed to stand.

All this compares unfavourably with an appeal following *summary* conviction in the magistrates' court (para 6.2.1.1 above). Here, an appeal against conviction lies to the Crown Court as of right in all cases where the defendant originally pleaded not guilty, there is a complete rehearing with witnesses, and the burden of proof is on the prosecution to establish the defendant's guilt beyond reasonable doubt.

The traditional reluctance of the Court of Appeal to quash convictions or order retrials (amounting to an admission that something had gone seriously wrong before or during the trial) is partly explained by the desire of senior judges to maintain public confidence in the criminal justice system and to lend continued support to the role of the jury as the body solely responsible for determining guilt.

Section 17 of the Criminal Appeal Act 1968, which, as noted in para 6.3.3 above, conferred a discretion upon the Home Secretary to refer a case for review by the Court of

Appeal at any time, was a useful provision. However, it had two serious limitations. First, the Home Secretary appeared reluctant to refer cases out of a fear that he may be perceived to be interfering with the work of the courts, and whether he did refer cases may have depended too much on the amount of media attention generated by a particular case and on the amount of pressure exerted on him by people of influence. Mr Douglas Hurd, a former Home Secretary, said in evidence to Sir John May's inquiry that he had learned as the result of a rebuke from Lord Lane CJ during the first reference back of the case of the 'Birmingham Six' that any 'lurking doubts' harboured by Home Secretaries about potentially unsafe or unsatisfactory convictions were 'not welcomed' by the Court of Appeal (see *The Independent,* 3 October 1991). Secondly, the Court of Appeal (at least until a spate of serious miscarriages of justice) was reluctant to allow an appeal on a reference under s. 17 of the Criminal Appeal Act 1968 when it had previously dismissed a normal appeal in the same case under s. 2.

The House of Commons Select Committee on Home Affairs (*Sixth Report,* 1981–82, *Miscarriages of Justice,* HC Paper 421) recommended the setting up of an independent review body to investigate alleged miscarriages of justice. It was envisaged that the new procedure would replace the Home Secretary's reference to the Court of Appeal under s. 17 of the Criminal Appeal Act 1968. The government rejected the notion of an independent review body. It was envisaged, however, that the Home Secretary would in future be prepared more readily to exercise his power to refer cases to the Court of Appeal under s. 17 of the Criminal Appeal Act 1968, and that the court would be prepared to make greater use of its powers to admit fresh evidence and order a retrial (*Miscarriages of Justice: Government Reply to the Sixth Report from the Home Affairs Committee, Session 1981 to 1982,* Cmnd 8856, 1983). In November 1985, the Home Secretary announced that he did not intend to put the scheme of *ex gratia* payments on to a statutory footing but that he would for the future consider himself bound by the decisions of the independent assessor on the *amount* of compensation to be offered in particular cases. By 1988, however, he had changed his mind on the first point for the Criminal Justice Act of that year created a limited *statutory* scheme of compensation for victims of miscarriages of justice (see para 6.3.4 above). According to a report by a Committee of Justice under the chairmanship of Sir George Waller, a former Lord Justice of Appeal, the government's declaration of 1983 that the Home Secretary would more readily refer cases to the Court of Appeal and the court would make greater use of its powers to admit fresh evidence and order retrials was not acted upon (*Miscarriages of Justice,* Justice, 1989). Justice concluded that what was required was an independent review body to investigate allegations of serious miscarriages of justice, as proposed by the House of Commons Select Committee on Home Affairs in 1982 (*op. cit.*).

As a result of the successful appeal of the 'Guildford Four' in October 1989, a committee of inquiry was established under Sir John May, a retired judge of the Court of Appeal, to investigate the circumstances surrounding their convictions and those of the 'Maguire Seven'. In an interim report exonerating the 'Maguire Seven', Sir John May's inquiry was highly critical of the trial judge, Donaldson J (later Lord Donaldson MR, now retired), the three Court of Appeal judges who dismissed the appeal in 1977, and the conduct of certain scientists employed at the Royal Armament Research and Development Establishment (see *The Independent,* 13 July 1990). The report concluded, first, that both the trial judge and the Court of Appeal had failed to appreciate that new scientific evidence which had emerged on the last day of the trial removed the whole basis of the prosecution's case against the defendants; secondly, that the trial judge had allowed the jury to hear inadmissible evidence;

and, thirdly, that the scientists acting for the prosecution had presented misleading evidence and suppressed other evidence which may have cast doubts on the prosecution's case. Most of Sir John's findings were, by implication, rejected when the Court of Appeal quashed the convictions of the 'Maguire Seven' in June 1991. Their appeals were allowed on the narrow ground that their hands could have been innocently contaminated by nitroglycerine. In particular, the Court of Appeal, while accepting that the scientists were wrong to have withheld evidence and that doing so could amount to a material irregularity in the course of a trial, nevertheless concluded that no miscarriage of justice had resulted from the non-disclosure (*R* v *Maguire and others* [1992] 2 All ER 433, CA).

Mr Douglas Hurd, a former Home Secretary, in evidence to Sir John May's inquiry expressed his opinion that current arrangements were inadequate to deal with miscarriages of justice. In place of the Home Secretary's power to make references under s. 17 of the Criminal Appeal Act 1968, he advocated the creation of an independent tribunal with power to investigate, and refer direct to the Court of Appeal, potentially wrongful convictions (see *The Independent*, 3 October 1991). Liberty (formerly the National Council for Civil Liberties) put forward a similar proposal to the May inquiry (see (1990) 140 New LJ 1298).

The final report of Sir John May's inquiry into the case of the 'Maguire Seven', published in December 1992, confirmed that they had been the victims of a serious miscarriage of justice. Most criticism was reserved for the scientists whose reliability and credibility were highly suspect and who had misled prosecuting counsel and Sir Sam Silkin, who, as Attorney-General, authorised the prosecution in 1975. Sir John was unable to reach a definite conclusion as to why the hand-swab tests on the 'Maguire Seven' had proved positive for nitroglycerine. He recommended the setting up of a new body with wide powers to investigate alleged miscarriages of justice. This was endorsed by the then Home Secretary, Kenneth Clarke, who, like Douglas Hurd, favoured taking the task away from the Home Office (see *The Independent*, 4 December 1992). Sir John May's final report into the case of the 'Guildford Four' was published in June 1994 and, although critical of Surrey police and the prosecution lawyers, was a grave disappointment to those who expected names to be named and blame to be apportioned (see *The Times*, 1 July 1994).

On the same day that the convictions of the 'Birmingham Six' were quashed in March 1991, the Home Secretary announced the appointment of a Royal Commission on Criminal Justice to 'examine the effectiveness of the criminal justice system in England and Wales in securing the conviction of those guilty of criminal offences and the acquittal of those who are innocent, having regard to the efficient use of resources'. These terms of reference were wide enough to permit a review of the whole criminal process, including police investigation of crime, the interrogation of suspects, the reliability of scientific evidence, the right to silence, the provision for appeals, and the facilities for reviewing alleged miscarriages of justice after the appellate process has been exhausted. The Royal Commission, which was under the chairmanship of Lord Runciman of Doxford and had Sir John May among its membership, reported in July 1993 (see para 6.3.6 below).

There are two situations in which the victim of an injustice has no prospect of even an *ex gratia* award of compensation and may also be left without any legally-enforceable remedy. First, the case of the person who has been prosecuted and acquitted either by a magistrates' court or the Crown Court. Acquittals affect a significant proportion of defendants, especially in the Crown Court. For example, in 1998, the proportion of defendants acquitted in the Crown Court out of all those sent there for trial was 18 per cent. In the case of those who pleaded not guilty to all charges, the proportion acquitted was 64 per cent (*Judicial Statistics 1998*, Cm 4371, 1999, p. 65). It goes without saying that not all acquitted defendants are victims of injustice. However, those who *are* have no legal remedy unless they can succeed against the police in a civil action for damages for malicious prosecution, a tort which is notoriously difficult to prove. Secondly, a person who has been kept in custody and then released later without being prosecuted has no legal remedy unless he can succeed against the police in a civil action for the tort of false imprisonment. In recent years there appears to have been an increase in the number of out-of-court settlements agreed by police authorities in actions against them for false imprisonment and/or malicious prosecution.

6.3.6   Report of the Royal Commission on Criminal Justice, 1993

6.3.6.1   Introduction
While the Royal Commission was sitting, expectations were high that it would ultimately make radical proposals for root and branch reform of the criminal justice system. In particular, it was anticipated in some quarters that there would be support for a move towards an inquisitorial trial model as a replacement for the adversarial system, that uncorroborated confession evidence would be condemned, and that the creation of a new independent body to investigate alleged miscarriages of justice would be suggested. In the event, only the latter turned out to have been a realistic expectation and it seems that the inquisitorial model of trial was never considered to be a serious proposition (see Zander, 'Where the Critics Got It Wrong', (1993) 143 New LJ 1338 at p. 1341).

The much awaited Report was generally well received by the police and the prosecuting authorities. The then Lord Chief Justice, too, welcomed the Report while not agreeing with everything it proposed. At a conference on 'Criminal Justice after the Royal Commission', Lord Taylor CJ said that the overall impact of the 352 recommendations, which seemed modest when looked at individually, could be profound if they were viewed as an integrated package (see *The Times*, 28 July 1993).

Other interested parties were disappointed and the Report was criticised for being somewhat bland, unadventurous, and even naive. An attempt to answer some of the criticisms was made by an erstwhile member of the Royal Commission (Zander, *op. cit.*, at pp. 1338 and 1364). He argued that it was not reasonable to expect the Commission to give primary weight to the issue of avoiding the conviction of the innocent given that its terms of reference (see para 6.3.5 above) alluded to 'convicting the guilty' and 'the efficient use of resources' as well as to acquitting the innocent. He suggested that the critics' disappointment was due in part to their own unreal expectations and assumptions and to the mistaken view (fostered by the Press) that the Commission's task was to see that miscarriages of justice could never happen again.

The criticisms notwithstanding, the Royal Commission made a number of recommendations which, if implemented, would affect the roles of all the principal players in the criminal justice system — suspects and defendants, the police, the Crown Prosecution Service, expert witnesses, lawyers and judges — and would go some way towards preventing or rectifying the commonest causes of miscarriages of justice.

Recommendations were made, *inter alia*, on such matters as identification evidence, police investigations, safeguards for suspects, the right of silence, confession evidence, disclosure, forensic evidence, appeals, and the mechanisms for detecting and correcting miscarriages of justice. Some of these recommendations are dealt with below. Others are noted at appropriate points throughout the book and are not repeated here.

6.3.6.2 Appeals

Section 2(1) of the Criminal Appeal Act 1968 was criticised by the Royal Commission on the basis that it created overlapping between the grounds of appeal and caused confusion over the scope of the proviso to the subsection. Its redrafting was recommended. The majority of the Commission thought that the then existing grounds of appeal should be replaced by a single broad ground which would give the court flexibility to consider all categories of appeal. They identified the correct approach as being for the court to decide whether a conviction 'is or may be unsafe'.

Where an appeal is based on an alleged error by the trial lawyers, it was proposed that the test of 'flagrantly incompetent advocacy' (para 6.3.4 above) should be extended to a consideration of whether the lawyers' particular decision (be it reasonable or unreasonable) caused a miscarriage of justice.

6.3.6.3 Correction of miscarriages of justice

Abolition of the Home Secretary's power to refer cases to the Court of Appeal under s. 17 of the Criminal Appeal Act 1968 was recommended.

In its place there was proposed the creation of a new body (the 'Criminal Cases Review Authority') to consider allegations put to it that a miscarriage of justice may have occurred, to ensure that any further investigation called for was launched, to supervise that investigation if conducted by the police, and, where there were reasons for supposing that a miscarriage of justice might have occurred, to refer the case to the Court of Appeal.

It was envisaged that the Authority would be independent of the court structure and that its decisions would be immune from any appeal or judicial review process.

6.3.6.4 The government's response to the Report of the Royal Commission

A partial government response to the Report was provided at the Conservative Party Conference in October 1993 as part of a wider package of measures designed to fight crime and to satisfy the party's law and order lobby. Some of the more contentious elements of the package had been widely leaked before the event.

The Home Secretary announced that it was the government's intention to establish a Criminal Cases Review Authority. More controversially, and in defiance of a majority of the Royal Commission, it was proposed to abolish a defendant's right of silence so that it would become possible at the trial to draw adverse inferences from his decision to remain silent under police questioning (see *The Times*, 7 October 1993).

The Home Secretary's Conference speech represented a significant shift in government policy on law and order. Among other changes announced were new measures to deal with persistent young offenders, bail bandits, terrorism, intimidation of witnesses and jury nobbling. It was revealed that the government also intended to change the law so as to provide harder work for persons serving community sentences and to extend the Attorney-General's power to seek a review of unduly lenient sentences.

Some of the changes mentioned in this paragraph were effected by the Criminal Justice and Public Order Act 1994. That Act, however, contained no provisions for the reform of s. 2(1) of the Criminal Appeal Act 1968 or for the establishment of a Criminal Cases Review Authority. These two matters were instead dealt with in the Criminal Appeal Act 1995. First, the 1995 Act substituted a new s. 2(1) of the Criminal Appeal Act 1968 (see para 6.3.2 above). Secondly, it repealed s. 17 of the 1968 Act and thereby abolished the Home Secretary's power to refer cases back to the Court of Appeal (see para 6.3.3 above). The responsibility for referring possible miscarriages of justice back to the court was taken over by a new body created by the 1995 Act, the Criminal Cases Review Commission, which came into existence on 1 January 1997 and began examining cases at the end of March of that year.

At the same time as implementing these reforms, the Criminal Appeal Act 1995 made it more difficult to appeal against a Crown Court conviction by substituting a new s. 1(2) of the Criminal Appeal Act 1968. The new s. 1(2) provides that leave of the Court of Appeal, or a certificate from the trial judge that the case is fit for appeal, is required in all cases before an appeal can be taken to the Court of Appeal (see para 6.2.2.1 above).

7

Trial by Jury

7.1 INTRODUCTION

Trial by jury is an ancient and democratic institution. It will be seen later that it is also a declining one, particularly in civil cases (para 7.6 below). But, while it lasts, it provides an opportunity for the layman to participate in the administration of the legal system, to reassure the rest of us that justice is being done in individual cases, and to act as a restraining influence on the professional judiciary.

It is said that in the judicial process the members of a jury are essentially judges of *fact*. But this is not the whole story because, in reality, a jury's verdict is a decision of *mixed fact* and *law*. In criminal prosecutions in the Crown Court the jury will listen to the evidence from both sides, to the trial judge's summing-up of the evidence, and to any directions on the law given by the judge. The members of the jury then decide, in the light of their understanding of the law as explained by the judge, whether, in fact, the accused is guilty or not guilty. In those civil cases where a jury is still available, the jury will consider the evidence and any directions on the law given by the judge. The members of the jury then apply their understanding of the law to the facts of the case and decide whether to find for the claimant or for the defendant. If judgment is given for the claimant, the jury also decides, as a question of fact, how much the damages should be.

The different roles of judge and jury in criminal cases are explained in the following model direction, issued by the Judicial Studies Board in 1991 and endorsed by the Lord Chief Justice, which a trial judge is encouraged to give to the jury:

> It is my job to tell you what the law is and how to apply it to the issues of fact that you have to decide and to remind you of the important evidence on these issues. As to the law, you must accept what I tell you. As to the facts, you alone are the judges. It is for you to decide what evidence you accept and what evidence you reject or of which you are unsure. If I appear to have a view of the evidence or of the facts with which you do not agree, reject my view. If I mention or emphasise evidence that you regard as unimportant, disregard that evidence. If I do not mention what you regard as important, follow your own view and take that evidence into account.

Failure to offer to the jury an explanation of their role along the lines of the model direction may amount to a misdirection which could result in the quashing of the defendant's conviction on appeal. (See, for example, *R* v *Jackson* [1992] Crim LR 214, CA, where the trial judge gave a wholly inadequate direction on the functions of judge and jury and on the manner in which the jury were to regard any comments that he might make during the summing-up.)

The respective functions of judge and jury in civil cases may be illustrated by reference to an action for the tort of defamation. It should be noted that there is a qualified right to trial by jury in defamation cases and that the majority of such actions are still tried by jury in spite of the decline of jury trials in civil cases generally. In 1975, the Faulks Committee on Defamation (*Report*, Cmnd 5909, 1975) recommended that a jury should be available in a defamation action only at the discretion of the judge on the application of either party. The recommendation has not been implemented. (See also para 7.6.2 below.) In a defamation action, if the judge decides, as a *matter of law*, that the offending statement is capable of being defamatory, he must explain to the jury what defamation means in law. The jury then decides, as a *matter of fact* but in the light of their understanding of the law, whether the particular statement is defamatory. If the judge is of the opinion that the statement is not capable of being defamatory in law, he must withdraw the case from the jury (*Capital & Counties Bank Ltd v Henty* (1882) 7 App Cas 741, HL).

Juries do not have to justify or explain their verdicts to anyone. In a criminal case there is no right of appeal by the prosecution against a jury's verdict of not guilty at the Crown Court, although the Attorney-General may refer the case to the Court of Appeal under the procedure contained in s. 36 of the Criminal Justice Act 1972 (para 6.2.2.5). In civil cases a jury's verdict can only be upset by an appeal court if it was perverse; i.e., so unreasonable that no jury properly directed could reasonably have reached it on the evidence (*Mechanical & General Inventions Co. Ltd v Austin* [1935] AC 347, HL; *Powell v Streatham Manor Nursing Home* [1935] AC 243, HL, *per* Viscount Sankey LC at p. 250; *Scott v Musial* [1959] 2 QB 429, CA, *per* Morris LJ at p. 437).

It is certainly not a sufficient ground for setting aside a jury's award to say that the damages are much more, or much less, than the appeal court itself would have awarded in the particular circumstances. In *Cassell & Co. Ltd v Broome* [1972] AC 1027, for instance, the House of Lords, by a majority of four to three, refused to interfere with a jury's award of £40,000 damages in a libel case even though all their Lordships considered the award excessive. Similarly, in *Blackshaw v Lord* [1983] 2 All ER 311, the Court of Appeal declined to interfere where a jury had awarded damages of £45,000 in a libel action even though all three members of the court considered the sum far too high. In *Lewis v Daily Telegraph Ltd* [1964] AC 234, however, the House of Lords ordered new trials of two libel actions in which juries had awarded a total of £217,000 in damages. The damages were so excessive that no reasonable jury could reasonably have awarded them. In *Riches v News Group Newspapers Ltd* [1985] 2 All ER 845, the Court of Appeal ordered a new trial on the issue of damages on the ground, *inter alia,* that no reasonable jury, properly directed by the judge, could have awarded such a high sum. The jury had awarded what were then record damages for libel, totalling £253,000, in an action brought by ten police detectives in respect of allegations of rape, assault and blackmail made against them in the *News of the World.*

In *Sutcliffe v Pressdram Ltd* [1990] 1 All ER 269, the Court of Appeal set aside an award of £600,000 damages made by a jury in a libel action brought by the estranged wife of the so-called 'Yorkshire Ripper' against the publishers of *Private Eye* (see further, para 7.9.2 below). Exceptionally in this case, a new trial before a different jury on the issue of damages was not ordered. The Court of Appeal, at the defendants' suggestion (with which the claimant concurred), agreed to reassess the damages itself at a later date. In the event, the Court of Appeal did not, in fact, reassess the damages since the parties agreed on a settlement of £60,000 (see [1990] 1 All ER 269 at p. 295).

In another case decided at about the same time as *Sutcliffe v Pressdram Ltd*, the Court of Appeal actually *increased* a jury's award of damages. Two sisters had successfully sued the Tesco supermarket chain, and a store detective employed by them, for libel, slander and false imprisonment following an incident in December 1984 in which they were detained and accused of dishonesty by switching price labels. Criminal charges against them were later dropped. The claimants were awarded damages of £800 each by a jury. Since this sum was less than the defendants' offer of £1,500 each of them had already rejected to settle the case out of court, they were liable to pay the defendants' costs as well as their own. The costs were estimated at £40,000. On appeal, the jury's award was set aside as being too low. Lord Donaldson MR said the size of the award provided some evidence that the jury had been misdirected by the trial judge, who had failed to make it sufficiently clear that *aggravated* damages could be awarded in view of the fact that the defendants had persisted in the allegation of dishonesty at the trial (see para 10.2.4 for the circumstances in which aggravated damages may be awarded). Instead of ordering a new trial on the question of damages, the Court of Appeal itself, at the invitation of the parties, reassessed the damages and awarded a sum of £7,500 to each claimant, thereby incidentally relieving the sisters of the costs burden. Lord Donaldson MR warned the legal profession that the figure assessed by the Court of Appeal was not to be treated as a precedent for guidance in future cases (*Warby* v *Cascarino* (1989) *The Times,* 27 October, CA).

The virtual inviolability of a jury's verdict makes it possible on occasions for juries to criticise by implication unsatisfactory laws and to assist in the shaping of future laws (para 7.9.1, below). Juries have, in effect, a power (albeit rarely exercised) to nullify the law.

7.2 QUALIFICATIONS FOR JURY SERVICE

By s. 1(a) and (b) of the Juries Act 1974, as amended, to qualify for jury service a person must:

(a)   be aged between 18 and 70 and be registered as a parliamentary or local government elector; *and*

(b)   have been ordinarily resident in the United Kingdom, Channel Islands or the Isle of Man for at least five years since the age of 13.

The property qualification was abolished in 1972 (Criminal Justice Act 1972) since when it has become noticeable that more women serve on juries and that the average age of jurors tends to be lower (see Baldwin and McConville, *Jury Trials,* 1979, pp. 94 et seq.). The law on jury service is now consolidated in the Juries Act 1974, as amended. By the Criminal Justice Act 1988, the upper age limit was raised from 65 to 70, although persons older than 65 are allowed to claim excusal as of right (see para 7.3.3 below).

7.3   INELIGIBILITY, DISQUALIFICATION, EXCUSAL AND DISCRETIONARY DEFERRAL

All persons who satisfy the above-mentioned conditions concerning age, residence and inclusion in the electoral register are prima facie qualified to serve as jurors. Any such person may, however, be ineligible, or be disqualified, or be excused, or have his attendance for jury service deferred until a future date. The difference between ineligibility and disqualification is that in the former case a person is prevented from serving by reason of his occupation or mental condition, while in the latter case he is prevented from acting on account of (for example) having been *sentenced* to life imprisonment or having *served* a term of imprisonment or youth custody. A person's occupation may also be relevant to excusal as of right, but here, unlike the case of ineligibility, a person may serve as a juror if he wishes.

7.3.1   Ineligibility

The persons who are *ineligible* for jury service are mainly those whose occupations are connected with the administration of justice and those whose religious vocation or function makes it desirable that they should be excluded (Juries Act 1974, s. 1 and sch. 1, pt 1). In the first category are, *inter alia,* judges, justices of the peace, the chairmen and vice-chairmen of tribunals, members of the legal profession (whether practising or not), solicitors' articled clerks, court officers, police officers, probation officers, members and employees of the Criminal Cases Review Commission, employees of any forensic science laboratory, and any person who has had such an occupation within the last ten years. It seems that close relatives of court officers will be regarded as within the spirit, if not the letter, of the ineligibility provisions if those relatives attend regularly as jurors. In *R* v *Salt* (1996) *The Times*, 1 February, CA, the defendant's conviction was quashed when it was discovered that the jury which had convicted him included the son of one of the court ushers and the son had sat as a jury member on five or six occasions during the previous year.

In the second category fall ministers of religion, monks and nuns. The *Report of the Royal Commission on Criminal Justice* (Cm 2263, 1993) recommended that clergymen and members of religious orders should cease to be ineligible for jury service. Also ineligible are persons who are mentally ill.

The lawfulness of a conviction is not affected by reason of the presence on the jury of an ineligible person (ibid., s. 18(1)(b)).

7.3.2   Disqualification

The following persons are *disqualified* from jury service:

(a)   a person who *at any time* in the United Kingdom, Channel Islands or Isle of Man has been sentenced to imprisonment for life, custody for life or to a term of imprisonment or youth custody of five years or more, or has been sentenced to be detained during Her Majesty's pleasure;

(b)   a person who *in the last ten years* has, in the United Kingdom, Channel Islands or Isle of Man, served any part of a sentence of imprisonment, youth custody or detention, or been detained in a borstal institution, or received a suspended sentence of imprisonment or order for detention, or had a community service order made against him;

(c)   a person who *in the last five years* has, in the United Kingdom, Channel Islands or Isle of Man, been placed on probation (Juries Act 1974, s. 1 and sch. 1, pt 2, as amended by the Criminal Justice Act 1982 and the Juries (Disqualification) Act 1984).

Such persons are disqualified because of the importance of maintaining public confidence in the administration of justice. It is felt to be unfair to entrust the fate of accused persons, and the fate of the parties in civil cases, to those whose own conduct has demonstrated a lack of any proper appreciation of decent behaviour (*Report of the Departmental Committee on Jury Service,* 1965, para 134).

The presence on the jury of a disqualified person does not affect the lawfulness of the jury's verdict (Juries Act 1974, s. 18(1)(b)).

(d) A person who is on bail in criminal proceedings is disqualified from jury service in the Crown Court (Criminal Justice and Public Order Act 1994, s. 40).

The Royal Commission on Criminal Justice (*Report*, Cm 2263, 1993) recommended that such a person be disqualified so as to avoid the possibility of a person sitting on a jury while on bail for the same offence for which he is to try the defendant.

7.3.3 Excusal

Certain persons are entitled, if they so wish, to be *excused as of right* from jury service (Juries Act 1974, s. 9(1) and sch. 1, pt 3, as amended). These are generally persons whose occupations involve them in duties to the state or its citizens or in the relief of pain and suffering. They include members of the House of Commons and the House of Lords, members of the Scottish Parliament and the Scottish executive, members of the National Assembly for Wales, members of the European Parliament, full-time serving members of the armed forces, practising doctors, dentists, nurses, midwives, vets and pharmaceutical chemists. To this list were added in 1995 practising members of religious societies or orders whose tenets or beliefs are incompatible with jury service (Juries Act 1974, sch. 1, pt 3, as amended by the Criminal Justice and Public Order Act 1994).

A person is also entitled to be excused as of right if he has (a) served on a jury (excluding a coroner's jury), or attended to serve on a jury, in the past two years, *or* (b) been excused from jury service by any court for a period which has not expired (Juries Act 1974, s. 8).

Persons more than 65 years old are entitled to be excused as of right (ibid., sch. 1, pt 3, as amended by the Criminal Justice Act 1988).

Discretionary excusal is also possible. A person may be excused from jury service on a particular occasion if he shows a 'good reason' (Juries Act 1974, s. 9(2)), such as illness or an arranged holiday commitment. There is a right of appeal against the refusal of the appropriate officer to excuse a person under s. 9(2) (ibid., s. 9(3)). The appeal will usually be heard by a Crown Court judge except in the case of a summons to attend before the High Court in Greater London, when the appeal will be heard by a High Court judge. Under rules of court, the appeal must not be dismissed unless the appellant has been given an opportunity of making representations. The court's power when hearing such an appeal is limited to excusing the appellant or refusing to excuse him. The court cannot excuse him and then impose an obligation on him to attend on a specified future date instead (*R* v *Crown Court at St Alban's (ex parte Perkins)* (1981) *The Times,* 12 December, DC; but see discretionary deferral, para 7.3.4 below).

Some guidelines on discretionary excusal are given in a *Practice Note* [1988] 3 All ER 177, which states that every application for excusal should be dealt with 'sensitively and sympathetically'. It lists the following circumstances as examples of 'good reasons' which may justify excusal under s. 9(2):

    (a)   personal involvement in the facts of the particular case;
    (b)   close connection with a party or prospective witness;
    (c)   personal hardship (this is not defined but presumably would include illness, holiday commitments and difficulty in making arrangements to have young children looked after);
    (d)   conscientious objection to jury service.

The *Practice Note* does not, of course, have the force of a statute. Although there is no *right* to legal representation for a person appealing against a refusal to excuse, the court has a *discretion* to allow it and should carefully and sympathetically consider exercising that discretion in cases involving conscientious objections to jury service (*R* v *Crown Court at Guildford (ex parte Siderfin)* [1989] 3 All ER 7, DC, *per* Watkins LJ at p. 12).

7.3.4 Discretionary deferral

A person summoned for jury service may have his attendance deferred if he shows a 'good reason' to the satisfaction of the appropriate court officer (Juries Act 1974, s. 9A, added by the Criminal Justice Act 1988). Where deferral is granted, the days of attendance will be varied. Discretionary deferral differs from discretionary excusal in that the person whose attendance for the time being is deferred will have to attend at some future date instead. If deferral is refused, there is a right of appeal to the court (ibid., s. 9A(3)).

7.3.5 Disabled persons

If there is doubt about a person's capacity to act effectively as a juror because of *physical disability* (such as deafness or blindness), the judge will decide whether or not that person should act as a juror. The judge must allow the person to act as a juror unless he is of the opinion that the person will not be capable of acting effectively by reason of his disability (Juries Act 1974, s. 9B, as inserted by the Criminal Justice and Public Order Act 1994).

7.3.6 Doubt about capacity

Any doubt about a person's capacity to act effectively as a juror because of *insufficient understanding of English* will be decided by the judge (Juries Act 1974, s. 10).

7.4 SUMMONING JURORS

The annual electoral register is the starting-point for the provision of jurors for both criminal and civil trials. The electoral register is compiled from information supplied by occupiers of houses. The information required includes the names of persons who live in a particular house and whether any such person is over the age of 18 or over the age of 70. Every electoral registration officer is under a duty to send to designated officers of the courts special copies of the electoral register. The copies are special in that they are marked so as to show which persons are under the age of 18 or over the age of 70 (Juries Act 1974, s. 3(1), as amended by the Criminal Justice Act 1988).

The court officer makes a random list, from his copy of the electoral register, of those aged between 18 and 70 whom he wishes to call for jury service on any particular occasion. Each person so listed is then summoned, by the court officer in the name of the Lord Chancellor, by written notice to attend for jury service (ibid., s. 2(1) and (4)). A notice, sent out with the summons, explains the grounds for ineligibility, disqualification and excusal. The court officer may *at any time* ask a person summoned such questions as he thinks fit in order to establish whether or not that person is qualified for jury service (ibid., s. 2(5), as amended by the Administration of Justice Act 1982). This provision is intended to facilitate the exclusion of disqualified persons at an early stage and to ensure that qualified persons do not evade jury service by pretending to be disqualified.

If at any trial the court is short of jurors it can require any qualified person who is in the vicinity to be summoned for jury service without any written notice (ibid., s. 6).

From those summoned, the court officer prepares lists (called panels) of jurors for the various courts. The information to be included in panels is determined by the Lord Chancellor (ibid., s. 5(1)). Reasonable facilities for inspecting a panel must be provided for a party to the proceedings and any person acting on behalf of a party. In addition, the court has a discretion to allow any other person to inspect the panel (ibid., s. 5(2) and (3)).

A particular jury is selected by ballot from the panel in open court. Each juror must be sworn separately (ibid., s. 11(1) and (3)).

The power to summon and empanel jurors is an administrative matter. The power has been conferred by statute specifically on the Lord Chancellor. It follows that a trial judge has no jurisdiction to order a multiracial jury to be empanelled for a particular trial (*R v Ford* [1989] 3 All ER 445, CA). Nor, for the same reason, can the judge order that jurors be brought in from outside the normal catchment area merely because he suspects that local jurors might be intimidated (*R v Tarrant* (1997) *The Times*, 29 December, CA, in which *R v Ford* was applied).

In relation to the summoning and empanelling of jurors, the Royal Commission on Criminal Justice (*Report*, Cm 2263, 1993) recommended that prospective jurors, on being summoned, should be required to declare that they do not have a disqualifying conviction and that jury summoning officers should take all practicable steps to minimise the risk that jurors serving on the same jury may know each other or the defendant. Some relaxation of the law so as to permit multiracial juries was recommended. It was suggested that, in exceptional circumstances, it should be possible for either the defence or the prosecution, first, to apply to the judge before the trial begins for the selection of a jury containing up to three members from ethnic minority communities, and, secondly, to argue the need for one or more of those three jurors to come from the same ethnic minority as the defendant or the victim.

7.5 JURIES IN CRIMINAL CASES

The jury is used in the Crown Court. There is no jury in the magistrates' courts, which try about 98 per cent of criminal cases. The jury is thus used (theoretically) in only the 2 per cent of criminal trials which take place at the Crown Court. In practice, however, the jury is used even less than this (in about 0.8 per cent of criminal trials) because 61 per cent of defendants at the Crown Court plead guilty and do not need a jury trial (*Judicial Statistics 1998*, Cm 4371, 1999, p. 64).

7.5.1 Challenging jurors

Before 1989, a person being tried on indictment could make a *peremptory challenge* (i.e., a challenge without cause) to not more than three jurors. This right was abolished by the Criminal Justice Act 1988 as a result of the government's concern that the right was being abused. The accused retains the right to challenge all or any of the jurors *for cause*. Any challenge for cause is tried as a preliminary matter by the trial judge (Juries Act 1974, s. 12(1)(a) and (b)). The challenge must be made after the juror's name has been drawn by ballot (ibid., s. 12(3)). It was held in *R v Comerford* [1998] 1 All ER 823, CA, that this provision does not, however, make it mandatory to call out jurors' names. It follows that where jurors are called by numbers, their names having been withheld to prevent jury-nobbling, the ensuing trial by anonymous jury is valid provided that the defendant's right of challenge is preserved. The purpose of s. 12(3) was held to be to define the time at which the challenge is to be made rather than to require the public announcement of jurors' names. (See further on this case, para 6.3.2.3.)

The prosecution can also challenge for cause and, in addition, has the right to 'stand by' any would-be juror and, if necessary, the entire panel. 'Stand by' is meant to be only a provisional challenge on the part of the prosecution. In theory, the prosecution can only challenge for cause and, when a juror is stood by, the inquiry into the cause is postponed until a later date. In practice, there will usually be sufficient other qualified persons in attendance from whom to form a jury, and to allow the trial to proceed, so that the prosecution's 'cause' is never investigated.

The Attorney-General's 'Guidelines on the Exercise by the Crown of its Right to Stand By' (published as a *Practice Note* [1988] 3 All ER 1086) reaffirm the principles of random jury selection and that no one should be treated as disqualified or ineligible except as provided for by Parliament in the Juries Act 1974, as amended. According to the 'Guidelines', it is accepted practice that the prosecution's right of stand by will be exercised sparingly, and only in exceptional circumstances, and that it will not be used in order to influence the overall composition of a jury or to obtain a tactical advantage over the defence. The circumstances in which it would be proper to exercise the right are listed as:

(a)   Where a jury check (see para 7.5.2 below) has revealed information which strongly suggests that, given the facts of the case and the offences to be tried, a particular juror might be a security risk, be susceptible to improper approaches or be influenced by improper motives in arriving at a verdict, and the Attorney-General has personally authorised use of the right of stand by.

(b)   Where a juror is about to be sworn in who is 'manifestly unsuitable' and the defence agrees that the exercise of the right of stand by would be appropriate. The 'Guidelines' give the example of an illiterate juror about to try a complex case.

When challenging for cause, counsel (whether for the prosecution or the defence) should not ask questions of the juror in order to establish the cause; any questioning should be left to the trial judge. Irregularities at the Angry Brigade trial in 1972 led to changes in procedure. At the suggestion of counsel for the defence, the trial judge asked would-be jurors to exclude themselves on a number of grounds; for example, if they were members of the Conservative Party or if they had relatives in the police or armed forces in Northern Ireland. *In toto,* 29 persons were challenged and another 19 admitted belonging to one or other of the judge's categories. The result was that, after the trial was concluded, the Lord Chief Justice issued a *Practice Direction* in which he emphasised that jurors should not be excused on account of race, religion, politics or occupation. By implication, the trial judge should not ask questions about such matters. A juror should be excused only on the more traditional grounds of personal connection with the facts of the case (or with a party or a witness), or personal hardship or conscientious objection to jury service (*Practice Direction* [1973] 1 All ER 240; see also *R* v *Broderick* [1970] Crim LR 155, CA; the 1973 *Practice Direction* was revoked and replaced in 1988 by *Practice Note (jury; juror; excuse)* [1988] 3 All ER 177, para 7.3.3 above). In 1973, the Lord Chancellor issued a directive that, in future, jury panels would not include the occupations of prospective jurors.

In *R* v *Andrews* (1998) *The Times*, 15 October, CA, the Court of Appeal held that the questioning of potential jurors by means of a questionnaire (or, *obiter*, orally) with a view to discovering whether they are biased is of doubtful efficacy and could be counterproductive in that it might bring to the attention of, or remind, jurors of some matter which the parties and the court would wish them to disregard. Such questioning should be avoided unless the circumstances are most exceptional. In all other cases, jurors must be trusted to be faithful to their oaths to return true verdicts in accordance with the evidence given in court.

7.5.2 Jury vetting

The practice of *jury vetting* (i.e., checking the background of jurors) appears to conflict with the Lord Chief Justice's *Practice Direction* of 1973 in which it was reaffirmed that a jury 'consists of 12 individuals chosen at random from the appropriate panel' ([1973] 1 All ER 240 *per* Lord Widgery CJ; see also *Practice Note (jury: juror: excuse)* [1988] 3 All ER 177 *per* Lord Lane CJ). It is also in defiance of Blackstone's caveat that the liberties of England depend upon the jury remaining 'sacred and inviolate; not only from all open attacks (which none will be so hardy as to make), but also from all secret machinations, which may sap and undermine it' (4 B1 Comm 350).

In 1978, at the trial of Messrs Aubrey, Berry and Campbell (the so-called ABC official secrets trial), two journalists and a soldier were charged with collecting secret information. Counsel for one of the defendants discovered that some weeks before the trial began the prosecution had been supplied with a list of potential jurors. Those on the list had been scrutinised so as to check their 'loyalty'. As a result of this discovery the trial was stopped and a new trial ordered before a fresh jury. All three defendants were ultimately acquitted (see Aubrey, *Who's Watching You,* 1981). In October 1978, pressure from MPs and the press led the Attorney-General to make public his 'Guidelines on Jury Checks', which, it was then admitted, had been in existence since 1974 following upon the Angry Brigade trial.

The Attorney's Guidelines have since been revised and the current version is open to inspection in the law reports (see *Practice Note (jury: stand by: jury checks)* [1988] 3 All ER 1086; for earlier versions see [1980] 3 All ER 786 and [1980] 2 All ER 457). The Guidelines first of all reaffirm three basic principles. They are that a jury should be chosen by random selection, that only those matters specified in the Juries Act 1974, as amended, should disqualify a person from jury service, and that the correct way for the prosecution to exclude a prospective juror is to stand him by, or challenge him for cause, in open court. However, the Guidelines highlight certain exceptional types of case of public importance in which the statutory safeguards of majority verdicts and the imposition of criminal liability on a disqualified person 'may not be sufficient to ensure the proper administration of justice'. These cases are identified as:

(a) Cases involving national security where part of the evidence is likely to be heard *in camera.*

(b) Terrorist cases.

In these exceptional cases it is felt that a potential juror's political beliefs may be so biased as to 'interfere with his fair assessment of the facts of the case or lead him to exert improper pressure on his fellow jurors'. And, in security cases, there is a danger that a juror, either voluntarily or under pressure, may reveal evidence given *in camera.*

The actual vetting is done by means of a check on police criminal records and police Special Branch records; in cases falling under (a) above the security services may also be involved. The involvement of Special Branches and the security services requires the personal authority of the Attorney-General on the application of the Director of Public

Prosecutions. The questioning of family, neighbours and friends is not in general permissible except where it is necessary to confirm the identity of a juror about whom doubts have been raised following the initial check on criminal or Special Branch records.

There is no statutory basis for the Attorney-General's Guidelines on Jury Checks and the authority of a judge is not required before vetting can take place. The prosecution can (though only with the personal authority of the Attorney-General) stand by a prospective juror who falls foul of the Guidelines without, in practice, any reason being given in open court. However, it is stated that a person should not be stood by unless the check has revealed a *strong* reason for believing that he might be a security risk or susceptible to improper approaches or be influenced in arriving at a verdict. There is no *duty* to communicate the reason for the stand by to the defence, although counsel may use his discretion to disclose it if its nature and source permit. If the prosecution do not stand by a juror but vetting has revealed that he may be biased against the accused, the Guidelines advise that defence counsel should be warned, even if only in a general way.

The question of jury vetting is controversial and has given rise to a conflict of judicial opinion within the Court of Appeal. The matter came before the Court of Appeal for the first time in *R* v *Crown Court at Sheffield (ex parte Brownlow)* [1980] 2 All ER 444, and the practice of jury vetting was condemned as unconstitutional in the civil division by Lord Denning MR and Shaw LJ. Two police officers had been committed for trial on charges of assault. Their solicitors wished to have the jury panel vetted for previous convictions but the prosecuting solicitor refused to do this. The defending solicitors therefore applied to a judge at the Crown Court and the judge ordered the police to vet the jury panel and to supply the defence with details of any convictions. The Chief Constable of South Yorkshire applied to the Divisional Court of the Queen's Bench Division for an order of certiorari to quash the judge's decision. The Divisional Court refused to interfere and the Chief Constable appealed to the Court of Appeal, which held, by a majority decision, that the court had no power to interfere with the judge's order.

Both Lord Denning MR and Shaw LJ, although differing on the question of the court's power to interfere, said that jury vetting was unconstitutional because it was not sanctioned by the Juries Act 1974 ([1980] 2 All ER 444 at pp. 453 and 455). They regarded it as a serious invasion of a person's privacy. The third judge in the appeal, Brandon LJ, while not directly condemning the practice, said that if jury vetting was permitted then the defence should be entitled to receive any resulting information (p. 456).

It is clear that, since the appeal in the *Sheffield* case was dismissed, what was said about jury vetting was strictly *obiter*. This fact was seized upon in the second case to reach the Court of Appeal (this time the criminal division), *R* v *Mason* [1980] 3 All ER 777. The defendant had been convicted in the Crown Court at Northampton of burglary and handling stolen goods. He appealed against conviction on the ground, *inter alia,* that the jury had been vetted for criminal convictions, a practice which appeared to be common at that time in Northampton. It was held that the appeal would be dismissed. The court said that some vetting of jurors was necessary in order to eliminate disqualified persons. There was some evidence that prospective jurors were not disclosing that they were disqualified, although since the Juries Act 1974 there had been only two prosecutions for serving on a jury while disqualified. One resulted in an acquittal and the other in a fine of £10.

Lawton LJ, delivering the judgment of the court, said that the principle of random selection of the jury had been qualified for centuries: certain persons were disqualified by statute; the defence has the right of peremptory challenge (since abolished in 1989); the prosecution has the right of stand by; and the judge can intervene to excuse a juror who, for example, cannot read or hear. His Lordship said that the only authority competent to check the criminal convictions of jurors are the police, and, since it is a criminal offence to serve on a jury while disqualified, the police are only performing their usual duty to prevent crime when they engage in jury vetting. He made it clear that his judgment was only concerned with the vetting of the jury panel for criminal convictions. He refused to comment on any information other than convictions or on the desirability of making other enquiries about jurors. He said that what was stated about jury vetting in the *Sheffield* case was *obiter* and not binding, and that in *Mason* the court had been able to examine the issue in greater depth. In *R v McCann and others* (1990) 92 Cr App R 239, the Court of Appeal, criminal division, preferring *Mason* to *ex parte Brownlow,* went further and declared that the practice of jury vetting in accordance with the Attorney-General's Guidelines, and the exercise by the Attorney-General of his right to 'stand by' prospective jurors (para 7.5.1 above), are constitutionally proper. (*R v McCann and others* is the case of the 'Winchester Three'; for the full story, see para 6.3.2.)

The legal position on jury vetting appears, then, to be this. The checking of criminal records for convictions is permissible and desirable in order to eliminate disqualified persons (*R v Mason* and *R v McCann,* above). The checking of police Special Branch records, and the making of other enquiries, in accordance with the Attorney-General's Guidelines, as outlined above, is also lawful (*R v McCann,* above). The jury which in 1984 convicted Michael Bettaney, an M15 officer, of charges under the Official Secrets Act had been vetted by M15 and Special Branch officers. However, jury vetting does not necessarily work to the advantage of the prosecution. In 1985, Clive Ponting, a senior civil servant with the Ministry of Defence, was *acquitted* of charges under the Official Secrets Act by a vetted jury.

7.5.3 Death or discharge of jurors

In a criminal case the trial (even if it is for murder) may continue if a juror *dies or is discharged* because of illness or any other reason, provided that the number of jurors does not fall below nine (Juries Act 1974, s. 16(1)). In the case of an offence punishable with death, this rule only applies if, in addition, there is the written consent of both the prosecution and the accused (ibid., s. 16(2), as amended by the Criminal Justice Act 1988). It should be noted that there are now no offences punishable with death. The death penalty for murder was abolished by Parliament in 1969 under the provisions of the Murder (Abolition of Death Penalty) Act 1965. The death penalty for setting fire to Her Majesty's ships and dockyards was abolished by the Criminal Damage Act 1971, s. 11(2). The death penalty for treason and piracy with violence was abolished with effect from 30 September 1998 by the Crime and Disorder Act 1998, s. 36.

The judge may discharge a juror otherwise than in open court if there is a good reason (*R v Richardson* [1979] 3 All ER 247, CA). The Court of Appeal has jurisdiction to review the trial judge's exercise of his discretion to excuse a juror under the Juries Act 1974 but will only interfere where the judge has been capricious or where injustice has resulted. Thus, in *R v Hambery* [1977] QB 924, the Court of Appeal refused to interfere where the trial judge had discharged a juror who was due to go on holiday the next day. It made no difference that the judge had not enquired of the juror whether it was important for her holiday to start on that day; the importance could be inferred. The judge had not been capricious and no injustice had resulted because a trial can continue with less than the maximum number of jurors present. Jurors are entitled to some consideration and if justice can be administered properly without undue inconvenience to jurors then it should be ([1977] QB 924, *per* Lawton LJ at p. 930).

In a *criminal* case, no appeal lies against the trial judge's decision to discharge the *whole jury*. This is because the Court of Appeal, criminal division, can only hear an appeal against a conviction on indictment (Criminal Appeal Act 1968, s. 2(1), as substituted by the Criminal Appeal Act 1995, para 6.2.2.1), and if the entire jury is discharged before a verdict is delivered there is no conviction against which to appeal (*R* v *Hambery*, above, *per* Lawton LJ at p. 929; *R* v *Gorman* [1987] 2 All ER 435, CA; *Gladding* v *Channel 4 TV Corporation* [1999] EMLR 475, CA). In a *civil* case, however, an appeal does lie against the trial judge's decision to discharge the whole jury because the civil division of the Court of Appeal is not subject to the same restriction as the criminal division, having jurisdiction, under s. 16(1) of the Supreme Court Act 1981, 'to hear and determine appeals from any judgment or order of the High Court' (*Gladding* v *Channel 4 TV Corporation*, above).

7.5.4 Majority verdicts

Majority verdicts, which were first introduced into English law by the Criminal Justice Act 1967, are now dealt with in s. 17 of the Juries Act 1974. In 1998, of those convicted in the Crown Court after a plea of not guilty 20 per cent were convicted on majority verdicts (*Judicial Statistics 1998*, Cm 4371, 1999, p. 66). In the Crown Court, a majority verdict is acceptable if:

  (a)   there are not less than eleven jurors and ten of them agree; or
  (b)   there are ten jurors and nine of them agree (Juries Act 1974, s. 17(1)(a) and (b)).

In either case the foreman of a jury which has reached a verdict of guilty must state in open court the number of jurors who agreed *and* disagreed with the verdict (without, of course, giving their names) (ibid., s. 17(3)).

Compliance with this requirement is mandatory (rather than merely directory) before a Crown Court judge can accept a majority verdict of guilty. If the requirement is not observed at all, the defendant's conviction may be quashed. Thus, in *R* v *Barry* [1975] 2 All ER 760, CA, where the judge accepted a majority verdict of guilty without the foreman of the jury stating, or even being asked to state, the number of jurors who agreed to or dissented from the verdict, the Court of Appeal allowed the defendant's appeal and quashed his conviction.

In *R* v *Reynolds* [1981] 3 All ER 849, in answer to a question by the clerk of the court asking how many agreed and how many disagreed with the verdict, the foreman said 'Ten agreed'. The Court of Appeal held that the appellant's conviction would be quashed. *R* v *Reynolds* was followed reluctantly in *R* v *Pigg* [1982] 2 All ER 591 in which the Court of Appeal, while accepting itself as bound by *Reynolds,* expressed the view (at p. 595) that it was absurd that it should be mandatory for the foreman to state how many jurors dissented when all that was required to find out was a simple arithmetical calculation.

The Crown appealed to the House of Lords in *R* v *Pigg* and the House ([1983] 1 All ER 56) reversed the decision of the Court of Appeal, overruled *R* v *Reynolds* and, at the same time, approved *R* v *Barry*. The House of Lords held that, although compliance with the requirement of s. 17(3) of the Juries Act 1974 was mandatory, the precise form of words used by the clerk of the court when asking the foreman of the jury the number who agreed and dissented, and by the foreman in his reply, was not an essential part of that requirement. Section 17(3) was satisfied as long as the words used by the clerk and the foreman made it clear to an ordinary person how the jury was divided. If, in the case of a jury of *twelve,* the foreman, on being asked how many jurors agreed with the verdict, replied that *ten* agreed,

s. 17(3) was satisfied because it was a necessary and inevitable inference which would be obvious to any ordinary person that *two* disagreed.

At the same time it was made clear in *R* v *Pigg* that if the requirement of s. 17(3) is not observed at all, as in *R* v *Barry,* the Crown Court judge cannot lawfully accept the jury's verdict. In *R* v *Mendy* [1992] Crim LR 313, CA, the foreman of the jury at the end of a lengthy trial of two counts of conspiracy to defraud answered a question put to him by the clerk of the court by saying (ambiguously) that, in respect of one count, the defendant had been found guilty 'by a majority of us all'. The professionals involved in the case (the clerk of the court, the trial judge, counsel and their instructing solicitors) seem to have simply assumed that this was a unanimous verdict. On appeal, however, the issue was raised as to whether the foreman was returning a majority verdict or a unanimous one. If his answer was meant to indicate a majority verdict then s. 17(3) had not been complied with because there was no statement about how many jurors agreed and disagreed with the verdict. Without needing to apply *R* v *Barry,* it was held that since the case was one involving the liberty of the subject the benefit of the ambiguity should be given to the appellant and his conviction on that count was quashed. The Court of Appeal stressed how important it was for counsel and solicitors to pay the closest attention to procedural matters in order to avoid for the future the 'horrifying possibility' of a verdict obtained in a long and expensive City fraud trial being set aside on a technicality.

Where the foreman of the jury fails to state the number of jurors who agreed and disagreed with a majority verdict of guilty, the verdict is not unlawful if the omission is corrected quickly by the foreman after the entire jury has been reassembled (*R* v *Maloney* [1996] 2 Cr App R 303, CA, in which the defective verdict was delivered on a Friday and corrected on the following Monday, the next working day).

In *R* v *Millward* [1999] 1 Cr App R 61, CA, the clerk of the court asked the jury whether they had reached a verdict on which at least ten of them were agreed, to which the foreman said: 'Yes'. The clerk asked the further question: 'Is that the verdict of you all or by a majority?', to which the foreman replied: 'All of us'. The clerk then said: 'You find the defendant guilty and that is the verdict of you all?', and the foreman answered: 'Yes'. A verdict of guilty was recorded. The next day the foreman wrote to the judge stating that she had made a mistake and that, in fact, only ten jurors had agreed and two had dissented. On appeal against conviction, it was argued that s. 17(3) had not been complied with.

The Court of Appeal dismissed the appeal, holding that the clerk had asked the right questions, the jury's answer was not ambiguous and there was a clear statement that the verdict was unanimous. The question whether the jury should be allowed to enter a different verdict did not arise, since it would be against the authority of *R* v *Young* [1995] QB 324, CA (para 7.7 below), for the court to inquire into what passed between jurors in the jury room. It was further held that, even if that conclusion was wrong, there was an acceptable majority verdict and there was nothing to indicate that the conviction was unsafe.

The cases of *Barry*, *Mendy* and *Maloney* were distinguished in *Millward* because, unlike *Barry* and *Maloney*, the clerk had asked the right questions, and, unlike *Mendy*, the jury's answer was not ambiguous. Unlike all three earlier cases, there was in *Millward* a clear and explicit statement of a unanimous verdict.

There is no requirement to state the number of jurors who agreed and disagreed in the case of a verdict of not guilty.

There are provisions designed to ensure that the jury does not resort to a majority verdict too hastily. The trial judge must encourage the jury to reach a unanimous verdict. In the Crown Court, at least two hours' deliberation must be allowed to the jury (Juries Act 1974,

s. 17(4)). In addition, Practice Directions issued by the Court of Appeal have said that if the members of the jury are not agreed after two hours they should be sent back to the jury room at least once with a view to reaching unanimity. And then (if necessary) they should be sent back at least once to see if they can reach the required majority (see [1967] 3 All ER 137 and [1970] 2 All ER 215). If all these efforts fail, the jury will be discharged and the case may be retried before a fresh jury. Although judges are meant to observe the Practice Directions they do not have the force of law. Accordingly, the acceptance of a majority verdict in contravention of them does not necessarily render the defendant's conviction unsafe so as to entitle him to have it quashed on appeal (*R* v *Trickett* [1991] Crim LR 59, CA; *R* v *S* (*a juvenile*), 10 February 1997, CA, unreported).

It may be mentioned here that in *civil* cases in the High Court the rules about majority verdicts are the same as in the Crown Court (Juries Act 1974, s. 17(1)). In the county courts, where there can be a jury of eight (County Courts Act 1984, s. 67), the verdict need not be unanimous if seven jurors agree (Juries Act 1974, s. 17(2)). They must, however, be given reasonable time for deliberation, although the two-hour rule does not apply in the civil courts (ibid., s. 17(4)).

7.5.5   Judicial pressure on the jury

It is generally accepted that a jury must be allowed to consider their verdict free from all external pressures, such as violence, threats, intimidation or attempted bribery. It is also important that a jury should not be subjected to undue pressure from the trial judge; if they are so subjected, this may lead to the defendant's conviction being quashed on appeal on the ground that it is unsafe (see para 6.3.2).

One of the most extreme examples of improper judicial pressure occurred in *R* v *McKenna* [1960] 1 QB 411, CCA, in which the trial judge, Stable J, threatened the jury that if they did not return a verdict within another ten minutes they would be locked up all night. Inside six minutes the jury brought in verdicts of guilty against the defendants, having spent the previous two and a quarter hours unable to agree. On appeal, the convictions were quashed because of a material irregularity in the course of the trial. The Court of Criminal Appeal said ([1960] 1 QB 411 *per* Cassels J at p. 422):

> It is a cardinal principle of our criminal law that in considering their verdict, concerning, as it does, the liberty of the subject, a jury shall deliberate in complete freedom, uninfluenced by any promise, unintimidated by any threat. They still stand between the Crown and the subject, and they are still one of the main defences of personal liberty. To say to such a tribunal in the course of its deliberations that it must reach a conclusion within ten minutes or else undergo hours of personal inconvenience and discomfort, is a disservice to the cause of justice . . .

Two points should be noted about the facts of *R* v *McKenna*. First, they arose in the days before majority verdicts were permitted. If, in more recent times, the trial judge considers that the jury are taking too long to reach a decision he can accept a majority verdict as long as they have been deliberating for at least two hours. Secondly, although until recently a jury were not allowed to separate once they had retired to consider their verdict, it became the usual practice to accommodate them in an hotel, rather than to lock them up in the jury room, if an overnight stay was necessary. When a jury are sent to an hotel for the night, the object is to give them a break from the case they are trying (*R* v *Young* [1995] QB 324, CA, para 7.7 below). They are not meant to continue their deliberations at the hotel and they should be directed against doing this by the trial judge. A failure on the judge's part so to do may lead to a successful appeal against conviction (*R v Tharakan* [1995] 2 Cr App R 368, CA, where a medical practitioner, who had been convicted of obtaining and attempting to obtain property by deception after a 24-day trial, had his convictions quashed because the judge had failed to direct the jury not to deliberate at the hotel).

A jury may now be allowed by the trial judge to separate at any time, whether before or after they have retired to consider their verdict (Juries Act 1974, s. 13, as substituted by the Criminal Justice and Public Order Act 1994). If the jury are unable to reach a verdict during a day's sitting, an overnight stay in an hotel away from family is no longer inevitable since, at the discretion of the judge, they may be permitted to separate and go home.

The Court of Appeal has provided guidance to judges on how to direct juries which are to be allowed to separate before reaching their verdicts. The direction should remind the jury of the following matters:

(a)   that they must decide the case only on the evidence and arguments presented in court;

(b)   that the evidence has been completed and it would be wrong to seek or receive further information of any sort about the case;

(c)   that they must not discuss the case with anyone except other members of the jury in the jury room;

(d)   that when they leave court they should try to put the case on one side until they return to court and get to the jury room to begin or continue their deliberations.

The direction should be given in full before the jury separate for the first time and a brief reminder should be given before each subsequent dispersal (*R v Oliver* [1996] 2 Cr App R 514, CA).

It is not to be regarded as improper pressure for the judge simply to ask the jury, as a practical administrative matter, whether they are likely to reach a verdict that evening (*R v Bean* (1991) *The Times*, 1 May, CA). In another case the jury were unable to agree on their verdict and the judge sent a message to them after 6 p.m. asking them to continue their deliberations. Within minutes thereafter the jury convicted the defendant by a majority verdict of 10–2. The judge's action was construed as improper pressure amounting to a material irregularity in the course of the trial. Instead of sending the offending message he should have brought the jury back into court and asked them about the prospects of reaching a verdict (*R v Wharton* [1990] Crim LR 877, CA; see also *R v Duggan* [1992] Crim LR 513, CA).

In *R v Walhein* (1952) 36 Cr App R 167, CCA, the trial judge said to a jury who were unable to agree:

. . . it makes for *great public inconvenience and expense* if jurors cannot agree owing to the unwillingness of one of their number to listen to the arguments of the rest . . . (Italics supplied.)

On appeal, this direction was upheld by the Court of Criminal Appeal. However, it has since been disapproved on the basis that reference to 'public inconvenience and expense' may amount to pressure on the jury to express agreement with a view they do not really hold. If this is the case, the defendant's conviction might be quashed on appeal on the ground that it is unsafe. In *R v Watson* [1988] 1 All ER 897, CA, Lord Lane CJ said (at p. 903):

One starts from the proposition that a jury must be free to deliberate without any form of pressure being imposed on them, whether by way of promise or of threat or otherwise. They must not be made to feel that it is incumbent on them to express agreement with a view they do not truly hold simply because it might be inconvenient or tiresome or expensive for the prosecution, the defendant, the victim or the public in general if they do not do so . . .

It is at the trial judge's discretion to decide whether to give a specific direction, and at what stage of the trial, to a jury who are, or might be, unable to agree. According to the Court of Appeal in *R* v *Watson,* such a direction is best given in the following form (*per* Lord Lane CJ at p. 903):

Each of you has taken an oath to return a true verdict according to the evidence. No one must be false to that oath, but you have a duty not only as individuals but collectively. That is the strength of the jury system. Each of you takes into the jury box with you your individual experience and wisdom. Your task is to pool that experience and wisdom. You do that by giving your views and listening to the views of the others. There must necessarily be discussion, argument and give and take within the scope of your oath. That is the way in which agreement is reached. If, unhappily, [ten of] you cannot reach agreement you must say so.

7.5.6 Communications between the jury and the judge

The trial judge must at all times be in a position to give proper and accurate advice to a jury on any matter of law or fact which is troubling them. At the same time it is important that, as a general rule and for the sake of impartiality and openness, there should be no private or secret communication between the jury and the judge.

During the jury's deliberations any communication from the jury should normally be dealt with by the judge in open court in the presence of the entire jury and of the defendant and his counsel. Failure to observe this practice may result on appeal in the quashing of the defendant's conviction on the ground that it is unsafe (see *R* v *Lamb* (1974) 59 Cr App R 196, CA (conviction quashed); *R* v *Townsend* [1982] 1 All ER 509, CA (conviction quashed); *R* v *Rose* [1982] 2 All ER 536, CA (conviction quashed); *R* v *Rose* gave rise to other proceedings in the House of Lords: see [1982] 2 All ER 731 and para 6.3.2.3; *R* v *Woods* (1988) 87 Cr App R 60, CA (conviction not quashed); *R* v *Sipson Coachworks Ltd* [1992] Crim LR 666, CA (conviction quashed); *R* v *Obellim* [1997] 1 Cr App R 355, CA (conviction quashed)). In *R* v *Gorman* [1987] 2 All ER 435 (conviction not quashed), the Court of Appeal laid down the following guidelines:

(a)   If the note from the jury is about some matter unconnected with the trial (e.g., a request to pass on a message to a juror's relative), it can be handled by the judge without involving counsel or bringing the jury back into court.

(b)   In other cases, the judge should state in open court, in the presence of the defendant and his counsel, the nature and content of the note and, if he considers it helpful, may seek the assistance of counsel before bringing the jury back into court in order to deal with the note.

(c)   If the note contains information which the jury need not and should not have disclosed (such as details of their voting figures), the judge should not read out that particular information.

7.5.7 Jurors' expenses and compensation for loss of earnings

A juror is not paid for his services but he is entitled to travelling expenses, subsistence expenses and compensation for loss of earnings. The amounts are fixed by the Lord Chancellor by statutory instrument and the money is provided by Parliament out of taxation (Juries Act 1974, s. 19(1), (3) and (4)). All of these allowances are tax-free. They are paid not only to jurors but to all those who perform unpaid public duties, such as justices of the peace and witnesses in criminal trials.

7.5.8 The representativeness of the criminal jury

The jury in criminal cases is frequently under attack. Its representativeness was called in question by some research carried out in Birmingham, where it used to be the practice (since discontinued) to summon for jury service only half as many women as men (see Baldwin and McConville, *Jury Trials,* 1979, p. 97). The jury is probably no longer 'predominantly male, middle-aged, middle-minded and middle-class'. The abolition of the property qualification in 1972 has led to working-class juries with no evidence of less willingness to convict. Members of juries also now tend to be younger than hitherto — again with no evidence that they are less willing to find guilt (ibid., pp. 101–2). But it was found that racial minorities were not adequately represented on juries in Birmingham. In the period investigated, only 0.7 per cent of jurors were from the West Indies, India and Pakistan. Again, although 10 per cent of the population of Birmingham is from Ireland, only 3.6 per cent of jurors were from there (ibid., p. 98).

7.6 JURIES IN CIVIL CASES

7.6.1 Introduction

In the county courts, a jury of eight may be called (County Courts Act 1984, ss. 66 and 67), although trial by jury is practically obsolete there. In the High Court, a jury of 12 may be called. In the Chancery Division and the Family Division, trial by jury is practically obsolete. In the Queen's Bench Division, a jury is used in perhaps only 1 per cent of all cases. (For the coroner's jury, see paras 2.5.4 and 2.5.6.) The use of the jury in civil cases has declined considerably over the past 145 years. Before 1854 all cases tried in the common-law courts were heard by a judge sitting with a jury. The Common Law Procedure Act 1854 then laid down that common law actions could be tried without a jury if the parties agreed. There was a further decline after the reorganisation of the structure of the courts effected by the Judicature Acts in 1875. Section 6 of the Administration of Justice (Miscellaneous Provisions) Act 1933 severely curtailed the use of the jury in civil cases. The provisions of the 1933 Act have been repealed and replaced by the Supreme Court Act 1981, s. 69.

7.6.2 The right to a jury in civil cases

The Supreme Court Act 1981, s. 69, provides that there is a *right* to trial by jury only where there is a charge of fraud against a party, and in claims for libel, slander, malicious prosecution or false imprisonment. A similar provision is contained in s. 66 of the County Courts Act 1984.

Juries today are most commonly used in defamation actions, although their virtual abolition in such actions was recommended in 1975 by the Faulks Committee on Defamation (*Report*, Cmnd 5909, 1975), which proposed that jury trial in defamation actions should be at the discretion of the judge. The proposal was not implemented. In 1981, during the passage of the Bill for the Supreme Court Act in the House of Lords, an amendment was defeated which would have implemented the Faulks Committee recommendation. The proposed amendment was a result of *Orme* v *Associated Newspapers Group Ltd* (31 March 1981, unreported), a libel action brought by the Unification Church (the 'Moonies') against the *Daily Mail*. The action was tried with a jury on more than 100 days between October 1980 and the end of March 1981. In December 1982 the Unification Church lost a two-week appeal before the Court of Appeal, based on alleged misdirections by the trial judge, and was left to pay the costs of the trial and appellate proceedings estimated at some £800,000.

Even in the four exceptional cases mentioned above, the right to a jury is qualified. The judge can refuse to allow trial by jury if the case 'requires any prolonged examination of documents or accounts or any scientific or local investigation which cannot conveniently be made with a jury' (Supreme Court Act 1981, s. 69(1); County Courts Act 1984, s. 66(3)). It has been held that the word 'conveniently' refers to the efficient administration of justice. If the administration of justice is likely to suffer by the presence of a jury, the judge should consider ordering a trial by judge alone (see e.g., *Goldsmith* v *Pressdram Ltd* [1987] 3 All ER 485, CA — order for trial by judge alone upheld; *Viscount De L'Isle* v *Times Newspapers Ltd* [1987] 3 All ER 499, CA — order for trial by judge alone reversed; *Beta Construction Ltd* v *Channel Four TV Co. Ltd* [1990] 2 All ER 1012, CA — order for trial by judge alone upheld; *Taylor* v *Anderton* [1995] 2 All ER 420, CA — order for trial by judge alone upheld; *Aitken* v *Preston and others* (1997) *The Times*, 21 May, CA – order for trial by judge alone upheld; *Oliver* v *Calderdale Metropolitan Borough Council* (1999) *The Times*, 7 July, CA — order for trial by judge alone upheld).

During the passage through the House of Commons of the Bill that became the Supreme Court Act 1981, the government proposed an amendment that jury trial should not be available in civil cases where the probable length of the trial made the action one which could not conveniently be tried with a jury. The proposed amendment, which was not accepted, was again a direct result of *Orme* v *Associated Newspapers Group Ltd*. In June 1981, Lord Lane CJ issued a *Practice Direction* [1981] 2 All ER 775 reminding lawyers that great care should be taken in estimating the length of civil trials so as to avoid hardship to jurors.

It has, in any event, been made clear by subsequent case law that the likely prolongation of a trial is a relevant factor, among others, to be taken into account under s. 69 of the Supreme Court Act 1981 as it stands. In *Goldsmith* v *Pressdram Ltd* [1987] 3 All ER 485, CA, Lawton LJ said (at p. 492) that

> [a] trial with a jury inevitably takes longer than a trial by a judge alone. If the trial is made much longer because of the time taken up by the jury examining documents, then an element of inconvenience arises.

In *Beta Construction Ltd* v *Channel Four TV Co. Ltd* [1990] 2 All ER 1012, CA, the defendants had admitted liability in a libel action and the only issue to be tried was the quantum of damages. This would involve a consideration of actual and estimated losses of net profits which could only be worked out by a long investigation of the claimants' accounts and other documents. The claimants wished damages to be assessed by a jury while the defendants wanted them assessed by a judge alone. At first instance it was decided that damages should be quantified by a judge alone and, on appeal, that decision was upheld. The Court of Appeal held that whether a libel action involving 'prolonged examination of documents or accounts' can conveniently be tried by a jury, so as to be consistent with the efficient administration of justice, depends upon a consideration of such factors as:

(a)   The extent to which the presence of a jury might add to the length of the trial.

(b)   The extent to which the presence of a jury might add to the cost of the trial by reason of its increased length and the necessity of photocopying a multitude of documents for use by the jury.

(c)   Any practical difficulties which a jury trial might cause, such as the physical problem of handling in the confines of a jury box large bundles of bulky documents.

(d)   Any special complexities in the documents or accounts which might lead a jury to misunderstand the issues in the case.

The longest trial in English legal history — the libel actions brought by the McDonald's Corporation and McDonald's Restaurants Ltd against two environmental activists over statements contained in a six-page leaflet entitled *What's wrong with McDonald's? Everything they don't want you to know* — was held without a jury. The writs were issued in 1990, the trial was originally estimated to last for five weeks, and at an early stage the trial judge decided that the case would not be suitable for trial by jury. In the event, the trial occupied 313 days between June 1994 and November 1996, the judge taking another seven months to consider his judgment. A major factor contributing to the length of the trial was that the defendants were not legally represented. Some of the allegations made against the claimants were held to be true; others were found to be untrue and defamatory. Damages totalling £115,000 were awarded to the claimants (*McDonald's Corporation and another* v *Steel and Morris*, 19 June 1997, unreported, but see *The Times*, 20 June 1997).

7.6.3   The judge's discretion to order trial by jury in civil cases

In all other civil cases in the Queen's Bench Division there is *no right* to trial by jury but the judge has a *discretion* to allow it (Supreme Court Act 1981, s. 69(3); a similar provision relating to trial in a county court is contained in the County Courts Act 1984, s. 66(2)).

The guidelines for the proper exercise of this discretion were laid down by a full Court of Appeal of five members in *Ward* v *James* [1966] 1 QB 273. This was an action for personal injuries sustained in a motor accident. The claimant sued the defendant in negligence and applied for trial by jury. The judge ordered a jury and the defendant appealed against this order to the Court of Appeal which held that, in the circumstances, there should be a jury to hear the case. The Court of Appeal laid down the following guidelines:

(a)   The judge's discretion is not absolute but must be exercised judicially.

(b)   Normally, personal injury cases should be tried by a judge sitting alone so as to achieve the three basic objectives of assessability, uniformity and predictability of awards of damages.

(c)   A jury in civil cases should be used only in exceptional circumstances, such as where there is a substantial dispute about the facts.

The effect of the decision in *Ward* v *James* has been significant in the Queen's Bench Division of the High Court. Before *Ward* v *James* about 2 per cent of personal injury cases were tried by jury ([1966] 1 QB 273 *per* Lord Denning MR at p. 290). After *Ward* v *James* the proportion has dropped to less than 1 per cent. The full effect of this decision on the trial of civil cases is difficult to predict, especially because no comprehensive guidance was given on what are 'exceptional circumstances'. But at least the Court of Appeal made it very clear that they were not seeking to abolish trial by jury. Lord Denning MR, in particular, made this clear in the following well-known passage ([1966] 1 QB 273 at p. 295):

> Let it not be supposed that this court is in any way opposed to trial by jury. It has been the bulwark of our liberties too long for any of us to seek to alter it. Whenever a man is on trial for serious crime, or when in a civil case a man's honour or integrity is at stake, or when one or other party must be deliberately lying, then trial by jury has no equal.

The question of whether a jury should be used in a personal injury case arose before the Court of Appeal again in *Hodges* v *Harland & Wolff Ltd* [1965] 1 All ER 1086. The claimant was injured at work by a spindle which caught his trousers and injured his penis. One result of the injury was that the claimant could no longer perform the sex act although he still retained his sexual urge. The judge ordered trial by jury after taking into account all the relevant factors, including the desirability of uniformity of awards. The defendant appealed. The Court of Appeal held that the judge was right and there should be a jury as the case was an exceptional one. This time Lord Denning MR (at p. 1087) emphasised that the decision in *Ward* v *James* had not taken away the right to trial by jury in civil cases:

> It was not this court but Parliament itself which years ago took away any absolute right to trial by jury and left it to the discretion of the judges. This court in *Ward* v *James* affirmed that discretion and . . . laid down the considerations which should be borne in mind by a judge when exercising his discretion.

In *Singh* v *London Underground* (1990) *The Independent,* 25 April, an application for trial by jury of a claim arising from the King's Cross underground fire disaster of November 1987 was refused on the ground that a case involving such wide issues and technical topics was unsuitable for a jury.

In another personal injury case, *H* v *Ministry of Defence* [1991] 2 All ER 834, CA, the claimant was a regular soldier diagnosed by the Army Medical Service as suffering from Peyronie's disease. This is a congenital disease resulting in curvature of the penis and making sexual intercourse difficult. He submitted to a test designed to assess the extent of the abnormality. The test involved injecting the penis with a saline solution; as a result of the test the claimant's penis became infected at the site of the injection. He was then advised to have a skin graft but while he was under the anaesthetic awaiting surgery it was discovered that a skin graft was impossible and, instead, a major part of his penis was amputated.

On discovering what had happened to him, the claimant suffered severe psychological trauma and brought an action for damages for personal injuries caused by the defendants' negligent medical treatment. The defendants admitted liability and the only issue remaining between the parties was the assessment of damages. On the claimant's application, the judge ordered trial by jury on the ground that the circumstances of the claimant's claim were exceptional.

The Court of Appeal allowed the defendants' appeal and held that, although the claimant's injuries were most unusual and distressing, the circumstances of his claim were not exceptional and did not, therefore, displace the legislative presumption contained in s. 69(3) of the Supreme Court Act 1981 against trial by jury in those civil cases not specified in s. 69(1). Applying *Ward* v *James,* the court said it was appropriate for there to be trial by a judge alone since it was important that an award of compensatory damages to the claimant should be compatible with the conventional scale of personal injury awards (see [1991] 2 All ER 834 *per* Lord Donaldson MR, delivering the judgment of the court, at p. 840).

7.7 SECRECY OF JURY DELIBERATIONS

In both civil and criminal cases the jury's actual deliberations take place in secret. What information is available about the practical workings of the jury system has come in general from more indirect sources (see Devons, 'Serving as a juryman in Britain', (1965) 28 MLR 561; letter in (1973) 123 New LJ 952; McCabe and Purves, *The Jury at Work,* 1972, and *The Shadow Jury at Work,* 1974; Barber and Gordon (eds), *Members of the Jury,* 1976; see also the series of articles in (1990) 140 New LJ 1257 and at pp. 1264–76). The question of the permanent preservation of the secrets of the jury room was raised for discussion in a case in 1979.

A politician, Jeremy Thorpe, was accused with others at the Central Criminal Court of conspiracy to murder Norman Scott, and separately accused of incitement to murder. The jury returned verdicts of not guilty in June 1979 (*R* v *Holmes and others,* 22 June 1979, unreported). Rumours about Mr Thorpe had begun to circulate after the earlier trial of a Mr Andrew Newton for shooting Mr Scott's dog on Exmoor. In addition, Mr Thorpe's committal proceedings at Minehead were reported extensively in the media because reporting restrictions had been lifted at the request of one only of the defendants.

In view of the massive publicity surrounding the case and the consequent difficulty of finding an unbiased jury, the verdicts of not guilty were seen by many as a remarkable vindication of trial by jury. It soon became clear that extraneous factors had been at work on the minds of the jurors, particularly the widely reported fact that the press had 'bought' some prosecution witnesses. The *Sunday Telegraph,* for instance, had agreed to pay one witness, Peter Bessel (who, incidentally, had been granted, by the state, immunity from prosecution even for perjury), the sum of £25,000 for his story, or £50,000 if Mr Thorpe were convicted! The contract was terminated after public criticism, especially from the trial judge, Cantley J.

Soon after the acquittal of Mr Thorpe the *New Statesman* published an interview with one of the jurors, who remained anonymous and was not paid for his cooperation (see 'Thorpe's trial: how the jury saw it', *New Statesman,* 27 July 1979). It was said in the published interview that the members of the jury had made up their minds to acquit on the first day of the trial.

The Attorney-General brought proceedings for contempt of court in the Divisional Court of the Queen's Bench Division against the *New Statesman.* In *Attorney-General* v *New Statesman* [1980] 1 All ER 644 it was held that the mere disclosure of the secrets of the jury room was not contempt unless it interfered with the finality of jury verdicts or with the attitude of future jurors towards their responsibilities. On the facts, the *New Statesman* had not committed contempt of court. It was said that each case of disclosure must be judged in the light of the circumstances in which the disclosure took place. The warning was given that care must be taken not to abandon totally the secrecy of the jury room because that would lead to the abandonment of trial by jury itself (*per* Lord Widgery CJ at p. 649).

The Contempt of Court Act 1981 sought to clarify the issue by making it a contempt to obtain, disclose or solicit any particulars of statements made, opinions expressed, arguments advanced or votes cast by members of a jury in the course of their deliberations in any legal proceedings, whether criminal or civil (Contempt of Court Act 1981, ss. 8(1) and 19). The prohibition thus extends to the deliberations of any jury, including a coroner's jury, and it is clear that these statutory provisions make the law of contempt much more restrictive in this area than was found to be the case at common law in *Attorney-General* v *New Statesman*. However, by s. 8(3) of the 1981 Act proceedings for this sort of contempt can only be brought by or with the consent of the Attorney-General or on the motion of a court having jurisdiction to deal with it, such as the trial court in the case of an attempt by a journalist to obtain particulars from a juror.

The purpose of s. 8(1) is to secure free and uninhibited jury deliberations. Section 8(1) prohibits disclosures both by a member of the jury and by a non-juror who has acquired information directly or indirectly from a juror (*Attorney-General* v *Associated Newspapers Ltd* [1994] 1 All ER 556, HL; see further on s. 8, para 5.2.1.5).

It is not a contempt under s. 8(1) to disclose particulars in the legal proceedings in question for the purpose of enabling the jury to arrive at their verdict, or in connection with the delivery of the verdict (ibid., s. 8(2)(a)), or to disclose them in evidence in subsequent legal proceedings for an offence alleged to have been committed in relation to the jury in the earlier proceedings (ibid., s. 8(2)(b)). However, there is no exception permitting disclosure of jury-room deliberations for the purpose of an appeal by the defendant against his conviction by the jury or for the purpose of research into the practical workings of the jury system. The *Report of the Royal Commission on Criminal Justice* (Cm 2263, 1993) recommended that s. 8 should be amended so as to permit research into how juries arrive at their verdicts.

Judges like everyone else are bound by s. 8 and cannot, therefore, inquire into events in the jury room without committing contempt of court. In *R* v *Young* [1995] QB 324, CA, the defendant had been convicted of murder. He appealed and his conviction was quashed and a retrial ordered. The Court of Appeal placed an embargo until after the retrial on publication of its reasons for allowing the appeal. At his second trial, the defendant was again convicted of murder and sentenced to life imprisonment. The Court of Appeal then made public its reasons for having quashed the first conviction. It transpired that the Court of Appeal had secretly ordered affidavits to be taken from each of the 12 jurors and from the two bailiffs looking after them in the hotel at which they had stayed. From these affidavits (limited by the Court of Appeal to events which took place at the hotel) it emerged that four members of the jury had used a makeshift ouija board, which had spelled out the name of the victim, the type of gun referred to in evidence as the murder weapon, and the message: 'vote guilty tomorrow . . .'. The incident was discussed with other jurors at breakfast the next morning. In court, the jury delivered a unanimous verdict of guilty. The Court of Appeal held that s. 8 precluded it from inquiring into events in the jury room but not from investigating what happened during the jury's retirement at the hotel. It was further held that the use of the ouija board by the jury amounted to a material irregularity in the trial.

7.8 FINALITY OF JURY VERDICTS

In both civil and criminal cases the jury's verdict is final and cannot be changed. To this end the Court of Appeal will not listen to evidence about what took place in the jury room or jury-box (*R* v *Thompson* [1962] 1 All ER 65, CA; *R* v *Bean* [1991] Crim LR 843, CA; *R* v *Less* (1993) *The Times*, 30 March, CA; *R* v *Miah* (1996) *The Times*, 18 December, CA).

It is in the interests of the public and of the proper efficient administration of justice that there should be finality of jury verdicts, a rule which also protects jurors themselves from pressures to explain or alter their verdicts. In *Boston* v *W.S. Bagshaw & Sons* [1966] 1 WLR 1135n the claimant sued the defendants for libel and the question of malice was raised. The jury found there was no malice and the claimant's case failed. The twelve jurors were surprised at this result and each swore an affidavit that he meant to find malice and wished to change his answer. The claimant moved for a new trial. The Court of Appeal refused the motion, Lord Denning MR saying (at p. 1136):

To my mind it is settled as well as anything can be that it is not open to the court to receive any such evidence as this. Once a jury have given their verdict, and it has been accepted by the judge, and they have been discharged, they are not at liberty to say they meant something different.

This dictum was applied by the Judicial Committee of the Privy Council in *Nanan* v *The State* [1986] 3 All ER 248 (an appeal from Trinidad and Tobago), where it was held that affidavit evidence from four jurors that they had been under a misapprehension in agreeing to a guilty verdict in a criminal trial was inadmissible. Evidence from a juror that he did not in fact agree with the verdict would be similarly inadmissible. It might be otherwise if the verdict was not pronounced in the sight and hearing of one or more members of the jury, who did not in fact agree with the verdict, or if a juror was not competent to understand the proceedings (ibid., *per* Lord Goff at pp. 253–4).

In *R* v *Froud* [1990] Crim LR 197, CA, the jury foreman mistakenly announced a verdict of not guilty. He realised his mistake immediately and corrected the verdict to one of guilty. The judge accepted this verdict and refused later to reopen the matter. The defendant's appeal against conviction was dismissed, the Court of Appeal holding that the jury were entitled to rectify their verdict before it was recorded, or promptly thereafter. Moreover, since the jury had been discharged the judge's later refusal to reopen the matter was held not to have been wrong. In *R* v *Aylott* [1996] 2 Cr App R 169, CA, owing to a misunderstanding on the part of the judge, the jury was discharged before it could deliver the verdict it had reached. Shortly thereafter the judge realised his mistake, reassembled the jury, and accepted its guilty verdict. The Court of Appeal, dismissing the defendant's appeal against conviction, held that the judge had acted correctly in the interests of fairness and justice.

In the somewhat unusual circumstances of *R* v *Bills* [1995] 2 Cr App R 643, CA, the judge was held to have been wrong to accept a changed verdict. The jury had found the defendant not guilty of wounding with intent but guilty of the lesser offence of unlawful wounding. They remained in the jury box while the defendant's previous convictions were read out and then they were discharged. Later the same day the jury purported to change their verdict, saying they had meant to find the defendant guilty of the graver offence of wounding with intent. The judge accepted the changed verdict. The Court of Appeal held that the changed verdict was unsafe since the jury had been influenced by hearing about the defendant's previous convictions and to allow that verdict to stand would be unfair to the defendant. The judge's summing-up had been clear, there was no evidence of any misunderstanding by the jury, their original verdict was plain, and there was no indication of dissent when it was announced. The Court of Appeal quashed the changed verdict and substituted the original verdict.

The swearing of affidavits by jurors, as in *Boston* v *W.S. Bagshaw & Sons,* would now be a contempt under s. 8(1) of the Contempt of Court Act 1981 since the narrow exceptions contained in s. 8(2) do not extend to disclosure of jury deliberations for the purposes of an appeal.

7.9 FUTURE OF THE JURY

7.9.1 Some advantages of trial by jury

Several advantages have long been claimed for trial by jury. In words which have become something of a cliché, the jury is a bastion of liberty against the state. It is, however, ironic that today some offences which involve the state are triable without a jury, i.e., summarily in the magistrates' court. Examples are assaulting the police and offences arising out of demonstrations and strikes.

Trial by jury involves ordinary people in the day-to-day administration of justice and thus prevents the domination of the system by professional judges. But the jury is used only in a very small proportion of cases, and the value of lay participation is effectively diminished in those cases where there is a jury by the great influence exercised by the judge over its members in the Crown Court; for instance, one-sixth of acquittals by juries is on the direction of the trial judge. The figures show that, of those acquitted on all charges in the Crown Court in 1998 after pleading not guilty, 35 per cent were acquitted by the jury alone after a full trial, 15 per cent were acquitted by the jury on the direction of the judge because, for example, the prosecution case was weak, and 50 per cent were discharged by the judge alone because, for example, the prosecution had offered no evidence (*Judicial Statistics 1998,* Cm 4371, 1999, p. 65).

The attitude of juries has been known to mitigate the harshness of the criminal law and to lead to its reform. In the early decades of the nineteenth century all felonies (some 146 of them, except petty larceny and mayhem) were, in theory, punishable by death. One of them was theft of goods or money above the value of one shilling. Juries would often find the value of the property to be less than one shilling and so avoid the imposition of the death penalty.

In the present century, jurors who were motorists themselves were reluctant to convict persons accused of motor-manslaughter, which carried a sentence of life imprisonment. In 1956, Parliament was moved to create the separate, less serious offence of causing death by reckless driving, which carried a sentence of up to five years' imprisonment (Road Traffic Act 1956, s. 8; later contained in the Road Traffic Act 1988, s. 1). In *Jennings* v *United States Government* [1982] 3 All ER 104 the House of Lords decided that, notwithstanding the existence of a separate statutory offence under the Road Traffic Act, causing death by reckless driving was still also the common-law offence of manslaughter because Parliament had not abolished motor-manslaughter either at the time the separate offence was created or later. However, it seemed fairly certain that the prosecuting authorities would not have brought a motor-manslaughter charge except in a very grave case (*Jennings, per* Lord Roskill at p. 117; by an amendment to s. 1 of the Road Traffic Act 1988 made by the Road Traffic Act 1991, the offence of causing death by *reckless* driving was abolished and replaced by the offence of causing death by *dangerous* driving for which the sentence is, under the Road Traffic Offenders Act 1988, sch. 2, pt 1 (as amended), imprisonment for up to 10 years).

The introduction in 1967 of the so-called 'breathalyser law', which is based on the presence in the bloodstream of a prescribed level of alcohol, was due in part to the reluctance of juries to convict motorists of drunken driving (Road Safety Act 1967; the relevant provisions may now be found in the Road Traffic Act 1988).

The acquittals of Jeremy Thorpe in 1979 (para 7.7 above), Clive Ponting in 1985 (para 7.5.2 above), and of Patrick Pottle and Michael Randle in 1991 — described in some quarters as perverse verdicts — have been explained as the reaction of a lay jury to an unsatisfactory law or to unfair treatment of the defendant. Twenty-five years after the event, Messrs Pottle and Randle were prosecuted for helping George Blake, the convicted MI6 double agent, to escape from Wormwood Scrubs prison. Despite admitting their guilt publicly, discussing the episode in the media, and publishing a book about it (*The Blake Escape: How We Freed George Blake, and Why*), they pleaded not guilty at their trial and were acquitted by a jury which was not only sympathetic (and no doubt unimpressed by the bunglings of the security services and the prosecuting authorities over the years) but was also prepared to ignore the direction of the trial judge that the defendants had no defence in law (see *The Independent*, 27 June and 5 July 1991).

7.9.2 Some disadvantages of trial by jury

There are disadvantages to trial by jury. Jurors can be intimidated, and this factor, *inter alia*, has led to the suspension of jury trial for terrorist offences in Northern Ireland. The fact that the composition of the jury is not known until the trial begins is nothing to the point. Nor is contempt of court, or the existence of criminal offences relating to interference with jurors, necessarily a deterrent to determined and unscrupulous people.

That jury nobbling remains a problem in the 1990s is evidenced by the fact that the *Royal Commission on Criminal Justice (Report*, Cm 2263, 1993) found it necessary to recommend that every effort should be made to protect jurors from intimidation, that they should be informed about what steps to take if they feel intimidated in any way, that 'sensitive' cases be tried in courtrooms where the positioning of the public gallery does not facilitate intimidation of jurors by members of the public, that in new courtrooms jury boxes should not be situated opposite the public gallery, and that, so far as practicable, jurors be given waiting and eating areas separate from the ordinary public. There is evidence that the intimidation or attempted bribery of jurors and witnesses participating in trials involving armed robbery or drugs offences is a highly organised activity carried on by criminal gangs (see *The Times*, 23 August 1993 and the comments of Lord Bingham CJ on jury-nobbling in *R v Comerford* [1998] 1 All ER 823, CA, at p. 827). The law was strengthened by s. 51 of the Criminal Justice and Public Order Act 1994, which created new offences of intimidating or harming, or threatening to harm, jurors, witnesses or persons assisting in the investigation of offences. Conviction on indictment for these offences carries a penalty of up to five years' imprisonment and/or an unlimited fine.

Jurors may not always be able to bring to bear that degree of objectivity which is essential to the impartial administration of justice. They may, for example, be prejudiced, albeit subconsciously, in favour of attractive members of the opposite sex, or against newspapers in libel suits (see, for example, *Lewis v Daily Telegraph Ltd* [1964] AC 234, HL, para 7.1 above), or against the police in actions for false imprisonment and malicious prosecution.

Jurors may be incapable of following the evidence in a long and complicated trial of libel or commercial fraud. Their inexperience and ignorance may mean that they are too easily influenced by what counsel says to them at the expense of the real issues in the case. In its Report published in 1986, the Committee on Fraud Trials under the chairmanship of Lord Roskill, a Lord of Appeal in Ordinary, recommended abolition of jury trial in complex criminal fraud trials (estimated at about 20 a year) in favour of a trial before a tribunal consisting of a judge sitting with two laymen with business, City or accounting skills.

The government rejected this central recommendation and decided instead to introduce statutory changes designed to make it easier for juries to follow the proceedings. These changes are contained in the Criminal Justice Act 1987. In a case of serious or complex fraud, a judge of the Crown Court can order the holding of a 'preparatory hearing' *before the jury are sworn* if he considers that such a hearing would produce substantial benefits (ibid., s. 7(1)). The benefits which may accrue from a preparatory hearing are listed as:

(a) identifying issues which are likely to be material to the verdict of the jury;
(b) assisting the jury's comprehension of the issues;
(c) expediting the proceedings before the jury; or
(d) assisting the judge's management of the trial (ibid.).

At the preparatory hearing the judge may, *inter alia,* decide any question of law relating to the case, including any question about the admissibility of evidence (ibid., s. 9(3)). He may order the prosecution to prepare its evidence in a form which is likely to aid comprehension by the jury (ibid., s. 9(4)). An order under s. 9(4) does not involve any question of law; no right of appeal against it is expressly provided and none can be implied (*R* v *Smithson* [1994] 1 WLR 1052, CA). The jurisdiction of the judge under s. 9(3) to decide at the preparatory hearing any question of law relating to the case includes the power to interpret, as a question of law, all forms of legislation and binding agreements between parties (*R* v *Spens* [1991] 4 All ER 421, CA, where it was held that the interpretation of the City Code on Takeovers and Mergers is a question of law to be decided by the judge and not a question of fact to be decided by a jury since, first, the Code bears a sufficient resemblance to legislation; secondly, the Code represents a consensual agreement as between affected parties; and thirdly, if juries were allowed to determine the meaning of the Code disastrous consequences would follow from inconsistent interpretations). The judge who presides at the preparatory hearing should normally also preside at the trial before the jury (*R* v *Southwark Crown Court (ex parte Commissioners for Customs and Excise)* (1992) *The Independent,* 15 December, DC).

The Royal Commission on Criminal Justice (*Report,* Cm 2263, 1993) made a number of recommendations with a view to increasing the assistance given to juries generally. Thus, it was suggested that the trial judge's opening remarks should indicate to the jury that they may take notes and the extent to which they may ask questions, that the provision of writing materials should be standard practice, that technological aids be provided if they would help with the presentation of complicated facts, and that the judge should consider whether documents might with advantage be given to the jury in complex cases and in all cases where there has been a preparatory hearing.

Jury awards of damages in civil cases may be unrealistic and too sympathetic towards the claimant. Appealing against the quantum of damages assessed by a jury is usually fruitless since the Court of Appeal will only interfere where the assessment is so high (or so small) as to be perverse (para 7.1 above). The generosity of juries in running-down cases led to the principles laid down in *Ward* v *James* [1966] 1 QB 273, CA (para 7.6.3 above), and exaggerated awards of damages were responsible, in part, for the abolition of the action for breach of promise in 1970 (Law Reform (Miscellaneous Provisions) Act 1970, s. 1, following recommendations of the Law Commission in Law Com. No. 26, 1969).

More recently, jury awards in libel cases have given increased cause for concern. It is always difficult to put a value on a person's reputation but awards appear to have got completely out of hand and seem to contain an element of punishment which, in general, is not justified in law (see para 10.2.2 for the circumstances in which punitive damages may be awarded). A jury awarded what were then record libel damages of £500,000 in July 1987 to the novelist and politician, Jeffrey Archer, against whom it was alleged by *The Star* newspaper that he had paid a prostitute for sex. Costs (also payable by the unsuccessful defendants) were estimated at a further £670,000. (The sum of £1m paid to the 'pop' singer and composer, Elton John, by the *Sun* newspaper in December 1988 was part of an out-of-court settlement and was not awarded by a jury; the same is true of the £500,000 paid by British Airways to Richard Branson, chairman of Virgin Atlantic, in January 1993.) In November 1988, the actress Koo Stark received damages of £300,000 from the publishers of the *Sunday People* following allegations that she had resumed her relationship with the Duke of York after her marriage.

Sonia Sutcliffe, the estranged wife of Peter Sutcliffe (the so-called 'Yorkshire Ripper'), was awarded libel damages of £600,000 by a jury in May 1989. She had successfully sued the publishers of the satirical magazine, *Private Eye,* in respect of assertions that she was prepared to capitalise on her notoriety as the wife of a multiple murderer by selling her story to the Press. The jury's award was, however, set aside on appeal five months later (*Sutcliffe* v *Pressdram Ltd,* decided in October 1989 and reported at [1990] 1 All ER 269, CA. The action was eventually settled by the parties for damages of £60,000, one-tenth of the jury's original award: see [1990] 1 All ER 269 at p. 295). The Court of Appeal took the view that damages of £600,000 were so high as to be irrational. Invested at 10 per cent p.a., £600,000 would produce a weekly income in excess of £1,000 before tax with the capital sum left untouched and available for the claimant to leave to whomsoever she wished at her death.

Lord Donaldson MR (at pp. 283–4) said that juries, when assessing damages in libel cases, should be given improved guidance by the judge. He thought that referring them to awards made in other libel actions would confuse rather than assist them, and that any attempt by counsel or the judge to discuss figures would, in the case of counsel, lead to unseemly over-bidding or under-bidding, and, in the case of the judge, seem to be usurping the function of the jury. He suggested that guidance was required which was aimed at helping juries to appreciate the real value of large sums of money. The guidance could possibly take the form of inviting juries to consider what the result of their awards would be in terms of weekly, monthly or annual income if the damages were invested in a building society deposit account without touching the capital sum, or, in the case of a smaller award, to consider what could be bought with it. Nourse LJ (at p. 290) proposed that, if appropriate, the judge should warn juries that it might be a real disservice to make an award of damages which was at risk of being set aside on appeal with consequent exposure of the claimant to the expense, delay and anxieties of a retrial.

Before *Sutcliffe* v *Pressdram Ltd* went to the Court of Appeal, the disturbingly high level of jury libel damages had led both the Lord Chancellor and the Bar Council to set up (in the summer of 1989) separate reviews with the object, *inter alia,* of re-examining the role of juries in libel cases. Any hopes that the comments of the Court of Appeal in *Sutcliffe* v *Pressdram Ltd* would in themselves be enough to bring about a return to a saner level of awards were dashed just six weeks later when the jury in Lord Aldington's libel case awarded damages of £1.5m following a 41-day trial the costs of which were estimated as approaching a further £1m (*Aldington* v *Watts and Tolstoy,* 30 November 1989, unreported, but see *The Times,* 1 December 1989). The unprecedented sum of £1.5m was awarded in spite of the trial judge's efforts to advise the jury in accordance with *Sutcliffe* v *Pressdram Ltd.* Thus, he had warned them against giving 'grossly too much' (what he described as

'Mickey Mouse money') because to do so could simply lead to an appeal, had reminded them to pay no attention to any other case they may have heard about, and had pointed out that it was not their function to punish or 'fine' the defendants.

The *Aldington* case has a number of peculiar features. The defendants were not national newspaper proprietors but private individuals. The libel was contained in a pamphlet and did not, therefore, have the mass circulation of a newspaper, although 10,000 copies of the pamphlet were distributed to Members of Parliament, peers, staff, parents and boys at Winchester College where Lord Aldington was Warden, and to his neighbours. It has to be admitted that the libel was particularly grave, involving as it did allegations that Lord Aldington, as an officer in the second world war, had been responsible for the repatriation, torture and massacre of some 70,000 Cossacks and Yugoslavs. Nevertheless, an award of such massive proportions as £1.5m cannot be justified and, if taken to appeal, would almost certainly have resulted in a retrial or a substantial reduction of the damages if the parties had invited the Court of Appeal itself to reassess them. As it was, Count Tolstoy was ordered to pay into court the sum of £124,900 as security for costs if he wished to pursue an appeal (*Aldington v Watts and Tolstoy (No. 2)* (1990) *The Independent,* 20 July, CA). On his being unable to do so, no appeal was pursued in the case. Both defendants became bankrupt and it appears that Lord Aldington, who is on record as saying that he would be content with a payment of £300,000, has not received a penny of the damages and costs he was awarded in 1989. Mr Watts was given an 18-month prison sentence in 1995 for contempt of court in disobeying an injunction (imposed at the end of the trial) not to repeat the allegations (see *The Times,* 28 April 1995). In the same year, the European Court of Human Rights unanimously condemned the jury's award as disproportionate and a violation of Count Tolstoy's right to freedom of expression under art. 10 of the European Convention on Human Rights. By a majority decision the European Court of Human Rights decided that the Court of Appeal's order for security for costs did not violate Count Tolstoy's right of access to court under art. 6 (*Tolstoy Miloslavsky v United Kingdom* (1995) 20 EHRR 442, ECHR).

Towards the end of 1991, a jury awarded record damages of £150,000 for *slander* (defamation in temporary form, such as the spoken word). This was in a case where a female doctor was found to have slandered a male doctor by making, in front of patients, allegations of sexual harassment (*Smith v Houston,* 25 October 1991; the case is unreported but see *The Independent,* 26 October 1991). However, on appeal the damages were later reduced to £50,000 by the Court of Appeal (see *The Times,* 17 December 1993). The defendant became bankrupt and the claimant received very little in respect of damages or costs. Indeed, he ended up being sued by his solicitor for unpaid fees (see *The Times,* 13 January 1995). The defendant was later given a three-month prison sentence for contempt of court in disobeying a series of asset-freezing injunctions (see *The Times,* 8 July 1998).

William Roache, the actor who plays the part of Ken Barlow in the television series *Coronation Street,* was awarded libel damages of £50,000 by a jury after he was found to have been defamed in the *Sun* newspaper by a description that he was 'self-satisfied, smug and boring' (*Roache v News Group Newspapers Ltd,* 4 November 1991, unreported; see *The Times,* 5 November 1991). In addition, the claimant was granted an injunction to restrain further publication of the offending words and he was awarded his costs. On appeal by the defendants, the claimant was not only deprived of his costs from the date (three weeks before the trial began) when the defendants paid into court a sum of money to settle the action but was also ordered to pay the defendants' costs from that date. He effectively ended up as the loser since those costs, together with the costs of the appeal, exceeded the amount he was awarded as damages.

The damages awarded by the jury matched exactly the sum of £50,000 previously paid into court by the defendants (and rejected by the claimant) in an unsuccessful attempt to settle the case. The award of costs in civil litigation in the High Court is always a matter for the discretion of the trial judge (Supreme Court Act 1981, s. 51). The courts habitually exercise the discretion in accordance with two general rules. The first is that costs 'follow the event'; i.e., the 'winner' will normally be awarded his costs against the 'loser'. This rule is aimed at deterring claimants from bringing, and defendants from defending, actions which they are likely to lose. In straightforward cases the rule creates no problem, but in more complex cases it may be necessary to identify the 'event' which costs are to follow. This involves an investigation as to who is really the winner and who is really the loser. The second rule is that a successful claimant who has rejected a sum of money previously paid into court by the defendant which equals or exceeds the amount ultimately awarded as damages will not be granted his costs unless he has won something else of value (such as an injunction) which he could not have won without fighting the action through to the end.

The Court of Appeal regarded the defendants as the substantial winners at the trial since they had succeeded in keeping the damages down to a sum no larger than they had already offered in settlement. Furthermore, the injunction obtained by the claimant was not something of value but merely a token remedy. The defendants did not intend to repeat the libel anyway and it was 'overwhelmingly probable' that they would have been prepared to give an undertaking (equivalent, in effect, to an injunction) not to repeat it if the claimant had accepted the money paid into court instead of insisting on fighting the case to the end in order to obtain more than £50,000 by way of damages (*Roache* v *News Group Newspapers Ltd* (1992) *The Times*, 23 November, CA).

Mr Roache later unsuccessfully sued his solicitors for negligently failing to advise him fully about the financial risk of rejecting the defendants' payment into court and pursuing the libel case to the end (see *The Times*, 10 July 1998). This left him liable for further costs, and he eventually declared himself bankrupt with debts of some £500,000 (see *The Times*, 13 April 1999).

Libel damages of £250,000 were awarded by a jury to Esther Rantzen, the television presenter and founder of 'Child Line' (a charity established to help victims of abuse), as a result of allegations in *The People* newspaper that she had deliberately and improperly kept quiet about the activities of a suspected child abuser (*Rantzen* v *Mirror Group Newspapers*, 16 December 1991, unreported; see *The Times*, 17 December 1991). The damages were later described by the Court of Appeal as excessive and 'disproportionately large' in comparison to the harm suffered by the claimant and were reduced to £110,000 (*Rantzen* v *Mirror Group Newspapers (1986) Ltd* [1993] 4 All ER 975, CA; see further below).

Juries have continued to award large libel damages throughout the 1990s. In 1992, Sara Keays received £105,000 in respect of an article published in *New Woman* which alleged that she had written a book about her relationship with Cecil Parkinson, a prominent politician, solely in order to make money and to embarrass the government (*Keays* v *Murdoch Magazines (UK) Ltd*, 19 February 1992, unreported; see *The Times*, 20 February 1992). The Australian 'pop' star and actor, Jason Donovan, was awarded £200,000 against the publishers of *The Face* magazine in which it had wrongly been suggested that he was 'queer' (*Donovan* v *Wagadon Ltd*, 3 April 1992, unreported; see *The Times*, 4 April 1992). A Syrian financier was awarded £400,000 against a defendant who had alleged that in financial matters the claimant was not a man of his word. The judge had warned the jury to be realistic in their award of damages (*Said* v *Baki*, 21 May 1992, unreported; see *The Times*, 22 May 1992). In November 1993, a jury awarded damages totalling £350,000 (including an exemplary sum of £275,000) to Elton John against the publishers of the *Sunday Mirror* newspaper in which it had been alleged that at a Hollywood party he had spat out partially chewed food into a napkin and recommended the practice to guests as a good way to lose weight. The fictitious story was found to be libellous because it wrongly suggested that Mr John had relapsed after successfully overcoming drug and alcohol addiction and the eating disorder, *bulimia nervosa* (*John* v *Mirror Group Newspapers*, 4 November 1993, unreported; see *The Times*, 5 November 1993). The damages were later reduced to £75,000 by the Court of Appeal (see below).

In July 1994, libel damages totalling £1,485,000 were awarded by a jury in respect of an editorial and review in *Yachting World* which contained a scathing attack on a revolutionary trimaran design (*Walker* v *Sheahan and others*, 8 July 1994, unreported; see *The Times*, 9 July 1994). The damages were later reduced by agreement to £160,000 (see *The Times*, 23 August 1995). Later that year, a retired police superintendent was awarded £375,000 by a jury after being libelled by media allegations of sexual abuse at a children's home (*Anglesea* v *Newspaper Publishing plc and others*, 6 December 1994, unreported; see *The Times*, 7 December 1994).

Graeme Souness, the former manager of Liverpool Football Club, was awarded damages of £750,000 against the publishers of *The People* newspaper over an article in which his ex-wife made unflattering allegations about his parsimonious attitude towards money and the maintenance of their children (*Souness* v *Mirror Group Newspapers*, 15 June 1995, unreported; see *The Times*, 16 June 1995). The damages were later reduced by agreement to £100,000 (see *The Times*, 24 February 1996). In the early part of 1996, damages of £625,000 were awarded to a consultant orthopaedic surgeon against the publishers of the *Daily Mirror* after the newspaper had described him as 'Dr Dolittle' for allegedly failing to do more to find a hospital bed for a patient with serious head injuries who later died (*Percy* v *Mirror Group Newspapers*, 23 February 1996, unreported; see *The Times*, 24 February 1996).

It was announced in February 1990 that the Court of Appeal was to be given a statutory power to reassess of its own motion a jury's award of damages. This new power was conferred by s. 8 of the Courts and Legal Services Act 1990. Under the former law, the Court of Appeal itself could only reassess an irrational award made by a jury if both parties agreed to its doing so. (See, for example, *Lewis* v *Chief Constable of Greater Manchester* (1991) *The Independent*, 23 October, CA, where, with the agreement of the parties given in order to avoid a retrial some nine years after the events giving rise to the claim, the Court of Appeal reviewed a jury's award of damages for false imprisonment and reduced it from £17,500 to £5,000.) If the parties did not agree to this course of action, the Court of Appeal had no other alternative but to order a retrial — with consequent expense and delay. The new procedure applies only to appeals set down after 31 January 1991. (For this reason it was not available in *Lewis* v *Chief Constable of Greater Manchester*, above.) Under the new law, juries are still available in libel cases, and continue to be responsible for assessing any damages to be paid, but if, on appeal, it is shown that the damages awarded are excessive (or inadequate), the Court of Appeal can reduce (or increase) the damages (without being invited to do so by the parties) to 'such sum as appears to the court to be proper' (Courts and Legal Services Act 1990, s. 8(2)). It is anticipated that s. 8 will provide a cheaper and quicker procedure than a retrial on the issue of damages.

Gorman v *Mudd*, 15 October 1992, unreported, appears to be the first case in which the Court of Appeal exercised its new power under s. 8. Here, libel damages of £150,000 awarded by a jury to the Conservative Member of Parliament, Teresa Gorman, in respect of allegations in a 'mock press release' that she was vain and spiteful were reduced to £50,000 on appeal (see *The Times*, 16 October 1992). In *Clark* v *Chief Constable of Cleveland Constabulary* (1999) *The Times*, 13 May, CA, the Court of Appeal *increased* from £500 to £2,000 compensatory damages awarded by a jury in a malicious prosecution action against the police.

Given the terms and purpose of s. 8, it always seemed likely that the Court of Appeal would be expected in its judgments to give general guidance on levels of damages for use by trial judges in addressing juries in future cases. The opportunity to provide such guidance was taken by Neill LJ in delivering the judgment of the court in *Rantzen* v *Mirror Group Newspapers* [1993] 4 All ER 975, CA (see above), where the Court of Appeal stated its readiness to interfere more frequently with excessive jury awards.

It was said in the *Rantzen* case that the power under s. 8 is to be exercised in a way which attaches proper weight to the guidance given by the House of Lords in cases like *Attorney-General* v *Guardian Newspapers Ltd (No. 2)* [1988] 3 All ER 545 (especially *per* Lord Goff at p. 660) and *Derbyshire County Council* v *Times Newspapers Ltd* [1993] 1 All ER 1011 (especially *per* Lord Keith at p. 1021) on the relationship between the common law and art. 10 of the European Convention on Human Rights, and by the European Court of Human Rights on the proper scope of art. 10. Article 10 lays down that 'everyone has the right to freedom of expression . . . subject to such . . . restrictions . . . as are prescribed by law and are necessary [meaning that a pressing social need exists] in a democratic society . . . for the protection of the reputation or rights of others'. The Court of Appeal in the *Rantzen* case felt that investing a jury with an almost unlimited discretion to fix damages was an unsatisfactory measurement for deciding what was necessary in a democratic society or justified by a pressing social need (see [1993] 4 All ER 975 *per* Neill LJ at p. 994).

According to *Rantzen*, the question for the Court of Appeal to ask itself is whether a reasonable jury could have thought that the sum awarded was necessary to compensate the claimant and to re-establish his or her reputation. On the facts, Esther Rantzen was acknowledged as still being a distinguished and respected figure in broadcasting. She continued to have a successful career as a television presenter and her work in fighting child abuse had been widely acclaimed. It was held that the award to her of £250,000 libel damages could not be justified on any objective standard of reasonable compensation or necessity or proportionality.

On the question of guidance for jurors, the Court of Appeal decided that it was still not right to allow reference to be made to awards by juries in previous libel cases since they do not establish any meaningful norm or standard for use in future cases. (Nor, it may be added, is the jury entitled to hear details of any specific sums offered as damages by the defendant to the claimant in the case they are trying: *Kiam* v *Neil* (1994) *The Times*, 14 December, CA.)

While recognising the unsatisfactory nature of the present practice whereby a claimant in a libel action may recover much more by way of damages for a transient injury to his reputation than is awarded to the victim of a serious accident for a permanent injury, the suggestion that libel juries should be referred to awards made in personal injuries actions was also rejected as unsatisfactory.

It was further decided, however, that awards made or confirmed by the Court of Appeal in the exercise of its powers under s. 8 of the Courts and Legal Services Act 1990 were different and could be relied upon as establishing the correct norm or standard. This conclusion was reached by inferring that one of the purposes of s. 8 must have been to allow the Court of Appeal, over a period of time, to provide guidance for use in subsequent cases. Indeed, the Court of Appeal took the view that preventing reference to its awards under

s. 8 would conflict with the principle stated in art. 10 of the European Convention on Human Rights that restrictions on freedom of expression should be 'prescribed by law' (see [1993] 4 All ER 975 *per* Neill LJ at pp. 995–6). It was envisaged that any tendency towards over-citation of previous awards would be controlled by the trial judge.

Pending the development of a body of guidance under its new power, the Court of Appeal laid down (see [1993] 4 All ER 975 *per* Neill LJ at p. 997) that juries should be asked by the trial judge to consider:

(a)   the purchasing power of the sum they are minded to award;

(b)   whether the sum is proportionate to the damage suffered by the claimant; and

(c)   whether the sum is necessary in order to provide adequate compensation for, and to re-establish the reputation of, the claimant.

Within three years the Court of Appeal was persuaded to review *Rantzen* v *Mirror Group Newspapers (1986) Ltd* [1993] 4 All ER 975, CA, in view of the fact that, notwithstanding what was laid down in that case, juries continued to make libel awards so large as to be divorced from reality. The review of the *Rantzen* case was carried out in *John* v *MGN Ltd* [1996] 2 All ER 35, CA, where libel damages of £350,000 awarded by a jury to Elton John in November 1993 (see above) were reduced to £75,000, and what were described as 'modest but important' changes of practice were approved. The Court of Appeal, while endorsing the *Rantzen* view that juries should not be referred to awards made by other juries in previous libel cases but that they could be referred to awards approved or substituted by the Court of Appeal, departed from *Rantzen* in two important respects. First, it decided to allow juries to be referred to conventional personal injury awards as a means of checking the reasonableness of their proposed libel awards. Secondly, it decided to permit counsel and the judge to indicate levels of award which, in their opinion, would be appropriate for the libel in question.

The decision of the Court of Appeal in *John* v *MGN Ltd* to look again at the question of referring the jury to other awards of damages was influenced by a number of considerations: the body of guidance to be built up in the Court of Appeal, and referred to in *Rantzen*, had scarcely developed in practice; juries had continued to make what appeared to be 'grossly excessive' awards; the High Court of Australia was now in favour of allowing libel juries to be referred to personal injury damages (see *Carson* v *John Fairfax and Sons Ltd* (1993) 67 ALJR 634, HC of Australia); and since *Rantzen* the European Court of Human Rights had held in *Tolstoy Miloslavsky* v *United Kingdom* (1995) 20 EHRR 442, ECHR, above, that Count Tolstoy's rights under art. 10 of the European Convention on Human Rights had been violated.

The compensatory damages of £75,000 awarded by the jury to Elton John were held to be excessive because the newspaper article, though it was untrue, offensive and distressing, had not attacked his integrity or damaged his reputation as a performer. A compensatory award of £25,000 was substituted. The Court of Appeal further held that the case was a suitable one for the award of exemplary damages because the defendants had calculated to make a profit out of their story which would exceed any compensation paid to the claimant (see para 10.2.2) and, in the circumstances, a compensatory award by itself was not adequate to mark the gravity of the defendants' conduct, to punish them, or to deter them and others from behaving in the same way again. However, the jury's award of £275,000 as exemplary damages was considered excessive and a sum of £50,000 was substituted — sufficient, according to the Court of Appeal, to do justice to both parties.

Further measures proposed to tackle the problem of excessive jury libel awards won the support of the Lord Chancellor at the end of 1992. A new summary procedure was envisaged under which some libel actions would be tried, and any damages assessed up to a fixed limit, by a High Court judge sitting without a jury. It was also suggested that the limitation period for commencing defamation proceedings should be reduced from three years to one year.

These measures became law in the Defamation Act 1996, which reduced the limitation period to one year and introduced a summary procedure for disposing of libel and slander claims under which a judge *sitting without a jury* can (a) dismiss a claim if it appears that it has no realistic prospect of success and there is no reason why it should be tried, or (b) give judgment for the claimant and grant him summary relief if it appears that there is no defence to the claim which has a realistic prospect of success and that there is no other reason why the claim should be tried. 'Summary relief' means (i) a declaration that the defendant's offending statement was false and defamatory of the claimant, (ii) an order that the defendant publish or cause to be published a suitable correction and apology; (iii) damages not exceeding £10,000 or such other amount as the Lord Chancellor may prescribe by order; (iv) an order restraining the defendant from publishing or further publishing the matter complained of.

A provision allowing a defendant in a defamation action to introduce evidence before the jury showing that the claimant is disreputable and not deserving of damages was dropped during the passage of the Bill through Parliament (where the provision was described as a 'muckraker's charter') and is, therefore, not part of the Act.

Following a number of cases in which juries had awarded very large sums of exemplary damages in actions against the Metropolitan Police for malicious prosecution, false imprisonment, wrongful arrest, and assault, the Metropolitan Police Commissioner sought clarification from the Court of Appeal, in *Thompson v Commissioner of Police of the Metropolis* [1997] 2 All ER 762, CA, on the directions which the trial judge should include in his summing up to help the jury decide what to award by way of damages (including exemplary damages) in such actions. The Court of Appeal (*per* Lord Woolf MR, delivering the judgment of the court, at pp. 775–778) laid down that, where exemplary damages are claimed (e.g., because there has been oppressive or arbitrary behaviour; see para 10.2.2), the jury should be told that (a) they should be awarded only if the jury consider that the compensatory and aggravated damages they have already awarded are, in the circumstances, an inadequate punishment for the defendants; (b) exemplary damages are a windfall for the claimant and, if payable out of public funds, the sum awarded may no longer be available to the police to spend for the benefit of the public; and (c) the amount awarded as exemplary damages should be adequate to indicate their disapproval of the oppressive or arbitrary behaviour of the police, but no more. The sum is unlikely to be less than £5,000 and might be as much as £25,000. Exemplary damages of more than £25,000 should not be awarded, except in cases where officers of at least the rank of superintendent have been directly involved in the police misconduct. The absolute maximum is £50,000. These figures will be adjusted to take account of future inflation. In the two cases with which the Court of Appeal was concerned in *Thompson*, jury awards of exemplary damages were reduced from £50,000 to £25,000, and from £200,000 to £15,000, respectively.

7.9.3 Some alternatives to trial by jury

The question of whether the jury should be retained must be considered in the light of possible alternatives (see Cornish, *The Jury,* 1971, pp. 284–301). Trial by a single professional judge is the norm in civil cases, and in those areas where there is a stipendiary magistrate (para 1.7.2) *summary offences* are triable by him sitting alone. But in the more serious criminal cases heard in the Crown Court it may be considered undesirable to have guilt or innocence determined by one individual with his in-built prejudices and with no opportunity for discussion. Where there is trial by jury, at least ten persons have to be satisfied instead of just one.

Another alternative is trial by a *bench* of professional judges. This method is used when criminal *appeals* are heard in the Divisional Court of the Queen's Bench Division, the Court of Appeal and the House of Lords. But to resort to a plurality of judges to try criminal cases at first instance would necessitate the appointment of many more judges. This would be expensive financially and would leave the legal profession depleted of some of its best practising talent. Moreover, the idea is open to the objection that it would allow guilt to be decided solely by lawyers.

Trial by a combined bench of professional judges and laymen is already a reality in the Crown Court. Appeals from magistrates' courts to the Crown Court *must* be heard by two to four justices in addition to the judge or recorder (Supreme Court Act 1981, s. 74(1)). On appeals in licensing and gaming cases, four justices *must* be present, and on appeals and committals from youth courts two justices from the youth court panel *must* sit and the court must include a man and a woman (Crown Court Rules 1982, r. 3). Theoretically all members of the court are of equal status, but the influence of the professional judge over the lay members must be substantial and, when the voting is tied, the judge or recorder has a casting vote (Supreme Court Act 1981, s. 73(3)). Up to four justices *may* sit at a trial on indictment, except for cases listed for plea of not guilty (ibid., ss. 8(1) and 75(2); *Practice Note* [1995] 2 All ER 900, para 8). Thus their presence is effectively confined to the hearing of guilty pleas.

8

Legislation and Statutory Interpretation

8.1 INTRODUCTION

In the English legal system the law-making process is shared, not necessarily equally, by two bodies. While Parliament claims to be the sole domestic law-maker, its powers are supplemented by the activities of the judiciary, which traditionally has adopted a much less overt role. Parliament, consisting of the Queen (whose royal assent is necessary by constitutional convention before a Bill can become an Act), the House of Lords, and the House of Commons, passes legislation in the form of Acts of Parliament, alternatively called statutes. The interrelationship between legislation and the judiciary is of crucial importance, for the judges are the ultimate enforcers of the law, whether civil or criminal, and whether Parliamentary in origin or judge-made. A judge will spend approximately one-half of his judicial time on the interpretation of legislation, as a glance at the law reports will confirm.

Once a statute is in force it must be applied by the courts. The judges have 'judicial notice' of all public Acts whenever passed (Interpretation Act 1978, s. 3) and of all private Acts passed after 1850 (ibid., s. 22(1) and sch. 2, para 2). A private Act passed before 1851 must be pleaded and proved in evidence unless there is a deeming provision in it by which it is to be treated as a public Act and judicially noticed as such (1 Bl Com 85; *Greswolde* v *Kemp* (1842) Car & M 635). 'Judicial notice' is a convenient device whereby knowledge of certain matters is attributed to judges so that those matters do not need to be proved in evidence every time they arise in a particular case. (See *R* v *Simpson* [1983] 3 All ER 789, CA at pp. 793–4.) If a judge made a decision without reference to a relevant statute, either because he was ignorant of it or it was not cited to him by counsel, that in itself would provide a ground for appealing. The judges also have judicial notice of the European Union Treaties, the *Official Journal* of the Union, and decisions and opinions of the European Court of Justice or any court attached thereto (European Communities Act 1972, s. 3(2), as amended by the European Communities (Amendment) Act 1986).

If a statutory provision is ambiguous, the judge must *interpret* it before he can *apply* it. Statutory interpretation, which is by no means a precise art, involves the application of certain rules and presumptions (para 8.10 below). But before looking at the role of statutory interpretation in the judicial process it will be helpful to examine more closely Parliamentary and delegated legislation and the relationship between Parliament and the judiciary, especially in the light of the United Kingdom's membership of the European Union.

8.2 ADVANTAGES OF STATUTE LAW

Several advantages are claimed for statute law — usually at the expense of judge-made law. (The advantages of judge-made law are discussed in para 9.6.) Since Parliament is supreme, a statute can abrogate any rule of law, whether contained in a previous statute or a previous case. The judges have no reciprocal power to abrogate a statutory provision (see, e.g.,

British Railways Board v *Pickin* [1974] AC 765, HL, para 8.6 below). There are, however, some circumstances arising from our membership of the European Union in which the judges may be expected to disapply the provisions of a statute of the United Kingdom Parliament in order to give priority and effect to directly applicable Community law (see para 8.7 below).

Normally when Parliament abolishes a rule of law it will only do so for the future so that previous transactions based on the old rule are not affected. Occasionally, Parliament passes legislation which has retrospective effect (para 8.10.3.6 below). When an English court overrules a decided case it always does so with retrospective effect (para 9.3.1).

The constitutional doctrine of the separation of powers is to a greater extent satisfied by legislation than by judge-made law. Parliament *makes* law but does not *enforce* it, whereas judge-made law, or case law, is made by the very people who enforce it.

While statute law can be known in advance, case law can only be known at the same time that it is made. If there is no statutory provision covering a particular legal point, the parties may not know what their rights are until after the judge has decided the dispute between them. Of course, much of the advantage claimed here for statute law is lost if the particular statutory provision is ambiguous — a state of affairs which is very common. A clear, unambiguous statute can undoubtedly prevent much litigation. The proper develop-ment of case law is too often dependent on the 'accidents of litigation'. The courts are not allowed for the most part to give opinions on hypothetical cases as opposed to real cases involving actual litigation between citizens. Thus, unsettled points in the common law tend to remain unresolved for a long time, either because a similar factual situation has not arisen or because the parties cannot afford, or do not wish, to litigate because of the costs involved. A statute could settle such doubtful points of law immediately, although perhaps a more practicable solution would be the establishment of a suitors' fund to allow points of law of general public importance to be taken to the highest court at the public expense.

It should be possible for statutory provisions to be expressed, not only in authoritative form, but clearly. This is not always possible with judge-made law where it may often be necessary to separate the *ratio decidendi* from the *obiter dicta* in order to discover what the case actually decided (para 9.5).

Parliament is more in touch with the outside world than is the judiciary and can more quickly turn public opinion and social policy into new law. Although, since 1966, the House of Lords as a court has not been absolutely bound to follow its own previous decisions (para 9.3.2.2), it still does not enjoy the freedom to make new law possessed by Parliament. The legislature is free to make law on any subject it thinks fit while the courts are constrained by the facts of the cases before them.

8.3   CONSOLIDATING STATUTES AND CODIFYING STATUTES

8.3.1   Consolidation

Consolidation is the re-enactment in one statute of some topic in the law, previously contained in several different statutes, but without changing the law. 'All consolidation Acts are designed to bring together in a more convenient, lucid and economical form a number of enactments related in subject-matter . . . previously scattered over the statute book' (*Farrell* v *Alexander* [1977] AC 59, HL, *per* Lord Simon of Glaisdale at p. 82). Recent examples of consolidating statutes are the Education Act 1996 (with 583 sections and 40 schedules), the Justices of the Peace Act 1997 (75 sections and six schedules), and the Petroleum Act 1998 (53 sections and five schedules).

A consolidating statute is presumed not to change the law but only to re-enact it in a different place. It is therefore possible, when interpreting such a statute, to apply cases already decided on the meaning of the replaced Acts. In cases of difficulty or ambiguity, the Acts which have been consolidated may themselves be scrutinised (*Farrell* v *Alexander; R* v *Heron* [1982] 1 All ER 993, HL; *Cullen* v *Rogers* [1982] 2 All ER 570, HL; *Sheldon* v *R.H.M. Outhwaite Ltd* [1995] 2 All ER 558, HL). In *Epping Forest District Council* v *Essex Rendering Ltd* [1983] 1 All ER 359 — not, one would have thought, a case involving great difficulty or ambiguity — the House of Lords considered the legislative history of the Public Health Act 1936, a consolidating measure, before deciding that the requirement of the written consent of a local authority under that Act to the establishment of an offensive trade was mandatory and not merely directory. The legislative precursors of the Public Health Act 1936 were so emphatic that the requirement was mandatory that it was not permissible to construe a consolidating measure in such a way as to change the nature of the requirement from mandatory to directory, even though the 1936 Act was expressed in slightly different language. In *Sheldon* v *R.H.M. Outhwaite Ltd* [1995] 2 All ER 558, the House of Lords declined to look at the Acts consolidated by the Limitation Act 1980 in construing s. 32(1)(b) of that Act because the wording of paragraph (b) was clear and involved no difficulty or ambiguity.

Only corrections and minor improvements can be made during the process of consolidation (Consolidation of Enactments (Procedure) Act 1949). If a joint committee of both Houses of Parliament certifies that a Bill is a consolidating Bill (and does not change the law) it can expect a speedy passage through Parliament since full debate is largely unnecessary (for the various types of consolidating statute, see *R* v *Heron* [1982] 1 All ER 993, HL, *per* Lord Scarman at p. 999).

8.3.2 Codification

Codification is a restatement in one place of the law on a particular topic, which, if necessary, may also alter the law. It embraces not only previous statutes but also common-law principles derived from previous cases. There was a flurry of codification towards the end of the nineteenth century when certain commercial law topics were set down in codified form in, for example, the Bills of Exchange Act 1882, the Partnership Act 1890 and the Sale of Goods Act 1893. More recently, the Theft Act 1968, based on the *Eighth Report of the Criminal Law Revision Committee: Theft and Related Offences* (Cmnd 2977, 1966), attempted to codify the law relating to theft.

But these codifying statutes, which are proceeded with in a piecemeal fashion, are not 'codes' in the Continental sense because there is no attempt to put down in one place the whole of English law. They do, however, resemble the Continental type of code in that they put the law on a particular topic into a compact form which makes it easier to apply. Codification of the law is a difficult and long process (see Diamond, 'Codification of the law of contract', (1968) 31 MLR 361). It is one of the objectives of the Law Commission, a full-time law-reform body for England and Wales set up by the Law Commissions Act 1965. Codification of the law is expressly mentioned in s. 3(1) of the Act. One of the Law Commission's first tasks was to prepare a code of the law of contract, but the project soon ran into difficulties and had to be abandoned as a comprehensive exercise (see Diamond, op. cit., and Law Commission, *Eighth Annual Report* (for 1972–73)). Later, the Law Commission decided to abandon the proposed codification of the law of landlord and tenant and to proceed instead in a piecemeal way (see Law Commission, *Thirteenth Annual Report* (for 1977–78)).

Notwithstanding these disappointments, the Law Commission in 1981 asked a committee of four academic lawyers, under the chairmanship of Professor J.C. Smith QC, to make, invite and consider proposals for the codification of the general part of the criminal law; i.e., the general principles of criminal liability (see [1981] Crim LR 281). The committee completed its work (which included a draft criminal code bill) in 1985 (*Codification of the Criminal Law — A Report to the Law Commission,* Law Com. No. 143, 1985). The Law Commission then proceeded to revise and expand the committee's draft into a comprehensive criminal law code and this was published in two volumes in 1989 (*A Criminal Code for England and Wales,* Law Com. No. 177, 1989). Volume 1 comprises a report and a draft criminal code bill while Volume 2 is a commentary on the draft bill which, in 220 clauses, seeks to restate not only the general part of the criminal law but also the substantive law applicable to over 90 per cent of indictable offences.

8.4 PREPARATION OF LEGISLATION

The responsibility for initiating the vast majority of modern legislation rests with the government. Private members' Bills are unlikely to become law because of shortage of parliamentary time, although there have been some notable exceptions where the government has been prepared to cooperate and make time available. Some examples are the Matrimonial Causes Act 1937 (A.P. Herbert MP); the Obscene Publications Act 1959 (Roy Jenkins MP); the Abortion Act 1967 (David Steel MP); the Forfeiture Act 1982 (Leo Abse MP, see para 8.10.2.2 below); the Computer Misuse Act 1990 (Michael Colvin MP).

The legislative proposal of a particular government department may be approved in principle in the cabinet and then handed to the Parliamentary draftsman ('Parliamentary Counsel to the Treasury') to be put into legal language in the form of a Bill. Sometimes the Bill is preceded by a White Paper containing the government's proposals for legislation.

Legal language is used because the English practice is to legislate by using precise words seeking to cover every conceivable situation and allowing of no loopholes. Complaint is frequently made that the use of legal language makes the legislation unintelligible to the layman. And there is sufficient evidence of this; indeed, some legislation is unintelligible to lawyers. Displays of judicial exasperation with legislative drafting are not uncommon. In *Davis* v *Johnson* [1979] AC 264, HL, at p. 333, Viscount Dilhorne said of s. 1 of the Domestic Violence and Matrimonial Proceedings Act 1976 (now repealed and replaced by the Family Law Act 1996) that 'Few, if any, sections of a modern Act can have given rise to so much litigation in so short a time and to such a difference of opinion'. It has also been said that the Housing (Homeless Persons) Act 1977 (now part III of the Housing Act 1985) is not an easy statute to interpret and the judge expressed 'a fervent hope that it will not be allowed to give rise to the sort of running battles which occurred 150 years ago with regard to paupers, itinerants and the inmates of workhouses' under the old poor-law (*R* v *Slough Borough Council (ex parte London Borough of Ealing)* [1981] 1 All ER 601, DC, *per* Comyn J at p. 610). In *Cocks* v *Thanet District Council* [1982] 3 All ER 1135, HL, Lord Bridge (at p. 1136) described the 1977 Act as a 'fruitful source of litigation'. The Landlord and Tenant Act 1987 has been branded as 'ill-drafted, complicated and confused' (*Denetower Ltd* v *Toop* [1991] 3 All ER 661, CA, *per* Sir Nicolas Browne-Wilkinson V-C at p. 668), while the Dangerous Dogs Act 1991 has been said to bear 'all the hallmarks of an ill-thought out piece of legislation' (*R* v *Ealing Justices (ex parte Fanneran)* (1995) *The Times,* 9 December, DC, *per* Rougier J).

In 1975, the *Report of the Committee on the Preparation of Legislation* (Cmnd 6053) recommended that legislation should be arranged to suit the convenience of users, not legislators. It was said that the modest system of issuing explanatory notes with new Bills should be extended and that statements of purpose and principle should be encouraged. It was recommended that there should be more Parliamentary draftsmen and more and quicker consolidation of statutory provisions.

It is important for democracy that the law should command the respect of the people who are expected to abide by 'the rules'. It is equally important that they should know what 'the rules' are. Legislation expressed in vague and cumbersome language is likely to bring the law into disrepute because it cannot be understood by those whose duty it is to observe it. Clarity and simplicity of expression should be the objectives of the draftsman.

Difficulties often arise where one statute is amended by a subsequent statute in a *non-textual* way; i.e., where the amending provision simply refers to the previous statute without setting out the law as amended. Sometimes statutes are amended more than once in this way so that it becomes increasingly difficult and time-consuming to discover what the relevant law is. It is necessary to read two or more statutes side by side. In the absence of regular consolidation, *textual* amendment is to be preferred; i.e., where the amending provision actually sets out the amended law. In *Merkur Island Shipping Corporation* v *Laughton* [1983] 2 All ER 189, HL, Lord Diplock made a plea for greater clarity and simplicity in legislative drafting. This was in a case where the House of Lords had to consult three Acts of Parliament, none of them intelligible by itself, in order to decide whether some secondary industrial action by employees was actionable in tort. His Lordship said (at pp. 198–199):

> I see no reason for doubting that those on whom the responsibility for deciding whether and if so what industrial action shall be taken in any given circumstances wish to obey the law, even though it be a law which they themselves dislike and hope will be changed through the operation of this country's constitutional system of parliamentary democracy. But what the law is, particularly in the field of industrial relations, ought to be plain. It should be expressed in terms that can be easily understood by those who have to apply it even at shop floor level. . . . Absence of clarity is destructive of the rule of law; it is unfair to those who wish to preserve the rule of law; it encourages those who wish to undermine it. The statutory provisions which it became necessary to piece together into a coherent whole . . . are drafted in a manner which, having regard to their subject matter and the persons who will be called on to apply them, can in my view, only be characterised as most regrettably lacking in the requisite degree of clarity.

8.5 COMMENCEMENT OF AN ACT OF PARLIAMENT

A Bill consists of clauses, subclauses and paragraphs. After it has been through its Parliamentary stages and has received the royal assent it is an Act, consisting of sections, subsections and paragraphs. The royal assent to a Bill has not been refused since Queen Anne refused to assent to the Scottish Militia Bill in 1707. There is no law which requires the royal assent to be given, although there is probably today a constitutional convention that it will not be withheld.

An Act comes into force on the date specified in the 'commencement section', if any, situated usually towards the end of the statute. If there is no commencement section, there may be an 'appointed day section', authorising a Secretary of State or the Lord Chancellor to implement the Act by means of an order made by statutory instrument. The Act may provide that different parts can be brought into effect on different dates. An appointed day section gives the minister a discretion to bring the Act, or parts of it, into effect when he feels it is appropriate to do so. He cannot be compelled to implement the Act on any particular date. His discretion, however, is not completely unfettered. Parliament must be taken to intend that legislation will come into force at some time and that its commencement will not depend entirely upon ministerial whim. The minister will not be allowed to frustrate the intentions of Parliament by, for example, deciding not to implement the Act at all. Any such decision would be an abuse of power and unlawful. Thus, in *R* v *Secretary of State for the Home Department (ex parte Fire Brigades Union)* [1995] 2 All ER 244, HL, a decision by the Home Secretary never to implement certain parts of the Criminal Justice Act 1988 — which would have established a statutory Criminal Injuries Compensation Scheme in place of the non-statutory, prerogative-based scheme introduced in 1964 — was held to be unlawful. (Subsequently, the relevant parts of the Criminal Justice Act 1988 were repealed by the Criminal Injuries Compensation Act 1995 without ever having been brought into force. By the same Act, the prerogative scheme, under which compensation was assessed on common law principles, was replaced by an inferior statutory, tariff-based scheme.)

If there is no commencement section and no appointed day section, the Act comes into force on the day it receives the royal assent, which nowadays is normally signified simply by being announced to their respective houses by the Lord Chancellor and the Speaker (Royal Assent Act 1967). However, personal assent by the Queen (although this has not been done since 1854), or assent by Lords Commissioners (Royal Assent Act 1967), is still possible.

An Act of Parliament is deemed to have been in force for the whole of the day of its commencement (Interpretation Act 1978, s. 4, derived from the Interpretation Act 1889, s. 36(2), and the Acts of Parliament (Commencement) Act 1793). *Tomlinson* v *Bullock* (1879) 4 QBD 230, DC, concerned the Bastardy Laws Amendment Act 1872, which had laid down that any unmarried woman who had an illegitimate child 'after the passing of this Act' could apply for an affiliation order against the father. The royal assent to the Act was given on 10 August 1872 and the Act came into operation immediately. The applicant's illegitimate child was born on the same day. It was held that she could apply for an affiliation order. The actual hour of assent was irrelevant as the statute was deemed to have been in force for the whole of that day.

8.6 PARLIAMENTARY SOVEREIGNTY AND THE VALIDITY OF STATUTES

Because Parliament is supreme it is not possible for anyone to challenge the validity of a statute in the courts, even though it is unreasonable or its passage was produced by fraud or some other irregularity. There were suggestions down to the early seventeenth century that the judges could declare void an unreasonable statutory provision. In *Dr Bonham's Case* (1610) 8 Co Rep 114, Coke CJ said, at p. 118, that 'when an Act of Parliament is against common right and reason, or repugnant, or impossible to be performed, the common law will control it, and adjudge such act to be void'. (See also *Day* v *Savadge* (1615) Hob 85, *per* Hobart CJ at p. 97: 'Even an Act of Parliament, made against natural equity, as to make a man judge in his own cause, is void in itself'.) However, Coke's statement was *obiter* and is not consistent with his support of Parliamentary sovereignty expressed in the *Institutes* (4 Inst 36). If the judges were to arrogate to themselves such a power, conflict with Parliament would be inevitable. More recently Lord Denning MR has suggested, extra-judicially, that the courts may have power to strike down legislation on grounds of unconstitutionality along the lines of the function exercised by the Supreme Court of the USA (*The Misuse of Power: The Richard Dimbleby Lecture 1980*, reprinted in Denning, *What Next in The Law*, 1982, pp. 309–31).

Lord Denning's view on this occasion is not only unorthodox but also bereft of authority. The actual position is exemplified by the decision of the House of Lords in *British Railways Board* v *Pickin* [1974] AC 765, HL, where the respondent challenged the validity of a private Act alleging that British Rail had fraudulently concealed facts from Parliament. The respondent complained that the Act would deprive him of his land. It was held, applying in particular a dictum of Lord Campbell in *Edinburgh & Dalkeith Railway Co.* v *Wauchope* (1842) 8 CL & F 710, at p. 725, that the respondent could not challenge the validity of the statute and his claim was struck out as frivolous, vexatious and an abuse of the process of the court. The attitude of the House of Lords was summarised thus by Lord Morris of Borth-y-Gest (at pp. 788–9):

The question of fundamental importance which arises is whether the court should entertain the proposition that an Act of Parliament can be so assailed in the courts that matters should proceed as though the Act or some part of it had never been passed. I consider that such doctrine would be dangerous and impermissible. . . . When an enactment is passed there is finality unless and until it is amended or repealed by Parliament. In the courts there may be argument as to the correct interpretation of the enactment: there must be none as to whether it should be on the Statute Book at all.

(See also *Manuel* v *Attorney-General* [1982] 3 All ER 822, CA.)

8.7 PARLIAMENTARY SOVEREIGNTY AND THE EUROPEAN UNION

Section 2(1) of the European Communities Act 1972 provides as follows:

All such rights, powers, liabilities, obligations and restrictions from time to time created or arising by or under the Treaties, and all such remedies and procedures from time to time provided for by or under the Treaties, as in accordance with the Treaties are without further enactment to be given legal effect or used in the United Kingdom shall be recognised and available in law, and be enforced, allowed and followed accordingly.

The result of s. 2(1) is that European Community law, whether arising from the treaties or from Community regulations, and whether such law has already been made or is to be made in the future, is to be directly applicable in the United Kingdom without the need for the UK Parliament to pass a statute each time. In addition, by s. 2(4), any 'enactment' (which is wide enough to cover a statutory instrument as well as a statute) passed or to be passed in the United Kingdom must be construed with directly applicable European Community law in mind.

Thus, the 1972 Act lays down that European Community law overrides existing domestic law whenever the two conflict and the former is directly applicable (*Duke* v *GEC Reliance Ltd* [1988] 1 All ER 626, HL; *Factortame Ltd* v *Secretary of State for Transport (No. 1)* [1989] 2 All ER 692, HL, *per* Lord Bridge at pp. 700–1; *Factortame Ltd* v *Secretary of State for Transport (No. 2)* [1991] 1 All ER 70, HL, *per* Lord Bridge at p. 108), and it lays down a presumption of interpretation that future United Kingdom statute law is to be read subject to European Community law. It is anticipated thereby that Parliament will not pass legislation which is inconsistent with Community law. It is presumed that a United Kingdom statute is consistent with Community law unless and until it is declared by a court to be inconsistent (*Factortame Ltd* v *Secretary of State for Transport (No. 1)* [1989] 2 All ER 692, HL, *per* Lord Bridge at pp. 702–3).

Although the English courts will strive to achieve consistency with Community law where a United Kingdom statute has been passed in order to give effect to our Community obligations (*Pickstone* v *Freemans plc* [1988] 2 All ER 803, HL; *Litster* v *Forth Dry Dock and Engineering Co. Ltd* [1989] 1 All ER 1134, HL, para 8.10.6 below), they will not deliberately misconstrue the meaning of a United Kingdom statute in an effort to enforce against an individual some provision of Community law which is not directly applicable and which, therefore, creates no directly enforceable rights between individuals. In *Duke* v *GEC Reliance Ltd,* above, it was accordingly held that the claimant had not been unlawfully discriminated against when she was required to retire at the age of 60 while men were permitted to continue at work until the age of 65. The House of Lords decided that the claimant's employers were not liable to her under English law because the Equal Pay Act 1970 and the Sex Discrimination Act 1975 had not been passed by Parliament to give effect to the European Community Council Directive on equal treatment but in order to preserve discriminatory retirement ages. Nor were they liable to her under Community law since the equal treatment directive did not have direct effect as between individuals in the private employment sector.

Lord Templeman said (at p. 636, the other Law Lords expressly agreeing with him):

Section 2(4) of the European Communities Act 1972 does not . . . enable or constrain a British court to distort the meaning of a British statute in order to enforce against an individual a Community directive which has no direct effect between individuals. Section 2(4) applies and only applies where Community provisions are directly applicable.

(Note that the 1970 and 1975 Acts were amended by the Sex Discrimination Act 1986 so as to provide the same *retirement age* for both men and women while leaving the ages at which the State *retirement pension* is payable at 65 and 60 respectively. This change in the law was of no avail to Mrs Duke because the facts of her case arose before the change took effect in November 1987. *Duke* v *GEC Reliance Ltd* [1988] 1 All ER 626, HL, was reaffirmed by the House of Lords in *Finnegan* v *Clowney Youth Training Programme Ltd* [1990] 2 All ER 546, where, again, the claim failed on similar facts. Their Lordships made it clear that, so long as the UK legislation has not been enacted to give effect to a directive, it matters not whether the legislation was passed *before* adoption of the directive (as in *Duke*) or *after* it (as in *Finnegan*).)

The European Communities Act 1972 does not *expressly* forbid Parliament from amending or repealing that Act itself. The effect on Parliamentary sovereignty of the accession of the United Kingdom to the European Union was questioned in *Blackburn* v *Attorney-General* [1971] 2 All ER 1380, CA (see also *McWhirter* v *Attorney-General* [1972] CMLR 882, CA). Mr Blackburn applied for a declaration that the United Kingdom government would, by signing the Treaty of Rome, surrender in part the sovereignty of Parliament and would surrender that part for ever, which, he argued, would be in breach of the law. The Court of Appeal held that Mr Blackburn's statement of claim disclosed no cause of action and should be struck out. The court said that making treaties was not the function of Parliament but of the Crown acting through government ministers. It was a matter of the royal prerogative, the exercise of which could not be challenged in the courts. On the binding of Parliament's successors, the Court of Appeal said that in legal theory it was not possible but what the legal position would be if Parliament did try to bind its successors was a hypothetical question and should not be decided in the present case.

The point arose again in *Macarthys Ltd* v *Smith* [1979] 3 All ER 325, CA, a case in which for the first time the Court of Appeal referred a question of law to the Court of Justice of the European Communities in Luxembourg (para 2.1.3.3.3). This time, although the question of a possible conflict between Parliament and the European Union was still hypothetical, the Court of Appeal was much more vigorous in its response. Lord Denning MR said this (at p. 329):

> If on close investigation it should appear that our legislation is deficient or is inconsistent with Community law by some oversight of our draftsmen then it is our bounden duty to give priority to Community law. Such is the result of s. 2(1) and (4) of the European Communities Act 1972. . . .
>
> Thus far I have assumed that our Parliament, whenever it passes legislation, intends to fulfil its obligations under the Treaty. If the time should come when our Parliament deliberately passes an Act with the intention of repudiating the Treaty or any provision in it or intentionally of acting inconsistently with it and says so in express terms then I should have thought that it would be the duty of our courts to follow the statute of our Parliament. I do not however envisage any such situation.

Lawton LJ agreed (at p. 334):

> Parliament's recognition of European Community law and of the jurisdiction of the European Court of Justice by one enactment can be withdrawn by another.

In *R* v *Secretary of State for Foreign and Commonwealth Affairs (ex parte Rees-Mogg)* [1994] 1 All ER 457, DC, an unsuccessful attempt was made to demonstrate that the United Kingdom government's ratification of the Maastricht Treaty (the Treaty on European Union signed at Maastricht on 7 February 1992) would be unlawful on the grounds, *inter alia*, that it would be in breach of s. 6 of the European Parliamentary Elections Act 1978 and that it would involve transferring to Europe without statutory authority that part of the royal prerogative relating to the conduct of foreign and security policy.

These objections were dismissed by the court, which held that ratification of the Treaty would not be unlawful. Section 6 of the European Parliamentary Elections Act 1978 provides that a treaty increasing the powers of the European Parliament cannot be ratified by the United Kingdom unless it has been approved by an Act of the United Kingdom Parliament. It was held that ratification would not violate s. 6 of the 1978 Act because the Maastricht Treaty (including all its titles, protocols and declarations) had been approved for the purposes of that section by s. 1(2) of the European Communities (Amendment) Act 1993.

The court was doubtful whether the prerogative point was justiciable in the courts. It was decided that, in any event, the point was without merit since ratification of the Maastricht Treaty would not involve a *transfer*, but an *exercise*, of prerogative power similar to that involved in membership of bodies like the United Nations Organisation or the North Atlantic Treaty Organisation. To emphasise the fact that the prerogative was not being transferred or abandoned, the court said that it would presumably be open to the government, as a last resort, to denounce the Treaty or at least to fail to honour its obligations under the provisions concerning foreign and security policy.

Since a deliberately engineered conflict (of the type referred to by Lord Denning in *Macarthys* v *Smith,* above) between English domestic law and Community law (in which, for example, a statute of the United Kingdom Parliament *expressly* provides that it is to override Community law) has not yet arisen, its legal consequences remain unresolved. In the meantime, the supremacy of directly applicable Community law over what may be described (perhaps euphemistically) as 'inadvertently' inconsistent English domestic law is well illustrated by the *Factortame* litigation concerning the Spanish fishing industry.

In the field of employment, Community law makes directly effective provision for the removal of discrimination between citizens of member states on grounds of nationality. It also recognises the right of vessels registered in the Community to fish in any Community waters, but lays down a system of fishing quotas. Dissatisfied with the allocation of quotas to Spain, a number of Spanish fishing companies began 'quota-hopping'. They turned their attentions to British quotas by purchasing vessels already registered as British or by re-registering their own vessels under the British flag. The British Government reacted by securing the passage through Parliament of the Merchant Shipping Act 1988. Part II of the Act, and regulations made thereunder, introduced new registration conditions so that some of the fishing boats belonging to the Spanish companies no longer qualified for British registration — with potential disastrous consequences for the Spanish companies and their employees since the boats were not eligible to resume fishing against the Spanish quotas. The Spanish companies argued that the 1988 Act and the regulations made under it contravened their rights under Community law, and 95 of them applied to the High Court for judicial review of the validity of the legislation.

The High Court decided to request a preliminary ruling from the European Court of Justice under art. 177 (now art. 234) of the EC Treaty on, *inter alia,* the interpretation of Community law provisions relating to non-discrimination on grounds of nationality and the right to establish a business in another member state. Because it would take two years to get a ruling (by which time the Spanish companies could have suffered irreparable damage), the High Court also decided to grant an interim injunction against the Crown to prevent the application of the 1988 Act to the Spanish companies in the meantime.

The Court of Appeal allowed the Crown's appeal and set aside the interim injunction. On a further appeal, the House of Lords affirmed the decision of the Court of Appeal and held (in accordance with conventional constitutional wisdom) that English courts had no power to suspend the operation of a statute and no power to grant an interim injunction against the Crown (*Factortame Ltd* v *Secretary of State for Transport (No. 1)* [1989] 2 All ER 692, HL). However, the House of Lords itself referred the following question to the European Court of Justice under art. 177 (234): under Community law, must a national court ignore its own national law and provide interim relief for a person with directly enforceable Community law rights who would otherwise suffer irreversible damage because of delay in having those rights determined?

In *Factortame Ltd* v *Secretary of State for Transport (No. 2)* [1991] 1 All ER 70, CJEC and HL, the European Court gave an affirmative answer to the question referred. A principle found in earlier European Court case law (see, for example, *Amministrazione delle Finanze dello Stato* v *Simmenthal SpA* [1978] 3 CMLR 263, CJEC) was re-emphasised and applied: namely, that under Community law a national law (whether legislative, judicial or administrative in character) must be set aside by a national court if it prevents the application of Community law. This principle ensures that the operation of Community law is not frustrated by an inconsistent national law. The House of Lords implemented the European Court's decision by granting an interim injunction against the Secretary of State for Transport (in effect, the Crown) to last until such time as the European Court made a decision on the merits of the Spanish companies' case. This injunction meant that, for the first time ever, the operation of a statute of the United Kingdom Parliament had been suspended by an English court of law.

In *R v Secretary of State for Transport (ex parte Factortame Ltd)* [1991] 3 All ER 769, the European Court, in answer to the reference made to it by the High Court in 1989, held that the registration provisions contained in part II of the Merchant Shipping Act 1988, and in regulations made under it, were contrary to Community law and, therefore, ineffective against nationals of other member states. As a result of the decision of the European Court in *R v Secretary of State for Transport (ex parte Factortame) (No. 4)* [1996] QB 404, CJEC, the way is now open for the Spanish companies to claim compensation in the English courts (possibly running as high as £30m) from the United Kingdom Government. The principle that a member state may be liable to compensate an individual for loss caused to him through a breach of Community law committed by the state has been held by the European Court to be inherent in the scheme of the EC Treaty (*Francovich v Italian Republic* [1992] IRLR 84, CJEC; *Factortame (No. 4)*, above; see further, para 8.9 below).

The European Court gave its decision in *Factortame Ltd v Secretary of State for Transport (No. 2)* [1991] 1 All ER 70 in June 1990 and, in response to it, the House of Lords decided to grant the interim injunction in July 1990 but reserved its reasons for doing so until October 1990. In the intervening period, the decision of the European Court was subjected to considerable criticism. In view of its effect on the sovereignty of the United Kingdom Parliament, it was greeted with some disbelief at Westminster and in the media by those who were either anti-European or less than enthusiastically pro-European. In a famous dictum uttered in 1974, shortly after the United Kingdom became a member of the European Union, Lord Denning MR likened the impact of Community law to an incoming tide, flowing into our estuaries and up our rivers, which could not be held back (*H. P. Bulmer Ltd v J. Bollinger SA* [1974] Ch 401, CA, at p. 418). By 1990, in retirement and obviously concerned as the full implications of membership of the Communities became clearer from cases like *Factortame (No. 2)*, he had rephrased his dictum as follows:

> No longer is European law an incoming tide flowing up the estuaries of England. It is now like a tidal wave bringing down our sea walls and flowing inland over our fields and houses — to the dismay of all.
> (Quoted in *The Independent*, 16 July 1990; see also Crossick, 'The ebb and flow of Lord Denning' (1990) 140 New LJ 1431.)

He accused the European Court (which, he said, was manned by pan-Europeans whose ideology is allowed to influence their decisions; see Crossick, op. cit.) of interfering with parliamentary sovereignty in the absence of express authority conferred by the EC Treaty. He advocated the amendment of the European Communities Act 1972 to ensure that European Court decisions and Community directives would not be binding unless approved by, respectively, the House of Lords and the relevant British government minister.

Others accused the European Court of being a political institution guilty of abusing its powers by moving away from merely interpreting law to actually creating it in order to promote the ideal of European political union (see *The Independent*, 16 July 1990). Referring to the criticisms of the European Court's decision, Lord Bridge said in *Factortame (No. 2)* [1991] 1 All ER 70, HL, at pp. 107–8, that they were based on a 'misconception':

If the supremacy within the European Community of Community law over the national law of member states was not always inherent in the EEC Treaty it was certainly well established in the jurisprudence of the Court of Justice long before the United Kingdom joined the Community. Thus, whatever limitation of its sovereignty Parliament accepted when it enacted the European Communities Act 1972 was entirely voluntary. Under the terms of the 1972 Act it has always been clear that it was the duty of a United Kingdom court, when delivering final judgment, to override any rule of national law found to be in conflict with any directly enforceable rule of Community law. Similarly, when decisions of the Court of Justice have exposed areas of United Kingdom statute law which failed to implement Council directives, Parliament has always loyally accepted the obligation to make appropriate and prompt amendments. Thus there is nothing in any way novel in according supremacy to rules of Community law in those areas to which they apply and to insist that, in the protection of rights under Community law, national courts must not be inhibited by rules of national law from granting interim relief in appropriate cases is no more than a logical recognition of that supremacy.

Growing suspicion of the European Court, heightened by a number of adverse decisions given by it, led the United Kingdom government to propose a number of changes in a White Paper published in 1996. In particular, the Conservative government of the day was concerned to prevent the European Court from imposing disproportionate costs on governments and businesses, and from committing what the government saw as abuses of power by making (rather than interpreting) the law. It was, therefore, proposed that the retroactive capacity of the European Court's judgments should be restricted, and that the European Union should adopt, first, the principle that member states be liable in damages for violation of Community law only in cases of serious and clear breaches of their obligations, and, secondly, a mechanism for the rapid amendment of Community law which has been interpreted by the European Court in a way never intended by member states (*A Partnership of Nations*, Cm 3181, 1996).

8.8   DELEGATED (OR SUBORDINATE) LEGISLATION

8.8.1   Types of delegated legislation

Delegated legislation is law made by some person or body other than Parliament but with the authority of Parliament. It can be made by the following persons and bodies:

(a)   Ministers of the Crown, in the form of regulations made by statutory instrument. This is a particularly well-used method of making law, and statutory instruments are numerous. For example, in 1998 Parliament passed 49 public general Acts; in the same year, over 3,300 statutory instruments were made.

(b)   The Privy Council (in effect the government for this purpose), in the form of Orders in Council. Thus, law may be made by Orders in Council under the Emergency Powers Act 1920. This method of legislation was also used to impose economic sanctions under the Southern Rhodesia Act 1965, and to make the Iraq and Kuwait (United Nations Sanctions) Order 1990 under the United Nations Act 1946.

(c)   Local authorities, in the form of by-laws under such enabling statutes as the Public Health Act 1936 and the Local Government Act 1972.

(d)   Public corporations, in the form of by-laws.

(e)   Court rule committees, in the form of rules of court governing procedure. Examples of such committees are the Civil Procedure Rule Committee (Civil Procedure Act 1997, s. 2); the Crown Court Rule Committee (Supreme Court Act 1981, s. 86); the Family Proceedings Rule Committee (Matrimonial and Family Proceedings Act 1984, s. 40); the Rule Committee for Magistrates' Courts (Magistrates' Courts Act 1980, s. 144).

8.8.2   Reasons for delegated legislative powers

Delegated legislative powers are conferred by Parliament for a number of reasons. For example, Parliament does not have the time to discuss all Bills in detail. Members of Parliament may not have the necessary knowledge to deal with the details of technical Bills. In an emergency a law can usually be introduced more quickly by, say, ministerial regulation than by Act of Parliament. However, sometimes Parliament itself can act with surprising swiftness as in 1965, when the Southern Rhodesia Act went through all its legislative stages in one day in response to the illegal unilateral declaration of independence in what is now Zimbabwe. The Imprisonment (Temporary Provisions) Act 1980 was passed in one day to deal with the consequences of industrial action by prison officers.

8.8.3   Control of delegated legislation by the courts

One important difference between Parliamentary legislation and delegated legislation is that whereas a court of law cannot question the validity of an Act of Parliament (para 8.6 above), it *can* question the validity of delegated legislation. This is because of the doctrine of *ultra vires*. If, for instance, a minister acts *ultra vires* (beyond his powers) by making a regulation which he has no power to make, then that regulation can be declared void by the court, as in *Chester* v *Bateson* [1920] 1 KB 829, DC, and *Commissioners of Customs & Excise* v *Cure & Deeley Ltd* [1962] 1 QB 340 (para 11.5.2.3).

It should be noted that the court has the same power of control where the minister's excess of power arises out of a document which does not necessarily have the force of law. Thus, in *Laker Airways Ltd* v *Department of Trade* [1977] QB 643, CA, a minister was held by the Court of Appeal to have acted *ultra vires* when he issued a policy directive which had the effect of contradicting the express provisions of the statute that had given him the power to issue the directive. Similarly, it was held in *R* v *Secretary of State for the Environment (ex parte Lancashire County Council)* [1994] 4 All ER 165 that the Environment Secretary had acted *ultra vires* when he issued to the Local Government Commission policy guidance (on replacing the two-tier structure of local government with unitary authorities) which undermined the provisions of a statute. (A revised version of the policy guidance was upheld as lawful in *R* v *Secretary of State for the Environment (ex parte Lancashire County Council) (No. 2)* (1995) *The Times*, 9 December.) Regulations can also be declared *ultra vires* if they conflict with statutory rights already conferred by previous primary legislation (*R* v *Secretary* of *State for Social Security (ex parte Joint Council for the Welfare of Immigrants)* [1996] 4 All ER 385, CA; see further, para 11.5.2.3).

Statutory instruments are also void if they conflict with European Community legislation (European Communities Act 1972, s. 2(4)).

In addition, local authority by-laws can be declared void by the court if they are *uncertain* or *unclear* (*Percy* v *Hall* [1996] 4 All ER 523, CA), or if they are *unreasonable* (*Kruse* v *Johnson* [1898] 2 QB 91, DC). For examples of by-laws held to be unreasonable, see *Arlidge* v *Islington Corporation* [1909] 2 KB 127, DC; *Parker* v *Bournemouth Corporation* (1902)

86 LT 449, DC; and *Strickland* v *Hayes* [1896] 1 QB 290, DC, where a by-law prohibiting the singing or reciting of any obscene song or ballad, and the use of obscene language generally, was held to be unreasonable and void because it was drawn too widely in that it was not limited to public places and it did not require the prohibited acts to be done to the annoyance of the public.

8.9   EUROPEAN COMMUNITY LEGISLATION: PRIMARY AND SECONDARY

Much of English domestic law, such as land law, family law and criminal law, is not affected by United Kingdom membership of the European Union. European Community law is concerned mainly with restrictive trade practices, competition, consumer protection, employment, agriculture, fisheries, coal, steel, nuclear energy, the environment, and the free movement of labour, capital and services.

The *primary* European Community legislation consists, *inter alia*, of the three treaties that established the Communities, namely, the European Coal and Steel Community Treaty, the Euratom Treaty and the European Community Treaty, together with the Single European Act, the Treaty on European Union (the Maastricht Treaty), and the Treaty of Amsterdam. The provisions of these treaties are directly applicable in the United Kingdom, without the need for further legislation by the UK Parliament, by virtue of the European Communities Act 1972, s. 2(1) (para 8.7 above).

The *secondary* European Community legislation consists of regulations, decisions, directives, recommendations and opinions made or given by the Council of Ministers or the Commission.

Recommendations and opinions are not directly applicable in the United Kingdom but can be given legal effect by statute or by delegated legislation made under the European Communities Act 1972, s. 2(2).

In general, the same applies to directives, although they can sometimes produce direct legal effects and create rights without having been implemented by domestic legislation if they fulfil certain criteria, notably that their terms are unconditional and sufficiently precise (see, e.g., *Van Duyn* v *Home Office* [1975] Ch 358, CJEC). Furthermore, when directives *are* directly effective they have 'vertical direct effect' but not 'horizontal direct effect' (*Marshall* v *Southampton and South West Hampshire Area Health Authority (Teaching)* [1986] QB 401, CJEC; *Foster* v *British Gas plc* [1990] 3 All ER 897, CJEC). This means that they have direct effect in proceedings against a member state ('vertically') but not in proceedings between individuals or companies ('horizontally'). For this purpose the word 'state' has been given a wide meaning (*Foster* v *British Gas plc,* above; *Marshall* v *Southampton and South West Hampshire Area Health Authority (No. 2)* [1993] 4 All ER 586, CJEC) and in the United Kingdom would include local authorities and nationalised industries. Although an unimplemented directive may thus be enforced *against* a local authority as an emanation of the state, it cannot be enforced *by* a local authority since such a body is not an 'individual' for the purposes of Community law (*Wychavon District Council* v *Secretary of State for the Environment* (1994) *The Times*, 7 January).

A member state which is in breach of Community law by failing to implement a directive may, in certain circumstances, be liable to compensate an individual who has suffered loss as a result of the non-implementation even though the directive in question does not have direct effect (*Francovich* v *Italian Republic* [1992] IRLR 84, CJEC).

The purpose of this case-law development is to prevent member states from taking advantage of their own failure to comply with Community law. A member state may be so liable if three conditions are fulfilled (see, for example, *Francovich*, above; *Faccini Dori* v *Recreb Srl* [1995] All ER (EC) 1, CJEC; *Dillenkofer* v *Germany* [1997] QB 259, CJEC). First, the purpose of the directive must be to confer rights on individuals. Secondly, the content of those rights must be identifiable from the provisions of the directive. Thirdly, there must be a direct causal link between the breach of the member state's obligation and the damage sustained by the individual.

It is no defence to a member state which fails to implement a directive to claim that the period allowed for implementation was too short or that other member states did not implement the directive on time either (*EC Commission* v *Italy* [1976] ECR 277, CJEC). In the case of *Dillenkofer*, above, it was held that failure to implement a directive within the prescribed period is a serious breach of community law, and that neither liability for the breach nor the obligation to pay compensation depends upon proof of fault on the part of the guilty member state. Accordingly, the German Federal Republic was liable to compensate some holidaymakers who suffered loss resulting from Germany's failure to implement a Council Directive of 1990 on package travel, package holidays and package tours. The Directive was intended to and did, in a clearly identifiable way, confer upon purchasers of packages a right to the reimbursement of sums already paid, and repatriation costs, in the event of the insolvency of the travel organiser and/or retailer.

In *Marshall* v *Southampton and South West Hampshire Area Health Authority (No. 2)*, above, the European Court held that it was not a proper implementation of a directive designed to secure equality of treatment for men and women in employment matters for the national law to set an upper limit to the compensation available for discriminatory dismissal and to exclude any award of interest thereon. It was further held that a person injured by discriminatory dismissal can enforce the directive against an authority of the state, acting in its capacity as an employer, in order to have the relevant national law set aside. In the light of this ruling of the European Court, the Sex Discrimination and Equal Pay (Remedies) Regulations 1993 (SI 1993, No. 2798) were made, removing the upper limit on the amount of compensation an employment tribunal can award for unlawful acts of sexual discrimination. Furthermore, the House of Lords later set aside the decisions of the Court of Appeal and the Employment Appeal Tribunal and restored that of the employment tribunal where the case had begun (*Marshall* v *Southampton and South West Hampshire Area Health Authority (No. 2) (note)* [1994] 1 All ER 736, HL).

The principle that a member state which violates Community law must compensate an individual who suffers resultant loss applies equally to a breach of the Community *treaties*, whether that breach is perpetrated by the executive, the judiciary or the legislature. In *R* v *Secretary of State for Transport (ex parte Factortame Ltd)* [1991] 3 All ER 769, CJEC, it had been established by the European Court that the United Kingdom was in breach of the EC Treaty in its dealings with the Spanish fishermen (see para 8.7 above). In *R* v *Secretary of State for Transport (ex parte Factortame Ltd) (No. 4)* [1996] QB 404, CJEC, it was further held that the fishermen, who had sustained considerable financial loss, would be entitled to claim damages against the United Kingdom in the English courts — and it made no difference that it was Parliament which was responsible for the breach of the Treaty by passing the Merchant Shipping Act 1988 — if the necessary requirements for state liability (to which absence of fault is no defence) were satisfied: the relevant provision of the EC Treaty was intended to confer rights on the fishermen, the breach was sufficiently serious, and there was a direct causal link between the breach and the damage suffered by the fishermen. It was also laid down that exemplary damages can be awarded for breach of Community law if they could be awarded for similar claims founded on domestic law. Thus, in *R* v *Secretary of State for Transport (ex parte Factortame Ltd) (No 5)* (1997) *The Times*, 11 September, DC, the fishermen argued that they would be entitled to exemplary damages under English law if they could show that the United Kingdom had acted in an oppressive, arbitrary or unconstitutional manner (see para 10.2.2). It was held that they were entitled to claim *compensatory* damages because, subject to the issue of causation (which was left undecided pending a determination of the seriousness of the breach), the requirements for state liability had been satisfied. However, they were not entitled to *exemplary* damages because they would not have been awarded in a similar claim based on English domestic law. The court said that a breach of Community law was akin to a breach of statutory duty and, in English law, exemplary damages are not available for a breach of a statutory duty unless the particular statute expressly says so, and in the present case there was no such express statutory provision.

The fishermen's claim for *exemplary* damages was not pursued when *R* v *Secretary of State for Transport (ex parte Factortame Ltd)* (No. 5) subsequently went to the Court of Appeal and the House of Lords. On the claim for *compensatory* damages, both the Court of Appeal ((1998) *The* Times, 28 April, CA) and the House of Lords ([1999] 4 All ER 906, HL) were unanimous in holding that the breach was sufficiently serious to entitle the fishermen to compensation for loss directly caused by the breach. The issue of causation will be tried later.

Decisions *may* be, and regulations *are*, directly applicable in the United Kingdom by virtue of the European Communities Act 1972, s. 2(1). Moreover, they are published in the *Official Journal* of the Communities of which judicial notice (para 8.1 above) is taken in the United Kingdom. Judicial notice is also taken of the treaties and of decisions and opinions of the European Court of Justice or any court attached thereto (European Communities Act 1972, s. 3(2), as amended by the European Communities (Amendment) Act 1986, see para 8.10.7 below).

Secondary European Community legislation is analogous to domestic delegated legislation and it is subject to a similar method of judicial control. The *validity* of the *primary* European Community legislation (the treaties) is not subject to review either in national courts or in the European Court of Justice. The power of the courts in relation to the treaties is limited to *interpretation* (EC Treaty, art. 177 (now art. 234); see para 2.1.3.3). But the *validity,* as well as the meaning or effect, of *secondary* Community legislation can be challenged both in national courts and in the European Court of Justice (EC Treaty, art. 177 (234)). A court in the United Kingdom, instead of determining the point itself, may decide to refer any question of the validity of secondary Community legislation to the European Court of Justice (ibid.).

8.10 STATUTORY INTERPRETATION

8.10.1 Introduction

As was mentioned in para 8.1, the function of the judges in relation to legislation is to apply it. If, however, the wording of the legislation is ambiguous, or its extent uncertain, its meaning or scope will need to be interpreted or construed first. Legislation is expressed in words and words are an imperfect means of communication. Legislation may need interpretation because, for example, the Act is badly drafted, or because the subject-matter of the Act is so complex that errors are inevitable, or because the Act fails to provide for all possible contingencies.

In his task of statutory interpretation a judge is assisted by some so-called 'rules' and by some presumptions. In addition, there are available, within limits, some intrinsic and extrinsic aids to construction. These rules, presumptions and aids may together be referred to as the principles of statutory interpretation. They will be examined in the remainder of this chapter, which will end with a consideration of the different technique to be adopted by the English courts when interpreting European Community legislation.

8.10.2 Rules

8.10.2.1 The literal rule

By the literal rule the words used in a statute must be given their plain, ordinary or literal meaning. The objective of the court is to discover the intention of Parliament as expressed in the words used (*Stock* v *Frank Jones (Tipton) Ltd* [1978] 1 All ER 948, HL, *per* Viscount Dilhorne at p. 951; see also the explanation of the literal rule given by Lord Diplock in *Duport Steels Ltd* v *Sirs* [1980] 1 All ER 529, HL, at p. 541).

In *Cutter* v *Eagle Star Insurance Co. Ltd* [1998] 4 All ER 417, HL, the House of Lords was concerned with the meaning of the word 'road' in the Road Traffic Act 1988. Their Lordships rejected a purposive approach in favour of giving the word 'road' its ordinary, literal meaning. The claimant was sitting in the front passenger seat of his friend's car parked in a multi-storey car park. Inflammable gas leaked inside the car from a can of lighter fuel, and when the driver returned to the car and lit a cigarette the gas was ignited and the claimant was injured. The claimant sued the driver for negligence and won the case, but the driver had no money with which to pay damages.

As required by law, the driver was insured under a motor vehicle policy against any liability for death or bodily injury to any person arising out of the use of his car on a 'road'. The Road Traffic Act 1988 defines the word 'road' as 'any highway and any other road to which the public has access'. The House of Lords held that whether a particular place is a 'road' is always a question of fact. The car park was not a road within the definition because a road provides for cars to move along it to a destination. A car park simply enables cars to stand and wait. The fact that a car can be driven across a car park does not make it a 'road' because that is merely incidental to the main function of parking. Similarly, the fact that a car is parked on a road does not make the road a 'car park'. Accordingly, the claimant had not been injured due to the use of the car on a 'road', and the insurance company was not liable to pay out on the driver's policy. (See further on this case, para 8.10.6 below.)

If the words used are quite *clear* they must be applied even though the result is absurd, or even though one may dislike the statute (*Stock* v *Frank Jones (Tipton) Ltd*, *per* Lord Edmund-Davies at p. 954), or even though the interpretation may inflict hardship on those affected by the legislation. Thus in *Leedale* v *Lewis* [1982] 3 All ER 808, HL, the unanimous opinion of the House of Lords was that if the meaning of a taxation statute is *clear* it must be given effect to and the court should not seek to discover some alternative (*ex hypothesi* wrong) interpretation merely because the true meaning involves hardship for the taxpayer (or, it may be added, because it might leave a loophole for frauds against the revenue: *Barnard* v *Gorman* [1941] AC 378, HL, *per* Viscount Simon LC at p. 384).

Similarly, a person is not homeless for the purposes of the Housing (Homeless Persons) Act 1977 (now part III of the Housing Act 1985) if he is occupying 'accommodation' within the ordinary meaning of that word, even though the place which he occupies is lacking in cooking and washing facilities and he is thereby compelled to eat out and to use a launderette for washing his clothes (*Puhlhofer* v *Hillingdon London Borough Council* [1986]

1 All ER 467, HL). It might be otherwise where the 'accommodation' is not, by reason of its size, capable of accommodating a person together with others who normally reside with him as members of his family (ibid., *per* Lord Brightman at p. 474). Such a place could not be described as 'accommodation' in any meaningful sense.

Smith v *Director of Serious Fraud Office* [1992] 3 All ER 456, HL, was concerned with some of the provisions of the Criminal Justice Act 1987 relating to serious or complex fraud. By s. 2(13), a person who without reasonable excuse fails to answer questions or provide information on matters relevant to an investigation by the Director of the Serious Fraud Office is guilty of an offence and liable to be imprisoned, or fined, or both. The question arose whether a defendant can rely on the privilege against self-incrimination and refuse to answer questions.

It was decided unanimously by the House of Lords that the right to silence was not to be implied into the express, clear wording of the 1987 Act, which showed that Parliament had intended to establish an inquisitorial system in cases of serious or complex fraud whereby the Director of the Serious Fraud Office can, in the questioning process, *require* a defendant to provide answers which might be self-incriminating. It was held that the powers of the Director under s. 2 to question a person under investigation do not end when that person is charged. The defendant's right to silence has been removed in such cases with the result that the Director can continue to question him after he has been charged and without giving a further caution. (It should be noted that a statement made by the defendant in response to a requirement imposed on him under s. 2 is only later admissible in evidence against him in a prosecution for making a false or misleading statement or in a prosecution for some other offence where in his evidence he makes an inconsistent statement (s. 2(8)).)

Lord Mustill (with whose speech the other Law Lords agreed) pointed out that there is a strong presumption of interpretation against taking away the right to silence but that 'statutory interference with the right is almost as old as the right itself' (*Smith* v *Director of Serious Fraud Office* [1992] 3 All ER 456, HL, at pp. 471–2). Lord Mustill's opinion was much relied upon in *A. T. & T. Istel Ltd* v *Tully* [1992] 3 All ER 523, HL, another case in which the right to silence was under attack, where Lord Templeman (at p. 531) described Parliament's willingness to abrogate or modify the right as a recognition of the 'unsatisfactory results of the common law privilege against self-incrimination'. He went further (supported by Lord Griffiths) and suggested that the privilege against self-incrimination is only justifiable on the two grounds that it discourages the ill-treatment of a suspect and discourages the production of dubious confessions. In the view of Lord Templeman and Lord Griffiths, the privilege against self-incrimination in civil proceedings is an archaic and unjustifiable survival from the past and should not be available to allow a litigant to refuse production of relevant documents (*A. T. & T. Istel Ltd* v *Tully*, above, at pp. 530 and 534 respectively; see further on this case, para 8.10.2.4 below).

Sometimes the search for the ordinary, natural meaning of words can produce disagreement and surprising results at the highest level. The case of *R* v *Maginnis* [1987] 1 All ER 907, HL, was concerned with the interpretation of the Misuse of Drugs Act 1971, by s. 5(3) of which:

> . . . it is an offence for a person to have a controlled drug in his possession, whether lawfully or not, with intent to supply it to another . . .

The police had found a package of cannabis resin in the defendant's car. He said that the package was not his but had been left in his car by a friend for collection later. The defendant was convicted of the offence and appealed on the ground that his intention to return the drug to its owner did not amount to an intention to 'supply' the drug within the meaning of the statute. The Court of Appeal allowed his appeal and the Crown appealed to the House of Lords. Their Lordships held, by a majority of four to one (Lord Goff of Chieveley dissenting), that the defendant was guilty of the offence because a person in unlawful possession of a controlled drug left with him by another person for safekeeping had the necessary 'intent to supply it to another' (even though the supply was not being made from the provider's own resources) if his intention was to return it to the other person and for that other person's purposes.

The majority of their Lordships purported to apply the ordinary, natural meaning of the word 'supply'. Lord Goff of Chieveley, however, dissented on that very point and referred to definitions of the word given in *The Shorter Oxford English Dictionary*. In his view, which would seem clearly preferable to that of the majority, the word 'supply' was not apt to describe a transaction in which A handed back to B goods which B had previously left with A. Thus, the cloakroom attendant, left luggage officer, warehouseman and shoe repairer do not, in ordinary parlance, 'supply' their customers. Lord Goff was further of the opinion that the particular offence in question was aimed at drug 'pushers'; the defendant was not a 'pusher' and should have been charged with the lesser offence of 'unlawful possession'. If, he said, persons in the position of the defendant were to be convicted of 'possession with intent to supply', it was up to Parliament and not the courts to enlarge the definition of 'supply'. (See [1987] 1 All ER 907 at pp. 913–15.)

The application of the literal rule produced disagreement among their Lordships again in *R v Brown* [1996] 1 All ER 545, HL. Here, a majority of the House held that the offence under s. 5(2)(b) of the Data Protection Act 1984 (since repealed by the Data Protection Act 1998) of knowingly or recklessly using personal data other than for the purposes described in the relevant entry in the register of data users is not committed by a person who merely accesses information on a computer in order to read it on screen or by means of a print-out. The data is only 'used', and the offence committed, if the defendant thereafter goes on to make unauthorised use of it, such as by passing it on to someone else. This conclusion was reached by giving the word 'use' in s. 5(2)(b) its natural and ordinary meaning of 'make use of' or 'employ for a purpose'. Since there was no evidence that the defendant, a police officer who had twice used the police national computer to check the registration numbers of vehicles owned by debtors of clients of his friend's debt collection company, had passed on the data to his friend he was not guilty of the offence.

Lords Griffiths and Jauncey dissented on the ground that the word 'use' required a broad construction in order to achieve the purpose of the Data Protection Act 1984 and to prevent a serious gap in the protection it seeks to provide. The Act was passed to give effect to the United Kingdom's obligations under the Council of Europe Convention for the Protection of Individuals with regard to Automatic Processing of Personal Data. The two dissentients adopted a purposive approach, preferring an interpretation of s. 5 which accorded with the purpose of the Convention, namely, to secure respect for individual rights and fundamental freedoms (especially the right to privacy) in relation to the automatic processing of personal data. In their view, a person 'uses' data stored in a computer if he informs himself of its content, and the section should be construed widely so as to cover not only the use of data for an unauthorised purpose but also the invasion of privacy resulting merely from the unauthorised display of data about other people (see especially *per* Lord Griffiths at pp. 554–5).

It must be appreciated in relation to the literal rule of interpretation that the ordinary meaning of a technical word is something technical. In *Unwin v Hanson* [1891] 2 QB 115,

CA, the Highways Act 1835 empowered the borough surveyor to prune and lop trees which excluded light from the highway. The claimant sued a borough surveyor who had cut the tops off the claimant's trees. It was shown in evidence that in forestry terminology 'prune' meant removing surplus branches to improve growth and 'lop' meant to cut branches from the side of the tree. The defendant had done neither of these things. He had 'topped' the trees when he had no power to do so. In *Munby* v *Furlong* [1977] 2 All ER 953, the Court of Appeal held that the word 'plant' in a taxation statute covered books bought by a barrister for the purpose of his practice and that, therefore, he was entitled to an allowance for capital expenditure. Lord Denning MR said (at p. 956) that the word 'plant' in a taxation statute did not mean what the ordinary English person thought it meant. It had acquired a special meaning in tax cases. It was not limited to things used physically, like machinery, but covered the 'intellectual storehouse' which a professional person has in exercising his profession.

Unless it can be shown that the statutory framework or the legal context in which the words are used requires a different meaning, the words of the statute should be assigned their natural and ordinary meaning. This approach, in the words of Lord Scarman in *Shah* v *Barnet London Borough Council* [1983] 1 All ER 226, HL, at p. 237:

helps to prevent the growth and multiplication of refined and subtle distinctions in the law's use of common English words. Nothing is more confusing and more likely to bring the statute law into disrepute than a proliferation by judicial interpretation of special meanings, when Parliament has not expressly enacted any.

In order to arrive at the proper meaning of the words used in a statute a judge may have recourse to dictionaries, to the definition section (if any) in the particular statute, to the Interpretation Act 1978, and to previous cases decided on the meaning of similar words.

In *R* v *Inner London Education Authority (ex parte Westminster City Council)* [1986] 1 All ER 19, a *Shorter Oxford English Dictionary* definition was applied to the word 'information' in the Local Government Act 1972 (see further on this case, para 11.5.2.1).

But the use of dictionaries does not always yield helpful results. In *Coltman* v *Bibby Tankers Ltd* [1987] 3 All ER 1068, the House of Lords decided that a ship fell within the definition of 'equipment' given in s. 1(3) of the Employer's Liability (Defective Equipment) Act 1969, where the word 'equipment' is defined as including 'any plant and machinery, vehicle, aircraft and clothing'. In so holding, their Lordships unanimously reversed the decision of the majority of the Court of Appeal and expressed disagreement with the conclusion reached by O'Connor LJ in the court below on the dictionary definition of 'equipment'. Referring to the *The Oxford English Dictionary,* O'Connor LJ had held that 'equipment' denoted only 'something ancillary to something else' and did not, therefore, include an entire ship, though it would cover machinery attached to the ship. Speaking for the House, Lord Oliver of Aylmerton said (at p. 1071) that there was nothing in the *Oxford English Dictionary* definition which necessarily limited 'equipment' to 'parts of a larger whole'. One would, he said, refer without any misuse of language to a shipowner's fleet of ships as the 'equipment of his business'.

Coltman v *Bibby Tankers Ltd* was considered in *Knowles* v *Liverpool City Council* [1993] 4 All ER 321, HL, where it was held that it was consistent both with the purpose of the 1969 Act and with an ordinary interpretation of the word 'equipment' to construe that word as including the material with which an employee works in his employer's business. Accordingly, the defendant council was held liable when one of its employees who was employed to lay flagstones was injured by a defective flagstone supplied to the council by a third party. It was also said, *obiter*, that defective equipment which causes injury to an employee will be within the scope of the 1969 Act even though the employee was not required to use it and had not, in fact, used it since s. 1(1) of the Act does not require that the equipment has been provided for the employee's use but only that it has been provided 'for the purposes of the employer's business' (see [1993] 4 All ER 321 *per* Lord Jauncey at p. 327, the other Law Lords agreeing with him).

Where a statute defines a word in a certain way, Parliament is presumed to have intended that definition to be used in preference to the ordinary meaning of the word (as given, for example, in a dictionary) unless there is some clear indication to the contrary. Thus, in *Wyre Forest District Council* v *Secretary of State for the Environment* [1990] 1 All ER 780, HL, there being no clear indication to the contrary, a chalet structure was held by the House of Lords to come within the definition of 'caravan' given in s. 29(1) of the Caravan Sites and Control of Development Act 1960 even though a chalet structure is not a caravan within the ordinary meaning of that word.

The Interpretation Act 1978 provides definitions of many words and expressions. These definitions are to be used in construing any Acts which contain those words or expressions (Interpretation Act 1978, s. 5 and sch. 1). The 1978 Act also states that, unless the contrary intention appears, words in a statute importing the masculine gender include the feminine, and *vice versa,* and that words in the singular include the plural, and *vice versa* (ibid., s. 6).

If these various aids to construction are of little or no assistance to the judge in a particular case then he must simply decide for himself what the words mean. The case of *Mandla* v *Dowell Lee* [1983] 1 All ER 1062, HL (the 'Sikh turban case') turned on the meaning of the word 'ethnic' in s. 3 of the Race Relations Act 1976. The word is not defined in the Act itself and recourse was had, in both the Court of Appeal and the House of Lords, to dictionary definitions, all of which were rejected by the House of Lords which eventually held (reversing the Court of Appeal) that Sikhs are a racial, and not solely a religious, group for the purposes of the race relations legislation (see *per* Lord Fraser of Tullybelton at p. 1066; Lord Fraser's tests were applied in *Crown Suppliers (PSA)* v *Dawkins* (1993) *The Times,* 4 February, in which the Court of Appeal held that Rastafarians are solely a religious sect and not a racial group entitled to the protection of the legislation).

8.10.2.2 The golden rule

The golden rule may be used in two ways. It is mostly used in a narrow way to modify the literal rule in order to avoid an absurdity. In its narrow application, the golden rule lays down that if the words used are ambiguous the court should adopt an interpretation which avoids an absurd result. *Adler* v *George* [1964] 2 QB 7, DC, concerned a prosecution under the Official Secrets Act 1920 which made it an offence to obstruct HM Forces 'in the vicinity of' a prohibited place. The defendants had obstructed HM Forces *in* a prohibited place and the Divisional Court held they were guilty of the offence.

In its second, broader, application the golden rule is sometimes used in preference to the literal rule where the words used can have only one literal meaning. This is especially so where considerations of public policy intervene to discourage the adoption of an obnoxious interpretation. There is, for example, a principle grounded in public policy which precludes a murderer from benefiting under his victim's *will*. In *Re Sigsworth* [1935] Ch 89, the judge had to decide whether the same principle applied so as to preclude a murderer from claiming a benefit conferred on him *by statute* where the victim died *intestate.* By the Administration of Estates Act 1925 the residuary estate of a person dying intestate was to be divided among the 'issue'. Mrs Sigsworth died intestate leaving only a son who, a coroner's jury found, had murdered her. The question for the court was whether the son as 'issue' could succeed on the mother's intestacy. Clauson J held that he could not. He said that the principle of public policy which prevents a murderer from reaping the fruits of his crime must be applied in the construction of Acts of Parliament so as to avoid conclusions which are obnoxious to that principle. In reality, while not mentioning any so-called 'rule' of interpretation, Clauson J in *Re Sigsworth* in effect applied the golden rule *in preference* to the literal rule since the only possible literal interpretation of 'issue' must include a son.

The importance of considerations of public policy, exemplified in *Re Sigsworth,* was reaffirmed in two later decisions of the Divisional Court of the Queen's Bench Division. In both cases the wording of the relevant statute was clear and yet, on grounds of public policy, an alternative meaning was found. These cases show that a statute is to be construed in the light of the principles of public policy accepted by the courts at the time when the statute was passed and which the draftsman and Parliament must have had in mind.

In the first of these cases, *R v National Insurance Commissioner (ex parte Connor)* [1981] 1 All ER 769, DC, Mrs Connor had been acquitted by a jury of the murder of her husband but found guilty of his manslaughter and placed on probation for two years. She applied for a widow's allowance under the Social Security Act 1975, s. 24(1) (since substituted by the Social Security Act 1986), which provided that:

A woman who has been widowed shall be entitled to a widow's allowance . . . . if:

    (a)   she was under pensionable age at the time when her late husband died; . . . and
    (b)   her late husband satisfied the contribution condition for a widow's allowance.

In Mrs Connor's case the necessary conditions were satisfied but it was decided that public policy disentitled her from receiving a widow's allowance. The Divisional Court held that although the Social Security Act 1975 laid down a self-contained code, it was to be applied subject to the rules of public policy which demanded that she should not receive a widow's allowance on account of her deliberate and conscious killing of her husband, even though the punishment for that crime had been only a probation order. Lord Lane CJ said (at p. 774):

The fact that there is no specific mention in the Act of disentitlement so far as a widow is concerned if she were to commit this sort of offence and so become a widow is merely an indication . . . that the draftsman realised perfectly well that he was drawing this Act against the background of the law as it stood at the time.

R v National Insurance Commissioner (ex parte Connor) was applied by the Divisional Court in *R v Secretary of State for the Home Department (ex parte Puttick)* [1981] 1 All ER 776, DC. The question before the court in this case was whether Astrid Puttick (née Proll), who had contracted a valid marriage to a United Kingdom citizen by means of fraud, forgery and perjury, was entitled to be registered as a United Kingdom citizen under the British Nationality Act 1948, s. 6(2) (since repealed), which (as amended) provided that:

. . . a woman who has been married to a citizen of the United Kingdom and Colonies shall be entitled, on making application therefor to the Secretary of State in the prescribed manner, to be registered as a citizen of the United Kingdom and Colonies.

Mrs Puttick's circumstances fell fairly and squarely within s. 6(2). It was held that the Home Secretary was entitled, despite the mandatory wording of s. 6(2) of the 1948 Act, to refuse to register Mrs Puttick as a United Kingdom citizen. She had secured her marriage, and therefore her entitlement to registration under s. 6(2), by fraud, forgery and perjury, and public policy would not allow her to benefit from her own criminality.

Donaldson LJ (at p. 780) quoted the words (cited above) of Lord Lane CJ in the *Connor* case and said of that decision that it:

provides authority for the proposition that statutory duties which are in terms absolute may nevertheless be subject to implied limitations based on principles of public policy accepted by the courts at the time when the Act is passed.

Of the case before him Donaldson LJ said (at p. 781) that:

when the British Nationality Act 1948 was enacted it was well established that public policy required the courts to refuse to assist a criminal to benefit from his crime at least in serious cases and that Parliament must be deemed to have been aware of this.

R v *National Insurance Commissioner (ex parte Connor)* [1981] 1 All ER 769 and *R* v *Secretary of State for the Home Department (ex parte Puttick)* [1981] 1 All ER 776 were considered (and, in effect, extended) by the Court of Appeal in the highly unusual case of *R* v *Registrar General (ex parte Smith)* [1991] 2 All ER 88, CA. Section 51(1) of the Adoption Act 1976 provides that

. . . the Registrar General shall on an application made in the prescribed manner by an adopted person a record of whose birth is kept by the Registrar General and who has attained the age of 18 years supply to that person on payment of the prescribed fee (if any) such information as is necessary to enable that person to obtain a certified copy of the record of his birth.

The applicant was detained in a secure mental hospital, having been convicted of the murder of a stranger in a public park and of the manslaughter of a cellmate in prison. The applicant had been adopted when only a few weeks old. He had later expressed extreme hatred for his adoptive parents and had killed his cellmate while under the delusion that he was killing his adoptive mother. He now wished to obtain a copy of his birth certificate. He satisfied the statutory conditions but the Registrar General refused to supply him with the necessary information on grounds of public policy: the medical advice given to the Registrar General pointed to a possibility that the applicant's natural mother might be placed in danger if the applicant was ever released and he knew her identity. Counsel for the applicant argued that the statute conferred an absolute right to the information and sought to distinguish the *Connor* and *Puttick* cases on the ground that the public policy principle did not apply to possible *future* criminal conduct.

It was held that, notwithstanding the absolute nature of the duty in s. 51(1), the Registrar General had not acted unlawfully in refusing to supply the necessary information. An absolute duty was, as a matter of statutory interpretation, subject to the principle of public policy that performance of it was not required if to do so would enable a person to benefit from a serious crime already committed by him, or which he intended to commit, or if there was a significant risk that performance of the duty would facilitate future criminal conduct resulting in danger to life.

The cases of *Connor, Puttick* and *Smith* were applied in *Whiston* v *Whiston* (1995) [1998] 1 All ER 423, CA, where it was held that, as a matter of public policy, a person who knowingly contracts a bigamous marriage cannot, after the marriage is declared void, claim financial relief under the Matrimonial Causes Act 1973 (despite its clear wording) because a person cannot be allowed to benefit from his own crime and bigamy is a serious criminal offence which strikes at the root of the institution of marriage. In the later case of *S-T* v *J* (1996) [1998] 1 All ER 431, CA, which was concerned with a marriage contracted by a transsexual, a majority of the Court of Appeal restricted the effect of *Whiston* to the crime of bigamy where it is the marriage itself which constitutes the criminal act. It was held that the commission of other serious criminal offences in relation to the marriage, such as perjury, would not, on public policy grounds, automatically bar a claim for financial relief. The court was unanimous, however, in dismissing the transsexual's claim in the exercise of the statutory discretion conferred by the Matrimonial Causes Act 1973 to take into account all the circumstances of the case.

It was thought by some that the so-called forfeiture rule of public policy operated too harshly in cases like Mrs Connor's. Parliament passed the Forfeiture Act 1982 in an effort to mitigate some of its harshness in individual cases.

The Act confers a judicial discretion to modify the effect of the forfeiture rule in respect of specified property rights which may otherwise have been forfeited. The Act is very limited in scope and does not seek to *abolish* the forfeiture rule. The Act defines the forfeiture rule as 'the rule of public policy which in certain circumstances precludes a person who has unlawfully killed another from acquiring a benefit in consequence of the killing' (Forfeiture Act 1982, s. 1(1)). If this rule is applicable in any case coming before a court, the judge is given a discretion to modify its effect (ibid., s. 2). In deciding how to exercise the discretion, the test is whether the justice of the case requires the effect of the forfeiture rule to be modified after considering the conduct of the killer and the deceased, together with other material circumstances (ibid., s. 2(2)). The Act does not affect the application of the forfeiture rule to murderers (ibid., s. 5). It only applies to those persons whose unlawful killing of another falls short of murder.

In *Re K (deceased)* [1985] 2 All ER 833, CA, a woman was beaten by her husband on many occasions over a six-year period. During an argument the woman killed her husband with a shotgun. At her trial she pleaded guilty to manslaughter and was placed on probation for two years. The question arose whether she should be allowed to inherit her deceased husband's estate under his will. It was held that, on the facts, the forfeiture rule would be modified to allow her to take under the will. She had been a loyal wife who had suffered extreme violence from the deceased and it would be unjust for her to be deprived of the benefits conferred on her by the will.

It has since been held at first instance that public policy does not, in any event, require the forfeiture rule to apply in every case of manslaughter as there is an enormous range of such cases. In *Re H (deceased)* [1990] 1 FLR 441, a husband who was severely depressed and taking anti-depressant drugs killed his wife. He pleaded guilty to manslaughter on the grounds of diminished responsibility. The trial judge accepted that he was not responsible for his actions and made a hospital order. He was named as the sole beneficiary under his wife's will and the question arose whether the forfeiture rule applied and, if so, whether the court would exercise its power to modify its effect. Gibson J held that the forfeiture rule only applied to a case of manslaughter where there had been deliberate, intentional and unlawful violence. This was not such a case and, accordingly, the forfeiture rule did not apply to it. The judge made it clear that if the rule had been applicable he would have modified its effect in the husband's favour under s. 2 of the Forfeiture Act 1982.

The earlier Court of Appeal decision in *Re Royse (deceased)* [1984] 3 All ER 339, CA, was not cited in *Re H (deceased)* [1990] 1 FLR 441. The two cases appear to be incompatible (see, e.g., *Jones* v *Roberts* [1995] 2 FLR 422, like *Re H (deceased)* a decision at first instance, in which the latter was doubted). Gibson J's conclusion in *Re H (deceased)* that the forfeiture rule does not apply unless the death has been caused by a deliberate and intentional act was disapproved by the Court of Appeal in *Dunbar* v *Plant* [1997] 4 All ER 289, CA. Here it was held that the forfeiture rule applied to the survivor of a suicide pact who had aided and abetted the suicide of her fiancé, even though the death was not caused by her deliberate and intentional act. On the facts, however, the forfeiture rule was modified under the 1982 Act to allow her to succeed to her fiancé's interest in their jointly owned house and to claim the proceeds of an insurance policy on his life.

The Social Security Commissioners have the same power to modify the effect of the forfeiture rule in relation to social security benefits as the courts have in relation to property rights (ibid., s. 4(1A)–(1H), as inserted by the Social Security Act 1986).

It must be stressed that the golden rule is used in most cases in its first, narrower, sense. And, in this application, the golden rule can only be used where there is a sensible alternative interpretation. If there is only one interpretation, or the second interpretation is as absurd as the first, the literal rule must be applied even though the result might be ridiculous, unless, that is, the result would be so undesirable that the court can be persuaded to adopt the golden rule in its broader sense.

8.10.2.3   The mischief rule

The mischief rule, sometimes referred to as the rule in *Heydon's case* (1584) 3 Co Rep 7a, allows the court to look at the state of the former law in order to discover the *mischief* in it which the present statute was designed to remedy. The mischief was, in former times, usually referred to in the preamble to the statute (*Black-Clawson International Ltd* v *Papierwerke etc. AG* [1975] AC 591, HL, *per* Lord Diplock at p. 638; *Sussex Peerage Case* (1844) 11 Cl & F 85, HL, *per* Tindal CJ, at p. 147; on the preamble, see further, para 8.10.4.3 below). In *Heydon's case* the position was explained thus by the court:

[F]our things are to be discerned and considered:

    1st   What was the common law before the making of the Act.

    2nd   What was the mischief and defect for which the common law did not provide.

    3rd   What remedy the Parliament hath resolved and appointed to cure the disease of the commonwealth. And

    4th   The true reason of the remedy; and then the office of all the Judges is always to make such construction as shall suppress the mischief, and advance the remedy.

In *Corkery* v *Carpenter* [1951] 1 KB 102, DC, a man was arrested without a warrant for being drunk in charge of a bicycle on the highway. By the Licensing Act 1872, s. 12, a person found drunk in charge of a 'carriage' on the highway may be arrested without a warrant. The Divisional Court held that a bicycle was a 'carriage' for the purposes of the 1872 Act and so the defendant had been properly arrested. The mischief aimed at by the Act was drunken persons on the highway in charge of some form of transport. If the court had applied the literal rule instead of the mischief rule the result might well have been different since it is arguable that a bicycle is not a 'carriage' within the ordinary meaning of that word.

The mischief rule was applied, and the presumption in favour of *mens rea* for criminal liability was rebutted, in *Maidstone Borough Council* v *Mortimer* [1980] 3 All ER 552, DC (for *mens rea* and the presumption in favour of it, see para 8.10.3.5 below). The defendant cut down an oak tree which, unknown to him, was protected by a tree preservation order under the Town and Country Planning Act 1971 (now the Town and Country Planning Act 1990). The local council prosecuted him for an offence in the magistrates' court. The justices dismissed the case on the ground that knowledge of the preservation order was an essential element of the offence. On appeal by the council, the Divisional Court allowed the appeal and held that the offence was committed whether or not the accused had knowledge of the preservation order. The mischief which the statute, read as a whole, was designed to prevent was the cutting down of protected trees without the consent of the local planning authority.

The House of Lords applied the mischief rule in *Royal College of Nursing of the United Kingdom* v *DHSS* [1981] 1 All ER 545, HL, a case which provoked considerable judicial disagreement.

By the Abortion Act 1967, s. 1(1), it is provided that no criminal offence is committed 'when a pregnancy is terminated by a registered medical practitioner' in specified circumstances. In 1972, surgical abortions in hospitals were replaced by medically induced abortions, which were not within the contemplation of Parliament in 1967. They involved pumping a chemical fluid into the mother's womb to induce premature labour. The medical induction was in two stages. First, the insertion, *by a doctor*, of a catheter into the womb. Secondly, the administration of the fluid into the womb via the catheter by means of a pump or drip. This second stage was what actually caused premature labour and termination of the pregnancy. However, the second stage was not carried out by a doctor but *by nurses* under the doctor's instructions while the doctor was absent but on call.

The question for the court was whether, in a medically induced abortion, the pregnancy was terminated 'by a registered medical practitioner'. At first instance, Woolf J granted a declaration that it was but the Court of Appeal unanimously reversed his decision. On a further appeal, the House of Lords, by a majority of three to two, held that the procedure was lawful. The decision of the Court of Appeal was reversed and that of the trial judge restored. On a count of heads, five out of the nine judges who sat in the three courts thought the medical induction procedure was unlawful while only four considered it to be lawful.

The decision of the majority of the House of Lords was based on two grounds. The first ground was the mischief which the Abortion Act 1967 was intended to remedy, (see especially [1981] 1 All ER 545, *per* Lord Diplock at p. 567). The mischief was the unsatisfactory and uncertain state of the law prior to 1967. The second ground was the policy of the 1967 Act (see especially *per* Lord Diplock at pp. 568–9 and Lord Keith of Kinkel at p. 575). This was to broaden the basis on which abortions might lawfully be obtained and to ensure that abortions were performed with proper skill in hygienic hospital conditions. These two grounds led the majority of their Lordships to the conclusion that s. 1(1) of the 1967 Act was satisfied so long as a doctor prescribed the treatment, remained in charge and accepted responsibility throughout, and the treatment was carried out in accordance with his directions. If these conditions were fulfilled it did not matter that the doctor was not actually present when the pregnancy was terminated.

The case of *Royal College of Nursing of the United Kingdom* v *DHSS* was one of considerable public importance. It does seem that the statutory language was strained so as to avoid the conclusion that since 1972 large numbers of doctors and nurses had been unwittingly performing illegal abortions. (Note the relief expressed by Lord Keith at p. 575.

See also Glanville Williams, 'The meaning of literal interpretation', (1981) 131 New LJ 1128, 1150.) Lord Wilberforce and Lord Edmund-Davies dissented on the ground that it could not be said that a pregnancy was terminated 'by a registered medical practitioner' when it was plainly not terminated by a registered medical practitioner. They felt that the majority in the House were not engaged in interpretation but in rewriting, or, as Lord Edmund-Davies put it, in 'redrafting with a vengeance' (p. 573).

By s. 1(1) of the Street Offences Act 1959, it is an offence for a 'common prostitute to loiter or solicit in a street or public place for the purpose of prostitution'. In *Director of Public Prosecutions* v *Bull* [1994] 4 All ER 411, DC, it was held that the term 'common prostitute' is limited to female prostitutes and does not include male prostitutes. This conclusion was reached in part by an application of the mischief rule. In identifying what mischief the 1959 Act was intended to remedy, the court relied upon the *Report of the Committee on Homosexual Offences and Prostitution* (the Wolfenden Report, Cmnd 247, 1957) which had led to the passing of the Act. This *Report* clearly saw the relevant mischief as one created by women.

The application of the mischief rule was preferred to a literal approach in *Director of Public Prosecutions* v *Johnson* [1995] 4 All ER 53, DC. Here it was decided that in the context of s. 5(1) of the Road Traffic Act 1988 (part of the breathalyser law by which it is an absolute offence to drive on a road while over the prescribed alcohol limit), the expression 'consuming alcohol' is wide enough to cover the ingestion of alcohol by any method notwithstanding the fact that the primary meaning of that expression is consuming it by mouth. The mischief at which s. 5 is aimed (identified with the help of the marginal note to the section) is the danger caused by drunken driving, and the court was of the view that that mischief is better remedied by an interpretation of s. 5 which renders irrelevant the route by which alcohol reaches a driver's body, whether it be by drinking, eating, injecting, sniffing, rubbing or in the form of a suppository.

In *Manchester City Council* v *McCann* [1999] 2 WLR 590, CA, the Court of Appeal applied the mischief rule when it decided that a threat is an 'insult' within the meaning of s. 118(1)(a) of the County Courts Act 1984 (first enacted in the County Courts Act 1846), which enables the county courts to deal with any person who 'wilfully insults the judge . . . or any juror or witness, or any officer of the court . . .'. The mischief was identified as the need to protect the persons mentioned as participants in the court process. It was said that if the court could deal with 'insults' but not 'threats', it would not be able to give immediate protection from interference to those who need it most (see [1999] 2 WLR 590, *per* Lord Woolf MR at p. 598). Although, literally, an 'insult' is not necessarily a 'threat', Parliament was taken to have intended that the protection should extend to both. (See further on this case, para 5.4.3.)

By ss. 37(5) and 40(1)(b) of the Police and Criminal Evidence Act 1984, a person who has been arrested but not yet charged must have his detention at a police station reviewed periodically. The review officer is required to make a written record of the grounds for detention 'in the presence of the person arrested', and, at that time, to inform the detainee of those grounds. In *R* v *Chief Constable of Kent Constabulary (ex parte Kent Police Federation Joint Branch Board)* (1999) *The Times*, 1 December, DC, the Chief Constable had proposed that such reviews should be conducted by video link in the majority of cases. It was held that this would be unlawful since video link reviews would not take place 'in the presence of' the detainee. In so holding, the court identified the mischief as the prolonged detention of suspects without periodic reviews of their detention and emphasised the need to give a meaning to the statutory language which best effected the intention of

Parliament. Although the statute did not refer to 'physical presence', 'presence' in ordinary parlance meant 'physical presence' and the court was not prepared to hold, even taking a modern and progressive approach, that a record was made by a review officer 'in the presence of' the detainee if they were not in the same place and in each other's company at the time. Parliament, it was said, had provided for a face-to-face confrontation, and if it was felt desirable to make use of modern technology it was for Parliament to make the change and not for the courts.

8.10.2.4   The statute must be read as a whole

The words used in a statute must not be interpreted out of their context, for *noscitur a sociis,* a word is known by the company it keeps. Each section in a statute must be read subject to every other section, which may explain or modify it. If there is an irreconcilable conflict between two sections in the same statute, or between two subsections within the same section, the correct test to be applied is to determine which is the leading provision and which the subordinate provision. The statute will then be interpreted so as to give effect to the leading provision. The principle of interpretation (if it ever existed) that the provision occurring later in the statute prevails over that occurring earlier is long since obsolete (*Re Marr and another (bankrupts)* [1990] 2 All ER 880, CA, *per* Nicholls LJ at p. 886, applying a dictum of Lord Herschell LC in *Institute of Patent Agents* v *Lockwood* [1894] AC 347, HL, at p. 360 and disapproving a dictum in *Wood* v *Riley* (1867) LR 3 CP 26 at p. 27).

Where the statute to be construed is ambiguous and forms part of a statutory code intended by Parliament to achieve a distinct purpose, the other statute(s) in the code should be looked at as well. In *Oliver Ashworth (Holdings) Ltd* v *Ballard (Kent) Ltd* [1999] 2 All ER 791, CA, it was found that s. 18 of the Distress for Rent Act 1737 was ambiguous about the extent of a landlord's right to double rent and that, consequently, the 1737 Act and the Landlord and Tenant Act 1730, which together constituted a single code, should be read collectively as a whole. (See further on this case, para 8.10.6 below.)

The rule of interpretation that the statute must be read as a whole gives rise to a presumption that, so far as possible, every word used in the statute is to be given some effective meaning. If, however, there is a word or phrase for which no sensible meaning can be found the court may disregard it if to do otherwise would render the statute absurd or incapable of achieving its evident purpose. (For a recent example where the House of Lords dismissed statutory words as mere surplusage, see *R* v *R (rape: marital exemption)* [1991] 4 All ER 481, para 9.3.2.7.)

One particular application of the general rule that the statute must be read as a whole is *expressio unius est exclusio alterius* — the express mention of a person or thing excludes by implication other persons or things not mentioned. In *Tempest* v *Kilner* (1846) 3 CB 249, it was held that the Statute of Frauds 1677, s. 17 (now repealed), which required a contract for the sale of 'goods, wares and merchandise' for £10 or more to be evidenced in writing, did not apply to a contract for the sale of stocks and shares. The latter were not 'goods, wares and merchandise' and were excluded by implication because they received no express mention.

Another particular, and more common, application of the general rule is the so-called *ejusdem generis* ('of the same kind') rule. This provides that general words which follow particular words must be limited to meanings similar to those of the particular words. *Powell* v *Kempton Park Racecourse Co.* [1899] AC 143, HL, concerned the Betting Act 1853, which had prohibited the keeping of a 'house, office, room or other place' for the purpose of betting with people who called there. The question for the House of Lords was whether

Tattersall's ring, an outdoor place at a racecourse, fell within the words 'other place'. It was held that it did not because the specific places mentioned were indoor places and the words 'other place' must be construed *ejusdem generis*. (The 1853 Act has been repealed and the absolute prohibition replaced by a system of licensing governed by the Betting, Gaming and Lotteries Act 1963.)

In *DPP* v *Jordan* [1977] AC 699, HL, the appellant was charged with possessing obscene films, books, and magazines for publication for gain contrary to the Obscene Publications Act 1959. The appellant wished to rely on the defence of 'public good' and sought to adduce expert evidence that the articles, though obscene, had some psychotherapeutic value for sexual deviants. The House of Lords held that such evidence had been rightly excluded at the appellant's trial. The defence of 'public good' is contained in s. 4(1) of the 1959 Act which says that there should be no conviction if it is proved that publication of an obscene article

is justified as being for the public good on the ground that it is in the interests of science, literature, art or learning, *or of other objects of general concern* (italics supplied).

It was not suggested that the obscene articles in question had any scientific, literary or artistic merit, and the House of Lords decided that they did not fall within the italicised words, which must be construed as falling within the same field or dimension as 'science, literature, art or learning'.

In *Wood* v *Commissioner of Police of the Metropolis* [1986] 2 All ER 570, DC, it was held that a piece of glass accidentally broken was not an offensive weapon within the meaning of the words 'any gun, pistol, hanger, cutlass, bludgeon, or other offensive weapon' in s. 4 of the Vagrancy Act 1824. The general words 'other offensive weapon' had to be construed *ejusdem generis* with the preceding words, which comprised a list of articles made or adapted for the purpose of causing injury. (The words of s. 4 of the Vagrancy Act 1824 considered in *Wood* v *Commissioner of Police of the Metropolis* were repealed by the Public Order Act 1986, s. 40(3) and sch. 3.)

In *Williams* v *Williams* [1987] 3 All ER 257, CA, it was held that paying-in slips and paid cheques kept by a bank after the conclusion of a banking transaction, were not 'other records', and, therefore, not 'bankers' books', within the definition 'ledgers, day books, cash books, account books and other records used in the ordinary business of the bank' given in the Bankers' Books Evidence Act 1879 s. 9, as amended. In consequence, the paying-in slips and paid cheques could not be made the subject of a court order for inspection under the 1879 Act for the purpose of legal proceedings.

In *A. T. & T. Istel Ltd* v *Tully* [1992] 3 All ER 523, HL, the claimants brought proceedings against the defendants claiming, *inter alia*, damages for fraud, and were granted a freezing injunction (*Mareva* injunction) (see para 10.4.2.6) in wide terms. The defendants success-fully applied for a variation of the injunction on the ground that compliance with it might tend to incriminate them. The claimants appealed against the variation, arguing that the proceedings were for the infringement of rights pertaining to intellectual property, namely commercial information, and that the defendants had accordingly lost their privilege against self-incrimination by virtue of s. 72 of the Supreme Court Act 1981 (see para 10.4.2.5). By s. 72, in civil proceedings in the High Court for 'infringement of rights pertaining to any intellectual property' a person is not excused from answering questions or from complying with any order made in those proceedings (such as an order for discovery of documents) by reason of the fact that his answers or information might tend to incriminate him or his spouse. By s. 72(5) '"intellectual property" means any patent, trade mark, copyright, registered design, technical or commercial information or other intellectual property . . .' Although the claimants' appeal was allowed on other grounds, the House of Lords held that the words 'commercial information' in s. 72(5) had to be construed *ejusdem generis* with the other examples of 'intellectual property' listed in the subsection, and since the information sought by the claimants was not concerned with the 'infringement of rights pertaining to any intellectual property', but with their claim for damages for fraud, they could not rely on s. 72.

It should be noted that the *ejusdem generis* rule cannot apply if the particular words do not belong to any category (*R* v *Payne* (1866) 35 LJMC 170). It was for that reason that the House of Lords held that the *ejusdem generis* rule did not apply in *Re C (a minor) (interim care order: residential assessment)* [1996] 4 All ER 871, HL, in which the question arose whether the court has power under s. 38(6) of the Children Act 1989 to direct a local authority to carry out, and pay for, a residential assessment of a child and the parents together. Section 38(6) provides:

> Where the court makes an interim care order, or interim supervision order, it may give such directions . . . as it considers appropriate with regard to the medical or psychiatric examination or other assessment of the child . . .

This provision is ambiguous. The Court of Appeal adopted a narrow interpretation and held that the court has no such power because the words 'other assessment of the child', when construed *ejusdem generis* with the words 'medical or psychiatric examination', exclude an examination or assessment of any person other than the child. The House of Lords, however, rejected this approach, holding that the *ejusdem generis* rule did not apply to the case. The subsection refers not to the 'medical, psychiatric or other *examination* of the child' but to 'other *assessment* of the child'. There was, therefore, no category or 'genus' on which the rule could operate. A wider interpretation commended itself to the House of Lords based upon the purpose of the subsection, viz., to allow the court to gather whatever information is necessary to enable it to decide later whether to make a final care order. This purposive interpretation led their Lordships to the conclusion that the power of the court under s. 38(6) includes the power to order or prohibit any assessment which involves the participation of the child and the parents together.

It is not easy to apply the *ejusdem generis* rule if the general words are followed by a word like 'whatsoever' because such a word indicates that the general words are intended to be completely general and open-ended.

There must be at least two particular words to constitute a category or *genus*. Thus, in *Allen* v *Emmerson* [1944] KB 362, DC, it was held that a funfair was a place of amusement, within the statutory expression 'theatres and other places of amusement', even though not *ejusdem generis* with the word 'theatres'.

8.10.3   Presumptions

8.10.3.1   Against an alteration of the common law
Parliament is supreme and can, therefore, alter the existing common law but an intention to change it will not be implied. If a statute is capable of two interpretations, one involving an alteration of the common law and the other one not, the second interpretation will be preferred. The Criminal Evidence Act 1898 allowed an accused's spouse to be called as a

witness for the prosecution or the defence if the accused was charged with certain offences listed in the Schedule to the Act. It also provided that the consent of the accused was not required. In *Leach* v *R* [1912] AC 305, HL, the question arose whether this meant that a spouse in such a case could be *compelled* to be a witness for the prosecution. The House of Lords held that the spouse was merely competent, not compellable, as a witness. To have decided that the spouse was compellable would have involved too fundamental a change in the pre–1898 law, under which a spouse was simply not competent to give evidence for the prosecution. (Note that under s. 80 of the Police and Criminal Evidence Act 1984 the accused's spouse became, by express words, a compellable witness for the prosecution in cases involving violence to the spouse, or violence to or a sexual offence against a person under 16, or attempts or conspiracies to commit such offences.)

8.10.3.2   Against deprivation of liberty

It is presumed that Parliament does not intend to deprive a person of his liberty. If it does so wish, then clear, express words must be used. Thus, in defence of individual freedom, the House of Lords, in *R* v *Secretary of State for the Home Department (ex parte Khawaja)* [1983] 2 WLR 321, was prepared to depart from its own earlier decision in the *Zamir* case ([1980] AC 930; paras 4.5 and 9.3.2.2). In *Khawaja,* Lord Scarman said (at p. 344):

> If Parliament intends to exclude effective judicial review of the exercise of a power in restraint of liberty, it must make its meaning crystal clear.

Their Lordships were of the opinion that the immigration statute with which they were concerned did not have the effect of placing the burden of proof upon an immigrant to show that the decision of the Home Office to detain him was unjustified.

Even in cases where Parliament has expressly provided for deprivation of liberty, as in the Mental Health Act 1983, the words used will be construed in a way which permits the least possible interference with the liberty of the subject (*R* v *Hallstrom (ex parte W) (No. 2)* [1986] 2 All ER 306; see also *R* v *Governor of Durham Prison (ex parte Singh)* [1984] 1 All ER 983 — Home Secretary's power to detain a person under the Immigration Act 1971 pending deportation is subject to implied limitations).

8.10.3.3   Against deprivation of property or interference with private rights

Statutes which encroach on the rights of subjects should be interpreted wherever possible so as to respect such rights (*Glassbrook Bros* v *Leyson* [1933] 2 KB 91, CA). To this end there is a presumption of interpretation that Parliament does not intend to deprive a person of his property or interfere with his private rights — at least, not without compensation. In *Managers of the Metropolitan Asylum District* v *Hill* (1881) 6 App Cas 193, HL, the appellants had been given statutory authority under the Metropolitan Poor Act 1867 (since repealed) to provide asylums for the reception and relief of the sick, insane or infirm. Acting under this authority, they built a smallpox hospital in Hampstead where it caused a nuisance to the respondent and other residents of the neighbourhood. The statute contained no provision for compensation. The House of Lords held that the appellants would be restrained by an injunction from using the hospital in such a manner as to create a nuisance. The appellants' statutory authority was permissive, not mandatory, and must be exercised so as not to interfere with private rights.

In *British Airports Authority* v *Ashton* [1983] 3 All ER 6, DC, it was held that the Trade Union and Labour Relations Act 1974, s. 15(1), which, as amended, declares when picketing is lawful, did not authorise picketing on land against the owner's wishes. Such action is not *expressly* authorised by the section and the court said it would be 'astonishing if Parliament intended that such a right should be *implied*' (ibid., *per* Mann J at p. 13).

Cases like *Managers of the Metropolitan Asylum District* v *Hill* will be rare in contemporary society because a statute will not easily achieve its object unless it confers the right to interfere with private interests. The clear wording of a statute can deprive the citizen of the full and proper enjoyment of his land by authorising the commission of a nuisance without any compensation. Where the statute is sufficiently clear, the citizen is expected simply to put up with the infringement of his rights without any financial recompense. (See, e.g., *Allen* v *Gulf Oil Refining Ltd* [1981] 1 All ER 353, HL; but cf *Tate & Lyle Industries Ltd* v *Greater London Council* [1983] 1 All ER 1159, HL.)

In a modern, controversial instance — the War Damage Act 1965 (para 8.10.3.6 below) — the words used were clear enough to abolish (and retrospectively at that) any common-law right the citizen may have had to claim compensation from the Crown in respect of lawful destruction of, or damage to, his property caused on behalf of the Crown during, or in contemplation of, a war.

Subjects can only be deprived of their property by the Crown in the form of taxation under the authority of a statute expressed in clear words (*Bowles* v *Bank of England* [1913] 1 Ch 57; *Attorney-General* v *Wilts United Dairies* (1922) 91 LJKB 897, HL). If the meaning of the statute is clear the tax must be paid, even though this may result in hardship to the individual taxpayer, for Parliament must be taken to have been aware that some hardship might be involved (*Leedale* v *Lewis* [1982] 3 All ER 808, HL; para 8.10.2.1 above). If, however, the meaning of the statute is *not* clear it may possibly be legitimate for the court to choose an interpretation favourable to the taxpayer on the ground that he can only be taxed by *clear* words (*Leedale* v *Lewis* [1982] 3 All ER 808, *per* Lord Wilberforce at p. 816).

8.10.3.4   That the Crown is not bound unless the Act says so expressly or by necessary implication

This presumption applies whether or not the statute in question is one which was passed for the public benefit (*Lord Advocate* v *Dumbarton District Council* [1990] 1 All ER 1, HL, where it was held that the Crown was not bound, either expressly or by necessary implication, by the relevant Scottish planning and roads legislation to obtain local authority consent before closing a stretch of road and storing building materials thereon during the construction of an improved security fence at the Faslane submarine base).

It has been said to be desirable for the sake of clarity that statutes should state expressly (rather than leaving it to necessary implication) whether the Crown is to be bound by any, and if so which, of their provisions (*Lord Advocate* v *Dumbarton District Council,* above, *per* Lord Keith at p. 18).

Clarity in this matter is particularly important in those areas of law where the potential legal liability of the Crown is very wide, as in occupier's liability and employer's liability. The Crown is the occupier of a great deal of land and the employer of a great number of people; it is expressly bound by the Occupiers' Liability Acts of 1957 and 1984, by the Equal Pay Act 1970, by important parts of the Health and Safety at Work etc. Act 1974, by the Sex Discrimination Act 1975, and by some important parts of the Employment Rights Act 1996 (including the provisions on unfair dismissal but excluding the provisions on redundancy payments).

8.10.3.5 That mens rea is required in criminal offences

All common-law offences require proof of *mens rea* (guilty mind or intention) before a person can be convicted. In the case of statutory offences it is *presumed* that Parliament intended no liability without proof of *mens rea*. For the vast majority of offences a person cannot be properly convicted unless he committed the *actus reus* (forbidden act) with *mens rea*.

When creating new statutory offences, Parliament regularly provides definitions which are confined to the *actus reus* and are silent about *mens rea*. Here, '[t]he common law presumes that, unless Parliament indicated otherwise, the appropriate mental element is an unexpressed ingredient of every statutory offence' (*B (a minor)* v *Director of Public Prosecutions* [2000] 1 All ER 833, HL, *per* Lord Nicholls at p. 836). The weight to be given to the presumption increases with the seriousness of the offence since the punishment is more severe and the stigma of a conviction is graver (ibid., per Lord Nicholls, at p. 839). Parliament has been criticised for failing to state in clear terms whether or not *mens rea* is required when creating or restating offences (ibid., *per* Lord Hutton, at p. 856).

In *Harding* v *Price* [1948] 1 KB 695, DC, a motorist was prosecuted for failing to report an accident contrary to the Road Traffic Act 1930, s. 22 (see now Road Traffic Act 1988, s. 170, as amended by Road Traffic Act 1991, sch. 4). He did not know about the accident and the Divisional Court held he was not guilty of the offence because he lacked *mens rea*. In *Sweet* v *Parsley* [1970] AC 132, HL, a schoolteacher was convicted of being concerned in the management of premises used for the smoking of cannabis contrary to s. 5 of the Dangerous Drugs Act 1965 (see now Misuse of Drugs Act 1971, s. 8). The cannabis was used by her tenants and she knew nothing about it. The House of Lords held she was not guilty of the offence, and her conviction was quashed, because she did not *know* the premises were being used for the unlawful purpose and did not *intend* them to be so used. In *R* v *Phekoo* [1981] 3 All ER 84, CA, it was held that the offence of harassment of a residential occupier, under s. 1(3) of the Protection from Eviction Act 1977, is not committed unless the accused *knows* that the victim is a residential occupier and not, for example, a squatter. In *B (a minor)* v *Director of Public Prosecutions*, above, the House of Lords decided that in the offence of inciting a child under 14 to commit an act of gross indecency, contrary to s. 1(1) of the Indecency with Children Act 1960, the prosecution is required to prove that the defendant lacked an honest belief that the child was aged 14 or over. Accordingly, the defendant, a 15 year-old boy who had repeatedly asked a 13 year-old girl to perform oral sex with him, was held not to have committed the offence since he honestly believed that the girl was over 14.

The presumption that proof of *mens rea* is required in statutory offences can be rebutted either by express words in a statute or by implication. Offences which do not require proof of *mens rea* are called crimes of *strict liability* and are usually created in the public interest. The question whether *mens rea* is required or not must be determined by interpretation of the language of the particular statutory provision taken in conjunction with the subject matter and the structure of the statute as a whole (*Wings Ltd* v *Ellis* [1984] 3 All ER 577, HL, *per* Lord Scarman at p. 589). The presumption that *mens rea* is required is particularly strong where the offence is truly criminal in character, as in *Sweet* v *Parsley*, above, and *B (a minor)* v *Director of Public Prosecutions*, above. Indeed, it seems that the only situation in which the presumption can be rebutted is where (a) the particular statute deals with an issue of social concern, such as public safety, health or morals, *and* (b) it can be shown that the creation of strict liability will be effective to promote the objects of the statute by encouraging greater vigilance to prevent the commission of the forbidden act (*Gammon*

(Hong Kong) Ltd v *Attorney-General of Hong Kong* [1984] 2 All ER 503, PC, *per* Lord Scarman at p. 508).

In *Customs and Excise Commissioners* v *Air Canada* [1991] 1 All ER 570, CA, cargo unloaded at Heathrow Airport from a Tristar aeroplane making a regular scheduled flight was found to contain a large quantity of cannabis resin with an estimated street value of £800,000. Under s. 141(1)(a) of the Customs and Excise Management Act 1979, using an aircraft for the carriage of a thing liable to forfeiture (in this case the cannabis resin) renders the aircraft itself liable to forfeiture. The preliminary issue arose, *inter alia,* whether the defendants' lack of knowledge of the presence of prohibited drugs on their aeroplane would be a defence to the Customs and Excise Commissioners' claim for forfeiture of the aeroplane. Tucker J held that it would. In unanimously reversing his decision, the Court of Appeal was of the firm opinion that the wording of s. 141(1)(a) clearly and unambiguously allowed for forfeiture of the aeroplane without proof of *mens rea* on the part of the defendants. The dictum of Lord Scarman in *Gammon (Hong Kong) Ltd* v *Attorney-General of Hong Kong* [1984] 2 All ER 503, PC, at p. 508 (see above) was distinguished on the ground that breach of s. 141(1)(a) of the Customs and Excise Management Act 1979 does not in itself constitute a criminal offence but gives rise instead to *civil* proceedings. Reference, therefore, to cases on the presumption of *mens rea* in relation to criminal offences is misleading (see [1991] 1 All ER 570, CA, *per* Purchas LJ at p. 586 and Balcombe LJ at pp. 587–8).

When Air Canada later took its case to the European Court of Human Rights it was held that the seizure of the aeroplane and its subsequent release on payment of £50,000 did not amount to an unjustified interference with the peaceful enjoyment of possessions as guaranteed in art. 1 of the First Protocol of the European Convention on Human Rights. It was further held that there had been no violation of Air Canada's civil rights, guaranteed under art. 6 of the Convention, because the airline had not been denied access to a fair hearing before an independent and impartial tribunal (*Air Canada* v *United Kingdom* (1995) *The Times,* 13 May, ECHR).

Parliament has created a number of offences which do not require proof of *mens rea;* for example, speeding and parking offences and the offence of selling liquor to a person who is already drunk.

In *R* v *Hussain* [1981] 2 All ER 287, CA, it was decided that possessing a firearm without a certificate is, under s. 1(1)(a) of the Firearms Act 1968, an offence of strict liability and that the prosecution does not have to prove the accused knew that the article was a firearm. It was held in *R* v *Bradish* [1990] 1 All ER 460, CA, that the offence of being in possession of a prohibited weapon (a spray canister containing CS gas) contrary to s. 5(1) of the Firearms Act 1968 is one of strict liability. It was, therefore, no defence for the defendant to attempt to show that, by reason of the fact that the gas was concealed within the canister, he did not know, and could not reasonably have been expected to know, that the article in his possession was a prohibited weapon. It was, in any event, further held that the weapon consisted of the canister and gas *in combination* and not merely the noxious gas by itself. The imposition of strict liability in these circumstances furthers the purpose of the firearms legislation, namely the tight control of dangerous weapons in the public interest, and is in line with the interpretation adopted by the Court of Appeal in *R* v *Hussain,* above, in relation to s. 1 of the same Act.

In *R* v *Heron* [1982] 1 All ER 993, HL, the House of Lords held that the offence of falsely making or counterfeiting coin, contrary to s. 1(1) of the Coinage Offences Act 1936, does not depend on any intention to deceive and defraud in addition to an intention to make the coins in question. In *Chilvers* v *Rayner* [1984] 1 All ER 843, DC, the offence created by

s. 1(1)(b) of the Hallmarking Act 1973 of supplying or offering to supply an unhallmarked article to which is applied a description indicating that it is wholly or partly made of gold, silver or platinum, was held to be an offence of strict liability. In *Wings Ltd v Ellis* [1984] 3 All ER 577, HL, it was decided that since the purpose of the Trade Descriptions Act 1968 is the protection of the public through the maintenance of trading standards it followed that the offence, created by s. 14(1)(a) of that Act, of making a statement knowing it to be false does not require proof of *mens rea*. In *Pharmaceutical Society of Great Britain v Storkwain Ltd* [1986] 2 All ER 635, HL, s. 58(2)(a) of the Medicines Act 1968, which prohibits the retail sale or supply of certain medicinal products except in accordance with a prescription given by an appropriate practitioner, was held to have created an offence of strict liability. It follows that a pharmacist who supplies prohibited drugs on a forged prescription and without any fault on his part nevertheless commits an offence. In *Kirkland v Robinson* [1987] Crim LR 643, DC, it was decided that possession of a live wild bird, contrary to s. 1(2)(a) of the Wildlife and Countryside Act 1981, is an offence of strict liability which does not require proof of knowledge that the bird was a wild bird protected by the Act.

In *R v Brockley* (1994) 99 Cr App R 385, CA, it was held that the offence, created by s. 11 of the Company Directors (Disqualification) Act 1986, of acting as director of a company while an undischarged bankrupt except with leave of the court was one of strict liability. It followed that a mistaken but genuine belief that the bankruptcy had been discharged was no defence to the crime. Applying Lord Scarman's dictum in *Gammon (Hong Kong) Ltd v Attorney-General of Hong Kong* [1984] 2 All ER 503, PC, at p. 508 (see above), it was said that the mischief aimed at by s. 11 was clearly one of social concern and that the creation of strict liability would promote the object of the section by obliging bankrupts to ensure that their bankruptcy was in fact discharged before they acted as company directors. Lord Scarman's dictum was applied again in *R v Bezzina* [1994] 3 All ER 964, CA, where it was held that s. 3(1) of the Dangerous Dogs Act 1991 is aimed at securing public safety and creates an offence of strict liability committed by the owner or handler of a dog which is 'dangerously out of control in a public place'. It was also applied in *R v Blake* [1997] 1 All ER 963, CA, in which it was decided that the offence under s. 1(1) of the Wireless Telegraphy Act 1949 of using a wireless telegraphy station or apparatus without a licence was created in the interests of public safety and is, therefore, one of strict liability. It follows that a person may be convicted of the offence where he knew he was using the station or apparatus but had no intention of, and was unaware that he was, broadcasting anything.

The offence of selling tobacco 'to a person apparently under the age of 16 years', contrary to s. 7(1) of the Children and Young Persons Act 1933, was held to be one of strict liability in *St Helen's Metropolitan Borough Council v Hill* (1992) 156 JP 602, DC, where a boy aged 12 had been sold a packet of cigarettes by a shop assistant while the shopowner was in the stockroom and unaware of the sale. The shopowner was charged with an offence. As a general rule an employer is not liable for his employee's crimes committed in the course of his employment but there is an exception in the case of crimes of strict liability and the shopowner was held to have committed the offence. (Note that s. 7 of the Children and Young Persons Act 1933 has been amended by the Children and Young Persons (Protection from Tobacco) Act 1991. The word 'apparently' is removed from s. 7(1) and a new s. 7(1A) is added, creating a defence for a person charged under s. 7(1) if he can prove that he 'took all reasonable precautions and exercised all reasonable diligence to avoid the commission of the offence'. At the same time, the 1991 Act increased the penalties for selling tobacco to persons under the age of 16.)

In *Harrow London Borough Council* v *Shah* [1999] 3 All ER 302, DC, a 13 and a half year-old boy was sold a National Lottery ticket by an employee of a shopowner, who, at the time, was not in the shop but was working in a back room. The employee reasonably, but mistakenly, believed that the boy was at least 16 years old. The shopowner was charged with the offence, created by s. 13 of the National Lottery etc Act 1993 and reg. 3 of the National Lottery Regulations 1994 (SI 1994, No. 189), of selling a National Lottery ticket to a person under the age of 16.

In reaching the conclusion that the offence is one of strict liability, the court applied the *dictum* of Lord Scarman in *Gammon (Hong Kong) Ltd* v *Attorney-General of Hong Kong* [1984] 2 All ER 503, PC, at p. 508 (see above), and decided that the offence is not truly criminal in character, the statutory provisions deal with gambling, an issue of social concern, and the imposition of strict liability will encourage greater vigilance in preventing the commission of the *actus reus* (see [1999] 3 All ER 302, DC, *per* Mitchell J. at pp. 306–7). Since the offence is one of strict liability, it follows that the prosecution need only prove a sale to a particular person who was under 16 at the time; it does not have to prove that the defendant or his agent was aware of the buyer's age or was reckless as to his age. Moreover, as in *St Helen's Metropolitan Borough Council* v *Hill*, above, it is no defence to the shopowner that the ticket was not sold by him but by his employee.

There is little or no moral stigma attached to offences of strict liability and, although ignorance of the facts will not prevent conviction, it can be reflected in the sentence imposed. In *Maidstone Borough Council* v *Mortimer* [1980] 3 All ER 552, DC, in which the defendant was held guilty of the offence of cutting down a protected tree even though he had no knowledge of the tree preservation order, the court emphasised the public interest in preserving protected trees and that the defendant's moral innocence could be reflected in the penalty imposed on him by the magistrates, to whom the case was sent back with a direction to convict. (See also *R* v *Wells Street Metropolitan Stipendiary Magistrate (ex parte Westminster City Council)* [1986] 3 All ER 4, DC, *per* Watkins LJ at p. 8.) In *St. Helen's Metropolitan Borough Council* v *Hill*, above, the Divisional Court did not consider the case a suitable one to be sent back with a direction to convict even though it was held that the magistrates were wrong to have acquitted the defendant in the first place. In the court's view, the penalty would have been a modest one as it was nearly two years since the offence was committed and the local authority's appeal had been brought solely to establish the principle that the offence in question was one of strict liability. In *Harrow London Borough Council* v *Shah*, above, the Divisional Court sent the case back to the magistrates' court with a suggestion that leniency in sentencing would be appropriate given the employee's state of mind and the obvious care with which the shopowner conducted the sale of National Lottery tickets.

8.10.3.6   Against retrospective effect

There is a presumption of interpretation that statutes do not operate retrospectively. This presumption is particularly important in Acts creating crimes for it would be oppressive and abhorrent for a statute to make criminal retroactively an act which was quite lawful at the time it was done.

At the same time, if an Act abolishes a crime by repealing a statutory provision the repeal does not affect the institution or continuation of legal proceedings in respect of offences alleged to have been committed before the date of the repeal unless a contrary intention appears in the repealing Act. This rule is contained in s. 16(1) of the Interpretation Act 1978 and means, in other words, that the repeal does not automatically legalise conduct which was unlawful before the repeal took effect. The rule was relied upon by the House of Lords in *Commissioner of Police of the Metropolis* v *Simeon* [1982] 2 All ER 813, HL, a case which arose out of the repeal of the 'sus' law in 1981. By the Criminal Attempts Act 1981, that part of s. 4 of the Vagrancy Act 1824 which applied to suspected persons and reputed thieves frequenting or loitering in certain places with intent to commit an arrestable offence was repealed. The question before the House was whether the repeal affected the position of a person charged, but not tried, under the 'sus' law before the repeal took effect. The House of Lords, unable to discover any 'contrary intention' in the Criminal Attempts Act 1981, applied the normal rule and held that the accused's position was not affected by the repeal. Mr Simeon was not punished, however, as the Metropolitan Police Commissioner had made a policy decision not to proceed any further against him or against any other person in a similar position within the Metropolitan Police District. The Commissioner had appealed to the House of Lords merely in order to have an important point of principle clarified.

It is, of course, quite competent for Parliament to pass retrospective legislation, but clear, express words must be used. Retrospective tax legislation is perhaps the commonest example. Another notable example is the War Damage Act 1965, which was passed specifically to overrule retroactively the decision of the House of Lords in *Burmah Oil Co. Ltd* v *Lord Advocate* [1965] AC 75, and to deprive Burmah Oil of the victory gained therein. The company's oil installations in Burma (then a British colony) had been destroyed by the British forces in 1942 to prevent them being captured by invading Japanese forces. The company, which was registered in Scotland, now sued the Crown for compensation. The Crown argued that no compensation was payable when property was destroyed under the royal prerogative. The House of Lords held that compensation was payable. An inquiry as to damages was ordered but, in the end, the taxpayer was relieved by Act of Parliament of the burden of having to pay compensation.

The War Crimes Act 1991 is expressly made retrospective in operation. This statute allows the Attorney-General to authorise proceedings for homicide committed in Germany or German occupied territory during the Second World War to be brought against a person in the United Kingdom regardless of his nationality at the time of the alleged offence. The Act applies only:

(a) to offences which were committed between 1 September 1939 and 5 June 1945 and which were war crimes in that they violated the laws and customs of war; and

(b) to persons who were on 8 March 1990, or have subsequently become, British citizens or resident in the United Kingdom, the Isle of Man or the Channel Islands.

There is power by Order in Council to extend the provisions of the statute to the Isle of Man, any of the Channel Islands or any colony.

There was formerly no presumption against retroactivity as regards *procedural* matters. Indeed, there was authority for the view that since statutory changes in procedure are beneficial they are always to operate retrospectively unless there is a good reason why they should not. A good reason might be that retroactivity would cause unfairness or injustice.

Doubt was cast on this authority in *L'Office Cherifien des Phosphates* v *Yamashita-Shinnihon Steamship Co. Ltd* [1994] 1 All ER 20, HL, where the House of Lords was critical of an approach for ascertaining the retrospective effect of statutes which depends upon a distinction between accrued substantive rights on the one hand (where the presumption against retroactivity applies) and procedural rights on the other (where the presumption does not apply). As Lord Mustill pointed out (at p. 32, the rest of their Lordships agreeing with him), this distinction is both misleading (since some procedural rights are more valuable than some substantive rights) and difficult to apply in practice (since it proceeds on the assumption that every right is capable of classification as either substantive or procedural).

While reaffirming the existence of the presumption against retroactivity (the basis of which was described as 'simple fairness'), the House was concerned that the mechanical application of 'generalised presumptions and maxims' when seeking to discover the intention of Parliament would merely lead the court to treat all statutes, and all situations in which they apply, as if they were the same ([1994] 1 All ER 20 *per* Lord Mustill at p. 29). Their Lordships preferred an approach whereby the individual statute is scrutinised with a view to determining whether the consequences of retroactivity would be so unfair that the words used by Parliament cannot have been intended to mean what they appear to say. In determining this, several factors must be weighed together. These factors, each of which is capable of varying from one case to another, are the degree of suggested retroactivity, the value of the right affected, the clarity of the statutory language and the circumstances in which the statute was passed.

L'Office Cherifien des Phosphates v *Yamashita-Shinnihon Steamship Co. Ltd* was concerned with whether, under the Arbitration Act 1950, s. 13A (inserted with effect from 1 January 1992 by the Courts and Legal Services Act 1990), an arbitrator could take into account a claimant's 'inordinate and inexcusable delay' occurring before 1 January 1992. A shipowner's complaint about damage to a vessel caused by a charterer was referred to arbitration in 1985, but neither party took any major step in the proceedings between 1986 and 1991. In 1992, the charterer applied under s. 13A to have the shipowner's claim dismissed for want of prosecution.

By s. 13A, an arbitrator was given power to make an award dismissing a claim if 'there has been inordinate and inexcusable delay' by the claimant in pursuing the claim and either (a) the delay will give rise to a 'substantial risk' that a fair resolution of the claim is not possible, or (b) the delay has caused, or is likely to cause or to have caused, 'serious prejudice' to the other party.

In the view of the House of Lords, the real issue was not whether s. 13A was retrospective in the ordinary sense but whether it enabled the power it conferred to be exercised by reference to events which had taken place before it came into force. Their Lordships held, reversing the decision of the Court of Appeal, that s. 13A was partially retrospective in the sense that it was intended to allow an arbitrator to dismiss a claim by taking into account *all* the 'inordinate and inexcusable delay' which had caused the 'substantial risk' of unfairness, including the delay which had occurred before s. 13A came into force. The House reached this conclusion by reference to the crucial words, 'there has been inordinate and inexcusable delay', taken together with the legislative background to s. 13A (as to which see further, para 9.3.2.2).

The *L'Office Cherifien* decision was applied by the Court of Appeal in *Antonelli* v *Secretary of State for Trade and Industry* [1998] 1 All ER 997, CA, which was concerned with the interpretation of s. 3 of the Estate Agents Act 1979 under which the Director General of Fair Trading has power to make an order disqualifying from acting as an estate agent a person who, *inter alia*, 'has been convicted of . . . an offence involving fraud or other dishonesty or violence . . .' and is, in the Director's opinion, 'unfit to carry on estate agency work . . .' The Act came into force in May 1982; some ten years earlier Mr Antonelli had been convicted in the United States of the crime of 'burning real estate other than a dwelling house'. It was held that s. 3 applies to conviction for an offence committed abroad before the Act came into force and that the Director's disqualification order had been lawfully made. It was said to be 'quixotic' to suppose that Parliament intended to protect the public from an estate agent convicted a week *after* the Act came into force but not from one convicted a week *before* (*per* Beldam LJ at p. 1006).

8.10.4   Intrinsic aids to construction

8.10.4.1 Short title
The short title of an Act is not of much use for interpretation purposes. It does not enact anything and is merely descriptive.

8.10.4.2   Long title
The long title of an Act is part of the Act and may be looked at *in cases of ambiguity* (see, e.g., *Manuel* v *Attorney-General* [1982] 3 All ER 822, CA, *per* Slade LJ at p. 831). If, however, there is no ambiguity in the body of the Act because the words employed are clear, the long title cannot be used to restrict the scope of those words merely because they seem to be unduly wide (*R* v *Galvin* [1987] 2 All ER 851, CA, *per* Lord Lane CJ at p. 855). Whilst the long title may provide a useful guide to the general objectives of the Act it is less helpful on specific provisions.

In *Black-Clawson International Ltd* v *Papierwerke etc. AG* [1975] AC 591, HL, Lord Simon of Glaisdale said (at p. 647) he could see no reason for resorting to the long title only in cases of ambiguity when the long title provided the 'plainest of all guides to the general objectives of a statute'. In *Royal College of Nursing of the United Kingdom* v *DHSS* [1981] 1 All ER 545, HL (para 8.10.2.3 above), the long title of the Abortion Act 1967 was specifically referred to by four of the five Law Lords who decided the appeal.

8.10.4.3   Preamble
A preamble, which sets forth (sometimes at great length) the need for and the intended effect of the legislation, is not commonly found in modern public statutes. If there is a preamble it may be looked at for guidance in cases of ambiguity, subject to the caveat that it may be found to be narrower or wider than the operative words of the Act.

8.10.4.4   Punctuation
Punctuation was not used in old statutes but modern statutes use normal punctuation. Formerly, punctuation was not regarded as part of the statute but, more recently, there have been signs that this approach has been relaxed and that punctuation may be used as an aid to interpretation where a statutory provision is ambiguous (see *DPP* v *Schildkamp* [1971] AC 1, HL, *per* Lord Reid at p. 10).

8.10.4.5   Headings
In some statutes headings are given to particular sections or parts. Strictly speaking, headings are probably not part of the Act, although they may be used as an aid to construction in cases of ambiguity (*DPP* v *Schildkamp* [1971] AC 1, HL).

8.10.4.6   Marginal or side-notes
Marginal notes in the printed copies of Acts are not discussed in Parliament and are not part of the Acts. Their use as an aid to construction is limited; the danger lies in the fact that, although they indicate conveniently and pithily the main purpose of a section, they are not

of much help in interpreting the *precise scope* of a section (*DPP* v *Schildkamp* [1971] AC 1, HL; *Prior (Valuation Officer)* v *Sovereign Chicken Ltd* [1984] 2 All ER 289, CA, *per* Lawton LJ at p. 295). They may, however, be useful indicators of the *general purpose* of a section and the *mischief* at which it is aimed (*Stephens* v *Cuckfield RDC* [1960] 2 QB 372, CA; *Tudor Grange Holdings Ltd* v *Citibank NA* [1991] 4 All ER 1, *per* Sir Nicolas Browne-Wilkinson V-C at p. 13; *Director of Public Prosecutions* v *Johnson* [1995] 4 All ER 53, DC, where a marginal note was used to confirm the mischief intended to be remedied by the breathalyser law; see further on this case, para 8.10.2.3, above).

8.10.4.7   Schedules

Schedules to an Act are undoubtedly part of the statute and may be looked at to cast light on any uncertainty thrown up in the main body of the legislation. Schedules are placed at the end of an Act and their principal purpose is to prevent the main body from becoming too cluttered and complex. They usually consist of transitional provisions, minor and consequential amendments, forms, and a list of enactments repealed, although, occasionally, there is evidence of operative legislative words occurring in a schedule. Examples are the annual Finance Act and several schedules in the Access to Justice Act 1999.

8.10.4.8   Examples

Occasionally a statute gives examples to illustrate the working of the Act or the use of the new terminology created by it. These examples, whether contained in sections or in schedules, are part of the statute. The Law of Property Act 1925 (schs. 3, 4 and 5) and the Settled Land Act 1925 (sch. 1) give many examples of specimen forms and instruments which may be used to satisfy the terms of the Acts. The examples are part of the legislation and may be used as they stand or with appropriate variations or additions. The Consumer Credit Act 1974 created a new terminology for money-lending, pawning and hire-purchase transactions and the statute provides 24 illustrations of its use (sch. 2). Although the examples are part of the legislation, the statute makes it clear that they are not exhaustive and that they cannot prevail in any conflict with any other provision of the Act (s. 188(2) and (3)). Nevertheless they are of substantial persuasive authority in the construction of the new terminology.

8.10.5   Extrinsic aids to construction

Extrinsic aids are those which are not contained in the Queen's Printer's copy of the statute. The use of extrinsic material, including *travaux préparatoires* (preparatory works leading to legislation), as an aid to statutory interpretation is restricted. The strict practice was that, since the judges are not allowed to inquire into the social or political history of an Act, they would not look at the reports of Parliamentary debates contained in *Hansard,* ministerial pronouncements, explanatory memoranda issued with the Act, reports of commissions and official committees, or international conventions. For example, in *Ellerman Lines Ltd* v *Murray* [1931] AC 126, the House of Lords refused to look at an international convention (set out in a schedule to the statute) when interpreting the Merchant Shipping (International Labour Conventions) Act 1925 which had been passed to give effect to the convention. (For the more modern approach to the use of international conventions, see *Fothergill* v *Monarch Airlines Ltd* [1980] 2 All ER 696, HL, below.)

In recent years the strict practice has been relaxed and extrinsic material is now regularly consulted, especially in order to discover the mischief which the Act was intended to remedy. (See, e.g., *Pickstone* v *Freemans plc* [1988] 2 All ER 803, HL, where Lord Oliver (at p. 818) quoted from the explanatory note issued with the statutory regulations he was seeking to construe.) Thus reports of the Law Commission, royal commissions, the Law Reform Committee and other official committees have all been looked at by the judges (see *Black-Clawson International Ltd* v *Papierwerke etc. AG* [1975] AC 591, HL, *per* Viscount Dilhorne at p. 621). In the *Black-Clawson* case, the House of Lords said unanimously that where a statute is ambiguous the court is entitled to look at the report of an official committee, presented to Parliament and containing proposals for legislation, for the purpose of discovering the *mischief* which the resulting statute was designed to remedy. But there was disagreement among their Lordships as to whether the report could be considered for any other purpose. Lord Reid (at p. 614) and Lord Wilberforce (at p. 629) said it was not permissible to look at the report as a guide to the *meaning* of the legislation, even though the report contains a draft bill which is later enacted without amendment. Viscount Dilhorne and Lord Simon of Glaisdale disagreed, the latter saying (at p. 646) that:

Where Parliament is legislating in the light of a public report I can see no reason why a court of construction should deny itself any part of that light and insist on groping for a meaning in darkness or half-light.

The view of Lords Reid and Wilberforce has prevailed over that of Viscount Dilhorne and Lord Simon (see *Attorney-General's Reference (No. 1 of 1988)* [1989] 2 All ER 1, HL, *per* Lord Lowry at p. 6). In *R* v *Ayres* [1984] 1 All ER 619, HL, their Lordships looked at a report of the Law Commission and in *R* v *Allen* [1985] 2 All ER 641, HL, they considered a report of the Criminal Law Revision Committee. In each case this was done as an aid to discovering the mischief in the criminal law which the subsequent statute was designed to remedy. In the latter case, Lord Hailsham of St Marylebone LC made it clear (at p. 644) that the report had been looked at solely for that purpose and that it had not been used as a guide to the meaning of the statute. In *Duke* v *GEC Reliance Ltd* [1988] 1 All ER 626, HL, Lord Templeman (at pp. 629–30 and 634) referred to the White Paper, *Equality for Women* (Cmnd 5724, 1974), as a guide to the intention of Parliament in enacting the Sex Discrimination Act 1975. In *R* v *Burke* [1990] 2 All ER 385, HL, Lord Griffiths (at p. 389), in determining the 'social evil' which had led Parliament to create the criminal offence of unlawful harassment of a residential occupier (formerly s. 30(2) of the Rent Act 1965, now s. 1(3) of the consolidating Protection from Eviction Act 1977), and in concluding that the offence is committed notwithstanding that the harassment does not constitute a civil wrong known to the law, derived assistance from the *Report of the Committee on Housing in Greater London* (the Milner Holland Report), Cmnd 2605, 1965. The *Report of the Committee on Homosexual Offences and Prostitution* (the Wolfenden Report, Cmnd 247, 1957), was relied upon in a case where it was decided that the term 'common prostitute' in s. 1(1) of the Street Offences Act 1959 does not include a male prostitute. This *Report* had led to the passing of the Act and had identified the mischief associated with loitering or soliciting for the purpose of prostitution as one caused by women (*Director of Public Prosecutions* v *Bull* [1994] 4 All ER 411, DC; see further on this case, para 8.10.2.3. above).

In *Anderton* v *Ryan* [1985] AC 560, HL, the House of Lords virtually ignored the report of the Law Commission which preceded the Criminal Attempts Act 1981 (*Criminal Law: Attempt and Impossibility in Relation to Attempt, Conspiracy and Incitement*, Law Com. No. 102, 1980). This error led to a bad decision which the House found it necessary to overrule at the earliest opportunity in the case of *R* v *Shivpuri* [1986] 2 All ER 334 (see further, para 9.3.2.2.).

In the construction of purely *domestic* legislation, *Hansard* remained a closed book for much longer although its use was advocated in 1974 by Lord Simon of Glaisdale in *Race Relations Board* v *Dockers' Labour Club & Institute* [1976] AC 285, HL, at p. 299, albeit only for the purpose of discovering the mischief of the former law and not the meaning of the present statutory language. Lord Denning MR went the whole way in *Davis* v *Johnson* [1979] AC 264, CA and HL. In construing s. 1 of the Domestic Violence and Matrimonial Proceedings Act 1976, he looked at both the *Report of the House of Commons Select Committee on Violence in Marriage (H. of C. Papers* (1974–75) 553-i) and the reports of Parliamentary debates in *Hansard (H. of C. Official Report (1975–76) Standing Committee F, Domestic Violence Bill)*. On the latter his Lordship said (at pp. 276–7):

> Some may say — and indeed have said — that judges should not pay any attention to what is said in Parliament. They should grope about in the dark for the meaning of an Act without switching on the light. I do not accede to this view . . . . And it is obvious that there is nothing to prevent a judge looking at these debates himself privately and getting some guidance from them. Although it may shock the purists, I may as well confess that I have sometimes done it. I have done it in this very case. It has thrown a flood of light on the position.

Goff and Cumming-Bruce LJJ expressly dissociated themselves from Lord Denning's 'heresy'. Cumming-Bruce LJ said (at p. 316):

> I am not alarmed by the criticism that I am a purist who prefers to shut his eyes to the guiding light shining in the reports of Parliamentary debates in *Hansard*.

When *Davis* v *Johnson* went to the House of Lords all five Law Lords disagreed with Lord Denning's view. Lord Scarman's opinion (at pp. 349–50) is particularly interesting:

> There are two good reasons why the courts should refuse to have regard to what is said in Parliament or by ministers as aids to the interpretation of a statute. First, such material is an unreliable guide to the meaning of what is enacted. It promotes confusion, not clarity. The cut and thrust of debate and the pressures of executive responsibility . . . are not always conducive to a clear and unbiased explanation of the meaning of statutory language. And the volume of Parliamentary and ministerial utterances can confuse by its very size. Secondly, counsel are not permitted to refer to *Hansard* in argument. So long as this rule is maintained by Parliament (it is not the creation of the judges), it must be wrong for the judge to make any judicial use of proceedings in Parliament for the purpose of interpreting statutes.

After the decision of the House of Lords in *Davis* v *Johnson*, given in March 1978, the matter was thought to be closed; but Lord Denning reopened it. He found a way round the prohibition on the use of *Hansard* as an aid to construction. Direct reference to *Hansard* was forbidden, but indirect reference was not. Thus, if *Hansard* was quoted in a textbook or published speech, the textbook or speech may, according to Lord Denning, legitimately be looked at by the judge. In *R* v *Local Commissioner for Administration (ex parte Bradford Metropolitan City Council)* [1979] 2 All ER 881, CA, heard in July 1978, Lord Denning consulted a textbook quotation of a public address, which itself contained quotations from *Hansard*, in order to clarify the meaning of 'maladministration' in the Local Government Act 1974, s. 26(1). He justified his action in these words (at p. 898):

According to the recent pronouncement of the House of Lords in *Davis* v *Johnson*, we ought to regard *Hansard* as a closed book to which we as judges must not refer at all. . . .

By good fortune, however, we have been given a way of overcoming that obstacle. For the ombudsman himself in a public address to the Society of Public Teachers of Law quoted the relevant passages of *Hansard* as part of his address: and Professor Wade has quoted the very words in his latest book on administrative law [4th ed., 1977, p. 82.] And we have not yet been told that we may not look at the writings of the teachers of law. . . . I hope therefore that our teachers will go on quoting *Hansard* so that a judge may in this way have the same help as others have in interpreting the statute.

The parliamentary rule which prevented counsel from citing *Hansard* in court was abolished in 1980. However, this fact made no immediate difference to the use of *Hansard* as an extrinsic aid to the construction of United Kingdom domestic legislation. Lord Scarman's first objection to its use remained valid (see *Davis* v *Johnson* [1979] AC 264 at pp. 349–50, quoted above). It was argued by some that prohibiting citation from *Hansard* conflicted with the duty of our courts to discover and give effect to the intention of Parliament when interpreting statutes, although it will be appreciated that extensive reference to *Hansard* could add considerably to the length (and, therefore, the cost) of litigation without any guarantee that it would assist in resolving the problem before the court. The immediate post-1980 position was illustrated in the opinions of the Law Lords in *Hadmor Productions Ltd* v *Hamilton*. When that case was before the Court of Appeal (see [1981] 2 All ER 724), Lord Denning, without any reference to the criticism of the practice made by the House of Lords in *Davis* v *Johnson,* proceeded to refer once again to *Hansard* (at pp. 731 and 733). He was criticised for his approach when the *Hadmor* case reached the House of Lords ([1982] 1 All ER 1042). Lord Diplock said (at p. 1055):

There are a series of rulings by this House, unbroken for a hundred years, and most recently affirmed emphatically and unanimously in *Davis* v *Johnson,* that recourse to reports of proceedings in either House of Parliament during the passage of the Bill that on a signification of the royal assent became the Act of Parliament which falls to be construed is not permissible as an aid to its construction.

The process of legitimising reference to *Hansard*, which culminated in *Pepper (Inspector of Taxes)* v *Hart* [1993] 1 All ER 42, HL (below), began when the House of Lords took the lead in adopting a more relaxed approach towards its use in cases involving the construction of delegated legislation approved by the United Kingdom Parliament and designed to give effect to our European Union obligations. The justification for this development was that proposed delegated legislation, in the form of draft regulations, is not (unlike a Bill) subject to the Parliamentary process of consideration and amendment in committee.

In *Pickstone* v *Freemans plc* [1988] 2 All ER 803, the House of Lords was concerned with the interpretation of the Equal Pay Act 1970, s. 1(2)(c), which had been added to the 1970 Act in 1983. The addition had been made, not by primary legislation but by regulations made under the authority of s. 2(2) of the European Communities Act 1972 and approved by Parliament, in order to comply with a decision of the Court of Justice of the European Communities that English law did not accord with a European Community Council Directive on equal pay for work of equal value. Lord Templeman (at pp. 814–5) quoted from the *Hansard* report of the House of Commons' debate on the draft regulations. He did so as an aid to discovering, from 'the explanations of the government and the criticisms voiced by members of Parliament', what was the true intention of Parliament in approving the regulations. Lord Keith (at p. 807) adopted a similar stance, saying that, in the circumstances, it was

> entirely legitimate for the purposes of ascertaining the intention of Parliament to take into account the terms in which the draft was presented by the responsible minister and which formed the basis of its acceptance.

It was finally held that reference to *Hansard* was to be allowed as an aid to the interpretation of United Kingdom domestic primary legislation in *Pepper (Inspector of Taxes)* v *Hart* [1993] 1 All ER 42. Here, the House of Lords sitting seven-strong declined to follow, by a majority of six to one (Lord Mackay of Clashfern LC dissenting), three of its earlier decisions on the use of Hansard — *Beswick* v *Beswick* [1968] AC 58, *Black-Clawson International Ltd* v *Papierwerke Waldhof-Aschaffenburg AG* [1975] AC 591, and *Davis* v *Johnson* [1979] AC 264. Their Lordships held that the exclusionary rule against the use of Hansard would be relaxed so as to permit reference to parliamentary materials subject to the following conditions:

(a) the legislation is ambiguous, or obscure, or its literal meaning leads to an absurdity;
(b) the material relied upon consists of statements by a Minister or other promoter of the Bill; and
(c) the statements relied upon are clear.

Pepper (Inspector of Taxes) v *Hart* concerned the interpretation of s. 63 of the Finance Act 1976 (now s. 156 of the Income and Corporation Taxes Act 1988) on the taxation of in-house benefits, with specific reference to the concession enjoyed by teachers at Malvern College, an independent school for boys, to have their children educated there for only one-fifth of the fees charged to the public. This concession was undoubtedly a taxable benefit under s. 61 of the 1976 Act (now s. 154 of the 1988 Act). The taxpayers were assessed to income tax on the 'cash equivalent' of the concession on the basis that they were liable for a rateable proportion of the expenses of running the school as a whole for all the boys and that that proportion was roughly equal to the amount of the ordinary school fees. The taxpayers challenged this assessment.

Section 63, which defined 'cash equivalent' as 'an amount equal to the cost of the benefit', and the 'cost of the benefit' as 'the amount of any expense incurred in or in connection with its provision', was ambiguous. It could mean that the benefit was to be taxed on either:

(a) the marginal (or additional) cost to the employer of providing it to the employee (which, on the facts, was nil); or
(b) the average cost of providing it to both the employee and the public.

When the case reached the House of Lords, submissions were made on the appropriateness of modifying the prohibition on the use of parliamentary materials and on whether the use of *Hansard* in the courts would amount to a violation of the Bill of Rights 1688 or a breach of parliamentary privilege. The House decided to modify the existing practice (as explained above). Reference to *Hansard* revealed clear statements, made by the Financial Secretary to the Treasury during the committee stage of the Bill which became the Finance

Act 1976, that the intention was to tax employees on in-house benefits on their marginal cost to the employer, and it was held that the statutory provision should be given that meaning.

The Attorney-General, appearing on behalf of the Crown, had argued that using *Hansard* would infringe s. 1, art. 9, of the Bill of Rights 1688 ('That the freedome of speech and debates or proceedings in Parlyament ought not to be impeached or questioned in any court or place out of Parlyament'). But the House of Lords unanimously disagreed, holding that the courts, by making use of *Hansard*, would not be 'questioning' or criticising what was said in Parliament but trying to implement what was said there (see [1993] 1 All ER 42 especially *per* Lord Mackay of Clashfern LC, Lord Griffiths, Lord Oliver and Lord Browne-Wilkinson at pp. 47, 50, 53 and 67–9 respectively). The House further held that it was not inhibited from deciding the case before it by any general considerations of parliamentary privilege because no such privilege extending beyond the Bill of Rights had been identified (see especially *per* Lord Browne-Wilkinson, ibid., at pp. 73–4).

The dissent of Lord Mackay of Clashfern LC on the use of *Hansard* is perhaps not surprising in view of his role as the government minister responsible for public expenditure on legal aid. In his opinion (expressed at p. 48), the new approach introduced 'the possibility at least of an immense increase in the cost of litigation in which statutory construction is involved'. The rest of their Lordships, however, regarded this and other objections to the use of *Hansard* as exaggerated and were prepared to sweep them aside. Lord Bridge said (at p. 49) that he found it

difficult to suppose that the additional cost of litigation or any other ground of objection can justify the court continuing to wear blinkers which, in such a case as this, conceal the vital clue to the intended meaning of an enactment.

While recognising that practitioners would in some cases incur fruitless costs in search of the 'vital clue' where none existed, he implied that there could be many more cases where the cost of litigation would be avoided because *Hansard* provided the answer.

Lord Griffiths, agreeing, said (at p. 51) that the case before him was a 'dramatic vindication of the decision to consult *Hansard*' for, if it had not been looked at, a heavy burden of taxation would have been placed on a large number of people which it was not Parliament's intention to impose.

Lord Browne-Wilkinson (at p. 63) summarised the reasons put forward for the prohibition on the use of *Hansard*. First, it preserves the 'constitutional proprieties' whereby Parliament legislates in words and the courts interpret the meaning of the words. Secondly, it avoids the practical difficulty of an expensive researching of parliamentary materials. Thirdly, *Hansard* does not provide the citizen with an accessible and defined text regulating his legal rights. Fourthly, it is in any event improbable that any helpful guidance will be found in *Hansard*.

These objections notwithstanding, Lord Browne-Wilkinson was convinced that, as a matter of law, there were now sound reasons for modifying the prohibition in a limited way. Among those reasons (explained at pp. 64–5) was that reference to *Hansard* could allow the courts more regularly to get at the underlying parliamentary purpose of specific legislation, his acceptance of the view that 'clear and unambiguous statements made by ministers in Parliament are as much the background to the enactment of legislation as white papers and parliamentary reports', and his opinion that looking at ministerial statements made in introducing regulations which cannot be amended by Parliament (authorised by

Pickstone v *Freemans plc* [1988] 2 All ER 803, HL, above) is 'logically indistinguishable' from looking at ministerial statements made in introducing *primary* legislation which, though capable of amendment, was not amended in fact.

There is some evidence that the cost of litigation has increased after *Pepper (Inspector of Taxes)* v *Hart* [1993] 1 All ER 42, HL, as lawyers increasingly feel obliged to spend expensive time combing through *Hansard* in appropriate cases in order to avoid the risk of being sued in negligence by their clients (see *The Times*, 6 July 1993).

In *Warwickshire County Council* v *Johnson* [1993] 1 All ER 299, the House of Lords followed the new practice in relation to *Hansard* approved only two weeks earlier in *Pepper (Inspector of Taxes)* v *Hart*. *Warwickshire County Council* v *Johnson* was concerned with the interpretation of s. 20(1) of the Consumer Protection Act 1987, which makes it an offence for a person to give 'in the course of any business of his' a misleading indication about the price of goods. The words 'any business of his' were ambiguous. The question was whether they meant that a branch manager of Dixons (the electrical goods retailers) who was responsible for a misleading price advertisement could be guilty of the offence as well as the company. A literal approach, simplicity and common sense suggested that he could.

The leading opinion was delivered by Lord Roskill. He looked at the internal evidence and the legislative history of the provision, and concluded that the words 'any business of his' were meant to refer to the business of the employer. Since the employee did not have a business he could not be guilty of the offence. This view was confirmed by reference to *Hansard* where there were clear statements by the Minister at the Report stage of the Bill in the House of Lords that the intention of the proposed legislation was to catch employers and not employees.

Subsequent cases in which the House of Lords has applied the new practice include *Stubbings* v *Webb* [1993] 1 All ER 322 (where Lord Griffiths, at pp. 328–9, referred to debates in *Hansard* on s. 2(1) of the Law Reform (Limitation of Actions etc) Act 1954 as an aid to the construction of s. 11 of the Limitation Act 1980, which contained without alteration (via the Limitation Act 1975) the wording of the 1954 Act), *Chief Adjudication Officer* v *Foster* [1993] 1 All ER 705 (in which Lord Bridge, at pp. 715–17, resorted to *Hansard* in confirmation of his interpretation of s. 22 of the Social Security Act 1986), *Steele Ford & Newton* v *Crown Prosecution Service* [1993] 2 All ER 769 (where Lord Bridge, at p. 777, consulted *Hansard* when construing certain statutory provisions relating to the payment of costs; see further on this case, para 5.2.2.4.5), and *Scher* v *Policyholders Protection Board (No. 2)* [1993] 4 All ER 840 (in which Lord Mustill, at p. 852, referred to debates at the committee and report stages of the passage of the Policyholders Protection Act 1975). In *Secretary of State for Social Security* v *Remilien* [1998] 1 All ER 129, the House of Lords did not find 'clear', within the meaning of *Pepper (Inspector of Taxes)* v *Hart* [1993] 1 All ER 42, HL, and derived no assistance from, a statement about the Income Support (General) Regulations 1987 made to the House of Commons Second Standing Committee on Statutory Instruments by the Parliamentary Under-Secretary of State for Social Security.

The Queen's Bench Divisional Court declined to use *Hansard* in *Director of Public Prosecutions* v *Bull* [1994] 4 All ER 411, DC, because the legislation to be interpreted (s. 1(1) of the Street Offences Act 1959) was not ambiguous, obscure, or literally absurd within the meaning of *Pepper (Inspector of Taxes)* v *Hart* [1993] 1 All ER 42, HL. (See further on *Director of Public Prosecutions* v *Bull*, para 8.10.2.3 above.) In *R* v *Deegan* (1998) *The Times*, 17 February, CA, the Court of Appeal, when called upon to interpret the statutory expression 'folding pocketknife', found ministerial statements (made during debates on the Bill which became the Criminal Justice Act 1988) to be not clear in the sense required by *Pepper (Inspector of Taxes)* v *Hart* and declined to take them into account.

The relaxed rule sanctioned in *Pepper (Inspector of Taxes)* v *Hart* allows reference to be made to parliamentary materials which provide evidence of the purpose behind legislation then going through Parliament. It does *not* permit the citation of parliamentary materials which merely evidence a minister's understanding of the current state of the law (*Hillsdown Holdings plc* v *Pensions Ombudsman* [1997] 1 All ER 862, in which Knox J declined to take into account a ministerial statement made two years after the relevant statutory provision came into force).

Nor is it permissible to refer to ministerial or other statements recorded in *Hansard* which are not directly concerned with the specific statutory provision under consideration or to the problem raised by the litigation. Such statements do not assist the court, and attempts to widen the category of materials to which reference may be made can simply cause extra delay and expense (*Melluish (Inspector of Taxes)* v *BMI (No. 3) Ltd* [1995] 4 All ER 453, HL, where the House of Lords refused to allow the Crown to introduce ministerial statements which were not directly in point).

A more flexible approach to the admissibility of parliamentary materials than that applicable when construing purely domestic legislation may be desirable where (a) the court is trying to interpret a statute purposively and consistently with any relevant European Community legislation, or (b) the object of the statute is to introduce into English domestic law the provisions of an international convention or a European Community directive. Under such an approach, the court would be allowed to look at parliamentary materials for assistance in discovering the purpose of a statute even though no question of its interpretation had arisen at that stage. In *Three Rivers District Council* v *Bank of England (No. 2)* [1996] 2 All ER 363, Clarke J, applying and extending the approach adopted in *Pickstone* v *Freemans plc* [1988] 2 All ER 803, HL, para 8.10.6 below, and *Litster* v *Forth Dry Dock and Engineering Co. Ltd* [1989] 1 All ER 1134, HL, para 8.10.6 below, held on a preliminary application that there was nothing in *Pepper (Inspector of Taxes)* v *Hart* [1993] 1 All ER 42, HL, or *Melluish (Inspector of Taxes)* v *BMI (No. 3) Ltd* [1995] 4 All ER 453, HL, which prevented him from looking at ministerial statements in *Hansard* with a view to deciding the purpose behind the Banking Acts 1979 and 1987 and the extent to which, if at all, those Acts were intended to, and did, implement a Council Directive of 1977.

If it is intended to refer to *Hansard* in a case before the Court of Appeal, the High Court, the Crown Court or the county courts, copies of the relevant extract and a brief summary of the argument to be based upon the extract must, unless the judge directs otherwise, be served on all other parties and on the court (*Practice Note (procedure: reference to Hansard)* [1995] 1 All ER 234). A failure to do this may be penalised in costs (ibid.).

In view of its historically more liberal approach to statutory interpretation, it is perhaps surprising to find that the Court of Justice of the European Communities probably operates under a disability similar to that suffered by the English courts prior to *Pepper (Inspector of Taxes* v *Hart* [1993] 1 All ER 42, HL. In *National Panasonic (UK) Ltd* v *Commission of the European Communities* [1981] 2 All ER 1, CJEC, at p. 7, it was the clear opinion of the Advocate-General in the case (J-P Warner, now a High Court judge) that the European Court is not entitled to look at reports of debates in the European Parliament as aids to the interpretation of European Community legislation. This question, however, was not dealt with in the judgment of the Court itself and cannot, therefore, be regarded as settled.

Lord Denning was also instrumental in concentrating judicial attention on the use of *travaux préparatoires* as aids to the construction of an *international convention*. In

Fothergill v *Monarch Airlines Ltd* [1979] 3 All ER 445, one question before the Court of Appeal was whether the court could consider *travaux préparatoires* in construing the Carriage by Air Act 1961 which contained, in a schedule, the Warsaw Convention of 1929 as amended in 1955. The *travaux* included the minutes of 34 meetings held at an international conference at the Hague in 1955. Lord Denning said (at p. 451) that:

> These *travaux préparatoires* can be used not only to see what was the mischief needing to be remedied, not only to see what was the purpose or object of the draftsmen, but also to find out what they really meant to convey by the words they used.

Browne and Geoffrey Lane LJJ disagreed. Browne LJ said (at p. 456) that the court's power was limited to discovering the mischief of the old law. The court cannot take into account direct statements of what the Act was intended to mean.

Lord Denning's approach was completely vindicated, for when *Fothergill* v *Monarch Airlines Ltd* went to the House of Lords ([1980] 2 All ER 696, HL) a majority of four to one of their Lordships were of the opinion that, in interpreting international conventions, the court could look at *travaux préparatoires* in a general way and not merely for the specific purpose of discovering the mischief of the former law.

Their Lordships were convinced that a more liberal rule of interpretation was justified in the interests of universal uniformity of application. However, *travaux préparatoires* should be used with caution. In particular, they should be considered only where, first, they are publicly accessible, *and*, secondly, they clearly point to a definite legislative intention (*per* Lord Wilberforce at p. 703). These *travaux* are *aids* to the interpretation of, and not *substitutes* for, the terms of a convention. Their use is not mandatory. The court has a *discretion* whether to look at them and what weight to attach to them (*per* Lord Scarman at p. 715; note that the House of Lords unanimously reversed the *decision* of the Court of Appeal in the case but this does not affect the comments in the text). Thus, Bingham J in *Data Card Corp.* v *Air Express International Corp.* [1983] 2 All ER 639, Hirst J in *Cia Portorafti Commerciale SA* v *Ultramar Panama Inc.* [1989] 2 All ER 54, Lord Oliver in *Hiscox* v *Outhwaite (No. 1)* [1991] 3 All ER 641, HL, and Lord Hope in *Sidhu* v *British Airways plc* [1997] 1 All ER 193, HL, looked at the relevant *travaux préparatoires* but found them of no assistance whatever, while in *Gatoil International Inc.* v *Arkwright-Boston Manufacturers Mutual Insurance Co.* [1985] 1 All ER 129, HL, a majority of the House of Lords found the relevant *travaux* helpful as an external aid to construction.

8.10.6 Reform of the principles of statutory interpretation: the 'literal' approach v the 'purposive' approach

There has been much criticism of the English principles of interpretation. In particular, too much use has been made in the past of the literal rule at the expense of a more purposive approach. The three so-called 'rules' — literal, golden and mischief — are not rules at all since there is no compulsion to apply them. Moreover, there is no consistency of application when they *are* applied. There is no set order of priority. In one case the court will apply the literal rule, while in another it will apply the mischief rule. Sometimes the court does not identify which rule it is applying. The presumptions may be similarly criticised. For instance, there is no rule about which presumption should be applied where two of them conflict. Some of the limitations on the use of extraneous material have been felt to be unduly restrictive.

As long ago as 1969 the Law Commission published its report on *The Interpretation of Statutes* (Law Com. No. 21). Its proposals have not been implemented by legislation. The Law Commission was most impressed by the mischief rule but said that it needed to be adapted to modern conditions. It recommended the passing of a short statute setting out the extrinsic material which the court would be entitled to consider in interpreting legislation. The report of the Law Commission included some draft clauses (Law Com. No. 21, App. A). Their effect would be as follows:

(a)   Aids to interpretation available to the court would include:
   (i)   punctuation, side-notes, and short title;
   (ii)   reports of royal commissions or official committees presented to Parliament before the Act was passed;
   (iii) any relevant treaty or other international agreement referred to in the Act or presented to Parliament before the Act was passed;
   (iv) command papers on the subject-matter;
   (v)   any document declared to be relevant by the Act.
The amount of weight to be given to any of these matters should be no more than is appropriate in the circumstances. Reports of Parliamentary proceedings are expressly excluded.

(b)   The principles of interpretation would include:
   (i)   the preference of a construction which would promote the general legislative purpose over one which would not;
   (ii)   the preference of a construction which is consistent with the international obligations of the United Kingdom over one which is not.

(c)   The above provisions would apply also to the interpretation of delegated legislation.

Attempts have been made by Lord Scarman, a former Lord of Appeal in Ordinary, to secure legislation which would give effect to these proposals of the Law Commission, of which, at the time of its report in 1969, he was the first chairman. Lord Scarman's attempts have failed owing to opposition from judges and laymen alike. In 1980, his Interpretation of Legislation Bill was withdrawn after opposition from his judicial colleagues in the House of Lords. Only the Lord Chancellor, Lord Hailsham of St Marylebone, gave any encouragement to the Bill. In 1981, Lord Scarman introduced a more comprehensive Bill which passed through the House of Lords but was rejected by the House of Commons.

Some judicial efforts, notably by Lord Denning, have been made to improve interpretative technique. Writing extra-judicially, Lord Denning agrees that the object of statutory interpretation is to discover the intention of Parliament. But he argues that the actual words used in the statute are only the starting point and not the finishing point (*The Discipline of Law*, 1979, p. 9; see also *The Closing Chapter*, 1983, pp. 94–107 and 110–14). He prefers the 'purposive' approach to the literal approach. He is an 'intention seeker' rather than a 'strict literal constructionist'. The purposive approach is the European approach to statutory interpretation and he recommends its extension to Acts of the United Kingdom Parliament. Lord Denning has also aired his view from the bench in *Nothman v London Borough of Barnet* [1978] 1 All ER 1243, CA, at p. 1246:

The literal method is now completely out of date. . . . In all cases now in the interpretation of statutes we adopt such a construction as will 'promote the general legislative purpose underlying the provision' [quoted from the Law Commission report No. 21 cited above].

It is no longer necessary for the judges to wring their hands and say: 'There is nothing we can do about it.' Whenever the strict interpretation of a statute gives rise to an absurd and unjust situation, the judges can and should use their good sense to remedy it — by reading words in, if necessary — so as to do what Parliament would have done had they had the situation in mind.

When the *Nothman* case reached the House of Lords ([1979] 1 All ER 142), Lord Denning's approach was criticised. In particular, his attempt, single-handed and without legislation, to implement the Law Commission's recommendations of 1969 was too much for Lord Russell of Killowen, who expressly disclaimed Lord Denning's 'sweeping comments' (p. 151). Lord Denning's purposive approach to the interpretation of *domestic legislation* received little judicial support at the time.

A unanimous House of Lords had no hesitation in preferring a purposive approach to a literal interpretation in *R v Pigg* [1983] 1 All ER 56 (para 7.5.4). It was held there that, despite the clear mandatory wording of s. 17(3) of the Juries Act 1974, the foreman of a jury when announcing a majority verdict need not state expressly how many jurors *dissented from* the verdict provided that that was clear from his statement of how many *agreed with* it. Their Lordships said it was the *substance* of the requirement that had to be complied with rather than the precise form of words by which such compliance was to be achieved.

R v Pigg was clearly an exceptional case, however; the House of Lords later said that a judge may adopt a purposive interpretation only if he can find in the statute, or in permitted extrinsic material, an expression of Parliament's purpose or policy (*Shah v Barnet London Borough Council* [1983] 1 All ER 226, HL). The judge is not permitted to interpret legislation in the light of his own views about policy. In essence, this represented a reaffirmation of the literal approach to statutory interpretation by which judges are positively discouraged from seeking to discover the policy underlying a piece of legislation. The only concession granted to judicial creativity by the *Shah* case was that judges may adopt a purposive approach to interpretation if the purpose or policy of Parliament is discernible from the statute itself or from material to which they are permitted by law to refer as an aid to the construction of the statute.

The House of Lords moved towards a purposive approach in the interpretation of *international conventions and treaties* (para 8.10.5 above) in *Fothergill v Monarch Airlines Ltd* [1980] 2 All ER 696, HL, where Lord Wilberforce, Lord Diplock and Lord Scarman gave overt support to such a move (at pp. 700, 704 and 713 respectively). Their Lordships later demonstrated a willingness to adopt a purposive, as opposed to a literal, approach when construing legislation of the United Kingdom Parliament passed to give effect to our obligations under European Community law (see also para 8.10.5, above, on the use of *Hansard*).

Thus, in *Pickstone v Freemans plc* [1988] 2 All ER 803, HL, regulations approved by Parliament and designed to fill a gap (identified by a decision of the Court of Justice of the European Communities) in the English equal pay legislation were found, on a literal reading, to be inadequate for filling that gap. A *literal* approach would have left the United Kingdom in breach of its treaty obligations to give effect to European Community directives. The House of Lords held that, in the circumstances, it was permissible to give a *purposive* construction to the regulations so as to make them comply with European Community law. In order to achieve the manifest purpose of the regulations, and to give effect to the clear but inadequately expressed intention of Parliament, it was decided that certain words must be read into the regulations by necessary implication — even though that entailed departing from the strict, literal application of the words which Parliament had chosen to use. It was accordingly held that a female employee, employed on work of equal value to the work of a male employee doing a different job for the same employer, was entitled, under the Equal Pay Act 1970, to claim equal pay with that man notwithstanding the fact that there was another male employee doing the same work as her for the same pay.

Pickstone v *Freemans plc* was applied in *Litster* v *Forth Dry Dock and Engineering Co. Ltd* [1989] 1 All ER 1134, HL. This case was concerned with the construction of statutory regulations approved by Parliament in order to give effect to a European Community Council Directive. The regulations provided that the transfer of a business did not terminate the contracts of employment of employees who were employed in the business 'immediately before the transfer' and that those contracts were to be treated after the transfer as if they had originally been made between the employees and the transferee of the business. Some employees who had been dismissed one hour before the transfer of an insolvent business to new owners claimed compensation for unfair dismissal. The transferees argued that the employees' claim must fail since, having already been dismissed, they had not been employed in the business 'immediately before' its transfer.

If this argument, based on a literal interpretation of the regulations, had prevailed, the employees in question would have been left without any effective remedy for unfair dismissal. They would have no remedy for compensation, reinstatement or re-engagement against the transferees, and their remedy for compensation against the insolvent transferors would be worthless. The House of Lords was unanimous in preferring a purposive to a literal construction. It was held that the regulations applied not only to employees who were employed in the business immediately before the transfer in point of time but also to employees who would have been so employed had they not been unfairly dismissed before the transfer for a reason connected with it. The House of Lords was prepared to achieve this result by reading words into the regulations by necessary implication (see [1989] 1 All ER 1134 *per* Lord Keith, Lord Templeman and Lord Oliver at pp. 1136, 1139 and 1153 respectively). Moreover, this construction accorded with the relevant European Community Council Directive, whose object was to protect the rights of employees on a change of employer, and made it impossible for the transferor and transferee of a business to arrange for the transferor to dismiss the workforce shortly before the transfer took effect solely for the purpose of enabling the transferee to avoid liability for unfair dismissal or redundancy claims. *Litster* v *Forth Dry Dock and Engineering Co. Ltd* was applied in *Morris Angel & Son Ltd* v *Hollande* [1993] 3 All ER 569, CA, in which the Court of Appeal adopted a purposive approach to the construction of the same regulations in relation to their application to restraint of trade clauses in contracts of employment.

At first, this new approach only applied to the construction of primary or delegated legislation of the United Kingdom Parliament which was designed to give effect to European Community law. Accordingly, it was held that where the Parliamentary legislation in question was not passed for the purpose of implementing Community law the English courts would continue to prefer a literal to a purposive approach (*Duke* v *GEC Reliance Ltd* [1988] 1 All ER 626, HL, para 8.7 above).

The new approach was extended to *all* legislation of the United Kingdom Parliament by the decision of the House of Lords in *Pepper (Inspector of Taxes)* v *Hart* [1993] 1 All ER 42, HL (para 8.10.5 above). The resolution of the entire case proceeded on the basis of the purposive approach to statutory interpretation which, according to a majority of their Lordships, the courts had now adopted in order to give effect to the true intention of Parliament. Thus, in construing any domestic legislation the courts may now (subject to the limitations noted in para 8.10.5 above) refer to *Hansard* and other parliamentary materials. Moreover, they may do so not only for the limited purpose of discovering the mischief which the legislation was designed to cure but also for the purpose of discovering the general legislative intention. Their Lordships' support in *Pepper (Inspector of Taxes) v Hart* for the purposive approach was somewhat unexpected and surprising given the previous history of the subject in the House of Lords (see above and para 8.10.2.1).

Both Lord Griffiths and Lord Browne-Wilkinson in their speeches stressed the merits of the purposive, as opposed to the literal, approach to statutory interpretation. According to Lord Griffiths ([1993] 1 All ER 42 at p. 50),

> [t]he days have long passed when the courts adopted a strict constructionist view of interpretation which required them to adopt the literal meaning of the language. The courts now adopt a purposive approach which seeks to give effect to the true purpose of legislation and are prepared to look at much extraneous material that bears on the background against which the legislation was enacted.

Lord Browne-Wilkinson (with whose opinion Lords Keith, Bridge, Ackner and Oliver expressly agreed) said (ibid., at p. 65):

> [g]iven the purposive approach to construction now adopted by the courts in order to give effect to the true intentions of the legislature, the fine distinctions between looking for the mischief and looking for the intention in using words to provide the remedy are technical and inappropriate.

According to Laws LJ in *Oliver Ashworth (Holdings) Ltd v Ballard (Kent) Ltd* [1999] 2 All ER 791, CA, at p. 805 (Robert Walker LJ expressly agreeing with him at p. 803), it is misleading to make any rigid distinction between a literal and a purposive approach to statutory interpretation:

> The difference . . . is in truth one of degree only. On received doctrine we spend our professional lives construing legislation purposively, inasmuch as we are enjoined at every turn to ascertain the intention of Parliament. The real distinction lies in the balance to be struck, in the particular case, between the literal meaning of the words on the one hand and the context and purpose of the measure in which they appear on the other. Frequently there will be no opposition between the two, and then no difficulty arises. Where there is a potential clash, the conventional English approach has been to give at least very great and often decisive weight to the literal meaning of the enacting words. This is a tradition which I think is weakening, in face of the more purposive approach enjoined for the interpretation of legislative measures of the European Union and in light of the House of Lords' decision in *Pepper (Inspector of Taxes) v Hart* [1993] 1 All ER 42 . . . [T]he . . . virtue [of this shift in emphasis] is that the legislator's true purpose may be more accurately ascertained. Its vice is that the certainty and accessibility of the law may be reduced or compromised. The common law, which regulates the interpretation of legislation, has to balance these considerations.

(See further on this case, para 8.10.2.4 above.)

Since *Pepper (Inspector of Taxes) v Hart* [1993] 1 All ER 42 not every opportunity has been taken to further the purposive approach to interpretation. In *R v Brown* [1996] 1 All

ER 545, HL, for example, a purposive approach to the construction of s. 5 of the Data Protection Act 1984 (since repealed by the Data Protection Act 1998) was preferred only by a minority of their Lordships (including, it must be said, Lord Griffiths). The majority decided the appeal on a literal interpretation of the section (see further on this case, para 8.10.2.1 above). In *Re C (a minor) (interim care order: residential assessment)* [1996] 4 All ER 871, HL, the House preferred a wide, purposive construction of s. 38(6) of the Children Act 1989 to a narrow construction based upon the *ejusdem generis* rule (see further on this case, para 8.10.2.4 above).

The Court of Appeal in *Jones v Tower Boot Co. Ltd* [1997] 2 All ER 406, CA, noting that the purpose of the Race Relations Act 1976 was the eradication of racial discrimination, interpreted s. 32 of the Act in a liberal way so as to advance that purpose. The complainant was of mixed ethnic parentage and had been subjected to severe verbal and physical racial abuse at work by two fellow employees. After four weeks in the job, he resigned and made a complaint to an employment tribunal against his former employers, alleging that his fellow employees' conduct amounted to racial discrimination for which the employers were liable under the Race Relations Act 1976, s. 32(1), which provides that:

Anything done by a person in the course of his employment shall be treated for the purposes of this Act (except as regards offences thereunder) as done by his employer as well as by him, whether or not it was done with the employer's knowledge or approval . . .

The employers argued that they were not liable because the employees' acts of discrimination were not committed 'in the course of their employment' since, according to the common law principles for determining an employer's vicarious liability in the law of tort, the employees were not specifically employed to engage in the racial abuse of their colleagues, and their behaviour was not merely an improper mode of performing the duties of their employment but was completely outside the scope of those duties.

It was held that the words 'in the course of his employment' are to be given their natural everyday meaning and are not to be construed restrictively in accordance with the common law principles of vicarious liability. Waite LJ ([1997] 2 All ER 406 at p. 415) referred to the result of upholding the employers' contention, namely 'the more heinous the act of discrimination, the less likely it will be that the employer would be liable', and concluded that such a result ran counter to the whole legislative scheme and underlying policy of s. 32 of the 1976 Act. (See further on *Jones v Tower Boot Co. Ltd*, para 9.3.2.3.1.)

When later construing s. 7(1) of the same statute in *Harrods Ltd v Remick* [1998] 1 All ER 52, CA, the Court of Appeal applied the purposive approach adopted in *Jones v Tower Boot Co. Ltd* [1997] 2 All ER 406, CA, so as to achieve the perceived statutory objective of providing a remedy to victims of discrimination who would otherwise be without one.

In *Re Ismail* [1998] 3 All ER 1007, HL, which was concerned with an application for a writ of habeas corpus, the House of Lords noted that the purpose of the Extradition Act 1989 is to facilitate the bringing to justice of persons accused of serious crimes, and proceeded to adopt a 'broad and purposive approach' in holding that the appellant was an 'accused' person within s. 1(1) of that Act, and, therefore, subject to extradition proceedings.

In *Cutter v Eagle Star Insurance Co. Ltd* [1998] 4 All ER 417, HL, the House had to construe the word 'road' in the Road Traffic Act 1988 in order to determine whether a car park is a road. Some doubt was expressed about the true purpose of this statute, although their Lordships were prepared to accept that it was designed to protect the public from dangers arising from the use of motor vehicles. In any event, they eschewed a purposive approach in favour of giving the word 'road' its ordinary, literal meaning (see para 8.10.2.1, above).

Lord Clyde, with whom the rest of their Lordships agreed, said (at [1998] 4 All ER 417, 425):

> It may be perfectly proper to adopt even a strained construction to enable the object and purpose of legislation to be fulfilled. But it cannot be taken to the length of applying unnatural meanings to familiar words . . . This must particularly be so where the language has no evident ambiguity or uncertainty about it . . . [I]t has to be remembered that in many instances the purpose of the legislation is achieved by the creation of an offence. Against the employment of a broad approach to express the purpose of the Act must be put the undesirability of adopting anything beyond a strict construction of provisions which have penal consequences.

In *Fitzpatrick* v *Sterling Housing Association Ltd* [1999] 4 All ER 705, HL, the House of Lords held unanimously that a same-sex partner cannot succeed to a statutory tenancy on the death of the original tenant under para 2 of sch. 1 to the Rent Act 1977 because, in the case of unmarried couples, that provision necessitates 'living with the original tenant as his or her wife or husband'. These words are gender-specific and contemplate only a relationship between a man and a woman. However, adopting a purposive approach, it was further decided, by a majority of three to two, that a same-sex partner is capable of succeeding to an assured tenancy on the death of the original tenant as a 'member of the original tenant's family' under para 3 of sch. 1.

Lord Nicholls (at p. 722) identified the 'underlying legislative purpose' of this provision as the desire to 'provide a secure home for those who share their lives together with the original tenant in the manner which characterises a family unit', and continued:

> This purpose would be at risk of being stultified if the courts could not have regard to changes in the way people live together and changes in the perception of relationships. This approach is supported by the fact that successive Rent Acts have used the same undefined expression despite the far-reaching changes in ways of life and social attitudes meanwhile. It would be unattractive, to the extent of being unacceptable, to interpret the word 'family' in the 1977 Act without regard to these changes.

8.10.7   Interpretation of European Community legislation

The traditional English principles and technique of interpretation are not suitable for the construction of European Community legislation. The latter is drafted in Continental form, which is to state broad principles and leave the details to be filled in later by the judges, who are expected to promote the general legislative purpose. Lord Denning MR compared the English style and the style of the EC Treaty in *H.P. Bulmer Ltd* v *J. Bollinger SA* [1974] Ch 401, CA, at p. 425:

> The draftsmen of our statutes have striven to express themselves with the utmost exactness. They have tried to foresee all possible circumstances that may arise and to provide for them. They have sacrificed style and simplicity. They have forgone brevity. They have become long and involved. In consequence, the judges have followed suit. They interpret a statute as applying only to the circumstances covered by the very words.

They give them a literal interpretation. If the words of the statute do not cover a new situation — which was not foreseen — the judges hold that they have no power to fill the gap . . .

How different is this treaty! It lays down general principles. It expresses its aims and purposes . . . It uses words and phrases without defining what they mean. An English lawyer would look for an interpretation clause, but he would look in vain. There is none. All the way through the treaty there are gaps and lacunae. These have to be filled in by the judges, or by regulations or directives. It is the European way.

In *Macarthys Ltd* v *Smith* [1979] 3 All ER 325, CA, a case which involved a conflict between s. 1 of the Equal Pay Act 1970 and art. 119 (now art. 141) of the EC Treaty, Lord Denning compared the two models again (at p. 329):

Article 119 [141] is framed in European fashion. It enunciates a broad general principle and leaves the judges to work out the details. In contrast the Equal Pay Act is framed in English fashion. It states no general principle but lays down detailed specific rules for the courts to apply . . . without resort to considerations of policy or principle.

Legislation in European form cannot be interpreted literally. The mischief rule is more helpful, but Continental judges go further and adopt the *purposive* approach. The aim is to apply the 'spirit' rather than the 'letter' of the law. The Court of Justice of the European Communities has made it clear in its judgments that Community legislation should be interpreted in this fashion (*Da Costa en Schaake NV* v *Nederlandse Balastingadministratie* [1963] CMLR 224, CJEC; *Van Duyn* v *Home Office* [1975] Ch 358, CJEC). The Court of Appeal in *H.P. Bulmer Ltd* v *J. Bollinger SA* [1974] Ch 401 has said, through Lord Denning MR (at pp. 425–6), that English judges must do likewise:

Beyond doubt the English courts must follow the same principles as the European court. Otherwise there would be differences between the countries of the nine. That would never do. All the courts of all nine countries should interpret the [EC Treaty] in the same way.
. . .
Likewise the regulations and directives . . .
[The English courts] must follow the European pattern. No longer must they examine the words in meticulous detail. No longer must they argue about the precise grammatical sense. They must look to the purpose or intent . . . They must divine the spirit of the treaty and gain inspiration from it. If they find a gap, they must fill it as best they can. They must do what the framers of the instrument would have done if they had thought about it.

Lord Denning's approach here received tacit approval from Lord Scarman in *Fothergill* v *Monarch Airlines Ltd* [1980] 2 All ER 696, HL, at p. 712. Later, in *Macarthys Ltd* v *Smith* [1979] 3 All ER 325, CA, Lord Denning (at p. 329) went so far as to state that in interpreting a statute of the United Kingdom Parliament:

[W]e are entitled to look to the [EC Treaty] as an aid to its construction; but not only as an aid but as an overriding force.

However, the other two judges in the appeal apparently disagreed with this statement. Lawton and Cumming-Bruce LJJ said it was not permissible to look outside the Act at the terms of the treaty (pp. 332 and 335 respectively). When *Macarthys Ltd* v *Smith* came back to the Court of Appeal after its journey to the Court of Justice of the European Communities in Luxembourg, Cumming-Bruce LJ took the opportunity to explain that what he had said earlier was on the assumption that there was no ambiguity about the United Kingdom statute. If there is such ambiguity, then it *is* appropriate to look at the treaty in order to resolve it ([1981] 1 All ER 111 at p. 121).

When an English judge is interpreting Community legislation he must follow decisions and opinions of the Court of Justice of the European Communities. This is made clear by s. 3 of the European Communities Act 1972 (as amended by the European Communities (Amendment) Act 1986):

(1)   For the purposes of all legal proceedings any question as to the meaning or effect of any of the Treaties, or as to the validity, meaning or effect of any Community instrument, shall be treated as a question of law (and, if not referred to the European Court, be for determination as such in accordance with the principles laid down by and any relevant decision of the European Court or any court attached thereto).
(2)   Judicial notice shall be taken of the Treaties, of the Official Journal of the Communities and of any decision of, or expression of opinion by, the European Court or any court attached thereto, on any such question as aforesaid.

Section 3 of the European Communities Act 1972 itself must be read in conjunction with art. 177 (now art. 234) of the EC Treaty (para 2.1.3.3). Under art. 177 (234), a judge at first instance and the Court of Appeal (unless its decision would be final in the case) have a *discretion* to refer any question of the interpretation of European Community legislation to the Court of Justice of the European Communities for a ruling. The discretion arises if a decision on the question is necessary to enable the domestic court to give judgment in the case (para 2.1.3.3.2). On the same conditions, the House of Lords *must* refer such a question to the European Court.

When the European Court gives a ruling on the reference, its decision is then binding in that particular case. But it is not binding in future cases because the European Court is not bound by its own decisions (see, e.g., the *Da Costa* case, above). This freedom from the rigidity of any strict doctrine of precedent is necessary to enable the European Court to take into account future policy considerations (*H.P. Bulmer Ltd* v *J. Bollinger SA* [1974] Ch 401, CA, *per* Lord Denning MR at p. 420). It also means that if the House of Lords considers that an earlier decision of the European Court is wrong or unsatisfactory in some way it can refer the point again to the European Court for reconsideration in a later case.

It is also made clear by s. 3(1) of the European Communities Act 1972 that any question arising in an English court concerning the meaning or effect of any of the Community Treaties is to be treated as a question of *law*. Accordingly, such a question arising in a criminal trial should be decided by the *judge alone* and may properly be determined by him in the absence of the jury (*R* v *Goldstein* [1983] 1 All ER 434, HL).

8.10.8   Interpretation of United Kingdom legislation after the Human Rights Act 1998

The European Convention on Human Rights (*Convention for the Protection of Human Rights and Fundamental Freedoms, agreed by the Council of Europe at Rome on 4th November 1950*) guarantees certain fundamental rights and freedoms, including the right to life, the right to liberty and security, the right to a fair trial, the right to respect for private and family life, freedom of thought, conscience and religion, freedom of expression, and freedom of assembly and association. The United Kingdom has since 1951 been a signatory to the Convention and subject to the jurisdiction of the European Court of Human Rights at Strasbourg. The Convention, however, has never been part of English domestic law and, consequently, has not been *directly* enforceable in our courts. This is about to change under the Human Rights Act 1998, which is based upon the Labour Government's White Paper, *Rights Brought Home: The Human Rights Bill* (Cm 3782, 1997), published in October 1997.

When the Act is fully in force in England and Wales (probably in October 2000):

(a)   the rights and freedoms (referred to as 'Convention rights') will be incorporated into English law;

(b)   primary and delegated legislation, whenever made, will as far as possible be interpreted and applied in a way which is compatible with the Convention rights, although the validity, continuing operation or enforcement of any incompatible legislation will, in general, be unaffected;

(c)   if a legislative provision is found by the House of Lords, the Judicial Committee of the Privy Council, the Courts-Martial Appeal Court, the Court of Appeal or the High Court to be incompatible with one or more of the Convention rights, that court will be able to make a declaration of incompatibility;

(d)   a declaration of incompatibility will not affect the validity, continuing operation or enforcement of the incompatible provision, and will not be binding on the parties to the proceedings in which it is made;

(e)   where a court is considering whether to make a declaration of incompatibility, a Minister of the Crown, or a person nominated by him, will be entitled to be joined as a party to the proceedings;

(f)   a Minister of the Crown will be able to remove the incompatibility by making a remedial order which amends the offending legislation (and any other affected legislation);

(g)   as a general proposition, Parliament will be expected not to pass legislation which interferes with the Convention rights, and a Minister of the Crown in charge of a Bill in either House of Parliament will be required to make in writing, before Second Reading of the Bill, either a statement of compatibility to the effect that in his view the provisions of the Bill are compatible with the Convention rights or a statement that, although he is unable to make a statement of compatibility, the government nevertheless wishes the House to proceed with the Bill;

(h)   it will, in general, be unlawful for a public authority (which includes a court, a tribunal exercising functions in relation to legal proceedings, and any person with some functions of a public nature, but does not include Parliament) to act in a way which is incompatible with the Convention rights;

(i)   a court or tribunal deciding a question in connection with a Convention right will take account of relevant judgments, decisions, declarations and opinions made or given by the European Commission and Court of Human Rights and the Committee of Ministers of the Council of Europe.

The requirement that legislation is to be interpreted as far as possible so as to achieve compatibility with the Convention goes further than the principle of interpretation applicable hitherto, namely that the courts can take the Convention into account in resolving any legislative ambiguity.

In the White Paper, the government concluded that the doctrine of Parliamentary sovereignty was too important for our courts to be allowed to nullify statutes. Accordingly, the Human Rights Act 1998 does *not* give the courts the power to set aside Acts of Parliament which are inconsistent with the Convention rights but merely allows certain courts to make declarations of incompatibility. In Canada, the courts can strike down any legislation which is inconsistent with the Charter of Rights and Freedoms 1982, unless the legislation expressly states that it is to apply 'notwithstanding' the provisions of the Charter. In New Zealand, the Bill of Rights Act 1990, while requiring the courts as far as possible to interpret legislation consistently with the rights contained in the Act, provides that the legislation stands if that is impossible. The Human Rights Act 1998 prefers the New Zealand model to the Canadian model. The European Communities Act 1972 provides for that part of Community law which has 'direct effect' to take priority over inconsistent English domestic law. In the White Paper, however, the government dismissed this precedent on the 'essential difference' that giving such priority is a requirement of membership of the European Union whereas there is no such requirement in the European Convention.

In addition, the Human Rights Act 1998 does *not* entrench its own provisions to protect them from subsequent amendment or repeal. The model provided by the Constitution of the United States of guaranteeing certain rights which can be amended or repealed only by qualified majorities in the legislature and in the States themselves was rejected by our government as irreconcileable with United Kingdom constitutional convention, which allows any statute to be amended or repealed by a subsequent statute.

The Convention rights were made applicable to the Scottish Executive created by the Scotland Act 1998 as from 1 July 1999. One of those rights, the right to a fair trial, is enshrined in art. 6 of the Convention:

> In the determination of his civil rights and obligations or of any criminal charge against him, everyone is entitled to a fair and public hearing within a reasonable time by an independent and impartial tribunal established by law.

In *Starrs v Procurator Fiscal, Linlithgow* (1999) *The Times*, 17 November, it was held by the High Court of Justiciary in Scotland, sitting as the Court of Criminal Appeal, that a judge (in this case, a temporary sheriff) who has no security of tenure and whose appointment is subject to annual renewal by the Executive is not 'independent' within the meaning of art. 6. It follows that it is unlawful for the Crown in Scotland to prosecute a person before such a judge since a member of the Executive 'has no power . . . to do any act . . . incompatible with any of the Convention rights' (Scotland Act 1998, s. 57(2)).

In *Smith v Secretary of State for Trade and Industry* (1999) *The Times*, 15 October, EAT, the Employment Appeal Tribunal granted permission to appeal so that the Court of Appeal would have an opportunity to consider (before the Human Rights Act 1998 comes into force in England and Wales) whether employment tribunals are 'independent and impartial' within art. 6 of the Convention in view of their link with the Secretary of State for Trade and Industry.

The Lord Chancellor's reaction to the *Starrs* decision, above, was to review the terms of service of part-time judicial office-holders in England and Wales. In April 2000, new arrangements were announced guaranteeing their independence. The changes took immediate effect. Part-time appointments are now for a period of not less than five years, subject to the relevant upper age limit. Renewable appointments are normally to be renewed automatically, except for limited and specified grounds, and removal from office is only on limited and specific grounds. Whenever it is administratively possible, the offer of a minimum number of sitting days will be guaranteed. Subject to statutory provision, the specified grounds for *non-renewal* are:

(a)   misbehaviour;

(b)   incapacity;

(c)   persistent failure (without good reason) to comply with sitting requirements;

(d)   failure to comply with training requirements;

(e)   sustained failure to observe the standards reasonably expected from a holder of such office;

(f)   a reduction in numbers because of changes in operational requirements; and

(g)   a structural change to enable recruitment of new appointees.

The grounds for *removal* are those in (a)–(e), above.

Decisions not to renew, or to remove on grounds (a)–(e), above, are taken by the Lord Chancellor only with the agreement of the Lord Chief Justice and following an investigation conducted by a judge nominated by him.

9

Judicial Precedent

9.1 THE MEANING OF JUDICIAL PRECEDENT

At the beginning of Chapter 8 the superiority of Parliamentary legislation over judge-made law was noted (para 8.2). Despite its subservient position, however, there is still considerable scope for judicial law-making in the English legal system. When a judge applies or extends an established rule to new facts, or decides that the rule does not apply in a certain situation, he is making or changing the law. Of course, he does not have the same freedom as the legislature and must not be seen to be usurping its powers. All judge-made law is inferior to, and can be overruled by, Parliamentary or delegated legislation. But, unless and until they are overruled, judicial decisions on the interpretation of legislation are precedents just as much as decisions on non-statutory points of law, and, as such, are subject to the same rule of *stare decisis*. Most of English law derives from statute and the common law. The function of the judges is to interpret the one and evolve the other.

The term 'judicial precedent' has at least two meanings. First, it may mean the process whereby judges follow previously decided cases. Secondly, it may refer to the decided case itself — a 'precedent' which may be relied on in the future. The term is mainly used in the first sense and is to be so understood for most of this chapter.

The doctrine of judicial precedent is one which in English law involves an application of the principle of *stare decisis*; i.e., to stand by cases already decided. In practice, this element of compulsion means that the Court of Appeal is generally bound to follow its own previous decisions and that each court is bound to follow the decisions of a court above it in the hierarchy. (For the position of the House of Lords, see para 9.3.2.2 below.)

It is important to appreciate that the limitations placed on the courts by the principle of *stare decisis* are self-imposed. With the exception of the requirement that our courts must follow decisions of the European Court, or of any court attached thereto, on Community Law (European Communities Act 1972, s. 3(1), as amended, para 8.10.7), there are no *legislative* provisions on the application of judicial precedent. After the Human Rights Act 1998 is fully in force, when our courts and tribunals decide questions in connection with rights guaranteed under the European Convention on Human Rights, and given effect to by the 1998 Act, they will be required to take account of relevant judgments, decisions, declarations and opinions made or given by the European Commission and Court of Human Rights and the Committee of Ministers of the Council of Europe (see further, para 8.10.8).

9.2 *RATIO DECIDENDI* AND *OBITER DICTUM*

The decision or judgment of a judge may fall into two parts: the *ratio decidendi* and *obiter dictum*. When a judge delivers judgment in a case he outlines the facts which he finds have been proved on the evidence. Then he applies the law to those facts and arrives at a decision, for which he gives the reason (*ratio decidendi*). More precisely, the *ratio decidendi* of a case is the principle of law on which the decision is based. The judge may go on to speculate about what his decision would or might have been if the facts of the case had been different. This is an *obiter dictum* ('something said by the way').

The binding part (if any) of a judicial decision is the *ratio decidendi*. An *obiter dictum* is not binding in later cases because it was not strictly relevant to the matter in issue in the original case. However, an *obiter dictum* may be of *persuasive* (as opposed to *binding*) authority in later cases. This matter is examined later (para 9.4.2), as is the difficulty involved in discovering the *ratio decidendi* of a case (para 9.5).

Sometimes opinions delivered in the House of Lords contain statements which look at first sight as though they are *obiter* because of the way in which the case has been decided. But on a closer examination these statements are seen not as mere *obiter dicta* but as forming part of a *ratio decidendi*. Important examples of such cases are *Rondel v Worsley* [1969] 1 AC 191, HL, para 9.4.2 below; *Hedley Byrne & Co. Ltd v Heller & Partners Ltd* [1964] AC 465, HL, para 9.4.2 below; and *National Carriers Ltd v Panalpina (Northern) Ltd* [1981] 1 All ER 161, HL, para 9.4.2 below. Such instances are rare and occur usually where the House of Lords does not wish to lose a present opportunity for clarifying the law or providing guidance for lower courts in the future. Moreover, the House will only act in this way after full legal argument and mature consideration of the points at issue. This matter also is dealt with in more detail later (para 9.4.2).

Since the only binding part (if any) of a decided case is the principle of law contained within its *ratio decidendi*, it follows that cases are not binding on questions of *fact*. Nor are they binding on questions of law which were merely assumed to be correct without argument by counsel and without full consideration by the court. This is so regardless of the status of the court which decided the case. Thus, although normally bound by decisions of the House of Lords, a High Court judge need not follow one of their Lordships' decisions which is either essentially one of fact or is based upon an unargued assumption (see, for example, *Re Hetherington (deceased)* [1989] 2 All ER 129, para 9.3.2.6 below). And, in *R v Secretary of State for the Home Department (ex parte Ku)* [1995] 2 All ER 891, the Court of Appeal, which (as will be seen in para 9.3.2.3.1 below) is normally bound by its own previous decisions, declined to follow *R v Immigration Officer (ex parte Chan)* [1992] 2 All ER 738, CA, on the ground that it was decided on both a question of fact and on an assumption.

9.3 JUDICIAL PRECEDENT IN PRACTICE

9.3.1 Reversing, overruling and distinguishing

Reversing occurs where a court higher up in the hierarchy overturns the decision of a lower court on appeal in the same case. *Overruling* is where a principle laid down by a lower court is overturned by a higher court in a different, later case. Thus, in 1963 the House of Lords held unanimously in *Hedley Byrne & Co. Ltd v Heller & Partners Ltd* [1964] AC 465, HL, that there could be liability in English law for negligent misstatements. In so holding, the House of Lords overruled *Candler v Crane, Christmas & Co.* [1951] 2 KB 164, CA, which had represented the Court of Appeal's view of the law since 1951. At the same time, the dissenting judgment of Denning LJ in *Candler* was vindicated in *Hedley Byrne*. In domestic matters, while the House of Lords can now *overrule* itself it is not possible, strictly speaking, to *reverse* itself.

English courts have always followed the practice of retrospective overruling. This means that the overruled case is regarded as never having been law and will not be applied either in later cases or in the instant case. Retrospective overruling accords with the declaratory theory of the common law that the judges do not make or change the law but merely declare it. As Brett MR once put it (*Munster* v *Lamb* (1883) 11 QBD 588, CA at pp. 599–600):

> The judges cannot make new law by new decisions; they do not assume a power of that kind: they only endeavour to declare what the common law is and has been from the time when it first existed. But inasmuch as new circumstances, and new complications of fact, and even new facts, are constantly arising, the judges are obliged to apply to them what they consider to have been the common law during the whole course of its existence, and therefore they seem to be laying down a new law, whereas they are merely applying old principles to a new state of facts.

In more modern times, the declaratory theory has been described as a 'fiction' by Lord Simon of Glaisdale (*Jones* v *Secretary of State for Social Services* [1972] AC 944, HL, at p. 1026), and as a 'fairy tale' by Lord Reid ((1972–73) JSPTL 22). (See also *R* v *Governor of Brockhill Prison (ex parte Evans) (No. 2)* [1998] 4 All ER 993, CA, *per* Lord Woolf MR at p. 1002; *Kleinwort Benson Ltd* v *Lincoln City Council* [1998] 4 All ER 513, HL *per* Lord Browne-Wilkinson, Lord Goff, Lord Lloyd and Lord Hope at pp. 518, 535, 548 and 563, respectively.) Lord Browne-Wilkinson has explained the modern judicial function thus (*Kleinwort Benson Ltd* v *Lincoln City Council*, above, at p. 518):

> The theoretical position has been that judges do not make or change law: they discover and declare the law which is throughout the same. According to this theory, when an earlier decision is overruled the law is not changed: its true nature is disclosed, having existed in that form all along. This theoretical position is, as Lord Reid said, a fairy tale in which no one any longer believes. In truth, judges make and change the law. The whole of the common law is judge-made and only by judicial change in the law is the common law kept relevant in a changing world.

Now that the declaratory theory is generally regarded as old fashioned, and it is generally accepted that judges do make new law, the injustice arising from the practice of retrospective overruling is compounded. This injustice is that the parties in the instant case will have relied on what they understood the law to be, only to be told now that it is not, and never has been, the law.

Thus, in *R* v *Governor of Brockhill Prison (ex parte Evans)* [1997] 1 All ER 439, DC, where a prison governor had calculated a prisoner's release date in accordance with an approach sanctioned by three decisions of the Queen's Bench Divisional Court, and the court later held that its three previous decisions were wrong and should not be followed, it transpired that the prisoner, who should have been released earlier under the new approach sanctioned by the court, had been detained unlawfully for 59 days. In *R* v *Governor of Brockhill Prison (ex parte Evans) (No. 2)* [1998] 4 All ER 993, CA, she claimed damages for false imprisonment. It was argued on behalf of the prison governor that he had had lawful justification for the detention because, at the time he relied on them, the earlier decisions had not been held to be wrong. The Court of Appeal decided that when an earlier decision is effectively overruled by a later decision the earlier decision cannot be relied upon as a correct statement of the law because the later decision operates retrospectively. It followed that the governor had had no lawful justification for the detention since, from his point of view, it was as if the earlier decisions had never existed.

In *Kleinwort Benson Ltd* v *Lincoln City Council* [1998] 4 All ER 513, HL, the House of Lords abolished the common law rule that money paid under a mistake of law is not recoverable. It was appreciated that the retrospective effect of the decision would allow claims to be made for the recovery of money paid under a mistake of law in earlier transactions (see *per* Lord Goff, Lord Hoffmann and Lord Hope at pp. 535, 554 and 563, respectively). Lord Lloyd, dissenting, was alarmed by this consequence (p. 552), and Lord Browne-Wilkinson was similarly critical in his dissenting opinion (see especially at pp. 519 and 523). (See further on this case, para 9.3.2.2 below.)

In the interests of justice the practice of *prospective* overruling has been developed in the courts of some countries, notably in the US Supreme Court (see, e.g., *Linkletter* v *Walker* (1965) 381 US 618, USA). Prospective overruling means that the overruled case is applied in the instant case and is inapplicable in future cases only.

In *Jones* v *Secretary of State for Social Services* [1972] AC 944, HL, Lord Simon of Glaisdale suggested (at p. 1026) that the English courts should be given, by statute, the power of prospective overruling. (Lord Simon of Glaisdale made the same suggestion in an afterword to his opinion in *Miliangos* v *George Frank (Textiles) Ltd* [1976] AC 443, HL, at p. 490.) Lord Diplock agreed in principle ([1972] AC 944 at p. 1014). Lord Devlin, however, has expressed opposition to such a power on the ground that it 'turns judges into undisguised legislators' ('Judges and lawmakers', (1976) 39 MLR 1 at p. 11). The injustice arising from prospective overruling is that people are treated differently. Under this system of overruling there is also a disincentive to litigate. No one will volunteer to be the guinea-pig — that is, to take the risk of finding out whether an overruled decision will or will not apply in his case. The practice of prospective overruling appeared to commend itself to Lord Woolf MR in *R* v *Governor of Brockhill Prison (ex parte Evans) (No. 2)* [1998] 4 All ER 993, CA, at p. 1003, but in *Kleinwort Benson Ltd* v *Lincoln City Council* [1998] 4 All ER 513, HL, Lord Goff (at p. 536) said that its adoption elsewhere had had 'somewhat controversial results' and that it 'has no place in our legal system'.

Distinguishing a case on its facts, or on the point of law involved, is a device resorted to by judges usually in order to avoid the consequences of an inconvenient decision which is, in strict practice, binding on them. Distinguishing is discussed again in para 9.6.

9.3.2 Judicial precedent in individual courts

9.3.2.1 Court of Justice of the European Communities
As was seen in para 8.10.7, decisions of the European Court are binding on all English courts, including the House of Lords, on the interpretation of the Community treaties and on the validity and interpretation of secondary Community legislation. The European Court is not bound by its own decisions.

9.3.2.2 House of Lords
Decisions of the House of Lords are binding on all courts in the country except the House itself. Until 1966 the House of Lords was bound by its own decisions. This practice was established in the mid nineteenth century and reaffirmed in 1898 in *London Tramways Co. Ltd* v *London County Council* [1898] AC 375, HL. The reason was that it was felt that decisions of the highest appeal court should be final in the public interest so that there would be certainty in the law and an end to litigation. (See especially the speech of the Earl of Halsbury LC in the *London Tramways* case.) There was increasing judicial criticism of the practice from the 1930s. In particular, it was said that the rule did not produce the desired

certainty in the law and it had become too rigid (see, e.g., Lord Wright, 'Precedent', [1944] CLJ 118; Lord Denning, 'From precedent to precedent' (The Romanes Lecture, 1959, quoted in *The Discipline of Law,* 1979, pp. 291 et seq.); *Midland Silicones Ltd* v *Scruttons Ltd* [1962] AC 446, HL, *per* Lord Reid at p. 475). But the practice was not changed until 1966, when, in July of that year, Lord Gardiner LC made a statement on behalf of himself and the Law Lords. The *Practice Statement* [1966] 3 All ER 77; [1966] 1 WLR 1234 is here set out in full.

> Their Lordships regard the use of precedent as an indispensable foundation upon which to decide what is the law and its application to individual cases. It provides at least some degree of certainty upon which individuals can rely in the conduct of their affairs, as well as a basis for orderly development of legal rules.
>
> Their Lordships nevertheless recognise that too rigid adherence to precedent may lead to injustice in a particular case and also unduly restrict the proper development of the law. They propose, therefore, to modify their present practice and, while treating former decisions of this House as normally binding, to depart from a previous decision when it appears right to do so.
>
> In this connection they will bear in mind the danger of disturbing retrospectively the basis on which contracts, settlements of property, and fiscal arrangements have been entered into and also the especial need for certainty as to the criminal law.
>
> This announcement is not intended to affect the use of precedent elsewhere than in this House.

(On the 'especial need for certainty as to the criminal law', see *R* v *Cunningham* [1981] 2 All ER 863, HL, *per* Lord Hailsham of St Marylebone LC at p. 870 and Lord Edmund-Davies at p. 871.)

Lord Gardiner's statement was accompanied by a press release which emphasised the importance of and the reasons for the change in practice ([1966] *Public Law* 348). It would enable the House of Lords to adapt English law to meet changing conditions. It would enable the House to pay more attention to decisions of superior courts in the Commonwealth. The change would bring the House into line with the practice of superior courts in many other countries. In the USA, for instance, the US Supreme Court and state supreme courts are not bound by their own previous decisions.

The change in practice was approved by lawyers generally. But some were surprised that such an important alteration in the judicial process was brought about by a mere practice statement. It was suspected that this could only be done by legislation. Instead, the House of Lords freed itself from a self-imposed restraint by exercising its inherent jurisdiction as a court to change its own practice. It would certainly not have been appropriate to effect the change in an actual case on appeal because that case would have had no greater authority than, say, *London Tramways Co.* v *London County Council* [1898] AC 375, HL.

A party to an appeal who intends to ask the House of Lords to depart from its own previous decision must draw special attention to this in the appeal documents (*Practice Direction (House of Lords: Preparation of Case)* [1971] 1 WLR 534).

Developments since 1966 have indicated that the new freedom of the House of Lords to review its previous decisions will be used sparingly, particularly in cases involving the construction of statutes and documents (*Jones* v *Secretary of State for Social Services* [1972] AC 944, HL, *per* Lord Reid at p. 966, Lord Morris of Borth-y-Gest at p. 973, Lord Pearson at pp. 996–7 and Lord Simon of Glaisdale at p. 1024; but see *Vestey* v *Commissioners of*

Inland Revenue [1979] 3 All ER 976, HL, below). The House will not refuse to follow its earlier decision merely because that decision was wrong. And it is nothing to the point that the earlier decision was by a narrow majority. A material change of circumstances will usually have to be shown (*Fitzleet Estates Ltd* v *Cherry* [1977] 3 All ER 996, HL; *Jones* v *Secretary of State for Social Services*, above; *R* v *Knuller* [1973] AC 435, HL). Nor will the House reconsider its own previous decision merely because that decision has caused grave concern. In *Food Corp of India* v *Antclizo Shipping Corp* [1988] 2 All ER 513, HL, it was said that, in order to justify a review, the judges must feel that they are free to depart from both the reasoning and the decision in the previous case, *and* they must be satisfied that a departure from the earlier decision would help to resolve the dispute in the case presently before them. This latter point reinforces the general approach of the House of Lords (and other courts) that issues concerning private law rights which are only of academic interest will not be entertained (*Sun Life Assurance Co. of Canada* v *Jervis* [1944] AC 111, HL; *Ainsbury* v *Millington* [1987] 1 All ER 929, HL). In *Food Corp of India* v *Antclizo Shipping Corp,* the House of Lords, although tempted to do so, refused to conduct a review of the earlier authorities on the ground that the occasion was not appropriate because of the findings of fact in the case (see [1988] 2 All ER 513 *per* Lord Goff of Chieveley at pp. 516 and 520–1).

The House has a discretion to hear an appeal concerned with an issue of *public law* involving a *public authority* even though by the time the appeal is heard there is no longer a dispute to be resolved between the parties. This discretion is, however, exercised with caution. In particular, there must be some good reason in the public interest for hearing the appeal, such as the involvement of a discrete point of statutory interpretation not requiring a detailed consideration of the facts, and it is likely that the point will need to be resolved in the near future because of the existence or anticipation of a large number of similar cases (*R* v *Secretary of State for the Home Department (ex parte Salem)* [1999] 2 All ER 42, HL, distinguishing *Sun Life Assurance Co. of Canada* v *Jervis,* HL, above, and *Ainsbury* v *Millington,* HL, above; on the facts of the *Salem* case, the House declined to entertain the appeal).

Two years passed before the House of Lords first exercised the power to depart from its own previous decision. That was in *Conway* v *Rimmer* [1968] AC 910, HL, unanimously overruling *Duncan* v *Cammell, Laird & Co,* [1942] AC 624, HL, on a question of the discovery of documents. In *Duncan,* which was decided in wartime and was probably correct on its facts, the House of Lords had held that an affidavit sworn by a government minister was sufficient to enable the Crown to claim privilege not to disclose documents in civil litigation without those documents being inspected by the court (the so-called 'public interest immunity'). In *Conway* v *Rimmer,* their Lordships held that the minister's affidavit was not binding on the court. The position now is that it is up to *the court* to decide whether to order disclosure. This will involve balancing the possible prejudice to the state if disclosure is ordered against the possible injustice to the individual litigant if disclosure is withheld. The minister's affidavit is entitled to full consideration but is no longer final. If it is necessary to assist him in reaching a conclusion, the trial judge may read the documents in private. Disclosure should be ordered only if the party seeking access to the documents satisfies the court that they are likely to support his case. It is not enough merely to show that the documents are likely to affect the outcome of the case one way or the other (*Air Canada and others* v *Secretary of State for Trade* [1983] 2 WLR 494, HL; *Evans* v *Chief Constable of Surrey Constabulary (Attorney-General intervening)* [1989] 2 All ER 594).

In *Herrington* v *British Railways Board* [1972] AC 877, HL, the House of Lords overruled (or, at least, modified) *Addie & Sons* v *Dumbreck* [1929] AC 358, HL. In *Addie,* the House of Lords had held that an occupier of premises was only liable to a trespassing child who was injured by the occupier intentionally or recklessly. In *Herrington,* their Lordships held that a different approach was appropriate in the changed social and physical conditions since 1929. They propounded the test of 'common humanity' which involves an investigation of whether the occupier has done all that a humane person would have done to protect the safety of the trespasser.

In *Miliangos* v *George Frank (Textiles) Ltd* [1976] AC 443, HL, the House of Lords overruled *Re United Railways of the Havana & Regla Warehouses Ltd* [1961] AC 1007, HL. In the *United Railways* case, it had been held that damages in an English civil case could only be awarded in sterling. In *Miliangos,* the House of Lords held that damages can be awarded in the currency of any foreign country specified in the contract. A new rule was needed because of changes in foreign exchange conditions, and especially the instability of sterling, since 1961.

In *Vestey* v *Commissioners of Inland Revenue* [1979] 3 All ER 976, HL, an income tax case, the House of Lords overruled its own decision in *Congreve* v *Commissioners of Inland Revenue* [1948] 1 All ER 948, HL, which had stood for some 30 years. This action was all the more surprising because *Vestey* was a case involving the interpretation of a statute. In the earlier case of *Jones* v *Secretary of State for Social Services* [1972] AC 944, HL (decided on the construction of the National Insurance (Industrial Injuries) Act 1946), the House of Lords, by a majority of four to three, held that one of its own decisions of only five years' standing was wrong. Nevertheless, that decision was not overruled. All three dissentients, and one of the majority, took the view that they should not depart from it and so outvoted the remaining three members of the majority on this point. Lord Reid said (at p. 966) that it should only be in rare cases involving some broad issue of justice or public policy that the House should reconsider one of its own decisions involving the interpretation of a statute. In the *Vestey* case, the decision to overrule *Congreve* v *Commissioners of Inland Revenue* was unanimous. Their Lordships felt not only that the *Congreve* case was wrong but also that it would produce 'startling and unacceptable consequences' when applied to circumstances never contemplated when it was decided ([1979] 3 All ER 976 *per* Lord Edmund-Davies at p. 1003). This consideration brought the situation within Lord Reid's dictum about broad issues of justice or public policy (at p. 1005 *per* Lord Keith of Kinkel).

In *Jobling* v *Associated Dairies Ltd* [1981] 2 All ER 752, a case concerning damages for personal injuries, the House of Lords doubted and did not follow its own decision given ten years earlier in *Baker* v *Willoughby* [1970] AC 467. In *M.V. Yorke Motors* v *Edwards* [1982] 1 All ER 1024, the House did not follow (but did not expressly overrule) its own decision in *Jacobs* v *Booth's Distillery Co.* (1901) 85 LT 262. In *Paal Wilson & Co. A/S* v *Paartenrederei Hannah Blumenthal* [1983] 1 All ER 34, HL, a case on frustration of contract, the House declined an invitation to depart from its previous decision given only two years earlier in *Bremer Vulkan* v *South India Shipping Corporation* [1981] AC 909, HL. Their Lordships were resolved that the opposition of commercial people and of the majority of the Court of Appeal to the *Bremer Vulkan* decision did not constitute a material change of circumstances such as to justify the House in overruling it. The opposition amounted merely to what Lord Wilberforce, in *Fitzleet Estates Ltd* v *Cherry* [1977] 3 All ER 996 described (at p. 999) as 'doubts as to the correctness' of the *Bremer Vulkan* decision. In the interests of certainty in the field of commercial law the *Bremer Vulkan* decision was allowed to stand (see especially *per* Lords Brandon of Oakbrook and Roskill, [1983] 1 All ER 34 at pp. 47 and 54 respectively). The efforts of the majority of the Court of Appeal in the *Paal Wilson* case [1982] 3 All ER 394 to circumvent the *Bremer Vulkan* decision were said to reflect 'greater credit on their independence of mind than on their loyalty to the established and indispensable principle of judicial precedent' ([1983] 1 All ER 34 *per* Lord Brandon at p. 46).

A second attempt to persuade the House of Lords to depart from the *Bremer Vulkan* decision was unsuccessful in *Food Corp of India* v *Antclizo Shipping Corp* [1988] 2 All ER 513, HL (see above). The facts of the *Food Corp of India* case were such that the appeal was bound to fail. To have conducted a review of the earlier authorities in those circumstances would, therefore, have been a mere academic exercise and anything their Lordships said about *Bremer Vulkan* would have been *obiter* (see [1988] 2 All ER 513 *per* Lord Goff of Chieveley at p. 516). (The *Bremer Vulkan* and *Paal Wilson* decisions were ultimately modified by the Arbitration Act 1950, s. 13A, added with effect from 1 January 1992 by the Courts and Legal Services Act 1990, which gave an arbitrator power to dismiss a claim for want of prosecution where the claimant is guilty of 'inordinate and inexcusable delay' in pursuing it. Section 13A has partial retrospective effect in the sense that it allows an arbitrator to dismiss a claim by taking into account *all* 'inordinate and inexcusable delay', including that which occurred prior to s. 13A coming into force: *L'Office Cherifien des Phosphates* v *Yamashita-Shinnihon Steamship Co. Ltd* [1994] 1 All ER 20, HL. When this case was before the Court of Appeal (see [1993] 3 All ER 686), the mischief at which the section is directed was described by Sir Thomas Bingham MR (at p. 690) as a 'significant blemish on the English arbitration regime' and identified as the 'powerlessness of arbitrators . . . to dismiss claims without a hearing on the merits where the claimants had been guilty of gross and unjustified delay in pursuing their claims and the effect of such delay was such as to jeopardise the prospects of a fair trial or to cause the other parties at least a real risk of serious prejudice'. See further, para 8.10.3.6.)

In *R* v *Secretary of State for the Home Department (ex parte Khawaja)* [1983] 2 WLR 321, a case on illegal immigration, the House of Lords declined to follow its own decision given in a case two and a half years earlier, *R* v *Secretary of State for the Home Department (ex parte Zamir)* [1980] AC 930. (See further, paras 4.5 and 8.10.3.2.) The feeling of the House in the *Khawaja* case was that the power of the courts to review the detention and summary removal of an alleged illegal immigrant had been defined too narrowly in the *Zamir* case, which, in fact, had cast the main burden of proof upon the immigrant to show that his detention was not justified. In *Khawaja* Lord Scarman said (at p. 339) that the *Practice Statement* of 1966 indicated that the House of Lords, before departing from a precedent of its own making, must be satisfied on two counts. First, that continued adherence to the precedent would involve the risk of injustice and would obstruct the proper development of the law. Secondly, that a departure from the precedent is the safe and appropriate way of remedying the injustice and developing the law. Lord Bridge of Harwich said (at p. 356) that the case did not fall into any of the categories mentioned in the *Practice Statement* as requiring special caution before departing from precedent. There was no question of altering the criminal law or disturbing retrospectively the basis of any contract, settlement of property or fiscal arrangement. Moreover, as Lord Bridge of Harwich pointed out (at pp. 356–7), the case concerned both a matter of 'high constitutional principle affecting the liberty of the subject and the delineation of the respective functions of the executive and the judiciary' and a broad issue of justice and public policy, within the meaning of Lord Reid's dictum in *Jones* v *Secretary of State for Social Services* [1972] AC 944 at p. 966.

It is not at all decisive one way or the other that the precedent from which the House is invited to depart is relatively recent. In *Khawaja* Lord Bridge of Harwich described it (at

p. 356) as a 'neutral factor', while Lord Scarman (at p. 339) inclined to the view that it did not matter at all. In *R* v *Shivpuri* [1986] 2 All ER 334, in which the House of Lords overruled within 12 months its own earlier decision in *Anderton* v *Ryan* [1985] AC 560, Lord Bridge (who sat in both appeals) said (at p. 345):

> . . . I am undeterred by the consideration that the decision in *Anderton* v *Ryan* was so recent. The 1966 *Practice Statement* is an effective abandonment of our pretention to infallibility. If a serious error embodied in a decision of this House has distorted the law, the sooner it is corrected the better.
>
> (See also the same judge's equally frank admission of fallibility in *Patel* v *Immigration Appeal Tribunal* [1988] 2 All ER 378, HL, at pp. 383–4.)

In *Anderton* v *Ryan* the appellant, on a construction of the Criminal Attempts Act 1981, was held not guilty of attempting dishonestly to handle a stolen video recorder. She thought the goods had been stolen but, in fact, there was no evidence that they had been. In *R* v *Shivpuri,* another case on the Criminal Attempts Act 1981, the appellant was held to be guilty of attempting to commit a drugs offence. He had been caught with a suitcase which he thought contained prohibited drugs whereas, in fact, it contained snuff or some other harmless vegetable matter. It was, therefore, impossible for him to have committed the full offence involved but he was charged with *attempting to commit* the offence of being knowingly concerned in dealing with and harbouring prohibited drugs. His conviction was upheld by the House of Lords because he had intended to commit the full offence and had done acts which were 'more than merely preparatory to' the commission of the intended offence within the meaning of s. 1(1) of the 1981 Act. Mrs Ryan had escaped conviction in spite of the clear words of s. 1(2) of the Act that 'a person may be guilty of attempting to commit an offence to which this section applies even though the facts are such that the commission of the offence is impossible'. In *Anderton* v *Ryan* the House of Lords had held, in effect, that these plain words did not mean what they said (see further, para 8.10.5).

In *R* v *Howe* [1987] 2 WLR 568, the House of Lords decided that the defence of duress is not available to a person charged with murder, whether as a principal in the first degree (the actual killer) or as a principal in the second degree (an aider and abettor). In so holding, the House overruled its earlier decision in *Director of Public Prosecutions for Northern Ireland* v *Lynch* [1975] AC 653 that duress was available as a defence to a person who had participated in a murder as an aider and abettor. Their Lordships' decision in *R* v *Howe* was based on a desire to restore this part of the criminal law to what it was generally understood to be prior to *Lynch,* even though to do so produced the illogical result that, while duress is a *complete* defence to all crimes less serious than murder, it is not even a *partial* defence to a charge of murder itself (see [1987] 2 WLR 568 *per* Lord Hailsham of St Marylebone LC, Lord Brandon and Lord Griffiths at pp. 579–80, 585 and 592 respectively, but note that in *R* v *Gotts* [1992] 1 All ER 832, the House of Lords extended the decision in *R* v *Howe* by holding, albeit by a bare majority of 3–2, that duress is not a defence to *attempted* murder).

Elements of public and social policy are clearly discernible in the opinions in *R* v *Howe.* Lord Hailsham, referring to the existing *administrative* mechanisms (such as the availability of parole and the royal prerogative of mercy) which might be used in appropriate cases to alleviate any hardship suffered by persons convicted of murder committed while acting under duress, said (at p. 581):

It may well be thought that the loss of a clear right to a defence justifying or excusing the deliberate taking of an innocent life in order to emphasise to all the sanctity of a human life is not an excessive price to pay in the light of these mechanisms . . .

. . . We live in the age of the holocaust of the Jews, of international terrorism on the scale of massacre, of the explosion of aircraft in mid air, and murder sometimes at least as obscene as anything experienced in Blackstone's day.

Lord Griffiths said (at p. 590):

We face a rising tide of violence and terrorism against which the law must stand firm recognising that its highest duty is to protect the freedom and lives of those that live under it. The sanctity of human life lies at the root of this ideal and I would do nothing to undermine it, be it ever so slight.

In *Murphy* v *Brentwood District Council* [1990] 2 All ER 908, the House of Lords overruled its earlier decision in *Anns* v *Merton London Borough* [1978] AC 728 on the common law liability of local authorities for the inspection of building foundations. In *Anns,* the House had held that a local authority was under a common law duty to take reasonable care to ensure that the foundations of a building complied with building regulations. This duty was owed to the owner and occupier of the building, who, if the duty was broken, could sue the local authority for negligence. Any damages awarded would include a sum to cover the cost of putting right the defect. The decision in *Anns* v *Merton London Borough* was not greeted with universal acclaim throughout the common law world. In particular, doubts were expressed about its consistency with established principles of the law of tort. The Australian courts refused to follow it on the ground that the duty it created was too wide, while courts in Canada and New Zealand not only followed it but considerably extended it. The Australian courts later changed their minds (see below).

In *Murphy* v *Brentwood District Council,* the House of Lords was invited to reconsider *Anns* and, having done so, decided unanimously to overrule it. The principal factor which drove the House to this conclusion was the reluctance of English judges to provide a remedy in tort for pure *economic* loss (i.e., loss which is 'pecuniary', 'monetary' or 'financial') as opposed to *physical* loss (i.e., damage to persons or property). (There is no such reluctance where the economic loss results from negligent misstatements. The law laid down in *Hedley Byrne & Co. Ltd* v *Heller & Partners Ltd* [1964] AC 465, HL, para 9.4.2 below, is unaffected by *Murphy* v *Brentwood District Council* [1990] 2 All ER 908; see *Spring* v *Guardian Assurance plc* [1994] 3 All ER 129, HL.) In *Anns* v *London Borough of Merton* [1978] AC 728, the House of Lords appears to have proceeded on the mistaken assumption that the contemplated loss was physical. In reality, the loss was economic — namely, the cost of putting right the defect in the building — no person or property having been injured (see [1990] 2 All ER 908 *per* Lord Keith at p. 919 and Lord Oliver at p. 932).

Murphy v *Brentwood District Council* has been rejected by the Supreme Court of Canada (*Canadian National Railway Co.* v *Norsk Pacific Steamship Co.* (1992) 91 DLR (4th) 289; *Winnipeg Condominium Corpn No. 36* v *Bird Construction Co.* (1995) 121 DLR (4th) 193), the High Court of Australia (*Bryan* v *Maloney* (1995) 128 ALR 163), and by the New Zealand Court of Appeal (*Invercargill City Council* v *Hamlin* [1996] 1 All ER 756, PC; see further, para 9.3.2.9 below).

Smoker v *London Fire and Civil Defence Authority* [1991] 2 All ER 449 raised the question whether the amount of a disablement pension received by a claimant who is disabled from earning his living by an accident caused by his employer's negligence or breach of statutory duty should be deducted from any award of damages for loss of earnings. Although expressly invited to do so, the House of Lords refused to overturn the negative answer to this question given 20 years earlier in *Parry* v *Cleaver* [1970] AC 1. Their Lordships could not detect any material change of circumstances during the intervening years and were satisfied with the logic and effect of *Parry* v *Cleaver* (see *Smoker* v *London Fire and Civil Defence Authority*, above, *per* Lord Templeman at pp. 457–8, the other Law Lords agreeing with him).

An attempt to persuade the House of Lords to overrule its decision in *R* v *Lawrence* [1982] AC 510 (which had attracted considerable academic criticism) — on the meaning of the words 'driving recklessly' in s. 1 of the Road Traffic Act 1972 — failed in *R* v *Reid* [1992] 3 All ER 673. (For the subsequent history of the Road Traffic Act 1972 and the offence of causing death by reckless driving, see para 7.9.1.) However, in the later case of *R* v *Adomako* [1994] 3 All ER 79 the House declined to follow the requirement laid down in *R* v *Lawrence*, above, that the trial judge in manslaughter cases should give the jury detailed directions on the word 'reckless', and, at the same time, overruled another of its decisions, *R* v *Seymour* [1983] 2 All ER 1058. In *R* v *Gomez* [1993] 1 All ER 1 the House refused an invitation to depart from its decision in *Lawrence* v *Commissioner of Police for the Metropolis* [1972] AC 626 on the meaning of 'appropriates' in s. 1(1) of the Theft Act 1968.

In the historic case of *Pepper (Inspector of Taxes)* v *Hart* [1993] 1 All ER 42, the House of Lords declined to follow dicta in *Beswick* v *Beswick* [1968] AC 58, *Black-Clawson International Ltd* v *Papierwerke Waldhof-Aschaffenburg AG* [1975] AC 591 and *Davis* v *Johnson* [1979] AC 264 on the use of *Hansard* as an extrinsic aid to the interpretation of statutes (see further, para 8.10.5).

In *Moodie* v *Inland Revenue Commissioners* [1993] 2 All ER 49, a case on self-cancelling tax avoidance schemes, the House, without resorting to the *Practice Statement* of 1966, refused to follow its decision in *Inland Revenue Commissioners* v *Plummer* [1980] AC 896 because it was inconsistent with the later decision in *W. T. Ramsay Ltd* v *Inland Revenue Commissioners* [1982] AC 300. It was impossible to distinguish the two cases on the facts and it was clear that *Plummer* had been correctly decided on the arguments then put before the House (*Moodie*, above, *per* Lord Keith at p. 51 and Lord Templeman at p. 53). Nevertheless, *Plummer* would have been decided differently if the alternative arguments put in *Ramsay* had been advanced therein. Lord Templeman thought that it was not necessary to invoke the *Practice Statement* in order to depart from *Plummer*; it could, instead, simply be ignored as being inconsistent with *Ramsay* (*Moodie*, above, at p. 55). It was said that Hoffmann J, sitting at first instance when *Moodie* was before the High Court, had been right to ignore *Plummer*; when confronted by conflicting decisions of the House of Lords the courts are entitled and bound to follow the later decision (*Moodie*, above, *per* Lord Templeman at p. 55, the other Law Lords agreeing with him).

In *Westdeutsche Landesbank Girozentrale* v *Islington London Borough Council* [1996] 2 All ER 961, the House of Lords declined to follow its earlier decision in *Sinclair* v *Brougham* [1914] AC 398 on the nature of a claim for money had and received under an *ultra vires* contract. According to *Sinclair* v *Brougham*, such a claim is an *equitable proprietary* claim. This view was rejected by the majority in the *Westdeutsche* case, it being held that it is a *personal* action based upon a total failure of consideration. *Sinclair* v *Brougham* was variously described as 'controversial', 'bewildering', and 'wrongly decided' ([1996] 2 All ER 961 *per* Lord Goff, Lord Browne-Wilkinson, and Lord Lloyd at pp. 970,

996 and 1018 respectively), and two of their Lordships would have overruled it altogether (ibid., *per* Lord Browne-Wilkinson at pp. 993 and 996, and *per* Lord Lloyd at p. 1018). (See further on the *Westdeutsche* case, para 11.1.1.)

Being free of the shackles of binding precedent, the House of Lords is uniquely placed to develop English domestic law through its judicial decisions. Care must be taken, however, that evolution does not too often turn into the sort of reform which confuses the judicial function of a court of law with the legislative function enjoyed by Parliament.

To take a recent example, when in the momentous case of *R* v *R (rape: marital exemption)* [1991] 4 All ER 481 (para 9.3.2.7 below) the House abolished altogether a husband's 250 year-old immunity from criminal liability for raping his wife, their Lordships justified the decision on the basis that the case was not concerned with the creation of a new offence but with their duty to act in order to remove from the common law a fiction which had become unacceptable (ibid., *per* Lord Keith at pp. 489–90, quoting with approval from Lord Lane CJ's judgment delivered when the case was before the Court of Appeal). They saw the decision as an example of the ability of the common law to evolve 'in the light of changing social, economic and cultural developments' (ibid., *per* Lord Keith at p. 483). These explanations notwithstanding, some commentators viewed the decision in *R* v *R (rape: marital exemption)* as coming close to usurping the law-making functions of Parliament.

In three subsequent cases the House declined to change the law on the ground that to do so was the province of Parliament. In *R* v *Clegg* [1995] 1 All ER 334, it had been argued that the House should make new law by creating a new qualified defence which would have the effect of reducing murder to manslaughter. This defence, it was urged, would be one of using excessive force in self defence, or to prevent crime, or to make or assist a lawful arrest, and would be available to a soldier or police officer acting in the course of his duty. However, Lord Lloyd (speaking on behalf of their Lordships), though not averse to judicial law-making and citing *R* v *R (rape: marital exemption)* as a good recent example of it, declared that he had no doubt that they should abstain from law-making in the present case since the reduction of murder to manslaughter in a particular class of case was essentially a matter for Parliament, and not for them as a court, to decide upon (ibid., p. 346).

In *C* v *Director of Public Prosecutions* [1995] 2 All ER 43, the House referred to the anomalies and absurdities produced by the rebuttable common law presumption that a child between the ages of 10 and 14 is incapable of committing a crime (see further, para 1.7.6.2.4). Nevertheless their Lordships refused to abolish the presumption, preferring instead to call upon Parliament to review it. Lord Lowry discerned in the case law the following guidelines for judicial law-making (see [1995] 2 All ER 43 at p. 52):

(a) judges should exercise caution before imposing a remedy where the solution to a problem is doubtful;

(b) they should be cautious about making changes if Parliament has rejected opportunities of dealing with a known problem or has legislated while leaving the problem untouched;

(c) they are more suited to dealing with purely legal problems than disputed matters of social policy;

(d) fundamental legal doctrines should not lightly be set aside;

(e) judges should not change the law unless they can achieve finality and certainty.

(Parliament later abolished the presumption by s. 34 of the Crime and Disorder Act 1998 with effect from 30 September 1998.)

Under s. 14(1) of the Prevention of Terrorism (Temporary Provisions) Act 1989 a constable can arrest a person without warrant on reasonable suspicion that that person is guilty of certain offences, or is concerned in the commission, preparation or instigation of certain acts of terrorism, or is subject to an exclusion order. In *R* v *Chief Constable of the Royal Ulster Constabulary (ex parte Begley)* [1997] 4 All ER 833, it was argued that persons arrested and detained in Northern Ireland under s. 14(1) had a common law right to the advice and assistance of a solicitor during police interviews and that, if no such right existed, the House of Lords should create it. It was held unanimously that, although persons so arrested have the right to consult *privately* with a solicitor, there is no right to have a solicitor present *during police interviews*. Further, the House refused to create such a right since Parliament had clearly expressed its will in the relevant statutory provisions that persons arrested in Northern Ireland under s. 14(1) (as distinct from persons arrested under other provisions, or even under the same provisions if arrested in England and Wales) should not have it. Lord Browne-Wilkinson, delivering the leading opinion, emphasised that it is 'impermissible for the House to develop the law in a direction which is contrary to the expressed will of Parliament'. While acknowledging the power of the House of Lords as a court to develop the law, his Lordship described that power as a limited one to be 'exercised only in the gaps left by Parliament' ([1997] 4 All ER 833 at p. 838).

The House returned to judicial law-making in *Kleinwort Benson Ltd* v *Lincoln City Council* [1998] 4 All ER 513, HL, when, by a majority of three to two, it abolished the 200 year-old common law rule that money paid under a mistake of law is not recoverable. The majority decided that the mistake of law rule should no longer form part of English law because it did not sit well with the modern law of restitution based on the principle of unjust enrichment.

Lord Goff, an acknowledged expert on the law of restitution, noted how the rule had been criticised over the years (pp. 528–30), how it had already been abolished, either by judicial decision or by statute, in Australia, Canada, New Zealand, Scotland and South Africa (pp. 530–31), and how (p. 531) the Law Commission had recommended its abolition in 1994 in its report, *Restitution: mistakes of law and ultra vires public authority receipts and payments* (Law Com. No. 227, 1994). He concluded that there was 'no good reason for postponing the matter for legislation', especially as it was not known 'whether or, if so, when, Parliament may legislate' (p. 532).

The two dissentients, Lords Browne-Wilkinson and Lloyd, while agreeing that the law should be changed so as to allow the recovery of money paid under a mistake of law, were of the view, unlike the majority, that when the law is changed by a later decision of the courts any money paid under the former law is *not* recoverable since, at the time of payment, the payer was not acting under a mistake of law (pp. 517–19 and 546–48, respectively). They were disturbed by the retrospective effect of the majority decision (which would allow old transactions to be reopened: see para 9.3.1.2, above). In view of that, they thought that the correct course was to leave the mistake of law rule to be changed by Parliament, as recommended by the Law Commission (pp. 523 and 552, respectively).

Another piece of judicial law-making, at least as controversial as that in *R* v *R (rape: marital exemption)* [1991] 4 All ER 481, HL (above), occurred in *Fitzpatrick* v *Sterling Housing Association Ltd* [1999] 4 All ER 705, HL. Here, the House of Lords reversed the Court of Appeal and held – again by a bare majority – that a same-sex partner was capable of succeeding to an assured tenancy on the death of the original tenant as a 'member of the original tenant's family' under para 3 of sch. 1 to the Rent Act 1977, provided that the claimant could show that the homosexual relationship was characterised by features usually denoted by the word 'family'. These are that there should be 'a degree of mutual inter-dependence, of the sharing of lives, of caring and love, of commitment and support' (*per* Lord Slynn at p. 714). On the facts, the claimant was held entitled to succeed since he and the deceased had cohabited for many years in a stable, loving homosexual partnership.

Lord Lowry's guidelines for judicial law-making, proposed in *C* v *Director of Public Prosecutions* [1995] 2 All ER 43, HL, at p. 52 (above), were not cited in *Kleinwort Benson Ltd* v *Lincoln City Council* [1998] 4 All ER 513, HL, above, or in the *Fitzpatrick* case. In relation to those guidelines, it could be argued that the majority in *Fitzpatrick* ignored the fact that Parliament did not see fit to extend the right to succession to the survivor of a same-sex relationship when the Rent Act 1977 was amended as recently as 1988. By that amendment, the right to succession was extended to a person living with the tenant as his or her wife or husband, thereby putting the decision in *Dyson Holdings Ltd* v *Fox* [1976] QB 503, CA, on a statutory footing (see *per* Lord Hobhouse, dissenting, at [1999] 4 All ER 705, 744–45). It could be further argued that the majority were meddling in a disputed social policy matter which Parliament is more suited to formulate than the judges. The view that the matter is 'disputed' within Lord Lowry's guideline is supported by the presence of two dissenting House of Lords' opinions in *Fitzpatrick*, together with the judgments of the majority when the case was before the Court of Appeal ([1997] 4 All ER 991).

These criticisms notwithstanding, the majority in the *Fitzpatrick* case were convinced that they were right to make new law themselves rather than leave the matter to Parliament. Lord Slynn said (at p. 710):

It has been suggested that for your Lordships to decide this appeal in favour of the appellant would be to usurp the function of Parliament. It is trite that that is something the courts must not do. When considering social issues in particular, judges must not substitute their own views to fill gaps . . . It is, however, for the court in the first place to interpret each phrase in its statutory context. To do so is not to usurp Parliament's function; not to do so would be to abdicate the judicial function. If Parliament takes the view that the result is not what is wanted it will change the legislation.

Similarly, Lord Clyde (at p. 730) recognised that 'judicial activism certainly has to be tempered by due restraint' and that 'the drawing of the boundary of the judicial task is often delicate and sometimes controversial', but he did not consider that the boundary was being crossed in the decision of the majority. (See also *per* Lord Nicholls at p. 722.)

Lords Hutton and Hobhouse dissented on the ground that the matter should have been left to Parliament. Lord Hutton (at p. 742), while accepting the strength of the argument that the law should be changed so as to give protection to the homosexual partner of a deceased tenant, thought that such a change should only be made by Parliament. To Lord Hobhouse (at p. 743), it was 'an improper usurpation of the legislative function for a court to adopt social policies which have not yet been incorporated in the relevant legislation'. (See further on the *Fitzpatrick* case, para 8.10.6.)

9.3.2.3 Court of Appeal (civil division)

9.3.2.3.1 Circumstances in which the Court of Appeal is bound by precedent: Young v *Bristol Aeroplane Co. Ltd.* The Court of Appeal is bound by decisions of the House of Lords, even if it considers them to be wrong, unless they can be distinguished on the facts or on the law, or unless they were given *per incuriam* (*IM Properties plc* v *Cape &*

Dalgleish [1998] 3 All ER 203, CA, a somewhat controversial application of the *per incuriam* doctrine, as to which see below). The distinguishing of House of Lords' decisions by the Court of Appeal is dealt with in more detail later (para 9.3.2.3.2.2). Decisions of the Court of Appeal itself are binding on the High Court and the county courts but they do not bind the House of Lords.

The remaining question is whether the Court of Appeal is bound by its own previous decisions. In *Young* v *Bristol Aeroplane Co. Ltd* [1944] KB 718, CA, a 'full' Court of Appeal of six members decided that it was normally so bound subject to the following three exceptions:

(a) Where its own previous decisions conflict, the Court of Appeal must decide which to follow and which to reject. Thus, in *Tiverton Estates Ltd* v *Wearwell Ltd* [1975] Ch 146, the Court of Appeal refused to follow *Law* v *Jones* [1974] Ch 112, CA, which had been decided only six months earlier by a differently constituted Court of Appeal on the same point of law — the nature of the written memorandum required by s. 40 of the Law of Property Act 1925. *Law* v *Jones* was inconsistent with earlier decisions of equal authority. *Law* v *Jones* will probably not be followed in the future but, in strict theory, it is still open to the Court of Appeal to choose between *Law* v *Jones* and *Tiverton Estates* v *Wearwell Ltd*. *Law* v *Jones* was not followed by a Queen's Bench Division judge in *Cohen* v *Nessdale Ltd* [1981] 3 All ER 118. (Note that s. 40 of the Law of Property Act 1925 was repealed, as from 27 September 1989, by the Law of Property (Miscellaneous Provisions) Act 1989.)

In *National Westminster Bank plc* v *Powney* [1990] 2 All ER 416, CA, the Court of Appeal, faced with two irreconcilable decisions of its own on the question whether an application for leave to issue execution of a judgment was an 'action' capable of becoming statute-barred, chose to follow *W. T. Lamb & Sons* v *Rider* [1948] 2 KB 331 rather than *Lougher* v *Donovan* [1948] 2 All ER 11.

In *Finnegan* v *Parkside Health Authority* [1998] 1 All ER 595, CA, the Court of Appeal preferred its decisions in *Costellow* v *Somerset County Council* [1993] 1 All ER 952 and *Mortgage Corp Ltd* v *Sandoes* (1996) *The Times*, 27 December to its decision in *Savill* v *Southend Health Authority* [1995] 1 WLR 1254 on the relevance of prejudice in an application to the court for an extension of time for complying with procedural requirements.

(b) The Court of Appeal must refuse to follow a decision of its own which cannot stand with a decision of the House of Lords even though its decision has not been expressly overruled by the House of Lords. Thus, in *Family Housing Association* v *Jones* [1990] 1 All ER 385, CA, the Court of Appeal refused on this ground to follow three of its own recent decisions on the distinction between a tenancy and a licence. Although those decisions had not been expressly overruled by the House of Lords, one of them could not be reconciled with the subsequent decision of the House in *AG Securities Ltd* v *Vaughan* [1988] 3 All ER 1058, HL, while the other two could not stand with the later decisions in *Street* v *Mountford* [1985] AC 809, HL, and *AG Securities Ltd* v *Vaughan*, HL.

The Court of Appeal has taken the view that it is not bound by a decision of its own in a case where, on a further appeal, the House of Lords decided that an issue dealt with in the Court of Appeal did not arise for decision and expressed no opinion on the soundness of the Court of Appeal's reasoning on that issue. The decision of the Court of Appeal, though of persuasive authority, would not be binding (*R* v *Secretary of State for the Home Department (ex parte Al-Mehdawi)* [1989] 1 All ER 777, CA, not following *R* v *Diggines (ex parte Rahmani)* [1985] 1 All ER 1073, CA. Note that the *Al-Mehdawi* decision was reversed, and the *Rahmani* decision overruled, by the House of Lords in *Al-Mehdawi* v *Secretary of State for the Home Department* [1989] 3 All ER 843, HL (see further, para 11.8.3.2.2), but this does not affect the statement in the text).

(c) The Court of Appeal need not follow a decision of its own if satisfied that it was given *per incuriam* (literally, by carelessness or mistake).

The usual ground on which a decision of the Court of Appeal is regarded as *per incuriam* is that it was given in ignorance or forgetfulness of a relevant statutory provision or binding decision of the House of Lords or Court of Appeal. Before the Court of Appeal rejects one of its own decisions on this ground, it has to be shown not only that the decision was given *per incuriam* but also that the Court of Appeal in the earlier case *must* have reached a different conclusion had it had the uncited statute or binding decision in mind (*Duke* v *Reliance Systems Ltd* [1987] 2 All ER 858, CA; the *per incuriam* doctrine did not need to be (and was not) considered on appeal to the House of Lords in this case, reported *sub nom. Duke* v *GEC Reliance Ltd* at [1988] AC 618, HL).

In *Rakhit* v *Carty* [1990] 2 All ER 202, the Court of Appeal declined to follow two of its earlier decisions on the Rent Act 1977 on the ground that the first of them was made in ignorance of a relevant provision of the Act while the second was based solely (and reluctantly) on the first, which had been given *per incuriam*. In *Wellcome Trust Ltd* v *Hammad* [1998] 1 All ER 657, the Court of Appeal declined to follow its earlier decision in *Pittalis* v *Grant* [1989] 2 All ER 622, CA, on the meaning of 'dwelling house' in the Rent Act 1977 on the ground that it was arrived at in ignorance of some relevant decisions referred to in the speech of Lord Wilberforce in the House of Lords' case of *Maunsell* v *Olins* [1975] AC 373, and was, therefore, given *per incuriam*.

Royal Bank of Scotland v *Etridge* [1997] 3 All ER 628, CA, a decision of a two-judge court at an interim stage on the principles for deciding whether legal advice provided to a wife has rebutted the presumption of undue influence which arises in her favour against her husband, was not followed by a three-judge Court of Appeal in *Royal Bank of Scotland* v *Etridge (No. 2)* [1998] 4 All ER 705 on the ground that it was wrongly decided, having been made *per incuriam* in ignorance of two of its earlier decisions, *Midland Bank plc* v *Serter* [1995] 1 FLR 1034 and *Barclays Bank plc* v *Thompson* [1997] 4 All ER 816. In *Wallcite Ltd* v *Ferrishurst Ltd* [1999] 1 All ER 977, the Court of Appeal refused to follow its earlier decision in *Ashburn Anstalt* v *Arnold* [1988] 2 All ER 147, CA, on the scope of overriding interests under s. 70(1)(g) of the Land Registration Act 1925, on the ground that if the court in the *Ashburn* case had been referred to the House of Lords' decision in *Williams & Glyn's Bank Ltd* v *Boland* [1981] AC 487, HL, the *Ashburn* case would have been decided differently.

Young v *Bristol Areoplane Co. Ltd* [1944] KB 718, CA, envisaged that there would be other grounds on which decisions might later be held to be *per incuriam*, even though those decisions do not fall strictly within the usual definition of decisions given *per incuriam* (see above). It was pointed out, however, that such cases will be 'of the rarest occurrence' ([1944] KB 718 *per* Lord Greene MR at p. 729; or 'rare and exceptional', as Evershed MR described them in *Morelle Ltd* v *Wakeling* [1955] 2 QB 379, CA, at p. 406). The Court of Appeal has consistently refused to define what these other grounds might be (see, e.g., *Rickards* v *Rickards* [1989] 3 All ER 193, CA, *per* Lord Donaldson MR at p. 199 and Balcombe LJ at p. 201). It is certainly no ground for arguing that a decision was *per incuriam* to show that a necessary party to the proceedings was not before the court on the earlier occasion (*Morelle Ltd* v *Wakeling,* CA, above), or that the court had not had the benefit of the best argument from counsel (ibid.), or that the court *might* have reached a different conclusion if other arguments or material had been placed before it (*Duke* v *Reliance Systems Ltd,* CA, above). It has, however, been held that a decision may be *per incuriam* through incomplete reference during argument to the reports of a particular case which is otherwise binding on the Court of Appeal (*Industrial Properties (Barton Hill) Ltd* v *Associated Electrical Industries Ltd* [1977] QB 580, CA).

Subsequent developments have shown that the *per incuriam* doctrine applies in exceptional circumstances where the Court of Appeal's earlier decision involved a 'manifest slip or error'. In *Williams* v *Fawcett* [1985] 1 All ER 787, CA, the Court of Appeal held in a contempt of court case that there were exceptional circumstances for treating as *per incuriam* (and, therefore, not following) two of its own previous decisions reported in 1984 and 1985. Those circumstances were (i) that the growth of the error in the previous cases could be clearly detected; (ii) that the cases concerned the liberty of the subject; and (iii) that the cases were of such a nature that it was unlikely that they would ever reach the House of Lords, which would not, therefore, have an opportunity to rectify the error which had crept into the law (see [1985] 1 All ER 787 *per* Sir John Donaldson MR at p. 795; *Langley* v *North West Water Authority* [1991] 3 All ER 610, CA, *per* Lord Donaldson MR at pp. 621–2; see also *R* v *Parole Board (ex parte Wilson)* [1992] 2 All ER 576 (para 11.8.3.2.3), a case involving the liberty of the subject, where the Court of Appeal applied *Williams* v *Fawcettt* in refusing to follow its decision in *R* v *Secretary of State for the Home Department (ex parte Gunnell)* (1984) *The Times*, 7 November).

In *Rickards* v *Rickards* [1989] 3 All ER 193, CA, the Court of Appeal held that it could treat as *per incuriam* one of its own earlier decisions reported in 1981 in which the court had misunderstood the effect of a House of Lords' decision reported in 1891 and had consequently wrongly decided that it had no jurisdiction to do what was asked of it. This was a 'rare and exceptional' type of case because (i) a wrongful denial of jurisdiction was a serious matter amounting to a breach of statutory duty on the part of the Court of Appeal, and (ii) it was most unlikely (because of the cost involved) that the House of Lords would be presented with an opportunity to correct the mistake. The same considerations apply to a case where the Court of Appeal is guilty of abuse of power by purporting to exercise a jurisdiction which it does not possess (ibid., *per* Lord Donaldson MR at p. 199).

The reasoning in *Williams* v *Fawcett* [1985] 1 All ER 787, CA, and *Rickards* v *Rickards* [1989] 3 All ER 193, CA, was applied in *Rakhit* v *Carty* [1990] 2 All ER 202, CA. Here, the Court of Appeal did not follow *Cheniston Investments Ltd* v *Waddock* [1988] 2 EGLR 136, CA, because it had been given in 'error' on the mistaken assumption that the court was bound by *Kent* v *Millmead Properties Ltd* (1982) 44 P & CR 353, CA, which itself had been given *per incuriam* in ignorance of a relevant statutory provision (see *Rakhit* v *Carty* [1990] 2 All ER 202 *per* Russell LJ at pp. 207–8, Sir Roualeyn Cumming-Bruce at p. 208 and Lord Donaldson MR at p. 208). The circumstances of *Rakhit* v *Carty* were 'exceptional' because the case concerned not only the rights of the immediate parties but also the rights of thousands of landlords and tenants throughout the country (ibid., *per* Lord Donaldson MR at p. 208).

Like other courts, the Court of Appeal is only bound, if at all, by the *ratio decidendi* of a case. It is not bound by a previous decision which is not authority for the proposition for which it is cited, or in which a proposition of law was merely assumed to be correct without the court addressing the issue. For example, in interpreting s. 32 of the Race Relations Act 1976 in *Jones* v *Tower Boot Co. Ltd* [1997] 2 All ER 406, CA, the Court of Appeal was confronted by its own earlier decision in *Irving* v *Post Office* [1987] IRLR 289, CA, in which the Post Office was held not liable for the act of a postman who wrote a racially offensive remark on the back of an envelope addressed to his neighbours, with whom he was in dispute. In *Jones*, however, the Court of Appeal was able to ignore *Irving*, without concluding that it had been decided *per incuriam* and without distinguishing it, on the ground that the court in *Irving* had not been referred to s. 32(1) of the 1976 Act but appeared to have decided the case on the unchallenged assumption that the common law principles of vicarious liability applied to it. It followed, therefore, that *Irving* did not support the contention of the employers in *Jones*. The authority of *Irving* v *Post Office* was thus considerably weakened and the case may now be regarded as having been wrongly decided. (See further on *Jones* v *Tower Boot Co. Ltd*, para 8.10.6)

A fourth exception appears to have been recognised since the *Bristol Aeroplane* case was decided in 1944, namely, that the Court of Appeal is not bound to follow a decision in an *interlocutory* matter made by *two* judges in the Court of Appeal (*Boys* v *Chaplin* [1968] 2 QB 1, CA). Thus, in *Welsh Development Agency* v *Redpath Dorman Long Ltd* [1994] 4 All ER 10, CA, it was held by a three-man Court of Appeal in an interlocutory matter that, applying *Boys* v *Chaplin*, an earlier decision of a *two-man* Court of Appeal given in an interlocutory matter (*Kennett* v *Brown* [1988] 1 WLR 582) was wrong and not binding upon it. However, the extent to which *Boys* v *Chaplin* remains authoritative is unclear following opinions expressed, *obiter*, in *Langley* v *North West Water Authority* [1991] 3 All ER 610, CA. (See also *Limb* v *Union Jack Removals Ltd* [1998] 2 All ER 513, CA *per* Brooke LJ at pp. 522–23.) One thing seems clear: when the Court of Appeal is dealing with *final*, as opposed to interlocutory, appeals, the authority of a two-judge court is to be regarded as the same as that of a three-judge court (*Langley* v *North West Water Authority* [1991] 3 All ER 610, CA, *per* Lord Donaldson MR at pp. 621–2, explaining *Boys* v *Chaplin*, above). In consequence, the decision of a two-man Court of Appeal given in a final appeal will be binding on a later three-man Court of Appeal subject to the exceptions laid down in the *Bristol Aeroplane* case.

It is at least arguable that a fifth exception exists (or ought to exist) consequent upon United Kingdom membership of the European Union. In order to give full effect to Community law it would seem desirable that the Court of Appeal, like the House of Lords and the High Court, should be free to depart from a previous decision of its own which is inconsistent with Community law. Furthermore, by s. 3(1) of the European Communities Act 1972, an English court faced with a question of Community law must either refer the question to the European Court or decide the question itself in the light of any relevant decisions of the European Court. In Community law cases it follows that, since the Court of Appeal is bound both by decisions of the European Court and those of its own making, there is scope for potential conflict between decisions of the two courts.

Not surprisingly, the principles laid down in 1944 in the *Bristol Aeroplane* case do not, as generally understood, provide a direct solution to the problem where the Court of Appeal is confronted with a binding decision of its own (or, for that matter, of the House of Lords) which is, at the same time, inconsistent with a decision of the European Court. The view of the European Court is that the duty of a national court to apply Community law may involve, if necessary, ignoring national laws and practices (*Amministrazione delle Finanze dello Stato* v *Simmenthal SpA* [1978] 3 CMLR 263, CJEC). On the other hand, in at least one English case it has been said that United Kingdom membership of the European Union has not abrogated the doctrine of *stare decisis* in the Court of Appeal (*Duke* v *Reliance Systems Ltd* [1987] 2 All ER 858, CA, *per* Sir John Donaldson MR at p. 860).

One answer is to extend or adapt the existing exceptions recognised in the *Bristol Aeroplane* case. It may be, however, that s. 3(1) of the European Communities Act 1972 itself provides the answer for it appears to imply that, in the event of conflict, priority should be accorded to decisions of the European Court. It will be readily appreciated that the precedent problem is one which does not affect only the Court of Appeal since courts and tribunals sitting at first instance (to which s. 3(1) is also applicable) must administer Community law where appropriate. It seems unlikely that s. 3(1) was intended to confer upon, say, the High Court *carte blanche* to ignore binding decisions of the Court of Appeal or House of Lords where individual judges on their own initiative consider that those decisions are in conflict with the case law of the European Court.

9.3.2.3.2   Lord Denning's approach to precedent in the Court of Appeal

9.3.2.3.2.1   Introduction.   From the time of the *Practice Statement* affecting *stare decisis* in the House of Lords in 1966 (para 9.3.2.2 above) Lord Denning MR carried on a one-man campaign to secure a change of practice in the Court of Appeal (see Carty, 'Precedent and the Court of Appeal: Lord Denning's views explored', (1981) 1 Legal Studies 68). The attack was on two fronts. First, he asserted that the Court of Appeal was no longer bound by decisions of the House of Lords. Secondly, he claimed that the Court of Appeal was no longer bound to follow its own decisions as a general rule and not just in the exceptional circumstances laid down in *Young* v *Bristol Aeroplane Co. Ltd* [1944] KB 718, CA. His views were based on the *Practice Statement* itself, which, he alleged, had transformed the *stare decisis* principle in the Court of Appeal as well as the House of Lords. But this approach ignored the closing words of the *Practice Statement* that it was not intended to affect the use of precedent elsewhere than in the House of Lords. Lord Denning understood (or misunderstood) those words to mean: 'We are only considering the doctrine of precedent in the Lords. We are not considering its use elsewhere' (*The Discipline of Law*, 1979, p. 297).

9.3.2.3.2.2   Decisions of the House of Lords.   When *Conway* v *Rimmer* [1967] 2 All ER 1260 was before the Court of Appeal in 1967 Lord Denning said, dissenting (at p. 1263):

> [M]y brethren today feel that we are still bound by the observations of the House of Lords in *Duncan* v *Cammell, Laird & Co. Ltd.* . . . . I do not agree. The doctrine of precedent has been transformed by the recent statement of Lord Gardiner LC. This is the very case in which to throw off the fetters.

When *Conway* v *Rimmer* reached the House of Lords ([1968] AC 910), *Duncan's* case was reconsidered and overruled but it was made clear that *Duncan's* case had been binding on the Court of Appeal all along.

In *Broome* v *Cassell & Co. Ltd* [1971] 2 QB 354, the Court of Appeal, led by Lord Denning, unanimously refused to follow the decision of the House of Lords in *Rookes* v *Barnard* [1964] AC 1129, HL, on the principles for the award of exemplary damages in tort. The refusal was based on the ground that *Rookes* v *Barnard* was wrong and was decided *per incuriam,* in ignorance of two previous decisions of the House. When *Broome* v *Cassell & Co. Ltd* reached the House of Lords (*sub nom. Cassell & Co. Ltd* v *Broome* [1972] AC 1027), the Court of Appeal was castigated for its disloyalty. Lord Hailsham of St Marylebone LC said (at p. 1054) that:

[I]t is not open to the Court of Appeal to give gratuitous advice to judges of first instance to ignore decisions of the House of Lords in this way and, if it were open to the Court of Appeal to do so, it would be highly undesirable . . . .

The fact is, and I hope it will never be necessary to say so again, that, in the hierarchical system of courts which exists in this country, it is necessary for each lower tier, including the Court of Appeal, to accept loyally the decisions of the higher tiers.

Lord Denning, writing extra-judicially, has since expressed regret for the approach he adopted in *Broome* v *Cassell & Co. Ltd*. Because counsel, at the invitation of Lord Denning, had argued that *Rookes* v *Barnard* was wrong, Commander Broome was later ordered to pay part of the costs of the hearing in the Court of Appeal (*The Discipline of Law,* 1979, p. 311).

Lord Denning returned to the attack in *Schorsch Meier GmbH* v *Hennin* [1975] QB 416, CA, a case in which the Court of Appeal held that an English court had power to award damages for breach of contract in a foreign currency which was the currency of the contract. In so deciding, the Court of Appeal did not follow a decision of the House of Lords — *Re United Railways of the Havana & Regla Warehouses Ltd* [1961] AC 1007, HL — in which it had been laid down that damages could be awarded only in sterling.

The *Schorsch Meier* case did not go to the House of Lords. But another case on the same point did. This was *Miliangos* v *George Frank (Textiles) Ltd* [1976] AC 443, in which the House of Lords, while overruling the *United Railways* case themselves, once again put Lord Denning in his place on the issue of *stare decisis*. Lord Cross was particularly scathing in his criticism (at p. 496):

> In the *Schorsch Meier* case, Lord Denning MR . . . took it on himself to say that the decision in the *Havana* case that our courts cannot give judgment for payment of a sum of foreign currency — though right in 1961 — ought not to be followed in 1974 because the 'reasons for the rule have now ceased to exist'. . . . [T]he Master of the Rolls was not entitled to take such a course. It is not for any inferior court — be it a county court or a division of the Court of Appeal presided over by Lord Denning — to review decisions of this House. Such a review can only be undertaken by this House itself under the declaration of 1966.

The Court of Appeal is not, of course, bound by a House of Lords' decision if it is distinguishable on the facts or on the law. But care must be taken in the Court of Appeal to avoid using the process of distinguishing too hastily as a means of circumventing a House of Lords' decision which is felt to be wrong or, at least, inconvenient. Mindful of Lord Hailsham's rebuke in *Cassell & Co. Ltd* v *Broome* (above), the majority of the Court of Appeal in *Paal Wilson & Co. A/S* v *Paartenrederei Hannah Blumenthal* [1982] 3 All ER 394, CA, sought to avoid the consequences of the House of Lords' decision in the *Bremer Vulkan* case [1981] AC 909, HL, by distinguishing it rather than openly declaring it to have been wrongly decided. Lord Denning MR and Kerr LJ held in *Paal Wilson* that an important passage in the speech of Lord Diplock, speaking on behalf of the other Law Lords in *Bremer Vulkan,* was *obiter dictum* and not part of the *ratio decidendi* of that case. Since the Court of Appeal is only bound by *rationes decidendi,* as opposed to *obiter dicta,* of the House of Lords, Lord Denning MR and Kerr LJ concluded that the *Bremer Vulkan* case was distinguishable. Griffiths LJ dissented. While not enthusiastic about the *Bremer Vulkan* decision, he thought that it was not legitimately distinguishable and should therefore be loyally followed.

When *Paal Wilson & Co. A/S* v *Paartenrederei Hannah Blumenthal* reached the House of Lords ([1983] 1 All ER 34), the decision of Lord Denning MR and Kerr LJ was reversed. The House held that *Bremer Vulkan* was binding on the Court of Appeal. It was not distinguishable because the relevant passage in Lord Diplock's speech was not merely *obiter* but formed part of the *ratio decidendi* of the case. Furthermore, the House of Lords in *Paal Wilson* refused to reconsider its decision in the *Bremer Vulkan* case (para 9.3.2.2 above).

9.3.2.3.2.3 *Decisions of the Court of Appeal.*

The second front of Lord Denning's attack on *stare decisis* was to assert that the Court of Appeal was no longer bound rigidly to follow its own previous decisions. In 1969, in the case of *Gallie* v *Lee* [1969] 2 Ch 17, CA, he said (at p. 37):

I do not think we are bound by prior decisions of our own, or at any rate, not absolutely bound. We are not fettered as it was once thought. It was a self-imposed limitation: and we who imposed it can also remove it. The House of Lords have done it. So why should not we do likewise?

But the other two judges in the appeal expressly disagreed with this statement. Russell LJ said (at p. 41) that the House of Lords existed to correct errors in the Court of Appeal and so it was unnecessary for the Court of Appeal to depart from the principle of *stare decisis*. Salmon LJ was more reluctant in his disagreement. He could see no valid reason why the Court of Appeal should not one day alter its practice. But he thought it could only be done by a pronouncement of the whole court and, in any case, that day had not yet arrived (at p. 49).

In *Tiverton Estates Ltd* v *Wearwell Ltd* [1975] Ch 146, CA, Lord Denning repeated the view he had expressed in *Gallie* v *Lee,* but added (at p. 161): 'I have not been able, however, yet to persuade my brethren — or, at any rate, not all of them — to agree with this view.' Stamp LJ confessed (at p. 171) that he remained 'one of the unpersuaded brethren of whom Lord Denning MR has spoken'. Scarman LJ was more lengthy in his disagreement (at pp. 172–3):

The Court of Appeal occupies a central, but . . . an intermediate position in our legal system. To a large extent, the consistency and certainty of the law depend upon it. It sits almost always in divisions of three: more judges can sit to hear a case, but their decision enjoys no greater authority than a court composed of three. If, therefore, throwing aside the restraints of *Young* v *Bristol Aeroplane Co. Ltd,* one division of the court should refuse to follow another because it believed the other's decision to be wrong, there would be a risk of confusion and doubt arising where there should be consistency and certainty. The appropriate forum for the correction of the Court of Appeal's errors is the House of Lords, where the decision will at least have the merit of being final and binding — subject only to the House's power to review its own decisions. The House of Lords, as the court of last resort, needs this power of review: it does not follow that an intermediate appellate court needs it.

By this time Lord Denning seemed to have learnt his lesson. He capitulated and accepted the orthodox view in *Miliangos* v *George Frank (Textiles) Ltd* [1975] QB 487, CA, at p. 503:

I have myself often said that this court is not absolutely bound by its own decisions and may depart from them just as the House of Lords from theirs; but my colleagues have not gone so far. So that I am in duty bound to defer to their view.

But the whole matter was reopened, and at a much more sophisticated level, in *Davis* v *Johnson* [1979] AC 264, CA and HL. This case concerned the application of s. 1 of the Domestic Violence and Matrimonial Proceedings Act 1976 (since repealed and replaced by the Family Law Act 1996). The parties, who were not married to each other, lived together with their baby daughter in a council flat of which the parties were joint tenants. There was violence and beatings on the part of the man. The woman fled with the child to a battered wives' refuge. She applied under s. 1 of the 1976 Act to have the man excluded from the flat and for her to be reinstalled. This problem had come before the Court of Appeal on two occasions only a few months earlier in *B* v *B* [1978] Fam 26 and *Cantliff* v *Jenkins* [1978] QB 47. The Court of Appeal had held that the 1976 Act did not protect a female cohabitee where the parties were joint tenants or joint owners but only where she was the sole tenant or sole owner of the property. These decisions would have had the effect of destroying what most people regarded as one of the main objects of the 1976 Act. In *Davis* v *Johnson,* Lord Denning called together a 'full' court of five judges, describing it as 'a court of all the talents'. It was held by a majority of three to two (Lord Denning MR, Sir George Baker P and Shaw LJ; Goff and Cumming-Bruce LJJ dissenting) that the 1976 Act does protect a female cohabitee even where she is not a tenant at all or only a joint tenant. *B* v *B* and *Cantliff* v *Jenkins* were declared to be wrong and were not followed. An injunction was granted to order the man out and reinstall the woman.

On the question of *stare decisis* in the Court of Appeal Lord Denning had this to say (at p. 278):

> On principle, it seems to me that, while this court should regard itself as normally bound by a previous decision of the court, nevertheless it should be at liberty to depart from it if it is convinced that the previous decision was wrong. What is the argument to the contrary? It is said that if an error has been made, this court has no option but to continue the error and leave it to be corrected by the House of Lords. The answer is this: the House of Lords may never have an opportunity to correct the error; and thus it may be perpetuated indefinitely, perhaps for ever.

Later in his judgment (at pp. 281–2) Lord Denning was more specific:

> To my mind, this court should apply similar guidelines to those adopted by the House of Lords in 1966. Whenever it appears to this court that a previous decision was wrong, we should be at liberty to depart from it if we think it right to do so. . . .
>
> Alternatively, in my opinion, we should extend the exceptions in *Young* v *Bristol Aeroplane Co. Ltd* when it appears to be a proper case to do so.

Sir George Baker P was even more inventive and precise. He said (at p. 290) that *Young's* case was binding on the Court of Appeal but he would like to see a further limited exception to it:

> I would attempt to define the exception thus: 'The court is not bound to follow a previous decision of its own if satisfied that that decision was clearly wrong and cannot stand in the face of the will and intention of Parliament expressed in simple language in a recent statute passed to remedy a serious mischief or abuse, and further adherence to the previous decision must lead to injustice in the particular case and unduly restrict proper development of the law with injustice to others.'

On a further appeal, the decision of the majority in the Court of Appeal was upheld ([1979] AC 264, HL) and the House of Lords overruled *B* v *B* and *Cantliff* v *Jenkins*. But their Lordships rejected most of what had been said about *stare decisis* in the Court of Appeal. Lord Diplock, with whom the other four judges — Viscount Dilhorne, Lord Kilbrandon, Lord Salmon and Lord Scarman — expressly agreed, was especially critical. He said (at pp. 325–8) that:

> [T]he rule as it had been laid down in the *Bristol Aeroplane* case had never been questioned thereafter until, following upon the announcement by Lord Gardiner LC in 1966 that the House of Lords would feel free in exceptional cases to depart from a previous decision of its own, Lord Denning MR conducted what may be described, I hope without offence, as a one-man crusade with the object of freeing the Court of Appeal from the shackles which the doctrine of *stare decisis* imposed upon its liberty of decision. . . .
>
> In my opinion, this House should take this occasion to reaffirm expressly, unequivocably and unanimously that the rule laid down in the *Bristol Aeroplane* case as to *stare decisis* is still binding on the Court of Appeal.

Lord Denning has described this decision as his 'most humiliating defeat' and a 'crushing rebuff' (*The Discipline of Law,* 1979, p. 299). But after *Davis* v *Johnson* it is beyond doubt that the true position with regard to *stare decisis* in the Court of Appeal is that, first, the Court of Appeal is bound by decisions of the House of Lords even if they are wrong, and, secondly, the Court of Appeal is bound by its own decisions subject only to the exceptions laid down in *Young* v *Bristol Aeroplane Co. Ltd* [1944] KB 718, CA (para 9.3.2.3.1 above).

9.3.2.4   Court of Appeal (criminal division)

In principle there is no difference in the application of *stare decisis* as between the civil and criminal divisions of the Court of Appeal (*R* v *Spencer* [1985] 1 All ER 673, CA, *per* May LJ at p. 678, not overruled on this point by the House of Lords at [1986] 2 All ER 928). In practice, however, because a person's liberty may be at stake, precedent is not followed as rigidly in the criminal division. The criminal division is not bound to follow its own previous decision if satisfied that the law was misapplied or misunderstood in it, even though the case is not within one of the exceptions in *Young* v *Bristol Aeroplane Co. Ltd (R* v *Taylor* [1950] 2 KB 368, CCA; *R* v *Gould* [1969] 2 QB 65, CA). The same flexibility is applied to decisions of the old Court of Criminal Appeal, which was created by the Criminal Appeal Act 1907 and abolished by the Criminal Appeal Act 1966 (*R* v *Gould,* above).

In *R* v *Chalkley* [1998] 2 All ER 155, CA, the court decided that the earlier case of *R* v *Bloomfield* [1997] 1 Cr App R 135, CA, on the 'unsafeness' of a conviction within the meaning of the amended s. 2(1) of the Criminal Appeal Act 1968, was wrongly decided and declined to follow it for that reason. (See further on *R* v *Chalkley,* para 6.3.2.) *R* v *Popat* [1998] 2 Cr App R 208, CA, a case on identity parades, was criticised and not followed in *R* v *Forbes* (1999) *The Times,* 5 May, CA. *R* v *Forbes* itself was then criticised in *R* v *Khan* (19 August 1999, CA, unreported) and *R* v *Popat (No. 2)* (1999) *The Times,* 7 September, CA. In *R* v *Ryan* (1999) *The Times,* 13 October, CA, it was again held that *R* v *Popat* was correct and was to be preferred to *R* v *Forbes*.

9.3.2.5   Divisional Courts

A Divisional Court is bound by decisions of the House of Lords and Court of Appeal in both civil and criminal cases unless it can distinguish them on the facts or on the law or it is convinced that a particular decision was given *per incuriam*. In *Hughes* v *Kingston upon Hull City Council* [1999] 2 All ER 49, DC, the Queen's Bench Divisional Court refused to follow the Court of Appeal case of *Thai Trading Co.* v *Taylor* [1998] QB 781, CA (on the enforceability of contingency fee agreements entered into by solicitors), on the ground that it was decided *per incuriam* in ignorance of the House of Lords' decision in *Swain* v *Law Society* [1983] 1 AC 598, HL.

A Divisional Court is also normally bound by its own previous decisions but subject to the same exceptions laid down for the Court of Appeal, civil division, in *Young* v *Bristol Aeroplane Co. Ltd* [1944] KB 718, CA (para 9.3.2.3.1 above). This means, for example, that, if its previous decisions conflict, a Divisional Court may choose which to follow and which to reject. It also means that it may refuse to follow a decision of its own if it is now satisfied that the earlier decision was given *per incuriam*.

The Queen's Bench Divisional Court has claimed that, like the Court of Appeal, criminal division, it can refuse to follow its own earlier decision, if convinced that the first decision is wrong, in two cases — (a) when hearing criminal appeals from magistrates' courts, and (b) when considering applications for judicial review. This power was claimed in *R* v *Greater Manchester Coroner (ex parte Tal)* [1984] 3 All ER 240, DC, not following *R* v *Surrey Coroner (ex parte Campbell)* [1982] 2 All ER 545, DC, on the ground that the earlier case was incorrectly decided.

In *R* v *Stafford Justices (ex parte Customs and Excise Commissioners)* [1991] 2 All ER 201, the Divisional Court, on the authority of *R* v *Greater Manchester Coroner (ex parte Tal)*, refused to follow *R* v *Ealing Magistrates' Court (ex parte Dixon)* [1989] 2 All ER 1050, DC, on the ground that it was wrongly decided. *Ex parte Tal* was applied by the Divisional Court in *R* v *Hendon Justices (ex parte Director of Public Prosecutions)* [1993] 1 All ER 411, DC, in order to disown part of the decision (which it now regarded as wrong) in *R* v *Sutton Justices (ex parte Director of Public Prosecutions)* [1992] 2 All ER 129, DC, to the effect that an acquittal by a magistrates' court cannot be quashed by certiorari (see further on these cases, para 11.8.3.2.2).

In *Shaw* v *Director of Public Prosecutions* [1993] 1 All ER 918, DC, the Divisional Court refused to follow *Director of Public Prosecutions* v *Corcoran* [1993] 1 All ER 912, DC, a decision of its own given only four months earlier, on the grounds that it was decided *per incuriam* (in ignorance of *Metropolitan Police Commissioner* v *Curran* [1976] 1 All ER 162, HL, and *Roberts* v *Griffiths* [1978] RTR 362, DC, neither of which was cited to the court in *Director of Public Prosecutions* v *Corcoran*), *and*, applying *ex parte Tal*, that it was decided wrongly.

In *Corcoran*, it had been held that s. 7(6) of the Road Traffic Act 1988, which makes it an offence to fail to provide, without reasonable excuse, a specimen of breath, blood or urine for analysis, in effect created two separate offences relating to, first, driving or attempting to drive while unfit through drink or drugs, and, secondly, being in charge of a motor vehicle while unfit. It followed that an information laid before magistrates which failed to indicate the purpose for which the specimen had been required was bad for duplicity and would be dismissed. The Divisional Court in *Shaw* held that s. 7(6) creates only a single offence and that an information which fails to indicate why the specimen was required is not bad for duplicity. By so holding, the court was able to close off the defence — based on a procedural technicality — which *Corcoran* had created for many hundreds of undeserving motorists.

The matter did not rest there because in the wake of *Shaw* a number of attempts were made in lower courts to persuade magistrates and others that *Corcoran* was still good law. One such attempt which reached the Divisional Court was in *Butterworth* v *Director of*

Public Prosecutions [1994] RTR 181. Here, the Divisional Court preferred *Shaw* to *Corcoran* and decided that in view of the confusion it was time for the relevant law to be clarified by the House of Lords. Accordingly, *Butterworth* was certified as involving points of law of general public importance but leave to appeal was not granted, it being left to the House itself to decide whether it wanted to entertain an appeal. The Appeal Committee of the House granted leave to appeal, and in *Director of Public Prosecutions* v *Butterworth* [1994] 3 All ER 289, the House of Lords affirmed the decision of the Divisional Court in *Butterworth* v *Director of Public Prosecutions,* approved *Shaw,* and overruled *Corcoran.*

9.3.2.6 High Court of Justice

Decisions of individual High Court judges are binding on the county courts but not on other High Court judges. However, they are of strong persuasive authority in the High Court and are usually followed. If a High Court judge feels that he cannot follow a colleague's decision it is always with reluctance and he will usually state his reasons clearly and fully. He cannot 'overrule' it but is limited to 'disapproving' or 'not following' it.

Conflict between High Court decisions produces uncertainty in the law. The Court of Appeal may resolve the conflict one way or the other, and thereby remove the uncertainty, but its ability to do this is dependent upon an appeal being taken there by a litigant. In the early 1970s, long before the wearing of seat-belts in cars became compulsory, the question arose whether the damages awarded to a passenger injured in a road accident caused by the driver's negligence should be reduced for contributory negligence in the case of a passenger who was not wearing a seat-belt. Between 1973 and 1975 there were a dozen or so decisions on this point. Some judges held that failure to wear a seat-belt was not contributory negligence at all; others held that it was, but disagreed about the percentage by which the damages should be reduced. Eventually, the difference of opinion was resolved by the Court of Appeal in 1975 in *Froom* v *Butcher* [1976] QB 286, where it was held that in most cases failure to wear a seat-belt is contributory negligence if use of a belt would have avoided or lessened the injuries sustained in the accident. It was further suggested that, in general, the appropriate reduction is 25 per cent if the injuries would have been prevented altogether by the use of a seat-belt or 15 per cent if they would nevertheless have occurred but would have been less severe.

A solution to the problem of conflicting High Court decisions was suggested by Nourse J in *Colchester Estates* v *Carlton Industries plc* [1984] 2 All ER 601, applying a *dictum* of Denning J (as he then was) in *Minister of Pensions* v *Higham* [1948] 2 KB 153. Nourse J said that when a decision of a High Court judge has been fully considered, but not followed, by a second High Court judge, the second decision should normally be preferred by a third High Court judge, except in the rare case where the third judge is convinced that the second judge was wrong not to follow the first judge. The 'rare case' might be, for example, where some binding or persuasive authority was not cited in either of the first two cases. In the ordinary case the second judge's decision will be regarded as conclusive of the point at first instance, and if a party in the third case is dissatisfied he will have to take the point on appeal to the Court of Appeal (see [1984] 2 All ER 601, at pp. 604–5).

A High Court judge is normally bound by decisions of the House of Lords, the Court of Appeal (including an *ex parte* decision of the Court of Appeal: *The Alexandros P* [1986] 1 All ER 278) and the Divisional Court of his particular Division. He is probably also bound by the decision of a Divisional Court of another Division. For instance, a decision of the Divisional Court of the Queen's Bench Division is probably binding on a judge of the Chancery Division.

A High Court judge is not bound to follow the earlier decision of a higher court if he can *distinguish* it on the facts or on the law. Nor is he bound by such a decision on a proposition of law which was merely *assumed* to be correct without the higher court addressing its mind to the issue (*Re Hetherington (deceased)* [1989] 2 All ER 129, in which Sir Nicolas Browne-Wilkinson V-C held that he was not bound by certain observations of the House of Lords in *Bourne v Keane* [1919] AC 815; see also *Baker v R* [1975] AC 774, JCPC, *per* Lord Diplock at p. 788; *Barrs v Bethell* [1982] 1 All ER 106 *per* Warner J at p. 116; *R v Secretary of State for the Home Department (ex parte Ku)* [1995] 2 All ER 891, CA, *per* Hobhouse LJ at p. 898).

A High Court judge confronted with *conflicting* decisions of the Court of Appeal, in the later of which the earlier decision was fully considered and rejected, is bound to follow the later decision. This is so even if he considers that the later decision is wrong and the earlier decision preferable. While he is free to reject the decisions of other High Court judges (see, e.g., *Colchester Estates v Carlton Industries plc*, above), he does not enjoy the same freedom in relation to Court of Appeal decisions which he considers to be wrong (*Re Smith (a bankrupt)* [1988] 3 All ER 203 *per* Warner J at p. 215).

9.3.2.7 Crown Court

Decisions made on points of law by judges sitting at the Crown Court, though they are of persuasive authority (especially when made by judges of the High Court), are not binding precedents. There is, therefore, no obligation on the part of other Crown Court judges to follow them. Since inconsistent Crown Court decisions may produce uncertainty in the criminal law it is desirable that any conflict be resolved by an appellate court as quickly as possible.

This process may be illustrated by the difference of judicial opinion which surfaced in relation to the controversial subject of marital rape. At the heart of the controversy was an extra-judicial statement of Sir Matthew Hale (Chief Justice of the Court of King's Bench between 1671 and 1676) contained in his *History of the Pleas of the Crown,* published posthumously in 1736, that a husband could not be guilty of raping his wife because on marriage she was deemed to have given him an irrevocable consent to sexual intercourse (1 Hale PC 629). For over 250 years Hale CJ's proposition, though doubted in 1888 by some of the judges who decided *R v Clarence* (1888) 22 QBD 23 (a case not directly on marital rape), was accepted as representing the common law of England and Wales. In order to mitigate the harshness of this rule, some exceptions to it were developed by the judges from 1949 onwards. While leaving the basic rule itself intact, the exceptions recognised that there were circumstances in which the wife's implied consent was terminated.

A similar marital exemption rule had operated in Scots law since 1797. The Scottish courts rejected the rule altogether in 1989 (*S v HM Advocate* 1989 SLT 469, High Court of Justiciary). In the following year, the English rule came under judicial attack in the Crown Court. In July 1990, Owen J reluctantly accepted that part of Hale CJ's proposition which laid down that consent to intercourse was to be implied from the fact of marriage, but he denied that that consent was irrevocable (*R v R (rape: marital exemption)* [1991] 1 All ER 747, Crown Court sitting at Leicester). In October of the same year, Simon Brown J went further and rejected Hale CJ's proposition in its entirety (*R v C (rape: marital exemption)* [1991] 1 All ER 755, Crown Court sitting at Sheffield). He declined to follow the decision of Owen J in *R v R (rape: marital exemption)* and held that a husband could be guilty of raping his wife. In the following month, Rougier J (to whom new arguments had been addressed) decided that the inclusion of the word 'unlawful' in the statutory definition of rape as 'unlawful sexual intercourse with a woman who at the time of the intercourse does not consent to it' (Sexual Offences (Amendment) Act 1976, s. 1(1)(a)) meant that Parliament had intended to preserve the marital immunity rule, which was, moreover, subject only to the exceptions existing at the time the statute was passed (*R* v *J (rape: marital exemption)* [1991] 1 All ER 759, Crown Court sitting at Teesside, not following *R* v *C (rape: marital exemption)* and doubting the correctness of *R* v *R (rape: marital exemption); R* v *J (rape: marital exemption)* was followed by Swinton Thomas J in *R* v *S,* 15 January 1991, unreported, Crown Court sitting at Stafford).

The case of *R* v *R (rape: marital exemption)* was taken on appeal. The House of Lords, following the Scottish case of *S* v *HM Advocate* 1989 SLT 469 and affirming the decision of a full Court of Appeal of five members (see *R* v *R (rape: marital exemption)* [1991] 2 All ER 257, CA), held that, although Hale CJ's proposition had become an accepted part of the common law and reflected the status of wives at the time it was put forward, the marital exemption rule no longer existed in English law since it was an anachronistic and offensive common law fiction which did not reflect the status of wives in contemporary society (see [1991] 4 All ER 481, HL).

In reaching this conclusion, the House of Lords decided that the word 'unlawful' in s. 1(1)(a) of the Sexual Offences (Amendment) Act 1976 did not mean 'outside marriage'. It was held that the word was, in effect, meaningless in the context, and was to be treated as mere surplusage, since it is clearly unlawful to have sexual intercourse with any woman without her consent (*R* v *R (rape: marital exemption)* [1991] 4 All ER 481, HL, *per* Lord Keith at pp. 487–9, the other Law Lords agreeing with him).

In the light of the House of Lords' decision in *R* v *R (rape: marital exemption)* [1991] 4 All ER 481 and a subsequent recommendation by the Law Commission in its Report, *Rape within Marriage* (Law Com No. 205, 1992), Parliament redefined rape by removing the word 'unlawful' — thus making it clear that rape within marriage is a crime (Criminal Justice and Public Order Act 1994, repealing s. 1(1) the Sexual Offences (Amendment) Act 1976 and substituting a new s. 1 of the Sexual Offences Act 1956). It was later held that the House of Lords' abolition of the marital exemption rule had not violated the rights of Mr R (the defendant in *R* v *R (rape: marital exemption)*) under art. 7.1 of the European Convention on Human Rights, which provides that no one should be held guilty of a criminal offence in respect of an act which was not classified as criminal at the time it was committed. The European Court of Human Rights said that the decision of the House of Lords was simply a continuation of a perceptible line of case law dismantling a husband's immunity from prosecution for raping his wife. Furnishing a gradual clarification of the rules of criminal liability through judicial decision on a case-by-case basis was declared not to be a breach of art. 7.1 so long as the resulting development is consistent with the offence and can reasonably be foreseen (*CR* v *United Kingdom* [1996] 1 FLR 434, ECHR).

The Crown Court is bound by decisions of the House of Lords, the Court of Appeal and the Queen's Bench Divisional Court.

9.3.2.8 County courts and magistrates' courts
The decisions of these courts are not binding. They are rarely important in law and are not usually reported in the law reports.

9.3.2.9 Judicial Committee of the Privy Council
Decisions (technically, 'advice') of the Judicial Committee are not binding on the English courts but they are of strong persuasive authority. Thus, the decision of the Judicial

Committee in *Mutual Life & Citizens' Assurance Co. Ltd* v *Evatt* [1971] AC 793 on the question of liability for negligent misstatements, was not followed by the Court of Appeal in *Esso Petroleum Co. Ltd* v *Mardon* [1976] 1 QB 801, CA. But the decision of the Judicial Committee in *Overseas Tankship (UK) Ltd* v *Morts Dock & Engineering Co. Ltd (The Wagon Mound)* [1961] AC 388 on the question of remoteness of damage in negligence was followed by the Court of Appeal in *Doughty* v *Turner Manufacturing Co. Ltd* [1964] 1 QB 518 in preference to one of its own decisions, *Re Polemis* [1921] 3 KB 560, which was regarded as no longer good law.

Decisions of the Judicial Committee are binding in the country from which the appeal came and, possibly, in other countries subject to its jurisdiction where the law on the particular point is the same (*Fatuma Binti Mohamed Bin Salim Bakhshuwen* v *Mohamed Bin Salim Bakhshuwen* [1952] AC 1, PC).

The Judicial Committee is not strictly bound by decisions of the House of Lords because the common law in the Commonwealth is not necessarily the same as in England. It would be wrong, for instance, for the Judicial Committee to inflict on, say, New Zealand, decisions of the House of Lords on the English common law. Thus, in *Invercargill City Council* v *Hamlin* [1996] 1 All ER 756, PC, the Court of Appeal of New Zealand was held to be correct in declining to follow *Murphy* v *Brentwood District Council* [1990] 2 All ER 908, a House of Lords' decision on the liability of local authorities at common law for economic loss caused by the negligent inspection of building foundations (see para 9.3.2.2 above). The Judicial Committee said that the New Zealand courts are entitled to develop unsettled areas of the common law of New Zealand in accordance with conditions and policy considerations existing locally, which it would be rash for the Judicial Committee to ignore. As Lord Lloyd put it ([1996] 1 All ER 756 at pp. 764–5):

The ability of the common law to adapt itself to the differing circumstances of the countries in which it has taken root, is not a weakness, but one of its great strengths. Were it not so, the common law would not have flourished as it has, with all the common law countries learning from each other.

In *Australian Consolidated Press Ltd* v *Uren* [1969] 1 AC 590, PC, it was held that the High Court of Australia was right not to follow *Rookes* v *Barnard* [1964] AC 1129, a House of Lords' decision on exemplary damages. In *Parker* v *R* [1963] Crim LR 569 the High Court of Australia refused to follow the notorious decision in *DPP* v *Smith* [1961] AC 290, HL, on the mental element in the crime of murder. Where, however, it is decided or accepted that English law *is* applicable in a particular case, the Judicial Committee will consider itself bound to follow the House of Lords' decision which covers the point in issue (*Tai Hing Cotton Mill Ltd* v *Liu Chong Hing Bank Ltd* [1985] 2 All ER 947, PC, at p. 958 *per* Lord Scarman, a case in which the Judicial Committee, in an appeal from Hong Kong, followed the House of Lords' decision in *London Joint Stock Bank Ltd* v *Macmillan* [1918] AC 777; *Invercargill City Council* v *Hamlin*, PC, above).

The Judicial Committee is not strictly bound by its own previous decisions, although it rarely refuses to follow them (the *Bakshuwen* case, above). When in *Pratt* v *Attorney-General for Jamaica* [1993] 4 All ER 769, PC (para 2.2.3.1), the Committee held that failure to carry out a death sentence as swiftly as practicable after sentence amounted to a violation of the Jamaican constitution in that it was 'inhuman or degrading punishment or other treatment', it declined to follow two of its own earlier decisions (*Abbott* v *Attorney-General of Trinidad and Tobago* [1979] 1 WLR 1342, PC, and *Riley* v *Attorney-General of Jamaica*

[1983] 1 AC 719, PC) which had held that prolonged delay in carrying out a death sentence did not contravene a person's constitutional rights.

Decisions of the English Court of Appeal have only persuasive authority in the Commonwealth (*Robins* v *National Trust Co.* [1927] AC 515, PC; *De Lasala* v *De Lasala* [1980] AC 546, PC). A decision of the House of Lords on the *common law* also has only persuasive authority, although the authority is very strong because of the common membership of the House of Lords and the Judicial Committee (*De Lasala* v *De Lasala,* at p. 557, *per* Lord Diplock). In *Badry* v *Director of Public Prosecutions of Mauritius* [1982] 3 All ER 973, PC, the Committee regarded the decision of the House of Lords in *Attorney-General* v *British Broadcasting Corporation* [1981] AC 303, HL, as 'conclusive authority' on a point in the common law relating to contempt of court (see para 1.1.4).

A decision of the House of Lords on the *interpretation of legislation* common to the overseas territory and England is also, in theory, persuasive only. But, realistically, it has the same practical effect as if it were absolutely binding (*De Lasala* v *De Lasala,* at p. 558). In the case of common legislation, unlike judge-made law, there has been no divergent development and the overseas legislation would be interpreted according to English principles of interpretation. In *De Lasala* v *De Lasala* [1980] AC 546, PC, an appeal from Hong Kong on the interpretation of a piece of legislation virtually identical to the English Matrimonial Causes Act 1973, the Judicial Committee held that the Hong Kong Court of Appeal was effectively bound by the decision of the House of Lords in *Minton* v *Minton* [1979] AC 593 on the point.

9.4 BINDING AND PERSUASIVE PRECEDENTS

9.4.1 Binding precedents

A *binding* precedent is a decided case which a court *must* follow even though it is considered to have been wrongly decided. But a previous case is only binding in a later case if the legal principle involved is the same and the facts are similar. An inconvenient precedent which would otherwise be binding can be circumvented by *distinguishing* it on the facts or on the legal principle involved.

9.4.2 Persuasive precedents

A *persuasive* precedent is one which is not absolutely binding on a court but which *may* be applied. The following are some examples of persuasive precedents:

(a)   Decisions of English courts lower in the hierarchy. For example, the House of Lords *may* follow a Court of Appeal decision, and the Court of Appeal *may* follow a High Court decision, although not strictly bound to do so. Thus, in *Bromley London Borough Council* v *Greater London Council* [1982] 1 All ER 129, the House of Lords followed the decision of the Court of Appeal in *Prescott* v *Birmingham Corporation* [1955] Ch 210 (para 11.5.2.1), and in *Z Ltd* v *A-Z & AA-LL* [1982] 1 All ER 556, the Court of Appeal approved and followed the decisions of Robert Goff J in *Searose Ltd* v *Seatrain (UK) Ltd* [1981] 1 All ER 806 and *Clipper Maritime Co. Ltd of Monrovia* v *Mineralimportexport* [1981] 3 All ER 664 (para 10.4.2.6).

(b)   Decisions of the Judicial Committee of the Privy Council (para 9.3.2.9 above).

(c)   Decisions of the courts in Scotland, Ireland, the Commonwealth (especially Australia, Canada and New Zealand), and the USA. It is permissible for counsel to cite decisions of courts outside England and Wales. This is particularly appropriate where there is a shortage or total lack of English authority on the point. In *Conway* v *Rimmer* [1968] AC 910, HL (para 9.3.2.2 above), Scottish, Australian and American decisions were cited. In *Murphy* v *Brentwood District Council* [1990] 2 All ER 908, HL (para 9.3.2.2 above), in which decisions of courts in Australia, Canada, New Zealand and the USA were cited, the House of Lords preferred the decision of the High Court of Australia in *Sutherland Shire Council* v *Heyman* (1985) 60 ALR 1 to its own decision in *Anns* v *Merton London Borough* [1978] AC 728, HL.

(d)   *Obiter dicta* of English judges. Dicta are of different kinds and of varying degrees of weight. Some are casual expressions of opinion on a point which has not been raised in the case. Other dicta, although not necessary for the decision of the case, are deliberate expressions of opinion given after consideration of a point clearly put and argued before the court. These dicta carry much greater weight than casual expressions of opinion (see *Slack* v *Leeds Industrial Cooperative Society Ltd* [1923] 1 Ch 431, CA, *per* Lord Sterndale MR at p. 451).

House of Lords' dicta are the most persuasive and especially so if there was general agreement on the point in question. In *Rondel* v *Worsley* [1969] 1 AC 191, the House of Lords, after seven days of legal argument and the citation of 92 cases, held unanimously that a barrister is not liable in tort for the negligent presentation of a case in court and the preliminary work connected therewith, such as the drafting of pleadings. Four of their Lordships said, *obiter,* that a solicitor acting as an advocate was entitled to the same immunity ([1969] 1 AC 191 *per* Lord Reid at p. 232, Lord Morris of Borth-y-Gest at p. 243, Lord Pearce at p. 267 and Lord Upjohn at p. 284). There were dicta to the same effect by three different Law Lords in the later case of *Saif Ali* v *Sydney Mitchell & Co.,* and they were accepted as accurately representing the law ([1980] AC 198, HL, *per* Lord Wilberforce at p. 215, Lord Diplock at p. 224 and Lord Scarman at p. 227). In *Rondel* v *Worsley,* three of their Lordships said, *obiter,* that a barrister would not be immune from an action in negligence in relation to matters unconnected with cases in court and the preliminary work connected therewith, although the point had not been fully argued by counsel ([1969] 1 AC 191 *per* Lord Reid at pp. 231–2, Lord Morris of Borth-y-Gest at p. 244 and Lord Upjohn at p. 286).

In *Saif Ali* v *Sydney Mitchell & Co.* [1980] AC 198, HL, these dicta were followed by the majority and elevated to the status of *ratio decidendi*. Lord Wilberforce said (at pp. 212–13) that:

not all *obiter dicta* have the same weight, or lack of weight, in later cases. Of those then made in the House [in *Rondel* v *Worsley*] two things may be said. First, they were considered and deliberate observations after discussion of the same matters had taken place in the Court of Appeal and in the light of judgments in the Court of Appeal. It may be true that the counsel in the case did not present detailed arguments as to the position outside the court room — they had no interest in doing so — but I cannot agree that this invalidates or weakens judicial pronouncements. Judges are more than mere selectors between rival views — they are entitled to and do think for themselves. Secondly, it would have been impossible for their Lordships to have dealt with the extent of barristers' immunity for acts in court without relating this to their immunity for other acts. . . . These factors, in my opinion, tell in favour of giving considerably more weight to their Lordships' expressions of opinion than *obiter dicta* normally receive. We may clarify them, but we should hesitate before disregarding them.

It may be noted here that the immunity rule, exemplified in *Rondel* v *Worsley* [1969] 1 AC 191, HL, and *Saif Ali* v *Sydney Mitchell & Co.* [1980] AC 198, HL, whereby barristers and solicitors are immune from liability for the tort of negligence arising out of the presentation of a case in court and the preliminary work connected therewith was put on a statutory basis by s. 62 of the Courts and Legal Services Act 1990. The immunity rule was, moreover, extended in two ways by s. 62. First, it was made applicable to *all* authorised advocates (including paralegal advocates). Secondly, it now operates so as to prevent an action for a *breach of contract* arising from the same circumstances. This is an important provision in view of the abolition (by s. 61 of the 1990 Act) of any rule of law which prevents a barrister from entering into a contract with his client for the provision of his services as a barrister. Section 62 of the Courts and Legal Services Act 1990 does not, however, provide any protection against 'wasted costs orders', which can be made by the court under the Supreme Court Act 1981, s. 51 (as substituted by the Courts and Legal Services Act 1990), against legal or other representatives in respect of improper, unreasonable or negligent acts or omissions (*Ridehalgh* v *Horsefield* [1994] 3 All ER 848, CA).

Some *obiter dicta* in House of Lords' cases are indistinguishable from *ratio decidendi*. In *Hedley Byrne & Co. Ltd* v *Heller & Partners Ltd* [1964] AC 465, the House of Lords said unanimously that there was a legal duty of care in making statements whenever there was a special relationship between the parties and the duty had not been excluded by a disclaimer of responsibility. But, on the facts, it was held that there had been an effective disclaimer of responsibility so that, on a strict application of the distinction between *ratio decidendi* and *obiter dictum,* what their Lordships said about the duty of care was *obiter.* Nevertheless, these dicta appear in the reserved opinions of five Law Lords delivered after listening to eight days of argument. It would be churlish to regard them as anything other than *ratio decidendi* and they have been followed as such in subsequent cases. The same considerations apply to the decision in *National Carriers Ltd* v *Panalpina (Northern) Ltd* [1981] 1 All ER 161, HL, concerning the applicability of the doctrine of frustration to leases of land. The House of Lords held unanimously that, on the facts, the lease had not been frustrated. Nevertheless, because the point had been fully argued, four out of five of their Lordships delivered reserved opinions holding that the doctrine of frustration is capable of applying to an executed lease of land.

9.4.3 The weight of persuasive precedents

The weight to be attached to any individual persuasive precedent will depend on several factors, such as the rank of the court in the hierarchy, the prestige of the judge(s) involved, the date of the case, whether judgment was reserved or given *ex tempore,* whether there was any dissenting opinion, whether the case was contested and whether the point in question was argued or merely conceded by counsel.

The higher the court the greater the weight given to its pronouncements. For instance, the House of Lords would normally find decisions of the Court of Appeal more persuasive than decisions of High Court judges. The prestige of individual judges is a factor which can only rarely be taken into account because, in theory, all judges are of equal status. Lord Diplock has described as 'invidious' any distinction made between individual judges which is based on their reputations as jurists (*Saif Ali* v *Sydney Mitchell & Co.* [1980] AC 198, HL, at p. 217). Nevertheless, in practice the judgments of an acknowledged master of the law are likely to be treated with more respect than those of judges in general. From the last century the judgments of Lord Eldon, Lord Bowen, Lord Esher, Lord Lindley and Sir George Jessell MR would fall into this category, and, from the present century, those of Lord Justice Scrutton, Lord Atkin, Lord Wright, Lord Reid and Lord Radcliffe.

A good example of a highly influential dictum is the statement of Lord Atkin in *Donoghue* v *Stevenson* [1932] AC 562, HL (the case of the snail in the ginger-beer bottle), at p. 580, where he attempted to lay down a general test for determining when a notional duty of care arises in the tort of negligence. His dictum has become known as the 'neighbour test' and was expressed in these words:

> You must take reasonable care to avoid acts or omissions which you can reasonably foresee would be likely to injure your neighbour. Who, then, in law is my neighbour? The answer seems to be — persons who are so closely and directly affected by my act that I ought reasonably to have them in contemplation as being so affected when I am directing my mind to the acts or omissions which are called in question.

This dictum, though clearly *obiter,* has been adopted in subsequent cases. In *Home Office* v *Dorset Yacht Co. Ltd* [1970] AC 1004, HL, Lord Reid said that it represented a statement of principle and should be applied unless there was some justification for its exclusion (at p. 1027). Lord Pearson agreed (at p. 1054), but Lord Diplock was more cautious, describing Lord Atkin's dictum as a guide rather than a principle of universal application (at p. 1060). The dictum was applied in the case to make the Home Office liable for damage done to neighbouring property by absconding borstal boys.

The date of a case is a factor which can be used to support or to weaken it as a precedent. If the case is old it can be argued that it has stood the test of time and now represents well settled law. On the contrary, it can be argued that it is now out of touch with changed conditions. If the case is recent it can be hailed as the most up-to-date pronouncement on the matter. On the contrary, it can be attacked as being of insufficient antiquity.

A considered judgment delivered after being reserved will usually carry more weight than one delivered 'off the cuff' at the conclusion of counsel's argument. The judge has had more time for reflection and the consideration of the authorities.

In the Court of Appeal and the High Court, judgment may be reserved or given *ex tempore* depending on the complexity or length of the case. A reserved judgment is signified in the law reports by the words *curia advisari vult* ('the court wishes to consider the matter'). The Latin words can often be seen abbreviated to *cur. adv. vult* or *C.A.V.*

Judgments in the House of Lords are always reserved, although sometimes their Lordships announce the actual decision at the end of counsel's argument without giving their reasons at that time. In *Royal College of Nursing of the United Kingdom* v *DHSS* [1981] 1 All ER 545, HL, a case concerning the legality of medically induced abortion carried out by nurses under the instructions of a doctor but in his absence, the House announced its decision immediately on the close of argument. Lord Wilberforce said the matter was urgent and it was in the interests of the Health Service to announce the decision quickly, although he stressed that it was an unusual course and not to be taken as a precedent. Two months later the written opinions revealed a majority of three to two in favour of the legality of this abortion practice. The unanimous decision of the Court of Appeal was reversed and the judgment at first instance affirmed (see para 8.10.2.3).

The weight to be given to a persuasive precedent will be reduced if any dissenting opinion was given in the case and, in particular, by a judge whose views command the highest respect. Persuasiveness is also affected if the case was not contested or if the point in issue was decided by the judge after being conceded by counsel. Such a case has not been subjected to the close scrutiny and refining process associated with skilled legal argument.

9.4.4   Other persuasive authorities

Where there is no direct authority in the form of decided cases, persuasive authority may
be found in Roman law or in legal writings in textbooks and periodicals. Roman law, and
especially the Digest of the Emperor Justinian (promulgated in AD 533), has been resorted
to on a number of occasions for a solution to English legal problems. The judgment of
Blackburn J in *Taylor* v *Caldwell* (1863) 3 B & S 826, which began the modern doctrine of
frustration of contract, was based largely on Roman doctrines. In *Kearry* v *Pattinson* [1939]
1 KB 471, CA, it was held, applying the Roman rule, that bees are animals *ferae naturae*
('wild by nature') so that, if they swarm, they belong to the first person who captures them.
A Roman rule was applied again in *Tucker* v *Farm & General Investment Trust Ltd* [1966]
2 QB 421, in which the Court of Appeal held that lambs born to ewes which are being
acquired on hire-purchase belong to the hirer and not to the owner of the ewes.

Legal writings have not played a particularly influential part in the judicial process in
England because of the attitude of the judges that English law should be found in statutes
and decided cases rather than in the writings of academic lawyers. Denning J (as he was
then) was probably exaggerating when in 1947 he wrote that the 'influence of the academic
lawyers is greater now than it has ever been and is greater than they themselves realise'
((1947) 63 LQR 516). (For a more recent assessment of the influence of academic legal
literature, see Birks, 'Adjudication and Interpretation in the Common Law', (1994) 14 Legal
Studies 156.) The English attitude contrasts with the position on the Continent of Europe
where academic commentaries on the Codes carry great persuasive weight. In France, for
example, the enacted law (*la loi*) is supreme. But it is often laconic and in need of
clarification and interpretation by cases and criticism. Decisions of the courts (*la jurisprudence*) are only persuasive. Legal scholarship is held in high regard and the opinions of
jurists (*la doctrine*) are as persuasive as decided cases. Judicial decisions are criticised by
academic writers in textbooks and periodicals and in case notes appended to law reports. In
the USA, too, legal writings are prestigious and academic commentaries are relied upon by
attorneys and judges alike.

It used to be the practice in England that only deceased authors could be cited in court
— presumably because they could no longer change their minds and could not be effectively
contradicted. This is no longer the practice as living authors may now be cited (Denning,
loc. cit.). A dead author may be referred to by his surname only whereas a living author
should be given his title.

The fact that the author happens to be a judge does not, in theory, give any added weight
to his extra-judicial writings. In *Cordell* v *Second Clanfield Properties* [1969] 2 Ch 9,
Megarry J, referring to the third edition of *Megarry and Wade's Real Property,* said this (at
pp. 16–17):

> It seems to me that words in a book written or subscribed to by an author who is or
> becomes a judge have the same value as words written by any other reputable author,
> neither more nor less. The process of authorship is entirely different from that of judicial
> decision. The author, no doubt, has the benefit of a broad and comprehensive survey of
> his chosen subject as a whole, together with a lengthy period of gestation, and intermittent
> opportunities for reconsideration. But he is exposed to the peril of yielding to preconcep-
> tions, and he lacks the advantage of that impact and sharpening of focus which the
> detailed facts of a particular case bring to the judge. Above all, he has to form his ideas
> without the aid of the purifying ordeal of skilled argument on the specific facts of a

contested case. Argued law is tough law . . . Today, as of old, by good disputing shall the law be well known.

Formerly, some authors were cited in court with such frequency that their works were regarded as 'authoritative' in a special sense. These authors were listed by Blackstone, writing in the eighteenth century (1 Bl Comm 72–3), as Glanville (twelfth century), Bracton, Britton, Fleta, Hengham (thirteenth century), Littleton, Statham (fifteenth century), Brooke, Fitzherbert, Staundforde (sixteenth century), and Coke, whose *Reports* and four volumes of *Institutes* were published in the seventeenth century. To this list may be added the names of Plowden (sixteenth century), Hale (seventeenth century), Hawkins, Foster (eighteenth century), and that of Blackstone himself. Sir William Blackstone (1723–80) became the first Vinerian Professor of English Law at Oxford in 1758. His *Commentaries* in four books were based on the lectures he gave at Oxford and were published between 1756 and 1769. He entered the House of Commons (1761), became Solicitor-General (1763), gave up his chair (1766), and was appointed a judge of the Court of King's Bench (1770) but in the same year transferred to the Court of Common Pleas.

Although these old works are undoubtedly still authoritative it is doubtful whether they now carry any greater weight than the works of more modern authors. The attitude of the Court of Appeal in *R* v *Richards* [1974] QB 776, CA, where Hawkins's *Pleas of the Crown* (8th ed., 1824) was preferred to Smith and Hogan's *Criminal Law* (3rd ed., 1973) even though Hawkins did not make sense, appears to have been an isolated incident. What appears to be more important today than the antiquity of the old books is the wisdom and correctness of what they say. They are certainly still cited occasionally, although not always with approval. Thus, Blackstone was criticised in *Button* v *Director of Public Prosecutions* [1966] AC 591, HL, on the definition of the crime of affray and in *Reid* v *Commissioner of Police of the Metropolis* [1973] QB 551, CA, on the market overt rule in the sale of goods. In *Attorney-General of the Duchy of Lancaster* v *G.E. Overton (Farms) Ltd* [1982] 1 All ER 524, 526–9, CA, Lord Denning MR quoted the definitions of treasure trove given by Bracton, Staundforde, Coke, Comyn and Blackstone and preferred Coke's definition to that of all the others.

In modern times the works of other authors have been cited frequently in court, both by counsel and by judges in judgments. Among the most influential of these works are Pollock's books on *Tort, Contract* and *Partnership*; Dicey's *Law of the Constitution* and *Conflict of Laws*; Kenny's *Outlines of Criminal Law*; the books of Salmond and Winfield on *Tort*; Cheshire on *Private International Law, Modern Real Property*, and (with Fifoot) the *Law of Contract*; Rayden on *Divorce*; Cross on *Evidence*; Professor H.W.R. Wade's *Administrative Law*; and the book (first published in 1965) by Professors Smith and Hogan on *Criminal Law*.

In addition to academic and practitioners' textbooks, citation is allowed from legal periodicals which publish, *inter alia*, learned articles suggesting what the law should be on contentious matters not covered by any statute or decided case. Among the periodicals most commonly relied on are the *Law Quarterly Review* (LQR, first published in 1885), the *Cambridge Law Journal* (CLJ, 1921), the *Modern Law Review* (MLR, 1937), and the *Criminal Law Review* (Crim LR, 1954).

9.5 DISCOVERING THE *RATIO DECIDENDI* OF A CASE

The *ratio decidendi* of a case is the principle of law which runs through the case and on which the decision is based. The *ratio* is not the decision itself. Only the litigating parties are bound by the actual decision in a case whereas the *ratio* of a case states the law for all persons and may be binding in later cases. The actual decision in *Ashton v Turner* [1980] 3 All ER 870, for example, is simply that the defendant was not liable to the claimant. The *rationes* on which that decision is based, three doctrines well known to the common law, are much more detailed in their articulation and far-reaching in their implications than the actual decision (see below).

The traditional view was that the *ratio decidendi* of a case was what it was perceived to be by the judge who decided the case. But the difficulty with this approach is that the judge may have expressed the principle too widely or too narrowly for it to be useful in a later case. Moreover, in appellate courts each judge may state the principle in different language and so it is not always easy to discover the *ratio* by a quotation from any one judgment.

The modern, generally accepted view is that the *ratio decidendi* of a case is what it is determined to be by a court in a later case and not what the judge in the original case considered it to be. This objective approach towards finding the *ratio* of a case makes it possible for a judge in a later case to relegate to the status of *obiter dicta* statements which had hitherto been thought to be *ratio*. It also means that, since the facts of two cases are unlikely to be identical, the judge in the later case usually has the task of either restricting or enlarging the *ratio* of the earlier case. If he decides that the *ratio* does not apply to the facts before him he is restricting its scope. If he decides that the *ratio* does apply to the different factual situation he is enlarging its scope.

Discovering the *ratio decidendi* of a case is often difficult because it may involve the separation of the relevant and irrelevant parts of a judgment. The *ratio* will hardly ever be stated explicitly in the judgment but will be found buried among a mass of dicta. In some respects the old cases are easier to read because the reporter did not always trouble to report what he considered to be mere *obiter dicta*. The *ratio* may not be accurately encapsulated in the headnote to the law report. The reporter may have misinterpreted the decision and attempted to state the *ratio* too widely or too narrowly.

The decision in a case and, therefore, the *ratio decidendi* must always depend on the particular facts of the individual case. To discover the *ratio* of a case all the facts found by the judge to be material must be considered. Whatever words are not necessary for the decision must be *obiter*. However, a judge may give two or more reasons for his decision in which event they are both or all *rationes decidendi* and not mere *obiter dicta*. As Lord Simonds said in *Jacobs v London County Council* [1950] AC 361, HL, at p. 369, the other Law Lords agreeing with him:

> [T]here is in my opinion no justification for regarding as *obiter dictum* a reason given by a judge for his decision, because he has given another reason also.

Thus, in *Ashton v Turner* [1980] 3 All ER 870, where the claimant had been injured due to the negligent driving of a known drunken driver with whom he was engaged in criminal activity, Ewbank J found against the claimant on three separate grounds. They were *ex turpi causa non oritur actio* ('no action can be brought on an illegal or immoral cause'), *volenti non fit injuria* ('no injury is done to one who consents'), and contributory negligence to the extent of 50 per cent. Either of the first two grounds by itself would have been sufficient to dispose of the claimant's claim without compensation while the third ground would have reduced his damages by one-half.

Lord Denning MR favoured a different approach to multiple *rationes* in the case of the Court of Appeal. His view was that where a Court of Appeal decision involves two or more *rationes,* that Court in a later case is not bound by all of them but may choose to ignore any particular *ratio* (*Dixon* v *British Broadcasting Corporation* [1979] 2 All ER 112, CA, at p. 116; *Ministry of Defence* v *Jeremiah* [1980] 1 QB 87, CA, at p. 98). This unorthodox view, which was not shared by Lord Denning's colleagues in the Court of Appeal, conflicts with the opinion of Lord Simonds in *Jacobs* v *London County Council,* quoted above, and with other dicta in the House of Lords.

All facts which the judge expressly or impliedly treats as immaterial must be regarded as immaterial. All facts which the judge expressly or impliedly treats as material must be regarded as material. There is a presumption against wide principles of law, and it must be remembered that the *ratio* widens or narrows according to how few or how many facts are considered to be material. If the judge decides that facts A, B, C, D and E exist but that only facts A, B and C are material, the *ratio* is wider than if he had decided that all the facts were material. For example, the judge decides that facts A, B, C, D and E exist. He then excludes facts D and E as immaterial. On the remaining facts, A, B and C, he reaches conclusion X. In any future case where the facts are A, B, C, D and E, conclusion X must be reached. But, in reality, the *ratio* is that where facts A, B and C exist the conclusion must be X, facts D and E having been discounted as immaterial.

The process of discovering the *ratio decidendi* of a case may be illustrated by reference to two well known decisions of the House of Lords: *Rylands* v *Fletcher* (1868) LR 3 HL 330 and *Donoghue* v *Stevenson* [1932] AC 562.

The facts of *Rylands* v *Fletcher* were that:

(a) the defendant (D) had a reservoir built on his land;
(b) the contractor was negligent in building the reservoir; and
(c) water escaped and flooded the mine of the claimant (C).

The conclusion on these facts was that D was liable to C for the damage. But the facts considered to be *material* by the court were only (a) D had a reservoir built on his land, and (c) water escaped and flooded C's mine. Fact (b) was considered immaterial and, by discounting it, the House of Lords formulated a wide *ratio* based on strict liability for the escape of water to which lack of negligence or the employment of a contractor is no defence.

Nor did the House stop there. It was made clear that the *ratio* was not limited to the building of reservoirs and the escape of water, although, in strict theory, a later court could have so restricted it but only by a rigid and mechanical application of the doctrine of precedent. The following statement of the rule was laid down by Blackburn J ((1866) LR 1 Ex 265 at pp. 279–80) and was approved by the House of Lords:

[T]he person who for his own purposes brings on his land and collects and keeps there anything likely to do mischief if it escapes, must keep it in at his peril, and, if he does not do so, is prima facie answerable for all the damage which is the natural consequence of its escape.

In subsequent cases, the rule in *Rylands* v *Fletcher* has been extended to escapes of fire, gas, oil, electricity, explosions, noxious fumes, colliery spoil, poisonous vegetation, and a 'chair-o-plane' at a funfair. (For a modern case on the rule in *Rylands* v *Fletcher* in which, on the facts, the defendants were held not liable, see *Cambridge Water Co. Ltd* v *Eastern Counties Leather plc* [1994] 1 All ER 53, HL.)

In *Donoghue* v *Stevenson* [1932] AC 562, a Scottish case which went to the House of Lords on a preliminary point of law, the assumed facts were as follows. The pursuer (the

Scots law equivalent of claimant) and a friend visited a café where the friend bought for the pursuer a bottle of ginger beer manufactured by the defender (defendant). The bottle was of opaque glass through which it was impossible to see the contents. The café owner opened the bottle and poured some of the ginger beer into a tumbler. The pursuer drank some of the ginger beer and the friend poured the remainder of the ginger beer into the tumbler from the bottle and with it emerged the decomposed remains of a dead snail. The pursuer suffered shock and gastric illness. Assuming these facts to be proved, the House of Lords held that the pursuer would be entitled to recover damages from the defender, even though there was no contract between them.

For the purposes of the decision, the House of Lords considered as *material* only that the pursuer had been injured through consuming ginger beer manufactured by the defender and bottled in glass through which the contents could not be seen and which contained a dead snail. It was *not material* that the ginger beer had been bought by the friend in a café or that it had been poured into the tumbler by the friend and the café owner. The House regarded as particularly *immaterial* the fact that there was no contractual relationship between the pursuer and the defender, and in this way a wider *ratio* was laid down.

It was made clear that the *ratio* was not to be limited to cases involving snails in ginger-beer bottles. The rule was laid down thus in the words of Lord Atkin (at p. 599):

> [A] manufacturer of products, which he sells in such a form as to show that he intends them to reach the ultimate consumer in the form in which they left him with no reasonable possibility of intermediate examination, and with the knowledge that the absence of reasonable care in the preparation or putting up of the products will result in an injury to the consumer's life or property, owes a duty to the consumer to take that reasonable care.

In subsequent cases, the *ratio of Donoghue v Stevenson* has been extended to motor cars, lifts, hair dye, industrial chemicals, and irritant chemicals in underpants. The category of persons potentially liable has been extended to include repairers, erectors and assemblers.

In appeal cases in the Court of Appeal and House of Lords, three or even five separate judgments may be given. It is possible for all the judges in an appeal to find for the same party but for different reasons. In this event, the *ratio decidendi* is whatever is agreed on by the majority. If there is no majority in favour of any one *ratio* the case loses much of its value as a precedent, and may not be considered binding, even if it is a decision of the House of Lords. A lower court faced later with the same issue can only discuss the different *rationes* of the higher court and then decide the matter for itself *de novo*. The House of Lords' decision in *Bell v Lever Bros Ltd* [1932] AC 161 is a notorious illustration of the problems involved in seeking to discover what a particular case actually decided. In that case, after wide divergences of opinion in the High Court and the Court of Appeal, the appellant ultimately secured judgment by a majority of three to two in the House of Lords. But only two (Lords Atkin and Thankerton) of the majority of three decided on the same *ratio,* namely, that there was, on the facts, no fundamental mistake to avoid the contract. The opinion of the third member of the majority (Lord Blanesburgh) was based on a different, procedural, ground.

The decision in *Bell v Lever Bros Ltd* has been considered in many subsequent cases but its true meaning is still not clear after 60 years. There are two possible interpretations. The first is that there is a common-law doctrine of operative mistake about the quality of the subject-matter of a contract, but in *Bell v Lever Bros Ltd* the mistake was just not fundamental enough to avoid the contract. The second is that there is no such doctrine at all. Lower courts in later cases have, for the most part, opted for the latter interpretation (see, e.g., the judgments of the Court of Appeal in *Solle* v *Butcher* [1950] 1 KB 671 and *Leaf* v *International Galleries* [1950] 2 KB 86; but cf *Associated Japanese Bank (International) Ltd* v *Crédit du Nord SA* [1988] 3 All ER 902 *per* Steyn J at pp. 909–13).

In recent years there has been a tendency in appeals before the House of Lords for only one speech to be delivered in which the other Law Lords simply concur. The object is to avoid the confusion which can result from different reasons contained in multiple judgments, as in *Bell* v *Lever Bros Ltd*. Nevertheless, the single-judgment approach itself may cause difficulties. In *Saunders* v *Anglia Building Society* [1971] AC 1004, at p. 1015, Lord Reid warned that 'there are dangers in there being only one speech in this House' because 'statements in it have often tended to be treated as definitions and it is not the function of a court or of this House to frame definitions'. Lord Denning MR spoke of the difficulties in *Paal Wilson & Co.* v *Blumenthal* [1982] 3 All ER 394, CA. He described the task of distinguishing between *ratio decidendi* and *obiter dicta* as 'formidable' and said that, occasionally, it is more difficult to distinguish them in a single speech than in multiple opinions. Lower courts are often tempted to treat the words of a single speech almost as if they were contained in a statute and, in so doing without attempting to distil the *ratio decidendi,* they are likely to be led astray (p. 400).

In an appeal case, if a judge says 'I agree' that means he agrees with the decision and proposed order but not necessarily that he agrees with the reasoning of his judicial colleagues. If a judge is silent about a statement of one of his colleagues, his silence does not imply agreement with it. Such short pronouncements, especially in unreasoned judgments, do not carry much weight.

9.6 ADVANTAGES AND DISADVANTAGES OF THE DOCTRINE OF JUDICIAL PRECEDENT

The following of precedent is a *convenient time-saving device*. If a problem has already arisen and been solved in a certain way it is natural in every walk of life to reach the same conclusion on the same problem without too much reconsideration. All legal systems follow precedent to a greater or lesser extent. The English legal system differs from most of the others in that we have a doctrine of *binding* precedent under which, more often than not, the previous case *must* be followed in the subsequent case.

But it must always be remembered that decided cases are illustrations of principles of law which a judge may turn to in deciding the case before him. Precedents should be used as 'stepping-stones' rather than as 'halting-places' (*Birch* v *Brown* [1931] AC 605, HL, *per* Lord Macmillan at p. 631). The convenience of following precedent should not be allowed to degenerate into a mere mechanical exercise performed without any thought. So, too, the citation of authority in court should be kept within reasonable bounds because it can be costly in terms of time and money. Lord Diplock has warned of the 'danger of so blinding the court with case law that it has difficulty in seeing the wood of legal principle for the trees of paraphrase' (*Lambert* v *Lewis* [1981] 1 All ER 1185, HL, at pp. 1189–90; see also *Pioneer Shipping Ltd* v *B.T.P. Tioxide Ltd* [1981] 2 All ER 1030, HL, *per* Lord Roskill at p. 1046, the other Law Lords agreeing with him on the point). The House of Lords has decided that it will not allow transcripts of *unreported* judgments of the Court of Appeal, civil division, to be cited before the House except with its leave. Leave will only be granted if counsel gives an assurance that the transcript contains a statement of some principle of law which is not to be found in any *reported* Court of Appeal decision (*Roberts Petroleum*

Ltd v *Bernard Kenny Ltd* [1983] 1 All ER 564, HL). The hard line thus taken by the House of Lords was in response to the citation of four unreported Court of Appeal decisions, none of which was of assistance to their Lordships in determining the appeal before them. None of these unreported decisions laid down any principle of law which could not be found in reported cases and the only result of referring to them had been to lengthen the hearing of the appeal unnecessarily. (See also *Stanley* v *International Harvester Co. of Great Britain Ltd* (1983) *The Times,* 7 February, CA, *per* Sir John Donaldson MR, and note that the Court of Appeal operates a similar practice: *Practice Direction (Court of Appeal: procedure)* [1999] 2 All ER 490.)

Greater *certainty* in the law is perhaps the most important advantage claimed for the doctrine of judicial precedent. From this advantage other benefits flow. If case X was decided in a particular way 20 years ago by the Court of Appeal or the House of Lords, the doctrine of *stare decisis* would normally demand that a court today faced with the same problem as in case X should decide it the same way. The existence of a precedent may prevent a judge making a mistake which he might have made if he had been left on his own without any guidance. It may also allow persons generally to order their affairs and come to settlements with a certain amount of confidence. But the advantage of certainty is lost where there are too many cases or they are too confusing. This can arise through the process of distinguishing cases and over-refining the principles embodied in them. Certainty in the law can only result from a large body of case law if the cases are uniform in outcome and not irreconcilable.

The doctrine of precedent may serve the *interests of justice.* If the decision in a case between A and B was X, it would be unjust to reach decision Y the next day in a similar case between C and D. This is one of the objections to the prospective overruling of cases, discussed earlier (para 9.3.1), but retrospective overruling is also affected by it. The overruling of an earlier case may cause injustice to those who have ordered their affairs in reliance on it. It is partly to prevent this sort of injustice that the Court of Appeal must normally adhere to its own previous decisions and the House of Lords should be circumspect in departing from its previous decisions. The problem is that the application of precedent may produce justice in the individual case but injustice in the generality of cases. It would be undesirable to treat a number of claimants unjustly simply because one binding case had laid down an unjust rule.

The interests of justice also demand impartiality from the judge. This may be assured by the existence of a binding precedent which he must follow unless it is distinguishable. If he tries to distinguish an indistinguishable case his attempt will be obvious.

Case law is *practical* in character. It is based on the experience of actual cases brought before the courts rather than on logic or theory. In this respect case law differs from statute law, which is often based on *a priori* theories. The doctrine of *stare decisis* is a limiting factor in the development of judge-made law. Practical law is founded on experience but the scope for further experience is restricted if the first case is binding.

The making of law in decided cases offers opportunities for *growth and legal development* which could not be provided by Parliament. The courts can more quickly lay down new principles, or extend old principles, to meet novel circumstances. There has built up over the centuries a mass of cases illustrative of a vast number of the principles of English law. The cases exemplify the law in the sort of detail that could not be achieved in a long code of the Continental type. But therein lies another weakness of case law. Its very *bulk and complexity* make it increasingly difficult to find the law.

The case-law method is sometimes said to be *flexible,* but this presupposes that a judge is free to lay down whatever rule he considers desirable in order to keep the law in step with changing social and economic conditions. But a judge is not thus free where there is a binding precedent. Unless it can be distinguished he must follow it, even though he dislikes it or considers it bad law. His discretion is thereby limited and the alleged flexibility of case law becomes *rigidity*. Judicial mistakes of the past are perpetuated unless bad decisions happen to come before the House of Lords for reconsideration. In any event, flexibility and certainty are incompatible features of judge-made law. A system that was truly flexible could not at the same time be certain because no one can predict when and how legal development will take place.

It has been seen that for almost every advantage claimed for the doctrine of precedent there is a corresponding disadvantage. This is not necessarily to say, however, that the advantages are outweighed by the disadvantages. The following of precedent is easier in England than in many other countries because England has a centralised legal system with only a small number of courts. In the USA, where there are federal and state courts and legislatures, the number of reported cases runs into millions and this has led to a modification there of the doctrine of *stare decisis* (see Cross and Harris, *Precedent in English law,* 4th ed., 1991, pp. 19–20). Decisions of the US Supreme Court are binding on courts other than itself, but the Supreme Court tends to decide only constitutional issues. In all other cases, US Federal and District Courts are not bound by precedent. Previous decisions are of persuasive authority only and may be rejected. Particularly persuasive is an established *line* or *trend* of decisions rather than a single decision.

The English doctrine of *stare decisis* is based on the binding effect of a single decision, which must be followed even when manifestly unjust or wrong. Such an approach is alien to Continental systems of law wherein no single decision, even of the highest court, is absolutely binding (Cross and Harris, op. cit., pp. 10–19; Goodhart, 'Precedent in English and Continental law', (1934) 50 LQR 40). Continental law tends to be codified and the code is all-important so that cases decided on the interpretation of the code are of persuasive authority only. In practice, however, a long line or trend of decisions (what the French call *la jurisprudence constante)* is highly persuasive and will rarely be departed from. Another reason for the relative unimportance of the single decision on the Continent is the great weight attached to *la doctrine*. The writings of jurists played a major part in the development of Roman law, which, in turn, influenced modern Continental systems of law. In England, because judges commanded greater respect than jurists, lawyers looked to judicial decisions rather than to textbooks for authority.

9.7 LAW REPORTING

9.7.1 Introduction

The effectiveness of a doctrine of precedent based on *stare decisis* depends in large measure on the availability of full and accurate reports of decided cases. There has never been in England any official or systematic attempt at compiling law reports. The law reporting that exists today has simply evolved by private enterprise through three periods of development.

9.7.2 Year Books (about 1275 to 1535)

The Year Books are anonymous reports, compiled annually, and written by hand in law French. Some were later printed but most remained in manuscript. The Year Books are rarely cited in court now as they are of no practical use in modern times. They are, however, useful in the study of the medieval common law.

9.7.3   Private (or named) reports (1535 to 1865)

The private reports were compiled by individuals for commercial publication. Most of the private reports are referred to by the name of the reporter. They are cited by recognised abbreviations. Thus the reports compiled by Sir Edward Coke between 1572 and 1616 are known as Coke's Reports, abbreviated to Co Rep.

The private reports show considerable variation in style and accuracy. The famous outburst of Holt CJ in *Slater* v *May* (1704) 2 Ld Raym 1071 exemplifies the judicial frustration with bad private reporting: 'See the inconveniences of these scrambling reports, they will make us appear to posterity for a parcel of blockheads'. The reports of Plowden, Coke and Burrow are regarded as among the most reliable, while the most vilified are probably those of Espinasse, who reported *nisi prius* cases between 1793 and 1807. As late as the present century Espinasse's reports have been criticised as 'imperfect and misleading' and one case reported by him in 1799 was disapproved on the ground that the report was probably inaccurate (*Wessex Dairies Ltd* v *Smith* [1935] 2 KB 80, CA, disapproving *Nichol* v *Martyn* (1799) 2 Esp 732).

The better private reports give the reasons for decisions, unlike most of the Year Books. Many of the private reports have been republished. Perhaps the best collection is the *English Reports* (ER, published between 1900 and 1932) containing in 176 volumes reprints of cases reported between 1220 and 1866. Volumes 177 and 178 are index volumes and there is an index wall-chart indicating where each volume of the old reports can be found reprinted in the *English Reports*. They are annotated with references to subsequent cases and this makes them more useful than the original reports.

9.7.4   Modern reports (1865 to the present)

The private reports were often criticised. They were expensive to buy. Some of them were never printed but had to be cited in manuscript form. There was too much overlapping in that the same case might be reported in two or more series. Their usefulness to the legal profession was reduced by the inordinate length of time taken to report some important decisions. They were, for the most part, unreliable.

As a result of dissatisfaction with the private reports, a council was established comprising representatives of the four Inns of Court and the Law Society with the Attorney-General and Solicitor-General as *ex officio* members. The council's reports, called *The Law Reports,* were first published in 1865 and eventually absorbed the private reports. In 1870 the Council was incorporated as a company limited by guarantee and became known as the Incorporated Council of Law Reporting for England and Wales.

The Incorporated Council employs paid law reporters and sells its reports to subscribers, but it is a non-profit-making, charitable association whose purposes are regarded as beneficial to the community and for the advancement of education (*Incorporated Council of Law Reporting for England & Wales* v *Attorney-General* [1972] Ch 73, CA). *The Law Reports* are not official or monopolistic. But they are usually more accurate and reliable than other series. Counsel's argument is summarised and the judgment is revised by the judge before publication. If a case is reported in *The Law Reports* it should, as a matter of practice rather than law, be cited in court from that series rather than from any other series in which it may be reported. However, counsel appearing in the *House of Lords* may, if they consider it more convenient to do so, cite a case from the Inland Revenue's series, *Reports of Tax Cases,* even though the case is also reported in *The Law Reports* as long as the reference to the case in *The Law Reports* is also given (*Bray (Inspector of Taxes)* v *Best* [1989] 1 All ER 969, HL, *per* Lord Mackay of Clashfern LC at p. 971).

In the *Court of Appeal* a similar practice exists in all cases. The general rule applies that citation from *The Law Reports* is preferred to citation from other series of reports where there is a choice because other series, although they provide a useful service (in, for example, reporting cases not reported elsewhere), do not contain a summary of counsel's argument and may not be readily available to the court (see *Practice Direction (Court of Appeal: procedure)* [1999] 2 All ER 490).

The Law Reports is a general series which reports decisions of the superior and appellate courts in England and Wales. The current series of *The Law Reports* began in 1891. The reports are issued in four parts per year:

AC	Appeal Cases in the House of Lords and the Judicial Committee of the Privy Council.
QB	Cases decided in the Queen's Bench Division of the High Court and on appeal therefrom to the Court of Appeal.
Ch	Cases decided in the Chancery Division and on appeal therefrom to the Court of Appeal.
Fam	Cases decided in the Family Division and on appeal therefrom to the Court of Appeal.

Since 1891, the year of publication of a volume of *The Law Reports* has appeared in square brackets and is part of the reference to that volume without which a case cannot be traced. Thus, the reference to the House of Lords' case of *Smith* v *Baker & Sons* is [1891] AC 325. The date given in the reference for a case is the year in which it is reported and not the year in which it is decided. Thus, the reference to the House of Lords' case of *Bell* v *Lever Bros Ltd*, which was reported in *The Law Reports* in 1932, is [1932] AC 161, although the case was actually decided at the end of 1931.

Since 1953 the Incorporated Council of Law Reporting for England and Wales has also published *The Weekly Law Reports* (WLR). This is another general series. The reports are published more quickly than *The Law Reports*, although it has not been possible to keep to the original aim of making reports available within about three weeks of judgment. The only decisions likely to be reported within three to four weeks are those of the House of Lords. In *The Weekly Law Reports* counsel's argument is left out and the judgments are not necessarily revised for publication. *The Weekly Law Reports* consist of three volumes per year. Volumes 2 and 3 contain reports of cases which will later appear in *The Law Reports*. Volume 1 contains reports of less important cases which are not intended for publication in *The Law Reports* and cases which are likely to go to appeal.

Another popular general series of reports is the *All England Law Reports* (All ER) published since 1936 by Butterworths. There are four volumes per year, containing in excess of 500 cases. Counsel's argument is not reported. Judgments are revised by the judges concerned before publication. Cases are usually reported within four or five months of judgment. Decisions of the House of Lords are often reported within three to four weeks of judgment. The *All England Law Reports Reprint* (All ER Rep) is a reprint of some 4,000 to 5,000 important cases from 1558 to 1935, contained in 36 volumes and an index volume.

Other general series of reports include those in the *Solicitors' Journal* (SJ or Sol Jo), which has been published since 1857, and *The Times, The Guardian* and *The Independent* newspapers. In common with the other law reports mentioned, these reports are authenticated by the signature of a reporter who was present throughout while judgment was delivered. They may be cited in court in the absence of any other approved report of a case, although they occasionally mislead by reason of their brevity (see, e.g., *Summers* v *Summers* (1987) *The Times*, 19 May, CA, referring to a misleading *Times* report). The rule that only reports of cases made by a barrister could be cited in court was abolished as from 1 April 1991 by s. 115 of the Courts and Legal Services Act 1990. Now reports of cases are citable if made by a barrister, a solicitor, or by a person who has a Supreme Court qualification within the meaning of s. 71 of the Act.

There are many specialist series of law reports which concentrate on decisions of specific courts or on specific areas of law. Some of these specialist series are official. Among these are *Reports of Tax Cases* (TC or Tax Cas) published by the Inland Revenue and *Reports of Patent, Design and Trade Mark Cases* (RPC) published by the Patent Office. The specialist series published privately include *Lloyds Law Reports* (Lloyd's Rep), *Knight's Local Government Reports* (LGR), *Knight's Industrial Reports* (KIR), *Industrial Cases Reports* (ICR, published by the Incorporated Council of Law Reporting), the *Common Market Law Reports* (CMLR), the *Criminal Appeal Reports* (Cr App R) the *Criminal Appeal Reports (Sentencing)* (Cr App R (S)), the *Family Law Reports* (FLR), and, beginning in 1988, the *Crown Office Digest* (COD, whose reports of cases in the Crown Office List include applications for judicial review). Legal periodicals such as the *Criminal Law Review* (Crim LR) and *Family Law* (Fam Law) report cases on all aspects of criminal law and family law respectively. Without discriminating between them, Lord Diplock has said that the various series of specialist reports are of limited value because they contain only a small minority of leading judgments in which some new principle of law is authoritatively propounded, as distinct from the application of some previously accepted principle to the facts of a particular case. In the main, their usefulness is restricted to helping lawyers to predict the likely outcome of future cases by showing how cases with analogous facts had actually been decided in the past (*Roberts Petroleum Ltd* v *Bernard Kenny Ltd* [1983] 1 All ER 564, HL, at p. 567).

Although, in general, the modern reports are far superior in quality and reliability than their predecessors, dissatisfaction with them is sometimes expressed (see, e.g., W. Goodhart, 'Law reporting and the computer revolution', (1982) 132 New LJ 643). The main criticisms are that too much is reported; too little is reported; there is too much overlapping in what is reported in the various series; and that the reports are not made available quickly enough. It is the duty of counsel to bring to the attention of the court all relevant authority, even if it is adverse to his case. The failure of counsel to cite to the trial judge a recent relevant decision of the Court of Appeal, reported some months earlier in the weekly parts of the *All England Reports* and *The Weekly Law Reports*, was criticised as a matter of 'very great concern' by Buxton LJ in *Copeland* v *Smith* [2000] 1 All ER 457, CA, at p. 459. Counsel were reminded by Brooke LJ (at p. 462) of their responsibility to bring and keep themselves up to date with new case law, not only in the specialist series of law reports but also in the general series, such as the *All England Reports* and *The Weekly Law Reports*. (Buxton LJ's reference (at p. 459) to *The Weekly Law Reports* as 'official' must be a slip of the tongue.)

The state of law reporting has not been officially investigated since 1940, when the *ad hoc* Law Reporting Committee, under the chairmanship of a High Court judge, Simonds J (as he then was), presented a report to the Lord Chancellor (*Report of the Committee on Law Reporting*, HMSO, Lord Chancellor's Office, 1940).

The report contained a concise account of the history of law reporting, and, although it discussed the main criticisms which have been made of the present system, the majority of the committee were unable to propose any positive solutions. They recommended rigid enforcement of the rule of practice that a case reported in *The Law Reports* should be cited in court from that series and from no other. They identified accuracy as the most important attribute of a law report. Speed of publication is also a consideration, and, while it is not as essential as accuracy, they said that something should be done to hasten publication of *The Law Reports*. They suggested that the editor of *The Law Reports* should take a more liberal view of what is reportable. Not only cases of a special character but also cases which throw light on general legal principles or the interpretation of statutes should be reported.

The committee rejected the suggestion that law reporters should be licensed in order to limit the number of cases being reported. Decisions of the courts must be available for public discussion and criticism, and it would be an adverse step to give a licence to report to one man but withhold it from another. They rejected the suggestion that a monopoly of law reporting should be granted to the Incorporated Council or to the publisher of any other series of reports. Such a monopoly would be difficult to maintain in practice. English law is what it is, not because it has been so *reported,* but because it has been so *decided.* To insist that only *The Law Reports* could be cited in court would be to deny the authority of cases not reported in that series. The majority of the committee rejected the suggestion that there should be a written record, to be revised by the judge, of every single judgment. This idea was dismissed on grounds of cost and the additional burden it would impose on the judiciary.

The late Professor Goodhart presented a strong dissenting report. He was particularly concerned that many reports were not revised by the judges, thus leading to published inaccuracies, and that many decisions were not reported at all but were nevertheless authoritative. He recommended that official shorthand writers should take down and transcribe all judgments in the superior courts. The transcripts should then be sent to the judges for revision and returned by them, preferably within one week, for filing in the records of the court. Copies of these transcripts would, on payment of a fee, be available to reporters and any other persons. Professor Goodhart did not consider that the cost of this service, or the burden it might impose on the judiciary, would be too great.

Professor Goodhart's proposal was never implemented in full, although an improvement was made in relation to the availability of Court of Appeal decisions several years later. In *Gibson* v *South American Stores (Gath & Chaves) Ltd* [1950] Ch 177, CA, Sir Raymond Evershed MR remarked (at p. 195) on the:

> [P]eculiar and unfortunate characteristic of our system that, although in the great majority of cases which come before it, this court is the final court of appeal for England, no provision whatever is made for taking a note or making a record of the judgments of the court.

This omission was rectified in 1951 since when transcripts of all judgments in the Court of Appeal, civil division, have been placed in the Bar Library or, since 1978, in the Supreme Court Library in the Royal Courts of Justice, where they are accessible to lawyers and litigants in person. The transcripts are properly indexed under case names and subject-matter. Copies may be bought on payment of a fee. The judgments are not revised by the judges. In 1986 all such cases (13,613 of them) decided between 1951 and the end of 1979 went on sale in microfiche form (see (1986) 136 New LJ 1045).

In addition, all *unreported* judgments of the Court of Appeal, civil division, delivered since the beginning of 1980 are stored in Lexis, a computerised data base operated by

Butterworth (Telepublishing) Ltd. The practice of citing unreported Court of Appeal decisions before the House of Lords and the Court of Appeal has been criticised by the House of Lords. Indeed, the House has gone so far as to prohibit their citation before itself except with leave, which will only be granted in limited circumstances (*Roberts Petroleum Ltd v Bernard Kenny Ltd* [1983] 1 All ER 564, HL, para 9.6 above; see also *Stanley v International Harvester Co. of Great Britain Ltd* (1983) *The Times,* 7 February, CA, *per* Sir John Donaldson MR, complaining about the indiscriminate citing of computer-recorded cases which contain no new law). The Court of Appeal also discourages the citation of unreported cases (*Practice Direction (Court of Appeal: procedure)* [1999] 2 All ER 490.)

Transcripts of cases decided after 10 April 1989 by the Court of Appeal, criminal division, are lodged in the Supreme Court Library in the Royal Courts of Justice.

Official shorthand notes are taken in all other courts except the county courts and magistrates' courts, but the transcripts are not officially deposited anywhere and the judgments are not revised. Unreported decisions of the House of Lords are deposited in the Record Office of the House of Lords. They are available to the public but, since they are indexed under case-names only, it is impossible to trace a particular decision without knowing the name of the case.

10

Remedies in Private Law

10.1 DISTINCTION BETWEEN COMMON-LAW AND EQUITABLE REMEDIES

At common law the normal remedy was damages. This was so even for a breach of a particular contract where damages might be inappropriate. Thus, if B contracted to sell to A a plot of land and then B broke the contract by refusing to convey the land to A, the common law would award only damages to A. This was an unsatisfactory remedy in cases where A preferred ownership of the land to money compensation. Equity was very inventive in providing a variety of new remedies: specific performance and the injunction, and also rescission and rectification. In this way, equity supplemented the common law.

The most important common feature of equitable remedies is that they are *discretionary*. At common law, if the claimant proved his case he was entitled to his remedy of damages and it mattered not that his own conduct had been bad, or that he had been dilatory in seeking relief, or that the outcome was unfair to the defendant. Equity, however, exercised a discretion over the granting of its remedies. In particular, equity was interested in the conduct of the parties — *the conduct of the claimant* as well as that of the defendant. A remedy would be refused to those whose conduct was inequitable, or who had delayed in seeking relief, or whose claims would produce unfair results. Such claimants would be left to pursue whatever remedy they might have at common law. If an adequate remedy existed at common law, that in itself was a ground for denying an equitable remedy to the claimant.

The position is the same today. Damages are available as of right while equitable remedies are granted or withheld on the judicial exercise of discretion.

Only the major equitable remedies are dealt with in this book. Details of other remedies, such as account, appointment of a receiver, discovery, and delivery up and cancellation of documents, can be found in other works (see especially, Snell, *Principles of Equity,* 29th ed., 1990; Spry, *Equitable Remedies,* 4th ed., 1990; Burrows, *Remedies for Torts and Breach of Contract*, 2nd ed., 1994).

10.2 DAMAGES

An award of damages is a common-law remedy available as of right. Damages are particularly important as a means of redress for breach of contract and the commission of a tort.

10.2.1 The object of damages

The object of damages for breach of contract is to place the claimant in the same position, as far as money can do it, as if the contract had been performed. The object of damages in the law of tort is to place the claimant in the same position, as far as money can do it, as if the tort had not been committed (i.e., *compensation* for the claimant). Thus, in contract and tort the common object of the remedy is *restitution*. In contract, the claimant is to be restored to the position he would have been in if performance had taken place. In tort, he is to be restored to the position he would have been in if no wrong had been done against him.

10.2.2   Types of damages

In both contract and tort the usual type of damages awarded is *compensatory* damages. But there also exist contemptuous, nominal and exemplary damages.

Compensatory damages provide compensation for actual loss suffered, no more and no less. Most torts are actionable only on proof of loss or damage so that no action will lie, and no damages are recoverable, without such proof. Breach of contract is actionable *per se*.

Contemptuous damages usually consist of the lowest coin of legal tender (currently 1p; formerly ½p and, before that, ½d and ¼d respectively). Contemptuous damages are awarded where the claimant proves his case but he has suffered no loss and the court has a low opinion of his claim. In tort they may be awarded because, morally at least, the claimant deserved what the defendant did to him. In *Dering* v *Uris* [1964] 2 QB 669, Dr Dering, an ex-prisoner at Auschwitz who had performed experimental surgical operations on inmates under Nazi pressure, sued Leon Uris for libel in respect of a reference to him in Uris's novel, *Exodus*. Libel is actionable without proof of damage. The trial of the action against the author and publisher of *Exodus* lasted for five weeks. The claimant's claim succeeded, but the jury, as an indication of their disapproval of his action, awarded him only a halfpenny in damages and he was ordered by the judge to pay the defence costs.

In a case decided towards the end of 1991, no damages at all were awarded to a successful libel claimant for what is believed to be the first time ever. A former teacher sued the publishers of *The People* newspaper over allegations that he was a sexual pervert and a danger to the boys he taught. The jury found that he had been libelled but awarded no damages, and the judge refused to order the claimant's costs to be paid by the unsuccessful defendants (*Standish* v *Mirror Group Newspapers*, 25 November 1991, unreported, but see *The Independent*, 26 November 1991; the founder of the 'ChildLine' charity, Esther Rantzen, fared considerably better when she later successfully sued the publishers of *The People* after it was alleged that she had kept quiet about Mr Standish's activities: see para 7.9.2). In 1996, a jury found in favour of the claimant, but awarded no damages, in a libel action brought by the former Irish Prime Minister, Albert Reynolds, against *The Sunday Times*, which had alleged that he had lied to the Irish parliament. The following day, the trial judge decided that the claimant was entitled to what were described as 'nominal damages' and awarded Mr Reynolds the sum of 1p (*Reynolds* v *Times Newspapers Ltd*, 19 November 1996, unreported, but see *The Times*, 20 and 21 November 1996). A new trial was later ordered on other grounds (see *Reynolds* v *Times Newspapers Ltd* [1999] 4 All ER 609, HL).

If the damages awarded to the claimant are of the contemptuous type, the chances are that he will not be given his costs even though, technically, he has won the case. Costs usually 'follow the event' so that the winner has his costs paid by the loser. But the judge always has a discretion in the matter of costs and the award of a derisory sum by way of damages is a material factor in exercising that discretion.

Nominal damages usually vary in amount between 5p and £2, although there is no conventional figure. They are awarded where the claimant proves his case but has suffered no loss and there is no moral blame attaching to him (although the claimant may still be deprived of his costs). Nominal damages are awarded, for example, in the case of torts which are actionable *per se* but where no loss has resulted, such as a technical trespass to land where no damage was done. The relatively large sum of five guineas was awarded as nominal damages in *Constantine* v *Imperial Hotels Ltd* [1944] KB 693 to the West Indian cricketer, Learie Constantine, who had been refused accommodation in one of the defendants' hotels. He was given accommodation in another of the defendants' hotels, but the defendants had broken their common-law duty as common innkeepers and the claimant was entitled to damages.

Exemplary (sometimes called *punitive or vindictive*) damages are sometimes awarded to the claimant in order to punish, or to make an example of, the defendant for what he has done and to deter him (and others) from doing the same in the future.

Exemplary damages cannot be awarded in contract but they can be awarded in tort in the following three circumstances (*Rookes* v *Barnard* [1964] AC 1129, HL; *Cassell & Co. Ltd* v *Broome* [1972] AC 1027, HL):

(a) Where they are authorised by statute.

(b) For oppressive, arbitrary or unconstitutional actions by servants of the government.

(c) Where the defendant calculated to make a profit out of the tort which would exceed any compensation payable to the claimant.

It has been held by the Court of Appeal that an exemplary award can only be made for torts in respect of which exemplary damages were available prior to 1964, the year in which *Rookes* v *Barnard* was decided (*AB* v *South West Water Services Ltd* [1993] 1 All ER 609, CA). Defamation, trespass to land, trespass to the person, false imprisonment and private nuisance are such torts. On the other hand, there appears to be no case prior to 1964 (or since) in which exemplary damages have been awarded for negligence, deceit, public nuisance, or misfeasance in public office. Accordingly, in *AB* v *South West Water Services Ltd*, above, a claim by 182 claimants for exemplary damages for public nuisance arising out of the contamination of their drinking water by large quantities of aluminium sulphate was struck out. And in *Kuddus* v *Chief Constable of Leicestershire* (2000) *The Times*, 16 March, CA, the claimant's claim for exemplary damages for misfeasance in public office committed by a police constable was struck out. It was emphasised that it made no difference that the particular circumstances of the tort of misfeasance in public office might include oppressive or arbitrary conduct, or might amount to, or include, the separate torts of trespass to the person or malicious prosecution for which exemplary damages were available before 1964.

This case is also authority for the proposition that the involvement of a large number of claimants would make a claim unsuitable for an exemplary award even where the tort concerned is one for which exemplary damages are normally available (see [1993] 1 All ER 609, CA, *per* Stuart-Smith LJ at p. 624 and Sir Thomas Bingham MR at p. 627).

Exemplary damages are normally awarded *in addition to* compensatory damages. The decision of a jury to award only exemplary damages without at the same time awarding compensatory damages will usually be regarded as perverse. Thus, in *Cumber* v *Chief Constable of Hampshire* (1995) *The Times*, 28 January, CA, the successful claimant in an action for false imprisonment was awarded £50 exemplary damages — but no compensatory damages — by a jury which appear to have totally misunderstood their function. On appeal, it was held that the jury's verdict was perverse and the Court of Appeal substituted a global award of £350 to cover both compensatory and exemplary damages.

(a) What appears to be the only statute authorising in terms the award of exemplary damages is the Reserve and Auxiliary Forces (Protection of Civil Interests) Act 1951. By

s. 13(2), in any action for damages for conversion or in other proceedings (which may be available in certain circumstances outlined in ss. 2 and 4) the court 'may take account of the conduct of the defendant with a view, if the court thinks fit, to awarding exemplary damages in respect of the wrong sustained by the plaintiff [claimant]'. There is no case law directly on s. 13(2) and it has been doubted whether the damages so mentioned are exemplary in the true sense. In *Cassell & Co. Ltd* v *Broome* [1972] AC 1027, HL, Lord Kilbrandon expressed the opinion (at p. 1133) that 'exemplary' really meant 'aggravated'.

Section 97(2) of the Copyright, Designs and Patents Act 1988 allows the court in an action for infringement of copyright to 'award such *additional damages* as the justice of the case may require' having regard to all the circumstances and, in particular, to the flagrancy of the infringement and any benefit obtained by the defendant as a result of the infringement. It is not at all certain, however, that the 'additional damages' mentioned in s. 97(2) can properly be described as 'exemplary'.

According to Lord Clyde, *obiter*, in the Scottish appeal case of *Redrow Homes Ltd* v *Bett Brothers plc* [1998] 1 All ER 385, HL, they are 'more probably' aggravated damages of a compensatory nature, and this seems to be confirmed by the history of the predecessor of s. 97(2). This was s. 17(3) of the Copyright Act 1956. In *Williams* v *Settle* [1960] 2 All ER 806, the Court of Appeal affirmed an exemplary award of £1,000 damages for breach of copyright. Although it is not clear from the report whether the damages were awarded at common law or under the statute, the 'additional damages' available under s. 17(3) of the 1956 Act were described in the Court of Appeal as 'exemplary'. In two subsequent cases in the House of Lords the view was advanced, *obiter*, that they are not true exemplary damages (*Rookes* v *Barnard, per* Lord Devlin at p. 1225; *Cassell & Co. Ltd* v *Broome, per* Lord Kilbrandon at p. 1133). In *Nichols Advanced Vehicle Systems Inc.* v *Rees* [1979] RPC 127, Templeman J held that the defendant's breach of copyright was flagrant enough to attract an additional award under the statute. He ordered an enquiry as to the amount payable, indicating that it should be a moderate, but not excessive, sum. Without citing any of the case law, Templeman J refrained from describing the additional damages as exemplary. Additional damages in the modest sum of £200 were awarded under s. 17(3) by Mervyn Davies J for breach of copyright in a Ph.D. thesis in *Sushil Kumar Goswami* v *Hammons and others*, 29 October 1982, unreported.

'Additional damages' under s. 97(2) of the Copyright, Designs and Patents Act 1988 are only available as an addition to normal compensatory damages; they are not available as an addition to other remedies for breach of copyright, such as an account of profits (*Redrow Homes Ltd* v *Bett Brothers plc* [1998] 1 All ER 385, HL).

It seems highly unlikely that an award of exemplary damages for unlawful discrimination is justified on the wording of the Sex Discrimination Act 1975, the Race Relations Act 1976, or the Disability Discrimination Act 1995 (see below).

(b) The expression 'servants of the government' includes the police, local government and statutory bodies. Thus, it has been held that exemplary damages may be awarded against a local authority in respect of unlawful discrimination in the selection of candidates for teaching posts in schools and colleges if the discriminatory acts are 'oppressive, arbitrary or unconstitutional'. In *Bradford Metropolitan City Council* v *Arora* [1991] 3 All ER 545, the Court of Appeal allowed an appeal from a decision of the Employment Appeal Tribunal and restored an employment tribunal's award of exemplary damages of £1,000 (made in addition to compensatory damages of £2,000) for the insulting manner in which a candidate had been treated.

Doubt has subsequently been cast on the correctness of *Bradford Metropolitan City Council* v *Arora* for two reasons. First, if the later case of *AB* v *South West Water Services*

Remedies in Private Law

Ltd [1993] 1 All ER 609, CA, is correctly decided it would follow that exemplary damages are not available in respect of unlawful discrimination since it was not a tort at the time *Rookes* v *Barnard* was decided in 1964. Sexual discrimination was made tortious by the Sex Discrimination Act 1975, racial discrimination became a tort actionable at the suit of the victim by the Race Relations Act 1976, and disability discrimination became tortious by virtue of the Disability Discrimination Act 1995. The point was not raised in *Arora*, where the arguments were presented on the *assumption* that exemplary damages could be awarded for a statutory tort created after 1964, and the case was decided solely on the issue as to whether employees of the local authority were acting privately or publicly. Because of this the Court of Appeal in *AB* v *South West Water Services Ltd* took the view that *Arora* was not binding on the point (see, for example, [1993] 1 All ER 609 *per* Stuart-Smith LJ at pp. 619–20). In *Deane* v *Ealing London Borough Council* [1993] ICR 329, the Employment Appeal Tribunal, in a judgment delivered by Wood J, refused to make an exemplary award for racial discrimination on the ground that it was bound by the decision of the Court of Appeal in *AB* v *South West Water Services Ltd* to hold that exemplary damages cannot be awarded for a tort which came into existence after 1964. (See also *Ministry of Defence* v *Meredith* [1995] IRLR 539, where the Employment Appeal Tribunal held that exemplary damages are not available for sexual discrimination for the same reason.)

Secondly, it seems likely that, in any event, the anti-discrimination legislation does not authorise the award of exemplary damages (see *AB* v *South West Water Services Ltd*, above, *per* Stuart-Smith LJ at p. 620). For example, s. 66(4) of the Sex Discrimination Act 1975 and s. 57(4) of the Race Relations Act 1976 (which deal with awards of damages in the county courts) are in identical terms:

For the avoidance of doubt it is hereby declared that damages in respect of an unlawful act of discrimination may include *compensation* for injury to feelings whether or not they include *compensation* under any other head. (Italics supplied.)

The wording of s. 25(2) of the Disability Discrimination Act 1995 is very similar. These three anti-discrimination statutes seem to contemplate the award of compensatory damages only; exemplary damages are not 'compensation'. This argument was not put forward in *Arora*.

The term 'servants of the government' does not include public or private bodies, such as nationalised or privatised water authorities, which carry on commercial operations without exercising any executive power derived from central or local government (*AB* v *South West Water Services Ltd*, CA, above). The term may possibly include solicitors since they are officers of the Supreme Court. This would mean, for example, that clients could be liable in exemplary damages if their solicitors execute *Anton Piller* orders in an excessive and oppressive manner (*Columbia Picture Industries Inc.* v *Robinson* [1986] 3 All ER 338 *per* Scott J at p 379; see para 10.4.2.5 below).

Actions against the police for wrongful arrest, false imprisonment, assault, and malicious prosecution are likely to raise allegations of oppressive or arbitrary behaviour. In *Thompson* v *Commissioner of Police of the Metropolis* [1997] 2 All ER 762, CA, the Court of Appeal laid down guidelines on how judges should instruct juries to help them decide what to award by way of damages in such cases (see para 7.9.2).

(c) In *Cassell & Co. Ltd* v *Broome*, the defendants published a book knowing that it was probably defamatory of the claimant, Commander Broome. The book, entitled *The Destruction of Convoy PQ17*, accused the claimant of disobeying orders and of cowardly desertion of the convoy he was escorting during the Second World War. The book was published in spite of a warning from the claimant that he would sue the defendants if they published it. The trial judge, Lawton J, was satisfied that the defendants had calculated that it was worth the risk of being sued because even the publicity value of litigation would help to sell more copies of the book. Accordingly the jury was directed that exemplary damages might be awarded in such a case. The jury awarded compensatory damages of £15,000 and exemplary damages of £25,000. All seven judges who heard the appeal in the House of Lords thought that the award of exemplary damages was excessive, but, by a majority of four to three, they refused to disturb the jury's verdict.

The profit motive is not limited to money-making in the strict sense. It also covers cases where the defendant is intent on securing, at the expense of the claimant, some other advantage which can only be obtained by paying a price he is not prepared to pay or by acting unlawfully (*Rookes* v *Barnard, per* Lord Devlin at p. 1227). Thus, in *Drane* v *Evangelou* [1978] 2 All ER 437, CA, an exemplary award of £1,000 for trespass to land made against a landlord who had engaged in 'monstrous behaviour' to secure the unlawful eviction of his tenant was upheld, and in *Guppys (Bridport) Ltd* v *Brookling* (1983) 14 HLR 1, CA, an award of a similar amount was affirmed in a case of private nuisance where reconstruction works had caused serious disruption to two tenants.

10.2.3 Difficulty of assessment of damages

Damages must still be awarded even though they are difficult to assess. For example, if an actor, through a breach of contract, loses the opportunity for publicity, damages must be awarded for this loss despite the fact that their quantification would be very difficult. In *Chaplin* v *Hicks* [1911] 2 KB 786, CA, the claimant was prevented from taking part in a beauty contest because of the defendant's breach of contract. It was held that although it was impossible to assess the damages with any precision, a sum should be awarded in accordance with the value of the chance which the claimant had lost. She had been deprived of the opportunity of competing as one of 50 final candidates for 12 prizes in the form of theatrical engagements. The jury had awarded £100 damages and the Court of Appeal refused to disturb this verdict.

In tort, damages are difficult to assess in defamation and personal injury cases but they must nevertheless be awarded.

10.2.4 Damages for mental distress

Damages may sometimes be awarded for mental distress as well as for the more common physical injuries or financial loss. Such damages are more likely to be awarded in tort than in contract.

The general rule in contract law is that damages are not recoverable for mental distress caused by a breach (*Addis* v *Gramophone Co. Ltd* [1909] AC 488, HL). For example, damages are not recoverable for mental distress, consisting of depression, frustration, anxiety and injured feelings, arising incidentally out of dismissal or demotion at work (*Bliss* v *South East Thames Regional Health Authority* [1985] IRLR 308, CA, applying *Addis* v *Gramophone Co. Ltd*, above, and overruling *Cox* v *Philips Industries Ltd* [1976] 3 All ER 161). Nor are damages available for anguish and vexation arising from the breach of a purely commercial contract (*Hayes* v *James & Charles Dodd* [1990] 2 All ER 815, CA, applying *Bliss* v *South East Thames Regional Health Authority*, above).

In some cases in recent years the courts have been prepared to compensate the claimant where the mental distress was a direct, as opposed to an incidental, result of the defendant's breach of contract. From these cases there has developed an exception to the general rule: where the contract is one whose very object is the provision of pleasure, relaxation, peace of mind, or freedom from harassment, damages for mental distress are recoverable upon breach (see *Watts* v *Morrow* [1991] 4 All ER 937, CA, *per* Bingham LJ at pp. 959–60).

For example, in *Jarvis* v *Swans Tours Ltd* [1973] 1 QB 233, CA, the claimant sued the defendants for failing to provide the houseparty holiday promised in their brochure. Among the claimant's disappointments in Switzerland were that there was no welcome party and no proper skiing facilities; the hotel owner did not speak English; the bar was open only on one evening; and the promised 'yodeller' consisted of a local man in his working clothes singing a few songs very quickly. It was held that the defendants were in breach of contract and, in the county court, the claimant was awarded as damages half the price of the holiday. The claimant appealed and the Court of Appeal held that he was also entitled to damages for mental distress, which the Court defined as including inconvenience, disappointment, annoyance and frustration. The claimant's damages were increased accordingly (see also *Jackson* v *Horizon Holidays Ltd* [1975] 3 All ER 92, CA). In another case, the Court of Appeal held the claimant to be entitled to damages for mental distress caused by the breach of contract of the defendant firm of solicitors in negligently failing to enforce a non-molestation injunction on her behalf (*Heywood* v *Wellers* [1976] QB 446, CA).

Jarvis v *Swans Tours Ltd*, above, and *Jackson* v *Horizon Holidays Ltd*, above, were approved by the House of Lords in *Ruxley Electronics and Construction Ltd* v *Forsyth* [1995] 3 All ER 268, HL. Here the builder of a swimming pool was in breach of contract in constructing a shallower pool than specified. The contract was treated as one to provide a 'pleasurable amenity', and a sum of £2,500 had been awarded as damages for loss of that amenity. Their Lordships thought that the sum was on the high side for a disappointed expectation but nevertheless refused to disturb it (see especially *per* Lord Lloyd at p. 289). On the other hand, damages for mental distress and inconvenience were refused in *Watts* v *Morrow* [1991] 4 All ER 937, CA, where the defendant's breach of an ordinary contract of survey had led the claimants to pay £15,000 more for their country house than it was really worth. The claimants were awarded compensatory damages of £15,000 on the diminution in value principle but were denied an additional sum by way of damages for mental distress and inconvenience because the 'very object' of a contract to survey the condition of a house for a prospective purchaser is not to provide 'pleasure, relaxation, peace of mind or freedom from molestation' (*per* Bingham LJ at p. 960).

Watts v *Morrow* was applied in *Alexander* v *Alpe Jack Rolls Royce Motor Cars Ltd* (1995) *The Times*, 4 May, CA, and in *Knott* v *Bolton* (1995) *The Independent*, 8 May, CA. In the *Rolls Royce* case, it was argued that damages for mental distress should be available for breach of a contract to repair a motor car because it is akin to a contract to provide a relaxing holiday (as in *Jarvis* v *Swans Tours Ltd*, above) or to provide freedom from worry and anxiety (as in *Heywood* v *Wellers*, above). It was held, however, that breach of a contract to repair a car, even one so prestigious as a Rolls Royce, does not give rise to a liability for damages for distress and inconvenience or loss of enjoyment in the use of the car. In *Knott* v *Bolton*, the claimants were unsuccessful in their attempt to obtain damages for mental distress from the defendant architect who had defectively designed their house so as to provide a much narrower staircase and smaller gallery than specified. The argument that the true nature of the contract entered into by the defendant was to provide pleasure for the claimants was rejected. The true nature of the contract was to design the house, and the provision of pleasure to the claimants was merely ancillary or incidental to that.

Watts v *Morrow*, above, and *Knott* v *Bolton*, above, were applied in *Farley* v *Skinner* (2000) *The Times*, 14 April, CA. Here, a contract to survey a house included an obligation to advise whether the property might be affected by aircraft noise. When the contract was broken by reason of the defendant's failure to ascertain this properly, it was held that damages for mental distress could not be awarded to the claimant because the contract was an ordinary contract of survey and not one to provide pleasure, relaxation or peace of mind. It was emphasised by the Court of Appeal that in deciding whether a contract comes within this exceptional category it is necessary to look at the contract as a whole and not simply one relatively minor aspect of it.

In *Malik* v *Bank of Credit and Commerce International SA (in liquidation)* [1997] 3 All ER 1, HL, the House of Lords held that *Addis* v *Gramophone Co. Ltd* [1909] AC 488, HL, does not prevent recovery of damages for *loss of reputation* caused by a breach of contract, including a breach of a contract of employment. Thus, where an employer carries on his business dishonestly or corruptly, and is thereby in breach of his implied duty not to conduct his business in a way likely to do serious damage to the relationship of confidence and trust between employer and employee, an employee who suffers loss in the form of damage to his future employment prospects in consequence of such breach can sue for damages if the loss was reasonably foreseeable. In the *Malik* case, two innocent former employees of BCCI, which ran its business fraudulently and collapsed in 1991, were accordingly held entitled to claim 'stigma compensation' arising from their difficulty in obtaining employment in the banking field because of their association with BCCI.

10.2.5   Aggravated damages

In tort, *aggravated* damages (which are compensatory in nature and are not to be confused with exemplary damages) may sometimes be awarded for injury to the claimant's dignity and pride. Such cases would include an 'insolent and high-handed trespass' to land (as in *Jolliffe* v *Willmett & Co.* [1971] 1 All ER 478, *per* Geoffrey Lane J at p. 485, and note the award of aggravated damages in *Columbia Picture Industries Inc.* v *Robinson* [1986] 3 All ER 338, para 10.4.2.5 below), or an attempted justification of a libel where the defendant repeats his statements but fails to prove the truth of them. In *W* v *Meah* [1986] 1 All ER 935, an action for trespass to the person (assault and battery), aggravated damages were awarded by Woolf J to two women, one of whom had been raped and the other seriously sexually assaulted in frightening and revolting circumstances. Aggravated damages were awarded in *Appleton* v *Garrett* [1996] PIQR P1, an action for trespass to the person where a dentist, for personal profit, had performed a large amount of unnecessary dental work on the claimants' teeth. Aggravated damages are available for the tort of malicious falsehood (*Khodaparast* v *Shad* [2000] 1 All ER 545, CA; this possibility had earlier been suggested, *obiter*, in *Joyce* v *Sengupta* [1993] 1 All ER 897, CA, para 1.9.1).

It seems that aggravated damages are not available in all torts. In *Kralj* v *McGrath* [1986] 1 All ER 54, the claimant contended that her compensation should include an award of aggravated damages for an obstetrician's 'horrific and wholly unacceptable' treatment of her while undergoing childbirth without an anaesthetic. Woolf J held that aggravated damages were not appropriate in medical negligence cases. Nor are they appropriate as compensation for anger and indignation in cases of public nuisance (*AB* v *South West Water Services Ltd* [1993] 1 All ER 609, CA).

10.2.6 Reform of aggravated and exemplary damages

In 1997, the Law Commission described the limited circumstances in which exemplary damages are available as 'plainly irrational' (*Aggravated, Exemplary and Restitutionary Damages,* Law Com No. 247, 1997). Under the Law Commission's recommendations, legislation would place exemplary damages on a 'clear, principled, but tightly controlled, footing'. At the same time, their availability would be extended to any legal wrong (other than breach of contract) where the defendant had 'deliberately and outrageously' disregarded the claimant's rights. Juries would no longer have the power to decide whether to award exemplary damages or to fix their amount; these matters would be for judges to determine. Exemplary damages would not be available where the defendant had been convicted of a criminal offence for the same conduct, or where another available remedy would be adequate punishment.

It was also recommended that, whenever exemplary damages are available, the court should also have the power to grant the less extreme remedy of restitutionary damages, which aim to deprive the defendant of any gains made by committing a legal wrong.

On aggravated damages, the Law Commission noted that they are really part of the law on damages for mental distress and referred to the confusion over whether aggravated damages contain a punitive, in addition to a compensatory, element. It was recommended that it should be made clear by legislation that they are intended only to provide compensation for the claimant's mental distress and not to punish the defendant for his conduct. To this end, it was proposed that they should go under the name of 'damages for mental distress' rather than the misleading name of aggravated damages.

10.3   SPECIFIC PERFORMANCE

10.3.1   Introduction

Specific performance is an order of the court directing the defendant to do what he has promised by contract to do. It is a creature of equity and is superior to the common-law remedy of damages in that it provides for the specific enforcement of a contract instead of merely giving money compensation to the claimant.

Like other equitable remedies, specific performance is awarded or withheld on a discretionary basis. This means that the court is not bound to grant it only because the conditions for it exist. Every breach of a binding contract entitles the injured party to the common-law remedy of damages, but not every breach of contract entitles him to the equitable remedy of specific performance. Thus, in *Wood* v *Scarth* (1855) 2 K & J 33 the claimant's action for specific performance failed, but three years later his action for damages on the same facts succeeded (*Wood* v *Scarth* (1858) 1 F & F 293).

Although specific performance is a discretionary remedy the discretion is exercised *judicially;* i.e., not according to the caprice of the individual judge but according to rules which have been settled in decided cases over the centuries.

10.3.2   Circumstances in which specific performance will not usually be decreed

10.3.2.1   Where the claimant's injury would be sufficiently remedied by damages
The court will not order a superior remedy where an inferior one will do. For example, if a contract for the sale of goods is broken, and the goods are ordinary commercial articles,

only damages will be awarded because similar goods can be obtained easily elsewhere. But specific performance may be granted where the goods are rare or unique or not easily obtainable elsewhere. Examples of such goods would be a rare jewel, an original painting by an old master, and even petrol during an oil shortage, as in *Sky Petroleum Ltd v VIP Petroleum Ltd* [1974] 1 All ER 954 in which an interlocutory injunction was granted to prevent an oil company from cutting off supplies of petrol to a garage when alternative supplies were not available because of the 1973 oil shortage. The injunction in these circumstances was tantamount to a decree of specific performance. In *Behnke v Bede Shipping Co. Ltd* [1927] 1 KB 649, specific performance was ordered of a contract for the sale of a ship (approved in *Astro Exito Navegacion SA v Southland Enterprise Co. Ltd (No. 2)* [1982] 3 All ER 335, CA, at p. 345). However, in *Cohen v Roche* [1927] 1 KB 169 specific performance was refused to the buyer of a set of Heppelwhite chairs on the ground that the chairs were not sufficiently rare or unique but were ordinary articles of commerce. The buyer was instead awarded £15 damages for breach of contract.

There seems to be no doubt that, historically, the whole basis of the equitable jurisdiction to decree specific performance rested on the inadequacy of the remedy at common law (*Harnett v Yielding* (1805) 2 Sch & Lef 549, *per* Lord Redesdale LC at p. 556; *Adderley v Dixon* (1824) 1 Sim & St 607, *per* Leach V-C at p. 610; Ingman and Wakefield, [1981] Conv 286, at p. 294). Specific performance was ideally suited to remedy the breach of a contract involving land because damages, even if substantial in amount, were not an adequate alternative since no single piece of land is exactly the same as any other. The claimant would much rather have the land he had contracted to buy than be fobbed off with a money judgment. Even so, specific performance is not always the appropriate remedy where the contract is for the sale of land. For example, in *Wroth v Tyler* [1974] Ch 30 specific performance of a contract for the sale of land was refused because, in the circumstances, it would have been unreasonable to decree it (see further, para 10.3.2.8 below).

At the same time there seems to be no good reason why in modern law the availability of specific performance should be deliberately restricted to contracts involving land. In the case of all contracts, whether for the sale of land or otherwise, a criterion based on what will produce the most just solution would perhaps be preferable to one based solely on the adequacy of damages as a remedy. Support for this approach can be found in *Beswick v Beswick* [1968] AC 58, in which the House of Lords ordered specific performance of a contract to pay a sum of money because, in the circumstances, that was the more just and appropriate remedy.

10.3.2.2 *Where constant supervision by the court would be necessary*

If the court were to enforce specifically a contract to do continuous successive acts it would not have the machinery for ensuring that the contract was performed. The court will not embarrass itself by making an order which, in practice, it cannot enforce. In *Ryan v Mutual Tontine Westminister Chambers Association* [1893] 1 Ch 116, CA, the lessor of a flat agreed in the lease that he would appoint a porter, who would be 'constantly in attendance' for the purposes of cleaning the common passages and stairs in the building, delivering letters and accepting articles for safe custody. The porter appointed was absent from the premises for several hours each day in order to act as a chef at a nearby club. The Court of Appeal held that, although the lessor had committed a breach of contract, the only remedy for the disappointed lessee was an action for damages. Such a contractual term, which was of a continuing nature and involved the daily performance of a series of acts, would not be enforced by an order for specific performance.

It is difficult to see why the court would have to become involved at all in daily or any other periodical supervision in a case like *Ryan.* If the court had decreed specific performance and the lessor had still ignored his responsibilities the lessee could have taken enforcement proceedings in the normal way against the lessor for breach of the court order. The authority of *Ryan's* case has been weakened by subsequent developments. In particular, it was distinguished on the facts in *Posner* v *Scott-Lewis* [1986] 3 All ER 513, where specific performance was decreed of a covenant in a lease to employ a resident porter in a block of flats. Mervyn Davies J's judgment implies that difficulty of supervision is not by itself a ground for withholding specific performance. He said (at p. 521) that the decision to grant or refuse a decree depends on (a) whether what has to be done in order to comply with the court order is sufficiently defined; (b) whether supervision by the court would be involved to an unacceptable degree; and (c) the respective prejudices or hardships likely to be suffered by the parties. In the *Posner* case the decree of specific performance simply ordered the lessor to employ a resident porter within a specified period. The making of the order would not involve the court in any protracted supervisory role.

Contracts to build or repair will not normally be specifically enforced. The reason is not so much that constant supervision of the work would be required but that damages would usually be an adequate remedy for breach of such contracts. If the defendant builder refuses to build, the claimant can employ another builder and recover any loss as damages from the defendant. Sometimes, however, building contracts have been specifically enforced. If the building work is clearly defined in the contract, if it is not possible for the claimant to employ another builder to build without committing a trespass because the defendant is in possession of the land, and if the work is not done the claimant will suffer a loss which cannot adequately be remedied by damages, then the contract may be enforced by means of an order for specific performance (*Wolverhampton Corporation* v *Emmons* [1901] 1 KB 515, CA; *Carpenters Estates Ltd* v *Davies* [1940] Ch 160). In *Rainbow Estates Ltd* v *Tokenhold Ltd* [1998] 2 All ER 860, a tenant's repairing covenant was specifically enforced because, on the facts, there was no adequate alternative remedy and the problems of defining the work required to be done and the need for supervision could be overcome by sufficiently defining in the decree of specific performance what had to be done in order to comply with it.

Similarly, the normal practice of the courts is not to compel retail premises to remain open, or to reopen, under a 'keep open' covenant in a lease because of difficulty of supervision or because damages would usually be an adequate remedy for breach of such a covenant. In *Co-operative Insurance Society Ltd* v *Argyll Stores (Holdings) Ltd* [1996] 3 All ER 934, CA, the Court of Appeal held that, on the facts, damages would not be an adequate remedy and the defendants were ordered to reopen one of their *Safeway* supermarkets at a cost of £1m and to keep it open for the remaining 29 years of a lease. On appeal to the House of Lords, this decision was reversed (see [1997] 3 All ER 297, HL). Their Lordships held that the normal, settled practice of the courts not to make orders compelling a person to run a business is based on sound sense. Although it is not a binding rule, and the grant or refusal of specific performance rests with the judge's discretion, the normal practice should only be departed from in exceptional circumstances. Disagreeing with the Court of Appeal, it was held that this was not a suitable case for specific performance because the defendants' contractual obligation to 'keep . . . open for retail trade during the usual hours of business in the locality . . .' was not sufficiently precise to be capable of specific performance since it left too much room for argument about whether the defendants were doing enough to comply with it. It would, therefore, require constant supervision by the court.

10.3.2.3   Where the contract is for personal work or services

The court is not a slave-driver and will not order a person to work against his will. In *Lumley v Wagner* (1852) 1 De GM & G 604, the defendant agreed to sing at the claimant's theatre for three months and 'not to use her talents' at any other theatre during that time. When the defendant broke her contract by singing elsewhere, Lord St Leonards LC refused to order her to sing for the claimant. He did, however, grant an injunction preventing her from singing elsewhere during the currency of the agreement (see further, para 10.4.2.2.3 below).

The judicial principle that specific performance will not be ordered of a contract for personal work or services has been given legislative force in the case of the contract of employment. By the Trade Union and Labour Relations (Consolidation) Act 1992, s. 236:

No court shall, whether by way of:

(a)   an order for specific performance . . . of a contract of employment, or
(b)   an injunction . . . restraining a breach or threatened breach of such a contract,

compel an employee to do any work or attend any place for the doing of any work.

The principle is reciprocal: the employee will not be compelled to work and the employer will not be compelled to employ. An employee who is *wrongfully* dismissed can sue his employer for breach of contract, claiming damages or a declaration that the dismissal was wrongful. He cannot claim specific performance to compel the employer to take him back. Under the code on *unfair* dismissal (which is not usually a breach of contract) contained in the Employment Rights Act 1996, an employment tribunal has power to recommend the reinstatement or re-engagement of the employee. But if the recommendation is not implemented there is no power of compulsion exercisable against the recalcitrant employer. He can only be ordered to pay extra compensation (Employment Rights Act 1996, ss. 113–117).

10.3.2.4   Where the contract is lacking in mutuality

The court will not grant specific performance to one party in a situation where it could not be granted to the other party. Thus, the court will not grant specific performance *to* a minor because it could not order specific performance *against* him (*Flight v Bolland* (1828) 4 Russ 298). It would be unfair to allow a minor to obtain specific performance against an adult in circumstances in which the contract is unenforceable by the adult against the minor.

As long as mutuality exists at the date of the trial it does not matter that there was no mutuality at the date when the contract was made. For example, an obligation to repair on the part of the claimant is not normally specifically enforceable at the suit of the defendant who has agreed to grant a lease. There is, therefore, a lack of mutuality at the inception of the contract. However, if by the time of the hearing the repairs have been carried out by the defendant, and the claimant is willing to pay for them, there is mutuality of remedy and the claimant could be awarded specific performance of the agreement to grant the lease (*Price v Strange* [1978] Ch 337, CA).

There are a number of exceptions to the mutuality rule. It is, for instance, possible for the victim of a misrepresentation to obtain specific performance of a contract which could not be enforced against him because of his ability to rescind it (*Winch v Winchester* (1812) 1 Ves & B 375).

10.3.2.5 *Where the contract is illegal or void*

Equity will not aid the enforcement of a contract which is illegal or for some reason void according to English law. Illegal contracts include those which offend public policy. A contract which, or the performance of which, is contrary to public policy cannot be enforced either at common law, by an action for damages or for an amount due, or in equity, by a decree of specific performance (*Cleaver* v *Mutual Reserve Fund Life Association* [1892] 1 QB 147, CA, *per* Lord Esher MR at p. 151). But if the contract, or its performance, is not illegal there may be compelling reasons of public policy why it should be specifically enforced, such as the protection of fundamental freedoms. In *Verrall* v *Great Yarmouth Borough Council* [1980] 1 All ER 839, the Court of Appeal ordered specific performance of a contractual licence of short duration to enable the National Front to hold its annual conference of 1979 at Great Yarmouth, as agreed with the council and in spite of fears about the likelihood of public disorder caused by opponents of the National Front. Specific performance would not have been decreed if the National Front itself had intended to engage in violence or other unlawful behaviour (*per* Lord Denning MR at p. 845). In this event, it would have been against public policy specifically to enforce the contract.

A void contract is no contract at all so that, in reality, there is nothing to enforce. In *Webster* v *Cecil* (1861) 30 Beav 62, the defendant vendor offered to sell land for £1,250 by mistake instead of £2,250. The claimant purchaser must have known the figure of £1,250 was a mistake because earlier the defendant had refused to sell for £2,000. The claimant accepted the offer of £1,250 by return of post. The defendant realised his mistake and immediately informed the claimant of it. The claimant claimed specific performance of the 'contract' but it was held that he could not have it and he was left to whatever remedy he might have at common law. In fact, there would be no remedy at law either since there was probably no binding contract due to operative mistake. Sir John Romilly MR said (at p. 64) that the court could not grant specific performance and compel a person to sell property for much less than its real value. In saying this, his Lordship must be taken to have assumed the existence of a mistake in addition to the low price because mere inadequacy of consideration does not of itself appear to be a ground for refusing specific performance. If there is no mistake on the part of the defendant, and no inequitable conduct on the part of the claimant, there is no reason why the court should not specifically enforce a contract to sell land at considerably less than its market value (*Collier* v *Brown* (1788) 1 Cox Eq Cas 428; *Coles* v *Trecothick* (1804) 9 Ves Jr 234, *per* Lord Eldon LC at p. 246).

10.3.2.6 *When an agreement is made without any consideration at all*

Equity will not aid a volunteer and so specific performance will not be granted of an agreement which is voluntary. This is so even if the agreement is binding at common law because it is contained in a deed (*Jefferys* v *Jefferys* (1841) Cr & Ph 138; *Re Pryce* [1917] 1 Ch 234).

10.3.2.7 *Where the claimant's hands are not clean*

This rule is based on the equitable maxim that 'he who comes into equity must come with clean hands'. It means that any conduct of the claimant which would make it inequitable to enforce the contract against the defendant will bar his action for specific performance. Such inequitable conduct covers not only actual fraud or innocent misrepresentation but also trickiness and unfairness falling short of those extremes. In *Webster* v *Cecil* (1861) 30 Beav 62 (para 10.3.2.5 above), for instance, the claimant's conduct in snapping at an offer which he must have known was made by mistake was inequitable and would of itself be a ground for refusing specific performance (see the explanation of *Webster* v *Cecil* given in *Tamplin* v *James* (1880) 15 ChD 215, CA, *per* James LJ at p. 221 and Brett LJ at p. 222).

In *Redgrave* v *Hurd* (1881) 20 ChD 1, CA, the defendant was induced into making a contract to buy the claimant solicitor's house and a share in his practice by an innocent misrepresentation of the value of the practice. When the defendant discovered the truth he refused to complete and the claimant brought an action for specific performance. The defendant counterclaimed for rescission of the contract. The Court of Appeal dismissed the claimant's claim for specific performance and ordered the contract to be rescinded. It would have been inequitable to allow the claimant specifically to enforce a contract which had been induced by a misrepresentation, albeit an innocent one, even though the defendant had not taken the opportunity presented to him to check the accuracy of the claimant's statements.

Since the court's discretion to grant or refuse the remedy of specific performance cannot be fettered by agreement between the parties, any attempt by them in their contract to exclude the 'clean hands' principle will not be binding upon the court. If the law were otherwise, the function of the court would be reduced to that of a rubber stamp (*Quadrant Visual Communications Ltd* v *Hutchison Telephone (UK) Ltd* (1991) [1993] BCLC 442, CA).

10.3.2.8   Where it would cause great hardship to the defendant

Specific performance as an equitable remedy is based on the desire to achieve fairness on both sides. It is not meant to be a punishment to the defendant and so it will not be decreed if it would involve the defendant in doing something unlawful or which he has no power to do or would otherwise inflict great hardship on him. In *Denne* v *Light* (1857) 8 De GM & G 774, specific performance of a contract to buy agricultural land was refused to the vendor on the ground that the land was completely surrounded by land belonging to other people over which there was no right of cartway for the purchaser.

In *Wroth* v *Tyler* [1974] Ch 30, the defendant contracted to sell his bungalow to the claimants. The defendant's title was registered as encumbered only by a building society mortgage but, on the day after exchange of contracts and unknown to the defendant, the defendant's wife entered in the charges register a notice of her rights of occupation under the Matrimonial Homes Act 1967 (now the Matrimonial Homes Act 1983). She refused to withdraw her notice to enable the defendant to complete the sale with vacant possession and he withdrew from the contract. The claimants claimed specific performance but it was refused by Megarry J on the ground that it would be highly unreasonable to compel the defendant to take legal proceedings against his own wife for an order terminating her rights of occupation under the 1967 Act. The claimants were instead awarded equitable damages under the Chancery Amendment Act 1858 (Lord Cairns's Act) (now s. 50 of the Supreme Court Act 1981) based on the difference between the market value of the bungalow at the date of judgment and the contract price.

The hardship need not have been caused by the claimant or be connected with the subject-matter of the contract. Thus, in the extreme circumstances of *Patel* v *Ali* [1984] 1 All ER 978 the claimants were refused specific performance of a contract to sell a house where, during a long delay (which was not the fault of any of the parties) following the making of the contract, the defendant had had a leg amputated due to bone cancer and had given birth to two children. Specific performance was refused because of the hardship the defendant would suffer if she had to leave the house and move to an area where she would be without the friends and relations on whose daily assistance she relied to look after her home and children. The claimants were left instead to pursue their remedy in damages.

10.3.2.9 Where it would seriously prejudice the rights of a third party

In *Watts* v *Spence* [1976] Ch 165, the defendant and his wife were joint owners of the matrimonial home. The defendant wished to sell the house and began negotiations with the claimant, who was interested in buying it. The defendant's wife knew nothing of this and had not consented to the sale of her share. The defendant, thinking he could persuade his wife to join in the sale by the date fixed for completion, represented to the claimant that he (the defendant) was the sole owner. This induced the claimant to enter into a contract with the defendant to buy the house. On discovering what had happened, the defendant's wife refused to consent to the sale. It was held that it would be unreasonable to grant specific performance against the defendant because a third party with an interest in the property (the defendant's wife) would be seriously prejudiced thereby. Instead, the claimant recovered damages for misrepresentation under s. 2(1) of the Misrepresentation Act 1967.

10.3.3 Damages in lieu of specific performance

When, before 1858, the Court of Chancery refused specific performance of a contract it normally had no power to award damages for the breach. The disappointed claimant was left to begin another action — this time in a common-law court — to recover damages. The law was changed by the Chancery Amendment Act 1858 (Lord Cairns's Act), s. 2, which gave the court a discretion to award damages in substitution for, or in addition to, specific performance. It should be noted that damages will be awarded *in addition to* specific performance only where there has been some special damage (*Jacques* v *Millar* (1877) 6 ChD 153, in which the claimant, in addition to specific performance, was awarded damages of £250 in respect of loss of business profits).

The 1858 Act itself was repealed in 1883, but the power it conferred by s. 2 survived by virtue of the general provision made for the powers of the Supreme Court in the Supreme Court of Judicature Act 1873, s. 24(6) and (7) (repealed and re-enacted as ss. 42 and 43 of the Supreme Court of Judicature (Consolidation) Act 1925). Despite the repeal in 1883, the 1858 Act has often been referred to as though it were still in force. The provision relating to damages in lieu of specific performance has been explicitly re-enacted in s. 50 of the Supreme Court Act 1981. The importance of the power is that a claimant whose claim for specific performance is rejected on some discretionary ground may, in the same action, be awarded damages instead.

Such damages are called *equitable damages* and must be distinguished from the *common-law damages* discussed in para 10.2 above. Common-law damages are available as of right to any claimant who establishes the breach of a binding contract. There is no such entitlement to equitable damages, which are awarded only on a discretionary basis and only under the jurisdiction originally conferred by the Chancery Amendment Act 1858. There is, however, no difference in the *measure* of common-law and equitable damages. Damages at common law and in equity are measured in the same way in respect of both the basis and the date of assessment (*Johnson* v *Agnew* [1979] 1 All ER 883, HL).

It would appear that the court has power to award equitable damages only for breach of a contract which is specifically enforceable. If there is no jurisdiction to grant specific performance of a particular contract, then there is no power to substitute equitable damages and the claimant will be left to his common-law remedy. Thus, equitable damages cannot be awarded in lieu of specific performance for breach of a contract for personal work or services (*Scott* v *Rayment* (1868) LR 7 Eq 112), or of a contract to sell or buy ordinary commercial goods (*Price* v *Strange* [1978] Ch 337, CA, *per* Buckley LJ at p. 369), or of a contract whose subject-matter no longer exists (*Hipgrave* v *Case* (1885) 28 ChD 356, CA;

Ferguson v *Wilson* (1866) LR 2 Ch App 77). These contracts are not specifically enforceable and so the power to award equitable damages in substitution for specific performance cannot be exercised. If, however, the court had jurisdiction to grant specific performance when the proceedings were begun, it retains the power to substitute equitable damages, even though, by the date of judgment, specific performance has become impossible (*Cory* v *Thames Iron Works & Shipbuilding Co. Ltd* (1863) 8 LT 237).

If a claimant claims specific performance of a contract that is specifically enforceable, the court can substitute equitable damages whether or not they have been asked for in terms by the claimant (*Crawford* v *Hornsea Steam Brick & Tile Co. Ltd* (1876) 45 LJ Ch 432, CA). On the other hand, if a claimant does not claim specific performance it would seem that equitable damages cannot be awarded because there is nothing for which they can be a substitute (*Horsler* v *Zorro* [1975] Ch 302).

In most cases the claimant will gain no advantage in seeking equitable damages because of the availability, as of right, of common-law damages. Since the Supreme Court of Judicature Act 1873, all divisions of the High Court have had power to grant both common-law and equitable relief in the same action. This means that if a court has no jurisdiction to decree specific performance in a particular case, or refuses to decree it in the exercise of its discretion, the court may nevertheless award *common-law damages* (*Johnson* v *Agnew* [1979] 1 All ER 883, HL).

But sometimes there is an advantage in seeking equitable as opposed to common-law damages. There are some circumstances in which common-law damages are not available because the claimant has no cause of action at common law. Yet in the same circumstances there may be a cause of action in equity justifying the exercise of the court's discretion to award equitable damages. For instance, if a defendant commits an anticipatory breach of contract, by saying *now* that he will not perform when the time for performance comes round, the claimant cannot be awarded damages at common law if he refuses to accept the breach. He may, however, sue immediately for specific performance (*Hasham* v *Zenab* [1960] AC 316, PC) and the court may then, if it wishes, award equitable damages in substitution (*Oakacre Ltd* v *Claire Cleaners (Holdings) Ltd* [1981] 3 All ER 667, following a dictum of Turner LJ in *Phelps* v *Prothero* (1855) 7 De GM & G 722, at p. 733).

10.4   INJUNCTIONS

10.4.1   Introduction

The injunction is an equitable remedy and is, therefore, discretionary. It is a particularly useful remedy in contract to restrain a breach, in tort to prevent the continuation of a nuisance, in family law to control domestic violence, and in administrative law to prevent public authorities from acting unlawfully. Breach of an injunction is a contempt of court.

The power to grant injunctions, which was originally an inherent power, is regulated by statute. By s. 37 of the Supreme Court Act 1981 the High Court may grant an interlocutory or a perpetual injunction (either unconditionally or on terms) 'in all cases in which it appears to the court to be just and convenient to do so'. The county courts may grant injunctions in actions within their jurisdiction by virtue of a statutory power to make any order which could be made in a similar case before the High Court (County Courts Act 1984, s. 38, as substituted by the Courts and Legal Services Act 1990). There are, however, strict limits on the power of the county courts to grant *Anton Piller* orders and *Mareva* injunctions (County Court Remedies Regulations 1991 (SI 1991, No. 1222) made under s. 38 of the County Courts Act 1984; see further, para 1.6.3.1).

A pre-existing cause of action at the suit of the claimant against the defendant is a prerequisite to an application for an injunction under s. 37 of the Supreme Court Act 1981 (*The Siskina* [1979] AC 210, HL, endorsed in *Mercedes-Benz AG* v *Leiduck* [1996] 1 AC 284, PC; but note *Channel Tunnel Group Ltd* v *Balfour Beatty Construction Ltd* [1993] 1 All ER 664, HL, where it was suggested (*per* Lords Goff, Browne-Wilkinson and Mustill at pp. 668, 670 and 685–86 respectively) that the case law may have unduly restricted the unfettered wording of s. 37).

Section 37 (quoted above) confers a very wide discretion to grant injunctive relief; that discretion must, however, be exercised judicially. As a judge once put it:

> . . . I have unlimited power to grant an injunction in any case where it would be right or just to do so; and what is right or just must be decided, not by the caprice of the Judge, but according to sufficient legal reasons or on settled legal principles.
>
> (*Beddow* v *Beddow* (1878) ChD 89, *per* Jessel MR at p. 93, commenting on s. 25 of the Supreme Court of Judicature Act 1873, one of the predecessors of s. 37 of the Supreme Court Act 1981.)

The wording of s. 37 authorises the granting of all the injunctions mentioned in the succeeding paragraphs, including *Anton Piller* orders (para 10.4.2.5 below) and *Mareva* injunctions (para 10.4.2.6 below). It is also wide enough to enable the court to grant an injunction freezing money in a person's bank account where the court is satisfied that the money has been obtained from another in breach of the criminal law (*Chief Constable of Kent* v *V* [1983] QB 34, CA). An injunction will not be granted, however, where the tainted money has been mixed in the account with untainted money and it is not possible to separate the two (*Chief Constable of Hampshire* v *A* [1985] QB 132, CA), or where the money in issue cannot be identified as having been obtained in breach of the criminal law (*Chief Constable of Leicestershire* v *M* [1988] 3 All ER 1015; injunction refused because the money sought to be restrained had not itself been obtained by fraud but was instead the profit made by the use of other money obtained by fraud).

The requirement of *The Siskina* [1979] AC 210, HL, above, that there must be a pre-existing cause of action to which an injunction can be attached appears to apply only in ordinary disputes concerning the alleged violation of *private* rights. As explained in *Morris* v *Murjani* [1996] 2 All ER 384, CA, *Chief Constable of Kent* v *V*, above, in which no pre-existing cause of action existed, was a case where the Chief Constable was acting under a general *public* duty to recover stolen property and restore it to the true owner. In *Morris* v *Murjani* itself, it was held that a trustee in bankruptcy was entitled to an injunction restraining a bankrupt from leaving the country on the ground that the bankrupt would otherwise not comply with his duty under s. 333 of the Insolvency Act 1986 to 'give to the trustee such information . . . as the trustee may for the purposes of carrying out his functions . . . reasonably require . . .' This section does not expressly create a cause of action. Nevertheless, and *The Siskina* notwithstanding, the Court of Appeal decided that injunctive relief was available for violation of the section because it imposed a type of public duty upon a bankrupt which was designed to help the trustee in bankruptcy to perform his statutory duties.

10.4.2 Types of injunctions

10.4.2.1 Prohibitory and mandatory injunctions

A *prohibitory* injunction is an order of the court to restrain the doing, continuance or repetition of some wrongful act. Most injunctions issued by the courts are of this type.

A *mandatory* injunction is an order of the court to undo some wrongful act; for example, to pull down buildings which interfere with an established right to light and which constitute, therefore, a legal nuisance. There are obvious similarities between a mandatory injunction and specific performance in that both require a positive act to be performed by the defendant. Specific performance, however, is available as a remedy only if there is a *contract* to enforce whereas, in most cases, the use of the mandatory injunction is confined to actions arising out of *tort*. But there is no reason why a mandatory injunction should not be used to order the defendant to undo what he has already done in breach of a contract (*Lord Manners* v *Johnson* (1875) 1 Ch D 673).

A mandatory injunction will not usually be issued where damages would be an adequate remedy or where it would involve constant supervision by the court. The reasonableness of the defendant's conduct is a relevant factor in deciding whether to order a mandatory injunction, as is the cost to the defendant of complying with it (*Redland Bricks Ltd* v *Morris* [1970] AC 652, HL, *per* Lord Upjohn at p. 665). The cost to the defendant is not such an important factor where he 'has tried to steal a march on' the claimant (ibid.). If the court decides to grant a mandatory injunction care must be taken to ensure that the defendant knows exactly what he has to do in order to comply with its terms (ibid.).

10.4.2.2   Interim and perpetual injunctions

10.4.2.2.1   Introduction.   An *interim* (formerly *interlocutory*) injunction may be granted before the trial of the action on the merits between the parties in order to preserve the *status quo*. It may last until the issue between the parties is finally decided. The object of an interim injunction is to prevent violation of the claimant's rights in a way for which he could not be adequately compensated in damages if his action succeeded at the full trial. Quite often the parties treat the interim application as the trial of the action if their respective cases are ready for presentation. If the case is one of great urgency the claimant can obtain an interim injunction *ex parte* in the absence of the defendant. The injunction will operate until there can be a hearing with the defendant present a few days later.

A *perpetual* injunction may be granted after the claimant has proved his case at the actual trial of the action. It is called 'perpetual' because it is granted after the final determination of the parties' rights and not because it will necessarily operate for ever. It may, however, be expressed to last for ever.

10.4.2.2.2   Interim injunctions   The decision whether to grant an interim injunction is usually a difficult one to make, involving a balancing of the parties' interests. The proceedings are conducted on affidavits only, without the benefit of oral evidence. To some extent the court must try to predict what is likely to happen later at the trial of the action because an interim injunction should not be granted on facts which would not justify the issue of a perpetual injunction. The court will rarely grant a *mandatory* injunction on an interim application (*Locabail International Finance Ltd* v *Agroexport* [1986] 1 All ER 901, CA) because to do so could be premature and oppressive and, in a contract case, would be tantamount to decreeing specific performance. Nevertheless, the court has done so in the past in cases where the defendant has tried to steal a march by hurrying on with building work after being served with notice of the proceedings (*Daniel* v *Ferguson* [1891] 2 Ch 27, CA; *Von Joel* v *Hornsey* [1895] 2 Ch 774, CA), or where the circumstances are so exceptional that to refuse the mandatory injunction would produce a greater risk of injustice than to grant it (*Films Rover International Ltd* v *Cannon Film Sales Ltd* [1986] 3 All ER 772).

If a claimant is granted an interim injunction he must give an *undertaking in damages*. This is an undertaking to pay damages to the defendant if at the trial it turns out that the injunction was wrongly granted, either because at the trial the claimant cannot prove the case he alleged in the interim proceedings or because the court, when it granted the interim relief, took a wrong view of the law (*Griffith* v *Blake* (1884) 27 ChD 474, CA). These damages are to compensate the defendant for any loss he has sustained by being prevented from doing what he wanted to do. The claimant's undertaking is given to the court. An undertaking in damages will not necessarily be required where the claimant is the Crown and the purpose of seeking the injunction is to enforce the law against the defendant (*F. Hoffman-La Roche & Co. AG* v *Secretary of State for Trade and Industry* [1975] AC 295, HL; *Director General of Fair Trading* v *Tobyward Ltd* [1989] 2 All ER 266).

This special privilege enjoyed by the Crown extends also to other public authorities in their role as law enforcers. It follows, therefore, that a local authority is not necessarily required to give an undertaking in damages if it wishes to obtain an interim injunction restraining a retailer from trading on Sundays (*Kirklees Metropolitan Borough Council* v *Wickes Building Supplies Ltd* [1992] 3 All ER 717, HL). Similarly, it has been held that the Securities and Investments Board, acting in its role as a law enforcer on behalf of the Secretary of State for Trade and Industry, need not necessarily give an undertaking in damages when seeking a freezing injunction in support of claims for compensation against a defendant alleged to have infringed the Financial Services Act 1986 (*Securities and Investments Board* v *Lloyd-Wright* [1993] 4 All ER 210, applying *F. Hoffman-La Roche & Co. AG* v *Secretary of State for Trade and Industry*, HL, above, and *Kirklees Metropolitan Borough Council* v *Wickes Building Supplies Ltd*, HL, above). Whether an undertaking in damages is required from a public authority in any particular case is a decision for the court in the exercise of its discretion (*Kirklees Metropolitan Borough Council* v *Wickes Building Supplies Ltd*, HL, above).

The principles to be taken into account by the court in deciding whether to grant an interim injunction are those laid down in 1975 by the House of Lords in *American Cyanamid Co.* v *Ethicon Ltd* [1975] AC 396, HL. Those principles have, however, been subjected to a process of refinement in recent years. It is important to remember that the sole source of the jurisdiction of the High Court to grant injunctions is s. 37 of the Supreme Court Act 1981 (para 10.4.1 above), which confers a wide discretion and contemplates taking into account all the circumstances of a case, and that any 'principles' set out in the case-law are merely guidelines which are not necessarily of universal application (*Factortame Ltd* v *Secretary of State for Transport (No. 2)* [1991] 1 All ER 70, HL, *per* Lord Goff at p. 118; *Lansing Linde Ltd* v *Kerr* [1991] 1 All ER 418, CA, *per* Butler-Sloss LJ at p. 434; in *Cambridge Nutrition Ltd* v *British Broadcasting Corporation* [1990] 3 All ER 523, CA, Kerr LJ said (at p. 535) that the '*American Cyanamid* case is no more than a set of useful guidelines which apply in many cases. It must never be used as a rule of thumb, let alone as a strait-jacket'; see also, ibid., *per* Ralph Gibson LJ at p. 538). The *American Cyanamid* principles are as follows:

(a) The court must normally be satisfied that there is 'a serious question to be tried' between the parties and that the claimant's claim is not frivolous or vexatious. In the event that there is no serious question to be tried, or if the claim is frivolous or vexatious, an interim injunction will be refused.

In at least one exceptional case an interim injunction may be granted even though there is no serious question to be tried. It is established that a landowner whose title is not at issue is prima facie entitled to an injunction to restrain a trespass to his land, whether or not the trespass is harmful, subject to any defence that may be put forward by the defendant. In these circumstances, if there is no serious question to be tried between the parties because the evidence before the court shows that the defendant has no valid defence to the trespass claim, then the issues (mentioned below) of the balance of convenience and the adequacy of damages as a remedy do not arise for consideration and the claimant may be granted his interim injunction (*Patel* v *WH Smith (Eziot) Ltd* [1987] 2 All ER 569, CA).

(b)   If there is a serious question to be tried the court will go on to consider 'the balance of convenience'. Whatever happens later at the trial of the action, one party will suffer a present disadvantage because of the grant or refusal of interim relief. With the interests of the parties and the public in mind, the court must consider the extent of the inconvenience likely to be suffered by each side. For example, in *Laws* v *Florinplace Ltd* [1981] 1 All ER 659, the balance of convenience was held to lie in favour of the claimants and, accordingly, an interim injunction was granted in the claimants' nuisance action restraining the defendants from carrying on the business of a sex shop.

In some situations, the existence of a serious question to be tried, and the fact that the balance of convenience lies in granting an injunction, will not necessarily be conclusive. If neither party is interested in damages and the court's decision on the application for an interim injunction would be equivalent to giving final judgment in the dispute between the parties (for example, where timing is crucial because the case concerns the transmission of a broadcast or the publication of a newspaper article), the court should be prepared to assess the relative strength of the parties' cases before deciding whether the injunction should be granted (*Cambridge Nutrition Ltd* v *British Broadcasting Corporation* [1990] 3 All ER 523, CA, where, in the claimants' breach of contract action, an interim injunction restraining the transmission by the defendants of a television programme about very low calorie diets was refused; see also *Lansing Linde Ltd* v *Kerr* [1991] 1 All ER 418, CA, but cf *Lawrence David Ltd* v *Ashton* [1991] 1 All ER 385, CA). The fact that an injunction would interfere with the public interest in freedom of speech is also a relevant consideration (*Cambridge Nutrition Ltd* v *British Broadcasting Corporation*, above, *per* Kerr LJ at p. 536 and Ralph Gibson LJ at p. 541; *Femis-Bank (Anguilla) Ltd* v *Lazar* [1991] 2 All ER 865).

(c)   If any damages awarded later to the claimant at the trial of the action would be an adequate remedy, an interim injunction should normally be refused. Where, however, damages would not adequately compensate the claimant, or where it is doubtful whether a remedy in damages exists at all, the court may be prepared to take a wider view of the 'balance of convenience' and grant an interim injunction (*Factortame Ltd* v *Secretary of State for Transport (No. 2)* [1991] 1 All ER 70, HL, a most exceptional case involving law enforcement by a public authority in which, pending final judgment, the balance of convenience was held to lie in favour of granting an interim injunction against the Secretary of State restraining him from withholding or withdrawing registration in the register of British fishing vessels in respect of certain fishing boats owned by British companies whose directors and shareholders were mainly Spanish nationals).

(d)   If damages would not be an adequate remedy for the claimant, an interim injunction may be granted if the claimant's undertaking in damages would give the defendant an adequate remedy should the claimant fail at the trial. Where, however, the defendant would not be adequately compensated by damages the court may refuse an interim injunction (*Cambridge Nutrition Ltd* v *British Broadcasting Corporation* [1990] 3 All ER 523, CA, above, in which one of the reasons for refusing an injunction was that damages could not provide adequate compensation if the claimant's claim failed at trial; while the defendants would be able to recover their lost production costs they would not be compensated for loss of their right to transmit a television programme on a topic of public interest in the form and at the time of their choice).

(e) If the inconvenience likely to be suffered by each party would not be widely different, the balance of convenience may be adjudged from the relative strengths of the parties' cases as revealed in the affidavits. But the claimant does not have to make out a prima facie case in order to obtain an interim injunction. At the interim stage the court will not embark on anything resembling a trial of the evidence on conflicting affidavits in order to evaluate the strength of either party's case. Nor is it appropriate at that stage for the court to decide difficult questions of law which call for detailed argument and mature consideration. However, it may be appropriate at the interim stage to decide less difficult questions of law, especially if that course would finally and quickly determine the issue between the parties (*Factortame Ltd* v *Secretary of State for Transport (No. 2)* [1991] 1 All ER 70, HL, *per* Lord Jauncey at p. 123).

(f) In the particular circumstances of individual cases there may be many other special factors to be taken into account in addition to those already mentioned (see, e.g., the cases cited above: *Cambridge Nutrition Ltd* v *British Broadcasting Corporation* [1990] 3 All ER 523, CA; *Lansing Linde Ltd* v *Kerr* [1991] 1 All ER 418, CA; *Femis-Bank (Anguilla) Ltd* v *Lazar* [1991] 2 All ER 865; *Factortame Ltd* v *Secretary of State for Transport (No. 2)* [1991] 1 All ER 70, HL).

An appellate court has only a limited function when reviewing the exercise of the judge's discretion to grant or refuse an interim injunction. The judge's exercise of his discretion cannot be interfered with, for example, merely because the members of the appellate court would have exercised the discretion differently if they had been sitting at first instance. It must be shown that the judge has misunderstood the law or the evidence before him, or that there has been a change of circumstances since the decision at first instance, or that the judge's decision is plainly wrong (*Hadmor Productions Ltd* v *Hamilton* [1982] 1 All ER 1042, HL, *per* Lord Diplock at p. 1046, with whom the other Law Lords expressly agreed; *Dimbleby & Sons Ltd* v *National Union of Journalists* [1984] 1 All ER 751, HL).

10.4.2.2.3 Perpetual injunctions. The jurisdiction of a court of equity to grant a *perpetual* injunction is discretionary, but, as in the case of specific performance, the discretion is exercised judicially in accordance with rules laid down in decided cases. A perpetual injunction will not normally be granted if damages would sufficiently compensate the claimant (*Wood* v *Sutcliffe* (1851) 2 Sim NS 163) or if it would require constant supervision on the part of the court (*Attorney-General* v *Colney Hatch Lunatic Asylum* (1868) LR 4 Ch App 146). It may also be refused on account of the claimant's own inequitable conduct (*Measures Bros Ltd* v *Measures* [1910] 2 Ch 248, CA).

Although the grant of an injunction is a matter of discretion, the court will rarely refuse an injunction to prevent the breach of a negative contractual term — even where damages would be an adequate remedy and the contract is one for personal work or services. In *Lumley* v *Wagner* (1852) 1 De GM & G 604 (para 10.3.2.3 above), specific performance was refused. But the contractual obligation which the defendant had broken was expressed in negative terms, and the court granted an injunction to restrain her from singing elsewhere than in the claimant's theatre during the currency of the contract.

The court will not grant an injunction to achieve a purpose which could not be achieved by a decree of specific performance (but see the exceptional case of *Sky Petroleum Ltd* v

VIP Petroleum Ltd [1974] 1 All ER 954, para 10.3.2.1 above). In *Page One Records Ltd
v Britton* [1967] 3 All ER 822, the claimants, who were the managers of 'The Troggs' pop
group, applied for an injunction to restrain the group from engaging another person as their
manager in breach of contract. Stamp J refused to grant the injunction as its effect would
have been the same as specific performance. It would have compelled the group to continue
to employ the claimants as their managers, and in a situation where they had lost all
confidence in the claimants. (This case was applied in *Warren v Mendy* [1989] 3 All ER
103, CA (boxer and manager), and see *Scandinavian Trading Tanker Co. v Flota Petrolera
Ecuatoriana* [1983] 2 All ER 763, HL *per* Lord Diplock at p. 766.)

But there is no objection to granting an injunction to restrain the breach of a negative
contractual term where its effect will be to encourage, but not force, the defendant to
perform the contract. In *Warner Brothers Pictures Inc. v Nelson* [1937] 1 KB 209, the
defendant (Bette Davis) had an 'exclusive' contract with the claimants by which she agreed
to act for them. She further agreed not to act for any third party, nor to engage in any other
occupation, during the currency of the contract, without the claimants' written consent.
There was a dispute between the parties over money and the defendant came to Britain to
make a film in breach of contract. Branson J granted an injunction against her but limited
it to stage and film activities. He said the injunction might 'tempt' her but would not 'drive'
her to perform her contract with Warner Brothers because she could earn her living, although
not as remuneratively, otherwise than by acting. The injunction was also limited to
preventing breaches of the contract within the jurisdiction of the court, i.e., England
and Wales. In *Lumley v Wagner,* above, Lord St Leonards LC was aware that his order
might tempt the defendant to fulfil her contract but he denied that it would compel her to
do so.

10.4.2.2.4   Damages in lieu of an injunction.   By virtue of s. 50 of the Supreme Court Act
1981 (para 10.3.3 above), the Court of Appeal or the High Court may award damages to a
claimant either in substitution for, or in addition to, an injunction. These damages are
awarded in equity and may be available when common-law damages are not. In tort, for
example, common-law damages cannot be ordered for an injury which has not yet been
inflicted but is only threatened or apprehended. However, as will be explained in para
10.4.2.3, an injunction *can* be ordered in such a situation, and, in the exercise of its equitable
jurisdiction, the court may substitute damages for that injunction in a proper case. Thus, in
Wrotham Park Estate Co. Ltd v Parkside Homes Ltd [1974] 1 WLR 798 damages were
awarded in lieu of a mandatory injunction in respect of the breach of a restrictive covenant;
in *Bracewell v Appleby* [1975] Ch 408, damages were awarded instead of an injunction in
respect of a trespass; in *Lyme Valley Squash Club Ltd v Newcastle under Lyme Borough
Council* [1985] 2 All ER 405, damages were awarded instead of an injunction in relation to
an interference with the claimant's right to light; and in *Jaggard v Sawyer* [1995] 2 All ER
189, CA, damages were awarded in lieu of an injunction in respect of both a continuing
trespass and the breach of a restrictive covenant.

If the court grants damages in lieu of an injunction the defendant is able to carry on as
before with what he was doing on payment of a sum of money to the claimant. The court
must take care that the substitution of damages for an injunction, and especially a *quia timet*
injunction, does not become simply a device which allows the defendant to buy a licence
to commit a wrong (*Shelfer v City of London Electric Lighting Co.* [1895] 1 Ch 287, CA;
Leeds Industrial Co-operative Society v Slack [1924] AC 851, HL, *per* Lord Sumner,
dissenting at pp. 867–8 and p. 872). In *Miller v Jackson* [1977] QB 966, CA, a majority of

the Court of Appeal held that the activities of a village cricket club, which had been established for over seventy years, were a legal nuisance to the claimants by reason of cricket balls landing in their garden. It was also decided by a majority that an injunction should not be granted. Instead, damages of £400 were awarded in respect of past and future damage. The majority, clearly not wishing to forbid the game on this particular cricket ground, said that the case was one where the public interest should prevail over the private interest. (Lord Denning dissented on liability. On the question of the appropriate remedy, Geoffrey Lane LJ would have granted an injunction.)

In *Kennaway* v *Thompson* [1981] QB 88, CA, the trial judge held that the defendant club's motor-boat races on a lake were a nuisance to the claimant, who lived nearby. But he refused to grant an injunction on the ground that it would spoil the enjoyment of the large numbers of people who attended the races. Instead he awarded damages of £15,000 under the equitable jurisdiction to compensate the claimant for damage likely to be suffered in the future. The Court of Appeal set aside the judge's order and granted an injunction restricting the defendants' racing activities in each year and limiting the noise levels of boats using the lake at other times. The court said the claimant was entitled to an injunction despite the public interest and tacitly disapproved of the refusal of an injunction by a differently constituted court in *Miller* v *Jackson,* a case which, it was said, was not consistent with earlier Court of Appeal authority. That was the case of *Shelfer* v *City of London Electric Lighting Co.* [1895] 1 Ch 287, in which the Court of Appeal granted an injunction restraining the defendants from causing excessive vibration in spite of the fact that the defendants were performing a public service and the injunction might have deprived a section of the public of its electricity supply. It was said that the court should not allow itself to be used, by too often substituting damages for an injunction, as a tribunal for legalising unlawful acts. In addition, the fact that the defendant is a public benefactor was stated not to be a sufficient reason for refusing an injunction and awarding damages instead. *Shelfer's* case was completely ignored in the judgments of two of the three members of the Court of Appeal in *Miller* v *Jackson.*

Kennaway v *Thompson* was distinguished on the facts in *Tetley* v *Chitty* [1986] 1 All ER 663 where an injunction was granted to *stop altogether* (and not merely to restrict) noisy go-karting activities which were a nuisance to the claimants. Damages were also awarded as compensation for past inconvenience.

10.4.2.3 Quia timet injunctions

A court of equity may grant a *quia timet* ('because he fears') injunction where a claimant's rights have not yet been infringed but they are being threatened. However, such an injunction is not commonly granted and a claimant must make out a strong case to obtain one. He must show that there is an imminent danger of very substantial damage or further damage occurring (*Crowder* v *Tinkler* (1816) 19 Ves Jr 617, *per* Lord Eldon LC at p. 622; *Attorney-General* v *Nottingham Corporation* [1904] 1 Ch 673). If the court refuses a *quia timet* injunction, this does not prejudice the claimant's right to apply later for an interim or a perpetual injunction when the damage does occur.

10.4.2.4 Ex parte ('without notice') injunctions

A 'without notice' injunction is an interim order which is obtained by one party without notice to, and in the absence of, the other party. The court must be satisfied that the case is one of urgency; for example, that the delay in using the normal procedure would cause irreparable damage. Such an injunction only operates until both parties can be heard.

10.4.2.5   Search orders (Anton Piller orders)

A search order is an interim mandatory injunction of recent origin (see Denning, *The Due Process of Law,* 1980, pp. 123–30).

It is obtained without notice to the defendant and its object is to prevent the defendant from removing, concealing or destroying evidence in the form of documents or movable property. (See *Crest Homes plc* v *Marks* [1987] 2 All ER 1074, HL, *per* Lord Oliver at pp. 1078–1081.) In an extreme case the court will order the defendant to permit the claimant to inspect, at the defendant's premises, the relevant documents and property.

A search order was originally called an *Anton Piller* order after the first case in which its use was sanctioned by the Court of Appeal — *Anton Piller KG* v *Manufacturing Processes Ltd* [1976] Ch 55, CA. The first reported case in the High Court appears to have been *EMI Ltd* v *Pandit* [1975] 1 All ER 418 in which Templeman J made an order and, in doing so, followed a House of Lords' decision of 1821 — *United Company of Merchants of England* v *Kynaston* (1821) 3 Bli 153. Before the *Anton Piller* case there were also a number of unreported High Court decisions (see *Anton Piller, per* Lord Denning MR at p. 58). In the *Anton Piller* case itself, the order was issued by the Court of Appeal so as to permit the claimants to enter the premises of the defendants, who were the claimants' English agents, in order to inspect, remove or make copies of documents belonging to the claimants. The defendants were planning to supply rival manufacturers with information belonging to the claimants and the claimants wished to prevent infringement of their copyright. The claimants did not wish to alert the defendants in case the documents were destroyed or sent out of the jurisdiction.

A search order will normally be obtained *before* final judgment in the action between the parties. It may, however, be granted *after* judgment to elicit documents which are essential to the claimant's efforts to execute the judgment (*Distributori Automatici Italia SpA* v *Holford General Trading Co. Ltd* [1985] 3 All ER 750).

Once obtained, a search order should be served in the presence of the claimant's solicitor and the defendant should be given an opportunity to consult his solicitor (*Anton Piller, per* Lord Denning MR at p. 61). Failure to comply with the order, either by refusing access or by destroying the evidence, is a contempt of court. (But note *Bhimji* v *Chatwani* [1991] 1 All ER 705 — not contempt where defendant, acting on legal advice, applies to court for discharge or variation of search order, and refuses access pending hearing of application, provided he makes reasonable offer to protect relevant documents in meantime and there is no evidence of impropriety on his part.)

A search order is obtained without notice so as to catch the defendant off guard. The court will only make such an order in an extreme case when there is a grave danger of vital evidence being destroyed or removed. However, if the danger exists the order may be made even though the item in question does not itself form the subject-matter of the action (*Yousif* v *Salama* [1980] 3 All ER 405, CA; *Sony Corporation* v *Time Electronics* [1981] 3 All ER 376).

It has been stressed that the order is not a search warrant authorising the claimant to enter the defendant's premises against the defendant's will (*Anton Piller, per* Lord Denning MR at p. 60). It is an order against the defendant *in personam* to permit the claimant to enter or, if he refuses permission, to be in contempt of court (*Anton Piller per* Ormrod LJ at p. 62). The courts are alive to the fact that the *ex parte* and draconian nature of a search order makes it a powerful weapon in the hands of claimants (see, e.g., *Columbia Picture Industries Inc.* v *Robinson* [1986] 3 All ER 338 *per* Scott J at p. 371; *Lock International plc* v *Beswick* [1989] 3 All ER 373 *per* Hoffman J at pp. 382–6; *Bhimji* v *Chatwani* [1991] 1 All ER 705 *per* Scott J at p. 712; *Universal Thermosensors Ltd* v *Hibben and others* [1992] 3 All ER 257 *per* Sir Donald Nicholls V-C at p. 275). To prevent the order from becoming too oppressive it should be drawn so as to extend no further than is necessary to achieve the purpose for which it was sought, namely, to preserve evidence which might otherwise be concealed or destroyed. Thus, although the claimant's solicitors may be allowed to retain documents for a short period for the purpose of taking copies, the documents should be returned to the defendant. Furthermore, during the execution of a search order the claimant or his solicitors must not remove any material (whether with or without the defendant's consent) unless it is clearly covered by the terms of the order (*Columbia Picture Industries Inc.* v *Robinson* [1986] 3 All ER 338: injunctions granted to claimants but defendant awarded damages of £7,500 for the 'excessive and oppressive manner' in which a search order had been executed by claimants' solicitors).

Concern that abuse of the search order procedure might result in this type of order falling into disrepute prompted Sir Donald Nicholls V-C to suggest in *Universal Thermosensors Ltd* v *Hibben and others* [1992] 3 All ER 257 at p. 276 that the following stricter safeguards in the execution of a search order were required for the protection of the defendant's rights:

(a)   the order should be served on the defendant, and its execution supervised, by a solicitor other than a member of the firm of solicitors acting for the claimant;
(b)   the solicitor should be experienced and be familiar with the workings of search orders and with judicial observations on the subject;
(c)   the solicitor should prepare a written report on what happened when the order was executed;
(d)   a copy of the report should be served on the defendant;
(e)   within the next few days the claimant should return to the court and present that report at an *inter partes* hearing, preferably to the judge who made the order.

Universal Thermosensors Ltd v *Hibben and others* was a case in which the defendants were awarded £20,000 on an undertaking (usually given when a search order is granted) by the claimants to pay damages if the court later considered that the defendants had suffered any damage by reason of the order. The order had been executed in a most unsatisfactory manner early in the morning at the defendants' homes and at business premises in the absence of any representative of the company. One of the defendants, alone in the house with her children in bed, had been called to the door in her nightclothes at 7.15 a.m. to be told by a strange man that he had a court order requiring her to permit him to enter her house and that she was entitled to seek legal advice forthwith but otherwise she was not allowed to speak to anyone. No list was made of what documents were taken from which premises, and at the defendants' business premises a director of the claimants had been allowed to carry out a thorough search of all the documents of a competing company. The order was found to have been drawn far too widely in that the restraint on informing others of its existence (normally imposed for a limited period to prevent one defendant from alerting others to what is happening) was expressed to last for a whole week.

Many of the procedural weaknesses identified in the *Universal Thermosensors* case have been dealt with by the promulgation of new standard forms (see *Practice Direction (Mareva and Anton Piller orders: new forms)* [1994] 4 All ER 52; *Practice Direction (Mareva and Anton Piller orders: forms)* [1997] 1 All ER 288).

The search order has been used often against so-called 'pirates' and 'bootleggers'. A 'pirate' includes a person who infringes the copyright in musical recordings and films by making and selling unauthorised copies, thus depriving the true owner of royalties. Orders have been granted to protect the copyright in recorded Indian music (*EMI Ltd* v *Pandit* [1975] 1 All ER 418), *Jaws* T-shirts (*Universal City Studios Inc.* v *Mukhtar & Sons* [1976] 2 All ER 330), and feature films which were being unlawfully reproduced on video cassettes (*Rank Film Distributors Ltd* v *Video Information Centre* [1981] 2 All ER 76, HL). A search order was made for the first time in a matrimonial case in *Emanuel* v *Emanuel* [1982] 2 All ER 342, in which the husband was ordered to permit the wife's solicitors to enter the husband's home to look for, inspect, photograph and remove all documents relating to his earnings and capital.

A twentieth-century 'bootlegger' is a person who records a live musical performance from the audience, or from the radio, and then makes and sells unauthorised copies. The performers are thus deprived of royalties on the sale of recordings. But they have no copyright in the music they perform and no copyright in their own performance. It has been held that they are nevertheless entitled to the protection of a search order (*Ex parte Island Records Ltd and others* [1978] Ch 122, CA: *Lonrho Ltd* v *Shell Petroleum Co. Ltd (No. 2)* [1981] 2 All ER 456, HL).

A search order can be used to compel the disclosure of material information, such as the names and addresses of persons who have supplied, or been supplied with, illicit films and recordings. In *Rank Film Distributors Ltd* v *Video Information Centre* [1981] 2 All ER 76, the House of Lords held that a search order should not be made for the purpose of eliciting information from the defendant which would tend to incriminate him. This decision would have had the effect of seriously diminishing the usefulness of the search order.

Their Lordships' decision in the *Rank* case was quickly overruled by s. 72 of the Supreme Court Act 1981, which withdrew the privilege against incrimination in certain types of civil proceedings. Section 72 provides that in civil proceedings in the High Court (and in any appeal thereon) for 'infringement of rights pertaining to any intellectual property' a person is not excused from answering questions under a search order or a freezing injunction (see para 10.4.2.6 below), or from complying with any order made in those proceedings (such as an order for discovery of documents), on the ground that he might incriminate himself or his spouse. 'Intellectual property' means 'any patent, trade mark, copyright, registered design, technical or commercial information or other intellectual property . . .' (s. 72(5); and note the restrictive interpretation placed on this subsection in *A.T. & T. Istel Ltd* v *Tully* [1992] 3 All ER 523, HL, para 8.10.2.4). At the same time, protection is given in any proceedings for a related criminal offence (such as conspiracy to defraud) in that the evidence obtained in the civil proceedings is not admissible in criminal proceedings with the exception of proceedings for perjury or contempt of court (s. 72(3) and (4)).

It may sometimes happen that the disclosure of material information under a search order (such as the names and addresses of other persons involved in unlawful activity) will expose the defendant and his family to the risk of violence. That risk, although a relevant factor for the court in deciding whether to order disclosure, will not usually prevail over any pressing need the claimant has for the information, especially where the defendant is principally implicated in the unlawful conduct and is not merely a person who has become innocently involved in the wrongdoing of others. It is in the public interest that threats of violence should not prevent the exposure of unlawful activity, and a defendant in this situation may have to rely upon police protection and the law of contempt if he is the recipient of such threats (*Coca-Cola Co.* v *Gilbey* [1995] 4 All ER 711).

Search orders have implications for civil liberties, and for this reason the government decided that it was desirable that they should have the express approval of Parliament.

Accordingly, they were placed on a statutory footing by s. 7 of the Civil Procedure Act 1997, which empowers the High Court to make an order for the purpose of securing in any existing or proposed proceedings (a) the preservation of evidence which is or may be relevant, or (b) the preservation of property which is or may be the subject-matter of the proceedings or about which any question arises or may arise in the proceedings. An application for an order can be made by a person who is, or appears to the court likely to be, a party to the proceedings.

An order under s. 7 can direct that any person described in the order be permitted to enter premises (including any vehicle) in England and Wales and to search for, or inspect, anything described in the order, and to make or obtain a copy, photograph, sample or other record of anything so described. An order can also direct that any information or article described in the order be provided and that anything described in the order be retained for safe keeping.

Technically, s. 7 of the Civil Procedure Act 1997 *confers* jurisdiction on the High Court to grant search orders. In practice, it simply *confirms* what has been happening since the mid-1970s without imposing any new limits.

10.4.2.6   Freezing injunctions (Mareva injunctions)

A freezing injunction is an interim injunction, of recent origin, granted often on a 'without notice' application. Its object is to prevent the defendant from removing his assets out of the jurisdiction of the English courts (i.e., England and Wales), or from otherwise dealing with them. The power to grant an interim injunction extends to cases where there is a danger that the assets will be dissipated *within the jurisdiction* as well as removed out of the jurisdiction (*Z Ltd* v *A* [1982] 1 All ER 556, CA, following a dictum of Lord Denning in *Prince Abdul Rahman* v *Abu-Taha* [1980] 3 All ER 409, CA, at p. 412 and disapproving a dictum of Ackner LJ in *A.J. Bekhor & Co. Ltd* v *Bilton* [1981] 2 All ER 565, CA, at p. 577; *Derby & Co. Ltd* v *Weldon (No. 2)* [1989] 1 All ER 1002, CA, *per* Neill LJ at p. 1017).

Breach of a freezing injunction by the defendant is a contempt of court. The order was originally called a *Mareva* injunction after one of the first cases in which it was used — *Mareva Compania Naviera SA* v *International Bulkcarriers SA* [1975] 2 Lloyd's Rep 509; [1980] 1 All ER 213, CA.

Like a search order, a freezing injunction is one of the most recent judicial developments in English Law, being first used in 1975. Attempts were made before that year to obtain such an injunction but they were unsuccessful, partly no doubt because of the oppressive nature of an order which restrains a person from dealing with his own property as he sees fit (the *Mareva* case [1980] 1 All ER 213 *per* Roskill LJ at p. 215; *Derby & Co. Ltd* v *Weldon (No. 2),* above, *per* Neill LJ at p. 1015 and Butler-Sloss LJ at p. 1022). The case of *Nippon YK* v *Karageorgis* [1975] 3 All ER 282, CA, appears to have been the first reported decision in which the freezing type of injunction was granted.

If a claimant issued a writ against a defendant for, say, debt, there was always a danger that the defendant would remove his assets from the jurisdiction so that they would not be available to satisfy judgment should the claimant win the action. Moreover, there was usually plenty of time for the defendant to act because of the delay of months or even years between the serving of the writ and the date of judgment. The freezing injunction is designed, *inter alia,* to obviate the risk of the defendant's assets disappearing out of the jurisdiction in such a situation. In the *Mareva* case itself, the claimant shipowners let their ship, the *Mareva,* to the defendant charterers. The hire money was to be paid in instalments.

The defendants defaulted on the third instalment and repudiated the contract. The claimants brought an action for unpaid hire of nearly US$31,000 plus damages for the repudiation. There was money in the defendants' name in a London bank and the claimants were fearful that it might disappear before the trial of the action. They applied, without notice to the defendant, for an injunction to restrain the disposal of the money pending the outcome of the trial. The Court of Appeal held that such an injunction would be granted to operate until judgment in the action or until the defendants made a successful application to have it set aside.

A freezing injunction will normally be obtained *before* final judgment in the action between the parties. It may, however, be granted *after* judgment to assist in execution of the judgment where there are grounds for believing that the defendant will dispose of his assets in order to frustrate execution (*Orwell Steel (Erection and Fabrication) Ltd* v *Asphalt and Tarmac (UK) Ltd* [1985] 3 All ER 747; *Babanaft International Co. SA* v *Bassatne* [1989] 1 All ER 433, CA). It may be granted or continued after judgment in support of any order made by the court for the payment of money, whether or not the precise sum payable has yet been fixed. Thus, it is available to assist in the enforcement both of a judgment in favour of the claimant for damages to be assessed at a later date and of a costs order against the defendant prior to taxation of costs (*Jet West Ltd* v *Haddican* [1992] 2 All ER 545, CA).

A freezing injunction may be granted against any defendant and not just a foreign or foreign-based person or company (Supreme Court Act 1981, s. 37(3); this statutory provision was anticipated in *Prince Abdul Rahman* v *Abu-Taha* [1980] 3 All ER 409, CA, approving the decision of Sir Robert Megarry V-C in *Barclay-Johnson* v *Yuill* [1980] 3 All ER 190).

Although freezing injunctions have been granted mostly in commercial actions, their use extends to other causes of action. A freezing injunction has been granted, for instance, in a personal injury action (*Allen* v *Jambo Holdings Ltd* [1980] 2 All ER 502, CA) and in matrimonial proceedings (*Ghoth* v *Ghoth* [1992] 2 All ER 920, CA, below).

The right to apply for a freezing injunction is not a cause of action in itself. It cannot stand on its own; as in the case of other injunctions, the application must be ancillary or incidental to a pre-existing cause of action which the claimant has against the defendant (*The Siskina* [1979] AC 210, HL). A freezing injunction cannot be granted unless the claimant has a legal or equitable right which has been violated, or threatened with violation, by the defendant (*The Siskina,* above; the *Mareva* case, above; *Derby & Co. Ltd* v *Weldon (No. 2)* [1989] 1 All ER 1002, CA, *per* Neill LJ at p. 1019; *Zucker* v *Tyndall Holdings plc* [1993] 1 All ER 124, CA). It has been held at first instance that a freezing injunction can be granted against a co-defendant (such as the main defendant's bankers or a company in which the main defendant has a majority shareholding) who has been joined as a third party to the proceedings, and against whom the claimant has no cause of action, provided that the application for the injunction is ancillary or incidental to a cause of action which the claimant has against the main defendant (*TSB Private Bank International SA* v *Chabra and another* [1992] 2 All ER 245).

It follows from the rule requiring a pre-existing cause of action that, if no cause of action has yet arisen, the court has no jurisdiction to grant *conditional* relief in the form of a freezing injunction made subject to a condition that it does not come into effect unless and until the cause of action arises. This is so even though the court is presently satisfied on the evidence before it that the case is an appropriate one for ordering freezing-type relief when the cause of action does arise.

Although it is recognised that the denial of conditional relief in such circumstances might enable the defendant to take steps, in the interval between the cause of action arising and the granting of a full freezing injunction, to defeat the purpose of the remedy, it has been held that the practical convenience attendant upon the invention of a conditional freezing injunction could only be achieved at the expense of inconsistency with the principle laid down by the House of Lords in *The Siskina (Veracruz Transportation Inc. v VC Shipping Co. Inc.* [1992] 1 Lloyd's Rep 353, where the Court of Appeal, first, set aside a conditional freezing injunction granted at first instance restraining the defendants from dealing with a substantial part of the purchase price of a cruise ship pending delivery of the ship which the claimants feared might not be in the state stipulated for in the contract, and, secondly, overruled *A v B* [1989] 2 Lloyd's Rep 423, the case in which the practice of granting conditional freezing injunctions appears to have been devised by Saville J).

There are three main issues for determination on an application for a freezing injunction (*Derby & Co. Ltd v Weldon (No. 1)* [1989] 1 All ER 469, CA):

(a) The claimant must have a good arguable case. In an application for an ordinary injunction the claimant need only establish that there is a serious question to be tried (para 10.4.2.2.2 above), whereas the applicant for a freezing injunction must go further and show a good arguable case that money is due to him and that he needs the protection of a court order to preserve the fruits of any judgment he might obtain against the defendant (*Derby & Co. Ltd v Weldon (No. 1)*, above, *per* Parker LJ at p. 475; *Derby & Co. Ltd v Weldon (No. 2)*, above, *per* Neill LJ at p. 1020 and Butler-Sloss LJ at p. 1022). However, he need not show, when applying for the injunction, a probability that he will succeed on the merits in the main action (*Rasu Maritima SA v Perusahaan* [1978] QB 644, CA; *Etablissement Esefka International Anstalt v Central Bank of Nigeria* [1979] 1 Lloyd's Rep 445, CA; *Derby & Co. Ltd v Weldon (No. 1)*, above, *per* Parker LJ at p. 475).

(b) The claimant must satisfy the court that the defendant has assets within or outside the jurisdiction. The term 'assets' includes cash and other property, such as an aeroplane (*Allen v Jambo Holdings Ltd*, above). The term is wide enough to cover motor vehicles, jewellery, *objets d'art* and other valuables as well as cash and securities (*CBS United Kingdom Ltd v Lambert* [1982] 3 All ER 237, CA, in which a husband and wife were ordered to deliver up, pending trial, the motor cars in their possession, to be kept in a garage chosen by the claimants' solicitors). Even a bank account which is overdrawn is sufficient evidence of assets within the jurisdiction since the overdraft may be presumed to be secured by other assets (*Third Chandris Shipping Corporation v Unimarine SA* [1979] QB 645, CA).

The standard form of freezing injunction, which refers to 'the defendant's assets', applies only to assets owned by the defendant beneficially and which are available to satisfy the claim against him. It does not apply to assets of which the defendant is bare legal owner as a trustee and in which he has no beneficial interest. Thus, a defendant whose assets were the subject of a freezing injunction was held not to be in contempt of court by authorising the transfer of funds out of bank accounts in his name but in which he himself had no beneficial interest (*Federal Bank of the Middle East Ltd v Hadkinson* [2000] 2 All ER 395, CA).

(c) The claimant must show that there is a real risk that the defendant's assets will be removed from the jurisdiction or that they will otherwise not be available when judgment is given. The mere fact that the defendant is abroad is not by itself sufficient for this purpose (*Third Chandris Shipping Corporation v Unimarine SA*, CA, above; *Z Ltd v A* [1982] 1 All ER 556, CA). If the claimant has already obtained a freezing injunction and/or a search order but there is a real risk that the order will be frustrated by the defendant leaving the jurisdiction, the court has power to grant further relief by, for example, ordering the defendant not to leave the country and to surrender his passport (*Bayer AG* v *Winter* [1986] 1 All ER 733, CA; *Re Oriental Credit* [1988] 1 All ER 892).

The claimant must normally give an *undertaking in damages* (see para 10.4.2.2.2 above) so as to protect the defendant if the claimant should fail in his claim or if the injunction turns out to have been wrongly granted (*Third Chandris Shipping Corporation* v *Unimarine SA,* above). But the decision whether to grant a freezing injunction rests on the balance of justice and convenience rather than on the financial standing of the claimant. An injunction should not, therefore, be refused merely because the claimant is unable to provide a satisfactory undertaking in damages (*Allen* v *Jambo Holdings Ltd* [1980] 2 All ER 502, CA, *per* Lord Denning MR at p. 505 and Templeman LJ at p. 506).

A claimant may also be required by the court to give an undertaking to pay any *expenses* reasonably incurred by an innocent third party, such as a banker, who is put to expense by the injunction in ascertaining whether any asset is within his possession or control (*Z Ltd* v *A* [1982] 1 All ER 556, CA, approving *Searose Ltd* v *Seatrain (UK) Ltd* [1981] 1 All ER 806). Furthermore, an innocent third party affected by a freezing injunction who successfully applies to the court for a variation of the order is entitled to have his legal *costs* paid by the claimant, provided that they are not unreasonable in amount or unreasonably incurred. The burden of proving that the costs were reasonably incurred and that their amount is reasonable rests on the third party (*Project Development Co. Ltd SA* v *KMK Securities Ltd and others (Syndicate Bank intervening)* [1983] 1 All ER 465).

If a third party has notice of a freezing injunction which affects assets in his hands, it is a contempt of court for him knowingly to assist in the disposal of the assets to others whether or not the defendant himself has knowledge of the injunction (*Z Ltd* v *A,* above). In *TDK Tape Distributor (UK) Ltd* v *Videochoice Ltd* [1985] 3 All ER 345, both the defendant and his solicitor were held to be guilty of contempt by dissipating the defendant's assets in breach of a freezing injunction even though the breach was merely 'negligent and inadvertent' rather than deliberate and intentional. A disposal by the third party to the defendant himself is not a contempt of court unless it is known to be probable that the defendant will dissipate the assets or otherwise dispose of them in breach of the injunction (*Bank Mellat* v *Kazmi* [1989] 1 All ER 925, CA, *per* Nourse LJ at pp. 928–9; in this case an order was made requiring the Secretary of State for Social Security to pay arrears of supplementary benefit into the defendant's account at a bank which had notice of the injunction).

In so far as it decided that a freezing injunction is available only as against assets which are situated within the jurisdiction of the English court, the case of *Ashtiani* v *Kashi* [1986] 2 All ER 970, CA, can no longer be regarded as good law. It has been overtaken by subsequent events in what is a rapidly developing area of the law (*Babanaft International Co. SA* v *Bassatne* [1989] 1 All ER 433, CA, *per* Kerr LJ at p. 440 and Neill LJ at p. 449; *Derby & Co. Ltd* v *Weldon (No. 1)* [1989] 1 All ER 469, CA, *per* May LJ at pp. 472–3; *Derby & Co. Ltd* v *Weldon (No. 2)* [1989] 1 All ER 1002, CA, *per* Lord Donaldson MR and Neill and Butler-Sloss LJJ at pp. 1007, 1019 and 1022 respectively; *Derby & Co. Ltd* v *Weldon (No. 6)* [1990] 3 All ER 263, CA, *per* Dillon LJ at p. 272).

Since *Ashtiani* v *Kashi* the Court of Appeal has held that a freezing injunction may be granted in respect of assets situated abroad, both *before* judgment (*Republic of Haiti* v *Duvalier* [1989] 1 All ER 456, CA; *Derby & Co. Ltd* v *Weldon (No. 1),* above; *Derby & Co. Ltd* v *Weldon (No. 2),* above) and *after* judgment (*Babanaft International Co. SA* v *Bassatne,* above). This is so where the purpose of the injunction is to prevent the frustration of a judgment of an *English* court. In matrimonial proceedings for financial relief, however, the court should not grant a worldwide freezing injunction. It is unlikely that the divorce court would ever award a spouse the whole of the other spouse's assets; the protection of a freezing injunction which extends to all of those assets wherever situated is, therefore, not needed. In *Ghoth* v *Ghoth* [1992] 2 All ER 920, CA, the wife had been granted an interim maintenance order for £500 per month which she wished to protect. The husband had jewellery in England, $200,000 in a New York bank account, and other property in various countries. It was held that the freezing injunction granted to the wife would be limited to the jewellery in England and $50,000 in the New York account.

In the case of a *foreign* judgment which an English court is being asked to enforce, any injunction granted will normally be limited to assets within the jurisdiction of the English court. The court will only grant a worldwide freezing injunction in support of a foreign judgment in very exceptional circumstances; to do otherwise could cause confusion in, and resentment by, foreign nations (*Rosseel NV* v *Oriental Commercial and Shipping (UK) Ltd* [1990] 3 All ER 545, CA, where *Republic of Haiti* v *Duvalier,* above, was distinguished as a special and unusual case). To assist in making the correct order, the court has power to require the defendant to disclose the whereabouts of his foreign assets, both before judgment (*Republic of Haiti* v *Duvalier,* above) and after judgment (*Interpool Ltd* v *Galani* [1988] QB 738, CA; *Maclaine Watson & Co. Ltd* v *International Tin Council (No. 2)* [1988] 3 All ER 257, CA). To protect the defendant against misuse of the information so obtained, the claimant will usually be required to give undertakings not to enforce the order in a foreign court or to use in foreign proceedings any information disclosed by the defendant about his overseas assets without first obtaining the leave of the English court (*Derby & Co. Ltd* v *Weldon (No. 1),* above). Breach of these undertakings would constitute a contempt of court.

A freezing injunction should not be granted over foreign assets if there are sufficient assets within the jurisdiction (*Derby & Co. Ltd* v *Weldon (No. 2),* above). By reason of its drastic and potentially oppressive nature, a pre-judgment injunction over foreign assets will usually only be granted in exceptional circumstances (*Derby & Co. Ltd* v *Weldon (No. 1),* above). Neither a pre-judgment nor a post-judgment freezing order granted in respect of overseas assets should be expressed to be unconditional (*Babanaft International Co. SA* v *Bassatne,* above, *per* Kerr LJ at p. 446 and Neill LJ at p. 450; *Ghoth* v *Ghoth* [1992] 2 All ER 920, CA, *per* Lord Donaldson MR at p. 922). In particular, it should be qualified, so as to afford protection for third parties abroad who are indirectly affected by the order, by the inclusion of a proviso that, in so far as it purports to have extra-territorial effect, no person should be affected by it until it is declared enforceable, or recognised, or enforced, by an appropriate foreign court. This can be achieved by incorporating in the order the so-called 'Babanaft proviso'. This is a term in the injunction named after the *Babanaft* case. As refined in *Derby & Co. Ltd* v *Weldon (No. 2),* the proviso is as follows:

PROVIDED THAT, in so far as this order purports to have any effect outside England and Wales, no person shall be affected by it or concerned with the terms of it until it shall have been declared enforceable or shall have been recognised or registered or enforced by a foreign court (and then it shall only affect such person to the extent of such declaration or recognition or registration or enforcement) UNLESS that person is (a) a person to whom this order is addressed or an officer or an agent appointed by power of attorney of such a person or (b) a person who is subject to the jurisdiction of this court and who (i) has been given written notice of this order at his or its residence or place of business within the jurisdiction and (ii) is able to prevent acts or omissions outside the jurisdiction of this court which assist in the breach of the terms of this order.

(*Derby & Co. Ltd* v *Weldon (No. 2)*, above, *per* Lord Donaldson MR at p. 1015. Such a proviso was included in the injunction granted by Sir Nicolas Browne-Wilkinson V-C in *Securities and Investments Board* v *Pantell SA* [1989] 2 All ER 673.)

The court should take particular care before imposing an injunction on assets the restraint of which would bring the defendant's business to a standstill or inflict on him great loss that might not be fully compensated for by the claimant's undertaking in damages (*Rasu Maritima SA* v *Perusahaan* [1978] QB 644, CA). The court should not order the delivery up of the defendant's clothes, bedding, furnishings, tools of his trade, farm implements, livestock or any machines or other goods which he uses for the purposes of a lawful business (*CBS United Kingdom* v *Lambert* [1982] 3 All ER 237, CA). Care should also be taken not to interfere substantially with an innocent third party's freedom of action generally or freedom to trade (*Galaxia Maritime SA* v *Mineralimportexport* [1982] 1 All ER 796, CA, distinguishing on the facts *Clipper Maritime Co. Ltd of Monrovia* v *Mineralimportexport* [1981] 3 All ER 664). Where a bank, building society or similar institution is involved in an application for a freezing injunction (whether as a defendant or as a third party), the court should give careful consideration to hearing the proceedings in private since public confidence in its finances is crucial to such an institution and the effects of publicity may harm not only the institution but also its innocent customers and depositors (*Polly Peck International* v *Nadir* (1991) *The Times,* 11 November, CA).

A freezing injunction must not be used as a means of exerting pressure on the defendant to settle the action (*Z Ltd* v *A* [1982] 1 All ER 556, CA; *PCW Ltd* v *Dixon* [1983] 2 All ER 158, below). Nor must it be used merely as an instrument of oppression or for improving the position of the claimant as against other creditors of the defendant. To allow the freezing injunction to be so used would be to ignore its real object, which is to prevent the claimant from being cheated out of the proceeds of his action against the defendant should it be successful (*PCW Ltd* v *Dixon,* below).

The court may afterwards *vary* the injunction so as to allow the restrained assets to be used, provided that the purpose for which they are to be used does not conflict with the policy underlying the freezing injunction, namely, to prevent the removal of assets from the jurisdiction (*Iraqi Ministry of Defence* v *Arcepey Shipping Co. SA* [1980] 1 All ER 480) or their dissipation within the jurisdiction (*Z Ltd* v *A,* above). Thus, in one case the defendants were permitted to use the restrained assets to repay to a third party a debt incurred in the ordinary course of business within the jurisdiction, even though what remained of the assets would not be sufficient to satisfy the claimants' claim (*Iraqi Ministry of Defence* v *Arcepey Shipping Co. SA,* above).

In another case a freezing injunction was varied so as to allow the defendant to withdraw from his bank account the sum of £1,000 per week instead of £100 per week for his living expenses, to pay pressing bills amounting to £27,500 and to pay his solicitors £50,000 on account of their costs in the litigation. Lloyd J said that justice and convenience demanded that the defendant should be allowed the means to defend himself, pay his ordinary bills and continue to live in the manner to which he had become accustomed. There was no evidence that the defendant, who was a wealthy man with five children to educate, was dissipating his assets by living as he had always lived and paying bills such as he had always paid. The original figure of £100 per week for the living expenses of a wealthy man was unrealistically low and suggested that it had been set deliberately so as to put pressure on the defendant to settle the claimants' actions against him (*PCW Ltd* v *Dixon* [1983] 2 All ER 158, varied by consent on appeal at ibid., p. 697, CA; see also *Customs and Excise Commissioners* v *Norris* [1991] 2 All ER 395, CA, where a restraint order made under the Drug Trafficking Offences Act 1986 (para 10.4.1 above) was held to be analogous to a freezing injunction and could, therefore, be varied so as to release funds to allow the defendant to appeal at his own expense against conviction for drug offences).

In *Camdex International Ltd* v *Bank of Zambia (No. 2)* [1997] 1 All ER 728, CA, a freezing injunction was varied on appeal so as to exclude from its scope a large quantity of Zambian bank notes which had been printed in the United Kingdom and paid for by, but not yet delivered to, the defendants, who wished to transfer them to Zambia for the purpose of allowing that country to repay debts to the World Bank and the International Monetary Fund. It was held that such a transfer would not be a dissipation of any assets available to the defendants' creditors since the bank notes had no value on the open market. Furthermore, not to exclude the bank notes from the scope of the injunction would amount to holding the defendants to ransom and would inflict great hardship on the Zambian people if Zambia was not able to honour its international debt obligations.

A variation of a freezing injunction will not be sanctioned where the purpose of the proposed variation is to facilitate repayment of a debt not incurred in the ordinary course of business and its effect would be to place assets out of the claimant's reach (*Atlas Maritime Co. SA* v *Avalon Maritime Ltd (No. 1)* [1991] 4 All ER 769, CA), or where its purpose is to allow a subsidiary company to meet legal expenses which the parent company could be expected to meet (*Atlas Maritime Co. SA* v *Avalon Maritime Ltd (No. 3)* [1991] 4 All ER 783, CA).

It is common for the court to specify in the order itself the maximum amount to be restrained and to leave the defendant free to deal with the rest of his assets (*Z Ltd* v *A* [1982] 1 All ER 556, CA, *per* Lord Denning MR at p. 565). Where the order allows the defendant to spend a specified amount on 'ordinary living expenses', such expenses are limited to ordinary recurrent expenditure required to maintain the defendant in the style to which he is reasonably accustomed. They do not cover exceptional expenses, such as legal costs incurred by the defendant in employing Queen's Counsel to defend him on serious criminal charges (*TDK Tape Distributor (UK) Ltd* v *Videochoice Ltd* [1985] 3 All ER 345). Authority to incur exceptional expenses would have to be sought from the court in the form of a variation of the freezing injunction (ibid.).

To obtain a variation of the injunction it is not enough for the defendant merely to state that he owes money to someone. He must produce evidence to show that he has no other (unrestrained) assets available out of which the debt could be paid (*A* v *C (No. 2)* [1981] 2 All ER 126).

If the claimant has obtained a freezing injunction without notice to the defendant and without proper disclosure of material facts the court will discharge the order where (a) the non-disclosure was not innocent (i.e., there was an intention to omit or withhold material information), and (b) the injunction would not have been granted in the first place if full disclosure had been made. If the non-disclosure was innocent, and the injunction could properly have been granted if there had been full disclosure, the court has a discretion to continue the order (*Behbehani* v *Salem* [1989] 2 All ER 143, CA, *per* Nourse LJ at p. 156; *Ali & Fahd Shobokshi Group Ltd* v *Moneim* [1989] 2 All ER 404). If new facts become known to the claimant, or if there is any material change in circumstances, after the grant of a freezing injunction without notice, the claimant is under a duty to inform the court of the new situation (*Commercial Bank of the Near East* v *A* [1989] 2 Lloyd's Rep 319).

10.5   RESCISSION

10.5.1   Nature and effect of rescission

Rescission is an equitable remedy and, therefore, discretionary.

The right to rescind is the right to set aside a transaction (usually a contract) and be restored to one's former position (*restitutio in integrum*). Rescission is not, strictly speaking, a judicial remedy because a party can rescind a contract without taking legal proceedings at all. A contract is rescinded if a party makes it clear that he refuses to be bound by it (*Abram Steamship Co. Ltd* v *Westville Shipping Co. Ltd* [1923] AC 773, HL, *per* Lord Atkinson at p. 781). He must usually give notice to the other party. If the other party cannot be communicated with (for example, where he has disappeared), the contract may be rescinded by the wronged party doing some overt act which is reasonable in the circumstances, such as asking the police to find his property, as in *Car & Universal Finance Co. Ltd* v *Caldwell* [1965] 1 QB 525, CA. This informal approach has not been followed in Scots law (see *MacLeod* v *Kerr* 1965 SC 253) and it was criticised by the Law Reform Committee, which recommended that until notice of rescission is communicated to the other party an innocent purchaser should acquire a good title to property (12th Report, *Transfer of Title to Chattels,* Cmnd 2958, 1966, para 16).

Although it is not essential to go to the court for rescission, it is desirable to do so for two reasons. First, a party who rescinds without good cause may be held to have repudiated the contract and be liable for breach. There may be a dispute over whether a party is or was entitled to rescind and this dispute may need to be resolved by the court. Secondly, the assistance of the court may be needed to obtain restitution of property which was handed over under the contract and which the other party now refuses to restore voluntarily.

In the absence of fraud, it is not possible to obtain damages as well as rescission. The reason is that the respective objects of rescission and damages are quite different. The object of rescission is to restore a party to the position he would have been in if the contract had not been made. The object of damages, on the other hand, is to place a party in the position he would have been in if the contract had been performed.

Sometimes, however, a party may be awarded a sum of money called an *indemnity* in addition to rescission where it would assist in restoring him more fully to his former position. An indemnity is an equitable remedy available to compensate a party for certain expenses incurred in performing obligations created by the contract.

The limited scope of the remedy of indemnity, and the distinction between damages and an indemnity, is illustrated in the case of *Whittington* v *Seale-Hayne* (1900) 82 LT 49. The claimant took a lease of the defendant's premises in order to breed poultry. The claimant, in entering into the lease, had relied on the defendant's innocent misrepresentation that the premises were in good sanitary condition. In fact, the water supply was poisoned and the claimant's manager became ill, most of the claimant's poultry died and the rest became useless for breeding purposes. In the lease the claimant had agreed to be responsible for rent, rates and repairs. The local authority declared the premises unfit for habitation and required the drains to be put in order by the claimant. The defendant submitted to rescission and agreed to pay £20 to the claimant in respect of rent, rates and repairs. In addition, the claimant claimed an indemnity against the following losses:

(a)   value of lost stock   £750
(b)   loss of profit on sales   £100
(c)   loss of breeding season   £500

(d)	removal expenses	£ 75
(e)	medical expenses for attention to the manager	£100

Farwell J held that the lease would be rescinded, but the claimant was entitled to an indemnity only in respect of rent, rates and repairs payable under the lease. Claims (a) to (e) were rejected; (a), (b) and (c) because they were clearly claims for damages, and (d) and (e) because such expenses were not created directly by the lease. The lease required the claimant to pay rent and rates and to do repairs. It did not require him to move in, stock the farm and employ a manager.

It should be noted that, as a result of s. 2(1) of the Misrepresentation Act 1967, damages can now sometimes be awarded for the sort of misrepresentation that occurred in *Whittington* v *Seal-Hayne*. Thus, in *Walker* v *Boyle* [1982] 1 All ER 634 a purchaser of land was held entitled to rescind the contract and, by virtue of s. 2(1) of the 1967 Act, to an inquiry into damage suffered from loss of interest on his deposit. But if the representor proves that he had reasonable ground to believe, and did believe up to the time the contract was made, that the facts represented were true, damages cannot be awarded and the representee would be able to claim only an indemnity.

10.5.2 Grounds for rescission

10.5.2.1 *Fraudulent misrepresentation*
A fraudulent misrepresentation is a false statement of fact which is made by the representor to the representee knowing it to be false, or without belief in its truth, or recklessly, without caring whether it is true or false, with the intention that it should be acted upon and which is in fact acted upon by the representee (*Derry* v *Peek* (1889) 14 App Cas 337, HL). In these circumstances, the representee, on discovering the truth, may rescind the contract he was induced into making. In addition, he may claim damages for the tort of fraud or deceit if he has suffered loss as a result of relying on the misrepresentation.

10.5.2.2 *Negligent misrepresentation*
A negligent misrepresentation is a false statement of fact which satisfies the same criteria as a fraudulent misrepresentation except that it has not been made fraudulently but, instead, with no reasonable ground for belief in its truth. A contract entered into on the faith of such a misrepresentation may be rescinded. In addition, the representee may claim damages under s. 2(1) of the Misrepresentation Act 1967, as in *Watts* v *Spence* [1976] Ch 165 (para 10.3.2.9 above), if he has suffered loss. Negligent misrepresentation is also actionable at common law as a *tort* (*Hedley Byrne & Co. Ltd* v *Heller & Partners Ltd* [1964] AC 465, HL).

It has been held that, by reason of the wording of s. 2(1), the measure of damages for a misrepresentation giving rise to an action under the subsection is the measure of damages in tort for fraud or deceit and not that applicable where the tort is negligent misrepresentation at common law. This means that the representee is not limited (as he would be in a common law action for negligent misrepresentation) to claiming for loss which could be foreseen but may also claim for that which was unforeseeable (*Royscott Trust Ltd* v *Rogerson* [1991] 3 All ER 294, CA).

10.5.2.3 *Wholly innocent misrepresentation*
A wholly innocent misrepresentation is a false statement of fact which is neither fraudulent nor negligent. It may have been made, for example, with an honest belief, and on reasonable

grounds, that it is true. A contract entered into in reliance on such a misrepresentation may be rescinded. There is no *right* to claim damages, although the court has a *discretion* to award damages in *lieu* of rescission. On a claim for rescission, the court may, under s. 2(2) of the Misrepresentation Act 1967, declare the contract to be still subsisting and award damages in *lieu* of rescission if it would be equitable to do so.

Section 2(2) has been interpreted as meaning that, so long as the claimant once had a right to rescind, damages can be awarded under the subsection even though by the time of the trial rescission is no longer a viable remedy and would not be granted (*Thomas Witter Ltd* v *TBP Industries Ltd* [1996] 2 All ER 573).

10.5.2.4 *Undue influence and unconscionable bargains*

Contracts, gifts and other transactions may be set aside by the victim of undue influence, which may be exerted *expressly,* as in *Williams* v *Bayley* (1866) LR 1 HL 200, HL (threat of prosecution of son for forgery), or may be *presumed* to have been exercised, as in *Re Craig* [1971] Ch 95 (domination of 84-year-old widower by his secretary/companion). Transactions of an improvident nature made by poor and ignorant persons acting without independent advice may be set aside unless the other party can show that the transaction is fair and reasonable (*Fry* v *Lane* (1888) 40 ChD 312: two poor and ignorant men, without independent advice, sold property at considerably below the real value; the transactions were set aside by the court).

By statute, the High Court and the county courts have power to reopen extortionate credit bargains, including those entered into with moneylenders and finance companies (Consumer Credit Act 1974, s. 137(1)). A credit bargain is 'extortionate' if the payments under it are 'grossly exorbitant' or if it 'otherwise grossly contravenes ordinary principles of fair dealing' (ibid., s. 138(1)). On reopening the transaction, the court is given a wide discretion to do justice between the parties (s. 137(1)). It may, *inter alia,* set aside the whole or part of any obligation imposed by the transaction on the debtor or a surety (s. 139(2)).

10.5.2.5 *Non-disclosure in contracts uberrimae fidei*

Contracts *uberrimae fidei* ('of the utmost good faith') are contracts in which there is a duty to make a full disclosure of material facts. By their nature they are contracts where one party alone has knowledge of facts which is denied to the other party (*Carter* v *Boehm* (1766) 3 Burr 1905, *per* Lord Mansfield at p. 1909). Examples are family arrangements (*Gordon* v *Gordon* (1821) 3 Swanst 400) and all types of insurance contract (*Lindenau* v *Desborough* (1828) 8 B & C 586, *per* Bayley J at p. 592). Thus, a proposer for insurance must disclose all material facts to the insurer. Facts are 'material' if they would influence the judgment of a prudent insurer in deciding whether to accept the risk and, if so, what the premium should be (*London Assurance* v *Mansel* (1879) 11 ChD 363). Failure to disclose all material facts will render the policy voidable at the option of the insurer, who may rescind it if he so wishes. (Note the warning given to the public about this by Fletcher Moulton LJ in *Joel* v *Law Union & Crown Insurance Co.* [1908] 2 KB 863, CA, at p. 885.)

10.5.2.6 *Mistake*

Before mistake will give rise to a right to rescind in equity it must be a fundamental mistake about the facts or about a party's rights. However, the mistake need not be so fundamental as to make the contract void at common law.

Since rescission is an equitable remedy and available only at the discretion of the court, it may be granted subject to conditions. In *Grist* v *Bailey* [1967] Ch 532, the claimant contracted to buy from the defendant a freehold house for £850 'subject to the existing tenancy thereof'. Later, the defendant refused to complete the contract on the ground that when the contract was made she thought there was a statutory tenant, X, in the house, whereas in fact there was no statutory tenant. The claimant also thought there was a statutory tenant (but a different one, Y) in the house. The value of the house with vacant possession was about £2,250. The claimant claimed specific performance and the defendant counter-claimed for rescission of the contract. It was held by Goff J that there had been a mistake about the existence of a statutory tenancy. Although the mistake was not fundamental enough to avoid the contract at common law, it was sufficiently fundamental to call for relief in equity. Neither party, knowing the true facts, would have negotiated for so small a price as £850. Specific performance was refused. The defendant's counterclaim succeeded and rescission was ordered but on condition that the defendant entered into a fresh contract with the claimant at a proper vacant-possession price. (See also *Solle* v *Butcher* [1950] 1 KB 671, CA, where a *lease* was set aside on equitable terms.)

10.5.2.7 Substantial misdescription of land

The purchaser under a contract for the sale of land may rescind if the vendor has substantially misdescribed the property; for example, where the land is described as registered freehold without disclosing that the title is only possessory and not absolute (*Re Brine and Davies's contract* [1935] Ch 388; see also *Walker* v *Boyle* [1982] 1 All ER 634). This rule is to ensure that the purchaser obtains what he bargained for and that he is not compelled to take something else (*Knatchbull* v *Grueber* (1817) 3 Mer 124 *per* Lord Eldon LC at p. 146; *Flight* v *Booth* (1834) 1 Bing NC 370). If the misdescription of the land is only slight and not material, so that the purchaser will obtain substantially though not exactly what he bargained for, the purchaser is not normally entitled to rescind but must be satisfied with financial compensation from the vendor (*M'Queen* v *Farquhar* (1805) 11 Ves Jr 467).

10.5.3 Loss of right of rescission

10.5.3.1 Restitutio in integrum impossible

A party may not be able to rescind a contract when the parties cannot be restored to their former positions; for example, where property has been consumed or destroyed and cannot, therefore, be handed back (*Clarke* v *Dickson* (1858) EB & E 148; *Vigers* v *Pike* (1842) 8 Cl & F 562). But *precise* restitution is not essential as long as *substantial* restitution is still possible so that equity can do what is just in the circumstances, including, if necessary, the ordering of financial adjustments between the parties (as in *Hulton* v *Hulton* [1917] 1 KB 813, CA, and *Cheese* v *Thomas* [1994] 1 All ER 35, CA). In *Erlanger* v *New Sombrero Phosphate Co.* (1878) 3 App Cas 1218, HL, a company formed by E bought the lease of a phosphate mine for £55,000. E then formed another company and sold the lease to it for £110,000 without telling the shareholders of the second company the facts about the purchase, including the profit being made by the first company. This was in breach of the fiduciary duty owed by the promoter of a company to its shareholders. By the time the true facts were discovered both the lease and the minerals were running out, although restitution was possible since the mine was not completely worked out. The House of Lords held that the sale of the lease to the second company would be rescinded on condition that the mine be handed back and an account rendered of the profits of working it.

In *O'Sullivan* v *Management Agency and Music Ltd* [1985] 3 All ER 351, CA, contracts entered into some years earlier by the 'pop' singer and composer, Gilbert O'Sullivan, with his managers, the defendants, were rescinded by the court (on the ground of undue influence) on terms which sought to do justice between the parties. The defendants were ordered to reconvey to the claimant the copyrights in his compositions, to deliver up to him the master tapes of his recordings, and to account for the profits due to him from the copyrights and recordings. However, the defendants were held to be entitled to an allowance representing reasonable remuneration (including a profit element) for work done by them in helping the claimant to enjoy a successful career.

10.5.3.2   By affirmation of the contract

The right to rescind will be lost if a party affirms the contract (whether by word or action) after learning the full facts. For instance, a party who, on discovering that he has been the victim of a fraudulent misrepresentation, takes a benefit under the contract will thereby lose his right to rescind it (*Clough* v *London & North Western Railway Co.* (1871) LR 7 Ex 26; *Urquhart* v *Macpherson* (1878) 3 App Cas 831, PC). But a party must be in possession of *all* the facts before it can be concluded that what he has said or done amounts to an affirmation of the contract (*Central Railway of Venezuela* v *Kisch* (1867) LR 2 HL 99, HL).

Lapse of time between the date of the contract and a purported rescission is evidence of affirmation (*Clough* v *London & North Western Railway Co.* (1871) LR 7 Ex 26). In the case of a fraudulent misrepresentation, time begins to run only from the discovery of the truth (*Armstrong* v *Jackson* [1917] 2 KB 822). In the case of innocent misrepresentation (and probably negligent misrepresentation, too), time begins to run as soon as the contract is made. In *Leaf* v *International Galleries* [1950] 2 KB 86, CA, the claimant was induced to buy a picture on the faith of an innocent misrepresentation that it was a genuine Constable. Five years later he discovered that the picture was not by Constable and he claimed rescission of the contract. The Court of Appeal held that he had lost his right of rescission by lapse of time, even though he had started his action immediately on discovering the truth.

Affirmation bars only the right to rescind. The party who affirms the contract, though he cannot set it aside, may still claim damages for misrepresentation or for breach of contract.

10.5.3.3   By the intervention of innocent third-party rights for value

The right to rescind a contract will be lost if, before rescission, an innocent third party acquires for valuable consideration an interest in the subject-matter of the contract (*Clough* v *London & North Western Railway Co.* (1871) LR 7 Ex 26). For example, X obtains P's goods under a contract induced by fraud. Before P discovers the fraud, X sells the goods to D, who is an innocent third party. It is too late for P to rescind his contract with X, and D obtains a good title to the goods. P loses his goods and must sue X, and not D, for damages in the tort of conversion — if X can be found and if he is worth suing.

In *Lewis* v *Averay* [1972] 1 QB 198, CA, a rogue, pretending to be Richard Greene, a well known film actor, offered to buy the claimant's car. The claimant accepted the offer and was given a cheque signed by 'R.A. Greene'. When the claimant said that he would like to clear the cheque before parting with the car, the rogue produced an admission pass to Pinewood Studios. The claimant was convinced that the rogue was Richard Greene and he parted with the car and its registration document forthwith. The cheque had been stolen and was worthless but, before the claimant discovered this, the rogue had sold the car and handed over the registration document to the innocent defendant. The claimant sued the defendant in conversion for the return of the car or its value. The Court of Appeal held that the claimant's action must fail because the defendant had acquired a good title to the car from the rogue. The original contract between the claimant and the rogue was voidable for fraud, but it was now too late for the claimant to rescind it because an innocent third party had already acquired for value an interest in the subject-matter. (See also *Phillips* v *Brooks Ltd* [1919] 2 KB 243 and cf. *Ingram* v *Little* [1961] 1 QB 31, CA.)

10.6 RECTIFICATION

10.6.1 Nature of rectification

Rectification is an equitable remedy and, therefore, discretionary.

Sometimes, by reason of an omission or a mistake or fraud, a written instrument does not represent the true agreement of the parties. There may, for example, have been a mistake in recording the agreed rent in a lease (*Murray* v *Parker* (1854) 19 Beav 305; *Thomas Bates & Son Ltd* v *Wyndham's (Lingerie) Ltd* [1981] 1 All ER 1077, CA). Or, by an oversight, some terms previously agreed upon orally may have been omitted from the later written instrument (as in *Joscelyne* v *Nissen* [1970] 2 QB 86, CA, para 10.6.3 below; *Craddock Bros Ltd* v *Hunt* [1923] 2 Ch 136, CA). A court of equity has power to rectify the instrument so that it does represent the true agreement of the parties.

The burden of proof, which rests upon the party seeking rectification, is that applicable in all civil cases, namely the balance of probability. The claimant must prove, on the balance of probability, that the written instrument does not reflect the common intention of the parties (*Thomas Bates & Son Ltd* v *Wyndham's (Lingerie) Ltd* [1981] 1 All ER 1077, CA, *per* Buckley LJ at p. 1085 and Brightman LJ at p. 1090). The claimant does not have to satisfy the higher burden, demanded in criminal cases, of proving the matter beyond reasonable doubt (*Earl* v *Hector Whaling Ltd* [1961] 1 Lloyd's Rep 459, CA; *Joscelyne* v *Nissen* [1970] 2 QB 86, CA). Nevertheless, in some circumstances a high standard of evidence may be required, especially where sharp practice is alleged (*Thomas Bates & Son Ltd* v *Wyndham's (Lingerie) Ltd* [1981] 1 All ER 1077, CA, *per* Buckley LJ at p. 1086).

10.6.2 Instruments subject to rectification

Instruments that may be rectified include contracts, leases, conveyances, bills of exchange, transfers of shares, policies of marine insurance, marriage settlements and wills. The court had no power to rectify a will before the Administration of Justice Act 1982 became law (*Harter and Slater* v *Harter* (1873) LR 3 P & D 11). Section 20 of the 1982 Act conferred that power, thus implementing belatedly the recommendation of the Law Reform Committee (19th Report, *The Interpretation of Wills*, Cmnd 5301, 1973, paras 17–33). By s. 20, if the court is satisfied that a will fails to carry out the testator's intentions, as a result of a clerical error or of a failure to understand his instructions, it may order rectification of the will so as to carry out the testator's intentions. (For the meaning of 'clerical error', see *Wordingham* v *Royal Exchange Trust Co. Ltd* [1992] 3 All ER 204; *Re Segelman (deceased)* [1995] 3 All ER 676.)

10.6.3 Conditions for rectification

(a) There must be a prior concluded agreement between the parties, although it is not necessary for it to be a legally enforceable contract as long as there is an outward expression of agreement. In *Joscelyne* v *Nissen* [1970] 2 QB 86, CA, the claimant applied for rectification of a written contract under which he had transferred his car-hire business to the defendant, who was his daughter. The parties shared a house and, before the written contract was entered into, it had been agreed verbally that the defendant would pay certain household expenses, including the gas, electricity and coal bills, in respect of the claimant's part of the house. But this agreement was not contained in the written contract. The defendant paid the bills for a while but then refused to pay any more and denied any liability to do so. The Court of Appeal held that the written contract would be rectified so as to include the defendant's liability for the agreed expenses. The oral agreement between the parties was not in itself a legally binding contract. Nevertheless, it did represent the common intention of the parties, who had reached an outward expression of agreement in respect of the household expenses.

(b)   This prior concluded agreement must have remained unchanged until it was put into writing in the instrument (*Marquis Townshend* v *Stangroom* (1801) 6 Ves Jr 328 *per* Lord Eldon LC at pp. 333 and 334). There can be no rectification if the parties deliberately changed the terms of their agreement or deliberately omitted a term from the written instrument.

(c)   By mistake the written instrument must fail to express the prior agreement of the parties. What is needed is a literal disparity between the language of the prior agreement and the later written instrument, as in *Joscelyne* v *Nissen* above. It is not enough to prove a misunderstanding of the language used where it is the same in both cases so that, in fact, the written instrument has accurately recorded the prior agreement. In *Frederick E. Rose (London) Ltd* v *William H. Pim Jnr & Co. Ltd* [1953] 2 QB 450, CA, the claimants, who were London merchants, received an order for 'Moroccan horsebeans described here as *féveroles*'. They asked the defendants what '*féveroles*' were and the defendants replied that they were just horsebeans and that they could obtain them for the claimants to resell. The parties orally agreed that the defendants would sell and the claimants would buy 'horse-beans'. The goods were also described as 'horsebeans' when the oral agreement was later embodied in a written contract. It turned out that there were three types of Moroccan horsebeans: *fèves*, *féveroles* and *fevettes*. The defendants supplied *fèves* and not *féveroles*. The claimants' customers claimed damages from the claimants, who now wished to claim damages from the defendants. The claimants, as a preliminary to claiming damages, first sought rectification of the written instrument so as to make it a contract for 'horsebeans described as *féveroles*'. The Court of Appeal held that the remedy of rectification was not available because both the prior oral agreement and the written contract were for 'horsebeans'. There had been a misunderstanding of the meaning of the word 'horsebeans' but there had been no mistake in recording the terms of the prior agreement. The parties all along had contracted to buy and sell 'horsebeans' and not '*féveroles*'.

Nor can mere confusion be used as the basis of a claim for rectification. Thus in *Cambro Contractors Ltd* v *John Kennelly Sales Ltd* (1994) *The Times*, 14 April, CA, rectification of a conveyance was refused where all that could be shown was that the parties and their solicitors had been confused about what land was included in the conveyance. This fell far short of establishing that the document contained a common mistake and failed to reflect the common intention of the parties.

10.6.4   Oral evidence

In a claim for rectification, oral evidence is admissible to prove that the intention of the parties was not properly expressed in the written instrument (*Marquis Townshend* v *Stangroom* (1801) 6 Ves Jr 328; *Craddock Bros Ltd* v *Hunt* [1923] 2 Ch 136, CA; *United*

States of America v *Motor Trucks Ltd* [1924] AC 196, PC). This is an exception to the parol evidence rule that evidence from witnesses will not be admitted to add to, vary or contradict a written instrument. The exception is justified on the ground that rectification could not be an effective remedy without evidence of the prior oral agreement being admitted.

10.6.5 Rectification for unilateral mistake

Normally, a claim for rectification is based on a *common* mistake; i.e., the written instrument fails to record the intention of *both* parties. However, rectification is also possible on the ground of *unilateral* mistake by the claimant alone on the following conditions (*Thomas Bates & Son Ltd* v *Wyndham's (Lingerie) Ltd* [1981] 1 All ER 1077, CA, applying *A. Roberts & Co. Ltd* v *Leicestershire County Council* [1961] Ch 555 and a dictum of Russell LJ in *Riverplate Properties Ltd* v *Paul* [1975] Ch 133, CA; see also *Paget* v *Marshall* (1884) 28 ChD 255):

(a) The claimant wrongly believed that the written instrument recorded the common intention of the parties.

(b) The defendant knew that the instrument did not record the common intention of the parties because of a mistake on the part of the claimant.

(c) The defendant failed to bring the mistake to the attention of the claimant.

(d) The claimant's mistake was favourable to the defendant (*Thomas Bates & Son Ltd* v *Wyndham's (Lingerie) Ltd, per* Buckley LJ at p. 1086) or, at least, was detrimental to the claimant (ibid., *per* Eveleigh LJ at p. 1090). As long as the defendant's conduct is such as to make it inequitable for him to object to rectification, it is not necessary for the claimant to prove that the defendant was guilty of any sharp practice (ibid., *per* Buckley LJ at p. 1086, Eveleigh LJ at p. 1090 and Brightman LJ at p. 1091).

In *Thomas Bates & Son Ltd* v *Wyndham's (Lingerie) Ltd* [1981] 1 All ER 1077, CA, two previous leases between the parties had contained an option giving the defendant tenants the right to take a further lease at a rent to be agreed between the parties or, in default of such agreement, at a rent to be fixed by an arbitrator. When a third lease was drawn up by the claimant landlords, they, by an oversight, omitted to include provision for the fixing of rent by an arbitrator in default of agreement. The parties had not agreed on this omission. The defendants were aware of the claimants' mistake at the time they executed the third lease but they did not bring it to the claimants' notice. When the rent came up for review there was disagreement and the defendants refused to go to arbitration, claiming to be entitled to pay only the old rent, or no rent at all, during the remainder of the lease. The claimants sought rectification of the lease so as to provide for determination of the rent by an arbitrator in default of agreement. The Court of Appeal held that the lease would be so rectified. The parties had a common intention to include in the third lease an arbitration clause similar to that in the two previous leases. The third lease did not accurately record that common intention owing to the claimants' mistake. The omission of the arbitration clause, which was contrary to the claimants' interests, was known to the defendants but they did not draw it to the attention of the claimants.

10.6.6 Defences to a claim for rectification

Generally, rectification is subject to the same limitations as the remedy of rescission (para 10.5.3 above). Thus, rectification will not be ordered where the written instrument has been affirmed or where a third party has acquired rights for value under the instrument and without notice of the mistake (*Bell* v *Cundall* (1750) Amb 101). One important difference, however, is that impossibility of *restitutio in integrum* is not normally a bar to rectification (*Cook* v *Fearn* (1878) 48 LJ Ch 63, in which a marriage settlement was ordered to be rectified *after* the marriage had taken place).

10.6.7   Effect of an order of rectification

A new instrument need not be prepared. A copy of the court order can be endorsed on the existing instrument and that is enough (*White* v *White* (1872) LR 15 Eq 247). The order of rectification works retrospectively in that the instrument is to be read as if it had been originally drafted in its rectified form (*Craddock Bros Ltd* v *Hunt* [1923] 2 Ch 136, CA). Rectification of a contract and specific performance of the contract as rectified can be decreed together in the same action (*Craddock Bros Ltd* v *Hunt*, above; *United States of America* v *Motor Trucks Ltd* [1924] AC 196, PC).

10.7   DECLARATIONS

A claimant may ask the High Court or a county court simply to declare the law on some disputed point. Alternatively, the court may make a declaration of its own motion even though not claimed by a party in the proceedings, as in *Cowan* v *Scargill* [1984] 2 All ER 750. Quite often a declaratory judgment can settle a dispute before the claimant's rights have been infringed.

The declaratory judgment is a relatively modern development. In general, the English courts had always denied any jurisdiction to make declarations without giving other relief (for example, damages or an injunction) at the same time. This attitude was possibly based on the unwillingness of the courts to try what they regarded as hypothetical cases. In Scotland, the courts had jurisdiction to make declarations by reason of the action of *declarator,* which had existed for hundreds of years (*Russian Commercial & Industrial Bank* v *British Bank for Foreign Trade Ltd* [1921] AC 438, HL, *per* Lord Dunedin at p. 448). In England, it seems that the old Court of Chancery had no *inherent* power to issue declarations without at the same time granting consequential relief (*Guaranty Trust Co. of New York* v *Hannay & Co.* [1915] 2 KB 536, CA, *per* Bankes LJ at p. 568). However, from the middle of the nineteenth century the Court of Chancery was given a *statutory* power to make declarations without granting consequential relief (13 & 14 Vict, c. 35 (1850) (Special Case Act); Chancery Procedure Act 1852, s. 50).

But the major change was brought about in 1883 when, pursuant to s. 17 of the Supreme Court of Judicature Act 1875, new Rules of the Supreme Court (RSC) were made. By them the power to make declarations of right was extended to all three divisions of the recently created High Court and could be exercised whether or not any other relief was claimed. In *F* v *West Berkshire Health Authority* [1989] 2 All ER 545, HL, Lord Brandon (at p. 557) said it was wrong to suggest that the jurisdiction to make declarations arose under the Rules of the Supreme Court. (See also *Re S (hospital patient: court's jurisdiction)* [1995] 3 All ER 290, CA, *per* Sir Thomas Bingham MR at p. 296: the 'jurisdiction . . . to grant declaratory relief is not conferred, but is regulated, by Ord. 15, r. 16'.) But his Lordship's view that the power is instead part of the inherent jurisdiction of the High Court seems to conflict with Lord Goff's opinion in the same case (see p. 570) and is difficult to reconcile with earlier dicta in the House of Lords (see *Russian Commercial & Industrial Bank* v

British Bank for Foreign Trade Ltd [1921] AC 438 *per* Viscount Finlay at p. 444 and Lord
Dunedin at p. 447; *Gouriet* v *Union of Post Office Workers* [1977] 3 All ER 70, HL, *per*
Lord Edmund-Davies at p. 110).

The rule is currently contained in RSC, Ord. 15, r. 16, which (substantially repeating the
language of s. 50 of the Chancery Procedure Act 1852) states that:

> No action or other proceeding shall be open to objection on the ground that a merely
> declaratory judgment or order is sought thereby, and the court may make binding
> declarations of right whether or not any consequential relief is or could be claimed.

The county courts have the same power to make declarations as the High Court (County
Courts Act 1984, s. 38, as substituted by the Courts and Legal Services Act 1990), including
the power to make declarations relating to land. Declarations, but not injunctions or specific
performance, are available against the Crown in private law proceedings (Crown Proceedings Act 1947, s. 21).

In the field of private law, declarations are often sought for a determination of the correct
interpretation of contracts, as in the case of *Eastham* v *Newcastle United Football Club Ltd*
[1964] Ch 413, in which a declaration was granted that the former 'retain and transfer'
system of the Football League, under which a player retained by his club could not obtain
a transfer without the consent of that club, was in unlawful restraint of trade. The declaration
was granted not only against the player's club (with whom he had a contract) but also
against the Football League Ltd and the Football Association Ltd (with whom he did not).

In *Consorzio Veneziano di Armamento e Navigazione* v *Northumberland Shipbuilding Co.
Ltd* (1919) 88 LJKB 1194, CA, Atkin LJ said (at p. 1201) that the action for a declaration
was one of the most valuable contributions to the commercial life of the country. It provides
a procedure whereby business people can go to court and have their disputes resolved
relatively quickly. In the *Consorzio Veneziano* case, the Court of Appeal upheld a judge's
decision to grant a declaration that certain contracts between the parties were still subsisting
and had not been repudiated. Furthermore, it was made clear that the very act of applying
for a declaration would not in itself usually amount to a repudiation of a contract (*per* Atkin
LJ at p. 1200).

The declaration is a discretionary remedy and the discretion is exercised with caution
(*Russian Commercial & Industrial Bank* v *British Bank for Foreign Trade Ltd* [1921] 2 AC
438, HL). The court will not entertain hypothetical questions (ibid., *per* Lord Dunedin at
p. 448 and Lord Sumner at p. 452). Despite the wide wording of RSC, Ord. 15, r. 16 (quoted
above), the power of the court will normally be limited to declaring contested legal rights,
subsisting or future, of the parties to the case before it (*Guaranty Trust Co. of New York* v
Hannay & Co. [1915] 2 KB 536, CA, *per* Pickford LJ at p. 562; *Gouriet* v *Union of Post
Office Workers* [1977] 3 All ER 70, HL, *per* Lord Wilberforce at p. 85 and Lord Diplock at
p. 100). There is, therefore, no jurisdiction to grant a declaration to a third party in
connection with a contractual dispute between two other parties, even though the third party
might be affected by the resolution of that dispute (*Meadows Indemnity Co. Ltd* v *Insurance
Corporation of Ireland Ltd* [1989] 2 Lloyd's Rep 298, CA). Where, however, the case
concerns a serious justiciable issue of a moral or social nature which is not merely of
academic interest, the court will be prepared to grant an appropriate declaration to a party
with a genuine and legitimate interest in that issue (as opposed to a stranger or officious
busybody) without insisting upon the demonstration of a specific legal right vested in that
party. To hold otherwise would be to 'confine the inherent jurisdiction of the court within

an inappropriate straitjacket'. Sir Thomas Bingham MR so said in *Re S (hospital patient: court's jurisdiction)* [1995] 3 All ER 290, CA, at p. 303. Here, the female companion of an elderly incapacitated patient was granted declaratory and injunctive relief against the patient's son and wife forbidding them to remove the patient from England to Norway. It was further said that, in any event, the companion had acquired a specific legal right which was liable to be infringed by the proposed action of the son and wife. This legal right had been obtained by assuming and discharging the responsibility for the patient's care and hospital treatment.

The declaration has become a valuable tool in determining personal status. Thus, under s. 45 of the Matrimonial Causes Act 1973 an application for a declaration could be made in order to determine, *inter alia,* whether a person was legitimate (note, however, that the court had no power to declare that a person was *illegitimate: B* v *Attorney-General* [1967] 1 WLR 776), or whether a person had been validly married. In *Puttick* v *Attorney-General* [1980] Fam 1, the marriage of the petitioner (nee Astrid Proll, the erstwhile terrorist) was held to be valid, but the judge, in his discretion, refused to make a declaration to that effect under s. 45 of the Matrimonial Causes Act 1973 because of the petitioner's fraud and other criminal activities. In another case it was held that if s. 45 of the 1973 Act was available any declaration should be made under that provision rather than under RSC, Ord. 15, r. 16 (*Vervaeke* v *Smith* [1981] 1 All ER 55, CA; not argued on appeal to the House of Lords ([1982] 2 All ER 144), although the opinion of the Court of Appeal received the approval of Lord Simon of Glaisdale at p. 160).

In 1988, s. 45 of the Matrimonial Causes Act 1973 was repealed and replaced by part III of the Family Law Act 1986, which makes fresh provision for declarations of status and incorporates earlier case-law developments. Thus, for example, a person may apply to the High Court or a county court for a declaration that a marriage was at its inception a valid one (Family Law Act 1986, s. 55), or that he is the legitimate child of his parents or that he has become or has not become a legitimated person (ibid., s. 56, as substituted by the Family Law Reform Act 1987). If the truth of the proposition to be declared is proved to the satisfaction of the court a declaration must be granted unless to do so would manifestly be contrary to public policy (Family Law Act 1986, s. 58(1), confirming *Puttick* v *Attorney-General,* above). No declaration available under the Family Law Act 1986 can be made by any court otherwise than under that Act (ibid., s. 58(4), confirming *Vervaeke* v *Smith,* above). No court has power, whether under the Act or otherwise, to declare that a person is or was illegitimate (ibid., s. 58(5), confirming *B* v *Attorney-General,* above).

In recent years applications for declarations under RSC, Ord. 15, r. 16 have been used as a means of testing the lawfulness of proposed surgical and medical procedures to be performed on adult mentally handicapped persons who are incapable of giving their own consent, and the courts have responded by making what are, in effect, *advisory* declarations. (See, for example, *T* v *T* [1988] Fam 62, where declarations were granted to the effect that it would not be unlawful to perform abortion and sterilisation operations on the defendant, a pregnant woman aged 19 who was epileptic and severely mentally handicapped.) In *F* v *West Berkshire Health Authority* [1989] 2 All ER 545, the House of Lords approved this practice. At the same time (Lord Griffiths dissenting on this point), their Lordships emphasised that a declaration is not essential in order to establish the lawfulness of such procedures since they may lawfully be performed at common law if they are in the best interests of the patient. According to their Lordships, the obtaining of a declaration is, however, *desirable* as a matter of good practice because a declaration of the court will establish whether the procedure is in the best interests of the patient and, therefore, lawful, and will protect the surgeon and others involved from subsequent criticism and legal action (see *per* Lord Brandon at p. 552). In determining whether the proposed procedure is in the best interests of the patient, the test is, applying *Bolam* v *Friern Hospital Management Committee* [1957] 2 All ER 118, whether it is accepted as appropriate treatment at the time by a reasonable body of medical opinion skilled in that particular form of treatment.

On the facts of *F* v *West Berkshire Health Authority,* the House of Lords affirmed the granting of a declaration that a proposed sterilisation operation, being in the existing circumstances in her best interests, could lawfully be performed on a severely mentally handicapped woman of 36 despite her inability to consent to it. The woman was a voluntary in-patient at a mental hospital who had formed a sexual relationship with a male patient and for whom ordinary methods of contraception were inappropriate and pregnancy would be disastrous. It was further ordered that, if there was any material change in the existing circumstances before the operation was carried out, any party would be able to apply to the Family Division of the High Court for such other declaration or order as might be just.

The case of *In Re D (medical treatment)* (1998) *The Times*, 14 January, concerned a 49-year-old mentally disabled man, with a history of alcohol and drug abuse problems, who suffered from chronic renal failure and high blood pressure and who required kidney dialysis three or four times a week lasting for four hours on each occasion. His mental disability rendered him incapable of consenting to or refusing treatment, and his general condition led to a lack of cooperation which meant that treatment could not be carried out without first anaesthetising him, which was both dangerous and impracticable. A declaration was granted that it was in the patient's best interests, and lawful, for the medical team involved not to impose treatment but to provide only such palliative care as the patient would accept.

In what is a rapidly developing area of law, the use of the declaration has been extended, first, to cover the situation where the patient is not mentally handicapped but is otherwise refusing consent to treatment, and, secondly, for the purpose of sanctioning the withdrawal of life-support facilities from a patient who is in a persistent vegetative state. In *Re T (adult: refusal of medical treatment)* [1992] 4 All ER 649, CA, it was declared that it would not be unlawful to administer a blood transfusion to the patient (who was in her early 20s) following an emergency Caesarian section because her apparent decision to refuse treatment was vitiated by her medical condition and by reason of the undue influence of her mother, a Jehovah's Witness who believed that the transfusion of blood was sinful. A declaration was granted in *Re S (adult: refusal of medical treatment)* [1992] 4 All ER 671 that a Caesarian section, together with any necessary consequential treatment, was in the vital interests of the patient, aged 30, and her unborn child and could lawfully be performed in spite of the patient's refusal on religious grounds (as a born-again Christian) to give her consent.

Airedale NHS Trust v *Bland* [1993] 1 All ER 821, HL, concerned Tony Bland, a young man who had been in a persistent vegetative state for three and a half years after suffering catastrophic and irreversible brain damage due to a severe crushed chest injury sustained in the Hillsborough football ground disaster of April 1989. His parents and family now wanted him to be allowed to die peacefully and with dignity. It was decided that in the best interests of the patient declarations would be granted to the health authority responsible for Tony Bland's care to the effect that all life-sustaining treatment could lawfully be discontinued and that there was no legal requirement thereafter to provide medical treatment, except for the sole purpose of allowing him to die peacefully with the greatest dignity and the least distress.

The House of Lords upheld these declarations but emphasised that the taking of positive steps to end a patient's life (euthanasia), such as by administering a drug to bring about death, remains unlawful. Applying *F* v *West Berkshire Health Authority*, above, their Lordships said that an application for a declaration is the appropriate means of seeking the guidance of the court before withdrawing life-supporting treatment from a patient in a persistent vegetative state. It was said that, for the time being at least, doctors should as a matter of practice (designed to protect patients and doctors and to reassure patients' families and the public) continue to seek that guidance. The hope was expressed that, in time, applications for declarations could be limited to special cases as and when a body of experience and practice was built up in the Family Division of the High Court. (See *Airedale NHS Trust* v *Bland* [1993] 1 All ER 821, HL, *per* Lords Keith, Goff and Lowry at pp. 862, 874 and 876 respectively.) A standard form of declaration is set out in *Practice Note (persistent vegetative state: withdrawal of treatment)* [1996] 4 All ER 766.

In addition to its important function in *private* law, the declaratory judgment also provides a useful remedy for keeping public authorities within their powers. The role of the declaration in *public* law is considered more fully in para 11.5.

11

Remedies against Public Authorities, Inferior Courts and Tribunals

11.1 INTRODUCTION

Some of the remedies discussed in Chapter 10 may be available in appropriate circumstances in private law proceedings against public authorities in order to prevent or redress wrongful conduct. In addition, the prerogative remedies, available in public-law proceedings and discussed later in this chapter, provide machinery for keeping public authorities, such as central government departments, local government authorities and statutory tribunals, within their powers and for ensuring that they observe the principles of natural justice.

In 1982, in the important case of *O'Reilly* v *Mackman* [1982] 3 All ER 1124, the House of Lords acknowledged that the distinction between public law and private law had assumed a new significance. This development has serious implications for the choice of remedies in cases involving public authorities and means that private-law and public-law remedies are to be more rigidly segregated than before.

The effect of *O'Reilly* v *Mackman* on the availability of private law and public law remedies against public authorities is noted at greater length later in this chapter (paras 11.5.1 and 11.11.2) but, in brief, it may be said here that where it is sought to protect a right conferred by *public,* as opposed to *private,* law then the appropriate relief should be claimed in an application for judicial review in public law rather than in an ordinary action in private law. The reasons for the procedural change ordered by the House of Lords in *O'Reilly* v *Mackman* are explained in para 11.11.2 below, together with the disadvantages of the change for the ordinary citizen and the advantages for public authorities. It is important, however, to appreciate from the outset that, on an application for judicial review, the applicant is not confined to the prerogative remedies but may claim in the same application appropriate *non-prerogative* relief in the form of a declaration, an injunction or damages (see further, para 11.11.6 below). The old remedies are still available; only the procedure for obtaining them against public authorities has changed.

11.1.1 *Ultra vires*

Ultra vires acts can take several forms, such as doing the wrong thing, acting in the wrong manner (e.g., by using the wrong procedure or behaving negligently), or abusing a discretion. For example, in *R* v *Port Talbot Borough Council (ex parte Jones)* [1988] 2 All ER 207, a decision to allocate a council house was quashed by certiorari on two grounds. First, the decision had not been reached in an authorised and lawful manner because the dominant role in making it had been assumed by the chairman of the housing tenancy committee whereas the council's standing orders delegated the making of the decision to the housing officer. Secondly, the decision amounted to an abuse of power because it was based on an irrelevant consideration, namely the chairman's wish to put the allottee, a fellow-councillor, in a better position to fight a local election, and it was unfair to others on the council housing list.

Prohibition, injunctions and declarations may be applied for in advance of, and certiorari and damages may be claimed after, the commission of the wrongful act.

An *ultra vires* act is *void*. One serious consequence of this rule is that money or property transferred under an *ultra vires* transaction may only be recoverable (if at all) with some difficulty. Thus, for example, since *ultra vires* transactions cannot be enforced by or against local authorities a creditor who lends money to an authority for an *ultra vires* object will be unable to recover the amount of the debt by suing on the void contract of loan. The money may be recoverable, however, by a process of restitution. In *Hazell v Hammersmith and Fulham London Borough Council* [1991] 1 All ER 545, HL, a declaration was granted to the district auditor that interest-rate swap transactions entered into by a local authority were *ultra vires* since they amounted to trading in the money market. This was held to be an activity which a local authority has no power (either express or implied) to engage in under the Local Government Act 1972. In the light of this decision, a bank in a separate case sought repayment of money paid to a local authority under an interest-rate swap transaction without attempting to enforce the *ultra vires* contract. It was held that the money was recoverable on the basis of restitution, either in an action at common law for money had and received by the authority to the use of the bank, or in an action in equity based upon unjust enrichment. It was said that the relevant principle was the same both at law and in equity, namely, that it was unconscionable for the authority to keep the money (*Westdeutsche Landesbank Girozentrale v Islington London Borough Council* [1994] 4 All ER 890, CA; this part of the Court of Appeal's decision was unaffected by the authority's subsequent appeal to the House of Lords ([1996] 2 All ER 961, HL) since the appeal was concerned only with whether the authority was liable to pay compound interest on the money).

11.1.2 Natural justice

The principles of natural justice, which apply to courts (see *B v W* [1979] 3 All ER 83, HL) and to tribunals as well as to public authorities, ensure that powers and duties are exercised in accordance with rules of 'fair play'. The principles of natural justice are, first, *nemo judex in causa sua potest* ('no man can be a judge in his own cause'), sometimes called 'the rule against bias', and, secondly, *audi alteram partem* ('hear the other side'), which insists that both parties to a dispute should be heard and that the hearing should be a fair one. The principles of natural justice and the doctrine of *ultra vires* will be explained and illustrated further in the course of this chapter.

A ORDINARY REMEDIES IN PRIVATE LAW

11.2 DAMAGES

A public authority which makes a contract of a type which it is within its powers to make may be sued in damages like a private individual if it commits a breach of that contract. If, on the other hand, an authority makes a contract which it has no power to make, the contract is *ultra vires* and void and neither party can sue on it (*North West Leicestershire District Council v East Midlands Housing Association Ltd* [1981] 3 All ER 364, CA; *Rhyl Urban District Council v Rhyl Amusements Ltd* [1959] 1 WLR 465).

A public authority which commits a tort while acting *ultra vires* or in violation of the principles of natural justice may be sued in damages. Thus, public authorities have been successfully sued in trespass (*Cooper* v *Wandsworth Board of Works* (1863) 14 CB NS 180); false imprisonment (*Percy* v *Glasgow Corporation* [1922] AC 299, HL); and nuisance (*Managers of the Metropolitan Asylum District* v *Hill* (1881) 6 App Cas 193, HL, para 8.10.3.3). In *Cooper* v *Wandsworth Board of Works,* a builder began to erect a house in London without giving seven days' notice to the local board of works as required by statute. The statute provided that the board could demolish the house if such notice was not given. When the building reached the second storey the board sent men late in the evening and they demolished it. The board had only done what the statute said it could do. Nevertheless, the builder succeeded in obtaining damages for trespass because the court construed the statute to mean that the board's power of demolition could only be exercised after giving the offending builder an opportunity to be heard in his own defence.

11.2.1 Action for damages for breach of statutory duty

In some cases an action for damages may be brought by a private individual against a public authority for breach of statutory duty. Whether such an action is available depends on the facts of each case and the interpretation of the particular statute (*Cutler* v *Wandsworth Stadium Ltd* [1949] AC 398, HL; *Lonrho Ltd* v *Shell Petroleum Co. Ltd (No. 2)* [1981] 2 All ER 456, HL; *Hague* v *Deputy Governer of Parkhurst Prison* [1991] 3 All ER 733, HL; *X (minors)* v *Bedfordshire County Council* [1995] 3 All ER 353, HL; *Stovin* v *Wise* [1996] 3 All ER 801, HL; *O'Rourke* v *Camden London Borough Council* [1997] 3 All ER 23, HL). The test is whether Parliament intended to confer on the claimant a private-law cause of action for breach of statutory duty.

The statute may, for example, expressly allow an action for damages. On the other hand, the statute may be completely silent about remedies. In *Reffell* v *Surrey County Council* [1964] 1 All ER 743, the claimant schoolgirl was injured at school when a cloakroom door swung towards her and her hand went through a glass panel in the door. The claimant was awarded damages against the local education authority for breach of statutory duty (imposed by the Education Act 1944 and the Standards for School Premises Regulations) in not using tougher glass in the door so as reasonably to ensure the claimant's safety.

In *Thornton* v *Kirklees Metropolitan Borough Council* [1979] 2 All ER 349, CA, the Court of Appeal had held that an action for damages for distress and inconvenience would lie against a local housing authority for breach of its statutory duty, imposed by the Housing (Homeless Persons) Act 1977 (now part III of the Housing Act 1985), to provide accommodation for certain persons in certain circumstances. The court said that it was to be presumed that Parliament intended an action for damages to lie because the 1977 Act had imposed a duty on a housing authority for the benefit of a specified category of persons and it provided no specific remedy for breach of that duty.

Although it appeared that this decision was approved in principle by the House of Lords in *Cocks* v *Thanet District Council* [1982] 3 All ER 1135, HL, their Lordships later overruled the *Thornton* case in *O'Rourke* v *Camden London Borough Council* [1997] 3 All ER 23, HL, in which it was held that the relevant provisions of the Housing Act 1985 reveal no legislative intention to create a private-law remedy in damages for breach of the statutory duty to provide accommodation for homeless persons.

An action for damages for breach of statutory duty against a public authority is not available to a private individual if, on the construction of the relevant statute, there is no indication (express or implied) that Parliament intended to confer such a private-law remedy. Thus, in *Hague* v *Deputy Governer of Parkhurst Prison* [1991] 3 All ER 733, HL, the House of Lords held that no action for damages lay against the prison authorities for breach of the Prison Rules 1964 (made by the Home Secretary under the authority of the Prison Act 1952, and since replaced by the Prison Rules 1999). The claimant, a convicted prisoner, had been ordered to be transferred to another prison and there to be segregated from other prisoners in purported reliance on r. 43 (now r. 45) of the Prison Rules. In fact, there had been a breach of r. 43 since the governor of one prison has no power to order the segregation of a prisoner after his transfer to another prison; that power is exerciseable by the governor of the receiving prison. Notwithstanding this irregularity, the claimant could not sue for damages for breach of statutory duty since r. 43 is a purely preventive measure adopted, *inter alia,* for the purpose of conferring a necessary power to segregate disruptive prisoners and there is nothing in the legislation to show that Parliament intended to confer on a prisoner a private-law remedy for breach of it. Similarly, it has been held that Parliament did not intend to confer upon a child a right of action against a local authority for breach of the statutory duties imposed by the child care legislation (*X (minors)* v *Bedfordshire County Council* [1995] 3 All ER 353, HL), the child-minding legislation (*T (a minor)* v *Surrey County Council* [1994] 4 All ER 577), or by the special educational needs provisions of the Education Acts (*E (a minor)* v *Dorset County Council* [1995] 3 All ER 353, HL).

In subsequent cases it has been held that no action for damages will lie at the suit of an individual in respect of a failure by the Crown Prosecution Service to perform its statutory duty under the Prosecution of Offences Act 1985, and regulations made thereunder, of ensuring that custody time limits are not exceeded (*Olotu* v *Home Office* [1997] 1 All ER 385, CA), a failure by a local authority under part III of the Public Health Act 1936 (now part III of the Environmental Protection Act 1990) to abate a statutory nuisance relating to the unhealthy state of its accommodation (*Issa* v *Hackney London Borough Council* [1997] 1 All ER 999, CA), a failure by a fire authority to provide an adequate water supply under s. 13 of the Fire Services Act 1947 (*Capital and Counties plc* v *Hampshire County Council* [1997] 2 All ER 865, CA), or a failure by a health authority to provide after-care services for a discharged mental patient under s. 117 of the Mental Health Act 1983 (*Clunis* v *Camden and Islington Health Authority* [1998] 3 All ER 180, CA).

The statute may expressly provide for some other remedy, such as a complaint to a government minister or the imposition of a fine payable to the state. In this case the court may decide that the specified remedy is exclusive of all other remedies so that an action for damages will not lie (*Pasmore* v *Oswaldtwistle Urban District Council* [1898] AC 387, HL; *London Borough of Southwark* v *Williams* [1971] 2 All ER 175, CA; *Clunis* v *Camden and Islington Health Authority,* CA, above). Damages may, however, be claimed where the specified remedy is inadequate for the protection of the person injured, as in *Reffell* v *Surrey County Council* [1964] 1 All ER 743 where the specified remedy of mandamus would have been useless in the circumstances (see also *Monk* v *Warbey* [1935] 1 KB 75, CA). And the remedy of a complaint to a minister does not exclude other remedies if a public authority is guilty of breach of its statutory duty by a decision taken *ultra vires* or by a positive act (*Meade* v *Haringey London Borough Council* [1979] 2 All ER 1016, CA).

In addition to those just discussed, other considerations apply in determining whether a private individual can succeed in an action for damages for breach of a statutory duty against a public authority. The damage suffered by the claimant must have been caused directly by the breach of statutory duty. The damage must be of the type contemplated by the statute (*Gorris* v *Scott* (1874) LR 9 Ex 125).

11.3 INJUNCTIONS

11.3.1 Nuisance

Injunctions are most commonly issued against public authorities to prevent the commission or continuance of nuisances. In *Pride of Derby Angling Association Ltd* v *British Celanese Ltd and others* [1953] Ch 149, CA, the owners of fishing rights in the Trent and Derwent sued three separate bodies for polluting the rivers with municipal and industrial effluent. The defendants were British Celanese Ltd, an industrial company which was discharging chemicals and overheating the water; Derby Corporation, a local authority which was discharging sewage into the water; and the British Electricity Authority, a nationalised undertaking which was overheating the water in the rivers. The decision of Harman J to grant injunctions against all three defendants was upheld by the Court of Appeal. The operation of the injunction against Derby Corporation was suspended for 16 months to allow time for the corporation to make alternative arrangements for sewage disposal.

11.3.2 *Ultra vires* acts

An injunction may be issued to restrain a public authority from committing or continuing to commit *ultra vires* acts. In *Attorney-General (on the relation of Yapp)* v *Fulham Corporation* [1921] 1 Ch 440, the corporation had a statutory power to set up public wash-houses where people could wash their own clothes. The corporation set up and ran a municipal laundry where people's clothes were washed by employees of the corporation. In an action brought by the Attorney-General on the relation of a ratepayer, Sargant J held that the corporation was acting *ultra vires*. He granted a declaration to that effect and issued an injunction restraining the corporation, its officers, servants and agents, from acting in contravention of the declaration. In *Bradbury* v *Enfield London Borough Council* [1967] 3 All ER 434, CA, a case of *procedural ultra vires,* the Court of Appeal granted an injunction against a local education authority which had not followed the correct statutory procedure in introducing comprehensive schools in its area.

11.3.3 Breach of statutory duty

An injunction may be issued against a public authority to restrain a breach of statutory duty. In *Attorney-General (on the relation of McWhirter)* v *Independent Broadcasting Authority* [1973] 1 QB 629, the Court of Appeal granted an interim injunction against the IBA to prevent the showing on ITV of a film about Andy Warhol, an American artist and film director. There was prima facie evidence that the showing of the film would amount to a breach of the IBA's statutory duty 'to satisfy themselves that, so far as possible . . . nothing is included in the programmes which offends against good taste or decency or is likely . . . to be offensive to public feeling' (Television Act 1964, s. 3(1)(a); see now s. 6(1)(a) of the Broadcasting Act 1990). At a further hearing nine days later the injunction was discharged on it appearing that, by then, the members of the IBA had viewed the film and satisfied themselves of the matters specified in the statute. (Lord Denning, writing extra-judicially, has described the film as 'dreary and dull'; see *The Discipline of Law,* 1979, p. 129.)

11.4 SPECIFIC PERFORMANCE

A public authority may be sued for specific performance if it refuses to perform a contract which is both *intra vires* and specifically enforceable. In *Storer* v *Manchester City Council*

[1974] 3 All ER 824, the Court of Appeal ordered specific performance against a local housing authority of a contract to sell a council house to one of its tenants. But ordinary contractual principles apply in such cases and, if there is no contract to enforce, specific performance will be refused. There must be a concluded contract, based upon offer and acceptance, between the parties. In *Gibson* v *Manchester City Council* [1979] 1 All ER 972, the House of Lords held that the local housing authority had never made any offer to its tenant. There was, therefore, nothing for him to accept and no contract to enforce.

11.5 DECLARATIONS

11.5.1 Nature and availability

As mentioned in para 10.7, an interested party can apply for a declaration of his rights under RSC Ord. 15, r. 16 in ordinary private-law proceedings without at the same time claiming any other relief. The declaration has proved to be a valuable remedy against public authorities in all manner of situations. In *Price* v *Sunderland Corporation* [1956] 3 All ER 153, for example, a declaration was granted that the dismissal of teachers who refused to collect school dinner money was unlawful, while in *Sim* v *Rotherham Metropolitan Borough Council* [1986] 3 All ER 387 declarations were granted *in favour of* the employers to the effect that teachers were in breach of contract in refusing to 'cover' for absent colleagues and that their employers were entitled to make deductions from salaries in such circumstances.

A declaration is available against the Crown in private-law proceedings whereas the remedies of injunction and specific performance are generally not (Crown Proceedings Act 1947, s. 21, and see *Dyson* v *Attorney-General* [1911] 1 KB 410, CA; *Congreve* v *Home Office* [1976] 1 QB 629, CA; *Factortame Ltd* v *Secretary of State for Transport (No. 1)* [1989] 2 All ER 692, HL; *Factortame Ltd* v *Secretary of State for Transport (No. 2)* [1991] 1 All ER 70, CJEC and HL; *M* v *Home Office* [1993] 3 All ER 537, HL, para 11.11.6.4 below).

As a result of *O'Reilly* v *Mackman* [1982] 3 All ER 1124, HL, declaratory relief is not now normally available in private-law proceedings under RSC Ord. 15, r. 16 against a public authority for infringement of a right protected by *public* as opposed to *private* law. Where it is desired to protect a *public-law* right, the aggrieved citizen must normally proceed by way of an application for judicial review under Ord. 53 rather than by way of an ordinary private law action. An attempt to protect a public-law right by proceeding against a public authority in an ordinary private-law action for a declaration under Ord. 15, r. 16 will in most cases be contrary to public policy and, as such, an abuse of the process of the court which will result in the action being struck out (*O'Reilly* at p. 1134 *per* Lord Diplock).

Clearly, the ordinary private-law action for a declaration remains available against a public authority where the right to be protected is exclusively a matter of *private law*. Furthermore, *O'Reilly* v *Mackman* itself envisaged at least two exceptional cases involving *public-law* rights where it may nevertheless be appropriate to use *private law* rather than judicial-review proceedings to seek a declaration. The first exception is where the invalidity of the impugned decision (i.e., the *public-law* element in the case) presents itself as a collateral issue in a claim for infringement of a right arising under *private law*. The second is where none of the parties objects to proceeding by way of an ordinary private law action instead of by way of an application for judicial review. Other exceptions may be developed in the course of time on a case-by-case basis (ibid., *per* Lord Diplock; see further, para 11.11.2 below).

It must be emphasised that the *substantive law* applied in the cases mentioned in this paragraph and in para 11.5.2 below is *not* affected by the new *procedural* approach sanctioned by the House of Lords in *O'Reilly* v *Mackman*. Most of those cases were decided before important amendments to Ord. 53 in 1978 made judicial review a more effective remedy than before (*O'Reilly* v *Mackman per* Lord Diplock at p. 1131). Moreover, cases like *Ridge* v *Baldwin* [1964] AC 40, HL (para 11.5.2.4 below) and *Vine* v *National Dock Labour Board* [1957] AC 488, HL (para 11.5.2.2 below) involved questions of *private* law as well as questions of public law, while *Price* v *Sunderland Corporation* [1956] 3 All ER 153 and *Sim* v *Rotherham Metropolitan Borough Council* [1986] 3 All ER 387 were concerned *exclusively* with questions of private law. These cases could, therefore, still be commenced by means of an ordinary private-law action.

O'Reilly v *Mackman* has, however, affected the *procedure* whereby cases involving public authorities are brought before the court. If cases like *Prescott* v *Birmingham Corporation* [1955] Ch 210, CA and *Congreve* v *Home Office* [1976] 1 QB 629, CA (para 11.5.2.1 below) were to arise again, proceedings would need to be started by way of an application for judicial review and not by means of an ordinary private-law action for a declaration.

11.5.2 Scope

11.5.2.1 To challenge or confirm the validity of an administrative decision
In *Prescott* v *Birmingham Corporation* [1955] Ch 210, the Court of Appeal granted to a ratepayer a declaration that the corporation's scheme to provide free bus travel for old people resident in the city was *ultra vires* and void. It was said that the corporation's scheme was an abuse of its statutory discretion to charge 'such fares as they may think fit'. The corporation's statutory power to operate a transport service on commercial lines may have anticipated financial loss but did not authorise the subsidisation of one class of the community at the expense of another merely out of benevolence or philanthropy. *Prescott* v *Birmingham Corporation* was applied by the House of Lords in *Bromley London Borough Council* v *Greater London Council* [1982] 1 All ER 129 (a case on certiorari rather than declaration), in which it was held that the GLC had acted *ultra vires* in issuing a supplementary rate precept to London boroughs in order to finance a 25 per cent cut in London Transport fares. The sequel to *Prescott's* case was that Parliament passed the Public Service Vehicles (Travel Concessions) Act 1955 in order to legalise travel concessions already in force throughout the country for old people, the disabled and children. The Travel Concessions Act 1964 authorised such concessions for the future. The Conservative government, however, refused to introduce legislation to neutralise the effect of the *Bromley* case.

In *Congreve* v *Home Office* [1976] 1 QB 629, CA, a private citizen obtained from the Court of Appeal a declaration that the Home Secretary's threat to revoke a television licence, bought at a fee of £12 before the expiry of an existing one and in anticipation of a rise in the fee to £18, was unlawful. The reaction of the Home Secretary to this decision was to change his practice: any increase in the television licence fee is not now announced until post offices are closed on the day before the increase is to take effect.

A declaration was granted on judicial review in *R* v *Inner London Education Authority* *(ex parte Westminster City Council)* [1986] 1 All ER 19. Section 142(2) of the Local Government Act 1972 provided that 'a local authority may — (a) arrange for the publication within their area of information on matters relating to local government. . .'. In 1984, ILEA took a decision to mount a media and poster campaign seeking not only to give information about the needs of the education service but also to persuade the public to support ILEA's views on rate-capping. One poster bore the slogan 'Education cuts never heal', and an advertisement declared 'What do you get if you subtract £75 million from London's education budget?'

It was held that ILEA's decision was invalid because the political part of it (which was not merely subsidiary to the informative part) was not authorised by s. 142(2)(a). 'Information' does not include propaganda. The applicant had claimed certiorari and an injunction in addition to a declaration, but the judge, in the exercise of his discretion, considered that a declaration alone was sufficient to dispose of the case. The *ILEA* case is also authority for the proposition that where a public body decides to pursue two primary objects at the same time, one of them authorised and the other not, the decision is *ultra vires* because in reaching it the body has taken into account an irrelevant consideration (see also *Westminster Corporation* v *London and North Western Rly Co.* [1905] AC 426, HL). One result of cases like that involving ILEA was s. 2(1) of the Local Government Act 1986, which expressly states that

> a local authority shall not publish any material which, in whole or in part, appears to be designed to affect public support for a political party.

Furthermore, by the same Act, the words 'on matters relating to local government' in s. 142(2)(a) of the Local Government Act 1972 (see above) were replaced by the words 'relating to the functions of the authority'. ILEA itself was abolished by the Education Reform Act 1988 with effect from 1 April 1990.

A declaration was refused in *Luby* v *Newcastle-under-Lyme Corporation* [1965] 1 QB 214, CA. The claimant had sought a declaration that the corporation's resolution to increase all its council house rents was *ultra vires*. The corporation had a statutory discretion to make 'such reasonable charges for the tenancy or occupation of the houses as they may determine'. The claimant tenant complained that the corporation had not taken into account the personal circumstances of individual tenants and that his rent was unreasonable. The corporation had no rent rebate or differential rent scheme in operation. This was a conscious decision, so that the burden of helping tenants who could not pay off their rents fell on the general body of taxpayers (through social security payments) and not on the general body of local ratepayers (through rent rebates). The Court of Appeal held that the corporation had not abused its statutory discretion but had exercised it reasonably in the circumstances.

It is clear that, in appropriate circumstances, an application for a declaration can be used to challenge the validity of non-statutory government advice. Thus, in *Royal College of Nursing of the United Kingdom* v *DHSS* [1981] 1 All ER 545 (para 8.10.2.3), the House of Lords granted a declaration that advice on medically-induced abortions contained in a DHSS circular did not involve the performance of unlawful acts by nurses. In *Gillick* v *West Norfolk and Wisbech Area Health Authority* [1985] 3 All ER 402 (para 11.11.2 below), the House of Lords was prepared to hear a case in which advice in a DHSS circular on contraception was challenged, although in the end the House set aside the declaration made in the Court of Appeal to the effect that the advice was unlawful. Lord Bridge, clearly perturbed by this new judicial incursion into the field of administrative discretion, gave a warning that in such cases the court must be careful to confine itself to deciding only whether the proposition of law contained in the non-statutory advice is erroneous. In particular, the court must 'avoid . . . expressing *ex cathedra* opinions in areas of social and ethical controversy in which it has no claim to speak with authority or proffering answers to hypothetical questions of law which do not strictly arise for decision' ([1985] 3 All ER 402 at p. 427).

In a case of great significance, *Council of Civil Service Unions* v *Minister for the Civil Service* [1984] 3 All ER 935 (the 'GCHQ case', para 11.11.4 below), the House of Lords held that judicial review is available to challenge the validity of an administrative decision where that decision is taken in the exercise of a delegated prerogative power. Although no declaration was granted in the GCHQ case, it was made clear that the minister's unilateral decision, taken under a delegated prerogative power, to withdraw trade-union membership from civil servants employed at GCHQ had prima facie infringed the legitimate expectation of consultation enjoyed by those concerned. Only the pressing issue of national security prevented their Lordships from granting a declaration that the minister's decision was unlawful.

The issue of whether a power exercised *directly* under the prerogative is subject to judicial review was left open. However, the conventional wisdom, expressed in such cases as *Attorney-General* v *De Keyser's Royal Hotel Ltd* [1920] AC 508, HL, to the effect that the courts will inquire into the existence and extent of a claimed prerogative power, but not into the way a prerogative power is actually exercised in individual cases, was seriously questioned in the GCHQ case (see especially *per* Lord Scarman at p. 948 and Lord Roskill at pp. 955–956). It was later held by the Court of Appeal in *R* v *Secretary of State for Foreign and Commonwealth Affairs (ex parte Everett)* [1989] 1 All ER 655, CA, that judicial review can be used to question whether the Foreign Secretary, in the direct exercise of a prerogative power, has wrongly refused to issue a passport to a citizen. Although on the facts of the case no relief was granted, the Court of Appeal made it clear that the courts do have jurisdiction to inquire into the manner of exercise of a prerogative power provided that the subject matter of the particular power is justiciable (*per* O'Connor LJ at p. 658 and Taylor LJ at p. 660).

It is thus now established that some aspects, at least, of the exercise of the royal prerogative are amenable to judicial review. Which aspects are reviewable will be for the courts to decide on a case by case basis. In *R* v *Secretary of State for the Home Department (ex parte Bentley)* [1993] 4 All ER 442, DC, it was decided that the exercise by the Home Secretary of the royal prerogative of mercy is reviewable by the courts. Although the court made no declaration or other formal order against the Home Secretary, it did suggest that he look again at the case of Derek Bentley with a view to deciding whether it would be right to grant him a partial posthumous pardon in recognition of the generally accepted view that he should not have been hanged in 1953. (For the background to this case, see para 6.3.4, and note that it was distinguished in the quite different circumstances of *Reckley* v *Minister of Public Safety and Immigration (No. 2)* [1996] 1 All ER 562, PC, where it was held that the exercise of the prerogative of mercy in death sentence cases under the constitution of the Bahamas is not justiciable.)

Delivering the judgment of the court in the *Bentley* case, Watkins LJ said (at pp. 452–3) that it would be regrettable if the exercise of the prerogative of mercy were to be immune from legal challenge, regardless of the gravity of any legal errors made by the Home Secretary, given that this particular prerogative power is exercised by the minister on behalf of society as a whole and is an important feature of our criminal justice system. He pointed out that the GCHQ case had shown that the powers of the court cannot be ousted simply by invoking the word 'prerogative' and that the court can intervene when the nature and subject matter of a particular ministerial decision is amenable to the judicial process. It is amenable when the court is qualified to deal with the matter. It is not amenable when it involves such questions of policy that the court should not intervene because it is ill-equipped to do so.

Watkins LJ concluded (at p. 453) that there must be cases in which the exercise of the royal prerogative of mercy is reviewable. He gave the example of a situation where it was clear that a pardon had been refused to a person solely on the ground of sex, race or religion; here, he said, the court would be expected, and entitled, to interfere. Lord Roskill's statement in the GCHQ case ([1984] 3 All ER 935 at p. 956) that the exercise of the prerogative of mercy was a non-justiciable issue was described by Watkins LJ as a 'passing reference' and was clearly *obiter*. (See further on justiciable issues, para 11.5.3 below.)

11.5.2.2   To challenge or confirm the validity of a judicial decision, whether of a statutory tribunal or of a voluntary tribunal

In *Barnard* v *National Dock Labour Board* [1953] 2 QB 18, the claimants were granted by the Court of Appeal a declaration that their suspension from work was *ultra vires* and void. The National Dock Labour Board had a duty under statutory regulations to delegate disciplinary functions to local boards. One such local board, the London Dock Labour Board, purported to sub-delegate these disciplinary functions, which included the power to suspend a worker, to the port manager. The port manager suspended the claimants from work and pay for refusing to obey instructions. They appealed to the statutory appeal tribunal, which dismissed their appeals. They then applied to the High Court for a declaration that their suspension was wrongful on the facts of the industrial dispute. When they later discovered that they had been suspended by the port manager and not by the local board, they claimed a further declaration that their suspension was *ultra vires* and void.

The Court of Appeal held that the local board had acted *ultra vires* because it had no power to delegate its disciplinary functions to the port manager. The power of suspension was a judicial and not an administrative function. Administrative functions can often be delegated but judicial functions can only be delegated by a judicial tribunal if it is empowered to do so expressly or by necessary implication, as in *Local Government Board* v *Arlidge* [1915] AC 120, HL (para 11.8.3.2.2 below). There was nothing in the dock labour scheme which expressly authorised delegation of the power of suspension and authorisation could not be implied. The *Barnard* case was followed by the House of Lords in *Vine* v *National Dock Labour Board* [1957] AC 488, although their Lordships were uncertain whether the function in question was judicial or administrative.

11.5.2.3   To challenge or confirm both the validity of delegated legislation and the legality of the exercise of delegated legislative powers

In *Agricultural, Horticultural & Forestry Industry Training Board* v *Aylesbury Mushrooms Ltd* [1972] 1 All ER 280, the Minister of Labour had purported to establish an industrial training board by means of an order made in 1966 under the Industrial Training Act 1964. He was under a statutory duty, before making any such order, to 'consult any organisation . . . appearing to him to be representative of substantial numbers of employers engaging in the activities concerned'. The minister did not consult the Mushroom Growers' Association, which represented about 85 per cent of all mushroom growers in England and Wales. Donaldson J granted a declaration that this omission rendered the minister's order invalid as against mushroom growers.

In *R* v *Customs and Excise Commissioners (ex parte Hedges & Butler Ltd)* [1986] 2 All ER 164, DC, a particular regulation made under the authority of the Customs and Excise Management Act 1979 was declared *ultra vires* the Act in an application for judicial review because it went further than was permitted by the Act.

In *R* v *Secretary of State for the Home Department (ex parte Leech) (No. 2)* (1993) *The Times*, 20 May, CA, a declaration was granted that r. 33(3) of the Prison Rules 1964 (SI 1964, No. 388), which allows a prison governor to read and stop any letter written by an inmate, was *ultra vires* s. 47(1) of the Prison Act 1952 in so far as it purported to apply to correspondence between inmates and their legal advisers. In *R* v *Secretary of State for the Home Department (ex parte Simms)* [1999] 3 All ER 400, HL, it was held that the Home Secretary's policy (adopted in the exercise of his powers under the Prison Act 1952 and the Prison Rules 1964) of imposing an almost blanket ban on oral interviews between journalists and prison inmates was *ultra vires* and unlawful. The House of Lords granted a declaration to that effect. The Home Secretary's policy was unlawful because it effectively deprived a prisoner of what was described as 'a fundamental right' to seek to persuade a journalist, by means of oral interviews, to investigate the safety of the prisoner's conviction and to publicise his findings in an effort to gain access to justice for the prisoner (see *per* Lord Steyn, Lord Hobhouse and Lord Millett at pp. 410, 422 and 424, respectively, and note that from 1 April 1999 the Prison Rules 1964 were replaced by the Prison Rules 1999 (SI 1999, No. 728)).

In *R* v *Secretary of State for Social Security (ex parte Joint Council for the Welfare of Immigrants)* [1996] 4 All ER 385, CA, the whole of the Social Security (Persons from Abroad) Miscellaneous Amendments Regulations 1996 (SI 1996, No. 30), made by the Secretary of State under the Social Security Contributions and Benefits Act 1992 in order to discourage asylum claims by economic migrants, were declared *ultra vires* because they conflicted with rights already conferred upon asylum seekers by another statute, the Asylum and Immigration Appeals Act 1993. (This case was reversed by the Asylum and Immigration Act 1996, which excluded from housing accommodation and social security benefits those asylum seekers who do not claim asylum at the port of entry. However, it was held by the Court of Appeal in *R* v *Hammersmith and Fulham London Borough Council (ex parte M)* (1997) *The Times*, 19 February, CA, that such asylum seekers were nevertheless still entitled to seek assistance from local authorities under the National Assistance Act 1948, as amended, if they satisfied the necessary criteria.)

In *R* v *Lord Chancellor (ex parte Witham)* [1997] 2 All ER 779, DC, a declaration was granted to the effect that art. 3 of the Supreme Court Fees (Amendment) Order 1996 (SI 1996, No. 3191) was *ultra vires* s. 130 of the Supreme Court Act 1981 because that statutory provision did not empower the Lord Chancellor to prescribe court fees which were so high as to abrogate a citizen's common law constitutional right of access to the courts. (This decision was referred to with approval by Lord Browne-Wilkinson in *Pierson* v *Secretary of State for the Home Department* [1997] 3 All ER 577, HL, at p. 592.) The *Witham* case, above, was distinguished in *R* v *Lord Chancellor (ex parte Lightfoot)* [1998] 4 All ER 764, where it was held that arts. 8(1) and 9(b) of the Insolvency Fees Order 1986 (SI 1986, No. 2030), which require a deposit of £250 to be paid to the court on the presentation of a winding-up or bankruptcy petition, were not *ultra vires* the Insolvency Act 1986. In *R* v *Secretary of State for the Environment, Transport and the Regions (ex parte Spath Holme Ltd)* [2000] 1 All ER 884, CA, the Rent Acts (Maximum Fair Rent) Order 1999 (SI 1999, No. 6) was held to be *ultra vires* the Landlord and Tenant Act 1985, and was quashed by certiorari, in that it had been made for a purpose not authorised by the Act.

It should be noted that it is possible to attack the validity of delegated legislation in other ways without seeking a declaration or otherwise resorting to judicial review. For example, it may be done by way of defence to a criminal charge in the magistrates' court or the Crown Court, in which event the trial court may be expected to decide the question of validity.

Whether this course is available depends upon the construction of the parent statute. If this indicates that judicial review is excluded, the criminal court can, in general, determine the question of validity. This was decided by the House of Lords in *R* v *Wicks* [1997] 2 All ER 801, HL, doubting the correctness of *Bugg* v *DPP* [1993] 2 All ER 815, DC, in which it had been held that whether a criminal court had jurisdiction to investigate the validity of a by-law depended upon the distinction between substantive invalidity (in which case the court could investigate) and procedural invalidity (in which case it could not).

Bugg v *DPP*, above, was finally overruled by the House of Lords in *Boddington* v *British Transport Police* [1998] 2 All ER 203, HL. Here, the defendant, Mr Boddington, had been convicted by a stipendiary magistrate of an offence contrary to the British Railways Board's by-laws made under statutory authority, namely smoking a cigarette in a railway carriage where smoking was forbidden. His appeal against conviction by way of case stated to the Queen's Bench Divisional Court was dismissed, and he appealed to the House of Lords.

Their Lordships confirmed what was said in *R* v *Wicks*, above, and held that in such cases no distinction is to be made between substantive and procedural invalidity. It was further held that there was nothing in the parent statute or the by-laws to indicate that Parliament had intended to deprive the smoker of the opportunity to defend himself in a criminal court by alleging the invalidity of the by-law. However, on the facts, the appeal was dismissed because the relevant by-law, being wide enough to allow the imposition of a ban on smoking in all carriages, was not *ultra vires*.

As a result of *Boddington*, unless the relevant statutory provisions indicate the contrary, it is open to a defendant in criminal proceedings to defend himself by challenging the *procedural*, as well as the *substantive*, validity of the delegated legislation under which he stands charged.

Boddington was considered in *Secretary of State for Defence* v *Percy* [1999] 1 All ER 732, where it was held that once a criminal court has decided that by-laws are invalid the maker of them must respect that decision and not put up, or keep up, notices of by-laws which are known to be invalid. It was further held, however, that members of the public are not entitled to go on to private land to remove such notices.

It has been said to be neither necessary nor appropriate for a criminal trial to be adjourned so that the validity of a by-law can be determined by way of judicial review in the High Court (*R* v *Crown Court at Reading (ex parte Hutchinson)* [1988] 1 All ER 333, DC, in which the Crown Court was directed to hear and determine whether the Royal Air Force Greenham Common Byelaws 1985 were *intra vires* the Military Lands Act 1892 under which they had purportedly been made).

Alternatively, the challenge to the validity of delegated legislation may be made on an appeal by way of case stated from the magistrates to the Queen's Bench Divisional Court, as in *Chester* v *Bateson* [1920] 1 KB 829, DC, in which reg. 2A(2) of the Defence of the Realm Regulations 1914 was held to be *ultra vires* the Defence of the Realm Consolidation Act 1914, or *Dunkley* v *Evans* [1981] 3 All ER 285, DC, where part of the West Coast Herring (Prohibition of Fishing) Order 1978 was held to be *ultra vires* the parent Act. Or, again, the challenge may be made in an ordinary civil action between the parties, such as a claim for a sum of money, as in *Commissioners of Customs & Excise* v *Cure & Deeley Ltd* [1962] 1 QB 340, in which reg. 12 of the Purchase Tax Regulations 1945 was held to be *ultra vires* the Finance (No. 2) Act 1940. In *Chief Adjudication Officer* v *Foster* [1993] 1 All ER 705, HL, it was held that, where it is alleged before the social security commissioners that a provision in the statutory regulations which they are called upon to apply is *ultra vires*, the commissioners have jurisdiction to decide the issue of validity if it is necessary to do so in order to determine whether a decision under appeal from a social security appeal tribunal is wrong in law. (The decision of the Court of Appeal [1991] 3 All ER 846 was reversed on this point, but its conclusion that, on the facts, the relevant regulation was *intra vires* was affirmed.) In *General Mediterranean Holdings SA* v *Patel* [1999] 3 All ER 673, it was held that r. 48.7(3) of the Civil Procedure Rules 1998 (on the disclosure of privileged documents in applications for wasted costs orders) was *ultra vires* the Civil Procedure Act 1997.

Instead of striking down a piece of delegated legislation *in toto* it may be possible in some cases to *sever* the bad part from the good part and leave the latter intact. Severance is not possible where the bad part is inextricably interconnected with the good part. Severance was achieved in the *Aylesbury Mushrooms* case, where the minister's order was invalid as against mushroom growers but valid in relation to others affected by it, and in *Dunkley* v *Evans* where the order was invalid in relation to 0.8 per cent of the sea area covered by the order but valid in relation to the remaining 99.2 per cent. In *DPP* v *Hutchinson* [1990] 2 All ER 836, HL, it was held that some of the Royal Air Force Greenham Common Byelaws 1985 were *ultra vires* the Military Lands Act 1892 and that their invalidity could not be cured by severance since that would result, in effect, in the enforcement of byelaws radically different from those in fact made. The appellants, who had been convicted of offences against the byelaws, were held to have been wrongly convicted and their appeals were allowed.

11.5.2.4   To clarify the rights of public employees

In *Ridge* v *Baldwin* [1964] AC 40, HL, the Brighton Watch Committee dismissed its Chief Constable, Ridge, following his trial at the Old Bailey for conspiracy to obstruct the course of justice. Ridge had been acquitted but his conduct was severely criticised by the trial judge. The Municipal Corporations Act 1882 gave power to the watch committee to dismiss 'any borough constable whom they think negligent in the discharge of his duty, or otherwise unfit for the same'. (The power of dismissal is now contained in the Police Act 1996 and regulations made thereunder.) Ridge was dismissed summarily without a hearing, although ten days later the watch committee did allow his solicitor to make representations. Ridge brought an action in the High Court against Baldwin and other members of the watch committee claiming a declaration that his dismissal, being in violation of natural justice, was unlawful, *ultra vires* and void. If he could show that his dismissal was of no effect then, as an employee, he could resign voluntarily and claim payment of back pay and his pension.

The case produced considerable judicial disagreement. At first instance, Streatfeild J held that the watch committee's statutory power of dismissal had to be exercised in accordance with natural justice and that it had been so exercised. The Court of Appeal held unanimously that natural justice did not have to be observed because the power of dismissal was an executive or administrative act. The House of Lords held, by a majority of four to one, that natural justice did apply to the situation and that the failure to give Ridge a hearing was a violation of natural justice which rendered the dismissal void. The subsequent hearing given to Ridge's solicitor did not rectify the earlier defect. Ridge should have been told what was alleged against him, notified of the date of the hearing, and allowed to put his defence or explanation to the watch committee. Ridge was granted a declaration that his dismissal was null and void. This meant that Ridge had been lawfully employed all the time. He had also claimed damages and, in a compromise settlement, he received some £6,500 in back pay from the date of the wrongful dismissal to the date of the settlement and, from that date, a pension of about £1,100 per annum.

One important effect of *Ridge* v *Baldwin* is that the applicability of natural justice no longer depends on any distinction between administrative, judicial or quasi-judicial acts (see *Leech* v *Parkhurst Prison Deputy Governor* [1988] 1 All ER 485, HL, *per* Lord Oliver at p. 505). A person is entitled to a fair hearing if he has some right, interest or legitimate expectation which it would be unfair to deprive him of without a hearing (see, further, *Breen* v *Amalgamated Engineering Union* [1971] 2 QB 175, CA, *per* Lord Denning MR at p. 191).

Ridge v *Baldwin* was applied by the House of Lords in *Chief Constable of the North Wales Police* v *Evans* [1982] 3 All ER 141, a case in which the treatment of the respondent, a probationer constable, was described by Lord Hailsham of St Marylebone LC as 'little short of outrageous' (p. 143). The Chief Constable, acting on rumours about the respondent's private life, decided to dispense with the respondent's services. Without putting the rumours to him or allowing him to make any representations, the Chief Constable told the respondent that if he did not resign he would be discharged under the Police Regulations 1971 (SI 1971, No. 156). The respondent resigned. He obtained leave to challenge the Chief Constable's actions by way of judicial review. The House of Lords held that the Chief Constable had acted unlawfully and in breach of his duty under the Police Regulations. He was wrong to assume that he had an absolute discretion under the regulations to dispense with the services of a probationer constable and he had totally failed to observe the rules of natural justice. The respondent was granted declarations to the effect that the Chief Constable had acted unlawfully and that the respondent, by reason of his unlawfully-induced resignation, was entitled to the same rights and remedies, not including reinstatement, as he would have had if the Chief Constable had unlawfully dispensed with his services under the regulations. An order of mandamus to compel the reinstatement of the respondent was refused (see para 11.10.1 below).

11.5.2.5   To secure the recognition of a right, which is being denied, to engage in a particular occupation or activity
Examples of declarations being sought for this purpose are *Associated Provincial Picture Houses* v *Wednesbury Corporation* [1948] 1 KB 223, CA; and *Pyx Granite Co.* v *Ministry of Housing & Local Government* [1960] AC 260, HL. The remedy of a declaration is available for this purpose against private bodies as well as public authorities. In *Nagle* v *Feilden* [1966] 2 QB 633, CA, the claimant, a female trainer of horses, sued the stewards of the Jockey Club, a private body, for a declaration that their practice of refusing a trainer's licence to a woman was void as against public policy. She also claimed a mandatory injunction ordering the stewards to grant her a licence. The stewards of the Jockey Club controlled horse-racing on the flat throughout Great Britain. They were responsible for making the rules of racing. No person was allowed to train horses for racing at their race meetings unless he held a licence from them. It was the practice of the stewards not to grant a trainer's licence to a woman under any circumstances. The claimant had frequently applied for, and been refused, a licence, although the stewards did grant licences to her male employees.

At first instance, the judge, acting under RSC, Ord. 18, r. 19, struck out the claimant's statement of claim, and dismissed the action, on the ground that it disclosed no reasonable cause of action. The claimant appealed on the preliminary issue of whether she had a cause of action. The Court of Appeal held that, although there was no contract between the parties, the claimant had an arguable case on grounds of public policy. The court said that the stewards' practice of discriminating against women applicants was arbitrary, absurd and out of touch with the present state of society in England. It was an abuse of a monopoly power which could be remedied, if necessary, by a declaration and an injunction ([1966] 2 QB 633 *per* Lord Denning MR at p. 647 and Danckwerts LJ at p. 651). The case did not proceed to full trial: the parties settled and the Jockey Club voluntarily changed its rules.

11.5.3 Disadvantages of declarations

A declaratory judgment merely states the legal position of the parties. It does not order or prohibit any action to be taken. It cannot quash a decision made by a public authority within its jurisdiction (*Punton* v *Ministry of Pensions & National Insurance (No. 2)* [1964] 1 All ER 448, CA). Being merely declaratory, it cannot be directly enforced. Disobedience to it is not contempt of court (*Webster* v *Southwark London Borough Council* [1983] 2 WLR 217). It is, however, always assumed that a public authority, especially the Crown, will not flout the law once it has been declared by the court.

The remedy is discretionary and will be granted only in exceptional circumstances (*Maxwell* v *Department of Trade & Industry* [1974] 2 All ER 122, CA). A declaration must be appropriate in the circumstances (*Williams* v *Home Office (No. 2)* [1981] 1 All ER 1211 *per* Tudor Evans J at p. 1248). The discretion should not be exercised so as to grant a declaration in a civil court to a defendant in criminal proceedings that the facts alleged by the prosecution do not in law prove the offence charged (*Imperial Tobacco Ltd* v *Attorney-General* [1980] 1 All ER 866, HL; *Attorney-General* v *Able* [1984] 1 All ER 277; *R* v *Director of Public Prosecutions (ex parte Camelot Group plc)* (1997) *The Independent*, 22 April, DC). Such a declaration would not be binding on the criminal court but would inevitably prejudice the criminal trial. Nor should a final declaration be made if there remains a dispute about the material facts of the case (*Commissioners of Inland Revenue* v *Rossminster Ltd* [1980] 1 All ER 80, HL).

The application for a declaration must raise a justiciable issue; i.e., an issue which is capable of determination by the application of legal principles. Questions of morality, as opposed to law, are non-justiciable in this sense. Thus, in *Cox* v *Green* [1966] 1 Ch 216, medical ethics were held not to be a justiciable issue. The question whether a government decision or act was in fact necessitated by the requirements of national security is a non-justiciable issue (*Council of Civil Service Unions* v *Minister for the Civil Service* [1984] 3 All ER 935, HL), as is probably also the exercise of such prerogative powers as the making of treaties, the grant of honours, the dissolution of Parliament and the appointment of ministers (*ibid., per* Lord Roskill at p. 956; *R* v *Secretary of State for Foreign and Commonwealth Affairs (ex parte Everett)* [1989] 1 All ER 655, CA, *per* O'Connor LJ at p. 658 and Taylor LJ at p. 660; in *R* v *Secretary of State for Foreign and Commonwealth Affairs (ex parte Rees-Mogg)* [1994] 1 All ER 457, DC (para 8.7) the court inclined to the view that a question relating to the transfer or exercise of the prerogative power to conduct foreign security policy was a non-justiciable issue).

There must be a real dispute between the parties; the action for a declaration cannot be used to seek an answer to hypothetical questions (*Russian Commercial & Industrial Bank* v *British Bank for Foreign Trade Ltd* [1921] AC 438, HL, *per* Lord Sumner at p. 452; *Blackburn* v *Attorney-General* [1971] 2 All ER 1380, CA).

The claimant must have *locus standi* ('a place of standing') in order to apply for a declaration in his own name against a public authority. *Locus standi* means, in effect, that the court will not grant the claimant a declaration unless he has a sufficient interest in the matter to which the application relates. It is a rule of procedure which is designed to discourage busybodies from meddling in other people's affairs and occupying the time of the courts. The question of *locus standi* is a fundamental one which affects the jurisdiction of the court. If the claimant has no *locus standi* then the court has no jurisdiction to hear the case and it is not open to the parties to purport to confer the necessary jurisdiction by agreeing to waive the issue of *locus standi* (*R* v *Secretary of State for Social Services (ex parte Child Poverty Action Group)* [1989] 1 All ER 1047, CA).

A person has *locus standi* to take proceedings against a public authority if his legal rights are likely to be affected by the activities of the authority (as in *Ridge* v *Baldwin* [1964] AC 40, HL, para 11.5.2 above; and *Anisminic Ltd* v *Foreign Compensation Commission* [1969] 2 AC 147, HL, para 11.13.3 below). Some other special interest falling short of a legal right will probably also suffice.

11.6 RELATOR ACTIONS

If a claimant's legal rights are not affected, and he has no special interest above that of the general public, he has no *locus standi* to apply for a declaration in his own name. He must use a different procedure called the relator action, which involves bringing in the Attorney-General. For example, in *Barrs* v *Bethell* [1982] 1 All ER 106 (para 11.5.3 above) the judge, having decided that the claimant ratepayers had no *locus standi,* encouraged them to seek the Attorney-General's consent to relator proceedings. This procedure is especially appropriate in the case of public wrongs because a private person is not entitled to bring an action in his own name, either for a declaration under Ord. 15, r. 16, or for an injunction, for the purpose of preventing or remedying a public wrong.

This was firmly established in *Gouriet* v *Union of Post Office Workers* [1977] 3 All ER 70, HL, in which the House of Lords held that the claimant (whom the Attorney-General had refused to assist) was not entitled to proceed with his application against the defendants for a declaration and an interim injunction to prevent the defendants' threatened boycott of mail to South Africa. In so holding, the House of Lords unanimously reversed a unanimous Court of Appeal. It should be noted, however, that the *Gouriet* case does not affect the alternative remedy of judicial review (para 11.11 below). A private citizen who is unable to obtain the appropriate relief in private law, and who cannot obtain the help of the Attorney-General, may nevertheless seek to prevent or remedy a public wrong by means of an application for judicial review under s. 31 of the Supreme Court Act 1981 (*Commissioners of Inland Revenue* v *National Federation of Self-Employed & Small Businesses Ltd* [1981] 2 All ER 93, HL, *per* Lord Diplock at p. 103, Lord Scarman at p. 110 and Lord Roskill at pp. 116–17). He may obtain a declaration under that section if he has a sufficient interest in the matter and the case is one in which a prerogative order could be granted.

A relator action is an action brought by the Attorney-General 'on the relation' (at the instance) of some other person. The Attorney-General, as an officer of the Crown, represents the public interest. The relator action derives from a special power exercised by the Crown to ensure that public authorities keep within their powers. The Attorney-General may bring proceedings *ex officio* on his own initiative but they are more often brought at the instance of a relator. In either case, the decision whether to proceed is within the Attorney-General's unfettered discretion. Thus, the refusal of the Attorney-General to give his consent to a relator action is not subject to review by the courts (*London County Council* v *Attorney-General* [1902] AC 165, HL; *Gouriet* v *Union of Post Office Workers* [1977] 3 All ER 70, HL).

The conduct of relator proceedings is under the control of the Attorney-General (*Gouriet's* case, *per* Lord Wilberforce at p. 80, Viscount Dilhorne at p. 94, Lord

Edmund-Davies at p. 106 and Lord Fraser of Tullybelton at p. 117). But the costs must be paid by the relator. Nevertheless, the relator action is a valuable procedure. The ordinary citizen, who may not have a sufficient interest to enable him to sue for a declaration or an injunction in his own name, may yet see justice done by calling in the Attorney-General. Relator actions were involved in some of the cases already mentioned, such as *Attorney-General* v *Fulham Corporation* [1921] 1 Ch 440, para 11.3.2 above, and *Attorney-General* v *Independent Broadcasting Authority* [1973] 1 QB 629, CA, para 11.3.3 above.

B THE PREROGATIVE REMEDIES AND NON-PREROGATIVE REMEDIES IN PUBLIC LAW

11.7 INTRODUCTION

The three prerogative remedies available against public authorities on an application for judicial review are certiorari, prohibition and mandamus. They were called 'prerogative writs' until their title was changed to 'prerogative orders' in 1938. Originally, they were writs brought by the King against his own officials to ensure that they exercised their functions properly and did not abuse their powers.

In modern times the prerogative orders are available to both private citizens and public authorities. Moreover, *non-prerogative* remedies in the form of a declaration, an injunction or damages may be claimed and granted on an application for judicial review.

Although set within the framework of *public* as distinct from *private* law, judicial review proceedings are essentially *civil* as opposed to *criminal* in character. The Crown is usually the nominal claimant but it is generally a private citizen who benefits from the proceedings if they are successful.

The power whose exercise it is sought to have reviewed will usually be derived from a statutory source; it may, however, be a common-law power (*Council of Civil Service Unions* v *Minister for the Civil Service* [1984] 3 All ER 935, HL). Perhaps the best known attempt to classify the circumstances in which the courts will intervene to prevent or remedy abuses of power by public authorities was in *Associated Provincial Picture Houses Ltd* v *Wednesbury Corporation* [1948] 1 KB 223, CA, one of the most often-cited cases in our courts today, in which Lord Greene MR laid down the so-*called 'Wednesbury* principles' of unreasonableness or perversity. However, since too much classification may hinder the growth of developing law, care must be taken not to treat Lord Greene's judgment as definitive and exhaustive (*Nottinghamshire County Council* v *Secretary of State for the Environment* [1986] 1 All ER 199, HL, *per* Lord Scarman at p. 203).

One of the most recent attempts at classification, though not meant to be exhaustive, is that contained in Lord Diplock's opinion in *Council of Civil Service Unions* v *Minister for the Civil Service* [1984] 3 All ER 935, HL, with which the other Law Lords expressly agreed. Lord Diplock said (at p. 950) that the grounds on which administrative action is subject to control by judicial review can be classified under three heads:

(a) *illegality* (covering substantive *ultra vires*), where the public authority has made an error of law such as purporting to exercise a power it does not possess;

(b) *irrationality* (in the *Wednesbury* sense of 'perversity'), where the authority has acted so unreasonably that no reasonable authority would have made the decision ('a decision which is so outrageous in its defiance of logic or of accepted moral standards that no sensible person . . . could have arrived at it': *per* Lord Diplock at p. 951);

(c) *procedural impropriety* (covering procedural *ultra vires* and violation of the principles of natural justice), where the authority has failed in its duty to act fairly.

Lord Diplock envisaged that further grounds might be added on a case-by-case basis. The three grounds he cites cover the matters dealt with in para 11.5.2 (above), and paras 11.8.3, 11.9.3 and 11.10.3 (below). Lord Diplock (at p. 950) suggested that English law might possibly adopt the principle of 'proportionality' at some time in the future. This principle, which is already recognised by the administrative law of several member states of the European Community, dictates that administrative action can be struck down (even though not perverse or absurd) if it is *disproportionate to the benefit it seeks to obtain or the mischief it seeks to avoid.* It is intended to cover the situation where a sledgehammer is taken to crack a nut when there is an efficient pair of nutcrackers readily available (*R v Secretary of State for the Home Department (ex parte Brind)* (1989) *The Times,* 30 May, DC, *per* Watkins LJ; decision affirmed by the Court of Appeal at [1990] 1 All ER 469; decision of the Court of Appeal affirmed by the House of Lords, *sub nom. Brind and others v Secretary of State for the Home Department* [1991] 1 All ER 720).

These words were spoken in a case in which several journalists challenged the legality of the restrictions imposed by the Home Secretary on the broadcasting of interviews with members and representatives of some named Northern Ireland extremist groups. One of the grounds of challenge was that the restrictions were a disproportionate response to the mischief they sought to control, namely the excessive amount of publicity given to such persons and groups. In upholding the legality of the Home Secretary's actions, the House of Lords made it clear that, while the principle of proportionality as understood elsewhere in Europe is not recognised by English law as a separate ground for reviewing administrative action, it is a relevant factor in a challenge based on *Wednesbury* unreasonableness or perversity. In other words, whereas administrative action which is not in itself irrational will not be struck down by the court merely because it is 'out of proportion' to the occasion, it may be struck down where that lack of proportion indicates irrationality (see, for example, [1991] 1 All ER 720 *per* Lord Ackner at p. 735).

The principle of proportionality as a separate ground of challenge to administrative decision-making was rejected by a majority of their Lordships on the facts of *Brind* v *Secretary of State for the Home Department* for the reason that it would require the judges to consider the merits of the decision under review and, if necessary, to substitute their own decision (although, presumably, Lord Templeman would have gone this far: see [1991] 1 All ER 720, 726). It was suggested by two of the Law Lords that rejection of the proportionality principle in the present case did not close the door to its possible development in future cases, as envisaged by Lord Diplock in *Council of Civil Service Unions* v *Minister for the Civil Service* [1984] 3 All ER 935, HL (see [1991] 1 All ER 720 *per* Lord Bridge and Lord Roskill at pp. 724 and 725 respectively). Another considered that the recognition of the proportionality principle was surrounded by disadvantages which made it an impractical proposition (*per* Lord Lowry at p. 739).

The grounds contained within Lord Diplock's tripartite classification are not mutually exclusive. This may be illustrated by reference to *Wheeler* v *Leicester City Council* [1985] 2 All ER 1106, HL, in which an administrative decision was condemned on a number of grounds. The council passed a resolution to ban the Leicester rugby club from using a recreation ground (on which it trained and played its club matches) for 12 months. The ban as imposed because the club, while opposing apartheid in South Africa, had refused the council's request to condemn the tour of an English rugby team to that country and to put pressure on three Leicester players not to join the tour. The council's resolution was quashed by certiorari, the House of Lords holding that the ban was unreasonable, unfair and a procedural impropriety in that the council had used illegitimate pressure in an attempt to coerce the club into accepting the council's own policy on the council's own terms. It was further held that the council had misused its power by punishing the club when it had done no wrong, as in *Congreve* v *Home Office* [1976] 1 QB 629, CA (para 11.5.2.1 above).

Wheeler v *Leicester City Council* was applied in *R* v *Lewisham London Borough Council (ex parte Shell UK Ltd)* [1988] 1 All ER 938, DC. Under s. 71 of the Race Relations Act 1976 local authorities have a duty to see that their functions are carried out with due regard to the need to eliminate unlawful racial discrimination and to promote good relations between different racial groups. Shell UK Ltd was a company registered and trading in the United Kingdom. It did not trade in South Africa but other subsidiaries of the same multinational group did carry on business there. The council decided, as part of its duty under the Race Relations Act 1976, to adopt a policy of boycotting Shell UK's products and of seeking to persuade other local authorities to do the same in order to put pressure on the parent companies of the group to give up their South African interests. Shell UK applied for a declaration that the council's decision was *ultra vires* and unlawful. A declaration to that effect was granted. The court held that the council's decision, although not unreasonable in the *Wednesbury* sense, was taken not merely to achieve a lawful object (the promotion of good race relations within its area) but also to achieve an extraneous and impermissible object (pressurising the group to sever trading links with South Africa). The lawful object of the council's decision was so inextricably bound up with, and tainted by, the unlawful object as to render the decision as a whole *ultra vires* its powers. It was observed that the scope of s. 71 of the Race Relations Act 1976 is wide and covers all the activities of a local authority, but that a council nevertheless cannot use its powers under that section to punish someone who has done nothing contrary to English law (see *per* Neill LJ at p. 951).

Lord Diplock's illegality ground covers a number of different issues which are often treated separately, such as excess of jurisdiction, misuse of power, error of law, failing to perform a statutory duty, fettering a discretion, taking into account irrelevant considerations and leaving out of account relevant considerations, and unauthorised delegation of the exercise of a discretion.

Misuse of power and taking into account irrelevant considerations were among the grounds upon which the local authority's ban on deer hunting on certain of its land was challenged in *R* v *Somerset County Council (ex parte Fewings)* [1995] 3 All ER 20, CA. The local authority had a statutory power to acquire land for the 'benefit, improvement or development of their area' (Local Government Act 1972, s. 120(1)(b)). The majority of the councillors who voted for the ban did so on the ethical ground of animal cruelty. The applicants, who were regular hunters on the land, argued that the ban was unlawful because it had been made on purely moral grounds and ignored the purpose of the local authority's statutory power. At first instance, it was held that the ban was an unlawful exercise of power because the view that deer hunting was morally repulsive was irrelevant. The local authority could only ban hunting if it was objectively necessary as the best way of managing the deer herd or if it preserved or enhanced the amenity of the area. The ban was quashed by certiorari. The local authority's appeal to the Court of Appeal was dismissed by a majority decision on the ground that the authority had failed to exercise its discretion in accordance with the stated statutory purpose. There was disagreement over the morality argument. Two of the three judges in the Court of Appeal thought that the cruelty argument is not necessarily irrelevant to a local authority's consideration of what is for the benefit of the area.

R v *Secretary of State for the Home Department (ex parte Venables)* [1997] 3 All ER 97, HL, was an application for judicial review by the two boys who were convicted at the age of ten of the murder of a two-year-old child, James Bulger. They were both subjected to the mandatory sentence of detention during Her Majesty's pleasure. The trial judge recommended that the 'penal' (or 'tariff') element in their sentence should be eight years. Later, the Lord Chief Justice recommended an increase to ten years and the Home Secretary decided that it should be increased to 15 years. The Home Secretary's decision was quashed by certiorari because (a) he had failed to take into account the possibility of early release based upon the progress and development of the applicants during their detention, and (b) he had taken into account irrelevant considerations, namely the public protests about the level of the tariff to be fixed in the case of the applicants. (See also *Pierson* v *Secretary of State for the Home Department* [1997] 3 All ER 577, HL, and *R* v *Secretary of State for the Home Department (ex parte Hindley)* [2000] 2 All ER 385, HL.)

A successful challenge to an administrative decision on the irrationality ground involves crossing, in every case, a high threshold. It is necessary to demonstrate that the decision is unreasonable in that it is 'beyond the range of responses open to a reasonable decision-maker' (*R* v *Ministry of Defence (ex parte Smith)* [1996] 1 All ER 257, CA, *per* Sir Thomas Bingham MR and Thorpe LJ at pp. 263 and 272 respectively, quoting from the submissions of counsel for the applicants). The threshold is lower where the decision affects human rights, especially the right to life. It is higher where the decision is of a 'policy-laden, esoteric or security-based nature' and remote from the ordinary experience of judges (ibid., *per* Sir Thomas Bingham MR at p. 264).

R v *Ministry of Defence (ex parte Smith)* involved a challenge, on the ground of irrationality, to the lawfulness of the government's policy (made under prerogative powers) prohibiting homosexual men and women from serving in the armed forces and requiring the discharge from the forces of any person found to be homosexual. The Court of Appeal held that the threshold of irrationality had not been crossed and that the policy was not unlawful. Although the human rights of the four applicants were in issue and the court had a constitutional duty to protect those rights, the Court of Appeal took the view that, at the time the applicants were discharged from the Royal Air Force and the Royal Navy between November 1994 and January 1995 on the ground of their homosexuality, the government's policy could not be classified as irrational. It had the support of both Houses of Parliament and of the defence ministry's professional advisers, and, at the relevant time, the different policy applicable in other NATO countries and in Australia, Canada and New Zealand had been adopted too recently to be of assistance to the United Kingdom government.

Criticism of the government's policy when the case was before the Divisional Court in June 1995 (see [1995] 4 All ER 427) led to a review, which, however, concluded that the policy should remain in place (see *The Times*, 5 March 1996).

It is proposed now to discuss certiorari, prohibition and mandamus in turn, to be followed by an account of the common procedure available for securing prerogative and non-prerogative relief on judicial review (para 11.11). The distinction between judicial review and an appeal will then be considered (para 11.12), and this is followed by an examination of the question of exclusion of judicial review (para 11.13).

11.8   CERTIORARI

11.8.1   Nature

Certiorari is short for *certiorari volumus* ('we wish to be informed'). It is a remedy which is used to bring before the High Court the decision of some inferior court, tribunal or authority so that its legality may be examined. The decision will be quashed if it is found to be invalid. Disobedience to an order of certiorari, as by refusing to submit the record of a case to the High Court for review, is punishable as a contempt of court.

11.8.2 Availability

11.8.2.1 Introduction
Certiorari has been sought successfully to quash the decision of, *inter alia,* the Crown Court, a county court, a magistrates' court, a coroner's court, the board of visitors of a prison, the Medical Appeal Tribunal, the Criminal Injuries Compensation Board, the Advertising Standards Authority, a mental health review tribunal, the registrar of companies, a local election court, a local valuation court, a local authority, an immigration officer, and of a government minister made after a public inquiry.

An applicant for certiorari must have sufficient interest in the matter to which the application relates (para 11.11.4 below).

11.8.2.2 Certiorari and bodies exercising a public function
Until recently, certiorari was not available to question the decisions of voluntary (i.e., non-statutory) domestic tribunals, whose powers generally exist within the field of private law and, therefore, outside the reach of prerogative remedies (*Ex parte Fry* [1954] 2 All ER 118, DC; *Buckoke* v *Greater London Council* [1971] 1 Ch 655, CA). By an oversight the Divisional Court was prepared to (but did not) grant prerogative relief in *R* v *Aston University Senate (ex parte Roffey)* [1969] 2 QB 538, DC (para 3.4.2). This preparedness to invoke the prerogative jurisdiction against a voluntary domestic tribunal was criticised by the Court of Appeal in *Herring* v *Templeman* [1973] 3 All ER 569, CA. However, now that it is clear that the jurisdiction to review judicially the decisions of inferior bodies depends not upon any distinction between their statutory or non-statutory method of creation but upon whether a particular body is exercising a sufficiently public function, there can be no doubt that the universities have a public character which is sufficient to bring their decisions within the High Court's supervisory jurisdiction in appropriate circumstances (*Page* v *Hull University Visitor* [1993] 1 All ER 97, HL; see further, para 11.11.2 below). Certiorari and mandamus were granted against a *statutory* disciplinary committee in *R* v *Statutory Committee of Pharmaceutical Society of Great Britain (ex parte Pharmaceutical Society of Great Britain)* [1981] 2 All ER 805, DC. It should be noted that although the prerogative remedies are not available against the members of a voluntary tribunal in respect of the exercise of a purely private function, the private law remedies of declaration and injunction *are* available.

Certiorari does not lie directly against the Crown, although, in practice, this limitation is not a serious obstacle since it *is* available against individual ministers of the Crown. It is also available against the Ombudsman (the Parliamentary Commissioner for Administration), a creature of statute (*R* v *Parliamentary Commissioner for Administration (ex parte Dyer)* [1994] 1 All ER 375, DC, where, however, relief was refused on the facts). It is not, however, available against the Parliamentary Commissioner for Standards (*R* v *Parliamentary Commissioner for Standards (ex parte Al Fayed)* [1998] 1 All ER 93, CA; see further, para 11.11.2 below). Certiorari probably cannot be used as a means of challenging delegated legislation. This is because certiorari applies to acts of a judicial nature as opposed to legislative or administrative acts (*R* v *Electricity Commissioners (ex parte London Electricity Joint Committee Co. (1920) Ltd)* [1924] 1 KB 171, CA; *R* v *Legislative Committee of the Church Assembly (ex parte Haynes-Smith)* [1928] 1 KB 411, DC; for legitimate methods of challenging delegated legislation, see para 11.5.2 above).

11.8.2.3   Certiorari and the Crown Court

Whether certiorari is available to question the decisions of the ordinary courts of law depends on the status of the individual court. The decisions of superior courts of record, which include the House of Lords, the Court of Appeal and the High Court itself are not subject to judicial review by the Queen's Bench Division. The Employment Appeal Tribunal is also a superior court of record and, as such, is not amenable to the prerogative jurisdiction of the Queen's Bench Division (Employment Tribunals Act 1996, s. 20). On the other hand, decisions of the county courts and magistrates' courts, which are inferior courts, can be challenged by means of judicial review.

The Crown Court is in an anomalous position as regards judicial review. It is a superior court of record (Supreme Court Act 1981, s. 45(1)) and yet, in some circumstances, its decisions are subject to judicial review. The Supreme Court Act 1981, s. 29(3) provides as follows:

> In relation to the jurisdiction of the Crown Court, other than its jurisdiction in matters relating to trial on indictment, the High Court shall have all such jurisdiction to make orders of mandamus, prohibition or certiorari as the High Court possesses in relation to the jurisdiction of an inferior court.

A 'helpful pointer' to the meaning of the phrase 'matters relating to trial on indictment' is to ask whether the decision in question is a 'decision affecting the conduct of a trial on indictment' (*Smalley* v *Crown Court at Warwick* [1985] 1 All ER 769, HL, *per* Lord Bridge at p. 780, the other Law Lords agreeing with him). No such decision of the Crown Court can be challenged in the High Court by means of certiorari. Thus, if a judge in the Crown Court at a trial on indictment should impose an *ultra vires* penalty, or act in violation of natural justice, or err in law, his action cannot be quashed by certiorari and the aggrieved party's only remedy will be an appeal against sentence to the Court of Appeal, criminal division, or against conviction on the ground that the conviction is unsafe. The object of s. 29(3) in exempting from challenge matters relating to trial on indictment is to prevent the delay that might otherwise occur in criminal trials if an application for judicial review were available (*Smalley* v *Crown Court at Warwick*, above, *per* Lord Bridge at p. 779; *DPP* v *Crown Court at Manchester and Ashton* [1993] 2 All ER 663, HL, *per* Lord Slynn at p. 669; *DPP* v *Crown Court at Manchester and Huckfield* [1993] 4 All ER 928, HL, *per* Lord Browne-Wilkinson at p. 933).

The following decisions of the Crown Court have been held also to affect the conduct of a trial on indictment and, as such, to be excluded from judicial review: an order refusing costs to an acquitted defendant (*Ex parte Meredith* [1973] 2 All ER 234, DC); a decision refusing to grant legal aid to defendants for their trial on indictment (*R* v *Crown Court at Chichester (ex parte Abodundrin)* (1984) 79 Cr App R 293, DC); a decision to revoke a previous order discharging a legal aid certificate (*R* v *Crown Court at Isleworth (ex parte Willington)* [1993] 2 All ER 390, DC); an order refusing the defendant his pre-trial costs (*R* v *Central Criminal Court (ex parte Spens)* [1993] COD 194: this aspect of *Ex parte Spens* was not discussed in *DPP* v *Crown Court at Manchester and Ashton* [1993] 2 All ER 663, HL, below; see also *R* v *Harrow Crown Court (ex parte Perkins)* (1998) *The Times*, 28 April, DC); a decision at the pre-trial stage not to disclose sensitive material to the defence (*R* v *Crown Court at Southwark (ex parte Johnson)* [1992] COD 364, DC); an order made at the trial for disclosure to the defence of inadmissible statements made during an informal complaints procedure (*R* v *Crown Court at Chelmsford (ex parte Chief Constable of the Essex Police)* [1994] 1 All ER 325, DC); a decision about the starting date of the trial (*R* v *Southwark Crown Court (ex parte Ward)* (1994) *The Times*, 19 August, DC); an order that an indictment should lie on the file and not be proceeded with without leave of the court (*R* v *Central Criminal Court (ex parte Raymond)* [1986] 2 All ER 379, DC — approved by the House of Lords in *DPP* v *Crown Court at Manchester and Ashton* [1993] 2 All ER 663 (see below)); an order lifting reporting restrictions previously imposed under s. 39 of the Children and Young Persons Act 1933 (*R* v *Crown Court at Winchester (ex parte B (a minor))* [1999] 4 All ER 53, DC, not following *R* v *Crown Court at Leicester (ex parte S (a minor))* [1992] 2 All ER 659, DC, and *R* v *Cardiff Crown Court (ex parte M (a minor))* (1998) *The Times*, 28 April, DC; note, however, that in *R* v *Crown Court at Manchester (ex parte H)* [2000] 2 All ER 166, DC, *R* v *Cardiff Crown Court (ex parte M (a minor))* was preferred to *R* v *Crown Court at Winchester (ex parte B (a minor))*, which was not followed); and a decision of the Crown Court at the conclusion of a trial whether or not to exercise its discretion under what is now s. 24(5) of the Legal Aid Act 1988 (para 1.9.7.3.2) to remit or order repayment of any contribution due from or paid by the defendant under a legal aid contribution order (*Sampson* v *Crown Court at Croydon* [1987] 1 All ER 609, HL, *per* Lord Bridge at pp. 613–614, the other Law Lords agreeing with him). Such a decision is to be regarded as an integral part of the trial process and is, therefore, not reviewable. On the other hand, the legal aid contribution order itself, made by the court before the trial begins under what is now s. 23(1) of the Legal Aid Act 1988 (para 1.9.7.3.2), does not affect the conduct of the trial and is not an integral part of the trial process. It is, therefore, reviewable by the High Court on an appropriate ground; for example, that it was made in spite of unchallenged evidence that the defendant's disposable income and capital did not exceed the prescribed limits (*Sampson* v *Crown Court at Croydon*, above).

The prohibition imposed by s. 29(3) of the Supreme Court Act 1981 against reviewing Crown Court decisions which relate to trial on indictment cannot be circumvented by using instead the general power of judicial review conferred by s. 31 of the same Act. This is because the Crown Court is a 'superior court', and the High Court has no jurisdiction to review the decisions of a superior court except where expressly granted by s. 29(3) (*R* v *Crown Court at Chelmsford (ex parte Chief Constable of the Essex Police)* [1994] 1 All ER 325, DC; see also *R* v *Director of Public Prosecutions (ex parte Kebeline)* [1999] 4 All ER 801, HL, below).

Section 29(3) of the Supreme Court Act 1981 clearly lays down that decisions of the Crown Court on other aspects of its jurisdiction, not concerned with trials on indictment, shall be capable of challenge by means of certiorari. In *Smalley's* case, for example, an order which caused the forfeiture of a recognisance given by a surety for a defendant who failed to surrender to his bail at the Crown Court was held to be reviewable. The House of Lords said that the order was not a 'matter relating to trial on indictment' within s. 29(3) since it did not affect the conduct of the trial in any way.

Smalley's case was applied in somewhat unusual circumstances in *R* v *Crown Court at Maidstone (ex parte Gill)* [1987] 1 All ER 129, DC, in which the applicant sought an order of certiorari to quash a forfeiture order made by the Crown Court in respect of two motor cars. The applicant had lent the cars to his son. Without the applicant's knowledge the son used the cars for two separate journeys to supply prohibited drugs. Later the son pleaded guilty to a charge of supplying heroin and was sentenced to a term of imprisonment; a second charge was not proceeded with.

The trial judge made an order under s. 27 of the Misuse of Drugs Act 1971 forfeiting the applicant's two cars. In judicial review proceedings in the High Court it was held that the forfeiture order was not a 'matter relating to trial on indictment' within s. 29(3) of the Supreme Court Act 1981 because it did not affect the conduct of the trial of the applicant's son in any way. It followed that the High Court was not precluded by s. 29(3) from considering the application to quash the forfeiture order. Having considered the merits, the court quashed the order on the ground that one of the cars had not, in fact, been used in the offence to which the son had pleaded guilty and that, although the other car had been so used, the applicant had had no reason to suspect that it would be used to transport prohibited drugs.

If the case of *Gill* had been decided the other way, and it had been held that the forfeiture order was a matter relating to trial on indictment, the implications would have been very serious. The applicant's remedy by way of judicial review would have been barred by s. 29(3) and, indeed, he would have had no remedy at all against the Crown Court's imposition of an unlawful order. There could be no appeal to the Court of Appeal, criminal division, because the applicant had been neither 'convicted' nor 'sentenced' (see [1987] 1 All ER 129 *per* Lord Lane CJ at p. 131 and para 6.2.2).

An application to stay criminal proceedings on the ground that they are an abuse of the process of the court has been held to be a 'matter relating to trial on indictment' within s. 29(3). It follows that the decision of the trial judge at the Crown Court on such an application is not subject to judicial review.

This was decided by the House of Lords in *DPP* v *Crown Court at Manchester and Ashton* [1993] 2 All ER 663, HL, reversing the Queen's Bench Divisional Court. Two earlier decisions to the contrary given by the Divisional Court — *R* v *Central Criminal Court (ex parte Randle)* (1990) [1992] 1 All ER 370, DC, and *R* v *Crown Court at Norwich (ex parte Belsham)* [1992] 1 All ER 394, DC, — were overruled. In addition, the correctness of two other decisions which had been influenced by the *Randle* and *Belsham* cases — *R* v *Crown Court at Southwark (ex parte Customs and Excise Commissioners)* [1993] 1 WLR 764, DC, and *R* v *Central Criminal Court (ex parte Spens)* [1993] COD 194, DC, — was doubted. *R* v *Central Criminal Court (ex parte Raymond)* [1986] 2 All ER 379, DC (see above), was approved.

The prohibition against reviewing the trial judge's decision to stay proceedings as an abuse of process cannot be circumvented by instead challenging a prosecutor's decision to prosecute. Thus, in *R* v *Director of Public Prosecutions (ex parte Kebeline)* [1999] 4 All ER 801, HL, it was held that a decision of the Director of Public Prosecutions to consent to a prosecution is not reviewable in the absence of dishonesty, bad faith or exceptional circumstances.

In *DPP* v *Crown Court at Manchester and Huckfield* [1993] 4 All ER 928, HL, it was held by the House of Lords, again reversing the Queen's Bench Divisional Court, that a decision of the Crown Court to quash an indictment for lack of jurisdiction is a 'matter relating to trial on indictment' and is, accordingly, not reviewable by the High Court.

Both in this case and in *DPP* v *Crown Court at Manchester and Ashton* [1993] 2 All ER 663, the House of Lords indicated that much difficulty had been caused in previous cases because the Divisional Court had treated Lord Bridge's 'helpful pointers' to the meaning of the statutory phrase 'matters relating to trial on indictment' as if they constituted a statutory definition or test. As mentioned above, in *Smalley* v *Crown Court at Warwick* [1985] 1 All ER 769 Lord Bridge suggested (at p. 780) that a 'helpful pointer' is to ask whether the decision in question is one 'affecting the conduct of a trial on indictment'. His second 'helpful pointer', suggested in *Sampson* v *Crown Court at Croydon* [1987] 1 All ER 609, 613, is to ask whether the decision is an 'integral part of the trial process'. An examination of the authorities in *DPP* v *Crown Court at Manchester and Huckfield* [1993] 4 All ER 928 led Lord Browne-Wilkinson to the conclusion (while eschewing any attempt to lay down a comprehensive definition of the meaning of the statutory phrase) that there may be a third 'helpful pointer', namely whether the decision arose in the issue (including the costs thereof) between the Crown and the defendant as formulated by the indictment (see [1993] 4 All ER 928 at p. 934). If it did, then it is probably excluded from review by s. 29(3) since review could delay the defendant's trial. If it did not, then the decision might well not be excluded from review by s. 29(3) since it is collateral to the indictment and reviewing it would not delay the trial.

The status of *R* v *Central Criminal Court (ex parte Director of Serious Fraud Office)* [1993] 2 All ER 399, DC, is uncertain following the decisions of the House of Lords in *DPP* v *Crown Court at Manchester and Ashton* [1993] 2 All ER 663 and *DPP* v *Crown Court at Manchester and Huckfield* [1993] 4 All ER 928.

In the *Serious Fraud Office* case, the Divisional Court held that a decision taken before the trial begins to dismiss fraud charges under s. 6 of the Criminal Justice Act 1967 (see para 1.7.6.3.5) is not a 'matter relating to trial on indictment' and is, therefore, reviewable in the High Court. According to the House of Lords in *Ashton*, the *Serious Fraud Office* decision was not based on the discredited cases of *Randle* and *Belsham*, which were merely 'referred to' therein, and, since the *Serious Fraud Office* case was not concerned with the same issues as *Randle, Belsham* and *Ashton* it was 'undesirable' to say anything about it (see *per* Lord Slynn at [1993] 2 All ER 663, 670). According to the House of Lords in *Huckfield*, however, 'much weight' was attached to *Randle* and *Belsham* in the *Serious Fraud Office* case, although again their Lordships were not prepared to express a view on the correctness of the latter decision but pointed out that it was concerned with a different issue and one which may raise special considerations (see *per* Lord Browne-Wilkinson at [1993] 4 All ER 928, 934).

Delay is the commonest ground for applying to stay criminal proceedings which are alleged to be an abuse of the process of the court. According to the Court of Appeal when issuing guidance to trial judges and lawyers in *Attorney-General's Reference (No. 1. of 1990)* [1992] 3 All ER 169, CA, proceedings should rarely be stayed on the ground of delay in bringing the matter to trial even where the delay is unjustifiable. They should rarely be stayed in the absence of any fault on the part of the prosecuting authorities and should never be stayed where the delay is due to the complexity of the case or to the actions of the defendant himself. When the judge is contemplating the imposition of a stay in an appropriate case, the correct test to apply is whether the defendant has shown on the balance of probabilities that the delay would cause him serious prejudice in that he could no longer receive a fair trial.

Delivering the judgment of the court in *Attorny-General's Reference (No. 1 of 1990)*, Lord Lane CJ expressed concern about the public suspicion and mistrust that would arise if stays became a matter of routine and he hoped that the court's decision would lead to a substantial reduction in the number of applications for stays on the ground of delay (see [1992] 3 All ER 169 at pp. 176–7).

R v *Bow Street Metropolitan Stipendiary Magistrate (ex parte DPP)* [1992] COD 267, DC, was concerned with the decision of a stipendiary magistrate that proceedings against three police officers for conspiracy to pervert the course of justice in the 'Guildford Four' case 17 years earlier were an abuse of the process of the court and should be stayed. This was not a case governed by s. 29(3) of the Supreme Court Act 1981 since it did not involve the Crown Court; the magistrate's decision was, therefore, reviewable. On judicial review, the decision was quashed because, in spite of the long delay and the adverse publicity the case had received, the Divisional Court was convinced that a fair trial was still possible. The three officers were acquitted by a jury at their subsequent trial at the Central Criminal Court. (See *The Times*, 20 May 1993. See also *R* v *Croydon Justices (ex parte Dean)* [1993] 3 All ER 129, DC, where on the facts it was held to be an abuse of process for the Crown Prosecution Service to prosecute a defendant who had been told by the police that he would not be prosecuted; the decision of the magistrates to commit the defendant for trial at the Crown Court was quashed by certiorari.)

When three former police officers involved in the 'Birmingham Six' investigation were prosecuted for conspiracy to pervert the course of justice and perjury, the case was withdrawn from the jury by the trial judge at the Crown Court on the ground that to proceed with the trial would amount to an abuse of process. The judge, Garland J, was of the opinion that the defendants would not receive a fair trial due to prejudicial publicity and due to the risk that the jury would be confused by the issues involved in the case. Since the decision was on a 'matter relating to trial on indictment' within s. 29(3) it was not, in the light of *DPP* v *Crown Court at Manchester and Ashton* [1993] 2 All ER 663, HL, reviewable. Garland J's decision caused considerable surprise and consternation; it raised the issues of public suspicion and mistrust of the criminal justice system about which Lord Lane CJ had spoken in *Attorney-General's Reference (No. 1 of 1990)*, above (see *The Times*, 8 and 16 October 1993).

The power of the High Court to review, where appropriate, decisions of the Crown Court by virtue of s. 29(3) of the Supreme Court Act 1981 is not limited to the ground of excess of jurisdiction. It extends to all grounds which are normally considered appropriate for the use of prerogative orders. Thus, in *R* v *Crown Court at Leeds (ex parte City of Bradford Chief Constable)* [1975] QB 314, DC, a decision of the Crown Court in a licensing appeal from the justices was quashed on the ground of error of law on the face of the record.

11.8.3   Scope

11.8.3.1   Where the decision is ultra vires
In *R* v *London Borough of Hillingdon (ex parte Royco Homes Ltd)* [1974] QB 720, DC, a planning permission was quashed by certiorari where the planning authority had attached conditions to the permission which were so unreasonable as to be *ultra vires* the planning legislation. The planning authority was held to have acted *ultra vires* in spite of the fact that there was a statutory power to impose 'such conditions as they think fit'. In *Westminster City Council* v *Greater London Council* [1986] 2 All ER 278, HL, decisions of the GLC (taken without consulting the London boroughs and to be implemented after its abolition on 1 April 1986) to provide grants totalling £76m for the ILEA, an arts centre and 900 voluntary organisations were quashed by certiorari on the ground that they were *ultra vires* the relevant legislation. (See also *Wheeler* v *Leicester City Council* [1985] 2 All ER 1106, HL, para 11.7 above.)

11.8.3.2   Where the decision was reached in violation of the principles of natural justice

11.8.3.2.1   The rule against bias.   This principle is expressed in the maxim *nemo judex in causa sua potest* ('no man can be a judge in his own cause'). In *R* v *Sunderland Justices*

[1901] 2 KB 357, CA, the local authority in Sunderland had bought a public house in order to demolish it so that a road could be widened. The local authority then made an agreement with a brewery under which the local authority would surrender the licence for the pub it had bought and would not object to the brewery's application for a licence relating to new premises nearby, provided the brewery paid the authority £10,000. The licensing committee of justices who heard the brewery's application included the chairman of the authority's highways committee, who had organised the agreement between the brewery and the local authority, and four other Sunderland councillors. The Court of Appeal ruled that the grant of the licence to the brewery would be set aside because of the committee's bias.

In *R* v *Hendon Rural District Council (ex parte Chorley)* [1933] 2 KB 696, DC, a ratepayer obtained an order of certiorari to quash the decision of the council which had voted to allow building to take place on a piece of land. The decision was made in violation of the rule against bias in that one of the councillors who voted on the resolution had a financial interest in the development of the land. He was the sole member of a firm which was currently advertising the land for sale.

In *R* v *Birmingham City Justices (ex parte Chris Foreign Foods (Wholesalers) Ltd)* [1970] 3 All ER 945, DC, certiorari was issued to quash a magistrate's decision that some imported sweet potatoes should be condemned as unfit for human consumption. At the conclusion of the case for the owners of the potatoes, the magistrate had retired to consider his decision with officers of the public health department, who had initiated the proceedings, saying that he wished to 'take advice' from them. This was held to be a breach of the requirement that proceedings should be conducted openly and fairly.

The rule against bias was violated again in *R* v *Barnsley Metropolitan Borough Council (ex parte Hook)* [1976] 3 All ER 452, CA. H was a trader with a stall in a Barnsley market. One evening, after the market and the public lavatories had closed, he satisfied an urgent need to relieve himself by urinating in a side street. His behaviour came to the attention of the local council, which decided to ban him for life from trading in the market. He was given an opportunity to put his case before the council meeting at which this decision was taken. But the market manager, who had brought the complaint before the council in the first place, was present throughout the meeting and in a position to give the council his view of the evidence.

H applied for an order of certiorari to quash the council's decision. The Court of Appeal was unanimous in holding that the order would be granted. The rules of natural justice applied to the situation because the council was determining questions affecting the rights of a citizen. And the rules had been violated as the council had heard the market manager's evidence in the absence of H or his representatives, and the market manager, who was in effect a prosecutor, had been present throughout the deliberations leading to the decision to ban H from the market. Two of the three judges in the appeal found an additional reason in favour of H. They said that the court could also interfere by means of certiorari to quash the council's decision on the ground that the punishment inflicted on H was excessive and out of proportion to the occasion (*per* Lord Denning MR at p. 457 and Sir John Pennycuick at p. 461).

One of the most serious aspects of bias is the existence of a *direct pecuniary interest* in the outcome of a case. Thus, in the well-known case of *Dimes* v *Grand Junction Canal Co.* (1852) 3 HL Cas 759, HL, a decision adverse to the defendant, given by no less a judicial figure than the Lord Chancellor himself, was set aside on it appearing that his Lordship was the owner of several thousand pounds' worth of shares in the claimant company. There was no evidence that the Lord Chancellor had been influenced in fact by his pecuniary interest in the company, but where a judge has a direct pecuniary interest in the outcome of a case bias is conclusively presumed and the maintenance of public confidence in the administration of justice demands that his decision should not be allowed to stand (*R* v *Gough* [1993] 2 All ER 724, HL, *per* Lord Goff at p. 730; see also *per* Lord Woolf at p. 740, and *R* v *Bow Street Metropolitan Stipendiary Magistrate (ex parte Pinochet Ugarte) (No. 2)* [1999] 1 All ER 577, HL, below).

There will not be an automatic breach of the rule against bias where the judge's interest in the case, whether pecuniary or otherwise, is merely *indirect* or *remote*. In this situation, bias is not presumed; a real danger of bias would need to be established in accordance with the test endorsed in *R* v *Gough* [1993] 2 All ER 724, HL (see below). In *R* v *Mulvihill* [1990] 1 All ER 436, CA, the defendant's sole ground of appeal against his conviction for conspiracy to rob was that the trial judge at the Crown Court had failed to disclose that he owned 1,650 shares in the National Westminster Bank plc, one of whose branches was involved in the charge against the defendant. The Court of Appeal had no difficulty in dismissing the appeal. It was said that, save possibly in very exceptional circumstances, a judge in a criminal trial is not bound to declare that he has a remote interest, such as a shareholding, in a company whose premises are alleged to be the scene of the crime (ibid., *per* Brooke J at p. 441).

The allegation of bias must be more than a flimsy pretext to have an inconvenient decision set aside (see e.g., *R* v *Mulvihill,* above). The proper test is whether the facts disclose that there was a *real danger of bias*. This was finally established by the House of Lords in *R* v *Gough* [1993] 2 All ER 724, HL, in which the previous case law was subjected to a detailed examination. This analysis disclosed two strands of authority on the correct test to be applied to alleged bias. First, some cases had laid down that the test was whether there was a 'real danger' (sometimes expressed as a 'real likelihood') of bias. (See, for example, *R* v *Sunderland Justices* [1901] 2 KB 357, CA, above; *R* v *Camborne Justices (ex parte Pearce)* [1955] 1 QB 41, DC, below.) Secondly, other cases had held that the test was whether a reasonable person might reasonably suspect bias (sometimes expressed as the 'reasonable suspicion' or 'appearance of bias' test). (See, for example, *Metropolitan Properties Co.* v *Lannon* [1969] 1 QB 577, CA; *R* v *Liverpool City Justices (ex parte Topping)* [1983] 1 All ER 490, DC, below; *R* v *Morris* [1991] Crim LR 385, CA, below.) The first test is the more rigid of the two; there is a danger that the second test can be used to overturn decisions on the flimsiest pretext of bias (see *R* v *Camborne Justices (ex parte Pearce),* above, *per* Slade J at pp. 51–2; *R* v *Gough,* above, *per* Lord Goff at p. 732 and Lord Woolf at p. 740).

In *R* v *Gough,* the House of Lords unanimously supported the first test and preferred to state it in terms of *real danger* rather than real likelihood in order to emphasise that the test is concerned with the *possibility* and not the probability of bias (see *per* Lord Goff at p. 737). Some of the previous case law had suggested that the test varied according to whether the person against whom bias was alleged was a justice of the peace or other judicial figure or whether he was a member of a jury. Their Lordships in *R* v *Gough* further held that the 'real danger of bias' test applies in like manner (with one exception noted below) in all cases of alleged bias on the part of justices of the peace, members of other inferior courts, and jurors.

The House affirmed the following principles. First, evidence of *actual* bias is not required (see the explanation of this given at [1993] 2 All ER 724 *per* Lord Goff at p. 728 and Lord Woolf at p. 740). Secondly, explaining and approving *Dimes* v *Grand Junction Canal Co.* (1852) 3 HL Cas 759, HL, above, in the exceptional case of a person acting in a judicial capacity who has a direct pecuniary or proprietary interest in the outcome of the proceedings before him, bias is assumed and his decision will be set aside without further inquiry. (See further, *R v Bow Street Metropolitan Stipendiary Magistrate (ex parte Pinochet Ugarte) (No. 2)* [1999] 1 All ER 577, HL, below.) Thirdly, expressly approving *R v Camborne Justices (ex parte Pearce)* [1955] 1 QB 41, DC, below, in all other cases the test to be applied is whether in the light of all the circumstances there was a real danger of bias in the sense that the person against whom bias is alleged might have unfairly disfavoured the claim of a party to the proceedings. Fourthly, in cases involving justices' clerks it must be shown that not only was there a real danger of bias on the part of the clerk but also that his participation in the decision-making process created a real danger that his bias would prejudice the justices against a party to the proceedings. This depends upon whether the clerk was requested to, and did, give advice to the justices. If he was so requested, the court of review may be prepared to infer from the facts that there was a real danger of the clerk's bias adversely infecting the justices' views. If he was not so requested, any bias on his part would not normally influence the outcome of the proceedings.

The case of *R v Gough* [1993] 2 All ER 724, HL, arose out of an appeal against conviction in a criminal case. Initially, the appellant and his brother had been charged with robbery but the brother was discharged at the end of committal proceedings and the appellant alone was indicted for conspiracy to rob. The brother was frequently referred to by name at the trial and the jury was shown his photograph and made aware of his address. One of the jurors was the brother's next door neighbour but she did not recognise him until he began shouting in court after the appellant had been found guilty and sentenced to 15 years' imprisonment. The appellant appealed on the ground that the presence on the jury of this particular juror amounted to a material irregularity in the course of the trial in that there was a reasonable suspicion that a fair trial had not been possible. The Court of Appeal, applying the real danger of bias test and holding that, in the circumstances, there was no danger that the appellant might not have had a fair trial, dismissed the appeal (see [1992] 4 All ER 481, CA).

The Court of Appeal refused leave to appeal to the House of Lords but certified that the case involved a point of law of general public importance (see para 6.2.2.4), namely, 'where a complaint is made after the conclusion of a trial that a juror may have been biased against the defendant, what is the proper test for the Court of Appeal to apply in deciding whether or not to order a retrial?' The House of Lords itself granted leave to appeal. Their Lordships did not confine themselves to a consideration of the certified question alone but conducted a fairly comprehensive review of the authorities on bias. The House affirmed the decision made below and dismissed the appeal for the reasons given above. The 'real danger of bias' test propounded in *Gough* was applied in *R v Inner West London Coroner (ex parte Dallaglio)* [1994] 4 All ER 139, CA, where decisions of the coroner inquiring into the disaster which befell the passenger launch *Marchioness* on the Thames in August 1989 were quashed by certiorari after he had described some relatives and survivors as 'mentally unwell' and referred to one bereaved mother as 'unhinged'. The coroner's language was held to have given rise to a real possibility that he had unconsciously allowed himself to become biased against the relatives. (See further on this case, para 2.5.5.) It was also applied in *R v Wilson* (1995) *The Times*, 24 February, CA, in which it was held that a real danger of bias had been caused by the presence on a jury of the wife of a prison officer who worked with the defendants while they were in prison on remand. The defendants' convictions were quashed and a retrial ordered.

Before the decision of the House of Lords in *R v Bow Street Metropolitan Stipendiary Magistrate (ex parte Pinochet Ugarte) (No. 2)* [1999] 1 All ER 577, HL, it had been assumed (wrongly, as it turned out) that the automatic disqualification rule (i.e., that bias is conclusively presumed) applied only to a judge who has a pecuniary or proprietary interest in the outcome of a case, as in *Dimes* v *Grand Junction Canal Co.* (1852) 3 HL Cas 759, HL, above. In *Pinochet (No. 2)*, the House of Lords extended the automatic disqualification rule to a judge with a non-financial interest whose decision may promote a cause in which he is involved together with one of the parties to the case. Lord Browne-Wilkinson said ([1999] 1 All ER 577 at p. 588) that there is 'no good reason' for limiting the automatic disqualification rule to cases of pecuniary or proprietary interest. He continued:

> The rationale of the whole rule is that a man cannot be a judge in his own cause . . . [I]f, as in the present case, the matter at issue does not relate to money or economic advantage but is concerned with the promotion of the cause, the rationale disqualifying a judge applies just as much if the judge's decision will lead to the promotion of a cause in which the judge is involved together with one of the parties.

(See also *per* Lord Goff, Lord Hope and Lord Hutton at pp. 591–92, 595–96 and 597, respectively).

Pinochet (No. 2) arose out of the attempt by the former head of state of Chile, Senator Pinochet, to avoid being extradited to Spain to face trial for crimes against humanity. In *R v Bow Street Metropolitan Stipendiary Magistrate (ex parte Pinochet Ugarte) (Amnesty International intervening)* [1998] 4 All ER 897, HL, proceedings in which Amnesty International was granted leave to take part, it had been held by a majority of three to two that the Senator could not claim immunity from the criminal processes, including extradition, of the United Kingdom in respect of acts of torture and hostage-taking since such acts were not a function of a head of state.

A few days after judgment was given it was discovered that one of the Law Lords in the majority, Lord Hoffmann, was a director and chairperson of Amnesty International Charity Ltd, which had been formed to carry out Amnesty International's charitable purposes, and the Senator petitioned the House of Lords to set aside its judgment. It was held unanimously by five Law Lords who had not been involved in the earlier appeal proceedings that Lord Hoffmann was automatically disqualified from hearing that appeal since, in effect, his failure to disclose his connection with Amnesty International meant that he was acting as a judge in his own cause. The judgment was set aside and the matter was referred to another appellate committee of the House for rehearing. (The rehearing, at which the Senator was again unsuccessful, took place before *seven* Law Lords and is reported as *R v Bow Street Metropolitan Stipendiary Magistrate (ex parte Pinochet Ugarte) (Amnesty International intervening) (No. 3)* [1999] 2 All ER 97, HL.)

In *Pinochet (No. 2)*, the House of Lords emphasised that the facts of the case were exceptional and that a judge is not expected to stand down, or disclose his position to the parties, in every case involving a charity with whose work he is connected. He need do this only where he has an active role as trustee or director of a charity which has a close connection with a party to the litigation (see, for example, *per* Lord Browne-Wilkinson at [1999] 1 All ER 577, 589).

Pinochet (No. 2) encouraged the making of allegations of judicial bias in a number of subsequent cases in which applications were made to the Court of Appeal for permission to appeal. Although these cases were not so much concerned with the automatic disqualification rule as with the real danger of bias test laid down in *R v Gough*, above, their potential impact on public confidence in the legal process led to them being dealt with by a particularly strong Court of Appeal comprising the Lord Chief Justice, the Master of the Rolls and the Vice-Chancellor. They are reported at [2000] 1 All ER 65, beginning with *Locabail (UK) Ltd* v *Bayfield Properties Ltd.*

The 28-page judgment in these cases emphasises, first, the fundamental nature of a litigant's right to a fair trial by an impartial tribunal, and, secondly, that a judge would be as wrong to accede to a tenuous or frivolous objection to his partiality as he would to ignore one of substance. Thus, it seems that no objection can ever be soundly based on the judge's religion, ethnic or national origin, gender, age, class, means, or sexual orientation, and only rarely can an objection be soundly based on the judge's educational, service or employment background, previous political associations, membership of social, sporting or charitable bodies, Masonic associations, previous judicial decisions or extra-judicial utterances (see [2000] 1 All ER 65 at p. 77).

On the other hand, a real danger of bias may well be thought to arise, for example, out of personal friendship or animosity between the judge and any member of the public involved in the case, or if for any other reason there are real grounds for suspecting that the judge's inability to ignore extraneous considerations and prejudices will prevent him from dealing objectively with the case before him. In these instances, the judge, although not automatically disqualified, will be expected to excuse himself from trying the case where there is real doubt over his impartiality (see [2000] 1 All ER 65 at pp. 77–78). Failure to do so will lead, on appeal, to the setting aside of his decision if a real danger of bias is established.

In the event, permission to appeal was granted in only one of the five cases; the defendant's appeal was allowed and a retrial ordered. This was a case in which the Court of Appeal concluded (reluctantly) that there was a real danger of bias on the part of a recorder who had decided a personal injury case in the county court in favour of the claimant. The recorder had views which were pro-claimant and anti-insurer, and had frequently expressed those views in legal publications. Taking a broad, commonsense approach, the Court of Appeal held that the possibility could not be excluded that the recorder might have unconsciously leant in favour of the claimant and against the defendant (who was supported by an insurance company) in deciding the factual issues between them (see [2000] 1 All ER 65 at pp. 92–93).

In *Seer Technologies Ltd* v *Abbas* (2000) *The Times*, 16 March, an application by an Arab defendant that an inquiry as to damages should not be heard by a Jewish judge was dismissed.

The status of some of the previous cases on bias is in doubt following *R* v *Gough* [1993] 2 All ER 724, HL. Insofar as they applied the 'reasonable suspicion'/'appearance of bias' test they are wrongly decided. In some of them, however, the conclusion on the facts may have been the same if the correct test, the 'real danger of bias' test, had been applied.

In *R* v *Sussex Justices (ex parte McCarthy)* [1924] 1 KB 256, DC, certiorari was issued to quash the applicant's conviction for dangerous driving on it appearing that the clerk to the justices was a member of a firm of solicitors acting for the claimant in a civil action against the applicant for damage sustained in the collision. This was in spite of the fact that, although he retired with them when they went to consider their decision, the clerk was not called upon to advise the magistrates and did not refer to the case. In *R* v *Essex Justices (ex parte Perkins)* [1927] 2 KB 475, DC, a maintenance order against a husband was quashed by certiorari where the justices' clerk was a solicitor with the firm acting for the wife, while in *R* v *Altrincham Justices (ex parte Pennington)* [1975] QB 549, DC, a conviction for selling vegetables under weight to a school was quashed because one of the magistrates was a member of the local education authority. In *R* v *Huggins* [1895] 1 QB 563, DC, the conviction of an unlicensed ship's pilot was quashed because one of the magistrates was a licensed pilot. In *R* v *Liverpool City Justices (ex parte Topping)* [1983] 1 All ER 490, DC, it was held that magistrates should not have proceeded to hear a charge against the applicant after they had been supplied with computerised court sheets disclosing the existence of other charges against the applicant. In *R* v *Morris* [1991] Crim LR 385, CA, *Topping* was applied when it was held that the defendant's conviction would be quashed since, on the facts, the trial judge was wrong to have refused to discharge a juror in a case where a Marks & Spencer store detective gave evidence and the juror declared herself to be a personnel assistant with Marks & Spencer, albeit at a different store.

All the cases mentioned in the preceding paragraph seem to have proceeded on the basis of the reasonable suspicion/appearance of bias test. If cases similar to these were to occur now, they would, in the light of *R* v *Gough* [1993] 2 All ER 724, HL, need to be decided in accordance with the real danger of bias test. It was in *R* v *Sussex Justices (ex parte McCarthy)* [1924] 1 KB 256, DC, that Lord Hewart CJ (at p. 259) uttered his famous dictum that 'it is not merely of some importance but is of fundamental importance that justice should not only be done, but should manifestly and undoubtedly be seen to be done'. According to their Lordships in *R* v *Gough* (repeating what was said earlier in *R* v *Camborne Justices (ex parte Pearce)* [1955] 1 QB 41, DC, *per* Slade J at pp. 51–2), Lord Hewart CJ's judgment in the *Sussex Justices* case was the cause of much misunderstanding and the continued citation of his dictum was in danger of giving the erroneous impression that 'it is more important that justice should appear to be done than that it should in fact be done' (see *R* v *Gough*, above, *per* Lord Woolf at p. 740).

In *R* v *Camborne Justices (ex parte Pearce)*, above, a county council had prosecuted a trader under the Food and Drugs Act 1938. The trader complained later that the justices' clerk, who had been invited to advise the magistrates in their private room, was a member of the county council and there was, therefore, a reasonable suspicion of bias. The Divisional Court refused to interfere because the justices' clerk, although a county councillor, was not a member of the council's health committee (which had initiated the prosecution) and in the circumstances there was no real danger of bias on his part. It was made clear that a mere suspicion or possibility of bias is not a sufficient basis on which to challenge the validity of a decision. In *R* v *Deal Justices* (1881) 45 LT 439, DC, it was held not to be an infringement of the rule against bias for a magistrate to hear a prosecution brought by a society for preventing cruelty to animals to which he was a subscriber.

Re Manchester (Ringway Airport) Compulsory Purchase Order 1934 (1935) 153 LT 219 arose out of a statutory application to quash and not an application for certiorari as such, but the principle involved is the same. A compulsory purchase order had been made by Manchester Corporation to assist the development of Manchester airport. Before the order was confirmed by the appropriate minister a public inquiry was held, during which the inquiry inspector was flown over the proposed site in an aeroplane piloted by one of the witnesses for Manchester Corporation, which supported the scheme. Those who objected to the scheme argued that they, too, should have been represented on the flight. It appeared that the witness pointed out some landmarks to the inspector but was unable to say much because of the noise. The minister subsequently confirmed the compulsory purchase order. It was held that there was no substance in the objectors' allegation that the minister was biased and the court declined to quash the order. It was pointed out, however, that the position might have been different if the inspector and the witness had discussed controversial matters on the flight without later giving the objectors a fair opportunity to comment on what was said.

The danger that he may appear to be biased against one side or the other makes it extremely unwise for a judge to refer in public outside court to a case he is currently trying. If his comments are reported in the media and he disagrees with the contents of the report he must make clear in court his disagreement, and what are the inaccuracies in the report, so as to remove any appearance of bias. This was decided in *R* v *Batth* [1990] Crim LR 727, CA, where the Recorder of London was reported in a newspaper as having referred in a public address to 'murderous Sikhs' involved in a case he was trying at the time. His explanation in court that the report was 'as usual inaccurate' was held not to be sufficient to dispel the appearance of bias raised on the facts, and his reported comments were described as 'deplorable'. The defendant's appeal against convictions for murder and manslaughter were nevertheless dismissed under s. 2 of the Criminal Appeal Act 1968 (see para 6.3.2) on the ground that no miscarriage of justice had actually occurred.

11.8.3.2.2 The duty to act fairly. There have been numerous cases involving a breach of the *audi alteram partem* rule of natural justice. This rule imposes a duty to act fairly and demands that a person should be told of the nature of the charges against him, that he should be allowed adequate time to prepare his defence, and that he should be given a fair hearing. However, the requirement of fairness does not demand that during the investigative process a person should be given particulars of the criminal conduct of which he is suspected by the police or other appropriate authorities. (See *R* v *Serious Fraud Office (ex parte Nadir)* (1990) *The Independent,* 16 October, where Asir Nadir, then chairman and chief executive of Polly Peck International plc, was refused leave to apply for judicial review to compel the Serious Fraud Office to provide him with brief details of the transactions which were suspected of involving criminality. Mr Nadir later absconded while on bail and flew to the Turkish Republic of Northern Cyprus (with which the UK has no extradition treaty) in May 1993. Note also that the public and the media have no right to be told the names of persons who are charged with, or under investigation for, criminal activity: *R* v *Secretary of State for the Home Department (ex parte Westminster Press)* [1992] COD 303, DC, in which an application for judicial review of the legality of a police circular advising use of the formula, 'a person has been charged', was dismissed).

A person is entitled to a fair hearing before a decision adversely affecting his interests is made by a public authority if, in the absence of any other more specific provision, he has a legitimate or reasonable expectation of being accorded such a hearing. The expectation may, for example, be based on some statement or undertaking by, or on behalf of, the public authority (*Attorney-General of Hong Kong* v *Ng Yuen Shiu* [1983] 2 All ER 346, PC; *Council of Civil Service Unions* v *Minister for the Civil Service* [1984] 3 All ER 935, HL), or it may arise by implication from the seriousness of the circumstances.

In *R* v *Norfolk County Council (ex parte M)* [1989] 2 All ER 359, it was held that a person is entitled to a fair hearing before having his name entered on a child abuse register since the decision to register his name is not merely an internal administrative procedure of the local authority but affects substantially the rights of the alleged abuser. On the facts, the decision of a child abuse case conference was quashed by certiorari on the ground that the conference had acted unfairly, unreasonably and in breach of natural justice in failing to consider whether the accusations of indecent assault and indecent exposure made against the applicant might be fantasy or fabrication, in deciding that the applicant was guilty after a brief and one-sided investigation, in failing to give the applicant an opportunity to object to the decision, and in secretly informing the applicant's employer of the decision. *R* v *Norfolk County Council (ex parte M),* above, was approved by the Court of Appeal in *R* v *Harrow London Borough Council (ex parte D)* [1990] 3 All ER 12, CA, although, on the facts, the court refused to quash the local authority's decision to place the applicant's name on the register as an abuser since she had been given an opportunity to give her explanation of how her children had come to be injured and had done so.

In *R* v *Secretary of State for Health (ex parte US Tobacco International Inc.)* [1992] 1 All ER 212, DC, the Oral Snuff (Safety) Regulations 1989 (made by the Secretary of State under the Consumer Protection Act 1987) were quashed by an order of certiorari. Before making regulations under the 1987 Act, it is the Secretary of State's duty (by virtue of s. 11(5)(a)) 'to consult such organisations as appear to him to be representative of interests substantially affected by' the proposed regulations. The Secretary of State, acting on the advice of a committee of experts set up to advise the government on the carcinogenicity of chemicals in food, consumer products and the environment, announced that he intended to make regulations banning oral snuff. The applicants, who were the only manufacturers of oral snuff products in the United Kingdom, were invited to make representations but were denied access to the text of the expert committee's advice. The Secretary of State made the regulations. On an application for judicial review, it was held that the Secretary of State had acted unfairly towards the applicants in not letting them see the committee's advice. His duty of consultation was said by the court to require him to demonstrate a high degree of fairness to the applicants since they were the only persons affected by the ban and their business would be devastated by it. The obligation to act fairly indicated that the applicants should have been given a full opportunity to read, and respond to, the scientific evidence.

Even the ordinary courts of law are capable, on occasions, of acting in breach of the fair hearing rule. In *Ex parte Bowgin* (1965) 109 SJ 76, DC, certiorari was ordered to quash the decision of a magistrates' court where the conviction of a person for careless driving had been announced before he had been given the opportunity to present his defence in full. In *R* v *Bradford Justices (ex parte Wilkinson)* [1990] 2 All ER 833, DC, the decision of a magistrates' court to convict the applicant of driving while the proportion of alcohol in his breath exceeded the prescribed limit was quashed by certiorari on the ground that the justices had failed to compel the attendance of witnesses crucial to his defence that he was not the driver at the relevant time. In *R* v *Marylebone Magistrates' Court (ex parte Perry)* [1992] Crim LR 514, DC, and *R* v *Marylebone Magistrates' Court (ex parte Joseph)* (1993) *The Times*, 7 May, DC, convictions were quashed on the ground that the defendants had not had a fair hearing where a stipendiary magistrate had failed to give their cases his undivided attention during the taking of evidence. In *Perry* he had signed warrants relating to other cases, while in *Joseph* he had read a newspaper law report, instead of devoting his full attention to the evidence in the proceedings before him.

In *R* v *Birmingham Justices (ex parte Lamb)* [1983] 3 All ER 23, DC, it was the *prosecutor* who sought judicial review after the magistrates had dismissed informations against the accused without a hearing! It was held that the magistrates had abused their powers, but the court, in the exercise of its discretion, declined to grant certiorari and mandamus because to have done so would have been unfair to the accused in the circumstances. (See also *R* v *Dorchester Justices (ex parte Director of Public Prosecutions)* [1990] RTR 369, DC, *R* v *Watford Justices (ex parte Director of Public Prosecutions)* [1990] RTR 374, DC, and *R* v *Milton Keynes Justices (ex parte Director of Public Prosecutions)* [1991] COD 498, DC, in all of which the magistrates were held to have wrongly dismissed informations without hearing any evidence; *R* v *Swansea Justices (ex parte Director of Public Prosecutions)* (1990) *The Times*, 30 March, DC, and *R* v *Sutton Justices (ex parte Director of Public Prosecutions)* [1992] 2 All ER 129, DC, where it was held that the magistrates had acted too hastily in dismissing informations — in the *Swansea* case simply because the prosecution witnesses had not appeared and the magistrates were not prepared to wait half an hour for them to arrive, and in the *Sutton* case because counsel for the prosecution was late and the magistrates were not prepared to wait another ten minutes for his arrival.)

Where the magistrates act unreasonably in dismissing an information (as in the *Sutton Justices* case, above), in consequence of which the defendant is acquitted, the acquittal is a nullity. Notwithstanding the fact that it appears to involve a contradiction in terms, the acquittal can be quashed by certiorari even though it is already null and void (*R v Hendon Justices (ex parte Director of Public Prosecutions)* [1993] 1 All ER 411, DC, not following the *Sutton Justices* case on this point; see further on the precedent issue, para 9.3.2.5). Where the prosecution still wishes to proceed on the information, an order of mandamus directing the magistrates to hear the information will usually be a more appropriate remedy than certiorari (*R v Hendon Justices (ex parte Director of Public Prosecutions)*, above, where the DPP sought certiorari but was granted mandamus instead).

The failure to provide a fair hearing (or any hearing at all) will usually be the fault of the court, tribunal or other public authority itself. Although unfairness to the defendant in criminal proceedings resulting from a failure by the prosecution to disclose the existence of witnesses who could have given evidence favourable to the defence may lead to the defendant's conviction being quashed on *appeal,* it is doubtful whether this unfairness is reviewable by means of *certiorari* (*Al-Mehdawi* v *Secretary of State for the Home Department* [1989] 3 All ER 843, HL, *per* Lord Bridge at p. 848, explaining and distinguishing *R v Leyland Magistrates (ex parte Hawthorn)* [1979] QB 283, DC; see also *R v West Sussex Quarter Sessions (ex parte Albert & Maud Johnson Trust Ltd)* [1974] QB 24, CA, approved by the House of Lords in the *Al-Mehdawi* case).

However, the unfairness may be reviewable by means of certiorari where the defendant has no right of appeal and he was convicted on the basis of flawed evidence unwittingly relied upon by the prosecution. In *R v Bolton Justices (ex parte Scally)* [1991] 2 All ER 619, DC, the applicant's conviction for driving while the proportion of alcohol in her blood exceeded the prescribed limit was quashed by certiorari on the ground that, after the conviction, it was discovered that the cleansing swabs used at the time the blood specimens were taken had been impregnated with alcohol in the same concentration as in beer and that this could have led to inaccurately high results when the specimens were subjected to laboratory analysis. At her trial, the applicant had pleaded guilty in the light of what appeared to be incontrovertible evidence; she was fined £200 and disqualified from holding a driving licence for twelve months.

There had been no unfairness towards the applicant on the part of the trial court or deliberate malpractice by the prosecutor (a combination of the police and the Crown Prosecution Service). Nevertheless, the process leading to the conviction was held to have been corrupted by the prosecutor in an unfair manner analogous to the fraud, collusion and perjury examples given in the *Leyland Magistrates case,* above, and approved in the *Al-Mehdawi* case, above. This defect in the pre-trial process had deprived the applicant of both a complete defence to the charge and a proper opportunity to decide whether to plead guilty or not guilty. It was held to entitle the court to intervene by way of judicial review, which in the applicant's circumstances was the only effective remedy available. She could not appeal against her conviction because she had pleaded guilty in the magistrates' court and no point of law was involved in the case (see para 6.2.1). A free pardon, even if forthcoming from the Home Secretary (which was doubtful) under his discretionary exercise of the royal prerogative of mercy, could excuse the sentence but would leave the conviction to stand (see [1991] 2 All ER 619 *per* Watkins LJ at pp. 625–6 and *R* v *Foster* [1984] 2 All ER 679, CA, para 6.3.4).

A failure to obtain a hearing (whether the case raises issues of *public* or *private* law) is not reviewable where it is due to the fault of the aggrieved party's own advisers rather than that of the court or tribunal. This is because the fault is outside the knowledge and control of the court or tribunal and does not, therefore, of itself involve any procedural impropriety or violation of natural justice on the part of the court or tribunal.

Thus, in a case where an immigration adjudicator had given an immigrant the opportunity of presenting his case against deportation but the opportunity was lost through the fault of the immigrant's solicitor, it was held that there had been no procedural impropriety or denial of natural justice and that, accordingly, the adjudicator's decision given in the absence of the immigrant was not reviewable (*Al-Mehdawi* v *Secretary of State for the Home Department*, above, HL, reversing the decision of the Court of Appeal in the case and also overruling *R* v *Diggines (ex parte Rahmani)* [1985] 1 All ER 1073, CA). This situation is akin to those wherein, owing to a solicitor's negligence, judgment is given in default of appearance, an action is dismissed for want of prosecution, or a claim becomes statute-barred (*Al-Mehdawi* v *Secretary of State for the Home Department* [1989] 3 All ER 843, HL, *per* Lord Bridge at p. 849). In these circumstances, the aggrieved person's remedy is to sue his solicitor for the tort of negligence.

In *R* v *Medical Appeal Tribunal (Midland Region) (ex parte Carrarini)* [1966] 1 WLR 883, DC, an applicant for a disability pension who wished to introduce in evidence a consultant's report favourable to himself was refused an adjournment. The tribunal decided the case against the applicant solely on the basis of the report of its own consultant. Certiorari was issued to quash the tribunal's decision because the tribunal had ignored the requirements of natural justice by refusing to let in expert evidence to controvert its own expert evidence.

There have been a number of cases where decisions have been quashed because the court of first instance had refused an adjournment and proceeded in the absence of one of the parties. See, for example, *R* v *Thames Magistrates' Court (ex parte Polemis)* [1974] 2 All ER 1219, DC (magistrates' court refusing an adjournment); *Priddle* v *Fisher & Sons* [1968] 1 WLR 1478, DC (employment tribunal refusing an adjournment). In *Ostreicher* v *Secretary of State for the Environment* [1978] 3 All ER 82 the Court of Appeal held that in deciding whether an adjournment should have been granted a distinction must be drawn between judicial proceedings before a court on the one hand and an administrative inquiry on the other. The court refused to quash an inspector's decision following a public inquiry (into a compulsory purchase order) which the Secretary of State had refused to adjourn.

In *R* v *Hull Prison Board of Visitors (ex parte St Germain and others)* [1979] 1 All ER 701, which arose out of the riot at Hull prison in 1976, the Court of Appeal decided as a preliminary matter that, in principle, certiorari is available to review the disciplinary decisions of a prison board of visitors. This decision was approved by the House of Lords in *O'Reilly* v *Mackman* [1982] 3 All ER 1124. In *R* v *Hull Prison Board of Visitors (ex parte St Germain and others) (No. 2)* [1979] 3 All ER 545, DC, the Queen's Bench Divisional Court actually ordered certiorari to quash some decisions of a prison board of visitors. One decision was set aside because the visitors had improperly refused a prisoner permission to call witnesses, and the others because prisoners were not given an opportunity to dispute the hearsay evidence of prison officers. Although not bound by the strict rules of evidence applicable in criminal cases in the courts, the board of visitors had an overriding duty to provide the accused with a fair hearing (see also *R* v *Blundeston Prison Board of Visitors (ex parte Fox-Taylor)* [1982] 1 All ER 646).

In *R* v *Deputy Governor of Camphill Prison (ex parte King)* [1984] 3 All ER 897, the Court of Appeal had held that certiorari was not available to review disciplinary decisions of the *prison governor* on the ground that, unlike a board of visitors, he was not an impartial and independent body but was instead a manager appointed by, and answerable to, the Home Secretary. That decision was, however, unanimously overruled by the House of Lords in the similar case of *Leech* v *Parkhurst Prison Deputy Governor* [1988] 1 All ER 485. Their Lordships took the view that a prison governor, when exercising his statutory power to find an offence proved and to make an award against a prisoner in disciplinary proceedings, is acting no less independently of the Home Secretary than a board of visitors (see *per* Lord Bridge at pp. 497–8 and Lord Oliver at p. 509). The fact that a governor can exercise a statutory power which affects the rights or legitimate expectations of citizens makes it imperative that the power be exercised in accordance with the principles of natural justice and that any allegation of abuse be subject to judicial review by the courts of law. As Lord Bridge put it (at p. 501):

> I cannot help reflecting . . . that it would be a very remarkable state of affairs if [a prisoner] were denied access to the courts to challenge the proceedings of an inferior judicial authority empowered, in effect, to deprive him of liberty by extending the term of his imprisonment.

The applicant's conviction for a prison disciplinary offence (being in possession of a device adapted for the smoking of a controlled drug), in respect of which he had been awarded 28 days' loss of remission, was accordingly quashed by certiorari where he had been found guilty by the deputy governor before being given any opportunity to state his defence or cross-examine the reporting prison officer.

Before *Leech* v *Parkhurst Prison Deputy Governor* reached the courts, the Home Office had informed Mr Leech that the finding of guilt against him was unsafe, that his record would be amended to show a finding of not guilty, and that the award against him would be remitted. Mr Leech wanted the finding of guilt to be totally quashed but, under the law as it then stood, the Home Secretary, while able to remit or mitigate any award, had no power to quash a finding of guilt. That could only be done by the court in judicial review proceedings and that was why Mr Leech made his application. The law has since been changed so that the Home Secretary does now have power to quash a finding of guilt. The terminology has also been changed; 'awards' are now referred to as what they really are — 'punishments'. (The terminology was changed in 1989; see now the Prison Rules 1999 (SI 1999, No. 728).)

The right to a fair hearing implicit in the rule, *audi alteram partem,* does not demand that a person should be heard orally; the making of written representations may satisfy the rule (*Board of Education* v *Rice* [1911] AC 179, HL, *per* Lord Loreburn LC at p. 182; *Local Government Board* v *Arlidge* [1915] AC 120, HL; *Lloyd* v *McMahon* [1987] AC 625, HL; *R* v *Army Board (ex parte Anderson)* [1991] 3 All ER 375, DC, *per* Taylor LJ at p. 387).

Nor does the requirement of a fair hearing necessarily demand legal representation by counsel or a solicitor before a tribunal or other hearing, even though it is available before the ordinary courts of law (*Pett* v *Greyhound Racing Association* [1969] 1 QB 125, CA; *Fraser* v *Mudge* [1975] 3 All ER 78, CA; *Maynard* v *Osmond* [1977] 1 All ER 64, CA; *Hone* v *Maze Prison Board of Visitors* [1988] 1 All ER 321, HL, approving *Fraser* v

Mudge). It has been said that in hearings before non-statutory domestic tribunals justice can often be done better by a good layman than by a bad lawyer (*Enderby Town Football Club Ltd* v *Football Association Ltd* [1971] Ch 591, CA, *per* Lord Denning MR at p. 605). Whether legal representation should be permitted as a matter of discretion will depend on the facts of each individual case. Relevant factors which may tip the scales in favour of permitting it are the gravity of the charge against a person or of the consequences to him should a decision go against him (*Pett* v *Greyhound Racing Association*). Thus, in *R* v *Secretary of State for the Home Department (ex parte Tarrant)* [1984] 1 All ER 799, DC, a prison board of visitors was held to have wrongly exercised its discretion by refusing a request for legal representation made by prisoners charged with the disciplinary offence of mutiny. The board had acted perversely in refusing the request having regard to the complexity of the offence and the gravity of the consequences to the prisoners if it was proved. Certiorari was granted to quash the board's decision.

A person is always free to represent himself at proceedings before a court or tribunal as a 'litigant in person'. In addition, of respectable antiquity is the right (recognised in *Collier* v *Hicks* (1831) 2 B & Ad 663) in civil proceedings to have the assistance of a 'McKenzie friend' (named after the case of *McKenzie* v *McKenzie* [1971] P 33, CA). A 'McKenzie friend' is a member of the public who accompanies a litigant in person in order to assist him by quietly making suggestions, quietly giving advice, or by taking notes. He does not have rights of audience and is, therefore, not entitled to address the court. A decision to deprive a litigant in person of his right to a McKenzie friend can be challenged in judicial review proceedings.

The right to a McKenzie friend is not an absolute one since the court may require the friend to leave if it becomes clear during the proceedings that his assistance is harmful to the efficient administration of justice, such as where the litigant in person is encouraged to waste time or is advised to ask immaterial questions or to raise irrelevant issues. In *R* v *Leicester City Justices (ex parte Barrow)* [1991] 3 All ER 935, CA, a magistrates' court refused to allow the applicants to be assisted by a member of an anti-poll tax organisation, acting as a McKenzie friend, in proceedings brought by a local authority for liability orders under the community charge legislation. The liability orders were made and the applicants sought judicial review. The Court of Appeal held that since there was no evidence that the applicants, or their chosen McKenzie friend, had any intention of disrupting or abusing the process of the court the magistrates were wrong to have denied the applicants the help of a friend. In the circumstances, that denial had created the appearance of unfairness and the liability orders made against the applicants were quashed by certiorari. (The *Barrow* case was followed in *R* v *Highbury Corner Magistrates' Court (ex parte Watkins)* (1992) *The Times*, 22 October, DC, and *R* v *Wolverhampton Stipendiary Magistrate (ex parte Mould)* (1992) *The Times*, 16 November, DC.) The Court of Appeal's plea in the *Barrow* case that the term 'McKenzie friend' no longer be used because, *inter alia,* it wrongly implies the status of an unqualified legal assistant known to the law (see [1991] 3 All ER 935 *per* Lord Donaldson MR at p. 947 and Staughton LJ at p. 948) has not been heeded (see *R* v *Bow County Court (ex parte Pelling)* [1999] 4 All ER 751, CA, *per* Lord Woolf MR at p. 757).

In the *Pelling* case, above, the Court of Appeal held that where the confidential nature of the proceedings makes it appropriate that they be heard in *private* (whether in court or in chambers), a judge may well be justified in concluding that it would be undesirable in the interests of justice for a McKenzie friend to assist. It was also held that a judge should give reasons for refusing the use of a McKenzie friend. The court said, *obiter,* that a person who earns his living by appearing regularly as a McKenzie friend must exercise considerable restraint in order to avoid abusing his true role (as an assistant to the litigant in person) by indirectly running the case instead (see *per* Lord Woolf MR at p. 758).

The right to a fair hearing does not entitle a citizen to have his case decided by the same person who heard the evidence initially. This limitation is particularly relevant in the case of statutory inquiries where the evidence is heard by an inspector appointed by the minister but it is the minister himself who makes the final decision. In *Local Government Board* v *Arlidge* [1915] AC 120, HL, the Hampstead Borough Council made a closing order against a house as being unfit for human habitation. The lessee of the house, A, appealed to the Local Government Board and a public inquiry, at which A presented his case, was held by one of the board's housing inspectors. The board confirmed the closing order and A applied for certiorari to quash its decision on the following grounds:

(a)   That the appeal had not been decided properly by the board because the decision did not disclose the identity of the officer of the board by whom the appeal was decided.
(b)   That he had not been allowed to be heard orally before the board.
(c)   That he had not been allowed to see the inspector's report.

The House of Lords held that certiorari would be refused. The board was bound to observe the principles of natural justice but had done so. The board had followed its customary procedure. It was entitled to act through delegates without revealing their identities. A was not entitled to an oral hearing before the board and the board was not obliged to disclose the inspector's report to A.

Their Lordships made it clear that the standards expected of public authorities when deciding questions affecting the rights and property of the individual are not as high as those expected of the ordinary courts of law. Thus, in *Bushell* v *Secretary of State for the Environment* [1980] 2 All ER 608, HL, the House of Lords held that the refusal of an inspector at a public inquiry to allow cross-examination of the Secretary of State's witnesses on traffic prediction methods did not amount to a denial of natural justice. In an ordinary court of law, such an omission would not be countenanced. Their Lordships in *Local Government Board* v *Arlidge* emphasised, however, that public authorities must act judicially at least to the extent of dealing with such questions impartially and of giving the parties the opportunity of adequately presenting their cases, unless, it may now be added, a party could have had no legitimate expectation of being heard in view of his own behaviour (*Cinnamond* v *British Airports Authority* [1980] 2 All ER 368, CA), or unless the requirement of a fair hearing has been waived by implication in an emergency which has led to the *provisional* suspension of a licence or permit in order to avoid the possible loss of many lives (*R* v *Secretary of State for Transport (ex parte Pegasus Holidays (London) Ltd)* [1989] 2 All ER 481 — Romanian organisation's permit to operate charter flights provisionally suspended pending an inquiry into the competence of their pilots).

11.8.3.2.3   The duty to act fairly: giving reasons for decisions
It is not, and never has been, a general requirement of natural justice that reasons for decisions should be given (*R* v *Gaming Board for Great Britain (ex parte Benaim and Khaida)* [1970] 2 QB 417, CA, *per* Lord Denning MR at p. 431; *R* v *Immigration Appeal Tribunal (ex parte Khan (Mahmud))* [1983] 2 All ER 420, CA, *per* Lord Lane CJ at p. 423; *Doody* v *Secretary of State for the Home Department* [1993] 3 All ER 92, HL, *per* Lord Mustill at p. 110; *R* v *Ministry of Defence (ex parte Murray)* (1997) *The Times*, 17 December, CA). In appropriate circumstances, however, a duty to give reasons may be

implied (R v Civil Service Appeal Board (ex parte Cunningham) [1991] 4 All ER 310, CA, below; *Doody v Secretary of State for the Home Department*, above, *per* Lord Mustill at p. 110; *R v Ministry of Defence (ex parte Murray)*, above).

The fact that natural justice does not generally demand that reasons be given means, first, that certiorari will not lie to quash a decision on the ground only that no reasons for it were given, and secondly, that mandamus is not available to compel the giving of reasons. In *R v Gaming Board for Great Britain (ex parte Benaim and Khaida),* the joint managing directors of Crockford's gaming club applied for certiorari to quash a decision of the Gaming Board refusing them a certificate of consent to apply for a gaming licence. They also sought mandamus to compel the board to give them sufficient further information to enable them to answer any case against them. By the Gaming Act 1968, gaming was prohibited except in premises licensed for the purpose by magistrates. Before a person could apply to the magistrates for a licence he first had to obtain a certificate of consent from the Gaming Board, a body established by the 1968 Act. Crockford's application for a certificate of consent was rejected without any reasons being given.

The Court of Appeal emphasised that the Gaming Board is bound to observe the principles of natural justice but held that it had done so. Both mandamus and certiorari were refused. Mandamus was refused because the board had given the applicants all the information which had led to doubts about their suitability for a gaming licence and had given them full opportunity to deal with it. The board was not bound to go further and disclose the sources of its information. Certiorari was refused because the board was not bound to give reasons for its decisions.

In *Payne v Lord Harris of Greenwich* [1981] 2 All ER 842, CA, it was held that the Parole Board was not under a duty to give reasons for not recommending the release of a person from prison. This was held to be so in the case of a prisoner serving a life sentence whether that life sentence was a mandatory one (as in *Payne v Lord Harris of Greenwich)* or a discretionary one (as in *R v Secretary of State for the Home Department (ex parte Gunnell)* (1984) *The Times,* 7 November, CA, and *R v Parole Board (ex parte Bradley)* [1990] 3 All ER 828, DC). In *R v Parole Board (ex parte Wilson)* [1992] 2 All ER 576, CA, in which the 76 year-old applicant had already served 20 years of a discretionary life sentence imposed for buggery, the Court of Appeal declined to follow its two earlier decisions in *Payne v Lord Harris of Greenwich* and *R v Secretary of State for the Home Department (ex parte Gunnell)* and held that a prisoner serving a discretionary life sentence who applies for release on licence is entitled to see any material to be placed before the Parole Board which suggested that he was still a danger to the public. It was said that fairness demands disclosure of the material because without knowing what is being said against him the applicant will be unable to make effective representations on the issue of dangerousness.

Payne was rejected as no longer reflecting established views on prisoners' rights and on the ground that, although it was a decision of the Court of Appeal, it was distinguishable (and, accordingly, not binding in the circumstances) since it concerned a *mandatory* life sentence. *Gunnell,* while not distinguishable, was rejected for the reason that, applying *Williams v Fawcett* [1985] 1 All ER 787, CA (para 9.3.2.3.1), in a case involving the liberty of the subject the Court of Appeal is not bound by an earlier decision of its own if following it might produce injustice. In effect, the Court of Appeal in *R v Parole Board (ex parte Wilson)* anticipated the coming into force of the new statutory arrangements (contained in part II of the Criminal Justice Act 1991) for the early release of prisoners.

Payne was eventually overruled by the House of Lords in *Doody v Secretary of State for the Home Department* [1993] 3 All ER 92, HL. Here it was held that in view of the fact that a discretionary life prisoner enjoyed certain rights as a result of *R* v *Parole Board (ex parte Wilson)* [1992] 2 All ER 576, CA, with which the House was in agreement, it was fair that a *mandatory* life prisoner should be entitled to certain rights in respect of the Home Secretary's decision about the penal element in his sentence. (The 'penal' (or 'tariff') element is that part of a life sentence, consisting of a determinate number of years, which is regarded as appropriate to the nature and seriousness of the offence and which covers the requirements of retribution and deterrence. The second element in a life sentence — the 'risk' element — consists of an indeterminate number of years reflecting the degree of danger to the public posed by the prisoner. It begins to run as soon as the penal element has been served.)

It was declared in *Doody* that a mandatory life prisoner has the right to put reasons to the Home Secretary for fixing a lower rather than a higher penal term, the right to know what the Home Secretary will take into account in determining the penal element of his sentence, and the right to be given reasons if the Home Secretary departs from the trial judge's recommendation about the penal element of his sentence. This latter right involves being informed of the *gist* of the advice and reasons given to the Home Secretary by the trial judge and the Lord Chief Justice; there is no right to insist upon production of the entire document in which the advice is given (see *Doody* [1993] 3 All ER 92, HL, *per* Lord Mustill at p. 109). (See also *Pierson* v *Secretary of State for the Home Department* [1997] 3 All ER 577, HL, and *R* v *Secretary of State for the Home Department (ex parte Hindley)* [2000] 2 All ER 385, HL.)

The reasoning in *Doody* has since been extended to cover category A prisoners. These are prisoners who are high security risks, whose escape would present great danger, and for whom release on licence by the Parole Board is virtually inconceivable. It follows that any decision to keep a prisoner in category A has serious implications for his liberty; a prisoner who aspires to release on licence will need to obtain classification in a lower category.

In *R* v *Secretary of State for the Home Department (ex parte Duggan)* [1994] 3 All ER 277, DC, it was held that a category A prisoner is entitled to be informed of the *gist* of any matter of fact or opinion to be relied upon by the Home Office in any subsequent review of his security classification and to be given reasons for a decision that he remain a category A prisoner. The applicant was granted declarations to that effect. The initial classification of a category A prisoner is not affected by this decision. Since he will be serving a substantial sentence anyway — so that initially placing him in category A will not materially affect his chances of release — it is not unfair that at that stage he is not provided with the gist of reports on him or furnished with reasons for his classification.

Not even the ordinary courts of law are generally bound to give reasons for their decisions, although the superior courts invariably do so in practice as a means of convincing the parties that justice has been done. Reasons for a decision may also provide grounds for a possible appeal to a higher court. (See *per* Rose LJ in *R* v *Snaresbrook Crown Court (ex parte Lea)* (1994) *The Times*, 5 April, DC; *Flannery* v *Halifax Estate Agencies Ltd* [2000] 1 All ER 373, CA. The present trend is towards *implying* a requirement that courts should give reasons (see, for example, *R* v *Warwick Crown Court (ex parte Patel)* [1992] COD 143; *R* v *Harrow Crown Court (ex parte Dave)* [1994] 1 All ER 315, DC; *R* v *Snaresbrook Crown Court (ex parte Input Management Ltd)* (1999) *The Times*, 29 April, DC; *Flannery* v *Halifax Estate Agencies Ltd*, above (county court); *Coleman* v *Dunlop Ltd* [1998] PIQR P398, CA (county court)).

By s. 10 of the Tribunals and Inquiries Act 1992, reasons must be given, if requested, for the decisions of tribunals listed in the Act and of ministers holding statutory inquiries. The reasons given must be proper, intelligible and adequate (*Re Poyser and Mills's Arbitration* [1964] 2 QB 467 *per* Megaw J at p. 478; this description was approved by the House of Lords in *Westminster City Council* v *Great Portland Estates plc* [1984] 3 All ER 744, HL, and in *Save Britain's Heritage* v *Secretary of State for the Environment* [1991] 2 All ER 10, HL, and see *Mountview Court Properties Ltd* v *Devlin* (1970) 114 SJ 474, DC, in which a case was sent back to a rent assessment committee with a direction to state its reasons fully and adequately). The reasons may be given in writing or orally but, even if oral, the reasons are taken to form part of the decision and accordingly are incorporated in the record of the proceedings (Tribunals and Inquiries Act 1992, s. 10(6)). The result of this rule is that decisions of these tribunals may be challenged by certiorari on the ground of error of law on the face of the record. This procedure is explained more fully in para 11.8.3.3 below.

A mental health review tribunal must give *written* reasons for its decisions (Mental Health Review Tribunal Rules 1983, SI 1983, No. 942, r. 23(2)). The reasons must be proper and adequate in the sense of enabling the patient to know whether the tribunal has made any error of law in reaching its decision (*Bone* v *Mental Health Review Tribunal* [1985] 3 All ER 330; *R* v *Mental Health Review Tribunal (ex parte Clatworthy)* [1985] 3 All ER 699). Under the Criminal Injuries Compensation Scheme 1990 (which is gradually being replaced by the tariff-based Criminal Injuries Compensation Scheme 1995 made by the Home Secretary under the authority of the Criminal Injuries Compensation Act 1995), the Criminal Injuries Compensation Board is bound to give reasons for a decision to refuse or reduce an award of compensation. In *R* v *Criminal Injuries Compensation Board (ex parte Moore)* [1999] 2 All ER 90, Sedley J commended it as good practice that the reasons should be given in writing. However, he refused to elevate this practice to the status of a principle of public law since to do so would come too close to usurping the Parliamentary function of legislating.

With regard to tribunals not covered by any statutory provisions, recent case law reveals a clearly discernible movement in favour of the giving of at least outline reasons for decisions. In *R* v *Civil Service Appeal Board (ex parte Bruce)* [1989] 2 All ER 907, the Court of Appeal said, *obiter,* that in order to create a greater sense of fairness in its proceedings it was desirable as a matter of policy and discretion for the Civil Service Appeal Board to give a brief statement of its reasons. In *R* v *Civil Service Appeal Board (ex parte Cunningham)* [1991] 4 All ER 310, the Court of Appeal went further and held that, in certain circumstances, the Board is bound by law to give reasons when deciding whether a dismissal is fair or unfair and, if unfair, when assessing the appropriate financial compensation. The approach adopted in this case was approved by the House of Lords in *Doody* v *Secretary of State for the Home Department* [1993] 3 All ER 92, HL, above.

Unlike internal, domestic appeal bodies established to deal with industrial relations problems within large companies or private organisations, the Civil Service Appeal Board, although non-statutory, is a body set up under the royal prerogative for the purpose of deciding, *inter alia,* unfair dismissal claims by those civil servants and others (such as prison officers) who are denied access to an employment tribunal. It is an independent public law body exercising judicial functions. There is no right of appeal against its decisions either on fact or law, although it is susceptible to judicial review in the High Court. In *R* v *Civil Service Appeal Board (ex parte Cunningham),* the Board had decided that the applicant's dismissal from his post as a prison officer was unfair and had assessed the compensation payable to him at £6,500. In comparable circumstances, an employment tribunal (to which the applicant was precluded from complaining) would have awarded more than twice as much. The Board refused to give reasons for its award, and the applicant sought judicial review of the Board's decision on the grounds that the refusal to give reasons was a violation of natural justice and that the award was prima facie irrational. The Court of Appeal decided, first, that the duty to act fairly demanded that reasons should be given in support of the way in which an award has been reached since in a similar case an employment tribunal is required by law to give reasons, and, secondly, that in the absence of any reasons the award was so low as to be prima facie irrational in view of what an employment tribunal would have awarded in a comparable case. The award was quashed and the case sent back to the Board for the amount of compensation to be reconsidered. It was made clear that the requirement to give reasons would be satisfied by a concise statement of the way in which an award had been arrived at; the reasons need not be set out at great length so long as they are sufficient to show that the correct issues have been addressed and that the Board has acted lawfully.

In deciding whether a particular tribunal should give reasons for its decisions when it is not obliged to do so by any statutory provisions, regard must be had to the nature and function of the tribunal and to its decisions. It has been said that a distinction must be made between those decisions which obviously demand the giving of reasons (as where personal liberty is involved) and those decisions where the giving of reasons would be completely inappropriate (*R v Higher Education Funding Council (ex parte Institute of Dental Surgery)* [1994] 1 All ER 651, DC, where it was held that the HEFC was not compelled to give reasons for its decision to lower the research rating of a London University dental college following a research assessment exercise; see also *R v English Nursing Board (ex parte Roberts)* [1994] COD 223, DC, in which the investigating committee of the English Nursing Board was held not to be obliged to give reasons for a decision to take no action on a complaint from a member of the public, and *R v University College London (ex parte Idriss)* [1999] Ed CR 462, where it was held that there was no requirement for a university to give reasons for refusing to admit an applicant to a course).

A duty to give reasons may be implied even where to do so runs counter to the express words of a statute. In *R v Secretary of State for the Home Department (ex parte Fayed)* [1997] 1 All ER 228, CA, the Fayed brothers' applications for naturalisation under the British Nationality Act 1981 had been refused by the Home Secretary. The brothers challenged his decision on the grounds, first, that they had not been given an opportunity to make representations, and, secondly, that the Home Secretary had given no reasons for his decision. At first instance, both grounds were rejected for the same reason: they were incompatible with the unequivocal language of s. 44(2) of the 1981 Act that the 'Secretary of State shall not be required to assign any reason for the grant or refusal of any application under this Act the decision on which is at his discretion . . .' On appeal, however, the Court of Appeal found in favour of the Fayeds. It was held that, notwithstanding the wording of s. 44(2), the Home Secretary must act fairly in exercising his discretion to grant or refuse citizenship, and fairness demands that the applicant should be given sufficient information about the Home Secretary's concerns as to enable the applicant to make what representations he can before the final citizenship decision is taken. The Home Secretary's decisions to reject the Fayeds' applications for citizenship were quashed by certiorari.

11.8.3.3 *Where there is an error of law*
The jurisdiction of the High Court to quash a decision by certiorari on this ground is quite independent of the two grounds already considered, namely, the doctrine of *ultra vires* and the principles of natural justice. A decision that is *ultra vires,* or one made in violation of the principles of natural justice, is void, whereas a decision containing an error of law is

merely voidable; i.e., it is valid until avoided by certiorari. Again, while there are several remedies available for challenging *ultra vires* actions (damages, injunctions, declarations, certiorari, prohibition, habeas corpus), the only remedy usually available for challenging error of law is certiorari. A declaration, for instance, is probably not available as a remedy for error of law (this question was raised but not answered in *Re Tillmire Common* [1982] 2 All ER 615).

Originally, the courts would only interfere on the ground of error of law where the error appeared on the face of the record. Thus, they would not interfere with the decision of an inferior tribunal if it had acted within its jurisdiction, observed the principles of natural justice, and the proceedings were regular on the face of them. However, a tribunal which acted within its jurisdiction and in accordance with natural justice may nevertheless have had its decision quashed if the proceedings were *not regular on the face of them;* that is, where the tribunal had erred in law and the error appeared on the face of the record of the proceedings.

The power of the courts to interfere on the ground of an error of law on the face of the record was reaffirmed for modern times by the Court of Appeal in *R v Northumberland Compensation Appeal Tribunal (ex parte Shaw)* [1952] 1 KB 338, CA, a case in which the judgment of Denning LJ gives a useful account of the history of this piece of jurisdiction. S, the clerk to a hospital board, lost his job on the introduction of the National Health Service. He was entitled by statute to compensation but there was some doubt about how it should be calculated. S claimed that his earlier service in local government should be taken into account as well as his service with the hospital board. The relevant statutory regulations required both to be taken into account but the Northumberland Compensation Appeal Tribunal decided that only S's service with the hospital board should count. This error of law did not actually appear on the face of the record because the record was incomplete in that it did not mention S's correct submission concerning the periods of employment that should be taken into account. The tribunal, however, admitted the error and the Court of Appeal quashed its order by certiorari. Denning LJ said (at p. 354):

> We have here a simple case of error of law by a tribunal, an error which they frankly acknowledge. It is an error which deprives Mr Shaw of the compensation to which he is by law entitled. So long as the erroneous decision stands, the compensating authority dare not pay Mr Shaw the money to which he is entitled lest the auditor should surcharge them. It would be quite intolerable if in such case there were no means of correcting the error. . . . If it had been necessary, the court could have ordered the record to be completed. But that is unnecessary, having regard to the fact that it was admitted in open court by all concerned that the decision was erroneous. I am clearly of opinion that an error admitted openly in the face of the court can be corrected by certiorari as well as an error that appears on the face of the record. The decision must be quashed, and the tribunal will then be able to hear the case again and give the correct decision.

In *R v Medical Appeal Tribunal (ex parte Gilmore)* [1957] 1 QB 574, CA, statutory regulations provided, in effect, that if a one-eyed man lost the sight of his good eye in an industrial accident his degree of disablement should be assessed at 100 per cent. The Medical Appeal Tribunal erred in law in assessing G's disablement at only 20 per cent. G applied for an order of certiorari to quash the tribunal's decision on the ground of error of law on the face of the record. His case was complicated by three factors:

(a)   The usual time-limit for applying for certiorari had expired.

(b) The error did not appear on the face of the record because the record made no mention of either eye.

(c) It was provided by statute that the decision of the tribunal 'shall be final'.

As to (a), the Court of Appeal exercised its discretion to extend the time-limit since G had not been guilty of any delay in claiming relief. As to (b), the tribunal's written decision had quoted from a specialist's report, which dealt with the injuries to G's eyes. The tribunal had thereby made the full report part of the record. Taken together, the decision and the specialist's report gave a full record, on the face of which was an error of law, for it was manifest that the statutory regulations had been misconstrued. As to (c), it was held that, although the words 'shall be final' successfully excluded an *appeal,* they were not explicit enough to preclude judicial review, by means of certiorari, for error of law on the face of the record (see further, para 11.12.1 below). The tribunal's decision was quashed and the value of the remedy of certiorari demonstrated once more. Since it was expressly provided that G had no right of appeal against the tribunal's decision, it was only by recourse to certiorari that he was able to obtain the industrial injuries benefit to which he was lawfully entitled.

The 'record' of proceedings includes the document which initiates the proceedings, the pleadings (if any), the decision of the tribunal (*R* v *Northumberland Compensation Appeal Tribunal (ex parte Shaw)* [1952] 1 KB 338 *per* Denning LJ at p. 352), and all those documents which appear from the formal order to have formed the basis of the decision (*Baldwin & Francis Ltd* v *Patents Appeal Tribunal* [1959] AC 663, HL, *per* Lord Denning at p. 690), such as the applicant's submission in *R* v *Northumberland Compensation Appeal Tribunal (ex parte Shaw)* and the specialist's report in *R* v *Medical Appeal Tribunal (ex parte Gilmore).*

In *R* v *Southampton Justices (ex parte Green)* [1976] QB 11, CA, affidavits sworn by the chairman of, and the clerk to, the justices were held by the Court of Appeal to be part of the record. The affidavits, which gave reasons for a decision, contained errors of law and the justices' decision was quashed by certiorari. The 'record' also extends to the reasons given in an oral judgment and set out in the official transcript of the proceedings (*R* v *Crown Court at Knightsbridge (ex parte International Sporting Club (London) Ltd)* [1981] 3 All ER 417, DC).

The record, however, does not include the evidence given before the tribunal unless the tribunal chooses to incorporate it as part of the record (*R* v *Northumberland Compensation Appeal Tribunal (ex parte Shaw), per* Denning LJ at p. 352; *Re Allen and Matthews's arbitration* [1971] 2 QB 518).

In more recent times, it has become clear that the jurisdiction of the High Court to interfere with the decision of an inferior court or other body on the ground of error of law is not limited to cases where the error appears on the face of the record of the proceedings. It extends to any error of law — whether or not it appears on the face of the record. In *Page* v *Hull University Visitor* [1993] 1 All ER 97, the House of Lords, although divided on some issues, was unanimous in the view that the distinction between errors of law on the face of the record and other errors of law had been swept away by their Lordships' decision in *Anisminic Ltd* v *Foreign Compensation Commission* [1969] 2 AC 147, HL (para 11.13.3 below), as explained by Lord Diplock in *Re Racal Communications Ltd* [1980] 2 All ER 634, HL (para 11.13.2 below), and by the whole House in *O'Reilly* v *Mackman* [1982] 1 All ER 1124, HL (see, for example, [1993] 1 All ER 97 *per* Lord Browne-Wilkinson at p. 107 and Lord Slynn at p. 111). The distinction was no longer meaningful following the extension of the *ultra vires* doctrine achieved in the *Anisminic* case.

As a result of *Page* v *Hull University Visitor*, above, the position now is that any error of law made by an inferior court or other body — whether acting within or outside its jurisdiction — is in general capable of correction by means of certiorari. However, according to the decision of the majority there is an exception in the case of the visitor to a university (or other educational or ecclesiastical foundation: [1993] 1 All ER 97 *per* Lord Browne-Wilkinson at p. 109, and see *R* v *Visitors to the Inns of Court (ex parte Calder)* [1993] 2 All ER 876, CA, para 11.11.2 below, in which *Page* v *Hull University Visitor* was applied). It was held that since the visitor has exclusive jurisdiction to decide disputes arising under the domestic law of the university, judicial review is not available to correct the visitor's decision, whether right or wrong, and whether on a question of fact or of law, so long as that decision was made within his jurisdiction and in accordance with the principles of natural justice. A review of the authorities convinced the majority in *Page* that this had been the position for 300 years. It followed that the High Court had no jurisdiction to review the Hull University Visitor's interpretation of the University statutes at the instigation of Mr Page, whose employment as a lecturer had been terminated (lawfully according to the Visitor) on the ground of redundancy. It was further held (unanimously) that, in any event, the visitor's decision contained no error of law.

The reasons given by the majority in *Page* were, first, that the visitor is not called upon to apply the common law familiar to the judiciary but, instead, a peculiar or domestic law of which he is appointed the sole judge, and, secondly, that the perceived advantages of the visitorial jurisdiction — swiftness, cheapness and finality — would be lost if the visitor's decisions could be challenged by judicial review.

After *Page* it is possible to challenge the visitor's decision by judicial review and have it quashed by certiorari in three cases. First, if the visitor has acted outside his jurisdiction (i.e., where he had no power to adjudicate upon the dispute in the first place). Secondly, if he has abused his powers by acting in a way which is incompatible with his judicial role. However, he is not to be regarded as having abused his powers simply by making a decision which a superior court might regard as containing a mistake of law (see [1993] 1 All ER 97 *per* Lord Griffiths at p. 100). Thirdly, if he has violated the principles of natural justice.

11.9 PROHIBITION

11.9.1 Nature

Prohibition is a remedy which is used to prevent inferior courts, tribunals and authorities from exceeding their jurisdiction and to prevent them from violating the principles of natural justice. It may be issued, for example, to prohibit a tribunal from exceeding, or continuing to exceed, its jurisdiction by hearing a case which it is outside its powers to hear.

Prohibition is in nature similar to certiorari, with the difference that the former is concerned with the future while the latter is concerned with the past. Although prohibition and certiorari may be sought separately, the two are often applied for together in the same proceedings. Thus, a decision may be set aside by certiorari, and further unlawful action, such as an attempt to implement the quashed decision, forbidden by prohibition. Like certiorari, prohibition is a discretionary remedy. Disobedience to an order of prohibition is punishable as a contempt of court.

11.9.2 Availability

Prohibition and certiorari are available against the same bodies. Prohibition has been sought successfully against an ecclesiastical court, a county court, a magistrates' court, Income Tax

Commissioners, rent tribunals, licensing authorities, police authorities and government ministers. An applicant for prohibition must have a sufficient interest in the matter to which the application relates (para 11.11.4 below). In one case prohibition is available where certiorari is not. Certiorari will not lie to challenge proceedings in ecclesiastical courts because ecclesiastical law is substantially different from the general law applied in the High Court. Prohibition, however, will lie against ecclesiastical courts to restrain excesses of jurisdiction and violations of natural justice (*R* v *North (ex parte Oakey)* [1927] 1 KB 491, CA).

Prohibition is not available against voluntary (i.e., non-statutory) domestic tribunals. It does not lie directly against the Crown since it emanates from the Crown, but it is available against individual ministers of the Crown. Prohibition will not lie against a deliberative body, such as the Legislative Committee of the Church Assembly, because it does not have the power to decide questions affecting the rights of subjects (*R* v *Legislative Committee of the Church Assembly (ex parte Haynes-Smith)* [1928] 1 KB 411, DC).

11.9.3 Scope

Prohibition will lie on two of the same grounds as certiorari.

11.9.3.1 To restrain an ultra vires act
In *R* v *Electricity Commissioners (ex parte London Electricity Joint Committee Co (1920) Ltd)* [1924] 1 KB 171, CA, the Electricity Commissioners had a statutory duty to make schemes for the supply of electricity. This involved the creation of electricity districts. For the London area, the commissioners proposed a scheme which was, in effect, for two electricity districts when the statute allowed only one. The Court of Appeal held that the scheme was *ultra vires* and issued prohibition to prevent the commissioners from going any further with it. Similarly, in *R* v *Minister of Health (ex parte Davis)* [1929] 1 KB 619, the Court of Appeal granted an order of prohibition to prevent confirmation by the minister of an *ultra vires* housing scheme.

Prohibition may be used to prevent a local authority from acting unlawfully. In *R* v *Greater London Council (ex parte Blackburn)* [1976] 3 All ER 184, CA, it was held by the Court of Appeal that the rules made by the GLC for the censorship of films were *ultra vires*. The GLC was applying the test of tendency to deprave or corrupt under the Obscene Publications Act 1959, which did not apply to films, instead of applying the test of indecency at common law. In consequence, films were being shown contrary to law. The court was minded to grant an order of prohibition but did not do so, preferring instead to give the GLC an opportunity either to change its rules so as to incorporate the proper test or to stop censoring films for adults altogether.

11.9.3.2 To restrain a violation of the principles of natural justice
In *R* v *Kent Police Authority (ex parte Godden)* [1971] 2 QB 662, CA, the police authority took steps compulsorily to retire G, a chief inspector of police, on medical grounds. The authority proposed to have G examined by the chief medical officer of the force. He was the same doctor who two years earlier had examined G for some other reason and had found him to be suffering from a paranoid mental illness. G himself went to a consultant psychiatrist who reported that G was mentally completely normal. The police authority refused to make available to G's doctors all the information which was available to its chief medical officer. G applied for orders of prohibition and mandamus.

The Court of Appeal granted both remedies. Prohibition was issued against the chief medical officer of the force to prevent him from deciding whether G was permanently disabled. The chief medical officer had already formed an opinion adverse to G and had thus committed himself to a view of G's mental condition which would preclude any appearance of impartiality at a second examination. Mandamus was issued against the police authority compelling it to supply to G's doctors all the information available to its own medical examiner. It should be noted that justice did not demand that G himself should be allowed to see all the material (*per* Lord Denning MR at p. 670).

In *R v Liverpool Corporation (ex parte Liverpool Taxi Fleet Operators' Association)* [1972] 2 QB 299, CA, the Court of Appeal issued prohibition against a taxicab licensing authority. The authority was prohibited from acting on a resolution to increase the number of taxicab licences without first considering representations from interested parties.

Prohibition was issued in 1990 in *R v Telford Justices (ex parte Badhan)* [1991] 2 All ER 854, DC, in order to stop committal proceedings in respect of a rape allegedly committed in 1973 or 1974 and which had not even been reported until 14 or 15 years after the event. It was held that, by reason of delay, the committal proceedings would be an abuse of the process of the court and the defendant would be so prejudiced in the preparation and conduct of his defence as to be unlikely to receive a fair trial in any subsequent proceedings.

11.10 MANDAMUS

11.10.1 Nature

Mandamus ('we command') is a royal command, issued in the name of the Crown from the Queen's Bench Division of the High Court, which orders the performance of a public legal duty. Mandamus is regarded as a residuary remedy with the result that it will not usually be granted where there is available some alternative remedy for enforcing a particular public legal duty (para 11.10.4 below).

Mandamus appears to be similar in nature to a mandatory injunction. The difference between the two is that an injunction is an equitable remedy which is normally available only in *private* law, while mandamus is a common-law remedy, based on royal authority, which is available only in *public* law (*Glossop v Heston & Isleworth Local Board* (1879) 12 ChD 102, CA).

Although mandamus may be sought separately, it is often applied for in the same proceedings together with certiorari. Thus, the decision of a tribunal which is *ultra vires* may be quashed by certiorari and the tribunal compelled to hold a proper rehearing by means of mandamus. However, if mandamus alone is ordered it is to be implied that the tribunal's decision was a nullity without its being quashed by certiorari (see, for example, *R v Hendon Justices (ex parte Director of Public Prosecutions)* [1993] 1 All ER 411, DC, para 11.8.3.2.2 above).

Mandamus, like certiorari and prohibition, is a discretionary remedy. In the exercise of its discretion, the court may refuse to grant it where the applicant has delayed unduly in seeking relief, or where the defendant public authority has tried but failed, through circumstances beyond its control, to perform its duty, or where it is unnecessary (*R v Commissioner of Police of the Metropolis (ex parte Blackburn) (No. 3)* [1973] QB 241, CA; *R v Bristol Corporation (ex parte Hendy)* [1974] 1 All ER 1047, CA, *per* Scarman LJ at p. 1051; *R v Northumberland Compensation Appeal Tribunal (ex parte Shaw)* [1952] 1 KB 338, CA, *per* Morris LJ at p. 357). Mandamus will not be granted to compel the performance of something which is impossible. Thus, in *R* v *London & North Western Railway Co.* (1851) 16 QB 864 the expiry of compulsory purchase powers was held to have barred the grant of mandamus to command the purchase of land necessary for constructing a branch railway line.

Mandamus may be refused if it is impractical to order it, even though it may be the only satisfactory remedy for the applicant in the particular circumstances of his case. In *Chief Constable of the North Wales Police* v *Evans* [1982] 3 All ER 141 (para 11.5.2.4), the House of Lords declined to order mandamus compelling the Chief Constable to reinstate a dismissed probationer constable on the ground, *inter alia,* that to do so would be tantamount to a usurpation by the courts of the powers of the Chief Constable. Instead, a declaration was granted that the Chief Constable had acted unlawfully. Sometimes the making of a declaration would amount to a usurpation of a public authority's function. In such a case mandamus should be preferred. Thus, in *Shah* v *Barnet London Borough Council* [1983] 1 All ER 226 the House of Lords held that where the court grants relief by way of judicial review of a decision of a local education authority to refuse an application for a grant for higher education, the appropriate remedies are certiorari to quash the decision and mandamus to compel the authority to reconsider the grant application. A declaration of the applicant's entitlement to a grant or of the authority's duty to bestow one should not be made since that would usurp the authority's function. The role of the court is limited to securing due observance of the law and does not extend to deciding that students are entitled to a grant or that the local education authorities are under a duty to bestow one. The power to decide whether to bestow or refuse a grant has been conferred by Parliament on the authorities. In exercising their power of decision they will be expected to follow the guidance on the law provided by the *Shah* case.

Disobedience to an order of mandamus is punishable as a contempt of court. In *R* v *Poplar Borough Council (ex parte London County Council) (No. 1)* [1922] 1 KB 72, CA, the borough council refused to pay a sum of money in respect of rates to the county council as required by statute. The Court of Appeal issued an order of mandamus against the borough council commanding it to pay over the money and, if necessary, to levy a rate for the purpose. When the borough council refused to obey the mandamus, the county council, in *R* v *Poplar Borough Council (ex parte London County Council) (No. 2)* [1922] 1 KB 95, CA, initiated contempt proceedings and some of the disobedient borough councillors were imprisoned.

11.10.2 Availability

Mandamus is available to the Crown, to the private citizen, and to one public authority against another, as in the *Poplar* cases discussed in para 11.10.1 above. Mandamus has been issued against the Crown Court; a county court judge; a magistrates' court; Income Tax Commissioners; a housing appeal tribunal; licensing authorities; planning authorities; local authorities; the Board of Trade; the registrar of companies; and against government ministers. The applicant for mandamus must have a sufficient interest in the matter to which the application relates (para 11.11.4 below).

Mandamus does not lie against the Crown since it emanates from the Crown. Moreover, unlike certiorari and prohibition, mandamus was not always available against servants of the Crown, such as individual ministers.

Mandamus would not lie against a Crown servant to compel him to perform, as an agent, a duty which was owed only to the Crown (*R* v *Lords Commissioners of the Treasury* (1872)

LR 7 QB 387, DC; *R* v *Secretary of State for War* [1891] 2 QB 326, CA). This was because a third party has no power to compel an agent to perform a duty which is owed only to the agent's principal. On the other hand, mandamus was held to lie (provided that the applicant had a sufficient interest) against a Crown servant to compel him to perform a statutory duty which was owed to a member of the public as well as to the Crown (see *M* v *Home Office* [1993] 3 All ER 537, HL, *per* Lord Woolf at p. 558). Thus, in *R* v *Commissioners for Special Purposes of the Income Tax* (1888) 21 QBD 313, the Court of Appeal issued mandamus against the Special Commissioners of Income Tax ordering them to make orders for the repayment of some income tax which a taxpayer had overpaid. It had been argued that mandamus would not lie against the Special Commissioners. The court held, however, that it would lie against them since they owed a statutory duty to the public, as well as to the Crown, to make orders for repayment of overpaid income tax.

According to the House of Lords in *M* v *Home Office*, above, the current position is that mandamus will lie against a Crown servant, such as a minister, without having to show that he was placed under some sort of statutory duty (see [1993] 3 All ER 537, HL, *per* Lord Woolf at p. 560).

11.10.3   Scope

Mandamus is used primarily to enforce the performance of a public *duty*, whether statutory or otherwise. But it may also be used to ensure that a *discretion* conferred by statute is exercised properly according to law. It may be granted, for example, where a minister is exercising his discretion in such a way as to frustrate the underlying policy of the statute (*Padfield* v *Minister of Agriculture, Fisheries & Food* [1968] AC 997, HL, below), or where irrelevant factors are taken into consideration (*R* v *Port of London Authority (ex parte Kynoch Ltd)* [1919] 1 KB 176, CA, in which, however, mandamus was refused on the facts).

Courts and tribunals are under a public duty to hear and determine all cases within their jurisdiction provided that those cases have been initiated according to the correct procedure. In *R* v *Huddersfield County Court Judge (ex parte Beaumont Ashton Ltd)* (1967) *The Times*, 24 October, DC, a county court judge refused to hear an application for the renewal of the tenancy of a shop on the ground that he did not have jurisdiction to do so. The Divisional Court held that he did have jurisdiction and granted an order of mandamus commanding him to hear and determine the application. But while mandamus may be issued to order a judge to hear and determine a case, it will not be issued so as to control the judge in his conduct of the case or to instruct him what evidence to admit or reject (*R* v *Sir Robert Carden* (1879) 5 QBD 1, DC, *per* Cockburn CJ at p. 5). In *R* v *Wells Street Stipendiary Magistrate (ex parte Seillon)* [1978] 3 All ER 257, the Divisional Court refused to interfere by means of mandamus where a stipendiary magistrate refused to allow a particular line of cross-examination by defence counsel during committal proceedings.

Mandamus is available to command the performance of the public duties owed by local authorities. Thus, in *R* v *Bedwellty Urban District Council (ex parte Price)* [1934] 1 KB 333, DC, a local authority was ordered by mandamus to produce its accounts for the inspection of the agent of a ratepayer. The applicant himself had been allowed access to the accounts but, being unable to understand them fully, he wished them to be examined on his behalf by his accountant. It was held that the statutory words, 'a person interested', included the agent of a ratepayer, such as an accountant.

Mandamus has also been used to ensure that a local authority abides by its own standing orders. In *R* v *Hereford Corporation (ex parte Harrower and others)* [1970] 1 WLR 1424,

DC, the local authority was bound, by statute, to make its contracts in accordance with its own standing orders. One standing order laid down that contracts which exceeded £50 in value should go out to tender unless the matter was one of urgency. The local authority did not go out to tender in respect of certain central heating installations because there was no heating design engineer on the staff to prepare the necessary specifications. The contract was placed with the electricity board. The local authority had the right to suspend standing orders but had not done so. The applicants, who were electrical contractors on the local authority's approved list and also ratepayers for the area, applied for mandamus to command the local authority to comply with its standing orders and put the contract out to tender. The court granted mandamus but suspended its operation for fourteen days to give the local authority an opportunity to resolve to suspend its standing orders. The authority had failed to comply with its own standing orders. The fact that there was no heating design engineer on the staff did not make the matter one of urgency. The applicants had a sufficient interest to enable them to apply for mandamus, not because they were approved electrical contractors but because they were ratepayers.

Mandamus may issue against a licensing authority to compel the proper performance of its public duties. In *R* v *Weymouth Borough Council (ex parte Teletax (Weymouth) Ltd)* [1947] KB 583, DC, a taxicab licensing authority misunderstood its statutory licensing powers and refused to transfer cab licences to a new owner of five cabs which had existing licences. The court held that the authority's power was to license cabs and not their owners or drivers. Accordingly, if a licensed cab was sold, the buyer was entitled to use the cab until the licence expired. Mandamus was granted commanding the authority to register the transfer of the licences.

Mandamus may lie against a police authority to compel the enforcement of the criminal law. In *R* v *Commissioner of Police of the Metropolis (ex parte Blackburn)* [1968] 2 QB 118, the Court of Appeal was prepared to issue mandamus against the police but did not do so. The remedy had become unnecessary because the Commissioner withdrew his instructions not to enforce the gaming laws in London. The Court of Appeal was of the clear opinion that mandamus would be available against the police in appropriate circumstances.

This view was repeated in *R* v *Commissioner of Police of the Metropolis (ex parte Blackburn) (No. 3)* [1973] QB 241, CA, in which the same applicant sought mandamus to compel the Commissioner to enforce the laws against pornography. The Metropolitan Police had been instructed by the Commissioner not to bring prosecutions or apply for destruction orders without the approval of the Director of Public Prosecutions. As a result, a great deal of pornographic material was openly on sale in London without any interference by the police. The validity of the Commissioner's instructions was questionable because the Obscene Publications Act 1959 required obscene articles to be brought before a magistrate, and not the DPP, for a decision on whether to destroy the articles.

The Court of Appeal held that it would interfere only in the extreme case where a police authority was not carrying out its duty of enforcing the law. It would not interfere with the discretion which the authority had in performing the duty of law enforcement as long as that duty was being carried out. On the facts, mandamus was refused, this time because the Commissioner was doing what he could to enforce the law under difficult conditions and no more could reasonably be expected of him. Although police efforts to control pornography had been notably ineffective, the Court of Appeal put most of the blame on the deficiencies of the Obscene Publications Act itself.

Mandamus may issue to order a public authority to exercise a *discretion* one way or the other where it has failed to do so, or to exercise it in a lawful manner (as by taking into account only relevant considerations and excluding irrelevant ones), or to give reasons for its decision to exercise the discretion in a particular way. The justification for the court's power to interfere in these circumstances is that a complete failure to exercise a discretion which is required by law to be exercised is unlawful, and that an improper or capricious exercise of a discretion is tantamount to a failure to exercise it at all (*Commissioners of Inland Revenue* v *National Federation of Self-Employed & Small Businesses Ltd* [1981] 2 All ER 93, HL, *per* Lord Scarman at p. 111). But the court will only compel the public authority to act; it will not substitute its own decision for that of the public authority. In *Padfield* v *Minister of Agriculture, Fisheries & Food* [1968] AC 997, it was held by the House of Lords that the minister had wrongfully refused to exercise a discretion to refer a complaint about the operation of a milk marketing scheme to a committee of investigation as required by statute. The case was sent back to the Divisional Court of the Queen's Bench Division for an order of mandamus to be issued commanding the minister to consider the complaint according to law.

In *Padfield*, a complaint could be referred to a committee of investigation for consideration and report 'if the minister in any case so directs'. The House of Lords emphatically denied that those words gave the minister a completely unfettered discretion to refer a complaint or not. The minister's discretion must be exercised in accordance with the intention of the statute which conferred it. The obvious intention of Parliament was that an independent committee, established for the purpose, should investigate complaints about the operation of the milk marketing scheme and that its reports should be available to Parliament. It was not a proper exercise of his discretion for the minister to take no action at all on a legitimate complaint, or to ignore the merits of the complaint and take into account irrelevant considerations (such as political embarrassment to himself if he later felt obliged to implement the committee's recommendations).

All the minister's reasons for refusing to order an inquiry into the complaint were held to be bad in law. It was argued on behalf of the minister that he was not bound to give reasons for refusing to refer a complaint and that if he had given no reasons his decision could not have been questioned. But the House of Lords made it absolutely clear that his decision could be challenged in those circumstances. If the minister failed or refused to give any reason for his decision, the court may infer that he had no good reason to give and may issue a prerogative order against him. 'Reason' means something more than a mere conclusion. If, however, an intelligible and salient reason is given, it is immaterial that matters of detail are not included (*Elliott* v *London Borough of Southwark* [1976] 2 All ER 781, CA). In *Padfield*, the House of Lords considered that the minister's silence would amount to an attempt to frustrate or thwart the underlying policy of the statute and, as such, would be an abuse of the discretion conferred on him by the statute.

11.10.4 Mandamus and alternative remedies

Mandamus is a discretionary remedy and will not normally be granted where there is some adequate alternative remedy or procedure available for enforcing a particular public legal duty. The alternative remedy or procedure may be provided by a particular statute or it may be available in the form of an action in tort.

In *Pasmore* v *Oswaldtwistle Urban District Council* [1898] AC 387, HL, a local authority had a statutory duty to provide such sewers as were necessary for draining their district. In default, the Act provided that a complaint could be made to the Local Government Board, which had power to order performance of the duty within a fixed time and to enforce its order by an application for mandamus. The owner of a paper mill applied to the court for mandamus to command the local authority to provide sewers adequate to carry effluent from the mill. The House of Lords held that the statute, by implication, had excluded an application for mandamus by a private person. The proper remedy, as provided by the statute, was to complain to the Local Government Board.

Before deciding whether mandamus is excluded by the availability of an alternative remedy, the court will consider carefully whether that other remedy is adequate in terms of convenience and effectiveness (*R v Poplar Borough Council (ex parte London County Council) (No. 1)* [1922] 1 KB 72, CA, *per* Scrutton LJ at p. 94; *R v Paddington Valuation Officer (ex parte Peachey Property Corporation Ltd) (No. 2)* [1966] 1 QB 380, CA, *per* Lord Denning MR at p. 400).

The alternative remedy was considered to be inadequate in three cases already discussed elsewhere. In *R v Poplar Borough Council (ex parte London County Council) (No. 1)* [1922] 1 KB 72, CA (para 11.10.1 above), mandamus was granted despite the existence of a specific statutory remedy. That remedy — the levying of distress on the goods of the council and/or those of its members — was held to be utterly inadequate for ensuring payment of the sum due to the county council. In *R v Bedwellty Urban District Council (ex parte Price)* [1934] 1 KB 333, DC (para 11.10.3), mandamus was granted even though the statute provided another remedy, namely, a criminal penalty not exceeding £5 to be imposed on the appropriate officer of the local authority for refusing to allow inspection of the accounts. It was held that such a remedy could lead the applicant no nearer to inspection of the accounts and was not, therefore, as convenient and effective as mandamus. In *R v Commissioner of Police of the Metropolis (ex parte Blackburn)* [1968] 2 QB 118, CA (para 11.10.3 above), it was argued that Mr Blackburn had an equally effective and convenient remedy in that he could himself seek to enforce the gaming laws by starting private prosecutions on his own. Mandamus was refused on the facts, but the Court of Appeal made it clear that they would not have regarded the alternative remedy as adequate. Salmon LJ (at p. 145) described it as 'fantastically unrealistic' and Edmund-Davies LJ (at p. 149) said that 'only the most sardonic could regard the launching of a private prosecution . . . as being equally convenient, beneficial and appropriate' as mandamus.

11.11 APPLICATION FOR JUDICIAL REVIEW: RULES OF THE SUPREME COURT, ORDER 53, AND SUPREME COURT ACT 1981, SECTION 31

11.11.1 Introduction

The common procedure for obtaining the prerogative remedies is now much simplified. Before 1933 the procedure was by means of 'rule nisi' and 'rule absolute'. A rule nisi issued by the court to the applicant compelled the other party to show cause why the prerogative remedy should not be granted against him. If sufficient cause was shown at the hearing, the rule nisi was discharged and the remedy was not granted. If sufficient cause was not shown, the rule nisi was made absolute and the remedy granted at the discretion of the court. This rule procedure was abolished by statute in 1933 and replaced by a new procedure under rules of court.

But other, more serious, deficiencies remained. In particular, it was not possible to claim an ordinary remedy, like damages or an injunction, in the same proceedings in addition to or instead of a prerogative remedy. And the *locus standi* required to apply for prerogative relief was not quite the same for each remedy, although there were signs that the differences were diminishing. In 1976, the Law Commission recommended a new procedure to be called 'application for judicial review' (Law Com. No. 73, *Remedies in Administrative Law,* Cmnd 6407, 1976). By 1978, most of the Law Commission's recommendations had been implemented, not by statute but by changes in the Rules of the Supreme Court. The new RSC, Ord. 53, came into force on 11 January 1978. Some of the more important provisions of Ord. 53 have since been put into statutory form, with effect from 1 January 1982, by s. 31 of the Supreme Court Act 1981.

The new Ord. 53 changed only procedure and practice, which includes the question of *locus standi (Commissioners of Inland Revenue v National Federation of Self-Employed & Small Businesses Ltd* [1981] 2 All ER 93, HL, *per* Lord Diplock at p. 102; and see para 11.11.4 below). The substantive law relating to the prerogative remedies, outlined above, remains the same, as does the jurisdiction of the High Court. The substantive law continues, therefore, to be capable of development by judicial decision.

It should be noted that, unless the circumstances are exceptional, an application for judicial review should not normally be made by the applicant, or entertained by the court, until *after* the objectionable decision has been reached or the impugned hearing concluded. To seek relief from the High Court too soon will in many cases turn out to be an unnecessary waste of time and money. Furthermore, for the High Court to entertain challenges to decisions made at the interlocutory stage of proceedings in inferior courts and tribunals could cause havoc there. (See, e.g., *R* v *Association of Futures Brokers & Dealers Ltd (ex parte Mordens Ltd)* [1991] COD 40, where an application for judicial review of two interlocutory decisions of a commissioner appointed to hear the applicants' appeal against the refusal of AFBD to admit them to membership of the Association was dismissed.)

11.11.2   Availability

The procedure by way of application for judicial review *must* be used in order to obtain the three prerogative orders of mandamus, prohibition and certiorari (RSC, Ord. 53, r. 1(1); Supreme Court Act 1981, s. 31(1)). In addition, the procedure *may* be used to obtain a declaration or an injunction (RSC, Ord. 53, r. 1(2); Supreme Court Act 1981, s. 31(2)), although these remedies continue to exist as private-law remedies also.

It was at first thought that a declaration in a matter of public law could be sought, according to the circumstances, *either* on an application for judicial review under the new Ord. 53 *or* in an ordinary private-law action under Ord. 15, r. 16. This was the intention of the Law Commission expressed in its *Report on Remedies in Administrative Law* (Law Com. No. 73, Cmnd 6407, 1976, paras 34 and 58(a)). However, in *O'Reilly* v *Mackman* [1982] 3 All ER 1124 the House of Lords held that a person seeking to challenge the decision of a public authority on the ground that it infringes a right protected by public law must, as a general rule, proceed by way of an application for judicial review under Ord. 53 rather than by way of an ordinary action for a declaration under Ord. 15, r. 16. Failure to use the correct procedure will result in the action being struck out as an abuse of the process of the court. *O'Reilly* v *Mackman* was applied immediately in *Cocks* v *Thanet District Council* [1982] 3 All ER 1135, a case decided by the House of Lords on the same day, in which it was held that the proper way to challenge the decision of a housing authority, under the Housing (Homeless Persons) Act 1977 (now part III of the Housing Act 1985), that a person became homeless intentionally and is therefore not entitled to permanent accommodation, is by way of an application for judicial review of the authority's decision under Ord. 53 and not by way of an ordinary action for a declaration (see also *Ali* v *Tower Hamlets London Borough*

Council [1992] 3 All ER 512, CA; *British Steel plc* v *Customs and Excise Commissioners* [1996] 1 All ER 1002).

The leading speech in *O'Reilly* v *Mackman* was prepared by Lord Diplock, with whom the other Law Lords expressly agreed. It is clear from Lord Diplock's opinion that the major grounds for the decision were, first, the improved usefulness of Ord. 53 since the changes introduced in 1978 and, secondly, the desire to protect public authorities from 'groundless, unmeritorious or tardy harassment' (at p. 1133). There can be no doubt that judicial review possesses safeguards against its abuse as a remedy which are not available in ordinary actions at law. These safeguards are the requirement of permission of a High Court judge to apply for judicial review, the limited form of discovery of documents, the fact that cross-examination will only be allowed when justice demands it, the three-month time-limit within which the application must be made, and the fact that any relief sought is granted only at the discretion of the court. (See, e.g., *R* v *Secretary of State for Social Services (ex parte Association of Metropolitan Authorities)* [1986] 1 All ER 164; *R* v *Monopolies and Mergers Commission (ex parte Argyll Group plc)* [1986] 2 All ER 257, CA; *R* v *Secretary of State for the Environment (ex parte Walters)* (1997) *The Times*, 2 September, CA, in which it was held on appeal that the judge, after taking into account all the circumstances, had correctly exercised his discretion in refusing relief to the applicant despite the judge's finding that the relevant statutory consultation process had not been properly followed.) While these safeguards may undoubtedly prevent abuse of the legal process and the unreasonable harassment of public authorities, they may also be seen as weapons with which to oppress the ordinary citizen seeking to remedy the excesses of the administration. Therein lies the danger to justice of the House of Lords' decision that Ord. 53 will in most cases exclude the ordinary action for a declaration under Ord. 15, r. 16.

In *O'Reilly* v *Mackman* it may well be that the disadvantages to the citizen of the procedure under Ord. 53 were played down and that his interests were placed a poor second best behind the desire to protect the administration. The advantages to the citizen (and corresponding disadvantages to public authorities) flowing from an ordinary action are real and well recognised. He does not require permission of anyone to commence his action; there is thus no judicial 'filter' at this stage. There are no special restrictions on the discovery of documents or on cross-examination. The limitation period is six years. The remedy of damages is not discretionary. In *Doyle and others* v *Northumbria Probation Committee* [1991] 4 All ER 294 (see further, below), Henry J (at p. 300) referred to the difficulties caused by *O'Reilly* v *Mackman*. The need to choose the correct procedure in litigation where public law and private law mix creates what he described as a 'formidable extra hurdle for plaintiffs [claimants]' and gives rise to the potential for expensive appeals. He said that the forms of action abolished in the nineteenth century appeared 'to be in danger of returning to rule us from their graves'.

That the rule in *O'Reilly* v *Mackman* involves a risk of creating procedural over-technicality was acknowledged by the House of Lords in *Roy* v *Kensington and Chelsea and Westminster Family Practitioner Committee* [1992] 1 All ER 705, HL (see further, below). Lord Lowry said (ibid., at pp. 729–30) that the rule in *O'Reilly* v *Mackman* is subject to exceptions based on the nature of the claim and on the undesirability of erecting procedural barriers, and that unless the procedure adopted in a case is ill suited to dispose of the issues raised in it there is much to be said for allowing the case to be heard rather than for the court to entertain a debate concerning the form of the proceedings. In *Roy*, it was held that the proceedings had been properly brought by ordinary action rather than by judicial review: the proceedings were dominated by the claimant's private-law rights; his claim might involve disputed issues of fact; the order sought (the payment of money due) could not be granted in judicial review proceedings; and it was said that, when individual private rights are claimed, there should not be a need for permission or a special time-limit and the relief should not be discretionary (see [1992] 1 All ER 705 *per* Lord Lowry at p. 729). In *Equal Opportunities Commission* v *Secretary of State for Employment* [1994] 1 All ER 910, HL, Lord Lowry referred to his criticism of *O'Reilly* v *Mackman* in *Roy* v *Kensington and Chelsea and Westminster Family Practitioner Committee* and expressed the hope (at p. 926) that *O'Reilly* v *Mackman* would one day be the subject of further consideration by their Lordships. A superficial re-examination was later conducted in *Mercury Communications Ltd* v *Director General of Telecommunications* [1996] 1 All ER 575, HL (see below).

It was recognised in *O'Reilly* v *Mackman* itself that neither Ord. 53 nor s. 31 of the Supreme Court Act 1981 makes judicial review the exclusive procedure for obtaining relief for the infringement of rights protected by public law. Lord Diplock himself identified two exceptions where an ordinary action may still be used but preferred to leave other exceptions to be developed on a case-to-case basis. The exceptions mentioned by Lord Diplock (at p. 1134) were, first, where the invalidity of the impugned decision arises as a collateral issue in a claim for infringement of a right arising under *private* law. Secondly, where none of the parties objects to proceeding by way of an ordinary action instead of by way of an application for judicial review.

The courts have had to consider the implications of *O'Reilly* v *Mackman* on a number of subsequent occasions. In *Davy* v *Spelthorne Borough Council* [1983] 3 All ER 278, the House of Lords upheld the claimant's right to bring an action for damages in negligence against a local planning authority. His action was concerned with infringement of his *private-law* rights and did not raise any issue of *public law*; he was not, therefore, obliged to use judicial review proceedings under Ord. 53. In *Wandsworth London Borough Council* v *Winder* [1984] 3 All ER 976, HL, the local authority brought a claim against the defendant for arrears of rent and possession of his flat on the ground that he had not paid the rent lawfully due. In his defence the defendant denied that he was in arrears because the local authority had exceeded their statutory powers in increasing his rent beyond what he was prepared to pay. He counterclaimed for a declaration that the notices of increase were void. The local authority applied to strike out the defence and counterclaim as an abuse of the process of the court. The House of Lords refused to do so on the ground that it was perfectly proper for the defendant, by way of reply to an action brought against him by a public authority, to claim that his existing *private-law* rights (arising under a contract with the authority) had been infringed by a decision of the authority. He was not obliged in such circumstances to mount his challenge to the decision by judicial review under Ord. 53. Where, however, the defendant's private-law rights have not been violated he will have no defence to the authority's possession proceedings. If he wishes to challenge the proceedings on the basis of an alleged infringement of some *public-law* right (for example, that it was unreasonable in the *Wednesbury* sense for the authority to apply for possession) he cannot do so in the authority's proceedings but must himself initiate a separate application for leave to apply for judicial review (*Avon County Council* v *Buscott* [1988] 1 All ER 841, CA, distinguishing *Wandsworth London Borough Council* v *Winder*, HL, above, and approving the decision of Scott J in *Waverley Borough Council* v *Hilden* [1988] 1 All ER 807). For the purposes of facilitating such an application, the defendant can apply to the trial court for an adjournment of the possession proceedings. However, an adjournment will only be granted where there is a real possibility that the defendant's application for leave to apply for judicial review will be successful (*Avon County Council* v *Buscott*, above).

In *Doyle and others* v *Northumbria Probation Committee* [1991] 4 All ER 294, the claimants were probation officers aggrieved at the decision of their employers to discontinue the payment of a daily home-to-office car mileage allowance as provided for in their contracts of employment. Just before the expiry of the six-year limitation period for bringing an action, they issued a writ claiming damages for breach of contract. The employers applied to the court to dismiss the action as an abuse of the process of the court on the ground that it raised issues of public law which should have been brought before the court by way of judicial review proceedings. The public-law element referred to was the employers' assertion by way of defence that they had no statutory power to pay the allowance. Applying the reasoning in *Wandsworth London Borough Council* v *Winder* [1984] 3 All ER 976, HL, Henry J held that the action would not be dismissed since it had been rightly commenced by writ. The claimants were seeking a *private-law* remedy in a genuine *private-law* claim; they were not alleging any breach of their public-law rights. Moreover, to dismiss their action and require them to proceed by way of judicial review would effectively deprive them of their private-law rights because, in view of the delay, it would be most unlikely that they would obtain permission to apply for judicial review.

In *R* v *East Berkshire Health Authority (ex parte Walsh)* [1984] 3 All ER 425, CA, a preliminary point was raised whether the purported dismissal of a senior nursing officer could be questioned in judicial review proceedings under Ord. 53 or whether the appropriate procedure was to make a private law complaint to an employment tribunal. The Court of Appeal held that public-law proceedings were inappropriate since a breach of an ordinary contract of employment with a public authority gives rise to private-law remedies only. It might be otherwise if there is a special statutory code of discipline governing the employment and dismissal of the employee. The existence of such a code might import a sufficient public law element into the purported dismissal to allow the employee to seek judicial review, as in *R* v *Secretary of State for the Home Department (ex parte Benwell)* [1984] 3 All ER 854 in which the *Walsh* case was distinguished. It is interesting to note that, unlike Mr Walsh, Mr Benwell, as a prison officer, was precluded from making a complaint about dismissal to an employment tribunal. Accordingly, unless he was able to have his unfair treatment remedied in judicial review proceedings he would be without a remedy at all, having exhausted the internal appeal procedures. The judge referred to this predicament in his judgment (see [1984] 3 All ER 854 at p. 866) but did not, of course, treat it as a ground for holding that he had jurisdiction in the circumstances to grant a declaration and certiorari against the Home Secretary.

It has been held that whether or not the relationship between a general medical practitioner and the family practitioner committee (later renamed 'family health services authority' by the National Health Service and Community Care Act 1990 and abolished by the Health Authorities Act 1995) could be described as 'contractual', a doctor's claim for unpaid practice allowances rested in private law and was rightly pursued by private-law action rather than judicial review notwithstanding the fact that it involved a challenge to a public law decision (*Roy* v *Kensington and Chelsea and Westminster Family Practitioner Committee* [1992] 1 All ER 705, HL, *per* Lord Bridge at p. 709 and Lord Lowry at p. 725; see also *Lonrho plc* v *Tebbit* [1992] 4 All ER 280, CA, in which *Roy* was applied).

Again, in a case brought by way of private-law action by a prison officer who refused to work on a new shift system, and in which he claimed a declaration that he was still employed on the old shift system, it was said to be at least arguable that the relationship between a prison officer and the Home Office is contractual and that, in any event, the issues raised were private-law ones. Accordingly, the claim was held to have been properly brought by way of private-law action rather than by application for judicial review (*McClaren* v *Home Office* [1990] ICR 824, CA). In *R* v *Derbyshire County Council (ex parte Noble)* [1990] ICR 808, CA, a deputy police surgeon's application for judicial review of the authority's decision to terminate his employment was dismissed on the ground that judicial review was inappropriate since the applicant's claim rested in the private law of contract and involved no sufficient public-law element.

Similarly, the dismissal of a barrister employed by the Crown Prosecution Service was held not to be a matter of public law in *R* v *Crown Prosecution Service (ex parte Hogg)* (1994) *The Times*, 14 April, CA, in which *McClaren* v *Home Office* was followed. In *R* v *Secretary of State for the Home Department (ex parte Moore)* [1994] COD 67, DC, the *Walsh, Noble* and *McClaren* cases were preferred to *Benwell* and it was held that the refusal of the Permanent Secretary at the Home Office to accept a recommendation of the Civil Service Appeal Board that the applicant, who had been unfairly dismissed from his employment, be reinstated as a prison officer was not a matter of public law and could not, therefore, be challenged in judicial review proceedings. On the other hand, in *R* v *Legal Aid Board (ex parte Donn & Co.)* [1996] 3 All ER 1 it was held that a decision — taken by a sub-committee of the Legal Aid Board — to award a contract for the management of the Gulf War Syndrome litigation to two particular firms of solicitors contained a sufficient public law element to justify allowing the decision to be challenged in judicial review proceedings.

In *Gillick* v *West Norfolk and Wisbech Area Health Authority* [1985] 3 All ER 402, HL, Lord Scarman (with whom Lord Fraser of Tullybelton expressly agreed) said that a parent who wishes to proceed against a public authority in respect of the threatened infringement of parental rights is entitled to proceed by way of an ordinary private-law action rather than by way of judicial review under Ord. 53. Such a claim has a sufficient private-law content in it not to make a private-law action an abuse of the process of the court. Lord Scarman was also of the opinion that, in any event, Mrs Gillick's case fell within both exceptions mentioned in Lord Diplock's speech in *O'Reilly* v *Mackman* [1982] 3 All ER 1124, at p. 1134, namely that her attack on the validity of the DHSS's contraceptive advice was collateral to her claim for infringement of her private-law rights and none of the parties to the case had objected to the use of the private-law procedure (see [1985] 3 All ER 402 at pp. 415–416).

O'Reilly v *Mackman* was considered by the House of Lords in *Mercury Communications Ltd* v *Director General of Telecommunications* [1996] 1 All ER 575, HL. Here, the importance of avoiding an over-rigid demarcation between procedures at the expense of maintaining flexibility of choice was again emphasised. It was held that the overriding consideration in deciding whether private-law or public-law proceedings are the more appropriate is whether the proceedings constitute an abuse of the process of the court. In accordance with a contract between Mercury Communications and British Telecom, the Director General of Telecommunications had determined some terms which the parties could not agree upon. Mercury's challenge to this determination was held to have been properly brought in an ordinary private-law action for a declaration. The argument of the Director General and British Telecom that the use of private-law proceedings was an abuse of the process of the court as any determination by the Director General was governed solely by public law, and could only be challenged by seeking judicial review in public-law proceedings, was unsuccessful. The House of Lords took the view that the Director General was not precluded under all circumstances from entering the realms of private law merely because he held a statutory office and performed public duties. Their Lordships cited with apparent approval *Wandsworth London Borough Council* v *Winder* [1984] 3 All ER 976, HL, *Gillick* v *West Norfolk and Wisbech Area Health Authority* [1985] 3 All ER 402, HL, and *Roy* v *Kensington and Chelsea and Westminster Family Practitioner Committee* [1992] 1 All ER 705 as examples of claims which arose in a public-law context but which were rightly dealt with in private-law proceedings.

In *Trustees of the Dennis Rye Pension Fund* v *Sheffield City Council* [1997] 4 All ER 747, CA, the claimants' applications for improvement grants were approved by the council under its statutory powers. When the council later refused to pay the grants, the claimants brought a private-law action claiming the sums (approaching £100,000) due under the grants. The council argued that private-law proceedings were an abuse of the process of the court since the appropriate remedy for the claimants was to apply for judicial review. The Court of Appeal disagreed, holding that in the circumstances an ordinary private-law action was the more appropriate and convenient procedure. It was decided that, although in general the council's function in relation to the making of grants is a public one, once an application for a grant has been approved the council's duty to pay it is enforceable in an ordinary private-law action. In addition, the claimants were seeking the payment of a sum of money, a remedy which is not available in judicial review proceedings.

In his judgment, Lord Woolf MR referred to the 'constant unprofitable litigation over the divide between public and private law proceedings' ([1997] 4 All ER 747, 754). He suggested that it was time to go back to first principles and the guidance given by Lord Diplock in *O'Reilly* v *Mackman* [1982] 3 All ER 1124, HL — in particular, first, the importance of recognising that, in the public interest, judicial review provides protection for public bodies (in the form of the requirement of permission to apply for it and the protection against delay) which is not available in a private-law action, and, secondly, that the *general* rule is that it is against public policy and, as such, an abuse of the process of the court to circumvent these protective measures by bringing a *private-law action* in order to enforce *public law rights*.

Lord Woolf proposed some guidelines for determining whether judicial review or a private-law action is, in general, the more appropriate procedure ([1997] 4 All ER 747, 755). First, if it is not clear which is the correct procedure it is 'safer' to use judicial review since the applicant cannot then be accused of evading the protection afforded thereby to public bodies. If it later turns out that judicial review should not have been used, the applicant is not necessarily prejudiced because the court is not bound to dismiss the application; it may instead order the proceedings to continue as if they had been private-law proceedings begun by claim (see further, para 11.11.6.3 below). Secondly, if a private-law action is brought and the defendant applies to have it struck out as an abuse of the process of the court, the court should consider whether the case is one in which leave to apply for judicial review would have been granted if the claimant had used judicial review proceedings instead of private-law proceedings. If such leave would have been granted, this indicates that the protection which judicial review is designed to provide to public bodies has not been compromised. The court should also consider at this stage which is the more appropriate procedure for trying the case. If a private-law action is equally appropriate, or is more appropriate than an application for judicial review, this indicates that the private-law action should not be struck out. Thirdly, if it is not clear whether proceedings have been correctly brought by means of a private-law action the court is not bound to strike it out. Although there is no power to order the action to continue as though it were an application for judicial review (para 11.11.6.3 below), an alternative to striking out is to transfer the case to the Crown Office List as a judicial review case.

In considering whether judicial review or a private-law action is the more appropriate procedure, a highly relevant factor is that judicial review 'is not a fact-finding exercise' (*R v Chief Constable of the Warwickshire Constabulary (ex parte Fitzpatrick)* [1998] 1 All ER 65, DC, *per* Jowitt J at p. 80). Judicial review is concerned with the *legality* of decisions, not with their *merits*. Any disputed questions of fact involved in a case are usually more appropriately resolved in private-law proceedings, where there can be a full-scale trial with no permission required, no special time limit, no special restrictions on the discovery of documents or on cross-examination, and where the relief granted is not necessarily discretionary. The presence of disputed questions of fact was another reason for holding in *Trustees of the Dennis Rye Pension Fund v Sheffield City Council* [1997] 4 All ER 747, CA, that a private-law action was a more appropriate and convenient procedure than judicial review, and in *R v Chief Constable of the Warwickshire Constabulary (ex parte Fitzpatrick)* above, it was stated (*per* Jowitt J at p. 80) that as a means for deciding whether there has been an unlawful seizure of material under a search warrant, judicial review in most cases 'has only disadvantages and no advantages when compared with the private law remedy'.

An application for judicial review, claiming any of the prerogative remedies or an injunction or declaration, is available to impugn only the decisions of a body which is performing a *public* function. It follows that judicial review is not available to challenge the decisions of a voluntary (i.e., non-statutory) domestic tribunal which is performing what are essentially *private* functions (*Law v National Greyhound Racing Club Ltd* [1983] 3 All ER 300, CA (company limited by guarantee established to enforce the rules of greyhound racing held not susceptible to judicial review), approving *R v British Broadcasting Corporation (ex parte Lavelle)* [1983] 1 All ER 241 (decision of disciplinary tribunal established by BBC for private internal purposes held not susceptible to judicial review); see also *R v Lord Chancellor's Department (ex parte Nangle)* [1992] 1 All ER 897, DC (internal disciplinary proceedings in government department held not amenable to judicial review); *R v Lord Chancellor (ex parte Hibbit and Saunders)* [1993] COD 326, DC (Lord Chancellor treated the applicants unfairly in the manner in which a contract for court reporting services was awarded, but his decision was held not to be reviewable because it lacked a sufficient public law element); *R v Fernhill Manor School (ex parte Brown)* (1992) *The Independent*, 25 June (decision of independent school to expel a pupil not amenable to judicial review)). The appropriate remedy against a voluntary domestic tribunal exercising purely private functions is to seek declaratory or injunctive relief in private law proceedings.

In *R v Panel on Takeovers and Mergers (ex parte Datafin plc)* [1987] 1 All ER 564, the Court of Appeal held that the decisions of the Panel on Takeovers and Mergers (the 'City Takeover Panel') are subject to challenge by means of judicial review. (See also *R v Panel on Takeovers and Mergers (ex parte Guinness plc)* [1989] 1 All ER 509, CA, and note that in both of these cases judicial relief was refused on the facts.) The City Takeover Panel is a non-statutory unincorporated association with no statutory, prerogative or common-law powers. It was established privately by financial institutions for the purpose, *inter alia*, of enforcing a City code of practice. Nevertheless, it performs a *public* function and makes decisions which may indirectly affect the rights of ordinary citizens. Similarly, the Advertising Standards Authority performs a *public* function (which, if the Authority did not exist, would be performed by the Director-General of Fair Trading). Accordingly, the Authority's decisions are susceptible to challenge by judicial review even though it has no statutory, prerogative or common-law powers (*R v Advertising Standards Authority Ltd (ex parte Insurance Services plc)* [1990] COD 42, DC, in which a decision of the Authority was quashed by certiorari where it had been reached without regard to a material consideration;

decisions of the Committee of Advertising Practice are likewise susceptible to judicial review: *R* v *Committee of Advertising Practice (ex parte Bradford Exchange)* [1991] COD 43, where, on the facts, it was held that the decision-making process had not been unfair.)

The question whether the decisions of particular non-statutory bodies are amenable to judicial review is a troublesome one which continues to occupy the time of the courts while the law is developed on a case-by-case basis. The position of the Jockey Club, for example, was considered by the Queen's Bench Divisional Court in two somewhat inconclusive cases decided in 1989 and 1990. In *R* v *Jockey Club (ex parte Massingberd-Mundy)* (1989) [1993] 2 All ER 207, DC, it was held by a two-man court consisting of Neill LJ and Roch J (with some reluctance on the part of the latter) that, applying *Law* v *National Greyhound Racing Club Ltd* [1983] 3 All ER 300, CA, above, the decisions of the Jockey Club are *not* susceptible to judicial review.

The second case, *R* v *Jockey Club (ex parte RAM Racecourses Ltd)* (1990) [1993] 2 All ER 225, DC, was also decided in favour of the Jockey Club — not on the jurisdiction point but on the doctrine of legitimate expectation — by a differently constituted two-man court. On the question of jurisdiction, Stuart-Smith LJ said, *obiter,* that it was clear that the decision in *Massingberd-Mundy* was not given *per incuriam,* and he felt bound by *Law* v *National Greyhound Racing Club Ltd* to hold that the decisions of the Jockey Club are not reviewable. In addition, neither he nor Simon Brown J was convinced that *Massingberd-Mundy* was wrongly decided (which, as noted in para 9.3.2.5, is an additional test, laid down in *R* v *Greater Manchester Coroner (ex parte Tal)* [1984] 3 All ER 240, DC, for determining whether the Queen's Bench Divisional Court may refuse to follow one of its own earlier decisions). Simon Brown J, however, expressed the opinion that *Law* v *National Greyhound Racing Club Ltd* was distinguishable and that, in the light of *R* v *Panel on Takeovers and Mergers (ex parte Datafin plc)* [1987] 1 All ER 564, *some* decisions of the Jockey Club *are* reviewable.

Some, at least, of the doubt surrounding the position of the Jockey Club was dispelled by the Court of Appeal in *R* v *Disciplinary Committee of the Jockey Club (ex parte Aga Khan)* [1993] 2 All ER 853, CA. Here it was held that the Jockey Club's decision to disqualify the applicant's horse, which had won a major race, following the detection of a prohibited substance (camphor) in its urine was not susceptible to judicial review. Applying *Law* v *National Greyhound Racing Club Ltd* [1983] 3 All ER 300, CA, above, and distinguishing *R* v *Panel on Takeovers and Mergers (ex parte Datafin plc)* [1987] 1 All ER 564, CA, above, the Court of Appeal decided that, although in its regulation of horse racing it exercises powers which affect the public, the Jockey Club is not a public body and its powers are not governmental. It is a private body whose powers emanate from the agreement of those who subscribe to its rules. This agreement creates private rights for breach of which judicial review is not, but private law remedies are, appropriate.

The question as to whether *all* decisions of the Jockey Club are similarly immune from judicial review was left open in *R* v *Disciplinary Committee of the Jockey Club (ex parte Aga Khan),* above. Sir Thomas Bingham MR declined (at p. 867) to speculate on the matter. Farquharson LJ (at p. 873) refused to dismiss the possibility that some decisions might be reviewable, as where the persons affected by them had no contractual relationship with the Jockey Club and their only remedy thus lay in public law. On the other hand, Hoffmann LJ (at pp. 875–6) was cautious about adopting an 'improvisatory' approach which pretends that domestic bodies are organs of government in order to give access to judicial review in public law as a means of supplementing inadequate or non-existent private law remedies.

Decisions of the following non-statutory bodies have been held to be susceptible to judicial review: the Professional Conduct Committee of the Bar Council (*R* v *General*

Council of the Bar (ex parte Percival) [1990] 3 All ER 137, DC, although, on the facts, it was decided that the Committee had acted properly); the Financial Intermediaries Managers and Brokers Regulatory Association (*R v FIMBRA (ex parte Cochrane)* [1990] COD 33, where, however, relief was refused on the facts); the Life Assurance and Unit Trust Regulatory Organisation Ltd (*R v LAUTRO (ex parte Ross)* [1993] 1 All ER 545, CA, where, on the facts, the application for judicial review was refused); the Code of Practice Committee of the British Pharmaceutical Industry Association, a voluntary self-regulating body but one which performs a public duty in the control of advertising and the promotion of medicines (*R v British Pharmaceutical Industry Association Code of Practice Committee (ex parte Professional Counselling Aids Ltd)* (1990) *The Independent,* 1 November; on the facts, relief was refused); the visitor of a university if he acts outside his jurisdiction, or abuses his powers, or violates the principles of natural justice (*Page v Hull University Visitor* [1993] 1 All ER 97, HL, where it was held that, on the facts, the visitor's decision was not reviewable); subject to the same conditions as apply to a university visitor, High Court judges acting as visitors to the Inns of Court in matters relating to the fitness of persons to become or remain barristers (*R v Visitors to the Inns of Court (ex parte Calder)* [1993] 2 All ER 876, CA).

On the other hand, decisions of the Chief Rabbi, of the Imam, and of a Beth Din have been held not to be subject to judicial review (*R v Chief Rabbi (ex parte Wachmann)* (1991) [1993] 2 All ER 249; *R v Imam of Bury Park Mosque, Luton (ex parte Sulaiman Ali)* (1993) *The Times,* 20 May, CA; *R v London Beth Din (Court of the Chief Rabbi) (ex parte Bloom)* [1998] COD 131). Their functions are essentially religious and spiritual ones lacking any public-law character. Furthermore, a secular court would not feel competent to adjudicate upon matters of religious law, customs and traditions.

It seems that the public function which a body must be exercising in order that the High Court's supervisory jurisdiction can be invoked against it must involve more than the mere fact that the decisions of that body might have consequences for the public at large. There must, according to some of the cases, be a potential *governmental* interest in the particular decision-making body in the sense that if the body did not exist the government might have to consider asking Parliament to impose a statutory regime of control. Some of the financial services cases, and the advertising cases, fall into this category, but the cases of the Chief Rabbi, the Imam, and the Beth Din clearly do not (see also *R v Football Association Ltd (ex parte Football League Ltd)* (1991) [1993] 2 All ER 833, where it was held that the Football Association is a body whose decisions are not subject to judicial review, and note that this case was heavily relied upon by the Court of Appeal in *R v Disciplinary Committee of the Jockey Club (ex parte Aga Khan)* [1993] 2 All ER 853, CA, above).

It has been held that, although the powers exercised by Lloyd's derive from a private Act of Parliament, the relationship between Lloyd's and the 'names' who join it in its insurance business is governed by the contract existing between the parties so that the relationship is a matter of private law and does not contain any public law element such as to make Lloyd's amenable to judicial review at the suit of 'names' (*R v Corporation of Lloyd's (ex parte Briggs)* (1992) *The Times,* 30 July, DC). Decisions of the Insurance Ombudsman Bureau, one of a number of non-statutory bodies established privately to assist with the resolution of disputes between providers and consumers of financial services, are likewise not susceptible to judicial review. The IOB's powers are derived entirely from the contract it has with member companies and it does not exercise governmental functions (*R v Insurance Ombudsman Bureau (ex parte Aegon Life Assurance Ltd)* [1994] COD 426, DC, distinguishing *R v LAUTRO (ex parte Ross)* [1993] 1 All ER 545, CA, above).

Decisions of the Parliamentary Commissioner for Administration (the Ombudsman) are reviewable (*R* v *Parliamentary Commissioner for Administration (ex parte Dyer)* [1994] 1 All ER 375, DC), but not those of the Parliamentary Commissioner for Standards (*R* v *Parliamentary Commissioner for Standards (ex parte Al Fayed)* [1998] 1 All ER 93, CA). This distinction is based upon a desire by the courts to leave Parliament to regulate its own internal affairs and not to be seen to be interfering with proceedings in Parliament. Both Parliamentary Commissioners have duties of a public nature, are subject to the supervision of standing committees of Parliament, and make reports to Parliament. However, while the Parliamentary Commissioner for Administration is concerned with the activities of the public service *outside* Parliament, the functions of the Parliamentary Commissioner for Standards relate directly to what happens *inside* Parliament and, in the performance of those functions, Parliament has placed him under the supervision of the Select Committee on Standards and Privileges of the House of Commons. In view of all this, the Court of Appeal decided in the *Al Fayed* case that it would be inappropriate for the activities of the Parliamentary Commissioner for Standards to be reviewable by the courts. Accordingly, Mr Al Fayed's application for judicial review of a report of the Parliamentary Commissioner for Standards, which had concluded that there was no basis for Mr Al Fayed's allegation that Mr Michael Howard (a member of Parliament and a government minister) had received a corrupt payment, was dismissed.

Decisions of the Criminal Cases Review Commission created by the Criminal Appeal Act 1995 are susceptible to judicial review (*R* v *Criminal Cases Review Commission (ex parte Pearson)* [1999] 3 All ER 498, DC, where, however, the challenge failed on the facts).

11.11.3 Permission to apply for judicial review

The continued discretionary nature of prerogative relief is emphasised by the rule that the applicant must obtain permission of the single judge to apply for judicial review (RSC, Ord. 53, r. 3; Supreme Court Act 1981, s. 31(3)). The application for permission to apply is made *ex parte;* i.e., without notice to the other side (Ord. 53, r. 3(2)). On the 'without notice' application, permission to apply for judicial review can be granted, deferred to the substantive hearing, or refused. If permission is granted, an application to set it aside can later be made by the other side.

Permission is required so that the court may act as a sieve to exclude unmeritorious claims at an early stage. It is thus possible to 'prevent the time of the court being wasted by busybodies with misguided or trivial complaints of administrative error' (*Commissioners of Inland Revenue* v *National Federation of Self-Employed & Small Businesses Ltd* [1981] 2 All ER 93, HL, *per* Lord Diplock at p. 105). It has already been noted that permission will be required if it is proposed to apply by way of judicial review for a declaration or an injunction whereas permission is not required if these remedies are sought as private-law remedies (para 11.11.2 above).

An application for permission to apply for judicial review is made by filing in the Crown Office a notice of application in a prescribed form accompanied by an affidavit. The notice sets out the name and description of the applicant, the relief sought and the grounds on which it is sought. The affidavit verifies the facts relied on by the applicant. The judge may determine the application without a hearing unless a hearing has been requested in the notice of application. The judge need not sit in open court (Ord. 53, r. 3(2) and (3)).

The application for permission is the first or 'threshold' stage in a two-stage procedure. The two stages are:

(a) the application for permission to apply for judicial review; and

(b) if permission is granted, the hearing of the substantive application itself on the merits.

If permission to apply for judicial review is granted, the substantive application is made to the Divisional Court in the case of a criminal cause or matter. In any other case, the application is normally made to a single judge sitting in open court. However, the court can instead order the application in a non-criminal case to be made to a single judge sitting in chambers or to the Divisional Court (Ord. 53, r. 5(1) and (2)).

Where permission to apply for judicial review is granted, the court may give interim relief pending the hearing of the application on the merits. If the applicant is claiming certiorari or prohibition, the grant of permission to apply operates, if the court so directs, as a stay of the impugned proceedings (Ord. 53, r. 3(10)). If any other relief (such as the non-prerogative remedy of injunction) is claimed, the court may grant such interim relief as could be granted in a private-law action begun by claim (ibid.).

Taken together with the wide jurisdiction to grant injunctions conferred by s. 37 of the Supreme Court Act 1981 (para 10.4.1), this means that the court has power to give, *inter alia*, a form of interim relief which is rarely granted, namely, an interim mandatory injunction (para 10.4.2.2.2). Such an injunction was ordered in *R* v *Kensington and Chelsea Royal London Borough Council (ex parte Hammell)* [1989] 1 All ER 1202, CA, where the applicant had been granted permission to apply for judicial review of the council's decision that it was not satisfied that she was homeless within part III of the Housing Act 1985. Taking into account the balance of convenience between the parties and the fact that the applicant had made out a strong prima facie case of breach of duty on the part of the council, the Court of Appeal held that there should be an interim mandatory injunction compelling the council to house the applicant and her children on a temporary basis pending the hearing of her application for judicial review.

Approving the *Hammell* case in *M* v *Home Office* [1993] 3 All ER 537, HL (para 11.11.6 below), the House of Lords confirmed that Ord. 53, r. 3(10) gives the court jurisdiction to grant interim injunctions in judicial review proceedings (see [1993] 3 All ER 537, *per* Lord Woolf at p. 563).

According to *R* v *Inspectorate of Pollution (ex parte Greenpeace Ltd)* [1994] 4 All ER 321, CA, where a stay is applied for under Ord. 53, r. 3(10) the court will apply the same principles as though the application had been for an interim injunction. Consequently, the factors to be taken into account (for example, as to where the balance of convenience lies) are those laid down in *American Cyanamid Co.* v *Ethicon Ltd* [1975] AC 396, HL (see para 10.4.2.2.2, and see also *R* v *Ministry of Agriculture, Fisheries and Food (ex parte Monsanto plc)* [1998] 4 All ER 321, DC).

11.11.4 *Locus standi*

Permission to apply for judicial review will not be granted unless the court considers that the applicant has a 'sufficient interest in the matter to which the application relates' (RSC, Ord. 53, r. 3(7); Supreme Court Act 1981, s. 31(3)). The requirement of *locus standi* affords protection against misuse of the legal process, enabling the court to 'prevent abuse by busybodies, cranks and other mischief makers' (*Commissioners of Inland Revenue* v *National Federation of Self-Employed & Small Businesses Ltd* [1981] 2 All ER 93, HL, *per* Lord Scarman at p. 113). *Locus standi* is not the same as capacity. A body may have capacity to apply for judicial review but it may later turn out that it has no *locus standi* in the proceedings. On the other hand, if capacity is found (at the permission stage) to be lacking, the proceedings will go no further (*R* v *Darlington Borough Council (ex parte Association of Darlington Taxi Owners)* [1994] COD 424, where it was held that an unincorporated association has no capacity to apply for judicial review).

The need to show *locus standi* arises initially at the first stage of the procedure; i.e., when applying for permission to apply for judicial review. Nevertheless, it is not usually possible to consider the question of whether the applicant has a 'sufficient interest' in total isolation from the merits of his claim. The court must first identify 'the matter' to which the application relates before deciding whether the applicant has 'a sufficient interest' in it (*Commissioners of Inland Revenue* v *National Federation of Self-Employed & Small Businesses Ltd*, above, *per* Lord Wilberforce at pp. 96–7, Lord Diplock at p. 106, Lord Fraser of Tullybelton at p. 107, Lord Scarman at p. 113 and Lord Roskill at p. 115). This will involve an examination of the legal powers or duties which are called in question, their alleged breach, and the position of the applicant in relation to those powers and duties (*ibid.*, *per* Lord Wilberforce at p. 96).

When applying for permission to apply for judicial review, the applicant must make out in his affidavit a prima facie case of illegality, irrationality or procedural impropriety. If he fails to do so, permission to apply will be refused. If he succeeds in making out such a prima facie case, the application may be adjourned pending a later hearing *inter partes* or permission to apply may be granted. If the evidence given later, either at the resumed hearing or at the hearing on the merits, shows that the applicant has no sufficient interest in the matter to which the application relates, the application for permission to apply, or the application for judicial review itself, will be dismissed.

In *Commissioners of Inland Revenue* v *National Federation of Self-Employed & Small Businesses Ltd* [1981] 2 All ER 93, the House of Lords was concerned with a long-standing practice in Fleet Street whereby casual employees on national newspapers received their wages without deduction of tax and, in order to avoid tax, supplied fictitious names and addresses (such as 'Mickey Mouse of Sunset Boulevard' and 'Sir Gordon Richards of Tattenham Corner') when drawing their pay. In order to prevent this evasion of tax for the future the Inland Revenue made an extra-statutory concession in 1979. The Fleet Street casuals were required to register with the Inland Revenue and to submit tax returns for the previous two tax years in exchange for an undertaking by the Inland Revenue not to investigate tax evasion prior to those two years. The applicant federation, which claimed to represent a body of 50,000 taxpayers and which was opposed to this new tax arrangement, applied for judicial review seeking (a) a declaration that the Revenue had acted unlawfully in declaring the amnesty, and (b) an order of mandamus commanding the Revenue to assess and collect tax on the Fleet Street casuals as required by law.

The Revenue opposed the application on the ground that the court could not grant permission to apply because the federation did not have a sufficient interest in the matter to which the application related. The Divisional Court ([1980] 2 All ER 378), treating the question of *locus standi* as a preliminary issue, agreed with the Revenue's argument and refused permission to apply, apparently on the ground that a taxpayer can never have a sufficient interest to apply for judicial review against the Revenue. The federation appealed to the Court of Appeal, which, by a majority of two to one, reversed the Divisional Court ([1980] 2 All ER 378 at p. 387). In the Court of Appeal, *locus standi* was again dealt with as a preliminary issue in isolation from the merits of the case. It was held, on the assumption that the Revenue had acted unlawfully, that the federation was not a mere busybody but had a genuine grievance and, therefore, a sufficient interest for the purposes of an application for judicial review. The Revenue appealed to the House of Lords, which unanimously reversed the decision of the Court of Appeal on other grounds.

Their Lordships held that both the Divisional Court and the Court of Appeal were wrong to treat the question of *locus standi* as a preliminary issue divorced from a consideration of the duty alleged to have been broken or not performed by the Revenue. There were two reasons why the federation had no sufficient interest to apply for judicial review. First, the tax legislation sought to achieve complete confidentiality of assessments, and no right on the part of one taxpayer to inquire about the tax affairs of another could be implied. Secondly, the evidence showed that the Commissioners of Inland Revenue had not acted *ultra vires* or unlawfully in granting the extra-statutory concession. They had acted properly in the interests of the good management of taxes under the statutory powers conferred on them.

Whether an applicant has a sufficient interest is not a question to be determined solely as a matter of discretion. It is a mixed question of law and fact ([1981] 2 All ER 93 *per* Lord Wilberforce at p. 97, Lord Scarman at p. 113 and Lord Roskill at p. 117). The court must exercise its discretion judicially; i.e., in accordance with legal principles.

Every applicant for judicial review, no matter whether he is seeking mandamus, prohibition, certiorari, a declaration or an injunction, must show the same *locus standi*. He must have a sufficient interest in the matter to which the application relates. But the fact that the same words are used to cover all the remedies available on an application for judicial review does not necessarily mean that the test is the same in all cases.

Thus, in an application for mandamus, where a person is seeking to compel a public authority to perform a public duty, the test of 'sufficient interest' may well be stricter than in an application for certiorari, where a person is claiming that some court or tribunal has wronged him by exceeding its powers or by disregarding the requirements of natural justice. In *R v Felixstowe Justices (ex parte Leigh)* [1987] 1 All ER 551, DC, a newspaper reporter claimed a declaration that the policy of a local bench of magistrates to withhold the names of justices from the public and the press during and after the hearing of cases was unlawful. He also claimed mandamus to compel the disclosure of the names of those magistrates who had tried a particular case. He was granted a declaration (see para 1.7.7) but mandamus was refused. As a public-spirited citizen and a representative of the press, he had a sufficient interest in the matter to which the application for a declaration related because the preservation of open justice in magistrates' courts was a subject of national importance and of vital concern in the administration of justice. It was held by the court, however, evidently applying a stricter test, that he did not have *locus standi* to apply for mandamus because he had not been present during the particular trial and the identity of the justices was not essential or even material to the newspaper article he intended to write.

In *Commissioners of Inland Revenue v National Federation of Self-Employed & Small Businesses Ltd* [1981] 2 All ER 93, the House of Lords suggested (not very helpfully) that *locus standi* for the purposes of an application for mandamus is tested by asking whether the definition (statutory or otherwise) of the public duty in question gives the applicant, expressly or impliedly, the right to complain to the court that that duty has been broken or has not been performed.

What constitutes a 'sufficient interest' will be decided on a case-by-case basis. It seems likely that the draftsman of RSC, Ord. 53, and s. 31(3) of the Supreme Court Act 1981, by choosing ordinary English words, was attempting to escape from the old technical rules about *locus standi*. He avoided using phrases such as 'a person aggrieved', 'a particular grievance', or 'a specific legal right'. All of these expressions have at some time been used in decided cases on mandamus, certiorari or prohibition, though there was evidence from more modern cases that they were being discarded in favour of a more liberal test — that of 'sufficient interest'.

In *Commissioners of Inland Revenue* v *National Federation of Self-Employed & Small Businesses Ltd* (at pp. 103, 104 and 107), Lord Diplock in particular welcomed the move away from the former technicalities. He regarded it as fundamental that there should be no reversion to the technical restrictions on *locus standi* which had allowed flagrant breaches of the law by public authorities to go unchecked. It is important that there should be as few restrictions as possible on the freedom of the ordinary private citizen to seek judicial review. The Attorney-General cannot always be relied upon to act for the protection of the public interest. As Lord Diplock pointed out (at p. 107), the Attorney-General in practice never seeks prerogative relief against central government departments. He will only proceed, if at all, against public authorities which are not part of central government.

Commissioners of Inland Revenue v *National Federation of Self-Employed & Small Businesses Ltd* was applied in *R* v *Secretary of State for the Environment (ex parte Rose Theatre Trust Co.)* [1990] 1 All ER 754, in which the judgment of Schiemann J (at pp. 766–8) contains a number of important observations on the requirement of *locus standi*. The case was a consequence of the Secretary of State's decision that the recently discovered remains of the Elizabethan Rose Theatre, acknowledged by him to be of national importance, should not be scheduled as a monument under the Ancient Monuments and Archaeological Areas Act 1979.

To the dismay of environmentalists, it was held, first, that the Secretary of State had not acted unlawfully in so deciding since he had not taken into account irrelevant factors when exercising his discretion, and, secondly, that, in any case, the applicant company had no *locus standi* to apply for judicial review. The company was said to lack standing because the decision not to schedule the theatre site was the type of governmental decision in which ordinary citizens (even distinguished archaeologists, actors and writers) did not have a 'sufficient interest' for the purposes of s. 31(3) of the Supreme Court Act 1981, and they could not acquire a 'sufficient interest' either by the expedient of incorporating themselves as a company with express power to press for scheduling or by making representations to, and receiving a considered reply from, the Secretary of State about scheduling.

In *R* v *Inspectorate of Pollution (ex parte Greenpeace Ltd) (No. 2)* [1994] 4 All ER 329, Otton J gave cursory treatment to, and declined to follow, the *Rose Theatre* decision in holding that Greenpeace had *locus standi* to challenge authorisations granted by the Pollution Inspectorate allowing BNFL to discharge liquid and gaseous radioactive waste from its premises. Among the factors taken into account were the nature of Greenpeace, the extent of its interest in the issues raised, and the nature of the remedy it sought.

The *Rose Theatre* case was not even cited, but *R* v *Inspectorate of Pollution (ex parte Greenpeace Ltd) (No. 2)* was applied, in *R* v *Secretary of State for Foreign Affairs (ex parte World Development Movement Ltd)* [1995] 1 All ER 611, DC. Here a non-partisan pressure group concerned with the misuse of overseas aid money wished to challenge the Foreign Secretary's decision to enter into an agreement with the Malaysian government to provide aid and trade support for the Pergau dam scheme. The Foreign Secretary argued that the World Development Movement had no *locus standi*, but it was held that it did in view of the importance of the issue raised and of safeguarding the rule of law, the fact that there was probably no other responsible challenger, and the Movement's prominent international role in promoting and protecting aid to underdeveloped nations. The Pergau dam scheme was uneconomic and the Foreign Secretary's decision to support it was declared unlawful because it was not concerned with promoting economically sound development as required by s. 1 of the Overseas Development and Co-operation Act 1980.

It has been held that a legally-aided client does not have a sufficient interest in the taxation of his solicitor's costs to enable him to apply to the High Court for judicial review of the Legal Aid Board's refusal to give authority to have the taxation reviewed by a judge under the civil legal aid regulations. Any application for judicial review should be made by the solicitor concerned rather than his client (*R* v *Legal Aid Board (ex parte Bateman)* [1992] 3 All ER 490, DC).

In *Equal Opportunities Commission* v *Secretary of State for Employment* [1994] 1 All ER 910, HL, it was held that the EOC has *locus standi* to bring proceedings for the purpose of determining whether the Secretary of State has acted in breach of European Community law. The EOC was created by the Sex Discrimination Act 1975. Its duties include working towards the elimination of discrimination, promoting equality of opportunity between men and women generally, and keeping under review the working of (and making proposals for amendments to) the Sex Discrimination Act 1975 and the Equal Pay Act 1970. The Court of Appeal had decided that the EOC did not have *locus standi*, but the House of Lords held that, looked at in the light of previous cases in which it had simply been assumed on all sides that the EOC had the necessary standing, it would be a retrograde step to deny it *locus standi* 'to agitate in judicial review proceedings questions related to sex discrimination which are of public importance and affect a large section of the population' (*per* Lord Keith at p. 919).

The Law Society has been held to have *locus standi* to challenge proposed cuts in legal aid provision (*R* v *The Lord Chancellor (ex parte The Law Society)* (1993) *The Times*, 25 June, DC, where, however, the challenge was unsuccessful; see also *R* v *The Lord Chancellor (ex parte The Law Society)* (1993) *The Times*, 11 August, CA, where an unsuccessful attempt was made to prevent the introduction of a standard fees scheme for solicitors doing criminal work in the magistrates' courts). It also has *locus standi* to appeal to the Master of the Rolls under the Solicitors Act 1974 against the restoration of a name to the roll of solicitors (*R* v *Master of the Rolls (ex parte McKinnell)* [1993] 1 All ER 193, DC).

It is well established that a council taxpayer has the necessary *locus standi* to take action, for example, to prevent his local council from overspending (*Prescott* v *Birmingham Corporation* [1955] Ch 210, CA, para 11.5.2.1 above), or to challenge (what are now) council tax assessments made on other taxpayers (*Arsenal Football Club Ltd* v *Ende* [1979] AC 1, HL). In *R* v *Bassetlaw District Council (ex parte Oxby)* (1997) *The Times*, 18 December, CA, it was held, applying *R* v *Port Talbot Borough Council (ex parte Jones)* [1988] 2 All ER 207 (para 11.1.1 above), that the leader of a local council has *locus standi* to apply for judicial review of planning decisions of his own council which turn out to have been tainted by actual or apparent bias on the part of the councillors who made them. Since it is not appropriate for the council itself to be both applicant and respondent in the proceedings, according *locus standi* to the council leader is a convenient way of avoiding this difficulty. (See further on the *Bassetlaw* case, para 11.12.3 below.)

It is clear that a person has a 'sufficient interest' to enable him to apply for judicial review where his *private-law* rights have been infringed, or are threatened, and there is an adequate public law element in the case (*Council of Civil Service Unions* v *Minister for the Civil Service* [1984] 3 All ER 935, HL, *per* Lord Diplock at p. 949; *Gillick* v *West Norfolk and Wisbech Area Health Authority* [1985] 3 All ER 402, HL, *per* Lord Scarman at p. 416).

What is more important is that it is also clear that judicial review may be available in cases where legal rights arising under private law are not involved at all. A person has a 'sufficient interest' to enable him to apply for judicial review of an administrative decision where he has a *legitimate expectation* that the public authority will act fairly towards him. The doctrine of legitimate expectation was explained in the following words by Lord Fraser of Tullybelton in *Council of Civil Service Unions* v *Minister for the Civil Service* [1984] 3 All ER 935 (the 'GCHQ case') at pp. 943–4:

> But even where a person claiming some benefit or privilege has no legal right to it, as a matter of private law, he may have a legitimate expectation of receiving the benefit or privilege, and, if so, the courts will protect his expectation by judicial review as a matter of public law . . . Legitimate . . . expectation may arise either from an express promise given on behalf of a public authority or from the existence of a regular practice which the claimant can reasonably expect to continue. Examples of the former type of expectation are *R* v *Liverpool Corporation (ex parte Liverpool Taxi Fleet Operators' Association)* [para 11.9.3.2] and *Attorney-General of Hong Kong* v *Ng Yuen Shiu* [para 11.8.3.2.2] . . . An example of the latter is *R* v *Hull Prison Board of Visitors (ex parte St Germain and others)* [para 11.8.3.2.2], approved by this House in *O'Reilly* v *Mackman* . . .

The doctrine of legitimate expectation was central to the *GCHQ* case. Although it was held on the facts that the minister had acted lawfully in withdrawing the right to trade-union membership without consulting the civil servants affected, it was made abundantly clear that the decision might have been different if the case had not involved national security at all or if the minister had failed to produce any evidence (beyond a bald assertion) that it did. The civil servants employed at GCHQ had no *legal right* to prior consultation. Nevertheless, their Lordships were unanimous in the view that the *regular practice* of consultation between management and the unions about changes in terms and conditions of employment had given rise to a *legitimate expectation* of consultation. In *O'Reilly* v *Mackman* [1982] 3 All ER 1124, HL, the prisoners who complained about unfair loss of remission could not point to the violation of any *private-law* right because, under the Prison Rules, remission of sentence is not a legal right but a matter of indulgence on the part of the prison authorities. Nevertheless, the prisoners did have a legitimate expectation of remission which, in *public law*, would give them a 'sufficient interest' for the purpose of challenging the validity of the board of visitors' decision in judicial review proceedings. (See also *Findlay* v *Secretary of State for the Home Department* [1984] 3 All ER 801, HL, *per* Lord Scarman at p. 830.)

In *R* v *British Coal Corporation and another (ex parte Vardy and others)* (1993) *The Independent*, 4 February, DC, it was held that the mineworkers' unions had a legitimate expectation that before pits were closed down and miners made redundant the Modified Colliery Review Procedure (the MCRP), which provides for consultation and an element of independent scrutiny, would be followed by British Coal unless and until notice to the contrary had been given. Decisions to close 10 pits were quashed by certiorari and the court further granted a declaration that British Coal should not reach a final decision on the closure of the 10 pits, and the President of the Board of Trade should not provide funds enabling British Coal to reach such a decision, until the MCRP or a procedure substantially similar thereto had been followed in respect of each pit.

In subsequent proceedings brought by the unions the court held that it had no jurisdiction to vary the earlier declaration, or to make further declarations, because its function had been discharged when it originally decided the issues between the parties (*R* v *British Coal Corporation and another (ex parte Price and others)* (1993) *The Independent*, 23 February).

The way was eventually cleared for the pits to be closed when British Coal, having satisfied the court that it had consulted the unions and allowed an independent scrutiny of its proposals, was granted a declaration that it would not be in breach of the earlier declaration if it now acted upon its closure decision (see *R* v *British Coal Corporation and another (ex parte Price and others) (No. 3)* (1993) *The Times*, 28 May, DC).

The Law Society has been held to have a legitimate expectation of consultation by the Lord Chancellor before he exercises his statutory power under the Legal Aid Act 1988 to introduce new regulations restricting eligibility for legal aid, advice and assistance. The legitimate expectation arises, *inter alia*, from the part played by the Law Society in the development of the legal aid scheme since its inception in 1949 and from the effect the proposed changes would have as a whole and on solicitor members of the Law Society (*R* v *The Lord Chancellor (ex parte The Law Society)* (1993) *The Times*, 25 June, DC; see also *R* v *The Lord Chancellor (ex parte The Law Society)* (1993) *The Times*, 11 August, CA, above).

In *R* v *Secretary of State for the Home Department (ex parte Hargreaves)* [1997] 1 All ER 397, CA, three prison inmates applied for judicial review of the Home Secretary's decision to implement a new home leave scheme under which eligibility to apply for home leave arose after serving one half of a sentence. When the applicants began their sentences, eligibility arose after serving one third of a sentence and they were given a notice confirming this and explaining that home leave was a privilege. They also signed an 'inmate compact,' under which the prison promised to consider them for home leave when they became eligible. The applicants' challenge to the Home Secretary's decision was based, *inter alia*, upon the doctrine of legitimate expectation. It was held, applying *Findlay* v *Secretary of State for the Home Department* [1984] 1 All ER 801, HL, that the applicants had no legitimate expectation of being considered eligible for home leave after serving one third of their sentences since, otherwise, the Home Secretary's unfettered statutory discretion to change policy would be restricted. Notwithstanding the notice and compact, the most they could legitimately expect was that their cases would be examined individually in the light of whatever policy the Home Secretary lawfully adopted for the time being.

The doctrine of legitimate expectation will continue to be developed by judicial decision. When it applies, it imposes a general duty to act fairly and is not confined to cases where the expectation is to be consulted or to be given an opportunity to make representations before a decision is made (*R* v *Secretary of State for the Home Department (ex parte Ruddock)* [1987] 2 All ER 518 *per* Taylor J at p. 531).

11.11.5   Delay in making an application

An application for permission to apply for judicial review must be made promptly and in any event within three months from the date when grounds for the application first arose (RSC, Ord. 53, r. 4(1)). The court has a discretion to extend this period if there is good reason for doing so (ibid.). 'Good reason' would include difficulty in obtaining legal aid which was not the fault of the applicant (*R* v *Stratford-on-Avon District Council (ex parte Jackson)* [1985] 3 All ER 769, CA). It is essential that the legal aid authorities should process legal aid applications for judicial review proceedings quickly because of the importance of promptness therein (ibid., *per* Ackner LJ, delivering the judgment of the court, at p. 773).

If certiorari is claimed, the date when grounds for the application first arose will be taken to be the date of the judgment, order, conviction or other proceedings which it is sought to quash (Ord. 53, r. 4(2)).

If the court considers that there has been undue delay in making an application for judicial review (which includes both an application for permission to apply and an application for substantive relief), the court has a discretion to refuse permission to apply, or to refuse a remedy if permission to apply has already been granted, where the granting of relief would be likely to cause substantial hardship to any person, or would be likely to prejudice his rights substantially, or would be detrimental to good administration (Supreme Court Act 1981, s. 31(6); *Caswell* v *Dairy Produce Quota Tribunal for England and Wales* [1990] 2 All ER 434, HL). A failure to apply promptly or within three months as required by r. 4(1) constitutes 'undue delay' for the purposes of s. 31(6) even though the court is satisfied that there is 'good reason' for the delay. Accordingly, the court may still refuse to grant relief, on the grounds mentioned in s. 31(6), at the hearing of the substantive application even though there was good reason for failing to apply promptly (*Caswell*, HL, above, approving *R* v *Stratford-on-Avon District Council (ex parte Jackson)*, above; *R* v *Secretary of State for Health (ex parte Furneaux)* [1994] 2 All ER 652, CA).

If, at the permission stage, the court grants permission to apply for judicial review notwithstanding the undue delay in applying for it, this has the effect of extending the application period. It follows that the court which later deals with the substantive application on the merits will not refuse to grant relief solely on the basis of the original delay. By that time the question of delay has already been resolved in the applicant's favour, and the court's powers are limited to refusing relief on the grounds contained in s. 31(6), namely hardship, prejudice or detriment to good administration. In *R* v *Criminal Injuries Compensation Board (ex parte A)* [1999] 2 WLR 974, HL, where permission to apply for judicial review had been granted by a judge despite the applicant's delay, the House of Lords held that the decision of the different judge who later dismissed the substantive application — solely on the ground of delay — was wrong. It is, moreover, probably the case that the court which later deals with the substantive application has no power to refuse permission to apply for judicial review on the basis of hardship, prejudice or detriment to good administration. Once permission to apply has been granted (and has not been set aside) it is too late to 'refuse' it, although the court at the substantive hearing would still have power under s. 31(6) to refuse to grant relief (ibid., *per* Lord Slynn at p. 979).

In *Caswell* v *Dairy Produce Quota Tribunal for England and Wales* [1990] 2 All ER 434, HL, the Dairy Produce Quota Tribunal in 1985 had fixed a farmer's quota on the basis of the expected production in 1985 from 70 cows and had indicated that the farmer could reapply to have his quota increased when, as anticipated, he expanded his herd to 150. The farmer later discovered that the quota set in 1985 could not be changed. Well over two years after the Tribunal's decision he applied for, and was granted, permission to apply for judicial review of it. At the hearing of the substantive application it was held that the Tribunal had misconstrued the relevant statutory regulations and should have set the quota on the basis of milk production from 150 cows. Notwithstanding the fact that the Tribunal's decision was wrong in law, the judge exercised his discretion under s. 31(6) to refuse relief because there had been undue delay in seeking permission to apply for judicial review and the granting of relief would be detrimental to good administration.

This decision was affirmed by the Court of Appeal and by the House of Lords. Their Lordships held, first, that there had clearly been undue delay in applying for permission, and, secondly, that granting relief would be detrimental to good administration within the meaning of s. 31(6) since it would be likely to lead to applications for permission to challenge the Tribunal's decisions by other disappointed applicants and to the reopening of the milk quota for previous years going back to 1984. This, according to Lord Goff (at pp. 440–1), delivering the leading opinion, was 'precisely the type of situation which Parliament was minded to exclude by the provision in s. 31(6) relating to detriment to good administration'.

The essence of r. 4(1) is that the application for permission must be made 'promptly'. The court has power to refuse permission to apply for judicial review under r. 4(1) even though the application for permission has been made within the three-month period (*R* v *Stratford-on-Avon District Council (ex parte Jackson)*, above, *per* Ackner LJ at p. 772). In *R* v *Herrod (ex parte Leeds City District Council)* [1976] 1 All ER 273, CA, which was decided when the time-limit was six months, the Court of Appeal held that, on the facts, a delay of five and a half months was fatal to an application for permission to apply for certiorari to quash a decision of the Crown Court. The Court of Appeal said that the time-limit was not an entitlement but a maximum rarely to be exceeded.

11.11.6   Non-prerogative relief

11.11.6.1   Declarations and injunctions
On an application for judicial review it is now possible, as previously noted, to obtain non-prerogative relief, although it is, of course, only granted at the discretion of the court. The court may grant a declaration or an injunction, if such a remedy is claimed, if it would be just and convenient to do so (RSC, Ord. 53, r. 1(2); Supreme Court Act 1981, s. 31(2)). In deciding on the justice and convenience of the matter, the court must apply the same rules relating to availability and scope as are applied in the case of applications for mandamus, prohibition and certiorari (ibid.). In addition, the court must take into account all the circumstances of the case. A declaration or an injunction may be claimed as public-law remedies by way of an application for judicial review without the applicant having to show that some legal right of his has been, or is being, infringed. He need only show that he has a 'sufficient interest' in the matter at issue.

Order 53, r. 1(2) does not say that in judicial review proceedings a declaration can only be granted instead of a prerogative remedy. Accordingly, it seems that a declaration can be granted to an applicant who has *locus standi* even though, on the facts, the court could not grant a prerogative remedy — for example, because there is no 'decision' to be quashed (*Factortame Ltd* v *Secretary of State for Transport (No. 2)* [1991] 1 All ER 70, HL; *Equal Opportunities Commission* v *Secretary of State for Employment* [1994] 1 All ER 910, HL, *per* Lord Browne-Wilkinson at pp. 926–28, supported by Lords Jauncey and Lowry at p. 925).

11.11.6.2   Damages
It is also now possible to obtain damages on an application for judicial review (RSC, Ord. 53, r. 7(1); Supreme Court Act 1981, s. 31(4)). This will save the expense and inconvenience of bringing a separate action. But damages can only be awarded if two conditions are satisfied. First, they must be claimed by the applicant in the notice of application for permission to apply. The court has no power to award damages of its own motion on an application for judicial review. Secondly, the court must be satisfied that the applicant's claim is such that he would have been awarded damages if he had begun an ordinary action instead of making an application for judicial review (Ord. 53 says '*could have been awarded damages*', but presumably the statute takes precedence over the order where the two conflict). This rule ensures that damages are not awarded on judicial review for causes of action which are unknown to the law and that the same principles (for example,

as to causation and remoteness of loss) are applied in applications for judicial review as are applied in ordinary actions for damages.

11.11.6.3   Allowing proceedings to continue as if private law proceedings begun by writ
If the applicant claims a declaration, an injunction or damages and the court considers that such relief should not be granted on an application for judicial review but might have been granted if it had been sought in an ordinary action begun by claim, the court may, instead of refusing the application for judicial review, order the proceedings to continue as if they had been private-law proceedings begun by claim (Ord. 53, r. 9(5)). This is a sensible provision which makes it unnecessary to condemn the applicant to the costly procedure of having to start his action all over again before a different court. The court has no power to take the opposite course, i.e., there is no power to permit an ordinary private-law action begun by claim to continue as though it were an application for judicial review.

In *R v South Glamorgan Health Authority (ex parte Phillips)* (1986) *The Independent,* 25 November, it was decided, for reasons similar to those in *R v East Berkshire Health Authority (ex parte Walsh)* [1984] 3 All ER 425, CA (para 11.11.2 above), that the court had no jurisdiction to deal with the case by way of judicial review. However, since the applicant had claimed a declaration as well as certiorari the judge exercised his discretion under Ord. 53, r. 9(5) to allow the case to proceed as if begun by claim. A declaration was granted. In *ex parte Walsh* itself it was not possible to allow the case to continue as if begun by claim because the applicant had not claimed a declaration, an injunction or damages (as required by r. 9(5)) but certiorari alone. Sir John Donaldson MR pointed out (at p. 432) that r. 9(5) is an 'anti-technicality' rule designed to preserve the position of an applicant who finds that the basis for *the relief he has claimed* is private law rather than public law. It is not designed to allow him to change to a claim for *different relief* which was not originally sought.

Rule 9(5) only operates where the applicant for judicial review has initially alleged a breach of his *public-law* rights. If the applicant has *prima facie* brought himself within the rule by claiming a declaration, an injunction or damages, r. 9(5) nevertheless cannot be used to order the proceedings to continue as if begun by claim where the applicant's complaint is essentially about a breach of his *private-law* rights and does not contain a *public-law* element. In *R v Secretary of State for the Home Department (ex parte Dew)* [1987] 2 All ER 1049, the applicant had received a bullet wound in the arm during the course of being arrested. While in prison on remand a bone graft was recommended by surgeons on two separate occasions but by the time of his trial (some 16 months after his arrest and at which he was sentenced to 18 years' imprisonment) he had still not received proper treatment. Thereafter he applied for judicial review. He claimed mandamus and/or an injunction, and certiorari, against the respondents (the Home Secretary and the governor and medical officer of Wandsworth Prison) to compel the provision of appropriate treatment for his arm. He also claimed damages for pain and suffering caused by the delay in treatment. Before his application was heard the applicant was given proper treatment so that his claim for mandamus, an injunction and certiorari was no longer relevant. He persisted with his claim for damages and sought an order under r. 9(5) that the proceedings should continue as if they had been begun by claim form. McNeill J held that the application for judicial review would be struck out as an abuse of the process of the court and that, accordingly, no order could be made under r. 9(5). The application for judicial review was held to be an abuse of the process of the court because the applicant's case did not allege any breach of his *public-law* rights but was essentially a *private-law* action for damages for the tort of negligence arising out of a failure to provide proper medical treatment. As such, it should have been commenced by claim and not by means of an application for judicial review.

11.11.6.4 Injunctions against the Crown in public law proceedings

Non-prerogative relief in the form of an interim injunction is not generally available against the Crown or its ministers in private-law proceedings begun by claim (see para 11.11.6.5 below). However, in *R* v *Licensing Authority (ex parte Smith Kline & French Laboratories Ltd) (No. 2)* [1989] 2 All ER 113, a majority of the Court of Appeal held, approving and applying the decision of Hodgson J in *R* v *Secretary of State for the Home Department (ex parte Herbage)* [1986] 3 All ER 209, that such relief was available in public-law proceedings for judicial review. On the facts, however, an interim injunction was not granted in either case. The reasoning behind these revolutionary decisions was, first, that s. 21 of the Crown Proceedings Act 1947, by which the court is prevented from granting an injunction against the Crown in civil proceedings, did not apply because, by s. 38 of the same Act, the expression 'civil proceedings' does not for this purpose include judicial review proceedings, and, secondly, that s. 31(2) of the Supreme Court Act 1981 had by implication extended the jurisdiction of the High Court so as to empower it to grant an interim injunction against the Crown in an application for judicial review.

Both the *Smith Kline & French* case and the *Herbage* case were overruled by a unanimous House of Lords in *Factortame Ltd* v *Secretary of State for Transport (No. 1)* [1989] 2 All ER 692, HL. Their Lordships decided that the courts below were erroneous in their interpretation of the relevant provisions of the Crown Proceedings Act 1947 and the Supreme Court Act 1981. The House held that the position at common law had always been that injunctions could not be granted against the Crown in what are now called judicial review proceedings, and that the absence from the Crown Proceedings Act 1947 of any express prohibition against the grant of injunctions against the Crown in judicial review proceedings was of no significance in view of the common law prohibition, which it would have been superfluous to repeat in the Act. In effect, according to *Factortame (No. 1)*, the Act had preserved the common law rule (see [1989] 2 All ER 692, HL, *per* Lord Bridge at p. 706). It was further held that s. 31(2) of the Supreme Court Act 1981 did *not* confer on the court a new jurisdiction to grant an interim injunction against the Crown because, among other reasons, if Parliament had intended to confer such a new and radical power it would have done so in express terms rather than leaving it to be created by mere implication (*per* Lord Bridge at p. 708).

In *M* v *Home Office* [1993] 3 All ER 537, HL, the whole question of the availability of injunctive relief against the Crown in judicial review proceedings was reopened. (For the facts of this case, see para 5.3.) The House of Lords retreated from the position it had adopted in the earlier case of *Factortame (No. 1)*, above, by holding that both final and interim injunctions are available against ministers acting in their official capacity as representatives of the Crown.

The leading judgment was delivered by Lord Woolf, with whose speech the other Law Lords expressed agreement. Lord Woolf pointed out that in *Factortame (No. 1)* the House had not been primarily concerned with the question as to whether injunctions were available against the Crown and its officers, and, accordingly, had not had the benefit of as full an argument on the history of both civil and prerogative proceedings involving the Crown as had been presented in the instant case (see [1993] 3 All ER 537 at pp. 549 and 561). In his view, the approach to the interpretation of s. 31 of the Supreme Court Act 1981 taken by Lord Bridge in *Factortame (No. 1)* (see above) was too narrow. In the opinion of Lord

Woolf, the unqualified language of s. 31(2) has succeeded in conferring upon the court jurisdiction to grant injunctions, including interim injunctions, against ministers and other officers of the Crown in judicial review proceedings (see [1993] 3 All ER 537 at pp. 562 and 564). In the light of this decision, the views on the effect of s. 31 expressed by Hodgson J and the majority of the Court of Appeal in, respectively, *R* v *Secretary of State for the Home Department (ex parte Herbage)*, above, and *R* v *Licensing Authority (ex parte Smith Kline & French Laboratories Ltd (No. 2))*, above, must be taken to have been rehabilitated.

Lord Woolf thought that the newly-discovered power to grant injunctions against the Crown in judicial review proceedings would be exercised only in 'the most limited circumstances', and he foresaw no change in the usual practice whereby *final* relief in the form of a declaration (which the Crown invariably respects) is granted as the appropriate remedy in judicial review proceedings involving Crown servants. With regard to *interim* relief against Crown servants, he thought that an interim declaration might have advantages over an interim injunction. The court now has power to grant an interim declaration by virtue of RSC, Ord. 53, and Part 25 of the Civil Procedure Rules.

The decision of the House of Lords in *M* v *Home Office* [1993] 3 All ER 537, HL, has the further effect of achieving a desirable harmonisation in the way rights are protected by means of injunctive relief. The same protection is now afforded to rights not derived from European Community law as is enjoyed by rights which are so derived. Although before 1993 interim injunctions were not generally available against the Crown in judicial review proceedings an exception had been established in *Factortame Ltd* v *Secretary of State for Transport (No. 2)* [1991] 1 All ER 70, CJEC and HL, to cover the situation where the case was governed by Community law and interim relief was required in order to protect a person's Community law rights pending the final outcome of the litigation. In *Factortame (No. 2)*, it was held by the European Court of Justice that a rule of national law must be set aside by a national court if it is the sole impediment to granting interim relief. In consequence, the House of Lords granted an interim injunction against the Secretary of State for Transport which had the effect of temporarily disapplying certain statutory regulations. (See further on this case, para 8.7.) Their Lordships held, first, that whether an interim injunction should be granted in this limited class of case will be determined according to the balance of convenience after taking into account the public interest in seeing that the law is upheld, and, secondly, that an apparently authentic law should not be disapplied unless the challenge to its validity is prima facie so firmly based as to justify the exceptional course of setting it aside by means of an interim injunction (see [1991] 1 All ER 70, HL, *per* Lord Goff of Chieveley at pp. 119–20).

This approach was applied in *R* v *HM Treasury (ex parte British Telecommunications plc)* (1993) *The Times*, 2 December, CA, albeit with a different result. The Court of Appeal refused an interim injunction to disapply some statutory regulations so as to relieve British Telecom from certain obligations pending a preliminary ruling from the European Court on a reference made to it under art. 177 (now art. 234) of the EC Treaty. It was said that the court should not adopt a formulaic approach to its assessment of the balance of convenience but should instead attach varying degrees of weight to all the relevant matters thrown up by the facts of the case. Thus, the court might be more reluctant to disapply a major piece of primary legislation than a minor piece of subordinate legislation. One of the relevant matters which weighed with the Court of Appeal in the *British Telecom* case was that, unlike the Spanish fishermen in *Factortame (No. 2)*, the survival of British Telecom was not put at risk by a denial of interim relief.

11.11.6.5 Injunctions against the Crown in private law proceedings
M v *Home Office* [1993] 3 All ER 537, HL, does not affect the availability or otherwise of injunctions against the Crown in *private-law* proceedings. This matter continues to be governed by s. 21 of the Crown Proceedings Act 1947, which (unlike s. 31 of the Supreme Court Act 1981) was not designed to extend the court's power to grant injunctions against the Crown (see [1993] 3 All ER 537 *per* Lord Woolf at p. 556). By s. 21(1)(a), the court is forbidden to grant an injunction against the Crown in any civil proceedings (defined in s. 38(2) in a way which excludes what are now called judicial review proceedings). Moreover, s. 21(2) forbids the court to grant an injunction against an *officer* of the Crown in any civil proceedings if its effect would be to circumvent s. 21(1)(a). Thus, if an officer of the Crown is sued in civil proceedings in a representative capacity no injunction can be granted against him because that would be tantamount to granting it against the Crown. If, however, the officer is sued in his personal capacity for some wrongdoing an injunction can be granted against him because to do so does not affect the Crown.

11.12 DISTINCTION BETWEEN JUDICIAL REVIEW AND AN APPEAL

11.12.1 Introduction

In essence, the distinction is that an appeal is concerned with the *merits* of the decision under appeal while judicial review is concerned only with the *legality* of the decision or act under review. The determination of an appeal is always a statutory function whereas judicial review is based on an inherent common-law power. It is implicit in the nature of judicial review that, so long as a public authority has acted *intra vires* and lawfully, the court will not interfere merely because it considers that the public authority came to a wrong conclusion. In the case of a successful appeal, however, the appellate body is called upon to substitute its own discretion for that of some inferior court or tribunal.

In *Chief Constable of the North Wales Police* v *Evans* [1982] 3 All ER 141, HL (para 11.5.2.4 above), the Court of Appeal had not only held that natural justice demanded a fair hearing but had also stated that the decision under review must itself be fair and reasonable. This confusion between the purposes of judicial review on the one hand and an appeal on the other was seized upon by the House of Lords. Their Lordships made it quite clear that judicial review is not an appeal from a decision but a review of the manner in which the decision was made. It follows that, on judicial review, the court is not entitled to consider whether the decision itself was fair and reasonable for that would be to usurp the power of the decision-making body under the pretence of preventing the abuse of power (see especially *per* Lord Hailsham of St Marylebone LC at pp. 143–4 and Lord Brightman at pp. 154–5).

The fact that a right of appeal exists against a decision does not prevent that decision being quashed by certiorari, following a judicial review, on the ground of excess of power, or violation of natural justice, or error of law. The difference in nature and purpose between an appeal and judicial review is re-emphasised by the fact that judicial review of a decision is still possible notwithstanding the existence of statutory words by which any right of appeal against that decision is successfully excluded (as in *R* v *Medical Appeal Tribunal (ex parte Gilmore)* [1957] 1 QB 574, CA, para 11.8.3.3 above). This matter will be examined more closely in para 11.13.

11.12.2 Overlap between judicial review and appeals

It is quite common for both an appeal and an application for judicial review to be available at the same time. And there is often a considerable overlap between the two procedures. The courts occasionally give guidance about which procedure is the more suitable in particular circumstances.

For example, both sides have a right of appeal by way of case stated to the Queen's Bench Division of the High Court from the decision of a magistrates' court (Magistrates' Courts Act 1980, s. 111) and of the Crown Court in a non-indictable matter, such as a decision on appeal from the justices (Supreme Court Act 1981, s. 28(1)). The grounds on which the appeal may be taken are that the decision was wrong in law or that it was made in excess of jurisdiction. Alternatively, either side may challenge the decision by way of an application for judicial review on slightly wider, but substantially the same, grounds, namely, error of law, excess of jurisdiction or violation of the principles of natural justice. In *R v Crown Court at Ipswich (ex parte Baldwin)* [1981] 1 All ER 596, the High Court said that the more convenient procedure where the facts of a case are complicated is an appeal by way of case stated. That procedure enables the High Court to get at the facts found by the justices more easily than in an application for judicial review. However, in *R v Hereford Magistrates' Court (ex parte Rowlands)* [1997] 2 WLR 854, DC, it was held that judicial review is a more appropriate procedure than appealing to the Crown Court where the complaint against the justices is one of procedural irregularity or bias (unless, it might be added, judicial review is applied for with the ulterior motive of causing delay which may thereby lead to the dropping of the prosecution before the defendant's appeal to the Crown Court is heard: *R v Peterborough Magistrates' Court (ex parte Dowler)* [1997] 2 WLR 843, DC). It was said in *ex parte Rowlands*, above, that it was important to retain the High Court's supervisory jurisdiction over magistrates' courts in order to ensure the maintenance of high standards of fairness and procedural propriety, having regard to the central role of those courts in the administration of the criminal justice system and to the fact that the Crown Court has no power to supervise their proceedings.

A challenge to a sentence imposed by a magistrates' court has been held to be better made by appealing to the Crown Court than either stating a case for the opinion of the High Court (*Tucker v Director of Public Prosecutions* [1992] 4 All ER 901, DC) or applying for judicial review (*R v Ealing Justices (ex parte Scrafield)* (1993) *The Times*, 29 March, DC, applying *Tucker*, above, and see para 6.2.1.2).

Similarly, it has been held that taxation issues, including the conduct of a hearing before General or Special Commissioners of income tax, are more properly dealt with by an appeal, by way of case stated to the Chancery Division of the High Court (under s. 56 of the Taxes Management Act 1970) than by an application for judicial review (*R v Commissioner for the Special Purposes of the Income Tax Acts (ex parte Napier)* [1988] 3 All ER 166, CA). Judicial review might, however, be the appropriate course where it is alleged that the commissioner's conduct of the hearing raised matters extraneous to taxation issues (ibid., *per* Purchas LJ at p. 171).

In *R v Birmingham City Council (ex parte Ferrero Ltd)* (1991) [1993] 1 All ER 530, CA, it was held that the better way of challenging a suspension notice served by a local authority under s. 14 of the Consumer Protection Act 1987 (prohibiting the supply of goods on the ground that a safety provision has been contravened) is by exercising the statutory right of appeal to a magistrates' court under s. 15 of the Act rather than by taking judicial review proceedings even where there are alleged defects in the local authority's decision-making process. In judicial review proceedings at first instance the judge had quashed the local authority's issue of a suspension notice which prohibited Ferrero Ltd from supplying 'Kinder Surprise' chocolate eggs containing kits for making Pink Panther toys. The notice had been issued following the death of a three-year-old child by asphyxiation after swallowing a toy foot which had come loose. The Court of Appeal allowed the local authority's appeal, holding that the applicants had adopted the wrong procedure in their challenge to the notice. The court held that the statutory appeal procedure is the more appropriate in the circumstances since it does not require permission, it is quicker and more suitable for getting at the facts, and there is provision (in s. 14(7)) for the payment of compensation to the trader if it transpires that no safety provision has been contravened.

On the other hand, it has been said that the proper way to challenge the validity of regulations and administrative directions made under the authority of a statute is by way of an application for judicial review rather than by the exercise of a right of appeal (*Moss of London* v *Commissioners of Customs & Excise* [1981] 2 All ER 86, CA, *per* Lord Denning MR at p. 90).

An application for judicial review will be more effective than a special case stated under s. 78(8) of the Mental Health Act 1983 as a means of challenging the reasons given by a mental health review tribunal for refusing to order the release of a mental patient (*Bone* v *Mental Health Review Tribunal* [1985] 3 All ER 330, *per* Nolan J at p. 334). This is because judicial review proceedings allow a broader consideration of the issues involved and provide more and varied remedies. For example, the High Court can quash the decision of a mental health review tribunal in judicial review proceedings but cannot do so under the special case-stated procedure.

11.12.3 Judicial review and alternative remedies

The granting of permission to apply for judicial review is, of course, discretionary. Until recently it could be said with some confidence that, with the exception of the remedy of mandamus (as to which see para 11.10.4 above), it did not matter as a general rule that an aggrieved citizen had not exhausted his rights of appeal, or whatever administrative procedures might be open to him, before seeking judicial review. Now, however, the general rule is that judicial review is to be regarded as a remedy 'of last resort' (*R* v *Inland Revenue Commissioners (ex parte Opman International UK)* [1986] 1 All ER 328, *per* Woolf J at p. 330) and leave to apply for it will not normally be granted where there exists an alternative remedy which has not been used (*Preston* v *Inland Revenue Commissioners* [1985] 2 All ER 327, HL, *per* Lord Scarman at p. 330 and Lord Templeman at p. 337; *R* v *Epping and Harlow General Commissioners (ex parte Goldstraw)* [1983] 3 All ER 257, CA).

Only in exceptional circumstances will judicial review be allowed where the alternative remedy has not been pursued or exhausted. What circumstances are 'exceptional' for this purpose will be developed on a case-by-case basis. In *R* v *Secretary of State for the Home Department (ex parte Swati)* [1986] 1 All ER 717, CA, at p. 724, Sir John Donaldson MR said that '[b]y definition, exceptional circumstances defy definition'. In the same case, Parker LJ said (at p. 728) that each case will depend on its own facts and that it would be impossible and legally wrong to attempt to define what are exceptional circumstances.

It is highly probable that no single circumstance by itself is sufficiently 'exceptional' to persuade the court to grant permission to apply for judicial review where there is an unused alternative remedy. Nevertheless, it is possible to distil from the cases some of the factors which may influence the court in the exercise of its discretion. Such factors include whether the alternative remedy would be quicker or slower than judicial review and whether the case involves some technical knowledge which the alternative appellate body is more likely to have than the High Court (*R* v *Hallstrom (ex parte W)* [1985] 3 All ER 775, CA, *per* Glidewell LJ at pp. 789–90), and whether the alternative remedy is as convenient and effective as judicial review.

In *R* v *Chief Constable of the Merseyside Police (ex parte Calveley)* [1986] 1 All ER 257, CA, Glidewell LJ (at p. 267) stood by his remarks in the *Hallstrom* case and they received the tacit approval of Sir John Donaldson MR (at p. 262). May LJ, however, was of the view (at p. 267) that the slowness of the alternative remedy should only be regarded as exceptional where it amounts to an abuse of process. He also doubted (at pp. 264–5) whether the fact that the alternative remedy is not as convenient and effective is in itself exceptional enough to justify giving permission to apply for judicial review. On the facts of *R* v *Chief Constable of the Merseyside Police (ex parte Calveley)* the Court of Appeal was unanimous that permission to apply should be granted and that the chief constable's decision should be quashed by certiorari. In proceedings under the statutory Police (Discipline) Regulations the applicants had been found guilty of disciplinary offences. Two of them were dismissed by the chief constable and the other three were required to resign. The applicants gave notice of appeal to the Home Secretary under the statutory disciplinary procedure. But before the hearing of the appeal they applied for certiorari to quash the chief constable's decision on the ground that the formal written notification, required by the regulations to be made 'as soon as is practicable', informing them of the allegations or complaints against them had been served so late as to prejudice their right to a fair hearing.

The Court of Appeal held that the circumstances were exceptional. There had been such a serious departure from the disciplinary procedure that the court should intervene even though the internal appeal machinery had not been exhausted.

In *R* v *Westminster City Council (ex parte Hilditch)* [1990] COD 434, CA, a ratepayer applied for permission to apply for judicial review of a local authority's policy on the sale of council flats. The relief claimed was a declaration. Permission to apply was refused because the applicant had already invoked an alternative statutory procedure by way of complaint to the auditor under the Local Government Finance Act 1982. The alternative remedy had not been exhausted and the court said that there were no exceptional circumstances to justify granting permission to apply for judicial review. The fact that only a declaration was sought meant that there was no urgency requiring judicial review proceedings to be given priority, and, in any event, the alternative procedure in question was more appropriate for resolving disputed issues of fact.

In *R* v *Director of Public Prosecutions (ex parte Camelot Group plc)* (1997) *The Independent*, 22 April, DC, Camelot, the organisers of the National Lottery, sought judicial review of the decision of the Crown Prosecution Service not to prosecute the promoters of another lottery scheme for running an illegal lottery. It was held that Camelot should make use of the alternative remedy of a private prosecution, which would be equally as effective as judicial review and would avoid the undesirable situation of inviting the court to declare in a civil case that a third party's actions are criminal. *R* v *Bassetlaw District Council (ex parte Oxby)* (1997) *The Times*, 18 December, CA, concerned planning decisions which were tainted by bias. The district council was held entitled to use judicial review proceedings to have the decisions declared illegal and void as an alternative to revoking them itself and paying compensation under the statutory procedure provided by the Town and Country Planning Act 1990. (See further on this case, para 11.11.4 above.) In *Scott* v *National Trust for Places of Historic Interest or Natural Beauty* [1998] 2 All ER 705, permission to apply for judicial review was refused on the ground that decisions of the National Trust, although it is a public body amenable to judicial review, are best challenged by means of the alternative remedy provided by Parliament ('charity proceedings' under the Charities Act 1993).

The new reluctance to make available the discretionary remedy of judicial review where an alternative remedy exists but has not been used can verge on the oppressive. In *R v Secretary of State for the Home Department (ex parte Swati)* [1986] 1 All ER 717, the Court of Appeal refused permission to apply for judicial review in an immigration case on the ground that the applicant ought first to exhaust the statutory right of appeal to an adjudicator and the immigration appeal tribunal as provided by the Immigration Act 1971. The court did not regard it as an 'exceptional' circumstance that, under the statute, a person who is refused permission to enter the United Kingdom must first leave the United Kingdom before exercising his right of appeal. It might be otherwise if the applicant's country of origin is hostile, as in *R v Chief Immigration Officer, Gatwick Airport (ex parte Kharrazi)* [1980] 3 All ER 373, CA, where permission to apply for judicial review was granted in the case of a 13 year old Iranian boy. If he had been forced to return to Iran in order to pursue his right of appeal, he would not have been allowed to leave that country again until he was much older.

It seems that the remedy of mandamus has always been subject to the rule that the discretion to grant it will not be exercised if there exists an adequate alternative remedy. This is dealt with in para 11.10.4 above.

11.13 STATUTORY EXCLUSION OF APPEAL AND JUDICIAL REVIEW

11.13.1 'Finality' or 'ouster' clauses

It is sometimes provided by a particular statute that a decision taken under it 'shall be final', or 'shall be final and conclusive', or 'shall not be appealable', or 'shall not be questioned in any legal proceedings whatsoever'. Such expressions are known as 'finality' or 'ouster' clauses because they make the original decision final by attempting to oust the jurisdiction of the courts.

Traditionally, the courts have interpreted these expressions narrowly so as to mean that, although there is to be no further appeal, the decision is still subject to judicial review, which, as noted in para 11.12.1 above, is not an appeal. In other words, the decision under attack may be final on the facts but it is not to be regarded as final on the law. For example, a finality or ouster clause will not necessarily prevent the quashing of a decision by certiorari on the grounds of excess or abuse of power, breach of the requirements of natural justice or error of law. Nor will it necessarily preclude the making of a declaration. In *R v Medical Appeal Tribunal (ex parte Gilmore)* [1957] 1 QB 574, CA (para 11.8.3.3 above), the tribunal's decision was quashed by certiorari for error of law even though the statute in question said that the tribunal's decision 'shall be final'. Denning LJ said (at p. 583): 'I find it very well settled that the remedy by certiorari is never to be taken away by any statute except by the most clear and explicit words'. In *South East Asia Fire Bricks Sdn Bhd v Non-Metallic Mineral Products Manufacturing Employees Union* [1981] AC 363, PC, it was held that words in a Malaysian statute that 'an award . . . shall be final and conclusive, and no award shall be challenged, appealed against, reviewed, *quashed* or *called into question in any court of law*' (italics supplied) were clear and explicit enough to exclude the remedy of certiorari for error of law. But, applying the *Anisminic* case (para 11.13.3 below), it was made clear that those words would not effectively exclude certiorari if the award was *ultra vires* or was a nullity because of violation of the principles of natural justice. In *R* v *Hallstrom (ex parte W)* [1985] 3 All ER 775, CA, the court had to construe s. 139(1) of the Mental Health Act 1983, which provides that 'no person shall be liable, whether on the ground of want of jurisdiction or on any other ground, to any civil . . . proceedings . . . in respect of any act purporting to be done in pursuance of this Act . . . unless the act was done in bad faith or without reasonable care'. It was held that those words were not sufficiently wide or clear to exclude judicial review by way of certiorari or a declaration.

The reason for the restrictive approach towards any attempt to exclude judicial remedies is the fear of the ordinary courts of law that public authorities and tribunals might otherwise acquire arbitrary and uncontrollable power. The courts seek to prevent this by means of a presumption that Parliament always intends statutory powers to be exercised lawfully.

Desirable though this approach is, it must be remembered that it can be adopted only against public authorities and tribunals. It probably cannot be used against an inferior *court of law* because Parliament must be taken to have assumed that a court of law is competent to decide questions of law as well as questions of fact. It cannot be used against a superior court for the same reason (*Re Racal Communications Ltd* [1980] 2 All ER 634, HL, *per* Lord Diplock at pp. 639–40). Moreover, the decisions of a superior court of record are not subject to judicial review, with the exception of decisions of the Crown Court on non-indictable matters (para 11.8.2 above).

It must also be remembered that the understandable judicial aspiration to prevent the acquisition and exercise of arbitrary and uncontrollable power by an unaccountable executive must yield to any express Parliamentary instruction to the contrary. The presumption that powers conferred by Parliament are intended to be exercised lawfully can be rebutted by express statutory words so that the exercise of particular powers becomes 'judge-proof'. For example, the Interception of Communications Act 1985 creates a Tribunal with the function, *inter alia,* of investigating and, if appropriate, remedying, complaints that postal or telephonic communications have been unlawfully intercepted. The Act provides that the

> decisions of the Tribunal (*including any decisions as to their jurisdiction*) shall not be subject to appeal or liable to be questioned in any court (s. 7(8); italics supplied).

There is an almost identical ouster clause in the Security Service Act 1989 with regard to decisions of the Security Service Tribunal and the Security Service Commissioner given on the investigation of complaints against the security service (s. 5(4)). The use of the word 'jurisdiction' appears to constitute a successful attempt to exclude even the effect of the *Anisminic* case (para 11.13.3 below) from the interpretation of these two statutes. The result is that the 'decisions' referred to, whether they are wrong or a complete nullity, are not only unappealable but also immune from challenge by way of judicial review and beyond the reach of certiorari. (This result was acknowledged in relation to the Interception of Communications Act 1985 by Taylor J, *obiter*, in *R* v *Secretary of State for the Home Department (ex parte Ruddock)* [1987] 2 All ER 518 at pp. 527–8.)

11.13.2   *Re Racal Communications Ltd*

In *Re Racal Communications Ltd* [1980] 2 All ER 634, HL, a High Court judge had refused to make an order under s. 441 of the Companies Act 1948 (now s. 721 of the Companies

Act 1985) authorising the inspection of a company's books or papers. It was provided by s. 441(3) of the 1948 Act (now s. 721(4) of the 1985 Act) that the decision of the High Court judge 'is not appealable'. Notwithstanding these clear words, the Director of Public Prosecutions, who had applied for the order, appealed. The Court of Appeal assumed jurisdiction, reversed the judge's decision and made the order sought. The reason given was that the judge had erred in law and the words, 'is not appealable', only excluded an appeal on the facts and not on the law.

On a further appeal, the House of Lords unanimously reversed the decision of the Court of Appeal. The House of Lords held that the words, 'is not appealable', mean exactly what they say. There was no right of appeal under s. 441 from the High Court judge's decision either on the facts or on the law. Therefore, the Court of Appeal had no jurisdiction under s. 441 to hear the appeal. In any case, the jurisdiction of the Court of Appeal is entirely statutory and the statute (now s. 18(1)(c) of the Supreme Court Act 1981) makes it clear that no appeal lies to the Court of Appeal from any decision of the High Court which by virtue of any statutory provision is final (see [1980] 2 All ER 634 *per* Lord Diplock at p. 638). Nor would it have any jurisdiction to reconsider a High Court judge's decision by way of judicial review. In the first place, the High Court is a superior court of record so that its decisions are not subject to judicial review. And, secondly, the jurisdiction of the Court of Appeal is entirely appellate. It has no original jurisdiction and cannot, therefore, hear original applications for judicial review but is limited to hearing appeals from decisions of the High Court made on such applications.

In *Re Racal Communications Ltd*, the earlier decision in *Pearlman* v *Keepers & Governors of Harrow School* [1979] QB 56, CA, in which it was held that the words 'shall be final and conclusive' did not preclude judicial review where a county court judge has exceeded his jurisdiction, was disapproved, as was Lord Denning's dictum in that case (at p. 71) that the operative words would exclude appeals from the county court to the Court of Appeal on questions of fact but not on questions of law.

One of the effects of *Re Racal Communications Ltd* is to make it clear that mistakes of law made by High Court judges can only be corrected by an appeal to an appellate court and that they cannot be corrected at all if the statute provides that the judge's decision shall not be appealable (see [1980] 2 All ER 634, *per* Lord Diplock at p. 640).

11.13.3 *Anisminic Ltd* v *Foreign Compensation Commission*

In *Re Racal Communications Ltd*, their Lordships were simply explaining and applying what had been laid down by the House of Lords in the earlier case of *Anisminic Ltd* v *Foreign Compensation Commission* [1969] 2 AC 147. The commission was set up by the Foreign Compensation Act 1950 to decide claims by British subjects to participate in compensation funds paid to Her Majesty's Government by a foreign government. The commission decided that the claimant company had failed to establish a claim for compensation for the loss of its Egyptian assets following the Suez crisis of 1956. This determination was based on a ground which the commission had no right to take into account. The 1950 Act provided that the commission's determination of an application 'shall not be called in question in any court of law'.

The claimant company applied for a declaration (under RSC, Ord. 15, r. 16) that the commission's determination was a nullity and that the company was entitled to participate in the compensation fund. The House of Lords held that it was only a real, and not a purported, 'determination' which could not be called in question. The commission's 'determination' was *ultra vires* and a nullity. It was no determination at all and could, therefore, be called in question in the courts of law. In the circumstances the declaration claimed by the claimant company was the appropriate remedy.

The importance of the *Anisminic* case is twofold. First, it is another example of the firm resolution of the courts to prevent the acquisition by public authorities and tribunals of arbitrary and uncontrollable power. Secondly, it provides an extended definition of 'jurisdiction' within which tribunals must confine themselves. The opinion of Lord Reid is particularly illuminating on this point. He said that the decision of a tribunal could be *ultra vires* and a nullity on many more grounds than simply lack of jurisdiction to consider the matter at issue in the first place. Lord Reid (at p. 171) listed the following additional grounds:

(a) Where its decision was given in bad faith.

(b) Where it has made a decision which it had no power to make.

(c) Where it has failed to comply with the requirements of natural justice.

(d) Where, in perfect good faith, it has misconstrued the provisions giving it power to act so that it failed to deal with the question remitted to it and, instead, decided some question which was not remitted to it.

(e) Where it has refused to take into account something which it was required to take into account.

(f) Where it has taken into account something which it had no right to take into account.

It is clear from the language used in the *Anisminic* case that their Lordships were confining their comments to the decisions of administrative tribunals as opposed to the ordinary courts of law. In the light of the decision in *Re Racal Communications Ltd* [1980] 2 All ER 634, HL, it is apparent that Anisminic Ltd would have had no remedy at all, either by way of appeal or judicial review, if the Foreign Compensation Act 1950 had provided for the 'determination' to be made by a High Court judge rather than by a statutory tribunal.

The *Anisminic* case was further explained by the House of Lords in *Page* v *Hull University Visitor* [1993] 1 All ER 97, HL (para 11.8.3.3 above).

11.13.4   Section 12 of the Tribunals and Inquiries Act 1992

As long ago as 1932 it was recommended that ouster clauses in statutes 'should be abandoned in all but the most exceptional cases' (*Report of the Committee on Ministers' Powers,* Cmd 4060, 1932, p. 65). But nothing was done by Parliament, in response to this proposal, to set aside such clauses, and continued reliance was placed on them. In 1957 a more fundamental recommendation was made to the effect that the prerogative remedies should not be ousted by statute (*Report of the Committee on Tribunals and Enquiries,* Cmnd 218, 1957, para 117). Legislation to implement this proposal was contained in the Tribunals and Inquiries Act 1958. But the legislation only applies to ouster clauses embodied in pre–1958 statutes. However, it does at least make ouster clauses clearer targets for attack. The rule is now to be found in s. 12 of the Tribunals and Inquiries Act 1992:

As respects England and Wales — (a) any provision in an Act passed before 1st August 1958 that any order or determination shall not be called into question in any court, or (b) any provision in such an Act which by similar words excludes any of the powers of the High Court, shall not have effect so as to prevent the removal of the proceedings into the

High Court by order of certiorari or to prejudice the powers of the High Court to make orders of mandamus.

Exceptional cases, where it is still possible for a pre–1958 statute to purport to oust the jurisdiction of the courts, are mentioned in s. 12(3) of the 1992 Act:

Nothing in this section shall apply — (a) to any order or determination of a court of law, or (b) where an Act makes special provision for application to the High Court . . . within a time limited by the Act.

Section 12 of the Tribunals and Inquiries Act 1992 seeks to prevent the exclusion of the prerogative remedies of certiorari and mandamus by pre–1958 statutes. Presumably, it is hoped that statutes passed after 1958 will not contain such ouster clauses in the first place, although there is nothing to stop Parliament resorting to them. If, however, an ouster clause in a statute passed after 1958 is simply a repetition of a pre–1958 clause, the courts will treat it as a pre–1958 clause and it will be caught by s. 12 (*R* v *Preston Supplementary Benefits Appeal Tribunal (ex parte Moore)* [1975] 2 All ER 807, CA).

The fact that the decisions of even inferior courts of law are expressly excluded indicates that s. 12 is intended to apply only to the decisions of public authorities and statutory tribunals.

The most significant exception to the operation of s. 12 of the Tribunals and Inquiries Act 1992 is the one relating to statutes which allow an application to the High Court only within a stated time-limit, usually six weeks. Provisions of this type are made in, for example, the Acquisition of Land Act 1981, the Housing Act 1985, the Town and Country Planning Act 1990, the Highways Act 1980, the Wildlife and Countryside Act 1981 and the New Towns Act 1981.

The time-limited procedure in the Acquisition of Land Act 1981 was previously contained in the Acquisition of Land (Authorisation Procedure) Act 1946. Under the procedure any person aggrieved by a compulsory purchase order who wishes to question the validity of the order on the ground that it was *ultra vires* the Act may apply to the High Court. But an application must be made within six weeks from the date on which notice of the confirmation or making of the order was first published. If an application is not made within the six-week period, then the order 'shall not . . . be questioned in any legal proceedings whatsoever'. 'Six weeks' means '42 days'; accordingly, the six-week period expires at midnight on the 42nd day following publication of the notice (*Okolo* v *Secretary of State for the Environment* [1997] 4 All ER 242, CA).

There is some justification for an ouster clause of this sort, although the time-limit of six weeks has been criticised as 'pitifully inadequate' (*Smith* v *East Elloe Rural District Council* [1956] AC 736, HL, *per* Lord Radcliffe at p. 769). Such a clause enables public authorities to proceed with confidence to commit public money after the expiry of the time-limit, knowing that the order cannot be invalidated or their title to the land called in question (*R* v *Secretary of State for the Environment (ex parte Ostler)* [1977] QB 122, CA, *per* Lord Denning MR at p. 136).

In *Smith* v *East Elloe Rural District Council* [1956] AC 736, the House of Lords, by a majority of three to two, held that once the six-week period had expired it was not possible to challenge the validity of the compulsory purchase order even on the ground that it had been obtained wrongfully and in bad faith. The argument that Parliament could not have intended to take away a remedy where powers had been exercised in bad faith was rejected.

Smith v *East Elloe Rural District Council* was criticised by three of the Law Lords who later decided the *Anisminic* case [1969] 2 AC 147. (The three were Lords Reid, Pearce and Wilberforce.) But the Court of Appeal has since held that the *East Elloe* case was not overruled by the decision in the *Anisminic* case. This was decided in *R* v *Secretary of State for the Environment (ex parte Ostler)* [1977] QB 122, CA, in which it was held that a provision in the Highways Act 1959 (since repealed and replaced by a similar provision in the Highways Act 1980) that a compulsory purchase order was not to 'be questioned in any legal proceedings whatever' after the expiry of a six-week time-limit was absolute. This was so even where bad faith and violation of natural justice were alleged. The *East Elloe* case was applied. The *Anisminic* case was distinguished on a number of grounds, two of which may be mentioned here.

First, it was said that the *Anisminic* case only applies where there has been a complete ouster of the jurisdiction of the courts. It does not apply where the ouster operates only after the expiry of a time-limit. Secondly, a distinction was drawn between an administrative decision, which involves considerations of policy and the public interest, and a judicial decision, which does not. The decision of the Secretary of State in the *Ostler* case to confirm the order after an inquiry was an administrative one whereas the decision of the Foreign Compensation Commission in the *Anisminic* case was a judicial one which could be challenged on the ground that it was *ultra vires* and a nullity.

The *Ostler* case was followed in *R* v *Secretary of State for the Environment (ex parte Kent)* [1990] COD 78, CA, where it was held that an appeal outside the six-week time-limit imposed by the planning legislation could not be allowed to proceed (see also *R* v *Secretary of State for the Environment (ex parte Upton Brickworks)* [1992] COD 301). In *R* v *Cornwall County Council (ex parte Huntington)* [1994] 1 All ER 694, CA, decided under the Wildlife and Countryside Act 1981, an attempt was made by counsel for the applicant to distinguish the *Ostler* case on the grounds that:

(a) it only applies to administrative decisions and not to judicial or quasi-judicial decisions; and

(b) it does not apply where the decision under attack is 'fundamentally invalid'.

The attempt failed. The distinction between administrative decisions and judicial or quasi-judicial decisions as a basis for ignoring a finality clause was rejected (despite what was said on this matter in the *Ostler* case (see above)), as was the notion that there are different degrees or grounds of invalidity. According to *R* v *Cornwall County Council (ex parte Huntington)*, above, the true position, applying the *Ostler* case, is that:

(a) an *Anisminic*-type statutory clause does not exclude challenges based on invalidity;

(b) an *Ostler*-type clause only allows questions of invalidity to be raised on the specified grounds, within the prescribed time and in the prescribed manner, but otherwise the clause successfully excludes the jurisdiction of the court in the interests of certainty.

In making use of the *Ostler*-type clause, it is taken to be the intention of Parliament that the statutory application to the High Court should be the exclusive remedy available to those affected by the impugned decision. The usual *Ostler*-type clause will additionally preclude any legal challenge whatsoever to a decision or order before it has had a chance to take effect or be confirmed. In *R* v *Cornwall County Council (ex parte Huntington)*, above, the local authority was required by the Wildlife and Countryside Act 1981 to keep under review, and make modifications to, the definitive map and statement of public rights of way. A modification order did not take effect until confirmed by the local authority or the Secretary of State. Any person aggrieved by an order which had taken effect could question its validity by making an application to the High Court within 42 days from the date of publication of notice of confirmation; otherwise, the validity of an order was not to be questioned 'in any legal proceedings whatsoever'. The applicant's challenge to the local authority's modification order failed because the order had not been confirmed and had not, therefore, taken effect within the meaning of the Act. Accordingly, the order could not be challenged in judicial review (or any other) proceedings at that stage. The applicant would have to wait for confirmation of the order and then impugn its validity — not in judicial review proceedings but by using the procedure prescribed by the Act, namely, a statutory application to the High Court.

The question has arisen of when the six-week period begins to run in these cases. For example, under s. 245 of the Town and Country Planning Act 1971 (now s. 288 of the Town and Country Planning Act 1990) a person aggrieved by the Secretary of State's handling of a planning application could apply to the High Court 'within six weeks from the date on which . . . [the Secretary of State's] action is taken'. In *Griffiths* v *Secretary of State for the Environment* [1983] 1 All ER 439, HL, the minister contended that the appellant's application to the High Court was out of time because the six-week limit began to run from the date on which the minister's letter of decision was signed or posted. The appellant argued that he had applied within the time-limit because it did not begin to run until he had received notification of the minister's decision.

Deciding the case in favour of the Secretary of State, the House of Lords, by a majority of four to one (Lord Scarman dissenting and Lord Elwyn-Jones reluctantly with the majority), held that the six-week time-limit began to run when the minister's letter of decision was typed, signed and date-stamped and not from the later date of receipt. Accordingly, the appellant's High Court application was time-barred and could not proceed. This decision has the curious result that a person to whom Parliament has given a right of access to the High Court is at risk of losing that right before he even knows that he has it where the Secretary of State's letter is never posted, or is lost, or delayed, in the post. It must be said, however, that a fresh application to the High Court is possible where the first one has become time-barred and that, in the *Griffiths* case itself, the appellant had *received* the Secretary of State's letter some five weeks before he became time-barred and was thus still afforded a reasonable opportunity to apply to the High Court in good time had he been so minded.

11.14   REFORM OF JUDICIAL REVIEW PROCEEDINGS

In October 1994, a number of procedural and substantive changes to judicial review were recommended by the Law Commission in its Report, *Administrative Law: Judicial Review and Statutory Appeals* (Law Com No. 226, 1994).

Under the Law Commission's proposals, the term 'permission to apply for judicial review' would be replaced by 'preliminary consideration' (at which interim relief would be available), and the test for allowing an application to go beyond the preliminary stage would no longer be whether the case is arguable but whether there is a serious issue to be tried. The test for *locus standi* would move away from 'sufficient interest' to whether the court considers either that the applicant has been, or would be, adversely affected or that he is acting in the public interest in applying for judicial review. Unincorporated associations (which include many interest or pressure groups) would be allowed to apply in their own name (cf. *R* v *Darlington Borough Council (ex parte Association of Darlington Taxi Owners)* [1994] COD 424, para 11.11.4 above). Applicants would not be compelled to take judicial review proceedings, as opposed to private-law proceedings, unless the matter in issue is solely concerned with public law (cf *O'Reilly* v *Mackman* [1982] 3 All ER 1124, HL, para 11.11.2 above), and it would be made possible to convert improperly-commenced private-law proceedings into judicial review proceedings without having to start all over again (cf para 11.11.6.3 above). The court would be given power to grant both interim and advisory declarations. The prerogative remedies of certiorari, mandamus and prohibition would be renamed 'quashing orders', 'mandatory orders' and 'prohibiting orders', respectively.

Lord Woolf's Final Report on civil justice (*Access to Justice: Final Report to the Lord Chancellor on the Civil Justice System in England and Wales*, HMSO, August 1996) also made a number of recommendations in relation to judicial review. Under the Woolf proposals, the permission stage would be renamed the 'preliminary consideration' stage, and would be conducted in writing. The court would be able to grant interim relief before the preliminary consideration of the claim. The test of standing in all cases would be that the claimant has been or will be adversely affected by the decision under review, or that it is in the public interest for the claim to be brought. The court would have a discretion not to order the unsuccessful party to pay the other party's costs if the proceedings have been brought in the public interest. Cases which involve local issues would be dealt with outside London. More judges from divisions other than the Queen's Bench Division would be nominated to hear cases for which they have relevant experience. Claimants would be encouraged to resolve their complaints whenever possible by using grievance procedures or ombudsmen, treating judicial review as a remedy of last resort.

By virtue of RSC, Ord. 53, and Part 25 of the Civil Procedure Rules 1998 (SI 1998, No. 3132), which came into force on 26 April 1999, the court now has power to grant interim declarations.

In April 2000, Sir Jeffery Bowman's *Review of the Crown Office List* was published (Lord Chancellor's Department, April 2000). This Review, which began in February 1999, recommended, *inter alia*, that the Crown Office List should be renamed the 'Administrative Court' in recognition of the value of a specialised court dealing with public law cases and as a more adequate reflection of the type of work done there. Various procedural changes were proposed for judicial review.

The government is anxious to implement any changes in time for the coming into force of the Human Rights Act 1998 in October 2000. It responded to the *Review* by appointing an additional four High Court judges to assist with the backlog of judicial review cases (especially on immigration and asylum), and by publishing a Consultation Paper, *New Rules and Procedures for Judicial Review Cases* (Lord Chancellor's Department, April 2000). This Paper invites comments on proposed new procedures and draft rules for judicial review cases. These procedures and rules aim to simplify procedure, to encourage parties to examine the strength of their case and to settle early, to reduce delay, to dispose of unmeritorious cases at an early stage, and to minimise costs.

Index